AN ENGLISH-SPEAKING HYMNAL GUIDE

AN ENGLISH-SPEAKING

HYMNAL GUIDE

Erik Routley

THE LITURGICAL PRESS

Collegeville   Minnesota

TABLE OF CONTENTS

To

FREDERICK PRATT GREEN

in whom the genius of Charles Wesley

lives again

INTRODUCTORY ESSAY
On the Pleasures of Hymnody

A man or woman who has one hymnal in the house, and who opens it occasionally, is already on the way to becoming an intelligent hymn singer. A man or woman who has two hymnals is on the way to becoming a hymnologist. He or she who has two hymnals and a *Companion* (such as this one) has advanced far enough along the road not to want to turn back.

It is one thing—and a not unpleasurable thing—to confine the hymnal to church, and to sing from it there without much thought. It is far better to have a copy at home and either occasionally or regularly to read from it, or to play from it (if you can play), and to become personally familiar with what it contains. It is, I think, a generation that has almost passed away that regularly did this; but I did in my own youth know seniors who kept their hymnal next to their Bible, read from both at their prayers, and snatched both if they were suddenly taken to hospital. The present book and its companion volumes, *A Panorama of Christian Hymnody* and *The Music of Christian Hymnody*, are designed to introduce readers to this almost forgotten pleasure, and to help them find their own way about in a country through which so many travel without ever really looking at the scenery.

Suppose, then, that there are two hymnals in the house. If you are English and Anglican, they may be the *English Hymnal* and *Hymns Ancient and Modern*; if you are Canadian and Protestant, perhaps the 1971 *Hymn Book* and the 1972 *Book of Praise*; if you are a citizen of the United States, perhaps the *Hymnal 1940* and the *Pilgrim Hymnal*, or the Lutheran *Service Book and Hymnal* and the *Methodist Hymnal*, 1966. Fairly soon you notice how they differ: what one chooses and the other omits; how differently they are arranged; how a hymn you thought you knew turns out to have a different text in one of the books, or a different tune. You hardly need to have more than one hymnal to notice the difference between the 17th century eloquence of Isaac Watts and the 20th century truculence of Fred Kaan. Thus, from one book alone you are already learning something about church history: from two, you begin to learn something about the different church traditions. Who can really explain the difference in England between 'high church' and 'low church'? Despairing of any reliable definitions, all you need do is open the *English Hymnal* and lay it alongside the *Anglican Hymnal* (1965), and there you have, if not a definition, at least a picture of the difference. You soon find that 'high church' means more than incense and vestments, and 'low church' more than powerful sermons and Gospel Songs. Many have only the obscurest notions of what is really different between American Methodists and American Presbyterians: you learn this quickest and most persuasively by putting the *Methodist Hymnal* alongside the *Worshipbook* (1972). Or you should be able to.

John Wesley called his first hymn book of 1780 'a little body of experimental and practical divinity'—and that is what a hymnal ought to be. In vulgar language Wesley's words mean, 'This is where we Methodists stand: books of discipline will tell you about us: here you will meet us.' No hymnal worth opening should aim to do less than that for its constituency; and no hymnal should be interpreted as doing less, however ill it may do it.

HYMNOLOGY IN THE PAST

Now the study of hymns, and the interpretation of history and churchmanship through them, is, for English-speaking people, about a century old. Apart from people who wrote prefaces to their own or others' hymnals, one of the first people to write generally about hymns in England was John Ellerton, whose essays on other and earlier hymn writers, written in the last quarter of the 19th century, are delightful reading. So far as I can discover, the first *Companion* on a large scale (that is, a book which explains the history and associations of every hymn in a parent hymnal) was *The Methodist Hymn Book Illustrated with Biography, History, Incident and Anecdote*, published in London in 1892 and compiled by George J. Stevenson.

Note that title—so redolent of 19th century expansiveness! The book dealt, in 597 pages of text, with the 1,026 hymns in the 1876 edition of the Methodist Hymn Book, familiarly known then simply as *Wesley's Hymns*. Not all the hymns were Wesley's, but about half of them were, and the substance of the book (which has no musical notes) is much given to 'incident and anecdote,' as, indeed, are many books about hymns still being published. The trouble with incident and anecdote is that the anecdote may be apocryphal and the incident a matter of receding interest as it fades into history.

But this was a start. It looks, however, as if a need for information more substantial and critical was being felt at that time; for 1891 was the year in which Dr. John Julian published the first edition of his *Dictionary of Hymnology*, a work which at a stroke raised hymnology from a hobby to a serious study. Julian—it seems incredible now—undertook to provide information about every hymn in English use available at that time, and he said that there were about 400,000 of them. The final edition of 1907, with two supplements, runs to 1,768 pages and is the nearest thing one is ever likely to see to a cubic book (The only comparable object is *Who's Who*). Those closely-printed, double-column pages distil all the scholarship that Julian could assemble, working with a devoted team of helpers; and surprisingly little of it needs revising now. Such a thing will never be done again; and the effect it had on hymnology was beneficent and irreversible.

The same year, 1891, brought from Scotland the first book of any importance about the music of hymns: James Love's *Scottish Church Music*. Hymnody in the Church of Scotland was at that date only about a generation old, but Scotland always did know what exact scholarship meant, and this book about psalm and hymn tunes remains a classic. Ten years later, with William Cowan, Love brought out the first *Companion* to deal with music. Known as Cowan and Love, *The Music of the Church Hymnary*, it was designed to go with the 1898 edition of the *Church Hymnary* (Church of Scotland); and very economically and devotedly, it dealt with all the tunes in that book. The texts had to wait for John Brownlie's *Hymns and Hymn Writers of the Church Hymnary* (1911).

Since the turn of the century, hymnology has ambled along a broad path bounded on the one side by the austere scholarship of *Julian*, and on the other, by books in the style of that classic, R. E. Prothero's *The Psalms and Human Life*. Now and again it has inevitably strayed into the jungle of 'incident and anecdote,' but on the whole the craft has been honestly pursued. The backbone of the study is to be found in a series of compendious *Companions*, bringing together information about all the texts and all the tunes in whatever parent book is under review; and a magnificent start was made along this road by W. H. Frere in his *Historical Edition of Hymns Ancient* and Modern (1909). This is another book of lexical proportions —1,022 pages, ten inches by seven, in which every text and tune, with the original of every translated piece, is printed out in full, with copious notes about their origins, many musical examples, and the whole preceded by over 100 double-column pages of Introduction, a preface which remains a classic in the whole field. Later on we shall refer the reader to other productions of this kind. Meanwhile we simply mention a few landmarks in the advance of hymnology in other forms.

One of the earliest large books of continuous text about the history and development of hymns (words only) was W. Garrett Horder's The Hymn Lover (London, 1889). The name of Horder will appear very frequently in the body of this present work; for it was he who introduced American hymnody of the highest standards to English singers, and his book was written partly in order to draw the attention of the English to the remarkable hymn texts which 19th century America had produced. Another great work—which is still a standard work in the field —was The English Hymn, by the American Presbyterian scholar Louis F. Benson, based on what must be the largest hymnological library ever personally assembled by one man. That appeared in 1915. Henry Wilder Foote's great work, Three Centuries of American Hymnody (1940) is worthy to stand beside it and remains the best conspectus of American hymnody available. That generation in England brought us Hymnody Past and Present, by C. S. Phillips (1937), a sound and solid work, and a smaller, but because of its size perhaps more brilliant, book written for the Church of Scotland by Millar Patrick, The Story of the Church's Song (1927). In its day this edition was sold for two shillings—now ten English pence or (at that date) forty cents. It ran 200 pages and told the story beautifully. An American edition, revised by Dr. James R. Sydnor, appeared in 1962.

Alongside these monuments of learning there have sprung up more modest memorials in more restricted styles—to which your present writer has in his day made some contribution. Among these perhaps the most brilliant and influential was a book of collected essays by Bernard Manning (1892-1941), The Hymns of Wesley and Watts. Manning was like C. S. Lewis in being both a first-rate scholar and a born story-teller (unlike him in that he loved hymns while Lewis loathed them), and he celebrated these authors to such effect that he stung the whole of English protestantism into a re-evaluation of Reformed orthodoxy in theology and in song. The Methodist scholar, Henry Bett, and the Congregationalist, Sydney Moore, made very valuable contributions in a specialized way, and of course Ernest Rattenbury's two magnificent studies in Wesley, The Evangelical Doctrines of Charles Wesley's Hymns, and The Eucharistic Hymns of John and Charles Wesley are the best things of their kind in Wesley studies. Along with these, many studies of hymn writers appeared in the second quarter of the 20th century, so that any reader who wished to study a great hymn writer in depth found what he needed. At the learned level, the Hymn Societies of American on the one side and of Great Britain and Ireland on the other (respectively founded in 1925 and 1936) have sought to keep the channel of scholarship and informed comment clear.

I suppose that I am beginning to help the reader to build up a shelf of good works on hymnology. I hope some readers may be tempted to do that, if they have not already done it. And of course, as soon as they begin to take the subject as seriously as that, the present book will begin to have less usefulness for them. But it is time to say what the purpose of the present book is.

This is intended to be a Companion book about hymns (not, for the moment, their music) for my friend who has two hymnals at home. As we shall see, many hymnals now have their Companions, and while any Companion of that kind may well be more substantial and readable than this one, it will deal only with the hymns in the parent book. This is designed to be used with whatever book you happen to have, and if that book is one of twenty-six hymnals I have chosen as the 'control books,' you will find most of what you want here.

But I must explain the method by which I have gone to work. If one is not limited by an editor's choices, how, if one is not to be faced with a job as daunting as Julian's, is one to proceed at all? My own answer was to assemble twenty-six hymnals: twelve from Britain, twelve from the U.S.A., two from Canada, which as far as I could judge represented the widest aggregate constituency. From these I culled all those hymns which appear in four or five of them, and that is my list. I am afraid that where anything appears in fewer than four books I have had to omit it; had I not cut it off at that point the book would have been twice as long. But experiments with charts and statistics showed that four or five is a practicable lower limit.

'Four or five—well, which?' you may well ask. The answer to that is that most of the time it is four. Had it been five, a number of pieces by successful modern authors, which have simply not had time to travel very far, would have been left out, and with them any mention of their authors. But I have allowed myself to pass up certain 'four-timers' about which there was really nothing to say which was not covered by other entries. If a computer-minded reader detects an omission which fell the wrong side of this deliberately blurred boundary, he may well find information about the author under another entry, if he looks in the authors' index and follows that.

But looked at in one way I have consulted far more than twenty-six sources, because I have allowed myself to regard a hymnal plus its 'supplement' as a single source. Supplements —small additional hymnals designed to be used alongside the parent book rather than supplanting it, have come into use on both sides of the Atlantic since 1969, and they contain much interesting and significant material which I certainly did not want to omit if, with this extension of my terms of reference, it qualified. On the other hand, where it is clear that two or more editions of the same basic hymnal are running in parallel, I have treated these editions as separate sources. In Scotland and England, for example, there are two editions of the Church Hymnary in use among Presbyterian or ex-Presbyterian congregations, and two editions of Hymns Ancient and Modern among Anglicans; in the U.S.A., while for the Methodists the 1966 hymnal has to all intents and purposes supplanted the 1935 edition, the Presbyterians are still using any one of three books, the Hymnal (1933), the Hymnbook (1955) and the Worshipbook (1972); and the American Baptists and Disciples of Christ are still using the 1941 and 1970 editions of Christian Worship.

Here then is the list of 'control hymnals.' References to these are given in what may appear to be the rather forbidding number-indexes at the end of each entry, against the initials shown. Do not be daunted by these index-lists: with a little alertness you will soon be able to use them to discover how a hymn has waxed or waned in popular favour. It will soon be obvious that E (English Hymnal) is the oldest source used (1906) and B (Baptist U.S.A. 1975) the newest. Those composite entries which represent successive editions of the same book provide a very ready guide to the way in which popularity has increased or diminished in any given case. The following entries are given in three groups—Canadian, United States and British, in alphabetical order within each group. In the number-indexes a bullet (●) separates the Canadian and U.S. entries from the British and an asterisk means that the source referred to is a Supplement to the parent book with the same initial. Two Catholic books appear at the end of the U.S. group and the British group.

Canadian: BP: *The Book of Praise*, 1972, of the Presbyterian Church of Canada
Can: *The Hymn Book*, 1971 of the United Church of Canada and the Episcopal Church in Canada

U.S.A.: B: *The Baptist Hymnal*, 1975, of the Southern Baptist Convention also published as the *New Broadman Hymnal* 1977
CW: *Christian Worship*, 1941 / *Hymns for Christian Worship*, 1970, in use in the American Baptist Churches and the Disciples of Christ churches in the U.S.A.
H: *The Hymnal-1940*, of the Episcopal Church in the U.S.A.
H*: *More Hymns and Spiritual Songs*, 1971 (Supplement to *H*)
L: The *Service Book and Hymnal* (1958) of the Lutheran Churches in America and the American Lutheran Churches
L*: (with number 700 +) *Worship Supplement*, 1969, Lutheran Church, Missouri Synod (a supplement to the *Lutheran Hymnal*, 1941, of that communion)
(in form '1-4') *Contemporary Worship I and IV*, 1969, 1972: supplemental to all Lutheran hymnals, roman figure indicating volume, arabic figure, number in that volume
M: *Methodist Hymnal*, 1966
P: Presbyterian *Hymnal*, 1933 / *Hymnbook*, 1955 / *Worshipbook*, 1972
Pm: *Pilgrim Hymnal*, 1958, published by American Congregationalists but in use in many interdenominational congregations.
CLB: *Catholic Liturgy* Book, 1975
W: *Worship - II*, 1975, revised edition of *Worship*, 1969

British: AM: *Hymns Ancient and Modern*, Standard edition (in text AM-S) 1922 / Revised edition (in text AM-R) 1950. Where, as often, a hymn has the same number in both it is indexed simply as, e.g., AM165
AM*: *100 Hymns for To-day*, 1969
An: *Anglican Hymn Book*, 1965
B: *Baptist Hymn Book*, 1962
B*: *Praise for To-day*, 1974
BB: *BBC Hymn Book*, 1951, prepared for use in daily broadcast services and the best current example of an English interdenominational hymnal
CH: *Church Hymnary* 1927/1973; Church of

Scotland and Presbyterian Churches elsewhere in association with it. The bibliographically tiresome title of the 1973 edition, *Church Hymnary, Third Edition* makes it necessary to refer to these in text as CH² and CH³, not, as might be expected, CH¹ and CH². CH¹ was published in 1898.
CP: *Congregational Praise*, 1951
CP*: *New Church Praise*, 1975 (Supplement, for the United Reformed Church in England and Wales, founded 1972, to the hymnals of the constituent churches, indexed above as CH², CH³ and CP)
E: *English Hymnal*, 1906; note that in the later edition of 1933 only very small adjustments were made to a very few texts, all other alterations being musical*
E*: *English Praise*, 1975 (numbers 1 - 106)
E*: *English Hymnal Service Book* 1962 (numbers 300-335, being those hymns in this abridged edition which were not in the parent book)
E*: *Hymnal for Scotland*, 1951 (numbers 745-759), a Scottish supplement bound in with the parent book for use in the Episcopal Church in Scotland
M: *Methodist Hymn Book*, 1933
M*: *Hymns and Songs*, 1969
NC: *New Catholic Hymnal*, 1971
PL: *Praise the Lord*, 1972 (Roman Catholic)

HOW TO USE THIS BOOK

The main body of the book, or reference section, is constructed on as consistent a pattern as, I think, can be achieved, to make it easy to use. Literary art follows the maxim that a foolish consistency is the hobgoblin of little minds—which is why other *Companions* are more readable than this one: but for quick reference, a predictable pattern is a help. So an entry in Part I (## 1 - 832) looks like this:

116. CHRIST WHOSE GLORY FILLS THE SKIES

3 st. 7.7.7.7.77
C. Wesley (1), *Hymns & Sacred Poems*, 1740. 'A Morning Hymn.'

That is a 'bare bones' entry. After the first line, the length and meter of the hymn are displayed; then the author's name. The (1) that here follows means that the author's biography will be found at entry #1. If this were the first time Charles Wesley had appeared, his biography would be found immediately below the data about the hymn, which finish always with the number-index (it is always worth looking the author up). After the author's name we give the original source, where ascertainable, and the author's title, if that is known. Any details of interest follow, including the first appearance as a hymn of a poem not originally so designed, and any textual matters that seem to be worth mentioning.

In the matter of variant texts, one cannot possibly do full justice in a book of this size to the complexity of this matter. Editorial alterations of non-copyright material abound—and in a medium so close to folk songs as hymnody it is not im-

---

*Abbreviated 'E' in the source references, the *English Hymnal* is abbreviated '*EH*' when referred to in the text.

proper that they should. I have simply had to judge what I thought the reader might want to know and what would cause his interest to flag. Broadly speaking, important alterations are noted, and in the case of well-known hymns important variations of stanza-selection. But in two cases I am altogether out of my depth. I refer to the *New Catholic Hymnal* in England and the *Worshipbook* in the U.S.A. Both these have followed a policy of wholesale and often idiosyncratic alteration of texts. In both cases one of the objects was to transpose most texts from the 'thou' to the 'you' form, but in neither was this the whole object, which is better described by the very suitably ugly word 'updating.' It would have been insufferably tedious to mention every case of this in those two books, and I simply have to tell the reader that neither of those books should ever be trusted if the reader is looking for an authentic text. This is not to make any blanket-judgment about the superiority or inferiority of the texts as altered, although I am prepared to say that in both books the alterations seem to me to have been unwise more often than wise.

Translated texts. Where a hymn is a translation, two patterns are followed. If the original is widely known in the control-hymnals in only one translation (whatever may be the case in hymnals outside our control-list), the hymn is in Part I under its English first line. That, for example is where you will find, 'O come, all ye faithful' and 'Now thank we all our God'; and although two of the control-sources do have different translations of 'O come, O come, Immanuel,' we include it in part I because all well-known translations begin with the same first line. But if an original is found in several translations, and these translations are importantly different, then we place it in Part II (833-88), which is arranged in alphabetical order of the *original* first lines, whatever the language. Entries in Part II are often rather complicated, and situations arise which are so different that a truly consistent pattern is impossible. I may say that the most intractable of all the entries in either section is the very last—which is a classic example of how popular taste takes over without considering the sensibilities of pedants. In the case of so great and venerable a piece as our (888) this is as it should be.

A book like this is, naturally enough, a hand-to-mouth affair; it is a book which you look up, rather than one which you read. Research in it will, however, gradually press upon the reader the fact that the story of hymnody is a continuous story. Since one cannot provide a reference book and a story book in the same composition, I am supplementing this work with another, *A Panorama of Christian Hymnody*, in which the story is told continuously with abundant textual quotations. Ideally, I suppose the reader should have both. The reference PCH after the meter (when no meter is given, after the title) refers to the place where the hymn at that entry will be found in the *Panorama*, and this means that the reader can there see its text (almost always in full) and can discover where this particular hymn fits into the total pattern. The matter of music, which, I have to say, has been continuously dealt with only in the work of Frere mentioned above (*Hymns Ancient and Modern, Historical Edition*, 1909, preface), in Maurice Frost's revision of that same work (*A Historical Companion to Hymns Ancient and Modern*, 1961) and in my own book, *The Music of Christian Hymnody*, 1957 (now out of print) I propose, should time be given me, to deal with in a third volume in the present series.

But one technical matter may baffle the reader who is com-

ing new to this study if it is not briefly explained, and that is *meter*.

METER

Meter (Englishmen write *metre*) is a subject upon which people ask questions which the usual books do not answer very fully. Meter is the pattern in which syllables are arranged in each of the stanzas that form a hymn. A stanza is a unit which is repeated, on exactly the same metrical pattern, through a hymn. (The Americans are right in calling this unit a *stanza*. The English say *verse*, which strictly should be used only in speaking of metrical psalms where the pattern of biblical verses does not always correspond with that of the stanzas into which the psalms are metricized.)

Most hymnals (the Lutheran *Service Book* oddly excepted) provide a metrical formula for each hymn, and a metrical index which gathers together tunes in the same meter. (The object of a metrical index is entirely to make it easy to substitute another tune for that set: since this practice is now scarcely ever followed in America there is little object there in printing metrical indexes.) This formula is expressed either in letters or in digits. The commonest meters use letters, and with these we will deal first.

C.M. (Common Meter) is the meter used for the earliest metrical psalms in English, from which the first metrical psalters deviated only seldom. The great success of the English metrical psalter, and the Scottish Psalter (see 42 and 323 for notes on these) was largely due to this fact, since it was possible for a congregation which knew only a few tunes to sing the whole psalter. In Scotland, indeed, theoretically the congregation need know only one tune since from 1650 onwards every psalm was in Common Meter, alternative meters appearing only in alternative versions. Common meter is based on the 14-syllable line made familiar in the English ballads which were well known in the 16th century:

> The King sate in Dunfermline towne,
> drinking his blude-red wine.

In the old psalters four, in the later ones, two such lines made up a stanza; and when the practice of associating a different tune with each psalm died out (the death, the British being what they are, was speedy), and the custom prevailed of providing a handful of tunes all of which could be sung to any psalm, these tunes were called 'common tunes' and hence the meter became Common Meter. The musical phrases, and the need to draw breath, naturally divided the long line at the eighth syllable, and the impatience of the British soon came to prefer a half-length tune, so that Common Meter became not, as originally, 14. 14. 14. 14, but 8.6.8.6 twice over which we now call Double Common Meter; and this appears in hymnals as D.C.M. or C.M.D. (for example in 'The Son of God goes forth to war.')

Occasionally, however, to make a special effect, the versifier dropped two syllables (or one 'foot') out of the first of the two lines that make Common Meter, so that this appeared on the page:

> Have mercy on us, Lord   and grant to us thy grace;
> so shew to us do thou accord   the brightness of thy face.

(That is how the early psalters were printed, with a visible *caesura* in the long lines). You have here then 6.6.8.6, and this came to be called Short Meter (S.M.).

One very famous psalm, with a tune from Geneva simple enough for the unmusical British to master, was in yet a third meter, being written in eight syllable phrases throughout. On the page of the old psalter this looked like 16.16, but of course it makes sense only as 8.8.8.8. This psalm was 'All people that on earth do dwell,' and that is the archetypal example in English of Long Meter (L.M.). It may be noted at this point that while the rhyme scheme of C.M. and S.M. is always *alternate*—that is, in modern form, rhymes between the second and fourth lines always and the first and third usually—the rhyme scheme in L.M. may be alternate or couplet (the difference between 'All people' and 'Ride on, ride on in majesty.'). Couplet rhyme is found in later Latin hymns using this meter, but not in the earliest English hymns using it. The reason for this is obvious: the Latin hymns were thought of, as were the later English ones, in units of eight syllables from the first; but the Long Meter metrical psalm was thought of in units of 16 syllables with what amounts to an 'internal rhyme' at the eighth. So far then we have C.M., S.M., and L.M., all of which (the last rarely) can appear as 'double.' 'Our God, our help in ages past,' 'Rise up, O men of God' and 'All people' are familiar examples of each.

We must dispose at once of the odd formula 'P.M.' which used to appear in very old hymnals and has been revived in the *Worshipbook*. This means 'Peculiar Meter,' and is strictly to be used for any hymn which is the only example of its meter in the book that contains it.

All other meters are expressed in figures in the manner we have already used: the digits represent the number of syllables in each line of a stanza. Thus, 'In the Cross of Christ I glory' is demonstrably 8.7.8.7, and 'The church's one foundation' is demonstrably 7.6.7.6 D. But there are traps for the unwary into which the most distinguished editors can fall. Of course, there is no consistent stanza-form which cannot be represented in a metrical formula, and certain well known German hymns produce quite remarkable patterns, like 8.7.8.7.6.6.6.6.7 ('A mighty fortress') and 14. 14. 4. 7. 8 ('Praise to the Lord the Almighty'). But there are three points at which one has to be vigilant.

(1) Consider the following four stanzas, all of which might carry the same metrical index.

(a) Eternal Father, strong to save,
   whose arm doth bind the restless wave,
   who bid'st the mighty ocean deep
   its own appointed limits keep;
   O hear us as we cry to thee
   for those in peril on the sea.

(b)Thou hidden love of God, whose height,
   whose depth unfathomed, no man knows,
   I see from far thy beauteous light,
   inly I sigh for thy repose;
   my heart is pained, nor can it be
   at rest till it finds rest in thee.

(c) I'll praise my Maker while I've breath,
   and when my voice is lost in death
   praise shall employ my nobler powers:
   my days of praise shall ne'er be past,
   while life and thought and being last,
   or immortality endures.

(d) Christ is the King! O friends, rejoice,
   brothers and sisters, with one voice
   make all men know he is your choice.
   Ring out, ye bells, give tongue, give tongue;
   let your most merry peal be rung
   while our exultant song is sung.

All these look like 8.8.8.8.8.8, but all are different. There is one kind of difference between (a) and (b) and between (c) and (d), another kind between (a), (b) and (c), (d).

The difference between (a) and (b) is in the rhyme scheme. In (a) the rhymes are lines 1-2, 3-4, 5-6: in (b), 1-3, 2-4, 5-6. The metrical formula can express this difference of phrasing, and does so, when possible, by the use of full points: the formula for (a) is 88.88.88 and for (b), 8.8.8.8.88. Two lines in a couplet-rhyme are represented by digits without the full point between.

Similarly, one would represent (c) by 88.8.88.8 and (d) by 888.888: but here we have exposed the other and much more dangerous difference. For both (a) and (b) are in three groups of two lines = ** ** **, while (c) and (d) are in two groups of three = *** ***. Now while it is possible to sing (a) and (b) to the same tune, since music doesn't have anything to do with rhyme, it is quite impossible, without alarming incongruity, to sing (c) to the same tune as (b). Try singing (c) or (d) to the tune of 'Eternal Father strong to save' and the dullest ear will detect something wrong. It is our grievous duty to report that Vaughan Williams (of all people) fell headlong into this trap in the later (1933) edition of the *English Hymnal* when at #539 he set a tune in 888.888 to a text in 8.8.8.8.88 (that is, a tune in (d) to a text in (b).

In those places where the barbarous custom of interlining texts within the music staves is not followed, meter is often reflected in the arrangement of the printed lines. We have intentionally printed two of the above stanzas incorrectly. Stanza (a) is all right, because the rhymes are alternate, even though sometimes the last two lines, which happen to be more or less a refrain, are indented. Stanza (d) is also correct because the rhymes are in triplets. But stanza (b) should have looked like this:

Thou hidden love of God, whose height,
   whose depth unfathomed, no man knows,
I see from far thy beauteous light,
   inly I sigh for thy repose;
my heart is pained, not can it be
   at rest till it finds rest in thee.

and stanza (c) like this:

I'll praise my Maker while I've breath,
and when my voice is lost in death,
   praise shall employ my nobler powers:
my days of praise shall ne'er be past,
while life and thought and being last,
   or immortality endures.

I cannot state too strongly my conviction that a great deal is lost when these subtle differences of stanza-shape are for any reason blurred; whether by writing all lines to the margin, as some modern hymnals do, or, worse, by splitting words into syllables and interlining them between music staves, a practice universal in the United States since about 1930.

If any sharp-eyed reader asks why in the above examples the first letter of each line is not capitalized, my answer is that this form of writing out hymns, which I think I invented in 1962, seems to promote a true apprehension of the sense of the lines, which is subtly held up by the old-fashioned capitalization. It is especially useful when a stanza does not end a sentence. The opening of the next with a lower-case letter imparts an immediate sense of the continuity of thought.

(2) Now we will take all this a step further, and expose a much more common error, which arises from the incapacity of a metrical formula to give all the needed information. Consider the following two pairs of stanzas; each pair of which could carry a similar metrical formula.

(e) In the cross of Christ I glory,
  towering o'er the wrecks of time;
 all the light of sacred story
  gathers round its head sublime.

(f) The King of love my shepherd is,
  whose goodness faileth never;
 I nothing lack if I am his
  and he is mine for ever.   (8.7.8.7)

(g) Lord God of hosts, whose purpose, never swerving,
  leads towards the day of Jesus Christ, thy Son,
 grant us to march among the faithful legions,
  armed with thy courage, till the world is won.

(h) Brightest and best of the sons of the morning,
  dawn on our darkness and lend us thine aid;
 Star of the East, the horizon adorning,
  guide where our infant Redeemer is born. (11.10.11.10)

Here we have stanzas of unequal lines, but of the same metric count. But try singing (e) to the tune of (f), or (g) to the tune of (h). What has happened is that the metrical formula has said nothing about the *rhythm*, or, in the language of prosody, the *feet* into which the syllables are distributed. Stanza (e) has this rhythm throughout:

 In the | cross of | Christ I | glory:

stanza (f), this:

 The King | of love | my she|pherd is.

The first is called *trochaic*, the second *iambic*; each 'foot' in the first has a heavy syllable followed by a light one: in the second they are the other way round. Similarly, in (g) the rhythm is basically iambic (despite the reversed opening foot) -

 Lord God | of hosts, | whose pur|pose ne|ver swer|ving:

but in (h) it is something different again—a triple rhythm in which a heavy syllable is followed by two light ones

 Brightest and | best of the | sons of the | morning,

the name of this rhythm being *dactylic*.

In forming the metrical formula for these you can do nothing about the digits: they remain 8.7.8.7 for the first two and 11.10.11.10 for the second two. But it is necessary to add 'iambic' to (f) and 'dactylic' to (h); a reasonable convention holds that you assume 'trochaic' in 8.7.8.7 unless the limiting word is added, because actually trochaic 8.7.8.7 is far commoner than iambic—and the same holds good with 'iambic' as assumed for the other meter unless 'dactylic' is added.

This is constantly overlooked by editors, who will include (e) and (f) in the same group, and (g) and (h), implying that a tune which fits one will fit the other. It happens again with the meter 10.10.10.10 (or of course 10 10. 10 10).

 Saviour, | again | to thy | dear name | we raise

is one kind of 'ten' (iambic) while

 Blessing and | honor and | glory and | power

is another (dactylic).

For completeness we may mention the one other 'foot' commonly found in hymnody—the *anapaest*, which is a dactyl beginning on the light syllable

 Immortal, | invisi|ble, God on|ly wise

(3) The other thing we have to mention is that while ninety per cent of the time (maybe more) the meter of the text is exactly the same as that of the tune, in the other ten per cent (or less) it is not the same.
Consider this:

 Guide me, O thou great Jehovah,
  pilgrim through this barren land;
 I am weak, but thou art mighty,
  hold me with thy powerful hand.
  Bread of heaven
 feed me till I want no more.

That is a meter of which 18th century writers were very fond, and it appears again in 'Praise, my soul.' Now there are tunes which follow that meter exactly, with its abrupt short line; but the best known tune to the hymn above is now not 8.7.8.7.4.7., as is the text, but 8.7.8.7.4.4.7.7. To accommodate it, lines have to be repeated in singing—which happens to be a device they were very fond of at the time when that hymn was written. There is a very fine tune which makes the 8.7.8.7.4.7 of 'Lo, he comes with clouds descending' into 8.7.8.7.444.7. 'Praise, my soul' was written as 8.7.8.7.4.7 (the fifth line was simply 'Praise him! Praise him!') but both well-known tunes to that hymn make it 8.7.8.7.8.7—more symmetrical, and it is just as well, when we have lost the curious and interesting effect of the short line, that both are fine tunes.

This happens more often than one might think. When a tune has a certain kind of flexibility it can go to more than one meter so long as the stresses are right. The tune FOREST GREEN, for example, is sung in England to 'O little town of Bethlehem,' in America to a variety of hymns in D.C.M., which is not exactly the meter of 'O little town.' ELLACOMBE can go equally well to 'The Son of God goes forth to war' (C.M.D.) and 'The day of resurrection' (7.6.7.6 D). This becomes especially useful when one is confronted with the odd handful of hymns whose meter is called 'Irregular.' This means that although the *stresses* in the successive stanzas always correspond, the number of syllables is not always exactly the same in corresponding lines. The most famous hymn of which this is true is a text which has no meter, but none the less a very strong rhythm: 'O come, all ye faithful.' In the usually received version the first stanza opens

  O come, all ye faithful
  joyful and triumphant

and the second

  God of God
  Light of light.

Yet the same tune goes equally well all through these irregular stanzas. This is because the tune has a *rhythm* that corresponds with that of the words. As Americans know, that tune can be equally conveniently (though I think not equally appropriately) sung to the two following highly contrasted stanzas:

  O come, all ye faithful,
  joyful and triumphant,
  O come ye, O come ye to Bethlehem;
  come and behold him,

born the King of angels,
O come, let us adore him Christ the Lord

and

How firm a foundation, ye saints of the Lord,
is laid for your faith in his excellent word:
what more can he say than to you he hath said,
you who unto Jesus for refuge have fled?

'Be thou my Vision' is 'irregular' in most books: its tune could be sung to 'Blessing and honor and glory and power,' which of course is not.

'God is working his purpose out' is very irregular; tunes which go to it could be sung to some hymns of Charles Wesley in the odd composite metre 7.6.7.6.7.6.8.6 (trochaic odd lines, iambic even lines). And so on. One has to take care, when using tunes that require word-repetition, that the repetitions do not make nonsense; but more flexibility is possible with many tunes, when irregular texts have to be handled, if one observes that regularity of stress is really more important than regularity of syllable-count.

But the purpose of this book is to promote intelligent pleasure in hymnody, and therefore we must go further and illustrate the *visual* pleasures of meter.

The interlined page destroys this pleasure. The two off-printed examples of consecutive hymns in a well known and typical American hymnal illustrate this at once. 'God the Lord a King remaineth' and 'A mighty fortress is our God' look the same shape. Printed as poetry a stanza of the first reads:

God the Lord a King remaineth
robed in his own glorious light:
God hath robed himself and reigneth;
he hath girt himself with might.
Alleluia!
God is King in depth and height.

and of the second:

A mighty fortress is our God,
a bulwark never failing;
our helper he amid the flood
of mortal ills prevailing.
For still our ancient foe
doth seek to work us woe;
his craft and power are great;
and, armed with cruel hate,
on earth is not his equal.

Poetry has always been to some extent visual and audible as well as intellectual. Lyric poetry in stanzas has three ways in which it makes its visible impact: in the stanza-shape, in the relative lengths of lines, and in the total design formed by a series of stanzas. This third point we need not take space to demonstrate here since the reader can see it exemplified in our *Panorama of Christian Hymnody*, or in any normal English hymn book. It will soon be obvious that if the total design is a horizontal oblong, the hymn will be a short one, and if it is a vertical oblong, the hymn will be a long one. Four stanzas of Long Meter produce what looks very close to a perfect square (as 'All people that on earth do dwell' if printed vertically). Three will make a horizontal oblong: five will make a vertical oblong. The lateral dimension of the frame represents the length of the longest lines: the vertical dimension, the number of repetitions of the stanza-shape. So much is very clear.

But now consider what happens if one studies, with the purpose of enjoying, the shapes of different stanza-forms. We will now give a series of these to show how different they can be.

Here first are the traditional English Psalm-meters: note the subtle differences in their visual impact.

COMMON METER
O God, my strength and fortitude
of force I must love thee;
thou art my castle and defence
in my necessity.
(rhyme always alternate)

LONG METER
All people that on earth do dwell,
sing to the Lord with cheerful voice;
him serve with mirth, his praise forth tell,
come ye before him, and rejoice.
(alternate rhyme)

another form:
The glory of these forty days
we celebrate with songs of praise;
for Christ, by whom all things were made,
himself has fasted and has prayed.
(couplet rhyme)

another (modern)
Strong Son of God, immortal love,
whom we, that have not seen thy face,
by faith, and faith alone, embrace,
believing where we cannot prove......
(abba rhyme)

SHORT METER
Lord Jesus, think on me,
and purge away my sin;
from earthborn passions set me free
and keep me pure within.

Sixes and fours
(6.6.6.6.4.44.4)
Ye holy angels bright   A
that wait at God's right hand   B
and through the realms of light   A
fly at your Lord's command: B
assist our song,   C
for else the theme   D
too high doth seem   D
for mortal tongue   E

(Note the special rhythmic effect of the abba rhymes in the short lines, and always distinguish it from the later development of this meter, 6.6.6.6.88:)

Rejoice, the Lord is King,   A
your Lord and King adore;
mortals, give thanks and sing,
and triumph evermore.   B
Lift up your heart, lift up your voice: C
rejoice, again I say, rejoice!   C

Tens and Elevens
(5.5.5.5.6.5.6.5)
O worship the King,
all glorious above,
O gratefully sing
his power and his love;
our Shield and Defender,
the Ancient of Days,
pavilioned in splendour
and girded with praise.

(Notice that if this were written out as 10 10. 11 11 it would turn out to be Long Meter in triple time, there being four stresses in each long line just as there are in L.M., but two beats between the strong syllables instead of one.)

God, the Lord, a King Remaineth

From Psalm 93
John Keble, 1839; alt.

BRYN CALFARIA: 8. 7. 8. 7. 4. 7.
William Owen (1814-1893)

1. God, the Lord, a King re-main-eth, Robed in His own glo-rious light;
2. In her ev-er - last-ing sta-tion Earth is poised, to swerve no more;
3. With all tones of wa-ters blend-ing, Glo-rious is the break-ing deep;
4. Lord, the words Thy lips are tell-ing Are the per-fect ver-i-ty;

God hath robed Him-self and reign-eth; He hath girt Him-self with might.
Thou hast laid Thy throne's foun-da-tion From all time where thought can soar.
Glo-rious, beau-teous, with-out end-ing, God, who reigns on heaven's high steep.
Of Thine high e-ter-nal dwell-ing, Ho-li-ness shall in-mate be:

Al - le - lu - ia! Al - le - lu - ia! Al - le - lu - ia!
Al - le - lu - ia! Al - le - lu - ia! Al - le - lu - ia!
Al - le - lu - ia! Al - le - lu - ia! Al - le - lu - ia!

God is King in depth and height! God is King in depth and height!
Lord, Thou art for-ev - er - more! Lord, Thou art for - ev - er-more!
Songs of o - cean nev-er sleep. Songs of o - cean nev-er sleep.
Pure is all that lives with Thee. Pure is all that lives with Thee. A-MEN.

A Mighty Fortress Is Our God

From Psalm 46
Martin Luther, 1529
Trans. by Frederick H. Hedge, 1853

EIN' FESTE BURG: 8. 7. 8. 7. 6. 6. 6. 6. 7.
Martin Luther, 1529

1. A might-y For-tress is our God, A Bul-wark nev-er fail - ing;
2. Did we in our own strength con-fide, Our striv-ing would be los - ing;
3. And though this world, with dev - ils filled, Should threat-en to un - do us,
4. That word a - bove all earth-ly powers, No thanks to them, a - bid-eth;

Our Help - er He a - mid the flood Of mor - tal ills pre - vail - ing.
Were not the right man on our side, The man of God's own choos - ing.
We will not fear, for God hath willed His truth to tri-umph through us.
The Spir - it and the gifts are ours Through Him who with us sid - eth;

For still our an - cient foe Doth seek to work us woe; His craft and power are
Dost ask who that may be? Christ Je - sus, it is He, Lord Sab - a - oth His
The prince of dark - ness grim, We trem-ble not for him; His rage we can en -
Let goods and kin - dred go, This mor-tal life al - so; The bod - y they may

great; And, armed with cru - el hate, On earth is not his e - qual.
name, From age to age the same, And He must win the bat - tle.
dure, For lo! his doom is sure; One lit - tle word shall fell him.
kill: God's truth a - bid-eth still; His King-dom is for - ev - er. A - MEN.

O worship the King, all glorious above.
All people that on earth do dwell.)

Those are the basic meters of the first English Psalter. Certain others occasionally appear in it, which were taken over from the much more complex meters of the Genevan Psalters (as indeed was that last one); but actually the psalms set out in those odd meters, with their peculiar tunes, soon went out of use in Britain, and the Scottish Psalter of 1564 never used them anyway.

Now in the *English Hymnal* there are 130 different meters, and in the *Hymnal-1940* of the U.S.A., 157 different meters, not counting Irregulars. One of the first influences to produce all these new stanza-forms was German hymnody imitated by the Wesleys. A favorite Wesley meter is that illustrated earlier on page *iv* at example (b), six eights arranged as 8.8.8.8.88; two pairs of alternate-rhyming lines, one of couplet rhyme. But look now at some of the others. Here is a tiny stanza in a German meter:

Ere I sleep, for every favour
    this day showed
    by my God,
I will bless my Saviour   (Cennick: 8.33.6)

Here is another (not used by the Methodists)

Glory be to Jesus
    who in bitter pains
poured for us the life-blood
    from his sacred veins.   (6.5.6.5)

That one can be extended to make 6.5.6.5 D, or, as in 'Onward, Christian soldiers,' 6.5.6.5. Ter., in which case the stanza becomes, unusually, a vertical oblong in its own right:

Onward, Christian soldiers,
    marching as to war,
with the cross of Jesus
    going on before.
Christ, the royal Master,
    leads against the foe;
Forward into battle
    see his banners go!
Onward, Christian soldiers,
    marching as to war,
with the cross of Jesus
    going on before.

(In printing this hymn, since the last four lines are a refrain, quite often they are indented, or printed only with the first stanza: but 'Who is on the Lord's side,' in exactly the same meter without a refrain, would have to be printed as above).

The most commonly used meters use lines that are equal, or nearly equal, in length. Such are 7.6.7.6 D, as 'The church's one foundation,' or 8.7.8.7 D, such as 'Glorious things of thee are spoken.' 7.6.7.6 and 8.7.8.7 are rather less common but are still quite often found. A longer line produces the ten and eleven syllable units we saw before in examples (e) to (h), page *vi*.

These are the normal meters; but variations on them produce special and often charming or massive effects just because they are abnormal. Large variations in line-length were much exploited by French and German hymn-writers and have had to be accommodated by later English translators. Look at the massive effect of the 'A mighty fortress' stanza we saw just now. Then look at this very eloquent and beautiful meter, given such dramatic effect by its short line at the end. (This is one of the very few meters from classical Latin that appear in

hymnody and is called *Sapphic*)

Sapphic Ah, holy Jesus, how hast thou offended,
        that man to judge thee hath in hate pretended?
    By foes derided, by thine own rejected,
            O most afflicted.
                            (couplet rhymes)

Father, we praise thee, now the night is over;
    active and watchful, stand we all before thee;
singing we offer prayer and meditation
            thus we adore thee.
                            (2/4 rhyme)

Let thine example, holy John, remind us
    ere we can meetly sing thy deeds of wonder,
hearts must be chastened, and the bonds that bind us
            broken asunder . . .
                            (alternate rhyme)

Christ, the fair glory of the holy angels,
    thou who hast made us, thou who o'er us rulest,
grant of thy mercy unto us thy servants
            steps up to heaven.
                            (unrhymed)

This is one of the very few meters which can be used successfully without rhyme.

Here are two contrasting Genevan meters, both exquisitely turned by Robert Bridges; in the first there is only rhyme between lines 3 and 6: in the second the rhyme-scheme is very subtle indeed. Both produce a captivating visual effect:

Love, unto thine own who camest
    condescending,
    whom thine own received not
Light, who shinedst in the darkness,
    but the darkness
thy splendour perceived not.   (8.4.7.8.4.7)

Thee will I love, my God and King,
    Thee will I sing
        my strength and tower:
For evermore thee will I trust,
    O God most just
        of truth and power.
Who all things hast
    in order placed,
Yea, for thy pleasure hast created;
    and on thy throne,
    unseen, unknown,
    reignest alone
in glory seated.   (84.5.84.5.44.9.444.5)

(Assonance, a device of using near-rhyme instead of exact rhyme, allows 'hast' to rhyme with 'placed' and 'created' with 'seated').

And here are some German examples which are very familiar. Consider the commanding effect of a stanza set out like this:

Wake, o Wake! with tiding thrilling
the watchmen all the air are filling,
    arise, Jerusalem, arise!
Midnight strikes! no more delaying
'The hour has come!' we hear them saying.
    Where are ye all, ye virgins wise?
        The Bridegroom comes in sight
        Raise high your torches bright!

> Alleluia!
> The wedding song
> swells loud and strong:
> Go forth and join the festal throng.
>
> (8.9.8.8.9.8.66.4.448)

Contrast the dancing effect of this, the most dramatic juxta-position of long and short lines in the whole repertory:

> Praise to the Lord, the Almighty, the King of creation;
> O my soul, praise him, for he is thy health and salvation;
> Come, ye who hear;
> Brothers and sisters draw near,
> Praise him in glad adoration!
>
> (14 14. 47.8)

Then there is the equally choreographic effect of this mini-ature meter, of which Charles Wesley was very fond:

> Come, let us anew,
> our journey pursue,
> roll round with the year,
> and never stand still till the Master appear.   (55.5 11)

Meters are usually consistent in their use of iambic, trochaic or dactylic feet, but Charles Wesley was ingenious in mixing iambics and trochaic feet, as here:

> Open, Lord, my inward ear,   (7 troch.)
> and bid my heart rejoice;   (6 iamb.)
> bid my quiet spirit hear
> thy comfortable voice;
> never in the whirlwind found,
> or where the earthquakes rock the place,
> still and silent is the sound,
> the whisper of thy grace.

The mixing of short and long lines, especially when the long line comes first, often has an effect of pathos, to which Victo-rian English women writers were often partial:

> My God, my Father, while I stray,
> far from my home, in life's rough way,
> O teach me in my heart to say,
> 'Thy will be done!'   (888.4)
>
> Charlotte Elliott

> Our blest Redeemer, ere he breathed
> his tender, last farewell,
> a Guide, a Comforter bequeathed
> with us to dwell.   (8.6.8.4)
>
> Harriet Auber

> Holy Father, in thy mercy
> hear our anxious prayer,
> keep our loved ones, now far absent
> 'Neath thy care.   (8.5.8.3)
>
> Isabella S. Stevenson

Newman, in a poem he never intended to be sung, uses this effect supremely well:

> Lead, kindly Light, amid the encircling gloom,
> lead thou me on;
> the night is dark, and I am far from home,
> lead thou me on.
> Keep thou my feet; I do not ask to see
> the distant scene; one step enough for me.
>
> (10.4.10.4.10 10)

The converse effect, with short lines leading to a long one, is seen in the exquisite translation of Littledale from an Italian poem:

> Come down, O love divine,
> seek thou this soul of mine,
> and visit it with thine own ardour glowing;
> O comforter, draw near,
> within my heart appear,
> and kindle it, thy holy flame bestowing.
>
> (66.11.66.11)

Something of the great popularity of the following hymn in America (apart from its being wed to a very effective tune) may well be in the energy imparted to it by a kind of inversion of the device Newman used above:

> Come, labour on!
> Who dares stand idle on the harvest-plain.
> while all around him waves the golden grain,
> and to each servant doth the Master say,
> 'Go work to-day!'

Stanza forms are the organization of sounds and rhythms transmitted visually. There may be, in a very short stanza, only twenty or twenty-four syllables to be organized (Common Meter handles twenty-eight). The longest stanza in normal use is that of the great German and Genevan tune, O MENSCH, BEWEIN' DUE SUNDE GROSS, which, displaying the formula 88.7 four times in a stanza, contains 92 syllables. It is, actually, rarely heard in full from congregations (but see *EH*544). The next longest is WACHET AUF ('Wake, O Wake' above), with 82 syllables, and certainly the longest really popular stanza among English speakers is that of 'We plough the fields, and scatter,' with 78. It is, of course, the artistry of musicians that makes such long stanzas manageable at all.

To end these illustrations I cannot forbear to quote the most remarkable stanza I know, from a song by the English musician David Goodall, whose music he himself provides, and which comes out with six short lines followed by a line twice as long as anything in the literature that has to be sung all in one breath. The metrical formula is almost beyond an editor's ingenuity to notate: (I quote the final stanza: the others are irregular only in one or two syllables in the long line:

> I want to get out,
> I want to stay here,
> I want to be welcomed,
> I want to stay clear;
> I want to believe,
> I want to be sure:
> Show me the man who knows the way, the truth, the life, and
> who is yesterday,
> to-day and everlastingly the same;
> Tell me his name!
>
> (5.5.6.5.5.5.28.4)

Such is the almost infinite variety which the modern printing of hymnals seeks to obscure.

Where to go from here? If this book has any use, it will be in arousing the reader to continue such researches for himself, and to be always critical, observant and sensitive about hymns. Before long, he will ask where he should look for the growing points, for the kind of portent which the rough and ready style of this book does not accommodate. The answer is to look in the Supplemental hymnals we quoted earlier, to look at the international explosion of hymnody illustrated in *Cantate Domino* (1974), and at the remarkable experimental material in *Ecumenical Praise* (Agape Publishing Co., 1977). See how the new hymn writers of Catholic France and of the countries which a century ago were mission fields have handled their new craft in the final section of the *Panorama*.

Hymns enshrine history, and close the gaps between culture and culture, and between past and present. Probably the best direction to follow is not exclusively into the future, but in a roaming line which includes those people and groups whose hymnody we have unconsciously enjoyed and taken for granted all our lives, but whom we have yet really to come to know. That, I think, is the kind of flesh which I hope to see forming on the dry bones which creak in these pages.

★   ★   ★

COMPANION BOOKS TO HYMNALS

If your hymn book has a *Companion* and it is obtainable, possess it. It will supplement this one by telling you about the hymns in your book which we have had to pass over, and about their tunes, with which we do not here deal at all.

(a) *Hymnals in the 'control' list*

American and Canadian

Can: *If Such Holy Song*, Stanley L. Osborne, Institute of Church Music, 705 Masson Street, Oshawa, Ontario, 1976

B: *Companion to Baptist Hymnal*, W. J. Reynolds, Broadman Press, 1975

CW²: *Companion to Hymnal for Christian Worship*, Arthur Wake, Bethany Press, 1970

H: *The Hymnal Companion*, Winfred Douglas and Compilers, Church Pension Fund, 1949

L: *Companion to the Hymnal of the Service Book & Hymnal*, William Seaman, Fortress Press and Augsburg Publishing House, 1975

M: *Companion to the (Methodist) Hymnal*, F. D. Gealy, Austin Lovelace and Carlton Young, Abingdon Press, 1968

Pm: *Guide to the Pilgrim Hymnal*, Ethel Porter and A. C. Ronander, United Church Press, 1966

English

AM: *Historical Companion to Hymns Ancient & Modern*, Maurice Frost, Wm. Clowes Ltd., London, 1961

B: *Baptist Hymnal Companion*, Hugh Martin, Psalms & Hymns Trust, London, 1962

CH²: *Handbook to the Church Hymnary*, James Moffatt (1930) rev. Millar Patrick (1936), Oxford University Press, London. (Possess rev. ed.)

CP: *Companion to Congregational Praise*, K. L. Parry and Erik Routley, Tavistock Bookshop, 86 Tavistock Place, London WH1H 9RT, 1953

M: *The Methodist Hymn Book Illustrated*, John Telford, Epworth Press, London, 1936
The Music of the Methodist Hymn Book, James T. Lightwood (1935) with additional material by F. B. Westbrook (1955). Epworth Press

M*: *A Short Companion to Hymns & Songs*, John Wilson,

privately printed 1970; Epworth Press or from the author, 30 East Meads, Guildford, England, GU2 5SP

(b) *Other Hymnals*

American

The Story of our Hymns (Hymnal of the Evangelical & Reformed Church), Armin Haeussler, Eden Publishing House, 1952 (very full and informative)

Hymns of our Faith (Baptist Hymnal, 1956), W. J. Reynolds, Broadman Press, 1964 (especially useful for identifying 'Gospel Songs')

A Short Companion to Westminster Praise (1976), Erik Routley, Hinshaw Music Inc., 1977

English

Hymns Ancient & Modern, Historical Edition, W. H. Frere, 1909. Now rare, being the original from which Frost (above) was revised, but basic; it contains full texts of hymn tunes, which Frost does not.

Songs of Praise Discussed (Songs of Praise, 1931 ed.), P. Dearmer and Archibald Jacob, Oxford University Press, 1933: the most readable and witty of all *Companions*

Companion to the School Hymnal of the Methodist Church, W. S. Kelynack, Epworth Press, 1950 (useful for unusual children's hymns)

Companion to the Baptist Church Hymnal (of 1933), Hugh Martin, Psalms & Hymns Trust, 1953

★   ★   ★

A NOTE ON HYMNS ANCIENT AND MODERN

In the material that follows, no hymnal is mentioned more often than *Hymns Ancient and Modern*, and for the sake of American readers a note about the place of this collection in the history of hymnody is probably not out of place.

Briefly: *Hymns Ancient and Modern* was the first successful hymnal of the *Oxford Movement* (see entry 83); it was the first widely used hymnal to print tunes alongside the hymns; it was almost the first, and certainly the first widely used hymnal to place *Amen* after every hymn (a custom now abandoned by its own communion and due for abandonment by all), and very often the tunes it set to hymns have remained with them in England, and the alterations their editors made to texts (which earned them the name of Hymns Asked for and Mutilated) have often become standard. It is also by far the longest-lived hymn book title, having survived through all its revised editions.

Hymns A & M, as we always call it, was a project founded by Sir Henry Baker (101) in 1858, and its first fruit was a trial edition of 160 hymns published in 1859 or early 1860. The first full music edition was of 273 hymns in 1861. Thereafter its bibliographical history is as follows:

First edition with supplement (total 386), 1868

Second edition wholly revised (473), 1875

Second Edition with Supplement (638), 1889
(I.e., ## 1-473 as before, with a Supplement 474-638 arranged in the same order)

Third Edition, wholly revised, 1904: 643 hymns

(This was the edition with which Frere's important *Historical Edition*, mentioned above, was associated)

Second Edition with First and Second Supplements, 1922
(The Third Edition having been judged unsuccessful, a Second Supplement to the 1889 edition was published separately in 1916 and bound in with it, the whole undergoing some musical revision, in 1922. The result was three series: 1-473; 474-638 and 639-779, all series being arranged in the same order)

Fourth Edition, called *Hymns Ancient and Modern Revised* (AMR), 1950: 636 hymns: total revision, although the numeration of many well known hymns was cunningly left unchanged from 1889 and 1875. Hereafter the 1922 edition was called *Hymns A & M, Standard Edition* (AMS)

In 1969 the Proprietors of *Hymns A & M* (they are never officially called Editors, but Proprietors and Assessors) issued *100 Hymns for To-day*, as an 'updating' supplement, which although it has its own name is part of the dynasty.

At the time of writing (1977) the 1922 and 1950 editions are still current.

★　★　★

A NOTE ON THE RELATIONS BETWEEN ENGLISH AND AMERICAN HYMN SINGING CUSTOMS AND THE IMPORTANCE OF WILLIAM GARRETT HORDER

The story of the relations between hymn singing customs in England and America falls broadly into the following historical sections.

(1) Between 1620 and 1776 successive waves of immigrants went from Britain to America to form the 'New World.' The earliest of these were idealistic Puritans who established a religious society in New England that was predominantly Congregationalist in style, and during the Colonial period used metrical psalmody for its public praise. Ainsworth's *Psalter* of 1612, compiled against a background of Dutch Puritanism, came over with the Pilgrim Fathers; in 1638 the *Bay Psalm Book*, a somewhat simpler and more manageable version, was the first book to be published on American soil (the 'Bay' being Massachusetts Bay). Episcopals used the Old Version of the Psalter (1562) or, when it was published, Tate & Brady's New Version of 1696 (see 323, 76). With one exception, no hymnody, nothing that has survived in present-day use, comes from this part of the U.S.A. before 1776. The exception is 'Great God of wonders,' by Samuel Savies, who died in 1761, which is known to the English now but not to the Americans.

But in 1735 John Wesley appeared in Georgia to establish his mission at Savannah, and produced in 1737 his Charlestown Hymn Book, which was the first hymnal (distinct from Psalter) to be published in America. Although this enterprise was the foundation of American Methodism, it remained local for two or three generations and its hymnody was not widely influential.

(2) The sociological development of the United States was totally unaffected by the Declaration of Independence, and 1776 is no more, in our story, than a convenient dividing date. But it was only after the Declaration that American hymnody began to develop independently of European influences; perhaps it is more accurate to say that after 1776 there was less importing of hymnody, more writing of hymnody by Americans, than before. The hymnody of the 19th century may be studied under four distinct heads.

(i) The developing 'Boston' style, which appeared when the psalm-singing Puritans, by now often Unitarians, began to write their own hymns in the high literary style which they had developed. Section 18 of the *Panorama* contains many examples of this style. Episcopals contributed to this, but on a smaller scale.

(ii) The Negro Spiritual, which is hardly an indigenous style, but certainly generated indigenous sacred song; this seems to have developed among negro slaves who found in evangelical religion a much needed solace. See 223 below for this.

(iii) The Southern Folk Hymnody, which is the hymnody of a social group very different from the New Englanders. This, which relied heavily on 18th century English evangelical and Calvinist hymnody for its texts, produced a musical heritage, closely associated with the Celtic styles of Scotland and Ireland, which has been shared with wider Christian groups only since about 1955. The people who generated this were whites, mostly English and Scottish, not a few of them victims of the Highland Clearances, who, having served their indentures with white masters in New England or Virginia (a condition sometimes hardly distinguishable from slavery) sought their own fortunes by going south, and ended up on one side or the other of the Southern Appalachians, that is, in N. Carolina or E. Tennessee. They were too poor ever to be slave-owners themselves, and existed on small holdings either in the unpromising countryside of N. Carolina, which has now become an unusually civilized state, or in the Appalachian valleys. (For a study of the origins of the Tennessee settlers, see *Neighbour and Kin*, by Elmore Matthews, Nashville University, 1971.) Their worship style has a good deal in common with that of Wales in the period 1850-1930 and their music mostly suggests Scottish folk song (See Amazing Grace, 37, for the most celebrated example of their style: an 18th century English hymn set to a clearly Scottish tune which was unknown until the music of these tiny inbred communities was released about twenty years ago).

(iv) The Gospel Song, the only truly American invention in hymnody, represents the fourth class, and was generated by the Second Evangelical Awakening of 1859, running in full spate by about 1870.

During the 19th century American hymnody was virtually unknown to the English, *Hymns Ancient and Modern* in 1861 included two American hymns in its collection (676 and 738 in our list). The first American hymnody to be widely heard in Britain was certainly class (iv) above, the Gospel Songs brought to Britain by the missions of Ira D. Sankey and Dwight L. Moody about 1872. Possibly British people were led to think that this represented all that the U.S.A. had to offer; certainly no more than a trickle of American hymnody entered the British vocabulary before 1884.

The fact that 'It came upon the midnight clear,' 'O little town of Bethlehem' and 'City of God,' to name but three, are among the favourite hymns of the English now is really due to the work of William Garrett Horder, an editor whose name will occur very frequently in the following pages.

Horder was born in 1838 at Salisbury, England, and ordained into the Congregationalist church in England, serving at St. Helens, Lancs (1866), Torquay (1869), Wood Green, London, 20 years from 1873, Bradford, Yorks, 1893, and Ealing (London) 1906. He was given the honorary D.D. by Howard University, Washington, D.C., in 1897 and died in 1919.

His chief interest was hymnology, and his first hymnal was *Congregational Hymns*, 1884, to which in 1889 he published a Companion called *The Hymn Lover*. This contained 841 hymns, of which a very large number were American. He reissued it with a Supplement (numbered from 1001 to 1242) in 1896 under the title of *A Treasury of Hymns*, including many more American pieces, especially the later work of F. L. Hosmer and that version of 'Once to every man and nation' (see 585 and *Panorama 370*) which has now become so famous. Finally he produced an edition with music called *Worship Song* in 1905, which reduced the contents to 803, but introduced about 25 pieces which were in neither of the previous books. He also issued in 1894 *A Treasury of American Sacred Song* and revised and enlarged that in 1900.

Now this work might have gone unacknowledged by any but the more liberal groups in Congregationalism had it not been that Percy Dearmer knew and admired Horder's work. But this meant that the *English Hymnal* of 1906, which did so much in other ways to enlarge the vocabulary of English hymn singers, included 32 hymns by 23 American authors, and by associating them with often excellent and appropriate tunes ensured that they would become popular in Britain. (The tunes chosen by Horder were sometimes enough to kill any hymn stone dead.) *Hymns Ancient and Modern* by 1906 (if we discount the 1904 edition which by then had not made much impact) permitted only six American hymns to be sung in its constituency. The result, however, of Dearmer's work was that in later generations we find the following figures: *Hymns Ancient and Modern* had in 1950 14 hymns by 11 American authors and Congregational Praise in 1951 has 45 by 32 American authors. Later English books show an increasing respect for American hymnody but it was Horder who began it.

All Horder's work was devoted, of course, to category (i) above, the educated New England style. For obvious reasons, Negro Spirituals do not yet appear in English books (there are a very few exceptions to that) and the mediation of the Southern Folk style to Britain must, in a much later era, be credited to Elizabeth Poston who first introduced it in her *Cambridge Hymnal*, 1967. Yet the tune PLEADING SAVIOR which appears in the *English Hymnal*, 1906 is actually from this background— a very early escape.

The use by English and Scottish editors of 'Gospel Songs' has always been a matter of debate and difficulty. Except for 'Rescue the Perishing,' *Hymns A & M* would never touch them. The *English Hymnal* included a few (one by Fanny Crosby herself) in a special section of Mission Hymns; other books tended to segregate them in this fashion. Horder had no interest in them. But in Britain the use of books very largely devoted to that style remains so common among certain groups that any who wanted it would be able to find it in abundance, and plenty of hymns by the great Gospel Song writers have been known in England for a hundred years. Only the Baptists and Methodists used them to any extent in their standard hymnals.

★　★　★

SIGNS AND ABBREVIATIONS

* - in index numbers: a *Supplement* to the parent book indicated by the initial
† - death, or died

Sch. - educated
Ord. - ordained (2 dates, where relevant, deacon/priest)
‡ - in index numbers, draws attention to important textual variant mentioned in entry above
Gbch - *Gesangbuch* (German for Hymn Book)
other verbal abbreviations are self-explanatory

ENGLISH COUNTIES. Social change has played havoc with topography in Britain. The counties are not now either part of a postal address or units of local government, and the names of several have been altered where two or three have been grouped. The traditional names, however, will continue to be a useful means of identifying a general area. English counties are usually mentioned, except where the city is a large and famous one; most of them have conventional abbreviations as set out below. The rest are written out in full, as are the Welsh and Scottish counties where they are mentioned.

BEDS - Bedfordshire
BERKS - Berkshire (pronounced *Barkshire*)
BUCKS - Buckinghamshire
CAMBS - Cambridgeshire
CHES - Cheshire
CUMB - Cumberland
DERBS - Derbyshire (pronounced *Darbyshire*)
GLOS - Gloucestershire (pronounced *Glostershire*)
HANTS - Hampshire
HEREFS - Herefordshire (pronounced *Herryfordshire*)
HERTS - Hertfordshire (*Hartfordshire*)
HUNTS - Huntingdonshire
LANCS - Lancashire
LEICS - Leicestershire (*Lestershire*)
LINCS - Lincolnshire
MIDDX - Middlesex
NFK - Norfolk
NORTHANTS - Northamptonshire
NOTTS - Nottinghamshire
OXON - Oxfordshire
SALOP - Shropshire
SFK - Suffolk
SOM - Somerset
STAFFS - Staffordshire
WARKS - Warwickshire (*Worrickshire*)
WESTM - Westmorland
WILTS - Wiltshire
WORCS - Worcestershire (*Woostershire*)
YORKS - Yorkshire

LONDON. Before 1889 what is now called London was a network of neighbourhoods, which had their own registries of birth and death. The most authoritative source for information on births and deaths is *British Hymn Writers and Composers— A Check List*, by A. Hayden and Robert Newton (British Hymn Society, 1976). Here the district of birth or death of people who would now be assigned to London is accurately given. But since the American reader may well be puzzled by some of these names, which have often disappeared from speech and maps, we add (London), or, where the district is central, simply say London. This explains occasional differences between the information given here and that in the authoritative book.

DATES: the form used on international documents of digital dating is here used: 8 February 1977 is written as 8 ii 1977, not (as in U.S.A.) 2. 8. 77.

AN ENGLISH-SPEAKING HYMNAL GUIDE

1. A CHARGE TO KEEP I HAVE

2 st. SMD PCH 71

C. Wesley, *Short Hymns on Select Passages of Holy Scripture*, 1762; 'Keep the charge of the Lord, that ye die not. Lev. 8:35', being a versification of Matthew Henry's commentary on that passage (see *Interpreter's Bible* II p. 46). In mod. use last st. norm. altd from orig.:
assured, if I my trust betray / I shall for ever die
to: and let me ne'er my trust betray/but press to realms on high.
Now norm. in SM.

US & CAN: B407: CW373/- : M150: P -/301/- • ENG: AM702/328: An602: B461: CH518/- : M578

THE WESLEYS. CHARLES, b. Epworth, Lincs, 18 xii 1707, Sch. Westminster and Christ Church, Oxf. Founder there of the Holy Club from which eventually the Methodist Society emerged. Ord. C/E 1735. After conversion experience 21 v 1738 joined his brother John in evangelism from London '38-9, then from Bristol '39-'56. Lived at Bath '61-71, London '71-†. Travelled less than John, but visited many parts of Britain, incl. Cornwall and Newcastle upon Tyne; also trav. in Wales. Often in controversy with John since he detected in him signs of separation from C/E of which he disapproved, esp. J's presumed ordaining of presbyters, '84. Father of two famous musicians, Charles Jr., b. 1757, Samuel, b. 1766, and grandfather of Samuel Sebastian, 1810-76. The poet of the Evangelical Revival, he wrote, acc. to best sources, 8,989 religious poems of which some 6,500 are commonly regarded as hymns. † London, 29 iii 1788 (80).

JOHN, b. Epworth 17 vi 1703, Sch. Charterhouse and Christ Church, Oxf. Tutor, Lincoln Coll., Oxf., '29-'35: Fellow, '26-'51. Took charge of Georgia (U.S.A.) Mission, '35 where he pub. first hymn book to be printed in America (earlier books were metrical psalm books); resigned '37 & returned to Eng. His conversion experience, 24 v '38, was largely due to his contacts with Moravians (see ZINZENDORF), whom he met in journey from America. Thereafter he instituted his historic evangelical mission wh. took him to every part of Britain. Founded Methodist system, but never personally wished to separate from C/E despite danger signals which alarmed Charles. Is not thought to have written original hymns, but made many trs. from German, most of wh. he did before Charles began writing. † London, 2 iii 1791 (87).

The Wesleys produced 63 hymnals between 1738 and 1786 of wh. the 58th was *Hymns for the Use of the People Called Methodists*, 1780, which is the first Meth. h. bk. J's preface to this remains a classic and is reprinted in most later eds. Relics and documents are to be seen in Wesley's Chapel, City Road, London, the New Room, Bristol, and elsewhere.

2. A GREAT AND MIGHTY WONDER

6 st. 7.6.7.6 PCH 186

Greek: μέγα καὶ παραδόξον Θαῦμα, St Germanus.

tr. J. M. Neale, *Hymns from the Eastern Church*, 1862.

L(US) has orig. form; all others re-shape text in 7.6.7.6.6.7.6 to carry tune ES IST EIN ROS' ENTSPRUNGEN (see 848), making a refrain out of lines 2-4 of orig. st. 3 and adding it to the other 5 sts. This apart, EH has authentic text; elsewhere often altd.

US & CAN: H18: L18‡ • ENG: AM -/68: An90: B87: BB41: CH -/192: E19

GERMANUS, b. Constantinople 634; Ord. Gk. Orth.; Bp. of Cyzicus, later (712) patriarch of Constantinople. Much involved in eccl. controversy in defence of icons against papal condemnation (at this date the Pope was technically in command of Eastern Ch); just before death expelled from patriarchal office. † 734 (100), and if dates authentic, longest-lived of all hymnographers.

JOHN MASON NEALE, b. London, 24 i 1818; Sch. Sherborne Gram. Sch., Trinity, Camb.; Fellow of Downing, Camb. Ord. C/E 1842; presented to living of Crawley, Sussex, but never instituted because of breakdown in health. Warden of Sackville Coll., E. Grinstead, Sussex (a home for indigent old men) '46-†. The most learned liturgist and hymnologist of his age, esp. in medieval Latin & Greek Christian literature. Founder of mod. Engl. carol culture. His advanced Tractarian views (see 83) caused Bp. of Chichester to inhibit him from ministry for 14 years. Best known publications, in addition to above source, *Medieval Hymns* '51, *Hymnal Noted*, '52 and '54. Most frequently mentioned in this book with 45 entries. † E. Grinstead, 6 viii 1866 (48).

3. A SOVEREIGN PROTECTOR I HAVE

2 st. 8.8.8.8.D anap.

This is the norm. 16-line cento from WHAT THOUGH MY FRAIL EYELIDS REFUSE (orig. in 6 st.) in *Gospel Magazine*, 1774. Uses sts. 1b, 2b, 4. In *An* has 5 st. 8.8.8.8 beg. INSPIRER AND HEARER OF PRAYER, using sts. 4, 5a, 6.

US & CAN: • ENG: An53‡: B570: CH560/651: CP399

AUGUSTUS MONTAGUE TOPLADY, b. 4 xi 1740, Farnham, Surrey; Sch. Westminster & Trinity, Dublin. Ord. C/E 1762, Vicar of Broadhembury, Devon, then to †. Engaged in continuous & heated controversy with J. Wesley (1) whom he once called a 'low and puny tadpole in divinity,' J. W. replying that he disdained dispute with chimney-sweepers. Fanatical calvinist, well-known preacher, wrote 114 hys. plus 7 'occasional pieces' as well as voluminous religious tracts and books. Best known as author of ROCK OF AGES (623). See Appendix p. 113. † London, 11 viii 1778 (37).

4. A STRANGER ONCE DID BLESS THE EARTH

8.8.8.8.88 PCH 439

John Clare, *The Village Minstrel*, 1821, 'The Stranger', beg. 'When trouble haunts me, need I sigh?' At #272 in *Oxford Book of Christian Verse* 7 st. are given, of which st. 3, immediately preceding our cento, reads:

> Though low and poor and broken down
>   am I to think myself distrest?
> No, rather laugh where others frown
>   and think my being truly blest;
> for others I can daily see
> more worthy riches, worse than me.

Then st. 4 begins 'Aye, once a stranger blest the earth.' The hymn, first appearing as such in *BBC* (1951) uses sts. 4-7 of the poem as given in above source.

US & CAN: H*56 • ENG: AM*2: B633: BB70

JOHN CLARE, b. 13 vii 1793, Helpstone, nr. Peterborough; began work as shepherd boy at 7, later under-gardener, militiaman and brickworker. Became well known Engl. poet: *Poems Descriptive of Rural Life*, 1820, *Shepherd's Calendar*, 1827, *Rural Muse*, 1835. Mental breakdown '37 sent him for the rest of his life into an asylum. † Peterborough, 20 v 1864 (70).

5. ABIDE WITH ME, FAST FALLS THE EVENTIDE

8 st. 10 10. 10 10 PCH 128

H. F. Lyte, prob. late August 1847 (see *Julian* p. 7), *Remains*, 1850; printed leaflet (Bristol), 1863, with auth's original tune, but by that time already well known as a hymn through inclusion of 5 st. in *Hymns A & M*, 1860, and in full music ed. of 1861 with Monk's now famous tune. Orig. ms handed to a friend after Communion service, 4 ix 1847, after sermon on Luke 14.29. Norm. vn. om. sts. 3-5.

US & CAN: BP533: Can180: B217: CW38/47: H467: L576: M289: P33/64/278: Pm209: CLB493 • ENG: AM27: An500: B686: BB298: CH286/695: CP622: E363: M948

HENRY FRANCIS LYTE, b. Ednam, Roxburghshire, 1 vi 1793; Sch. Portora (Ireland), Trinity, Dublin. Ord. C/E 1815, curate at Wexford (Ireland), then '17 Marazion, Cornwall, '19 Lymington, Hants, and '23-†, Lower Brixham, Devon. *Julian* lists 87 of his hymns in common use 1890. † Nice, France, 20 xi 1847 (54).

6. ACCORDING TO THY GRACIOUS WORD

6 st. CM

J. Montgomery, *The Christian Psalmist*, 1825; Luke 23:42, 1 Cor. 11:25, 'This do in remembrance of me.'

US & CAN: BP346: CW456/324: L266: M316: P358/444/- : Pm284 ●
ENG: An367: B306: BB196: CH313/585: CP301: E300: M763

JAMES MONTGOMERY, b. Irvine, Ayrshire, 4 xi 1771; moved with parents to Gracehill Moravian Settlement, nr. Ballymena (Ireland) '79. Sch. 2 years ('85-7) Fulneck (Moravian) Seminary, Yorks. Shop-assistant in 2 places, wh. work he soon abandoned to become a journalist. In '92 joined one Gales, printer, bookseller & newspaper owner (*Sheffield Register*) in Sheffield, Yorks; when Gales left country to avoid prosecution for sedition on the part of those who disapproved his radical views, JM took over the paper ('94), changed its name to *Sheffield Iris*, and remained editor 31 years. During '94-6 twice imprisoned, once for printing a song, 'The Fall of the Bastille' in sympathy with French revolution, then for printing factual account of a riot in Sheffield. Later his radical views mellowed & he became a powerful advocate, as many of his hymns testify, of evangelical foreign mission. Retired to private literary work 1825 and became well known for poetry and articles. Wrote about 400 hymns of which 18 appear in this book. † Sheffield, 30 iv 1854 (82).

7. AGAIN AS EVENING'S SHADOWS FALL

5 st. LM-coup.

S. Longfellow, *Vespers*, 1859

US & CAN: CW139/- : P -/62/- : Pm46 ● ENG: CH275/- : CP631

SAMUEL LONGFELLOW, b. Portland, Me, 18 vi 1819; Sch. Harvard (arts & theology); Ord. Unit. '48, Fall River, Ma; Brooklyn '53, Germantown, Pa, '60. Most famous publication, *Hymns of the Spirit*, 1864, with S. Johnson (121). Also pub. life of his more famous brother, H. W. L., '86. † Portland, 3 x 1892 (73).

8. AGAIN THE LORD'S OWN DAY IS HERE

5 st. LM-coup.

Latin: EN DIES EST DOMINICA, poem of 116 lines found in Karlsruhe ms., 15 c., but resembling, and poss. based on, earlier poem by St Thomas à Kempis (402)

Tr. J. M. Neale (2), *Hymnal Noted*, II, 1854, beg. THE SUNDAY MORN AGAIN IS HERE; version now familiar is by compilers of *Hymns A & M*, 1860, based on Neale.

US & CAN: ● ENG: AM35/40: An67: PL18

9. AH, HOLY JESUS, HOW HAST THOU OFFENDED?

5 st. 11 11. 11 5   **PCH 191**

German: HERZLIEBSTER JESU, WAS HAST DU VERBROCHEN? J. Heermann, *Devoti Musica Cordis*, 1630, based on *Meditations* VII, attr. to Augustine.

Par. R. Bridges, *Yattendon Hymnal*, 1899. (Tr. MY LOVING SAVIOUR . . . in NCH and CLB).

US & CAN: BP175: Can443: CW -/162: H71: L85: M412: P158/191/280: Pm163: CLB265: W6 ● ENG: An151: B137: BB500: CH -/251: CP775: E70: M177: PL175

JOHANN HEERMANN, b. 11 x 1585 Raudten; Sch. Wohlau, Fraustedt, Breslau, Brieg; Ord. Luth. 1611; Köben 1611-34, but ill health prevented his preaching after '23; † Posen 17 ii 1647.

ROBERT SEYMOUR BRIDGES, b. 23 xi 1844, Walmer; Sch. Eton & Corp. Chr., Oxf; qualified as physician & practised until '82, after wh. devoted himself to literature. Poet Laureate 1913-†. Most celebrated poetical work, *The Testament of Beauty* (1929). Pub. *Yattendon Hymnal* for parish ch. of Yattendon, Berks, wh. marked a new standard in scholarship for hymnody & had much influence on *English Hymnal* (see 88). † 21 iv 1930 (85).

10. ALAS, AND DID MY SAVIOUR BLEED?

6 st. CM

I. Watts, *Hymns & Sacred Songs*, 1707, Bk II; 'Godly Sorrow arising from the Sufferings of Christ.' Norm. vn. omits st. 2. Some U.S. bks (as *B*) use 4 st. only, adding to each a refrain by R. E. Hudson (1885).

US & CAN: BP183: B157‡: L486: M415: P249/199/- : W7 ● ENG: CP130

ISAAC WATTS, b. 17 vii 1674, Southampton; Sch. there and at Dissenting Academy of Th., Rowe (London). Many of his hymns were written 1694-6 at home. Spent 6 yrs, 1694-1700, as tutor to family of Sir John Hartopp at Freeby, Leics; Ord. Congl. 1702 Mark Lane Chapel, London (soon removed to Bury Street); illness 1712 made him unfit for full pastoral duties, so took up residence with family of Sir Thomas Abney at Theobalds, Herts '12-35, Stoke Newington (nr. London) '35-†. Auth. of many books, incl. *Improvement of the Mind*, 1741, and *Logic*, 1742; devotional works, incl. *Guide to Prayer*; 4 books of poetry & hymns— *Horae Lyricae*, 1705 (mostly not hymns), *Hymns & Spiritual Songs*, 1707, *Divine & Moral Songs for Children*, 1715, *The Psalms of David Imitated in the Language of the New Testament*, 1719. Sometimes called the Father of English hymnody; better, the liberator. Others before him had wrtn. New Testament hymns, but his were the first to gain wide acceptance in face of the official prohibition of any congregational song but metr. psalms; and the high quality of the best of them far outran anything done earlier. Total output was about 760 hymns of wh. *Julian* (1891) lists no fewer than 454 as in common use. † Stoke Newington, 25 xi 1748 (74).

11. ALL AS GOD WILLS, WHO WISELY HEEDS

CM   **PCH 362**

J. G. Whittier. The selections in BB and M below are from the poem *My Psalm* in *The Panorama and Other Poems*, 1856, using sts. 11-17, i.e. the last 7 of the poem. That in *CP* below uses sts. 11-12 and then sts. 16, 17, 19, and 20 from *The Eternal Goodness*, wh. appeared in *A Tent on the Beach, and Other Poems* (1867). Other centos from this poem are mentioned at (818). The homogeneous 7 st. vn. was first used by W. Garrett Horder in his *Congregational Hymns*, 1884.

US & CAN: ● ENG: BB1: CP407‡: M629

JOHN GREENLEAF WHITTIER, b. 17 xii 1807, Haverhill, Ma.; little formal ed.; poet & journalist, much involved in earlier years in speech and writing in support of abolition of slavery; regarded as second only to H. W. Longfellow in popularity in US. After 1866 settled at Amesbury, Ma. By inheritance he was a Quaker, and throughout his life cultivated their dress & speech. † 7 ix 1892, Hampton Falls, N.H. (84).

12. ALL BEAUTIFUL THE MARCH OF DAYS

3 st. CMD

F. W. Wile, *Unity Hymns & Carols*, ed. W. C. Gannett, 1911; wrtn. for First Unitarian Ch., Rochester, N.Y., at request of Gannett who was its minister for 'a winter hymn'.

US & CAN: Can388: CW588/- : M33: P471/96/281: Pm456 ● ENG:

FRANCES WHITMARSH WILE, b. Rochester, N. Y., 1878, lived most of her life there as a member of the Unitarian ch; writer, champion of women's rights, and, in later years, advocate of theosophy. Her husband, Abram Wile, was a teacher and for some years Sec. of the Young Men's Hebrew Ass'n. in Rochester. † Rochester 1939.

13. ALL CREATURES OF OUR GOD AND KING

7 st. 88.4.4.88.44.444

Italian: St. Francis of Assisi, 'Canticle of the Sun' in prose, tr. W. H. Draper, some time between 1906 & 1916; first app. in *Public School Hymn Book*, 1919 with tune LASST UNS ERFREUEN for wh. it was written (see 832). The orig. text clearly owes much to the *Benedicite*.

US & CAN: BP72: Can 1: B9: CW157/34: L173: M60: P -/100/282: Pm64: CLB423: W8 ● ENG: AM -/172: An251: B1: BB2: CH13/30: CP31:

E*299/84: M28: NC2: PL261

FRANCIS OF ASSISI, b. 1182, Assisi, s. of Pietro Bernardone; after an aristocratic upbringing recovery from a severe illness at 25 caused him to embrace ascetic life, out of which he formed a circle of men vowed to poverty, who became the Franciscan Order. Esp. celebrated for his love of nature in all its forms. When threatened with blindness near the end of his life he submitted to a cauterizing operation with the words, 'Brother Fire, you are beautiful and strong: be gentle with me.' † Assisi, 1226 (42).

WILLIAM HENRY DRAPER, b. Kenilworth, Warks, 19 xii 1855; Sch. Keble, Oxf., Ord. C/E 1880: Alfreton, (Staffs) Shrewsbury, (Salop) and, 1899-1919, Adel, Leeds; Master of the Temple, London (the chapel of the Inns of Court) 1919-30; Vicar of Axbridge, Som., '30-†. Musician and scholar, wrote a number of hymns of wh. this is the most famous. † Clifton, Bristol, 9 viii 1933 (77).

14. ALL GLORY BE TO GOD ON HIGH

4 st. 8.7.8.7.88.7

Low German: ALLEIN GOD IN DER HOGE SY ERE, N. Decius in Rostock *Gbch*, 1525.

High German: ALLEIN GOTT IN DER HOH' SEI EHR, in V. Schumann's *Gbch*, 1539, where it is associated with the tune now universally used with it. Text is framed on the liturgical canticle *Gloria in excelsis Deo*.

Tr. C. Winkworth, *Chorale-Book for England*, 1863.

US & CAN: CW -/58: L132: P -/-/283: Pm 2 ● ENG:

NICOLAUS DECIUS, birth date unknown, was a Catholic monk who under influence of Luther became an evangelical preacher in Stettin, Germany, where † 1525.

CATHERINE WINKWORTH, b. Saffron Walden, Essex, 13 ix 1827, lived for a time at Alderley Edge, near Manchester, and later in Bristol. Chiefly known for the many trslns. of German hymns which introduced German hymnody to England for the first time on a wide scale. These are in *Lyra Germanica* (2 vols. 1855, 1858) and *The Chorale Book for England* (1863), in wh. alone music is provided, and where some earlier trslns. appear revised to accommodate correct German meters. The idea of producing this musical edn., in wh. the music was edited by Sterndale Bennett and Otto Goldschmidt (husband of the singer Jenny Lind)—who were respectively the best English composer and the best English musicologist available—came from the Baron Bunsen, German Ambassador to England, 1841-54. The frequency with which she appears in these pages indicates the extent to which she made German hymnody part of English worship: among the pieces in the 1863 book for the first time are 'Now thank we all our God' and 'Praise to the Lord, the Almighty'. In '62 she moved to Bristol and became one of the founders of Clifton High School for Girls. She pub. *Christian Singers of Germany*, 1869, and † on a visit to Monnetin, Savoy, 1 vii 1878 (50).

15. ALL GLORY, LAUD AND HONOUR

9 st. 7.6.7.6

Latin: GLORIA LAUS ET HONOR, Theodulph of Orléans, in 78 lines of elegiac couplets, poss. wrtn. in prison at Angers, c. 820.

Tr. J. M. Neale (2), *Hymnal Noted* II 1854, orig. beg. 'Glory and laud and honour' and containing the verse, bracketed and never meant to be sung but rendering part of the orig. poem:

> Be thou, O Lord, the rider
>   and we the little ass,
>   that to God's holy city
>   together we may pass.

Neale notes that this was sung in Latin until 17c, but in his own time might 'produce a smile'. In *Medieval Hymns*, 1851, JMN made an earlier trsln., in orig. metre, in 2-line sts. thus:

Glory and honour and laud be to thee, King Christ the Redeemer!
       Children before whose steps raised their Hosannas of praise.

This is an English version of elegiac couplets, and his hymn, like the

orig., was designed to be sung with that opening st. repeated after all the others. This is preserved, with alts., at *AMR* 598. But in *Hymns A & M*, 1861, which invented the altd. first line, this stanza-chorus form was transferred to the 7.6.7.6 version, and the German tune now inseparable from it in Engl. use was associated with it, so that the stanzas are 7.6.7.6D, with half a stanza, and half the tune, at the end. While this was not exactly JMN's purpose in his 7.6.7.6 version it does actually preserve the ancient way of singing the hymn; not all hymnals now adopt it.

US & CAN: BP240: Can447: B39: CW221/155: H62: L74: M424: P146/187/284: Pm155: CLB253: W9 ● ENG: AM98 (AM -/598‡) An166: B114: BB77: CH91/233: CP120: E622: M84: NC2: PL261

THEODULPH OF ORLEANS was born in Italy but brought to France by Charlemagne († 814); he was suspected by Louis the Pious, Charlemagne's successor, of conspiracy against him, and imprisoned; legend says that as the King was passing the prison in the Palm Sunday procession he heard Theodulph singing this song from within, and was so well pleased that he ordered his release. That the plainsong tune preserved at *AMR* 598 is what he sang is improbable—but some such melody as that will have been used with the hymn as soon as it came into liturgical use. Theodulph at the time of his death, 821 A.D., was Bishop of Orléans.

16. ALL HAIL, ADORED TRINITY

4 st. LM

Latin: AVE COLENDA TRINITAS, anon., c. 11c, Anglo-Saxon origin, Trinity Office.

Tr. J. D. Chambers, *Lauda Sion*, Pt. 1, 1857 and incl. in *Hymns A & M*, 1861.

US & CAN: ● ENG: AM158/617: An228: E633

JOHN DAVID CHAMBERS, b. London, 1805; Sch. Oriel, Oxf.; called to the bar 1831, Recorder of New Sarum (Salisbury, Wilts), 1842. The above was his most important pubn., being trs. of ancient Latin hymns in successive vols., 1857-66. † Westminster (London), 22 viii 1893 (88).

17. ALL HAIL THE POWER OF JESUS' NAME

8 st. CM   **PCH 84**

E. Perronet, 1st st. with tune MILES LANE, *Gospel Magazine*, Nov. 1779; whole text in G. M. Apr. 1780. Most hyls. contain sel. of 5, 6 or 7 sts.; many end with that beginning 'O that with younder sacred throng' which is the last st. in a revision made by John Rippon in his *Selection of Hymns*, 1787. Text often altd. in details but *EH* has 7 st. in the nearest vn. to Perronet's original. (NOTE: the first line is often quoted, and even printed '. . . OF JESU'S NAME'; this is grammatically impossible. The form JESU is the vocative, a transliteration of that case in Greek: the genitive is the same in Greek as the nominative: in English an apostrophe *after* the Name is admissible, but not before its last letter.) The American tune CORONATION first app. in *Union Harmony*, 1793.

US & CAN: Can42: B42: CW253/284: H355: L426: M73: P192/132/284-5: Pm196: CLB453: W10 ● ENG: AM300/217: An265: B180: BB118: CH139/382: CP163: E364: M91: NC4

EDWARD PERRONET, b. Sundridge, Kent, c. 1726 where his father was Vicar and an enthusiastic collaborator with the Wesleys; he and his brother were Methodist preachers in 1746, but by '57 he had separated from the Methodists, and he later became minister of a Congl. ch. in Canterbury, where he was when he wrote this hymn. † 2 i 1792.

18. ALL MY HEART THIS NIGHT REJOICES

15 st. 8.33.6D

German FRÖHLICH SOLL MAIN HERZE SPRINGEN, P. Gerhardt, *Praxis Pietatis Melica*, 1653.

Tr. C. Winkworth (14) in 10 st., *Lyra Germanica* II, 1858. Norm. abr. to 6 st. or fewer. A free paraphrase of this text, 'Hearts at Christmas time were jolly', by P. Dearmer (88) is in *Songs of Praise*, 1931.

US & CAN: CW186/- : H32: L26: M379: P125/172/287: Pm 123: CLB221: W12 ● ENG: An92: B88: BB501: CH41/171: CP81: M121

PAULUS GERHARDT, b. Gräfenheinichen, nr. Wittenberg, 12 iii 1607; Sch. Univ. Wittenberg. Lived as tutor in Berlin until appointed chief pastor (Lutheran) at Mittenwalde, nr. Berlin, 1657. Archdeacon, Lübben, '69-†. Wrote 123 hymns, and is second only to Luther in the affection of German hymn singers. Many of the hymns used by J. S. Bach in his two Passions and in the Cantatas are his. † Lübben, 7 vi 1676 (69).

19. ALL MY HOPE ON GOD IS FOUNDED

5 st. 8.7.8.7.77   **PCH 200**

German: MEINE HOFFNUNG STEHET FESTE, J. Neander, pub. posth. in *Joachimi Neandri Glaub- und Liebesübung*, 1680, as a 'Grace before Meat'.

Par. R. Bridges (9), this being one of the German treasures that C. Wink-worth (14) missed. His vn. departs from orig. after st. 1. First appeared in *Yattendon Hymnal*, 1899.

US & CAN: BP104: Can134: CW354/20: Pm339 ● ENG: AM*3: B492: BB299: CH448/405: CP417: E*73: M70: PL278

JOACHIM NEANDER, b. Bremen, 1650, and Sch. there; Rector of Latin School, Düsseldorf, '74; but his zeal for pietism offended the Reformed school authorities, and he was suspended; lived for some months in a cave near Mettman on the Rhine, still called Neander's cave; appointed second preacher at St Martin's, Bremen, '79, but soon fell ill with tuberculosis and † Bremen, 1680, aged about 30. He wrote some 60 hymns and composed tunes for some of them.

20. ALL PEOPLE THAT ON EARTH DO DWELL

4 st. LM-alt.   **PCH 7**

W. Kethe, in *Anglo-Genevan Psalter*, 1561 & taken into the first English metrical psalter (the 'Old Version' of Sternhold & Hopkins) as Ps. 100. Wrtn. in imitation of Ps. 100 in *Genevan Psalter*, 1551, same meter but not same rhyme-scheme (Gen Psr. has LM-coup), to carry tune of Genevan Ps. 134 wh. therefore came in Engl. use to be called OLD HUNDREDTH.

Scot. Psalter 1650 altd. 'mirth' in st. 1 to 'fear,' and 'The Lord, ye know' to 'Know that the Lord' in st. 2. Doxology in EH, made very familiar through the festive setting of R. Vaughan Williams made for the Coronation of Queen Elizabeth II in 1953, is spurious, and it is a pity that R. V. W. gave it such wide currency.

US & CAN: BP42: Can12: B17: CW -/17: H278: L169: M21: P 1/24/288: Pm4: W14 ● ENG: AM166: An231: B2: BB450: CH229/1: CP 1: E365: M2: NC7: PL 11

WILLIAM KETHE, birth date unknown, was among Engl. Protestants exiled to Geneva and prominent member of John Calvin's congregation which during the period 1553-8 included many English people. Employed as envoy from Geneva to other Brit. congregations in Europe. Chaplain to the forces 1563 and 1569; therefore assumed to be Ord. C/E; Rector of Childe Okeford, Dorset. Contributed 25 psalms to *Old Version*, 1562, all of wh. were taken into Scot. Psr. 1564. But only this one came direct from France, being based on the French text of Theodore Beza. All Kethe's psalms except this one were ejected from the *Scot. Psalter* 1650. † prob. at Childe Okeford, 1594.

21. ALL POOR MEN AND HUMBLE

3 st. 66.8.66.8 anap.

Welsh: O DEUED POB CRISTION, anonymous.

Tr. K. E. Roberts, in *Oxford Book of Carols*, 1928, there set as one stanza to accommodate the Welsh tune. A second st. of same length added in CP by W. T. Pennar Davies.

US & CAN: Can417: P -/-/289 ● ENG: An94: CH -/185: CP721‡

KATHARINE EMILY ROBERTS, b. 1877, Leicester, Sch. Private; studied

singing in London & Paris; m. R. E. Roberts (839); became organizing Sec. Rutland Rural Community Council; writer of plays, pageants and a *History of Peterborough*. † Ashford, Middx., 12 iv 1962.

WILLIAM THOMAS PENNAR DAVIES, b. 1911, Aberpennar, Glamorgan; Sch. in Wales, Yale and Mansfield, Oxf.; Ord. Congl. (Wales); Minster Road, Cardiff 1943; Prof. Ch. Hist., Bala-Bangor Theol. Coll., N. Wales, '46; Vice-Principal, '50, Principal, '52, Memorial Coll., Brecon; Principal, Memorial Coll., Swansea, '59 (former institution removed). Welsh bard, poet and historian, and a leader in the revival of Welsh language and literature.

22. ALL PRAISE TO THEE, FOR THOU, O KING DIVINE . . .

5 st. 10 10 10. 4   **PCH 550**

F. Bland Tucker, 1938, pub. *Hymnal* 1940; Phil. 2:5-11. Wrtn. with tune SINE NOMINE ('For all the saints') in mind, but set otherwise on first pubn. and elsewhere.

US & CAN: Can107: B43: CW -/59: H366: M74: P -/-/290: Pm147: W15 ● ENG: AM*4: An253: B198: BB119: CH -/297: CP197: M*2

FRANCIS BLAND TUCKER, b. Norfolk, Va., 1895; Sch. Univ. Virginia, Virginia Theol. Sem; Ord. Episc., 1918/20; Rector of Grammer Parish, Va., '20; St. John's, Georgetown, Va., '25; Old Christ Ch., Savannah, Ga. (the parish served by J. Wesley), '45. Member of ed. cttee, *Hymnal 1940*, and the most sought-after author introduced by that hymnal.

ALL PRAISE TO THEE, MY GOD, THIS NIGHT
ALL PRAISE TO THEE, WHO SAFE HAST KEPT   see (63)

23. ALL THINGS ARE THINE: NO GIFT HAVE WE

5 st. LM-coup.

J. G. Whittier (11), for dedication of Plymouth Congl. Ch. in St. Paul, Minn., 1873; pub. *Hazel Blossoms*, 1875; introd. to Eng. by W. G. Horder in *Congl. Hymns*, 1884; the only hymn in common use by Whittier which was designed for congl. singing. St. 5 now always om. (Pm has st. 1 only).

US & CAN: CW606/262: H227: L244: M347: P475/313/- : Pm537‡ ● ENG: An658: CH254/610: E173

24. ALL THINGS BRIGHT AND BEAUTIFUL

7 st. 7.6.7.6 troch. and 7.6.7.6 iamb.   **PCH 308**

C. F. Alexander, *Hymns for Little Children, 1848* on the 2nd clause of the Apostles' Creed: 'Maker of heaven and earth.' The st. beginning 'The rich man in his castle' (3) survives in AM-S, but is elsewhere omitted.

US & CAN: BP105: Can86: CW -/2: H311: M34: P -/456/-: Pm478 CLB430: W17 ● ENG: AM573/442: An233: B733: BB3: CH18/154: E587: M851: CP684

CECIL FRANCES ALEXANDER (nee Humphreys), b. 1818, Redcross, Co. Wicklow (Ireland); m. 1850 Rev. William Alexander who became Bp. of Derry 1867 and (after her death) Abp. Armagh '96. She is the author of many celebrated children's hymns, all of wh. appeared in the source above (before her marriage); but she continued to write & publish later—see (626) † Derry (Londonderry), 12 x 1895.

25. ALL WHO LOVE AND SERVE YOUR CITY

6 st. 8.7.8.7   **PCH 504**

E. R. Routley, 1966 at Dunblane, Scotland; pub. *Dunblane Praises* II, 1967 and *New Songs for the Church* I, 1969; Luke 19:41; John 9:4; Ezek. 48:35. One orig. st. always om.

US & CAN: Can168: H*1: P -/-/293 ● ENG: B*3: M*3: CP*1

ERIK (REGINALD) ROUTLEY, b. Brighton, 31 x 1917; Sch. Lancing, Magdalen and Mansfield, Oxf; Ord. Congl., Wednesbury, Staffs, '43; Dartford, '45; Lecturer, later Mackennal Lecturer, Ch. Hist., Mansfield Coll., '48, also chaplain from '49 and director of music from '48; Augustine-Bristo Church, Edinburgh, '59; St. James's, Newcastle upon Tyne,

'67. President, Congregational Ch. in Eng. and Wales, '70-1; Chairman, Doctrine & Worship Cttee., United Reformed Church from foundation '72 to '74. Visiting Director of Music, Princeton Theol. Sem., U.S.A. Jan-June '75; Prof. Ch. Music, Westminster Choir Coll., Princeton, N.J. '75. Chief ed. consultant, *Cantate Domino*, '68-74; ed. *University Carol Book*, '61; joint-ed., *Hymns for Celebration*, '74; ed. *Westminster Praise*, '76.

26. ALL YE WHO SEEK A COMFORT SURE (CERTAIN CURE) (FOR SURE RELIEF)

5 st. CM

Latin, QUICUNQUE CERTUM QUAERITIS, 5 st. LM, uncertainly ascr. to Prudentius but not found earlier than *Roman Breviary* (Lisbon), 1786, where it is appointed for the Office of the Sacred Heart.

Tr. E. Caswall, *Lyra Catholica*, 1849 ('a certain cure'), later rev. in his *Hymns & Poems*, 1873 ('for sure relief') and rev. further in *Hymns A & M*, 1875 ('a comfort sure'), wh. is now the normal vn. Minor alts. introduced here & there.

US & CAN: P226/-/-: CLB430 ● ENG: AM 112/104: An466: BB289: E71: NC10: PL176

EDWARD CASWALL, b. 15 vii 1814, Yately Vicarage, Hants; Sch. Chigwell Sch., Marlborough Sch., Brasenose Oxf.; while an undergraduate pub. a satirical pamphlet—*A New Art Teaching How to be Plucked* for amusement of students ('plucked' or 'ploughed' at Oxford means failure in examination). Ord. C/E '38/39; 2 curacies in Somerset, then perpetual curate of Stratford-sub-Castle, nr. Salisbury. Resigned living '46, became R.C. '47 and joined the Oratory at Birmingham recently founded by J. H. Newman (196). On death of his wife, reordained R.C. All his hymnological work was done at the Oratory where he became one of the leading translators of Latin hymns. † at the Oratory, Edgbaston, Birmingham, 2 i 1878 (63).

27. ALLELUIA! ALLELUIA! HEARTS TO HEAVEN AND VOICES RAISE

3 st. 8.7.8.7 D

C. Wordsworth, *The Holy Year*, 1862; orig., 'HALLELUJAH! . . .' & wrtn. in 4-line sts. of 15 syllables (as set out in AM-S). St. 2 retained in *Church Hymns* (1903), otherwise om.

US & CAN: BP188: B117: CW -/175: H92: L108: Pm180 ● ENG: AM137: An178: BB98: E127

CHRISTOPHER WORDSWORTH, b. Lambeth Rectory, London, 30 x 1807; Sch. Winchester Coll., Trinity, Camb.; where became a Fellow; Head Master, Harrow, '36; Ord. C/E; Canon of Westminster '44; Bp. Lincoln '69-'84; nephew of Wordsworth the poet, and himself one of the best Anglican hymn writers of the later 19 c. † 20 iii 1885 (77).

28. ALLELUIA, SING TO JESUS

5 st. 8.7.8.7 D   **PCH 222**

W. C. Dix, *Altar Songs*, 1867; 'Redemption through the precious Blood.' St. 5 is the same as st. 1 and often om.

US & CAN: Can49: CW -/294: H347: L417: CLB463: W19 ● ENG: AM316/399: An383: B168: BB197: CH138/- : E301: PL66

WILLIAM CHATTERTON DIX, b. 14 vi 1837, Bristol; Sch. for mercantile life but after some years as manager of an insurance firm in Glasgow, Scotland, lived as a man of letters. † Cheddar, Som., 9 ix 1898 (61).

29. ALLELUIA, SONG OF SWEETNESS

4 st. 8.7.8.7.8.7

Latin: ALLELUIA DULCE CARMEN, in 11 c.ms. at Durham (England). Tr. J. M. Neale (2) in *Hymnal Noted* I, 1852. Medieval custom (preserved in some parts of the ch. today) forbade the use of the word *Alleluia* during Lent, and this hymn, a 'farewell to Alleluia' is designed for the Sunday or the day before Ash Wednesday. As late as 15 c. a ceremony of burying *Alleluia* in a coffin on Ash Wednesday was observed.

US & CAN: H54: L58 ● ENG: AM82: E63

30. ALMIGHTY FATHER OF ALL THINGS THAT BE

6 st. 10 10. 10 10   **PCH 254**

E. E. Dugmore, wrtn. 1884 for a village industrial exhibition in his parish, Parkstone (Dorset); pub. *Hymns of Adoration*, 1900. Text now used as modified in *Hymns A & M*, 1904.

US & CAN: BP475 ● ENG: B626: CH503/451: CP461

ERNEST EDWARD DUGMORE, b. Bayswater (London), 1843; Sch. Bruce Castle and Wadham, Oxf., Ord. C/E, curate St Peter's Vauxhall, London, '67; Vicar of Parkstone, Dorset, '72-1910; Canon of Salisbury, Prebendary of Gillingham Major; Warden, Salisbury Coll. of Missioners, 1910. † Salisbury 10 iii 1925.

31. ALMIGHTY FATHER, WHO DOST GIVE

4 st. LM-coup.

J. H. B. Masterman, *A Missionary Hymnbook*, 1922. In US, M and P[1,2] use sts. 2, 3, 1, beginning LIFT UP OUR HEARTS, O KING OF KINGS.

US & CAN: BP498: Can277: H530: M194‡: P405‡/481‡/- ● ENG: AM -/583: B675: CH491/508: M907

JOHN HOWARD BERTRAM MASTERMAN, b. Tunbridge Wells, Kent, 6 ii 1867; Sch. Weymouth Coll. and St John's Camb.; Ord. C/E 1894; Lect. Ch. Hist., St John's Camb., '93; Vicar of St Aubyn, Devonport (Devon) '96; Principal, Midland Clergy Coll., Edgbaston (Birmingham) '99; Warden, Queen's Coll., Birmingham, 1901; Vicar of St Michael's Coventry (later the first Coventry Cathedral) '07; Canon of Coventry '12; Vicar of St Mary le Bow, London '12; Rector of Stoke Damerel, Exeter, '22; Bp. Plymouth '23. † Devonport, 5 xi 1933 (65).

32. ALMIGHTY FATHER, WHO FOR US THY SON DIDST GIVE

4 st. 12 12. 12 12   **PCH 478**

G. B. Caird, wrtn. 1942 at Mansfield Coll., Oxf., as winning entry in the annual Scott Psalmody prize examination, the subject that year being 'a hymn on the social applications of the Gospel.' The other competitors were Pennar Davies (21) and R. T. Brooks (682) (neither with material shown in this book, although both were fine hymns). Meter was chosen at suggestion of a fellow-student (the present compiler) to carry tune ANNUE CHRISTE, to which it was set when first printed, in *Congl. Praise*, 1951.

US & CAN: Can291 ● ENG: AM*5: An591: B639: CP564

GEORGE BRADFORD CAIRD, b. Wandsworth (London), 19 vii 1917; Sch. King Edward's Sch. Birmingham, Peterhouse Camb., Mansf. Coll., Oxf.; Ord. Congl., Highgate '43; Prof. O. T., St Stephen's Coll., Edmonton, Alberta, '46; Prof. N. T. McGill Univ. Divinity School, Montreal, '50-9, and Principal, '55-9; Senior Tutor, Mansfield Coll., Oxf., '59, and Principal '70-77. Grinfield Lecturer, Univ. Oxf., '61-5. Dean Ireland Prof. N. T., Univ. Oxf. '77- . Biblical scholar, author of standard commentaries on Samuel, Luke, Revelation; many other books & articles. Member of panel of New English Bible translators.

33. ALMIGHTY GOD, THY WORD IS CAST

6 st. CM

J. Cawood, in T. Cotterill's *Selection of Psalms & Hymns*, 8th ed., 1819; norm. abr. in mod. use.

US & CAN: BP284: L196 ● ENG: An135: BB188: CH295/635

JOHN CAWOOD, b. Matlock, Derbs., 18 iii 1775, son of a small farmer; had little education but had conversion experience under a clergyman named Carsham at Sutton in Ashfield, Notts, while in his service, and entered St. Edmund Hall, Oxf. 1797. Ord. C/E 1801, curate at Ribbesford, then perpetual curate at St Anne's, Bewdley, Worcs. Intimate friend of the Havergal family (252). † Bewdley, 7 xi 1852 (77).

34. ALONE THOU GOEST FORTH, O LORD

4 st. CM   **PCH 551**

Latin: SOLUS AT VICTIMAM PROCEDIS, DOMINE, 4 st. iambic hexameters all rhymed, by P. Abélard in *Hymnarium Paraclitensis*, the hymnal he made for the convent of which Héloise was abbess, c. 1135. Tr. F. Bland Tucker (22), 1938; pub. *Hymnal-1940*. In some books, ALONE YOU JOURNEY FORTH . . . .

US & CAN: Can 454: CW -/169: H68: M427: P -/-/294: Pm159: CLB261 ● ENG: An169: B139: BB79: CH -/242

PETER ABÉLARD, b. Le Pallet, France, 1079, of the Breton aristocracy, became Lecturer in the Cathedral Sch. of Notre Dame, Paris, where he had international standing as theologian and philosopher. Controversial views (wh. today might be styled 'modernist') aroused fierce opposition. He fell in love with Héloise, niece of Fulbert (not he of Chartres mentioned at 827), a canon of Paris; he married her secretly and a son was born; the story of Fulbert's atrocious revenge, which separated them, is well known and told in many biographies. Thereafter Abélard became a monk, first founding a theological school at Nogent round his hermitage, then becoming Abbot of Gildas. His former school became then the House of the Paraclete under Héloise as Abbess. His enemies continued to hound him, and he was accused of heresy and denounced by Bernard of Clairvaux (857); he † at St. Marcel on the way to Rome to defend himself, 1142.

35. AM I A SOLDIER OF THE CROSS?

CM

I. Watts (10); this vn. is in *Sermons 1722-4*, at end of a sermon on 1 Cor. 16:13, entitled 'Holy Fortitude'; but it seems to be Watts' own revision of *Hymns . . . 1707*, I 37, in which he uses sts. 4, 7 and 8 of that hymn, transposing from 'Are we . . .' to 'Am I . . .' and adding 3 new sts. which are 2-4 in the norm. vn. now.

US & CAN: H550: L554: M239: P -/353/- ● ENG:

36. AM I MY BROTHER'S KEEPER?

3 st. 7.6.7.6 D PCH 503

John Ferguson, sent to & accepted by the second Dunblane Consultation, 1966 (cf. 25) and pubd. in *Dunblane Praises* II, 1967 and *New Songs for the Church* I, 1969. Based on Gen. 4:8-10 and Matt. 27:24-5.

US & CAN: P -/-/295: CLB500: W21 ● ENG: CP*2: E*99: PL293

JOHN (or IAN) FERGUSON, b. Manchester, 2 iii 1921; Sch. Bishop's Stortford Sch., St John's Camb.; classical scholar & prizewinner; taught at King's Coll. (now Univ.) Newcastle upon Tyne '48-53; Prof. Classics, Univ. Ibadan (Africa) '53-'66; Prof., Univ. Minnesota '66-9; Dean & Director of Studies, Open University (Gt. Britain) since '69. Chairman, Fellowship of Reconciliation since '69. Prolific author of books & articles.

37. AMAZING GRACE! HOW SWEET THE SOUND

6 st. CM

J. Newton, *Olney Hymns*, 1779; 'Faith's Review and Expectation,' 1 Chron. 16:16-17. The use of this hymn was until recently confined to evangelical congregations in Britain and to those of the Appalachian valleys in U.S. who associated the now very familiar tune with it. That tune, an American folk hymn based on a secular Scottish melody, is now indivorcible from the text, and since the late 1950's text and tune have leapt to popularity, not least through having been regularly featured in popular musical programs. Its first appearance with this tune in Britain was in *Hymns of the Faith*, 1964.

US & CAN: BP403: B165: M92: P -/275/296: CLB484: W22 ● ENG:

JOHN NEWTON, b. London, 24 vii 1725, joined his father at sea at age 11; at 17, conscripted into Royal Navy; deserted, taken back and punished; thereafter spent many years at sea with Royal and Merchant Navies, eventually commanding a ship engaged in the slave-trade. Turned to Christianity after reading *The Imitation of Christ*, by Thomas à Kempis (402), and after unsuccessfully seeking ordination from many authorities who suspected his background, eventually Ord. C/E, 1764

(aged 39), and became curate of Olney, Bucks, where he befriended William Cowper (235). Their collaboration produced *Olney Hymns* (1779) of which C. wrote 67 and N., 281. In '79 appointed Rector of St. Mary Woolnoth, London, where he remained until † 21 xii 1807 (82).

38. ANCIENT OF DAYS, WHO SITTEST THRONED IN GLORY

5 st. 11.10.11.10 PCH 389

W. C. Doane, 1886, wrtn. for the bicentennial of the granting of a charter to Albany, N. Y. (the first charter to be given to a city in the U. S.). Incl. with alterations in Episcopal *Hymnal*, 1892.

US & CAN: CW99/ -: H274: L137: M459: P58/246/297: Pm249 ● ENG:

WILLIAM CROSWELL DOANE, b. Boston, Ma., 2 iii 1832, son of G. W. Doane (197); Sch. Burlington Coll., Ord. Episc., asst at Burlington, N.J.; rector of St. John's, Hartford, Conn., then St. Peter's, New York; Bp. of Albany, 1869. Chairman of edit. cttee., *Hymnal*, 1892. † 17 v 1913 (81).

39. AND CAN IT BE THAT I SHOULD GAIN AN INTEREST IN THE SAVIOUR'S BLOOD?

6 st. 8.6.8.6.88 PCH 58

C. Wesley (1), wrtn. at Little Britain, London, May 1738 (the date of his conversion experience was 21 v 38); his journal notes that the hymn was begun on 23 May and sung, with his brother (whose conversion came on the 24th) on the 25th. First pub., *Psalms and Hymns*, 1738. It is highly probable that the tune sung 25 v 38 was VATER UNSER. In mod. use st. 5 always om. Acts 16:25.

US & CAN: BP173: CW -/241: M527 ● ENG: An 496: B426: CH110/409: CP472: M371

40. AND DID THOSE FEET IN ANCIENT TIME . . .

2 st. LMD-alt.

W. Blake, at end of Preface to his poem *Milton* (1804-8). The poem is preceded by a passage of invective against enslavement to the past, in the special shape of the classics of literature wh. he calls 'the silly Greek and Latin Slaves of the Sword.' The poem is followed by the quotation, 'Would that all the Lord's people were prophets' (Num. 11:29). The title *Jerusalem* is not in the original. In the poet's original intention the lines had no patriotic or social significance. The 'satanic Mills' are not factories but the systems of reason and logic which, in his view, smothered initiative and imagination. The long poem to which all this is a preface is regarded by most scholars as being in part unintelligible: but it is at least clear that the whole work is part of Blake's crusade against logic-chopping and sterile philosophizing, and is a major gesture in support of the romantic ideal of life.

Its subsequent history is therefore surprising. This 2-stanza fragment suddenly achieved popularity in Britain when set to music by Sir Hubert Parry (at the suggestion of Robert Bridges - 9) for a rally of Women's Institutes in the Albert Hall, London, in 1916. Since that date, which was in the darkest period of World War I, it became to all intents and purposes a second English National Anthem (or indeed, perhaps the only one, if 'God save the Queen' is allowed to be British, not only English). The original ms passed to Sir Walford Davies and is now in the possession of Mr. John Wilson, director of the Walford Davies Trust. The first regular hyl. to include it was *Songs of Praise*, 1925, but Sir Walford Davies had it in his *Students' Hymnal*, 1923.

US & CAN: Can157 ● ENG: AM -/578: BB387: CH640/487: CP754: E*100

WILLIAM BLAKE, b. 28 xi 1757, Soho (London); poet, painter, engraver, the prophet of the romantic movement in English life; all his books were engraved on copper by himself, with illustrations of his own, and bound by his wife. Hymnals contain a piece from his *Songs of Innocence* (1789) for which see (759). The early works (of which that was the first) have a tender and penetrating simplicity; the last works often dissolve into impenetrable obscurity. † London, 12 vii 1827 (69).

41. AND DIDST THOU LOVE THE RACE THAT LOVED NOT THEE?

5 st. 10.10.10.6   **PCH 286**

J. Ingelow: cento from 'On the Love of Christ' in her *Poems* (1863); first appeared as a 5 st. hymn in *Congregational Church Hymnal*, 1887.

US & CAN: P330/-/- • ENG: B140: CH144/- : CP109: M149

JEAN INGELOW, b. Boston, Lincs, 20 iii 1820, daughter of a banker; lived there or in Ipswich, Sfk, until moved to London '69. Poet, novelist and writer of very popular books for children. † Kensington (London), 20 vii 1897 (77).

42. AND NOW, BELOVED LORD, THY SOUL RESIGNING

6 st. 11.10.11.10

E. S. Alderson, 1868; pub. *Hymns A & M*, 1875. Norm. vn. now sts. 1,2, 5,6.

US & CAN: • ENG: AM121/123: CH103/250: E119

ELIZA SIBBALD ALDERSON (nee Dykes, sister of J. B. Dykes the famous ch. musician) b. Hull, Yorks, 16 viii 1818; m. 1850 Rev. W. T. Alderson, who was chaplain to Wakefield prison (Yorks), '33-76. Painter, linguist, poetess, wrote hymns all her life but early ones are lost and only 12 were printed, without date, as *Twelve Hymns*. † Heath, nr. Wakefield, 18 iii 1889 (70).

43. AND NOW, O FATHER, MINDFUL OF THE LOVE

6 st. 10.10.10.10.10 10   **PCH 249**

W. Bright, *The Monthly Packet* (ed. C. M Yonge), Nov. 1873; 'The Eucharistic Presentation'. Sts. 3-6 pub. in *Hymns A & M*, 1875, and this sel. has remained normal: therefore the initial 'And' was not the first word of the original hymn.

US & CAN: BP344: Can331: H189: L278: P355/-/-: Pm292 • ENG: AM 322/397: B307: BB198: CH320/580: E302: M759

WILLIAM BRIGHT, b. Doncaster, Yorks, 14 xii 1824; Sch. Univ. Coll., Oxf.; Fellow; Ord. C/E 1848; Theol. Tutor at Glenalmond Coll, Scotland; Canon of Cumbrae Cathedral '65; Canon of Christ Church Oxf. and Regius Prof. Eccl. Hist., Univ. Oxf., '68. † Oxford, 6 iii 1901 (76).

44. AND NOW THE WANTS ARE TOLD THAT BROUGHT THY CHILDREN TO THY KNEE

6 st. CM

W. Bright (43), *Hymns*, 1866 and *Hymns A & M*, 1875, where doxology was added.

US & CAN: H488 • ENG: AM32/- : CH296/636: CP283

45. ANGEL-VOICES, EVER SINGING

5 st. 8.5.8.5.84.3

F. Pott, wrtn. for dedication of an organ, 10 ii 1861, at Wingate (England) & incl. in his *Hymns Fitted to the Order of Common Prayer*, 1866, and *Hymns A & M*, 1875.

US & CAN: CW 101/- : L240: M2: P455/30/- • ENG: AM550/246: An234: B4: BB256: CH252/435: CP279: M668

FRANCIS POTT, b. 29 xii 1832, Southwark (London); Sch. Brasenose, Oxf.; Ord. C/E '56; curacies Bishopsworth, Som., '56; Ardingly, Sussex, '58; Ticehurst, Sussex, '61; Rector of Northill, Beds, '66-91. Ed. *The Free-Rhythm Psalter* '98. † Speldhurst, Kent, 26 xii 1909 (almost 77).

46. ANGELS FROM THE REALMS OF GLORY

5 st. 8.7.8.7.4.7

J. Montgomery (6) in *Iris* newspaper (Sheffield: see biography) for

24 xii 1816; 'Nativity.' Norm. vn. is sts. 1-4, but *Hymns for Church & School* (1964) has st. 5.

US & CAN: BP143: Can408: B87: CW192/124: H28: L31: M382: P124/ 168/298: Pm117: CLB211: W23 • ENG: AM482/64: An93: B89: BB42: CH65/182: E*320: M119: NC11

47. ANGELS HOLY, HIGH AND LOWLY

12 st. 8.7.88.7   **PCH 332**

J. S. Blackie, *The Inquirer*, 1840 and H. Bonar's *Bible Hymn Book*, 1845, as metr. vn. of the *Benedicite* pub. later in his *Lays and Lyrics of Ancient Greece*, 1857 (*Benedicite*'s oldest text is in Greek). Auth. notes that he wrote it for melody *Alles Schweigen* (in *Tait's Magazine*, 1840). 7 st. vn., now longest in use (sometimes further abridged) first introduced as a hymn in W. G. Horder's *Worship Song*, 1st ed., 1896. (*Songs of Praise* rearranges it in 5 st. 8.7.8.7.8.7.77).

US & CAN: P76/- /- : Pm73 • ENG: B5: CP39: M27

48. ANGELS WE HAVE HEARD ON HIGH

4 st. 7.7.7.7. with refrain *Gloria in excelsis Deo.*

French: LES ANGES DANS NOS CAMPAGNES, anon. in *Nouveau Receuil de Cantiques*, 1855.

Tr. in common use in USA, like that in 8.7.8.7 in *PL*, is based on an anon. tr. in *The Crown of Jesus*, 1862. In some later books it is altd. by E. Marlatt—or so the latest evidence suggests. A curious contradiction, however, appears in the sources, since A. Haeussler, in *The Story of our Hymns*, 1952 (p. 154), quotes a letter from Dr. Marlatt dated 1945 in which he says, 'I have no recollection of having written or even altered this hymn,' while W. A. Seaman in *The Companion to . . . the Service Book and Hymnal*, 1976 (written 1958), quotes a letter from the same author saying, 'The rumor that I "had nothing to do with the hymn" is a complete mystery to me,' and detailing, for the first time, the alterations which Dr. Marlatt made, which are in sts. 1 and 2.

US & CAN: B95: CW186/129: H42: L30: M374: P -/158/299: Pm116: CLB224: W24 • ENG: PL146‡

EARL BOWMAN MARLATT, b. Columbus, Ind., 24 v 1892; Sch. De Pauw Univ. and Boston Univ.; graduate work at Oxford and Berlin; Prof. Philosophy of Literature & Religious Education, Boston Univ. Sch. of Theol., 1923; Dean of that school, '38-'45; prof. Theol., Perkins School of Theol., Dallas, Tx., '45-'48 and prof. emeritus of Perkins after '58.

Nothing is known of the 'J. Chadwick' mentioned in *PL*.

49. APPROACH, MY SOUL, THE MERCY-SEAT

6 st. CM

J. Newton (37), *Olney Hymns*, 1779, the second of 2 hymns entitled 'The Effort.' In some editions of the book this is ascribed to Cowper (235), by the indication 'C' which distinguishes his hymns; and since it is a condensed version of the previous hymn, retaining many of that hymn's characteristic phrases, some have believed that either this or the other was revised by another hand. What seems to be at least possible is that N. rewrote the earlier hymn, which is 6 st. 10 10. 10 10, in an easier meter at C's suggestion and that C. may indeed have assisted in that process; but the ascription to N. stands.

US & CAN: BP438: Can70: L369: P -/386/- • ENG: AM626/345: An1: B332: CH451/667: CP769

50. AROUND THE THRONE OF GOD A BAND

10 st. LM-coup.

J. M. Neale (2) in *Hymns for Children*, first series, 1842—his first published hymn collection. As final st. he uses Ken's doxology, 'Praise God from whom all blessings flow' (63). Norm. vn. now has sts. 1, 2, 8, 9.

US & CAN: H120 • ENG: AM335/448: An452: BB237: E243

51. ART THOU WEARY? ART THOU LANGUID? (BURDENED?)

7 st. 8.5.8.3

J. M. Neale (2), *Hymns of the Eastern Church*, 1862; he there says that it is derived from a hymn of St. Stephen of Saba (725-94), but in 1866 he wrote that there is so little of the Gk. hymn in it that it shd. be regarded as original: see also 520. Penultimate line originally read 'Saints, Apostles, Martyrs, Virgins'; altd. in *Hymns A & M*, 1868. In modern books the last word of line 1 is often altd.

US & CAN: Can140: CW286/209: H406: L517: M99: P221/264/- • ENG: AM254/348: An467: B409: CH391/- : CP366: E366: M320

52. NOW AS THE SUN'S DECLINING RAYS

3 st. LM (CM)

Latin: LABENTE IAM SOLIS ROTA, C. Coffin, *Hymni Sacri*, 1736, 3 st. LM, for service of None (Office of approx. 3 p.m.)

Tr. J. Chandler, *Hymns of the Primitive Church*, 1837; vn. now in use as altd. in *Hymns A & M*, 1861, 1875. Not in orig. Latin meter.

US & CAN: P510/-/- • ENG: AM13/29: BB411: CH274/-: E265

CHARLES COFFIN, b. Buzancy (France), 1676; chief hymnographer of the R.C. 18th cent. liturgical revival; Principal, Coll., Dormans-Beauvais in Univ. Paris from 1712. The 1736 source above is a colln. of 100 of his hymns, all wrtn. in Latin. † Paris 1749.

JOHN CHANDLER, b. Witley Vicarage, Surrey, 16 vi 1806; Sch. Corp. Christi, Oxf.; Ord. C/E 1831; succeeded father as Vicar of Witley, '37. Chiefly known for trslns. of Latin hymns. † Putney (London), 1 vii 1876 (70).

53. AS PANTS THE HART FOR COOLING STREAMS

CM   **PCH 15**

Cento from Ps. 42 in the *New Version* of the English metr. psalter by Tate & Brady, 1696. Norm. seln., now sts. 1, 2, 11, with or without Gloria.

US & CAN: BP18: CW -/80: H450: L388: M255: P317/322/- : Pm390 • ENG: AM238/314: An516: B571: BB451: CP390: E367: M455

NAHUM TATE, b. Dublin 1652; Sch. Trin. Coll., Dublin; settled in London '72; became a poet and much sought-after; wrote revised vns. of Shakespeare incl. notorious updated *King Lear* in wh. Cordelia survives & marries Edgar; Poet Laureate, 1692; Historiographer Royal, 1702; largest original poem—*Panacea, or a Poem on Tea* (1700). † London, 12 viii 1715.

NICHOLAS BRADY, b. Bandon, Cork, 28 x 1659; Sch. Westminster; Oxford, Dublin; Ord. C/E; chaplain to William III and Queen Anne (†1714). From 1696-†, Vicar of Richmond, Surrey. † c. 1726.

These two Irishmen edited the *New Version* of the Psalter, to replace the *Old Version* of Sternhold and Hopkins (1562), which was until then the only authorized manual of praise for Engl. congregations of any kind. It did not succeed in supplanting the older version, but despite the unpromising literary antecedents of the two authors it was much less rugged and awkward in expression than the older. Nothing from the Old Vn. is now in standard hymnals (but see *Westminster Praise* #43); from Tate & Brady, however, the above hymn and also 747 & 826 are very familiar.

54. AS THE SUN DOTH DAILY RISE

5 st. 77.77

Latin, MATUTINUS ALTIORA, undated, pub. in 19 c. by J. Masters with a trsn. and the caption 'King Alfred's Hymn'; Latin is in 8.7.8.7 which in itself is suspicious, and ascription to King Alfred (d. 901 A.D.) need not be taken seriously.

Tr. in above source is attributed to an otherwise unidentifiable person called 'O. B. C.'; the tr. was recast by Earl Nelson in *Hymn for Saints Day and Other Hymns*, 1864.

US & CAN: CW114/24: P25/42/- : Pm33 • ENG:

HORATIO NELSON, was born 1823 Thomas Bolton, but changed his name when he succeeded to the title earned by his uncle, Admiral Viscount Nelson and became the second Earl. His contribution to hymnody could be called short and plump, in that the only original work of his now in currency is 'From all thy saints in warfare,' the 'Hymn for Saints Day' in the source above. This could be better described as a 'hymn kit for saint's day' because it contains 2 opening stanzas and one closing stanza between which are placed 16 optional stanzas, one for each major saint's day in the Anglican calendar and one only of which is sung on any given occasion. After falling fairly rapidly into disuse this has been surprisingly revived in the Missouri-Lutheran *Worship-Supplement* (1969) at #756. Nelson † 1913. But see 167.

Nothing is known of J. Masters.

55. AS WITH GLADNESS MEN OF OLD

5 st. 77.77.77   **PCH 221**

W. C. Dix (28) in *Hymns of Love & Joy*, 1861: wrtn. during an illness, 1860. Text sometimes revised and such alts. norm. taken from *Hymns A & M*, 1868. The author of one of the most famous of all hymns was about 23 when he wrote it.

US & CAN: BP153: Can435: CW196/141: H52: L52: M397: P135/174/302: Pm119: CLB234: W27 • ENG: AM79: An126: B90: BB62: CH63/200: CP95: E39: M132: NC15: PL159

56. ASK YE WHAT GREAT THING I KNOW?

6 st. 77.77.7

German: WOLLT IHR WISSEN WASS MEIN PREIS? J. C. Schwedler in *Hirschberger Gbch*, 1741.

Tr. B. H. Kennedy in his *Hymnologia Christiana*, 1863, in 77.77; based on 1 Cor. 2:2, Gal. 6:14. Norm. now in 4 st. U.S. Presbyterian *Hymnal* (1933) has this and also another trsln. in orig. meter by G. R. Woodward (737), from *Songs of Zion*, 1910, WHAT, YE ASK ME, IS MY PRIZE?—slightly altd.

US & CAN: B60: M124: P312 and 331‡/371/- • ENG:

JOHANN CHRISTOPH SCHWEDLER, b. Kronsdorf, Silesia, 21 xii 1672; popular preacher and poet in pietist tradition; friend of Zinzendorf (371); Sch. Univ. Leipzig; Ord. Luth., 1701. † Niederweise, Germany, 12 i 1730 (57).

BENJAMIN HALL KENNEDY, b. Summerhill, Warks, 6 xi 1804; Sch. King Edward's Sch., Birmingham: Shrewsbury Sch., St John's, Camb.; Ord. C/E; Fellow, St John's, 1828-30; asst. master Harrow Sch., '30; Head Master Shrewsbury Sch., '36; Prof. Greek, Univ. Cambridge, '67-†. Pub. many learned works & translations but best known for his Latin Primers (1843 onwards) wh. were used for over a century in Engl. schools. † Torquay, Devon, 6 iv 1889 (84).

57. AT EVEN WHEN THE SUN WAS SET (ERE THE SUN WAS SET)

8 st. LM-alt.   **PCH 241**

H. Twells, *Hymns A & M*, 1868. Orig. opening was '. . . ere the sun'; altd. in response to objection that in the Gospel story (Mk. 1:32-4) on wh. it is based, the sabbath did not end before sundown, before wh. people could not have been brought to our Lord for healing. Other minor alts. in most books, which often abr. to 6 sts. or fewer, but CH (1927) has full text. Author wrote it while invigilating an examination.

US & CAN: B555: H168: L232: M501: P43/55/- : Pm55 • ENG: An49: B688: BB412: CH277/52: CP632: E266: M689

HENRY TWELLS, b. 23 iii 1823, Ashted, nr. Birmingham; Sch. St. Peter's (Peterhouse), Camb.; Ord. C/E '49; Head Master, Godolphin Sch., Hammersmith (London), '56-'70: Rector of Waltham on the Wolds, Lincs, '71-90: Canon of Peterborough '84; retired to Bournemouth,

Hants, where he built & partly endowed St. Augustine's Ch. † Bournemouth, 19 i 1900 (76).

AT THE CROSS HER STATION KEEPING: see 876

AT THE LAMB'S HIGH FEAST WE SING: see 853

58. AT (IN) THE NAME OF JESUS EVERY KNEE SHALL BOW

7 st. 6.5.6.5 D   **PCH 289**

C. M. Noel, *The Name of Jesus, and Other Poems for the Sick and Lonely*, enlarged edition, 1870. (The first ed. of this was 1861). Auth. originally wrote 'In the Name . . .' but it was altd. as above for *Hymns A & M* 1875 to conform with the King James Version of Phil. 2:11, upon which the hymn is based. In *Church Hymns* 1903 at the request of her family, 'In the name . . .' was restored, and in a few current hymnals this version remains. Often abr., to 5 st. or fewer, but *A & M* and *EH* have full text.

US & CAN: BP234: Can39: B363: CW -/291: H356: L430: M76: P -/143/ 303: Pm197: CLB448: W30 ● ENG: AM306/225: An254: B199: BB120: CH178/300: CP167: E368: M249

CAROLINE MARIA NOEL, b. London, 10 iv 1817, youngest d. of Rev. G. T. Noel; lived all her life in London & suffered much illness in last 25 years; began writing hymns at 17, but this is from her later years, when she sought to assist other invalids through her writings. Last ed. of her collected works contained 78 pieces. † St. Marylebone (London), 7 xii 1877 (70).

AT THAT FIRST EUCHARIST BEFORE YOU DIED: see 568

59. AT THY FEET, O CHRIST, WE LAY

5 st. 77.77.77

W. Bright (43) in *The Monthly Packet*, Oct. 1867, his own *Hymns*, 1870 and *Hymns A & M*, 1875.

US & CAN: L203 ● ENG: AM6: An46: B671: BB402: CH265/- : CP597: E256: M933

60. AT THY FEET, OUR GOD AND FATHER

6 st. 8.7.8.7., but now always 3 st. 8.7.8.7 D

J. D. Burns, posth. *Psalms & Hymns*, 1867: 'New Year's Day Hymn': Ps. 65:2.

US & CAN: BP574: CW137/- : M498 ● ENG: B711: CH605/616

JAMES DRUMMOND BURNS, b. 18 ii 1823, Edinburgh; Sch. Univ. Edinburgh; Ord. Scot. Free Ch.; minister at Dunblane, '45-8; Scot. congn. in Funchal, Madeira, '48; Hampstead (London) Presb. Ch., '55-†. Pub. *Vision of Prophecy* '54, † Mentone, 27 xi 1864 (41).

61. AUTHOR OF LIFE DIVINE

2 st. 6.6.6.6.88

C. Wesley (1), in J. & C. Wesley's *Hymns on the Lord's Supper*, 1745.

US & CAN: BP347: L268: M315 ● ENG: AM319/394: BB199: CH317/ 587: CP299: E303: M764

62. AWAKE, AWAKE TO LOVE AND WORK

3 st. 8.6.8.6.8.6

G. A. Studdert-Kennedy, being sts. 4-6 of a 6 st. poem in *The Sorrows of God and other Poems*, 1921, and later incl. in collected poems, *The Unutterable Beauty*; 'At a Harvest Festival.' First as a hymn in *Songs of Praise*, 1931.

US & CAN: B413: CW323/- : H156: M190: Pm34 ● ENG: CP562: M588

GEOFFREY ANKETELL STUDDERT-KENNEDY, b. Leeds, 27 vi 1883; Sch. Trinity, Dublin, Ripon Coll., Oxf. Ord. C/E 1908, curate at St Mary's, Leeds; Vicar, St Paul's, Worcester, 1914; during World War I became celebrated as army chaplain, affectionately called 'Woodbine Willie'; decorated with Military Cross. From 1919 served in London parishes, founded Industrial Christian Fellowship, travelled incessantly on preaching missions, and wrote much incisive & penetrating poetry from which 2-3 pieces have been used as hymns, as well as several popular religious books incl. *I Believe*, *The Wicket Gate*, and *Food for the Fed-up*. In his time probably one of the six best known clergymen in England. † 7 or 8 iii 1929, Liverpool (45).

63. AWAKE, MY SOUL, AND WITH THE SUN

12 st. LM-coup., with doxology.   **PCH 29**

GLORY TO THEE, MY GOD, THIS NIGHT (ALL PRAISE. . . .)

10 st. LM-coup., with doxology.

PRAISE GOD, FROM WHOM ALL BLESSINGS FLOW

1 st. LM-coup., being the doxology appended to the above.

Thomas Ken, *Manual of Prayers*, for scholars of Winchester Coll., (England), ed. of 1695. Also in *A Conference between the Soul and Body*, 2nd ed. 1705 and in *A New Year's Gift*, 1709, in both of wh. revisions appeared wh. were incorporated in the 1709 ed. of the Winchester *Manual* & can be regarded as authorized by Ken. These include 'All praise' for 'Glory' at opening of st. 8 of the morning hymn, and st. 1 of the evening hymn. Modern books vary in their selns. from the 2 authorized texts.

Both were wrtn., with a 3rd for 'midnight,' for the devotions of the schoolboys at Winchester. The first appearance of the morning hymn in an authorized hymnal was in the 1782 (known as the 'University') edn. of Tate & Brady's *New Version* of the Psalms (53).

Both are always abridged now, and some books, esp. in the U.S., print the doxology, which ends all 3 hymns, as a separate piece: this is very widely used at the Offertory in U.S. churches. *EH* and others divide the morning hymn into 2 or more parts, and occasionally the 2 parts are given as separate hymns, the second beginning at st. 8, ALL PRAISE TO THEE WHO SAFE HAST KEPT (or 'GLORY . . .')

MORNING: US & CAN: BP547: Can357: H151-2‡: L202: M180: P278/ 50/-: Pm32 ● ENG: AM3: An34: B672: BB403, 402‡: CH256-7‡: CP590: E257: M931: PL302

EVENING: US & CAN: BP560: Can363: CW148/68: H165: L223: M493: P42/63/291: Pm56: W16 ● ENG: AM23: An64: B694: BB414: CH291/ 641: CP617: E267: M943: NC73: PL317

THOMAS KEN: b. Berkhamsted, Berks, vii 1637; Sch. Winchester & New Coll. Oxf.; Ord. C/E 1661; Rector of Brighstone 1667; Bp. of Bath & Wells 1685; imprisoned in Tower of London for political dissent, 1688, and deprived of see, 1691, for refusing to take the Coronation oath at the accession of King William IV; one of those therefore known to historians as 'non-jurors.' † Longleat, Warminster, Wilts, 19 iii 1711.

64. AWAKE, MY SOUL, STRETCH EVERY NERVE

5 st. CM

P. Doddridge, posth. *Hymns* (ed. Job Orton) 1755; 'Pressing onward in the Christian race: Phil. 3. 12-14.' Julian's comment that it is (1891) more pop. with C of E than nonconformist chs. in Britain, when compared with index below, shows a sharp change of custom.

US & CAN: CW369/- : H577: L552: M249: P -/346/- : Pm362 ● ENG: CP 491

PHILIP DODDRIDGE, b. London, 26 vi 1702; Sch. Kingston (Surrey) Gram. Sch., and Dissenting Academy at Knebworth, Herts; Ord. Congl., Knebworth 1723; Castle Hill Meeting, Northampton, '29, where in addition to his pastoral ministry he opened an academy for training ministers. Wrote *Rise and Progress of Religion in the Soul*, a noted religious classic, and over 300 hymns. These were collected after his death by Job Orton. † Lisbon (Portugal), 26 x 1751 (49).

65. AWAY IN A MANGER, NO CRIB FOR A BED

2 st. (1885) with 3rd st. added (1892), 11 11. 11 11 anap.

This is one of the more complicated stories in hymnology, and to follow it in detail, see A. Haeussler, *The Story of our Hymns*, 1952, pp. 159-161, or more briefly, Ronander & Porter, *Guide to the Pilgrim Hymnal*, 1966, p. 113.

Sts. 1-2 appear in *Little Children's Book for Schools and Family* (Philadelphia, 1885) and again in *Dainty Songs for Little Lads and Lassies* (ed. Murray, Cincinnati, 1887). Here the song was called 'Luther's Cradle Hymn.' Much time has since been spent in proving that it has nothing to do with Luther—whose family carol is at (884). No author is mentioned in either source, though the 1885 book came from a Lutheran publishing house.

St. 3 is also anonymous, though it was at one time falsely attributed to J. T. MacFarland, at first appearance in *Gabriel's Vineyard Songs*, 1892.

The tune best known in Britain is by W. J. Kirkpatrick, and first appeared in an American leaflet, 1895, *Around the World with Christmas*; this helped to perpetuate the Luther legend, and some even believed that the tune was by Luther. The tune familiar in U.S., MUELLER, is also anonymous, but again has suffered from mis-ascription. In the U.S. a total of 41 tunes to this carol, most pub. soon after the text's appearance, has been counted.

The first regular British hymnal to include it was the *Church Hymnary* (1927).

US & CAN: BP141: Can419: B80: CW199/128: H43: L47: M384: P126/157/- : Pm137: W34 ● ENG: B734: BB43: CH657/195: CP692: E*7: M860: PL152

66. AWAY WITH GLOOM, AWAY WITH DOUBT

3 st. 8.8.8.6.8.6

E. Shillito, *Jesus of the Scars and other Poems*, 1919, and *Methodist Hymn Book*, 1933.

US & CAN: ● ENG: B181: BB99: CH -/292: CP727: M231

EDWARD SHILLITO, b. Hull, 4 vii 1872; Sch. Silcoates Sch. and Owens College (now Univ.) Manchester; Ord. Congl., 1896, Ashton under Lyme (Lancs); Tunbridge Wells, Kent, '98; Brighton (Clifton Road), 1901; Harlesden (London), '06; Lyndhurst Road, Hampstead (London), asst., '09; Buckhurst Hill, Essex, '18-'27. Editorial Sec. London Missionary Society, '20-'32. After retiring from pastoral ministry '27 devoted himself to literary work. † Buckhurst Hill, Essex, 11 iii 1948 (75).

67. AWAY WITH OUR FEARS!

5 st. 5 5 5 11 D

C. Wesley (1), *Hymns of Petition & Thanksgiving for the Promise of the Father*, 1746. Norm. abr. and given in 4-line sts.

US & CAN: ● ENG: An213: B223: BB147: CP207: M278

68. BE KNOWN TO US IN BREAKING BREAD

2 st. CM

J. Montgomery (6), *Christian Psalmist*, 1825, 'The Family Table.' In some U.S. books, and one Eng., combined with 2 st. (anon.) found in *A Collection of Hymns* (United Brethren, Philadelphia), 1832, beginning SHEPHERD OF SOULS, REFRESH AND BLESS; this combination probably reflects a conventional dislike in U.S. for hymns unusually short or long, but M.'s original form seems to be returning to favour there.

US & CAN: CW465‡/311: H213‡: L269‡: M313: P356/446/- : Pm280: W242‡ ● ENG: B326‡: CP302: M766

69. BE PRESENT AT OUR TABLE, LORD

1 st. LM-coup.

J. Cennick, *Sacred Hymns for the Children of God in their Pilgrimage*, 1741. In that book #130 is this 4-line Grace before Meat and #131 is an 8-line Grace after Meat beginning WE BLESS (THANK) THEE LORD FOR THIS OUR FOOD. This fails to qualify, on the formula in our introduction, for inclusion here, but although it is disappearing from hymnals it is still very well known in English homes, and perhaps can be described as the best-known 'out of church' hymn. The Grace after Meat, where it is known, is now familiar in the form altd. by H. Bickersteth (517) in his *Collection* of 1833, where he substantially rewrites Cennick.

US & CAN: M518: Christian Hymnary (1972) 675 ● ENG: CH656/- Sunday School Praise (1955) 578

JOHN CENNICK (pronounced SENNICK) b. 12 xii 1718, Reading, Berks, of Quaker family, but at early stage joined C/E. Influenced by J. Wesley, appointed teacher at Kingswood School (a Wesley foundation) '39; left Wesleyans '41 and founded a short-lived society of his own; then for a while became an evangelist under Whitefield, but eventually joined the Moravians, visiting N. Ireland and Germany. Prolific hymnwriter and strenuous preacher. † London, 4 vii 1755 (36).

70. BE STILL, MY SOUL, THE LORD IS ON THY SIDE

6 st. 11.10.11.10.10 10   **PCH 334**

German: STILLE, MEIN WILLE, DEIN JESUS HILFT SEGEN; Katharina von Schlegel, in *Neue Sammlung geistlicher Lieder* (Wernigerode), 1752.

Tr. J. L. Borthwick in 5 st. 10.10.10.10.10 10, *Hymns from the Land of Luther*, 2nd series, 1855. Norm. now abr. to 4 st. (om. st. 5) or 3 (om. 2, 5). Now owes much of its appeal to tune FINLANDIA, first associated with it in *CH* (1927); the tune, by Jan Sibelius (1865-1957), became the national anthem of Finland in 1932.

US & CAN: BP417: L267: M209: P281/374/- : Pm77: W36 ● ENG: An520: CH556/673

KATHARINA von SCHLEGEL is known to have been born 22 x 1697, but apart from a conjecture that she was a court lady in the household of the Duke of Cothen no more is known, not even date of death.

JANE LAURIE BORTHWICK, b. Edinburgh, 9 iv 1813, d. of James Borthwick of the North British Insurance Office, Edinburgh; sister of Sarah Findlater (522), with whom she produced *Hymns from the Land of Luther* in 4 series, 1854, '55, '58, '62. This contained 61 pieces of hers and 53 of her sister's, and ranks almost level with C. Winkworth's 3 volumes (see 14) in importance as a mediator of German hymnody to Britain. † Edinburgh, 7 ix 1897 (84).

71. BE THOU MY (OUR) GUARDIAN AND MY (OUR) GUIDE

4 st. CM

I. Williams, *Hymns on the Catechism*, 1842; orig. vn. was in plural throughout, but *Hymns A & M*, 1861, popularized the singular vn.

US & CAN: ● ENG: AM282/300: An146: BB135: E369

ISAAC WILLIAMS, b. Cwmcynfelin, Cardiganshire (Wales), 12 xii 1802; Sch. Harrow and Trinity, Oxf., where he became a Fellow '29; Ord. C/E '25; influenced by Newman (196) and Keble (83), became a leader in the Oxford Movement; was Keble's curate at Bisley, '42-8; then retired to Stinchcombe, Glos., till †, devoting himself to writing and scholarly work. † 1 iv 1865 (62).

72. BE THOU MY VISION, O LORD OF MY HEART

5 st. 10 10.10 10 anap. irreg.   **PCH 324**

Irish: ROB TU MO BHOILE, A COMDI CRIDE, anonymous.

Tr. into Eng. prose by M. E. Byrne in *Erin*, vol. 2, 1905; versified by E. Hull in *Poem Book of the Gael*, 1912. First used as a hymn, with Irish tune

SLANE (which had no previous association with it) in *CH* (1927). In some books the irregular meter is straightened out, and in U.S. books norm. abr. to 4 st.

US & CAN: BP458: Can254: B212: CW321/90: M256: P325/303/304: Pm391 ● ENG: AM*10: An571: B462: BB316‡: CH477/87: CP432: E*75: M632: PL289

MARY ELIZABETH BYRNE, b. Dublin, 2 vii 1880; Sch. Dominican Convent, Dublin, and Univ. Dublin; became literary scholar; worked on the Catalogue of the Royal Irish Academy and compiled 3rd fascicle 1928; also worked on *Dictionary of the Irish Language.* † Dublin, 19 i 1931 (50).

ELEANOR HENRIETTA HULL, b. Manchester, 15 i 1860, was founder and first hon. Sec., of the Irish Text Society, from 1899, & became eminent scholar and interpreter of Irish language & culture. Was on staff of *The Literary World* & contributed to *Encyclopaedia of Religion and Ethics.* † Wimbledon (London), 13 i 1935 (almost 75).

BEAUTIFUL SAVIOR: see 873.

73. BEFORE JEHOVAH'S AWFUL THRONE

6 st. LM-alt.

I. Watts (10), Ps. 100 in *The Psalms of David Imitated . . .* , 1719. The first st. originally ran:

> Sing to the Lord with joyful voice;
> let every land his name adore;
> the British Isles shall send the noise
> across the ocean to the shore.

John Wesley, in his Charlestown *Hymn Book* (1737), edited during his American mission, understandably sought to rescue a fine hymn from the impression made by this unpromising and in any case (for his situation) inappropriate opening, and reconstructed the familiar first st. out of Watts' first two; he wrote his own first 2 lines, then used lines 3-4 of Watts' st. 2, so the familiar vn. is in 5 st. But *Hymns for Church and School*, 1964 (#235) has a 6 st. vn. using more of Watts.

US & CAN: Can13: CW -/48: L161: M22: P63/81/306: Pm9 ● ENG: AM516/370: An326: B6: BB452: CH230/2: CP2: M3

BEFORE THE ENDING OF THE DAY
BEFORE THE LIGHT OF EVENING FADES   see 878

74. BEGONE, UNBELIEF

7 st. 5.5.5.5.6.5.6.5   PCH 88

J. Newton (37), *Olney Hymns*, 1779; 'I will trust and not be afraid.' Bibl. refs. include Jer. 2:13 in st. 2; 1 Sam. 7:12 in st. 3 of modern version. Normally st. 4 of orig. now omitted.

US & CAN: ● ENG: An519: B573: CP396: M511

75. BEHOLD, A LITTLE CHILD

5 st. 6.6.6.6.88

W. W. How, in *Children's Hymns*, 1872.

US & CAN: H237 ● ENG: AM727/- : B116: CH76/207: E588: M164

WILLIAM WALSHAM HOW, b. Shrewsbury, 13 xii 1823, Sch. Shrewsbury and Wadham, Oxf.; Ord. C/E '46; curacies in Kidderminster & Shrewsbury; Rector of Whittington, '51; Bp. (suffragan) Bedford '79; Bp. Wakefield '88-†. One of the leading hymn-writers of England, and one of the editors of *Church Hymns*, 1871. † Leenane, Ireland, 10 viii 1897 (73).

76. BEHOLD THE AMAZING GIFT OF LOVE

5 st. C.M.

Scottish Paraphrases, 1781, revised by W. Cameron from vn. in *Paraphrases* of 1745 (see below), that vn. being itself rewritten from a hymn in I. Watts' *Hymn and Sacred Songs* (1707) in S. M. beginning 'Behold what wondrous grace.' 1 John 3:1ff.

US & CAN: BP224: Can151: P -/120/- ● ENG: An521: BB484: CH483/396: CP393: M*5: NC20

SCOTTISH PARAPHRASES. Until 1745 the only medium of congregational song in the Church of Scotland was the Book of Metrical Psalms, revised for the last time in 1650. Before that date five biblical canticles versified in the 1575 edition of the Psalter were also available, but in 1650 these were removed. General Assembly was asked in 1741 to rectify this situation, in which no Christian words could be used in public praise, and appointed a committee in 1742 to "make a Collection of Translations into English Verse . . . of passages of Holy Scripture, or receive (them) . . . from any who shall transmit them." In 1745 a collection of 45 such paraphrases, all in CM, was delivered to Assembly, but it aroused so much opposition that Assembly did not authorize it. The project was dropped until the question was raised again in 1775 by the Synod of Glasgow and Ayr. In that year another committee was appointed, to review the 1745 work, and in 1781 this committee delivered its complete work, consisting of 67 Paraphrases, to which were added 5 hymns—three by Addison (of which ## 1 and 2 are our 799 and 716) one by I. Watts (for which see PCH 32) and one by John Logan. The whole collection still survives in the *Scottish Psalter* of 1929 and many pieces from it found their way into general hymnody. The three chief writers in the Paraphrases, who either wrote their own or revised and adapted the work of others, are noted below.

WILLIAM CAMERON, b. Lochaber, 1751; Sch. Marischal Coll., Aberdeen; Ord. C/Scot. 1786 at Kirknewton, where he lived till †. Wrote much poetry; sole writer of Paraphrases 14 and 17, reviser of 33 others, chief editor of the collection. † Kirknewton, 17 viii 1811 (60).

JOHN LOGAN, b. Soutra, Midlothian, 1748; Sch. Musselburgh Sch. & Univ. Edinburgh; presented to parish of South Leith as licensed preacher 1771, but appointment was disputed, so not Ord. till '73. Attempted, but failed, to make a name in literature, fell into intemperate habits, resigned charge and went to live in London where † 28 xii 1788 (40).

MICHAEL BRUCE, b. Kinnesswood, Kinross, 27 iii 1746, of poor parents; Sch. there and Univ. Edinburgh; attended theol. Sem., which closed 6 months after he entered it; obtained employment as teacher in Forest Hill, Clackmannanshire; wrote a good deal of poetry and is usually thought to be author of Paraphrase 58 (814) and at least reviser of Par. 18 (79); but this remains obscure since Logan (above) pub. some of his poems after his untimely death without acknowledgment, and the authorship of these & others has remained in dispute. † 5 vii 1767 (21).

77. BEHOLD, THE GREAT CREATOR MAKES HIMSELF A HOUSE OF CLAY

5 st. CM   PCH427

Thomas Pestel, *Sermons and Devotions Old & New*, 1659; the hymn, first appearing as such in *EH*, 1906, is sts. 5-9 of a poem beginning FAIREST OF MORNING LIGHTS, APPEAR; full text in *Oxford Book of Christian Verse.*

US & CAN: ● ENG: AM -/69: BB44: CH -/107: CP79: E20

THOMAS PESTEL, b. about 1586, Sch. Queen's Coll., Camb; Ord. C/E, Vicar of Packington, Leics, but deprived 1646 by Westminster Assembly. The publication above is the only certain date, apart from that just mentioned, known in his biography; but he is presumed to have † some time thereafter.

78. BEHOLD, THE LAMB OF GOD

7 st. 4.66.4.88.4

M. Bridges, *Hymns of the Heart*, 1848. Text rev. in *Hymns A & M*, 1861, making opening line of each st. 'Behold the Lamb of God', altering it at other points and reducing it to 4 st. 6.66.4.88.4. In ed. of 1950 st. 2 was dropped, and this 3 st. vn. remains in use in U.S. With tune WIGAN, an unaccountably neglected masterpiece.

US & CAN: H338: L83: P153/-/307 ● ENG: AM187/212

MATTHEW BRIDGES, b. Maldon, Essex, 14 vii 1800; brought up in C/E but in 1848 became R. C. Lived as man of letters, and spent most of the latter half of his life in Canada. † on a visit to the Convent of the Assumption, Sidmouth, Devon, 6 x 1894 (94).

79. BEHOLD, THE MOUNTAIN OF THE LORD

6 st. (1745); 7 st. (1781) CM   **PCH 97**

Scottish Paraphrases (76). Sometimes ascr. to M. Bruce (*ibid.*), but if any of it is his, it must be only the added st. 3. Is. 2:2-5.

US & CAN: Can162 ● ENG:An416: B658: BB485: CH365/312: CP322: M904

80. BEHOLD US, LORD, A LITTLE SPACE

6 st. CM

J. Ellerton, *Church Hymns*, 1871, 'written for use at a midday service in a London city church'.

US & CAN: BP326: Can59: CW -/231: L213: M549: Pm395 ● ENG: AM475/13: An590: B627: BB349: CH242/453: CP277: M949

JOHN ELLERTON, b. Clerkenwell (London), 16 xii 1826; Sch. King William's Coll., Isle of Man, and Trinity, Camb. Ord. C/E 1850; various curacies & parishes until Rector of Barnes (London) '76, of White Roding, Essex, '86-93. The earliest modern critical hymnologist, wrote several essays on hymns and their writers as well as becoming a leading hymn writer in late 19c. Co-editor with W. W. How (75) of *Church Hymns*, 1871. † Torquay, Devon 15 vi 1893 (66).

81. BELOVED, LET US LOVE (FOR) LOVE IS OF GOD

5 st. 10 10   **PCH 338**

H. Bonar, Supplement to *Psalms & Hymns*, 1880; 1 John 4:10ff. Probably the last hymn he wrote, certainly the last in common use. 'For' in line 1 inserted in some books for musical reasons.

US & CAN: P500/-/- ● ENG:AM703/- : B591: BB373‡: CH488/- : CP539‡ : M444

HORATIUS BONAR, b. Edinburgh, 19 xii 1808; Sch. Royal High School and Univ. Edinburgh; Ord. Ch/Scot. Kelso, 1837; at Disruption of 1843 assisted in foundation of Free Ch. of Scotland (reintegrated with C/Scot. 1929). Minister of Chalmers Memorial Ch., Edinburgh, '66; Moderator of Free Church, '83; pub. *Hymns of Faith and Hope* in 3 series, '57, '61, '66, but continued to write hymns thereafter. † Edinburgh, 31 vii 1889 (80).

82. BENEATH THE CROSS OF JESUS

7.6.8.6. D Irreg.   **PCH 287**

E. C. Clephane, wrtn. at end of her short life & pub. posth. in *The Family Treasury*, 1872. Longest vn. of original poem in Eng. use is 5 st. (*AM, EH*) ; st. 3 of this seln. om. in some Eng. books, others also in U.S. *Worshipbook*, 1972, uses sts. 1 & 2 with a 3rd composed by members of ed. cttee., giving it a more universal sense.

US & CAN: BP185: Can440: B360: CW235/159: H341: L482: M417: P162/190/308‡: Pm160 ● ENG: AM667/- : AN152: B427: BB301: CH691/684: EH567: M197

ELIZABETH CECILIA CLEPHANE: b. 18 vi 1830, Edinburgh, d. of Alexander Clephane, Sheriff of Fife. Lived with family there and later at Melrose where † 19 ii 1869 (38).

BETHLEHEM, OF NOBLEST CITIES
BETHLEHEM, MOST NOBLE CITY   see 870.

83. BLESS'D (BLEST) ARE THE PURE IN HEART

4 st. SM   **PCH 123**

J. Keble, The Christian Year, 1827, has, under 'The Purification,' a poem of 17 st. SM, beginning 'Bless'd are . . .' In contemporary use the only hymnal to include even part of this in orig. vn. is *Westminster Praise* (#34) 1976, which uses sts. 1-5, 15-17 arranging in SMD. (Oxford Hymnal, 1908, had sts. 1-3, 15, 17). The familiar vn. in all books listed below consists of sts. 1 and 17 of orig., with 2 sts. interpolated by W. J. Hall in his *Mitre Hymn Book*, 1836; this was made popular by inclusion in *Hymns A & M*, 1868. In some books further alts. are made; and NC and CLB use a quite different hymn, with same opening line, by A. Petti, which stays closer than either to the thought of Matt. 5:1-12, but of course takes a quite different direction from Keble's.

US & CAN: BP413: Can58: H418: L394: M276: P-/276/-: Pm214: CLB 305‡ ● ENG: AM261/335: An638: B463: BB318: CH478/113: CP446: E370: M950: NC25‡: PL287

JOHN KEBLE, b. Fairford, Glos., 24 iv 1792; Sch. at home and Corp. Christi, Oxf.; Fellow of Oriel 1810 (age 18); Ord. C/E 1816; Vicar of Hursley, Berks, '25; pub. his celebrated *Christian Year* '27; Prof. Poetry, Univ. Oxf., '31; proceeds of *The Christian Year*, wh. was a best-seller in the first decade of legitimate hymn-singing in C/E, enabled him to rebuild his parish church. His assize sermon in St. Mary's, Oxford (the University Church) in 1833 marked the inception of the *Oxford Movement*, wh. transformed the C/E by recovering many medieval Catholic values, including a new view of priesthood and liturgy, east-end choirs, vestments and liturgical colors. Part of this movement was the translation of medieval hymns for English use, in which the leading artist was Neale (2). The most distinguished theologian of this movement was J. H. Newman (196), who, like many clergy influenced by it, later joined the R. C. church. Despite the extreme views of some of its promoters, many practices now taken for granted in the modern C/E (and in the Episcopal churches throughout the Anglican Communion) are traceable to this movement; and most evident of these is 'parish communion.' It wrought as radical and lasting a transformation in the C/E as did the Wesley's revival in the non-Anglican churches. Keble † Hursley, 29 iii 1866 (73).

84. BLESSED ASSURANCE! JESUS IS MINE

3 st. 9. 10. 9. 9 with refrain 99.99, dact. and troch.   **PCH 403**

Fanny Crosby, in J. R. Sweeney's *Gems of Praise* (Philadelphia), 1873. It is said that the tune was wrtn. first, and that the author, hearing it, and being asked what it suggested to her, spoke at once the words of st. 1, wh. remained unchanged when she developed this into the present hymn. First in a hymnal, *Hymnal* of the Methodist Episc. Church (South), U.S., 1889.

US & CAN: B334: CW412/- : M224: P -/139/- ● ENG: B493: M422

FANNY CROSBY, b. S-E Putnam City, N.Y., 24 iii 1820, was blind at 6 weeks, wrote hymns from age of 8; Sch. New York City Sch. for the blind, where later became a teacher. M. 1858 blind musician Alexander van Alstyne, but as hymn-writer always known by her maiden name. Said to have wrtn. 8,500 hymns, and became, so to say, the mother-superior of all Gospel-Song writers. Her work was introduced to England by Moody and Sankey. Lived all her life in New York as a Methodist. † Bridgeport, Conn., 12 ii 1915 (94).

BLESSED CITY, HEAVENLY SALEM: see 879.

BLESSED JESUS, AT THY WORD
BLESSED JESUS, HERE WE STAND   see 860.
BLESSED JESUS, WE ARE HERE

85. BLESSING AND HONOUR AND GLORY AND POWER

8 st. 10 10. 10 10 dact.

H. Bonar (81), *Hymns of Faith & Hope*, III, 1866, orig. beginning 'INTO THE HEAVEN OF THE HEAVENS HATH HE GONE.' Always in cento form, beginning with st. 8, 'Blessing and honour. . . .'; 3 st. vn. in this form first found in *Laudes Domini* (New York), 1884; 5 st. cento using sts. 8, 1, 4, 5, 7 in *Church Praise* (Free Ch/Scot.) 1885, and in all eds. of *CH* from 1898. U.S. books now norm. use sts. 8, 4, 5, 7.

US & CAN: BP241: CW -/185: L166: P196/137/311 ● ENG: CH169/299: CP168

86. BLEST BE THE EVERLASTING GOD

6 st. CM

I. Watts (10), *Hymns. . . .* 1707, Bk. I; 'Hope of Heaven by the Resurrection of Christ,' 1 Pet. 1:3-5; but now familiar as revised and abridged in *Scot. Paraphrases* (76) 1781; in *Sc. Par.* 1745 Watts' hymn was unchanged, and alts. are due to 1781 editors. In Scotland known as Paraphrase 61.

US & CAN: BP536: Can182 ● ENG: An517: BB486: CH137/530: CP392

87. BLEST BE THE TIE THAT BINDS

6 st. SM

J. Fawcett, *Hymns. . .* , 1782. The story that F. composed this after changing his mind about leaving his Baptist charge in Yorks. for a London charge (after preaching farewell sermon and loading luggage on removal-wagons) is often quoted, and from internal evidence believable, but unattested in biographical sources; if true the date of the incident & the hymn is 1772.

US & CAN: BP318: B256: CW476/273: H495: L543: M306: P343/473/- : Pm272 ● ENG: B355: CH490/- : CP245

JOHN FAWCETT, b. 6 i 1740, Lidget Green, nr. Bradford, Yorks; moved to Christian conviction by preaching of George Whitefield; Ord. Bapt., 1765. Minister at Waingate, Yorks, then Hebden Bridge, Yorks. Directed an Academy for training Bapt. ministers; declined invitation to become President of Bapt. Sem. at Bristol. D.D., Brown Univ., Providence, R.I., 1811. Wrote 160 hymns and important *Devotional Commentary on the Holy Scriptures*. † Hebden Bridge, 25 vii 1817 (77).

BLEST CREATOR OF THE LIGHT: see 861.

88. BOOK OF BOOKS, OUR PEOPLE'S STRENGTH

3 st. 7.8.7.8.77

P. Dearmer, *Songs of Praise*, 1st ed., 1925.

US & CAN: CW -/329: H403: M370: P -/248/- : Pm253: CLB482 ● ENG: B241: SP (1931) 457

PERCY DEARMER, b. 27 ii 1867, Kilburn (London); Sch. Westminster & Ch. Ch. Oxf.; Ord. C/E 1891/2; Vicar of St Mary's, Primrose Hill (London) 1901-15; Sec. London Branch of Christian Social Union, 1891-1912; chariman, League of Arts, 1919; chaplain to Brit. Red Cross in Serbia, '15-'18 (Serbian Red Cross Decoration); Prof. Eccl. Art, King's Coll., London, 1919-†; Canon of Westminster, '31-†. In early days a fervent & learned advocate of developed ideals of the Oxford Movement (83), and following these principles sought to raise and deepen standards of liturgy & hymnody; wrote *The Parson's Handbook* (1899), a manual for conduct of clergy of 'high church' manners in liturgy and life. With R. Vaughan Williams and a small circle of other friends edited *The English Hymnal* (1906) which, in seeking to furnish parishes with a complete liturgical system of praise, including full cycle of plainsong office hymns and of worship-material for the church's year did more than any one book of any kind to make the Tractarian ideals friendly to congregations. The book was banned by 2 bishops from their dio-

ceses, 1907, and an edition was published omitting 6 hymns to wh. special objection had been taken (worship of the Virgin, prayers for the dead); this book, widely successful during the next generation, also introduced many American hymns to Engl. congregations for the first time. Later, with R. V. W. and Martin Shaw, he edited *Songs of Praise*, 1925, enlarged 1931, a more liberal but equally fastidious book, mainly for schools and extra-liturgical congregations, and, most influentially of all, in 1928 the *Oxford Book of Carols*. By this time his own views had changed somewhat from their early liturgical center and were gathering round the literary, intellectual and liberal thought-forms largely popularized in England by the more learned nonconformists. He was, in all, the most colorful and original mind operating in the field of Anglican worship. He wrote many hymns himself, and while in *EH* his ideal was the preservation of classic texts unaltered, in *SP* he fairly often altered or abridged older hymns, esp. of the evangelical kind, to conform with modernist theology. In some cases he wrote new hymns taking the opening line from familiar ones, and for this encountered some surprised criticism. But nobody had a wider or more pervasive influence in 20th century English hymnody than he. † Westminster (London), 29 v 1936 (69).

89. BREAD OF HEAVEN, ON THEE I FEED

2 st. 77.77.77 PCH 134

J. Conder, *Star in the East*, 1824; from 1853 sometimes 'we feed,' and occasionally in older hymnals 3 st. 77.77.

US & CAN: Can340: H212: P -/-/3:3 : Pm281 ● ENG: AM318/411: An370: B309: BB200: CP304: E304: M769

JOSIAH CONDER, b. Aldersgate, London, 17 ix 1789, son of a bookseller; writer and editor. Ed. *Congregational Hymn Book*, 1836, first hymn book of the Congregational Union of England & Wales. In this work, designed as a supplement to Watts' hymns, he included 36 texts of his own: complete hymns pub. as *Hymns of Praise*, posth., 1856. † Hampstead (London), 27 xii 1855 (66).

90. BREAD OF THE WORLD, IN MERCY BROKEN

2 st. 9.8.9.8 PCH 118

R. Heber, posth. in *Hymns*, 1827; 'Before the Sacrament.' Often now as 1 st. 9.8.9.8 D.

US & CAN: BP358: Can326: CW453/303: H196: L279: M323: P353/445/- : Pm282 ● ENG: AM714/409: An371: B310: BB503: CH318/574: CP303: E305: M756: NC26

REGINALD HEBER, b. at Malpas Rectory, Ches., 21 viii 1783; Sch. Brasenose, Oxf.; Newdigate Prize for English Poem (Oxf.); Ord. C/E; Fellow of All souls, Oxf.; Vicar of Hodnet, Salop, 1807; Bp. Calcutta, '23-†. All his hymns wrtn. at Hodnet, in wh. he showed himself the leader of the new 'romantic' style, the style which allowed poetic imagination to question the supremacy of dogma. His *Hymns*, including a few not his but valued by him, pub. 1827. † Trichinopoly, 3 iv 1826 (42).

91. BREAK FORTH, O BEAUTEOUS HEAVENLY LIGHT

1 st. 8.7.8.7.88.77

German: BRICH AN DU SCHONES MORGENLICHT, being st. 9 of a 12 st. hymn by J. Rist beginning ERMUNTRE DICH . . ., a Christmas piece in *Himmlische Lieder*, 1641.

This st. tr. in Eng. vn. of Bach's *Christmas Oratorio* (Novello edn., undated) by J. Troutbeck. Modern hymnals have either that st. alone, or a 2 st. hymn made by adding a st. by A. T. Russell (which is not a trsn. of Rist); *Worshipbook* uses another, as st. 2, by Dalton Macdonald. Its inclusion in mod. hymnals is undoubtedly the consequence of its use for some years (later discontinued) in the celebrated King's College (Camb.) Service of Nine Lessons and Carols as an introit.

US & CAN: Can402: CW -/131: H25: L29: M373: P -/-/314: Pm118 ● ENG: In most Engl. carol collections after c. 1960

JOHANN RIST, b. Ottensee, Holstein, 8 iii 1607; Sch. Rinteln & Rostock;

Ord. Luth.; pastor and physician at Wedel. After much suffering in the Thirty Years' War (1618-48) in wh. he lost all his personal property, made Poet Laureate by Emperor Ferdinand III. Wrote many hymns (said to be about 680) wh. became popular during his last years. † 31 viii 1667.

ARTHUR TOZER RUSSELL, b. Northampton 20 iii 1806, son of a Congl. minister named Clout who changed his name to Russell; Sch. Merchant Taylors School (London), St John's Camb. Ord. C/E 1829; vicar of Craxton, '30, Whaddon '52; Toxteth Park, Liverpool, '66; Wrackwardine, Salop, '67; Southwick, Sussex '74, where † 18 xi 1874 (68).

92. BREAK FORTH, O LIVING LIGHT OF GOD

4 st. CM

F. von Christierson, in *Ten New Hymns on the Bible*, leaflet of hymns by various authors pub. by the Hymn Society of America, 1952, in celebration of pubn. of the R.S.V. of the Bible. First in a hymnal, *Methodist Hymnal* 1966.

US & CAN: CW -/343: M356: P -/-/316 • ENG: CH -/133

FRANK von CHRISTIERSON, b. Lovisa, Finland, 1900, came to America 1905; Sch. Stanford Univ., California, San Francisco Theol. Sem.; Ord. Pres. (U.S.) Calvary Pres. Ch., S. F., '29; Trinity Community Church, Hollywood, '44; Celtic Cross Ch., Citrus Heights, Cal., '61; Moderator of S. Francisco and Los Angeles presbyteries. From '66 asst. at First Pres. Ch., Marysville, Cal. Author of 7 prizewinning hymns in print; collected edition of 37 of his pieces, *Sing Your Faith* (1976).

93. BREAK THOU THE BREAD OF LIFE

2 st. 6.4.6.4 D

M. A. Lathbury, wrtn. 1877 for the Chautauqua Assembly (perhaps the pioneer of all summer religious conferences now so popular in U.S.) at request of its leader, Bishop Vincent, and sung there to tune BREAD OF LIFE wh. is, in U.S., inseparable from it. Brought to England by W. G. Horder in *Congregational Hymns*, 1884. After pubn. of extended version, with 16 new lines by A. Groves in *Wesleyan Magazine*, 1913, appeared in many books as a composite hymn. Composite form less used in U.S., but *CW²*, 1970, prints 8 lines of Groves after full vn. of Lathbury without acknowledgement. Often in 6.4.6.4 to make seln. of odd numbers of stanzas possible. The Lathbury stanzas begin 'Break thou,' 'Beyond,' 'Bless thou,' 'Then shall.' Composite vns. noted below with ‡.

US & CAN: BP285: B138‡: CW461/327‡: L491: M369: P216/250/317: Pm254 • ENG: An303‡: B243‡: CH202/- : CP233‡: M309‡

MARY ARTEMISIA LATHBURY, b. Manchester, N. Y., 10 viii 1841; d. of a Methodist minister; prof. artist and writer, contrib. to Methodist Sunday School periodicals; known as the 'Laureate of Chautauqua'; founder of the 'Look Up Legion,' a Meth. Sunday Sch. organization. † East Orange, N. J., 20 x 1913 (72).

ALEXANDER GROVES, b. Newport, Isle of Wight, 1842; † Henley on Thames, Oxon., 30 viii 1909.

94. BREATHE ON ME, BREATH OF GOD

4 st. SM   PCH 253

E. Hatch, leaflet, 'Between Doubt & Prayer,' 1878, then posth., *Towards Fields of Light*, 1890, and W. G. Horder's *Worship Song*, 1896.

US & CAN: BP259: Can240: B317: CW -/200: H375: L470: M133: P213/235/- : Pm233 • ENG: AM671/236: An287: B592: BB148: CH194/103: CP216: E*76: M300: NC27: PL6

EDWIN HATCH, b. Derby, 4 ix 1835, of nonconformist parents; Sch. King Edward's Sch., Birmingham and Pembroke, Oxf.; became Anglican '53 and Ord. C/E '59; served a short time in E. London, then prof. Classics, Trinity Coll., Toronto, '59-'62; Rector of a high school in Quebec, '62-6; Vice-Principal of St. Mary Hall, Oxf., '67-85; Reader in Eccl. Hist., Univ. Oxf., '84; first editor of Oxford Univ. Gazette, '70; Bampton Lecturer '78-9; many publications in field of ch. history. † Headington (Oxford), 10 xi 1889 (54).

BRIEF LIFE IS HERE OUR PORTION: see 850.

95. BRIGHT THE VISION THAT DELIGHTED

4 st. 8.7.8.7 D   PCH 206

R. Mant, *Ancient Hymns . . .*, 1837, Is. 6:3ff. St. 3 of orig. now always om., and most familiar form is in 6 st. 8.7.8.7, as first set in *Hymns A & M*, 1868. But also found omitting opening quatrain and beginning ROUND THE LORD IN GLORY SEATED, using orig. lines 9-12 as refrain after each of sts. 2, 4, 5 of 6 st. vn. This form first used in Thring's (191) *Collection*, 1853, therefore older than 4-line form; 8-line form noted below by †.

US & CAN: BP69‡: Can43: CW156‡/-: H269‡: L177†: P15†/-/: CLB413 • ENG: AM161: An15: B26‡: BB269: CH2‡/353‡: CO16: E372: M25‡

RICHARD MANT, b. Southampton 12 ii 1776; Sch. Winchester & Trinity, Oxf.; Ord. C/E; Fellow of Oriel; Bampton Lecturer, 1811; 3 Irish Bishoprics: Lillaloe, '20, Down & Connor '23; Dromore '42. † Ballymoney, Ireland, 2 xi 1848 (72).

96. BRIGHTEST AND BEST OF THE SONS OF THE MORNING

5 st. 11.10.11.10 dact. (sts. 1 and 5 identical).   PCH 117

R. Heber (90), Christian Observer, Nov. 1811, and posth. *Hymns*, 1827.

US & CAN: BP150: Can432: CW202/- : H46: L53: M400: P136/175/318: Pm126 • ENG: AM642/75: An125: B91: BB63: CH64/201: CP94: E41: M122

97. BRIGHTLY GLEAMS OUR BANNER

8 st. 6.5.6.5 Ter.

T. J. Potter, *Holy Family Hymnal*, 1860, for R. C. Sunday Schools. Text now fam. is drastically revised by compilers of *Hymns A & M* 1868 and of *Church Hymns*, 1871. Now in 5 st. or fewer.

US & CAN: CW485/- : H559: P457/-/- • ENG: AM390/- : An549: B464: CH538/- : M617

THOMAS JOSEPH POTTER, b. Scarborough, Yorks, 9 vi 1828; joined R. C. Church, and Sch. All Hallows College, Dublin. Ord. R. C. '57; Director of All Hallows and Prof. of Preaching and English. † Dublin, 31 viii 1873 (45).

98. BROTHER (LORD CHRIST) WHO ON THY HEART DIDST BEAR

6 st. LM-alt.   PCH 449

H. A. Thomas, *Congregational Hymnary*, 1916; appears with altd. first line and abr. to 5 st. in some books.

US & CAN: • ENG: AM*55‡: B636: BB380‡: CP556

HENRY ARNOLD THOMAS, b. Bristol 13 vi 1848; Sch. Mill Hill Acad. and Univ. Coll., London then Trinity Camb. Ord. Congl., Lee (Kent) 1873; Ealing (London), '74; Highbury, Bristol, succeeding his father, David Thomas, 1876-1923. Chairman Congl. Union of Eng. & Wales 1899-1900. † Bristol, 28 vi 1924 (76).

99. BY CHRIST REDEEMED, IN CHRIST RESTORED

6 st. 888.4

G. Rawson, *Psalms & Hymns*, 1858; 1 Cor. 11:26.

US & CAN: • ENG: AN372: B311: CH322/- : CP305: M773: NC30

GEORGE RAWSON, b. Leeds, 5 vi 1807; Sch. Manchester Gram. Sch.; practiced as solicitor in Leeds; active Conglst. layman and hymnwriter; ed. *Leeds Hymn Book*, 1853. † Clifton, Bristol, 25 iii 1889 (81).

100. BY JESUS' GRAVE ON EITHER HAND

5 st. 888

L. G. Smith (of whom nothing else is known), *Hymn Book for the Services of the Church*, 1858.

US & CAN: ● ENG: AM123/125: CH114/- : E121

101. CAPTAINS OF THE SAINTLY BAND

6 st. 77.77

Latin: CAELESTIS AULAE PRINCIPES, J. B. de Santeuil, *Cluniac Breviary*, 1686, in 6 st. LM.

Tr. H. W. Baker, *Hymns Ancient & Modern*, 1861.

US & CAN: ● ENG: AM432/507: CH -/539: E177

JEAN BAPTISTE de SANTEUIL, b. Paris, 12 v 1630; Canon of St Victor. Wrote many hymns under Latin name Santolinus Victorinus for liturg. revival in R. C. Church (cf. COFFIN, 52). † Dijon 1697.

HENRY WILLIAMS BAKER (Sir H. W. B. Bart), b. Lambeth (London) 27 v 1821; Sch. Trinity, Camb.; Ord. C/E 1844; Vicar of Monkland, Herefs., '51-†. He was chairman and principal promoter of *Hymns Ancient and Modern* from its inception, 1859 to † (see introduction). Wrote many well known hymns; the last words heard from him as he lay dying were 'Perverse and foolish oft I strayed' (698). † Monkland, 11 ii 1877 (55).

102. CHILD IN THE MANGER

PCH 326

Gaelic poem, LEANABH AN SIGH, Mary MacDougall.

Tr. L. McBean, 3 st. 5.5.5.4D in *Church Hymnary*, 1927.

US & CAN: BP136: B84 ● ENG: An96: B92: BB45: CH53/180: E*757

MARY McDOUGALL, later Mrs. MACDONALD, b. Ardtun, Isle of Mull, 1789; spent all her life on the island (Hebrides), where her husband, Neill Macdonald, was a crofter at Cnocan. She was a Baptist, and composed many Gaelic songs & poems. † Cnocan, 21 v 1872.

LACHLAN McBEAN, b. Kiltarlity, Inverness-shire, 1853; first businessman but later journalist, on staff of *The Highlander* '76, and from '77 on the *Fifeshire Advertizer* at Kircaldy, Fife, where he also was keeper of the Burgh records. One of the most zealous pioneers in the revival of Gaelic culture in Scotland. † Kirkcaldy, 24 i 1931.

103. CHILDREN OF JERUSALEM

3 st. 77.77.77, but last 2 lines extended as soon as familiar tune became associated with text.

J. Henley, posth. in *Sacred Songs for Children*, 1843. Refrain with added 'Hallelujahs' first pub. in undated leaflet *Tune Book to the Hymns and Chaunts for Sunday Schools* (presumably c. 1843) and then in *Juvenile Harmonist*, 1843. Orig. metre restored in most hymnals now.

US & CAN: BP246 ● ENG: An344: B755: CH658‡/236: M837

JOHN HENLEY, b. 18 iii 1800, Torquay, Devon; Ord. Meth. (Wesleyan) 1824, and quickly earned reputation for unusual gifts & faithfulness, especially in service of the poor. Last charge was at Manchester, but † Weymouth, Dorset, 2 v 1842 (42).

104. CHILDREN OF THE HEAVENLY FATHER

4 st. 88.88 troch.

Swedish, C. V. Sandell Berg, in *14 Hymns*, 1858; later in *Zions Harpen*, Swedish-American hymnal, 1890.

Tr. E. W. Olson, *Augustana Hymnal*, 1925.

US & CAN: B207: CW -/30: L572: M521 ● ENG:

CAROLINE V. SANDELL BERG, b. 3 ix 1832, Froderyd, Sweden, d. of a Swed. Luth. minister; on death of father began to write hymns & became known, under name Lina Sandell, as the Fanny Crosby (84) of Sweden. She completed c. 1650 pieces, writing under influence of the evangelical revival (pre-Moody) which from 1859 onwards swept America & Northern Europe. Her hymns became popular partly

through the musical settings of the guitarist Ahnfelt, the first edition of whose songs was underwritten by Jenny Lind (14). † 27 vii 1903 (71).

ERNEST WILLIAM OLSON, b. Skane, Sweden, 16 iii 1870, came to America with parents '75; Sch. Augustana Coll., Rock Island; ed. of Swedish weekly journals for 12 years; later office-editor of Engberg-Holmberg pub. company in Chicago, 1906, and ed. of Augustana Book Co., '11-49. Historian of Swedish-American immigrants, and translator of many Swed. poems & hymns. Member of ed. cttee., Lutheran *Service Book & Hymnal* (1958). † Chicago 6 x 1958 (88).

105. CHILDREN OF THE HEAVENLY KING

12 st. 77.77

J. Cennick (69). *Sacred Hymns for the Children of God*, 1742, pt. 3; 'Encouragement to praise.' Since 6 st. vn. pub. by George Whitefield, 1753, & M. Madan, 1760, always abr. to 6 st. or fewer.

US & CAN: BP506: CW267/- : H578: M300: P347/340/- ● ENG: AM 547/295: An550: CH574/- : CP242: E373: M696

CHRIST ABOVE ALL GLORY SEATED: see 834.

106. 'CHRIST FOR THE WORLD,' WE SING

4 st. 66.4.666.4   **PCH 385**

S. Wolcott, *Songs of Devotion for Christian Associations* (U.S.A.) 1870. Wrtn. Feb. 1869 after seeing a banner inscribed 'Christ for the World and the World for Christ' at a session of the Ohio State Convention of YMCAs in Cleveland, Ohio, which author was attending. Brought to England by W. G. Horder in *Worship Song*, 1896.

US & CAN: BP382: CW538/- : H537: L311: M292: P378/489/- : Pm295: CLB525 ● ENG: AM*11: B364: BB172: CH -/500: CP333: M805

SAMUEL WOLCOTT, b. S. Windsor, Conn., 2 vii 1813; Sch. Yale & Andover Theol. Sem., Ord. Congl.; Missionary to Syria, 1840-2, then in churches in R. I., Mass., Chicago, and Cleveland, Ohio. Sec. Ohio Missionary Society. Late in life (age 56 on) wrote 200 hymns. † Longmeadow, Mass., 24 ii 1886 (72).

107. CHRIST FROM WHOM ALL BLESSINGS FLOW

77.77 or 77.77 D

C. Wesley (1), *Hymns & Sacred Poems*, 1740. In its modern form it is a cento from a 39 st. poem beginning FATHER, SON AND SPIRIT, HEAR, and entitled 'The Communion of Saints.' In the first Methodist Hymn Book of 1780, J. Wesley organized 27 quatrains of this into 4 hymns, #501-4, calling them 'The Communion of Saints Parts 1-4,' and the 4th was CHRIST FROM WHOM ALL BLESSINGS FLOW, in 10 st. 77.77. Through later Meth. H. Books until 1933 this arrangement was followed, with only minor adjustments; but in the 1933 book only this, part 4, survives; other books base their selns. on this. Baptist *Psalms & Hymns*, 1858, uses sts. 1, 3, 5 (24 lines counting in 77.77 D), but begins LORD, FROM WHOM . . . , which has been followed by later Brit. Bapt. Hymnals.

US & CAN: M530 ● ENG: An417: B361‡: CP241: M720: PL270

CHRIST IS MADE THE SURE FOUNDATION
CHRIST IS OUR CORNER-STONE   see 879.

108. CHRIST IS THE KING! O FRIENDS, REJOICE

4 st. 888.888   **PCH 465**

G. K. A. Bell, *Songs of Praise*, 1931, wrtn. to celebrate the ecumenical movement at request of P. Dearmer (88), editor, who asked for it to be in this meter to carry the Welsh tune LLANGOEDMOR (see *SP* 242 and *CP* 365). In more recent use the hymn appears in 888. plus 3 Alleluias with tune GELOBT SEI GOTT, wh. English-speaking cogns. tend to find easier & which has assisted the hymn to great popularity; but since this produced 8st., text is now often abr. (This collocation of text and tune is believed to have been first thought of by the Rev. T. C. Micklem of London in the early 1950s). In H (U.S.), which has its own tune, the first 4 syllables are ingeniously attached to the last 4 of line 7, and the material from line 1 (second half) to the 4th syllable of line 7 omitted.

US & CAN: BP316: CW -/355: H543: CLB304: W44 ● ENG: AM812: B356: CH -/474: CP365

GEORGE KENNEDY ALLEN BELL, b. 4 ii 1883, Hayling Island, Hants; Sch. Westminster & Ch. Ch., Oxf., Wells Theol. Coll.; Ord. C/E; curate in Leeds, 1907; Student (Fellow), Ch. Ch., Oxf., 1911; Chaplain to Randall Davidson, Abp. Canterbury (whose *Life* he wrote), '14; Dean of Canterbury, '24; Bp. Chichester, '29-†. Since 1920 when he was asst. Sec. to the first Lambeth Conference his energies were especially given to the ecumenical movement, and he became one of the architects of the World Council of Churches. During World War II he and N. Micklem (724) were the two English clergy who had closest contact with the Confessional (anti-Establishment) Ch. in Germany. Ed. *Documents on Christian Unity*. † Canterbury, 3 x 1958 (75).

109. CHRIST IS THE WORLD'S LIGHT

4 st. 10.11.11.6 (quasi-Sapphic).   **PCH 505**

F. Pratt Green, *Hymns & Songs*, 1969. Included here as perhaps the most immediately successful hymn of the most recent wave of modern hymn-writing in Britain. Sung at the Inauguration of the United Reformed Church in England and Wales in Westminster Abbey, 5 x 1972.

US & CAN: Can119 ● ENG: CP*10: M*8

FREDERICK PRATT GREEN, b. 2 ix 1903, Roby, Liverpool; Sch. Rydal School, Colwyn Bay; Ord. Meth. 1924; ministered in various circuits, ending at York (Superintendent). Contributed 2 hymns to *Methodist School H. Bk.*, 1950, and best known as playwright and poet. After retirement turned again to hymn writing and at once became one of the leading hymn-writers of his generation in English. Pub. *The Old Couple*, collected poems, 2nd ed. 1976, and some collected hymns in *26 Hymns*, 1971: but since then has written many more.

CHRIST IS THE WORLD'S REDEEMER: see 855.

110. CHRIST IS THE WORLD'S TRUE LIGHT

3 st. 6.7.6.7.6.6.6.6   **PCH 461**

G. W. Briggs, *Songs of Praise*, enlarged ed. 1931 (see 88). Is. 2:5.

US & CAN: BP111: B274: H258: M408: P -/492/326: Pm198 ● ENG: AM*13: An418: B659: CH -/505: CP171: E*101: M*9

GEORGE WALLACE BRIGGS, b. 14 xii 1875, Kirkby, Notts; Sch. Emmanuel, Camb.; Ord. C/E 1899; curate, Wakefield, Yorks; then naval chaplain, '02-09; Vicar, St. Andrew's, Norwich, '09; Rector of Loughborough, '18; Canon of Leicester, '27, of Worcester, '34-†. Unquestionably the leading hymn writer of his generation in Britain. Special fields of interest, hymnology and religious education. Mostly responsible for *Prayers & Hymns for Use in Schools* (County of Leicester, 1927), wh. was based on the 1925 ed. of *Songs of Praise*; worked with Dearmer (88) on enlarged *Songs of Praise*; pub. *Songs of Faith* (his own hymns) 1945, and after 1945 edited a series of hymnals for County education authorities. Ed. *Hymns of the Faith* (1956) for Worcester Cathedral (only text-edition published). Also ed. many books of prayers, and wrote prayers, including one, 'Stablish our hearts, O God . . .' used at the promulgation of the Atlantic Charter, 1942. † Hindhead, Surrey, 30 xii 1959 (84).

111. CHRIST JESUS LAY IN DEATH'S STRONG BANDS

7 st. 8.7.8.7.7.8.7.4   **PCH 1**

German: CHRIST LAG IN TODESBANDEN, M. Luther, *Enchiridion*, 1524: for Easter based on VICTIMAE PASCHALI, the medieval Easter Sequence, but departing from it after st. 2 (cf. 883).

Tr. R. Massie, *Spiritual Songs* (trs. of Luther), 1854; norm. abr. to 4st. Not

in standard Eng. hymnals before *Methodist H.B.*, 1933.

US & CAN: BP191: CW -/177: H*60: L98: P -/-/327: CLB282: W45 ● ENG: B153: CH -/268: CP761: M210: NC33

MARTIN LUTHER, b. Eisleben, 10 vi 1483; Sch. Univ. Erfurt; Canon in Monastery, Erfurt, c. 1505, Ord. R. C. 1507; prof. at Univ. Wittenberg, 1508; stirred by disgust at preaching of John Tetzel, inaugurated the European Reformation by publishing his 95 theses, 1517. (Story of his nailing them to the church door at Wittenberg, though plausible, now doubted by historians who think he merely distributed copies). Theses condemned by the Pope; he defended his position in the 3 celebrated treatises of 1520 and was excommunicated in that year. Thereafter pursued a religious & political campaign to establish Protestant Reformation, and devoted years 1521-34 to hymn-writing and to perfecting his translation of the Bible, which became the foundation of the modern German language. Wrote 37 hymns, mostly on the Catechism, and composed or adapted many tunes for them. Texts and music of these, with commentary, accessible in English in Vol. 53 of *Luther's Works* (Fortress Press). † Eisleben 18 ii 1546 (62).

RICHARD MASSIE, b. Chester, 18 vi 1800, came of old Cheshire family, son of the Vicar of Coddington; himself a man of leisure; owner of two estates, devoted his life to literature, with special interest in Luther. † at one of his estates, Pulford Hall, Coddington, Ches., 11 iii 1887 (86).

112. CHRIST, THE FAIR GLORY OF THE HOLY ANGELS

6 st. 11.11.11.5 (Sapphic)   **PCH 150**

Latin: CHRISTE SANCTORUM DECUS ANGELORUM, Rabanus Maurus; appears in late medieval sources in four versions, but that in *Roman Breviary* 1632 generated the only trsn. in modern use.

Tr. A. Riley, *English Hymnal*, 1906.

US & CAN: Can506: H123 ● ENG:AM -/564: EH242

RABANUS MAURUS, b. c. 784, Sch. Fulda and Tours (under Alcuin); Ord. priest 814; abbot of Fulda, 822-42; resigned to lead a life of prayer & meditation; one of the most influential theologians and eccl. statesmen of his age; wrote many Scripture commentaries and a work *De Universo* about cosmology. Believed by some to have written VENI CREATOR SPIRITUS (880) but this cannot be proved. † Petersburg (nr. Fulda), 4 ii 856.

(JOHN) ATHELSTAN (LAURIE) RILEY, b. Paddington (London), 10 viii 1858; Ord. Eton & Pembroke, Oxf.; Seigneur de la Trinité, Isle of Jersey, and throughout most of his life member of the House of Laymen, Province of Canterbury (an Anglican body now replaced by the Synod). Member of ed. cttee. of *English Hymnal*. † Trinity, Jersey (Channel Islands), 17 xi 1945 (87).

113. CHRIST THE LORD IS RISEN AGAIN

7 st. 77.77.4

German: CHRISTUS IST ERSTANDEN, M. Weiss *Ein Neu Gesangbüchlein*, 1531, in 7 st. 6.6.88.4, suggested by late medieval hymn CHRIST IST ERSTANDEN.

Tr. C. Winkworth (14), *Lyra Germanica* II, 1858, without *Alleluia*, which however normally appears in mod. books (as in German orig.). Full Text, A & M; otherwise abr. to 6st or fewer.

US & CAN: CW -/176: L107: Pm183 ● ENG: AM136: An179: BB101: CP142: E129: M207: NC34: PL196

MICHAEL WEISSE, b. c. 1480, became a monk at Breslau, but later left to join the Community of Bohemian Brethren; learned Czech language & translated many Czech hymns into German. † 1534.

CHRIST THE LORD IS RISEN TO-DAY: CHRISTIANS, HASTE YOUR VOWS TO PAY: see 883.

114. 'CHRIST THE LORD IS RISEN TO-DAY', SONS OF MEN AND ANGELS SAY

11 st. 77.77

C. Wesley (1), *Sacred Poems*, 1739; always abr. in mod. books, many of which interpolate Alleluias after each line. In EM, AMR, begin with st. 2, LOVE'S REDEEMING WORK IS DONE, thus edited to avoid confusion with JESUS CHRIST IS RISEN TO-DAY (347); but now often in non-Anglican circles substituted for that hymn and sung to its traditional tune.

US & CAN: BP189: Can466: B114: CW239/180: H95: L99: M439: P165/-/330: Pm182: W46 ● ENG: AM -/141 : An180: B154: CH118/275: CP145: E135 : M204: PL192

115. CHRIST, WHO KNOWS ALL HIS SHEEP

66.6.5.6.5

R. Baxter, from a 31 st. poem, 'The Exit', in *Additions to Poetical Fragments*, 1683 (dated 19 xii 1682). As usually printed in hymnals the last 3 st. of the poem are used, as altd. by P. Dearmer (88) in *Songs of Praise*, 1925. Another vn. was made by F. Fletcher (561) for the *Clarendon Hymn Book*, 1936, and a third vn., based on these but using material from sts. 9, 11, 27, in 4 sts., is in *M** and *Hymns for Church & School*, 1964.

US & CAN: ● ENG: AM*14: BB507: CH -/672: CP757: M639: M*11‡: PL208

RICHARD BAXTER, b. 12 xi 1615, Rowton, Salop; Sch. Wroxeter Sch.; Ord. C/E 1640, curate at Kidderminster, Worcs; during Civil War, chaplain to one of Cromwell's regiments; chaplain to K. Charles II, 1660; nominated for bishopric of Hereford but refused it. After Act of Uniformity, '62, resigned his curacy and was for many years without a charge. Ministered in a dissenting ch. from '73, and tried for nonconformity before Judge Jeffries 1685 and imprisoned 18 months, Wrote more than 200 books and had one of the largest libraries in any clergy house of his time. † Charterhouse, Middx (London), 8 ii 1691 (75).

116. CHRIST WHOSE GLORY FILLS THE SKIES

3 st. 7.7.7.7.77   PCH 61

C. Wesley (1), *Hymns and Sacred Poems*, 1740. 'A Morning Hymn'.

US & CAN: BP149: Can362: CW -/285: H153: L208: M401: P26/47/332: Pm43 ● ENG: AM7: An36: B673: BB137: CH261/114: CP594: E258: M924

117. CHRISTIAN, DOST THOU SEE THEM?

4 st. 6.5.6.5 D

J. M. Neale (2), *Hymns of the Eastern Church*, 1862, founded on a Gk. poem by St. Andrew of Crete (7 c.). In orig. the cue verb in each st. was italicized: 'Christian, dost thou *see* them . . .?' &c.

US & CAN: CW -/248: H556: L68: M238: P275/360/-: Pm364 ● ENG: AM91: An137: B506: BB339: CP484: E72

ST. ANDREW OF CRETE, b. c. 660, Damascus, Abp. Gortyna (Crete), c. 692; Wrote 'hymns'—really Canons for Gk. Orthodox worship, the most famous of wh. ran 250 sts. (Another St. Andrew of Crete, known as 'the Colybite', sometimes confused with him). † 740.

118. CHRISTIAN, SEEK NOT YET REPOSE

6 st. 7.7.7.3   PCH 276

C. Elliott, *Morning and Evening Prayers for a Week*, 1839; 'Watch and Pray' for Wed. evening.

US & CAN: BP434 ● ENG: AM269/308: An573: B507: BB340: CH523/- : CP505: E374: M491

CHARLOTTE ELLIOTT, b. 18 iii 1789, Clapham, Surrey; a confirmed invalid through most of a long life, beginning 1821 she wrote well over 100 hymns, wh. were pub. in H. V. Elliott's *Psalms and Hymns*, 1838-48 (he being her brother) and in *The Invalid's Hymn Book*, wh. she took over from its editor & saw through several editions. † Brighton, Sussex, 22 ix 1871 (82).

119. CHRISTIANS, AWAKE: SALUTE THE HAPPY MORN

PCH 49

J. Byrom, 1749, written as a continuous poem in heroic couplets, 48 lines, (2 parts: 32 and 16), as a Christmas present for his daughter Dolly who, when asked what she would like for Christmas (1749) answered 'please write me a poem.' It was waiting for her on the breakfast table. Soon afterwards John Wainwright, a choirman in Manchester Collegiate Church (now Cathedral) and an organist of Stockport parish ch. wrote the famous tune, and on Xmas Eve 1750 it was sung by the Manchester choir under Byrom's window, and the following day in Stockport parish ch. (The custom of singing it in the streets in N. W. England at Christmas time survives to this day.) Presumably it was arranged in stanzas for the 1750 performances, but the arrangement now familiar in 6 st. 10.10.10.10.10.10. is chiefly the work of J. Montgomery (6). This was done in the 8th ed. of Cotterill's Selection (1819). Now often abr. to 4 st. in hymnals.

US & CAN: BP126: H16: L19: Pm127 ● ENG: AM61: An97: B393: BB46: CH54/190: CP83: E21: M120

JOHN BYROM, b. Manchester 29 ii 1692, Sch. King's Sch., Chester, Merchant Taylors Sch., London, Trinity Camb.; Fellow of Trinity 1714; resigned Fellowship because unwilling to take Holy Orders (necessary in those days for Fellowships). Studied medicine at Montpellier; taught shorthand in London, of which he was the inventor of the best system to date: taught it to the Wesleys who used it in their journals. Fellow of the Royal Society 1723; succeeded to family estates '24 and returned to Manchester area where family continued to live (Gee Cross, Hyde) into the mid 20th century. Poems first pub. posth. 1773. † Manchester 26 ix 1763 (71).

CHRISTIANS, TO THE PASCHAL VICTIM: see 883.

120. CITY OF GOD, HOW BROAD AND FAR   PCH 380

S. Johnson, wrtn. 1860 at Lynn, Mass., pub. 1864 in *Hymns of the Spirit*. Introduced to England by W. G. Horder in *The Treasury of Hymns*, 1896.

US & CAN: BP303: Can147: CW426/- : H386: L330: P338/436/- : Pm261 ● ENG: AM -/258: B255: BB173: CH209/422: CP253: E375: M703

SAMUEL JOHNSON, b. 10 x 1822, Salem, Mass.; Sch. Harvard and Cambridge (Mass.) Divinity Sch. Ord. Unit; formed Free Church congregation at Lynn, Mass., 1853 & remained there until '70. With S. Longfellow (7) ed. *Hymns of the Spirit*, 1864. † N. Andover, Mass., 19 ii 1882 (59).

121. COME, CHILDREN (CHRISTIANS) JOIN TO SING

C. H. Bateman, *Sacred Melodies for Children*, 1843, 'Praise to Christ.' Meter is peculiar, only expressible as 6. -6. 6.-6. 666.-6; 2nd and 4th lines always being 'Alleluia, Amen', others 1 dactyl and 1 amphibrach. A good example of the principle that a successful children's hymn at once becomes a successful adult hymn; in this case altn. of one word only was required, 'Children' to 'Christians', which is always found in U.S.

US & CAN: BP251: B61: CW -/295: M77: P191/131/333 ● ENG: CH177 /383

CHRISTIAN HENRY BATEMAN, b. Wyke, Halifax, 9 viii 1813; Sch. Moravian, later Congl.; served at Edinburgh (Richmond Place), Hopton, Yorks; Reading, Berks; later still Ord. C/E, St. Luke's, Jersey; chaplain to the forces, Childshill, Middx, and last St. John's, Penmynydd-Hawarden (Flints), thus ministering in England, Scotland, Channel Islands and Wales. Pub. a hymn book in Edinburgh in which this, his only well-known hymn is found. † Carlisle, 1889.

122. COME, DEAREST LORD, DESCEND AND DWELL

LM, sts. 1-2 alt., st. 3 coup.

I. Watts (10), *Hymns* . . . , 1707, Book I; 'The Love of Christ shed abroad in the heart,' Eph. 3:17-21.

US & CAN: P -/531/- ● ENG: B758: CH297/637: CP260

123. COME DOWN, O LOVE DIVINE
4 st. 66.11 D   **PCH 205**

Italian: *Discendi, Amor Santo*, by Bianco of Siena; text in *Laudi Spirituali*, ed. T. Bini, Lucca, 1851. The *Laudi* were vernacular hymns which appeared from mid-13 c. onwards in Italy and S. France, often among unorthodox or dissenting groups within the medieval church.

Tr. R. F. Littledale, *People's Hymnal*, 1867, but popular only after being set to music by Vaughan Williams in *EH*, 1906.

US & CAN: BP257: Can67: H376: L123: M466: P -/-/334: Pm239: CLB 296: W49 ● ENG: AM670/235: An214: B224: BB149: CH191/115: CP 204: E152: M273: NC42: PL7

BIANCO OF SIENA, b. Anciolina, date unknown: entered order of Jesuates (a small devotional order, not to be confused with 16 c. Jesuits). Believed to have lived in Venice, and † there 1434.

RICHARD FREDERICK LITTLEDALE, b. Dublin, 4 ix 1833, Sch. Trinity, Dublin; Ord. C/E 1856, curate of St Matthew's, Thorpe, Norwich '56; Vicar of St. Mary's, Soho, London, '57. Resigned charge '61 because of ill-health; devoted himself to literature & hymnology; translated hymns from 7 languages; compiled *Priest's Prayer Book* (with J. W. Vaux) '64 and *People's Hymnal* '67. † London 11 i 1890 (56).

124. COME, GRACIOUS (HOLY) SPIRIT, HEAVENLY DOVE
7 st. LM-coup.

S. Browne, *Hymns & Spiritual Songs*, 1720, Bk. I. Orig. vn. is in *Julian*, p. 246; wrtn. in first person sing. throughout. In later books much altd., notably Ash & Evans, *Collection* . . . , 1769, wh. transposed to first person plural; Toplady's *Psalms & Hymns*, 2nd (posth.) ed., 1787, wh. introduced 'gracious' in opening line; and Mercer, *Church Psalter & Hymn Book*, 1858, wh. abr. to 4 st. and whose vn. was taken with further small alts. into *Hymns A & M*, 1875; this is what all books now have.

US & CAN: Can266: H378: L127: P209/239/- : Pm238: CLB293 ● ENG: AM209/232: An215: BB150: CH188/116: CP205

SIMON BROWNE, b. Shepton Mallet, Som., c. 1680; Ord. Independent (Congl.); charges in Portsmouth and Old Jewry, London; contemporary & neighbor of I. Watts (10). One day he was attacked by a highwayman and in self-defence killed him, which induced severe mental trauma & temptation to suicide, with constant belief that he was in danger of insanity. Wrote many hymns which were among the first to be written in imitation of Watts. † Shepton Mallet, 1732.

COME, HOLY GHOST, CREATOR BLEST: see 880 d.

COME, HOLY GHOST, ETERNAL GOD: see 854 b.

COME, HOLY GHOST, IN LOVE: see 881 c.

125. COME, HOLY GHOST, OUR HEARTS INSPIRE
4 st. CM

C. Wesley (1), *Sacred Poems*, 1740, 'Before Reading the Scriptures.' In st. 3 'prolific Dove' altd. by J. Wesley in 1780 to 'celestial Dove.'

US & CAN: BP261: M131 ● ENG: AM599/- : An288: B244: CH196/ 122: CP226: M305

COME, HOLY GHOST, OUR SOULS INSPIRE: see 881.

COME, HOLY GHOST, WHO EVER ONE: see 854.

COME, HOLY GHOST, WITH GOD THE SON: see 854.

126. COME, HOLY SPIRIT, COME
9 st. SM

J. Hart, *Hymns* . . . , 1759. Norm. abr. 4 st. (1, 3, 6, 9).

US & CAN: BP264 ● ENG: AM673/- : An219: CH190/104: CP206

JOSEPH HART, b. London 1712; as recorded in Preface to his *Hymns* (1759), he underwent a series of dramatic religious experiences, being much depressed by repeated convictions of sin; in 1759 Ord. Congl. at Jewin St. Church, London. † London 24 v 1768.

127. COME, HOLY SPIRIT, GOD AND LORD
3 st. LMD-coup.

German: KOMM HEILIGER GEIST, adapted by M. Luther (111) from earlier form in 15th cent. ms. at Munich, wh. was itself an adaptation of an earlier Latin antiphon for Pentecost. In *Enchiridion*, 1524, Luther took st. 1 and expanded it into this hymn. The Lutheran melody is the subject of one of Bach's most impressive chorale-preludes (*S* 656).

Tr. C. Winkworth (14), *Lyra Germanica*, I, 1855, orig. met. In some U.S. books (‡ below) appears in 4 st. LM with altd. st. 3. In *L* and *CLB* a tr. beginning with the same line by E. Traill Horn III is used.

US & CAN: CW -/193: L122* P -/-/336‡ Pm235‡ CLB292* ● ENG: An 217: PL214

EDWARD TRAILL HORN, b. Ithaca, N.Y., 1909; Sch. Cornell Univ., and Luth. Sem., Philadelphia; Ord. Luth., succeeded his father at Luth. Ch., Ithaca, '34-43; then asst. prof., Philadelphia Luth. Sem., '43; pastor of Trinity Church, Germantown, Philadelphia, '46; member of Common Service Cttee., Lutheran Church, '37-52, and of committee producing Luth. *Service Book & Hymnal* (*L*), '52-58, also of many other bodies in the liturgical field.

129. COME, LABOUR ON
7 st. 4.10 10. 10 10. 4

J. Borthwick (70), *Thoughts for Thoughtful Hours*, 1859—rearranged as 7 st. 5 lines (4. 10 10. 10 4) in 1863 ed. of same work, which version is now always used, and always abr. to 4 st.

US & CAN: BP499: CW -/338: H576: P366/287/- : Pm 293 ● ENG: AM 738/339: An593: B511: BB388: CP542

130. COME, LET US ANEW
5 5. 5 11 anap.   **PCH 68**

Three hymns of Charles Wesley (1) begin with this phrase, all of wh. have been popular among Methodists in the past, but only one of wh. remains in common use (c below):

  (a) COME, LET US ANEW OUR PLEASURES PURSUE, *Hymns for the Watch Night*, 1744, 8 double sts. (80 lines).

  (b) COME, LET US ANEW OUR JOURNEY PURSUE: WITH VIGOUR ARISE . . . , 'On a Journey,' *Hymns & Sacred Poems*, 1749, 8 st. (40 lines).

  (c) COME, LET US ANEW OUR JOURNEY PURSUE, ROLL ROUND WITH THE YEAR . . . , in a tract sold for one penny, *Hymns for New Year's Day*, 1750, 6 st. (30 lines).

It is clear that all are related, and that the third one was suggested by the other two.

US & CAN: BP576 ● ENG: B712: CP639: M956

131. COME, LET US JOIN OUR CHEERFUL SONGS
5 st. CM

I. Watts (10), *Hymns . . .* , 1707, Book I, 'Christ Jesus the Lamb of God, Worshipp'd by all the Creation'; Rev. 5:11-13. St. 4 sometimes om. Appears in Scottish *Paraphrases* (76) embedded in Paraphrase 65, 'Hark how the adoring hosts above,' and in this form taken into *CH³* (1973).

US & CAN: Can247: B126: M413: W51 ● ENG: AM299/221: An16: B200: BB122: CH175/532‡: CP157: E376: M85: NC44

132. COME, LET US JOIN OUR FRIENDS ABOVE

5 st. CMD

C. Wesley (1), *Funeral Hymns*, 1759; sometimes found (‡ below) in abr. form as recast by F. H. Murray in *A Hymnal for Use in the English Church*, 1852, 5 st. CM, LET SAINTS ON EARTH IN CONCERT SING; this was taken into *Hymns A & M*, 1861. *Hymns A & M* included this in 1950 but also 8 lines of orig. at #628.

US & CAN: BP312‡: Can185‡: H397‡: M302: CLB531‡ ● ENG: AM 221‡/272‡: B402: BB249‡: CH227‡/543‡: CP361: E428‡: M824

133. COME, LET US TO THE LORD OUR GOD

6 st. CM   **PCH 99**

Scottish *Paraphrases* #30, 1781 (76): Hosea 6:1-4.

US & CAN:BP402: Can72: P -/125/- ● ENG: An113: BB487: CH400/69: CP386: M342

134. COME, LET US WITH OUR LORD ARISE

4 st. 88.88.88   **PCH 72**

C. Wesley (1), *Hymns for Children*, 1763; 'The Lord's Day.' St. 4 norm. om.

US & CAN: BP334 ● ENG: An69: BB397: CP606: E*60: M661: PL19

135. COME, MY SOUL, THOU MUST BE WAKING

14 st. 84.7 D

German: SEELE, DU MUST MUNTER WERDEN, F. Canitz, posth. in *Nebenstunden unterschiedener Gedichte*, 1700.

Tr. H. J. Buckoll, first pub. anon. in *British Magazine*, July 1838, later in his *Hymns Translated from the German*, 1842, 5 st. only. Versions now in use differ. Best seln. in *Hymns for Church & School* (1964), #327.

US & CAN: B542: CW134/32: H154: L207: M258: P487/44/337: Pm506 (1 st.) ● ENG: An38: B674: BB404: CP591: M929

FRIEDERICH RUDOLPH LUDWIG, Freiherr von CANITZ, b. Berlin 27 xi 1654; Sch. Univ. Leyden & Leipzig. Groom of the Bedchamber to Elector Frederick William of Brandenburg; Councillor of Legation, 1680, then privy councillor and Baron of the Empire. His poetry was ed. by J. Lange after his death, 11 viii 1699 (44).

HENRY JAMES BUCKOLL, b. Siddington, Glos., 9 ix 1903; Sch. Rugby and Queen's, Oxf.; Ord. C/E 1827; asst. master at Rugby Sch. for 44 years, until †. Edited first Rugby Sch. H. Bk. and also 2nd ed. † Rugby, Warks, 6 vi 1871 (67).

136. COME, MY SOUL, THY SUIT (PLEA) PREPARE

7 st. 77.77

J. Newton (37), *Olney Hymns*, 1779; 'Ask what I shall give thee,' 3 Kings 3:5. Norm. abr. to 5 st.

US & CAN: BP442: P -/529/- ● ENG: AM527/319: An607: B333; CH 450/- : CP264: E377: M540

137. COME, MY WAY, MY TRUTH, MY LIFE

3 st. 7.7.7.7   **PCH 415**

G. Herbert, *The Temple*, 1633; 'The Call.' First as a hymn in *Songs of*

Praise, 1925, but set to a hymn tune by Alexander Brent Smith (1889-1950) on leaflet privately printed at Lancing College c. 1919. (This setting is in M* and CP*).

US & CAN: Can258: H*3: W53 ● ENG: CP*15: M*12: PL110

GEORGE HERBERT, b. Montgomery Castle, Wales, 3 iv 1593; Sch Westminster & Trinity, Camb. Ord. C/E; Fellow of Trinity and Public Orator, Univ., Camb.; Prebendery of Leighton Ecclesia and Rector of Leighton Bromswold, Hunts, 1636; Rector of Bemerton, Wilts, 1630-†. His exquisite poems, among the profoundest devotional miniatures of his time, were gathered in *The Temple*, wh. he gave to Nicholas Ferrar about 3 weeks before his death, with permission to publish if he thought fit. This was done in 1633. † Feb. 1633 (39).

COME, O CREATOR-SPIRIT, COME: see 880.

138. COME, O THOU TRAVELLER UNKNOWN

14 st. 8.8.8.8.88   **PCH 62**

C. Wesley (1), *Hymns & Sacred Poems*, 1742. Gen. 32; 'Wrestling Jacob.' When his brother, J. Wesley, delivered his obituary tribute at Conference of 1788, he said, 'His least praise was his talent for poetry; although Dr. Watts did not scruple to say that "that single poem, *Wrestling Jacob*, was worth all the verse he himself had written." ' (This is in the Conference minutes of that session).

Longest vn. in a hymnal is the 12-st. version in M(Brit)339, wh. om. sts. 5, 7. Other selns. are (a) 1, 2, 8, 9; (b) 1, 3, 8, 9. (c) 1, 2, 3, 8, 9; (d) 1, 2, 4, 8, 9; (e) 1, 2, 11, 8, 9; (f) 1, 2, 3, 8, 9, 10, 11; (g) 1, 2, 4, 8, 9, 10, 11, 12.

US & CAN: L471 (e) M529 (a) ● ENG: AM774 (c) /343 (c) B767 (g) BB4 (b) CH416 (c) /- : CP495 (f) E378 (a) M339 (12st.) 340 (a)

139. COME, DEAREST LORD, AND DEIGN TO BE OUR GUEST

4 st. 10.10.10.10

G. W. BRIGGS (110), *Songs of Praise*, 1931. In st. 1 line 4, author wrote 'in thine own sacrament', but was persuaded by Dearmer (88), ed. of *SP*, to alter it to 'in this our sacrament.' He later wrote that he regretted the change.

US & CAN: BP349: CW -/305: H297: L*4-24: P -/-/340: Pm286 ● ENG: AM*16: An374: B312: CH -/572: CP311: E*61: M*13: PL67

140. COME, THOU ALMIGHTY KING

4 st. 66.4.666.4

Anon., date uncertain; first pub. in a leaflet by G. Whitefield containing 2 hymns, this and an altered one by C. Wesley (no date); so occasionally, but wholly improbably, this has been ascribed to C. W. Still very popular in U.S., it is clearly written on the pattern of the British National Anthem (whose tune is also used for one of the U.S. national songs [458], and may therefore be dated some time not too long after 1745, at about which date 'God save the King' first appeared (247). Although designed to be sung to the Anthem tune, it is now always set in U.S. to MOSCOW (or ITALIAN HYMN). During the American revolutionary battles (c. 1776) soldiers broke in on a congregation in Long Island and demanded that they sing the British National Anthem; the congregation satisfied both demand and honor by singing that tune to his text. The text is drastically recast in *Worshipbook*, 1972, and *CLB*, 1975; and it is not a text whose literary quality makes such recasting improper.

US & CAN: BP273: Cab62: B2: CW122/64: H271: L136: M3: P52/244/ 343‡: Pm246: CLB411‡: W55 ● ENG: CP221

141. COME, THOU FOUNT OF EVERY BLESSING

4 st. 8.7.8.7 D

R. Robinson, Ms. 1758 and *A Collection of Hymns . . .* , Angel Alley,

Bishopsgate (London), 1759. 24-line vn. now current in Britain, as found in Madan's *Psalms & Hymns*, 1760; other hymnals reduce to 16 lines, sometimes in 8.7.8.7. The reference in st. 2 is to 2 Sam. 7:12 ('Here I raise my Ebenezer'). It is one of those 18 c. evangelical hymns which contains too many fine thoughts to be dropped and too many roughnesses of style to be invulnerable to alteration. Those who can swallow 'Ebenezer' (and it is an over-sensitive stomach that cannot) will find the most satisfactory vn. at *CP* 442, *P²*379.

US & CAN: B13: CW111/- ; M93: P235/379/341 • ENG: An17: B444: CH435/- : CP442: M417

ROBERT ROBINSON, b. 27 ix 1735, Swaffham, Nfk; loss of his father at age 8 left family in poverty; he was indentured to a London barber, 1749, but resigned indentures '52; in that year, while he & some companions were making ill-natured fun of an old woman fortune-teller & attempting to make her drunk, she turned to R. R. and said he would live to see his children & grandchildren; this made such an impression on him that he took it to heart & began to study, and very soon afterwards he heard Whitefield preach on Matt. 3:7 on 'the wrath to come'; after 3 years of spiritual darkness and struggle he came to the Christian Faith in a new way, and for some years faithfully attended preaching of the leading evangelists, including J. Wesley himself. Ord. Calv. Meth. Mildenhall, Nfk, '58, a few months later to Bapt. Ch. Cambridge where in '61 he became full pastor. He remained there until he retired, adding much writing to preaching work. Very soon after retirement † 9 vi 1790 Birmingham (64).

COME, THOU HOLY PARACLETE
COME, THOU HOLY SPIRIT, COME   see 881.

142.   COME, THOU LONG-EXPECTED JESUS

2 st. 8.7.8.7 D

C. Wesley (1), *Hymns for the Nativity of our Lord*, 1744; more usually now in 4 st. 8.7.8.7. Text considerably altered in CLB.

US & CAN: BP114: Can389: B79: CW -/106: H1: L5: M360: P113/151/342: Pm103: CLB204†: W57 • ENG: AM640/54: An86: B78: BB152: CH150/320: CP159: E*303: M242: PL130

143.   COME TO OUR POOR (DARK) NATURE'S NIGHT

9 st. 777.5

G. Rawson (99), *Leeds Hymn Book*, 1853: vn. with 'dark' found elsewhere with other alts., first in *Hymnal Companion*, 1890, 8 st. (‡ below).

US & CAN: • ENG: AM524/- : An286‡: B229: M297

144.   COME UNTO ME, YE WEARY

4 st. 7.6.7.6 D

W. C. Dix (28), *People's Hymnal* 1867; Matt. 11:28.

US & CAN: CW277/- : P222/268/- : Pm315 • ENG: AM256/350: An 470: B412: CH390/- : CP372: E379: M328

145.   COME, WE (YE) THAT LOVE THE LORD

10 st. SM

I. Watts (10), *Hymns . . .* , 1707, Book II: 'Heavenly Joy on Earth.' In norm. use sts. 2, 4, 5, 7 om. *B* (U.S.) adds refrain by R. Lowry. 1867, to 4 st. vn.

US & CAN: B505‡: CW119/- : L165: M5: P -/408/- • ENG: B495: CH 447/- : CP391: M410

146.   COME, YE DISCONSOLATE, WHERE'ER YE LANGUISH

3 st. 11.10.11.10 dact.

T. Moore, *Sacred Songs*, 1816; sts. 1-2 altd. and st. 3 replaced by new st. by Thomas Hastings in *Spiritual Songs for Social Worship*, 1832 (U.S.); now always in that form.

US & CAN: B211: CW398/- : L569: M103: P293/373/- • ENG: CH688/-

THOMAS MOORE, b. Dublin, 28 v 1779; Sch. Trinity, Dublin; then studied law in Middle Temple, London; appointed Admiralty Registrar, Bermuda, 1803, but had to resign 1818 through dishonesty of his deputy, after which he travelled on the continent of Europe, returning to Britain '21 where he settled at Ashbourne, Derbs. Versatile & prolific writer, works include a *Life* of Byron (whom he knew) and much poetry; but most famous for his *Irish Melodies* (1807) and *Irish National Airs* in wh. he became known as the foremost promoter of Irish lyric and music. Himself a singer, he made them and himself much favored in London society. An unfavorable review of his *Epistles, Odes and Other Poems* (1806) caused him to challenge the reviewer to a duel, wh. was stopped literally at the last minute by the Bow Street Runners (forerunners of the London police). Spent final years in retirement at Sloperton, nr. Devizes, Wilts, where † 25 ii 1852 (72).

THOMAS HASTINGS, b. 15 x 1784, Washington, Conn., is more famous as musician than writer, being composer of over 600 tunes including the one famous in U.S. for 'Rock of Ages'; elder contemporary and friend of Lowell Mason, set himself to reform American church music, publ. a series of tune books from 1816 onwards, started a religious paper, 1823, in wh. he advocated good hymn singing; spent 40 years with church choirs in New York. The desk at which he wrote is now in possession of his distinguished descendant, Dr. Lee Hastings Bristol, Jr., of Princeton, N.J. † New York, 1872.

149.   COME, YE SINNERS, POOR AND WRETCHED

7 st. 8.7.8.7.4.7

J. Hart (127), *Hymns*, 1759. Now always abr. to 5 st. or fewer.

US & CAN: B196: M104 • ENG: An473: CH393/- : M324

150.   COME, YE THANKFUL PEOPLE COME

4 st. 77.77 D

H. Alford, *Psalms & Hymns*, 1844. Authorized text in his *Poetical Works*, 1865 wh. is used in most hymnals. But *Hymns A & M* in all editions persists in revision by its compilers of 1861 whose alterations the author repudiated with the remark that '*Hymns A & M*' should be interpreted, '*Hymns Asked for and Mutilated.*' None the less, it was *Hymns A & M* that made the hymn popular by associating it with the tune now inseparable from it, and it is still the best known of Engl. harvest hymns, and much used in Thanksgiving celebrations in U.S. (*Pm* has an alternative text, for a note on which see 602).

US & CAN: BP567: Can384: B233: CW593/101: H137: L363: M582: P460/525/346: Pm461: W59 • ENG: AM382/482: An648: B724: BB439: CH619/627: CP645: E289: M962: PL301

HENRY ALFORD, b. Bloomsbury, London, 7 x 1810; Sch. Ilminster Gram. Sch. & Trinity, Camb.; Ord. C/E '33; Incumbent of Quebec Chapel '53-7; Dean of Canterbury 57; † there 12 i 1871 (60).

151.   COMFORT, COMFORT YE, MY PEOPLE

4 st. 8.7.8.7.77.88

German: TROSTET, TROSTET, MEINE LIEBEN, J. Olearius, *Geistliche Singe-Kunst*, 1671.

Tr. C. Winkworth (14), *Chorale-Book for England*, 1863. St. 2 norm. om., at 3 slightly altd. Marked for St. John Baptist's Day and suitable also for Advent being based on Is. 40:1ff. Incomprehensibly absent from all English hymnals to this day.

US & CAN: B77: CW-/110: L12: P -/-/347: Pm104: W60 • ENG:

JOHANN OLEARIUS, b. 1611, was court chaplain at Halle, later at Weissenfels, and after that member of faculty of philosophy at Univ. Wittenberg. His 1671 hymnal (above) was regarded as one of the most influential in Germany at the time; it contained 1207 hymns, 302 being his own. † 1684.

152. COMMAND THY BLESSING FROM ABOVE

5 st. LM-alt

J. Montgomery (6), leaflet for Sheffield Sunday School Union, 3 vi 1816: *Evangelical Magazine*, Sept. 1816; *Cotterill's Selection*, 8th ed., 1819. Author made small alts. in text in his last book, *Hymns . . .*, 1853, which are now standard.

US & CAN: ● ENG: B357: CH241/117: CP269: M*14

COMMIT THOU ALL THAT GRIEVES THEE
COMMIT THOU ALL THY GRIEFS   see 840.

153. CONQUERING KINGS THEIR TITLES TAKE

6 st. 77.77

Latin: VICTIS SIBI COGNOMINA, 6 st. LM, anon. in *Paris Breviary*, 1736 (see 52).

Tr. J. Chandler (52), *Hymns of the Primitive Church*, 1837, orig., beginning 'TIS FOR CONQUERING KINGS TO GAIN; rewritten in *A & M*, 1861 by compilers who provided new vns. of sts. 1, 5, 6.

US & CAN: H324: L509 ● ENG: AM175/191: An552: E37

154. COURAGE, BROTHER, DO NOT STUMBLE

3 st. 8.7.8.7 D

N. McLeod, *Edinburgh Christian Magazine* (of wh. he was ed.), Jan. 1857.

US & CAN: ● ENG: B563: CH529/484: CP513

NORMAN MCLEOD, b. Campbelltown, Argyllshire, 3 vi 1812; Sch. Univs. Glasgow & Edinburgh; Ord. C/Scot., Loudoun, Ayrshire, 1838; minister at Dalkeith, Midlothian '43; Barony Ch., Glasgow, '51 to †; Chaplain to the Queen '57, Moderator of Assembly '69; ed. *Edinburgh Christian Magazine* '43; one of the foremost preachers of his day, was a founder of the Evangelical Alliance, a founder of the Glasgow Penny Savings Bank, and in '67 provoked controversy by his liberal views on use of the Sabbath. † Glasgow 16 vi 1872 (60).

155. CREATION'S LORD, WE GIVE THEE THANKS

4 st. LM-alt.

W. de W. Hyde, *The Outlook*, May 1903, beg. O LORD, WE MOST OF ALL GIVE THANKS; 'The Strenuous Life.' A longer poem from which hymnals select norm. 4 st. but differ in their seln. of lines. Familiar vn. of first line from *Unity Hymns & Carols*, 1911.

US & CAN: Can161: CW492/-.: H548: Pm303: CLB526 ● ENG:

WILLIAM DeWITT HYDE, b. Winchendon, Mass., 23 ix 1858; Sch. Exeter Academy & Andover Theol. Sem. Ord. Congl., Paterson, N.J., '82; President, Bowdoin Coll., '85 (age 28) where he remained till †. Fellow of American Academy of Arts & Sciences. † Bowdoin, 29 vi 1917 (58).

156. CREATOR OF THE EARTH AND SKIES

6 st. LM-alt.   PCH 487

D. Hughes, *Hymns for Church & School*, (1964), in some hymnals found with 'you' for 'thou' throughout, and sometimes abr. to 4 st. Full text in *HCS*, *PL*, and, with 'you,' *Westminster Praise*, 1976.

US & CAN: H*5: W61 ● ENG: AM*18: B*12: CP*17: M*15: PL99

DONALD HUGHES, b. Southport, 25 iii 1911, son of Dr. Maldwyn Hughes, the last President of the Wesleyan Methodist Conference (1932); Sch. Perse Sch., Cambridge, Emmanuel Coll., Camb., school-

master at The Leys Sch., Cambridge '34; Head Master, Rydal School, Colwyn Bay, Wales, 1946-†; his essays and poems are collected in *Donald Hughes, Head Master*, by P. Heywood, pub. at Rydal School, 1970. † in hospital at Welwyn Garden City, Herts, after a motor-accident following heart failure, 12 viii 1967 (56).

CREATOR OF THE STARRY FRAME
CREATOR OF THE STARRY HEIGHT   see 842.
CREATOR OF THE STARS OF NIGHT

CREATOR-SPIRIT, BY WHOSE AID: see 880.

157. CROWN HIM WITH MANY CROWNS

6 st. SMD   PCH 214

This appears in many difft. vns. because some hymnals take their text wholly from CROWN HIM WITH MANY CROWNS, by M. Bridges (78), *Hymns of the Heart*, 2nd ed., 1851, (a R. C. collection), while others mix it with sts. from CROWN HIM WITH CROWNS OF GOLD, by G. Thring (191), in. *Hymns & Sacred Lyrics*, 1874. The books which retain Bridges unadulterated are *AM* (om. st. 5b, 6a), *EH* (same), *NC* (om. st. 5) and (U.S.) *P¹*, *P²* (om. 2, 5b 6a). All hymnals use Bridges' st. 1, and all but *H* (U.S.) end with his last quatrain. All others use a seln. from Thring's stanzas—'Crown him the Son of God' (2), . . . 'the Lord of life' (4) '. . . the Lord of heaven' (5), and *H* (U.S.) also uses Thring's final st. (6). In *Songs of Praise* (1931) P. Dearmer (88) wrote a new hymn beginning CROWN HIM, using same meter, but after the first 2 words leaving the original altogether (SP480).

US & CAN: BP218: Can480: B52: CW250/184: H352: L431: P190/213/ 349: Pm199: CLB462: W63 ● ENG: AM304/224: An209: B182: BB124: CH136/298: CP166: E381: M271: NC47: PL223

158. DAY IS DYING IN THE WEST

4 st. 77.77.4 with ref. 7.7.7.4

M. A. Lathbury (93), for Chautauqua Convention, 1877; brought to England by W. G. Horder, *Congregational Hymns*, 1884.

US & CAN: CW144/53: L234: M503: P39/65/- : Pm45 ● ENG: B689

DAY OF WRATH AND DOOM IMPENDING
DAY OF WRATH AND DAY OF MOURNING   see 846.

159. DEAR LORD AND FATHER OF MANKIND

8.6.88.6

J. G. Whittier (11), being the last 6 st. (sometimes further abr.) of 17 st. poem, 'The Brewing of Soma,' pub. 1872, contrasting the Christian style with the Indian custom of drinking the intoxicating drug Soma to achieve communion with the Deity. 'Foolish' in line 2 is orig. First as a hymn in W. G. Horder's *Congregational Hymns*, 1884, wh. provided a tune that made the hymn v. popular both in Britain and in U.S.

US & CAN: BP424: Can249: B270: CW411/85: H435: L467: M235: P302/ 416/350: Pm341 ● ENG: AM -/184: An608: B50: BB351: CH245/76: CP408: E383: NC52: PL100

160. DEAR MASTER, IN WHOSE LIFE I SEE

2 st. LM-coup.

J. Hunter, in *Monthly Calendar* of Trinity Ch., Glasgow, then in his *Hymns of Faith & Life*, 1896.

US & CAN: CW318/- : M254: P507/-/-: Pm208 ● ENG: B465: BB319: CH460/691: CP462: M163

JOHN HUNTER, b. Aberdeen, 12 vii 1848; Sch. in Aberdeen; apprenticed to a draper at 13; affected by revival of 1859/61; attended Spring Hill Coll., Birmingham (wh. became in 1886 Mansfield Coll., Oxford); Ord. Congl.; Salem, York; Wycliffe Ch., Hull.; Trinity, Glasgow; then, after brief ministry at King's Weigh House Chapel, London, returned to Trinity, Glasgow, '04. Retired to London, '13. Liturgist and hymn writer. † London 15 ix 1917 (69).

161. DEAR SHEPHERD (GREAT SHEPHERD) OF THY PEOPLE, HEAR

7 st. CM

J. Newton (37), *Olney Hymns*, 1779, being sts. 2, 4, 5, 6 of hymn there beginning O LORD, OUR LANGUID SOULS INSPIRE. Circumstances of writing as 373, q.v.

US & CAN: ● ENG: AM690/- : BB259: CH246/- : CP265

DEAREST JESUS, WE ARE HERE: see 860.

DEAR MAKER OF THE STARRY SKIES: see 842.

162. DECK THYSELF, MY SOUL, WITH GLADNESS

8 st. 88.88D troch.   **PCH 196**

German: SCHMUCKE DICH, O LIEBE SEELE, J. Franck: st. 1, in Cruger's *Geistliche Kirchen-Melodien*, 1649; full text in Cruger & Runge, *Gesangbuch*, 1653, and in the 1653 and later eds. of *Praxis Pietatis Melica*.

Tr. C. Winkworth (14), *Chorale-Book for England*, 1863, 6 st.; this was a recasting of the vn. in *Lyra Germanica* II, 1858 which was in 88.88. 77.77. Now reduced to 4 st. or fewer for norm. use, sts. 2-3 being always omitted. *Worshipbook* has a substantially altd. trsln.

US & CAN: BP353: Can333: CW -/310: L262: M318: P -/-/351‡ ● ENG: AM -/393: B314: BB510: CH324/567: CP293: E306

JOHANN FRANCK, b. Guben, Brandenburg, 1 vi 1618; Sch. Univ. Konigsberg; lawyer in Guben from 1645; later burgomaster and ('71) deputy to the Landstag (parliament) of Lower Lausitz. † Guben 18 i 1677 (58).

163. DISMISS ME NOT THY SERVICE, LORD

6 st. 8.6.8.6.8.6

T. T. Lynch, *The Rivulet*, 1856. Norm. abr. to 3 st. (1, 3, 6).

US & CAN: ● ENG: B512: CH354/- : CP546: E555: M580

THOMAS TOKE LYNCH, b. Dunmow, Essex, 5 vii 1818; Sch. Islington and Highbury Congl. Sem.; Ord. Congl., Highgate (London), 1847; Mortimer St. (later Grafton St.), London, '49-'56 and '60-†, ministry interrupted by illness. Chiefly famous for *The Rivulet*, a book of 100 poems pub. 1856, of wh. some are hymns, wh. provoked a series of vituperative reviews in the religious press and gave rise to a theological controversy which brought the Assembly of the Congl. Union of England & Wales (founded 1832) as near as it ever came to dissolution, the dispute being between Calvinists and those who, upholding Lynch, approved of naturalistic imagery in hymns & theology. The dispute was quieted as much by the intervention of T. Binney (171) as by any decisive theological argument. Lynch † 9 v 1871 (52).

164. DISPOSER SUPREME AND JUDGE OF THE EARTH

6 st. 10.10.11.11   **PCH 170**

Latin: SUPREME QUALES, ARBITER, J. B. de Santeuil (101) in *Cluniac Breviary*, 1686, 6 st. LM.

Tr. I. Williams (71) in *British Magazine*, June, 1836, in the first phase of the Oxford Movement (83), when translators did not feel obliged to preserve orig. meters and tunes; then in *Hymns Translated from Parisian Breviary*, 1839. *Hymns A & M*, 1861, made alterations in text which

are usually now kept, but *EH* has full orig. text. *Can* uses st. 6 only as a doxology.

US & CAN: (Can 53) ● ENG: AM431/506: An459: BB226: CP654: E178: M788

DIVINE CRESCEBAS PUER: see 334.

165. DO NO SINFUL ACTION

7 st. 6.5.6.5

Mrs. Alexander (24) in *Hymns for Little Children*, 1848, on the text from the Catechism, 'to renounce the devil. . . .'

US & CAN: ● ENG: AM569/433: CH663/- : E589

166. DRAW NIGH AND TAKE THE BODY OF THE LORD

10 st. 10 10

Latin: SANCTI VENITE, CHRISTI CORPUS SUMITE, 10 st. 12 12 (5.7.5.7). *Antiphonarium Banchoriense*, a ms. written between 680 and 691 at Bangor, Ireland.

Tr. J. M. Neale (2), *Medieval Hymns*, 1851; full text in *EH* in 4-line sts. Altd. in *Hymns A & M*, 1868.

US & CAN: L273: CLB355 ● ENG: AM313/386: An373: E307: NC54: PL68

167. DRAW NIGH TO THY JERUSALEM, O LORD

5 st. 10 10. 10 10   **PCH 425**

Jeremy Taylor, *The Golden Grove*, 1655, in the Appendix of 'Festive & Penitential Hymns,' as a poem of 20 lines of varying length. A vn. in 4-line sts. appeared in *Leeds Hymn Book*, 1853, beginning DESCEND TO THY JERUSALEM. . , in 5 st. 10 10.10 10; a rev. 5 st. vn., clearly based on this, was in *Sarum Hymnal*, 1868, and this is what now appears in *CP* and *An*. In *Church Hymns*, 1871, this version, which makes a magnificent hymn, is credited to Earl Nelson (54). U.S. books noted hereunder use a 3 st. vn. which has Nelson's st. 1, 2, 3a, then 2 lines which depart from him & from Taylor. *AM-R* has an 8-line cento beginning RIDE ON IN TRIUMPH. Thus it remains a piece to which justice has not really yet been done.

US & CAN: CW -/154‡: P148‡/-/-: Pm156/‡ ● ENG: AM -/599‡: An 168: CP121

JEREMY TAYLOR, b. Cambridge, Aug. 1613; Sch. Caius Coll., Camb.; Ord. C/E, Fellow of Caius, and ('35) of All Souls, Oxf.; Rector of Uppingham, Rutland, '38; chaplain to Royalist army, '42; chaplain to Lord Carbery at Golden Grove, Wales, '45; lecturer at Lisburn, Ireland, '58; Bp. Down & Connor '61, and Vice-Chancellor, Univ. Dublin. † Lisburn 13 vii 1667 (53).

DRAW US IN THE SPIRIT'S TETHER: see 416.

EARTH HAS MANY A NOBLE CITY: see 870.

168. ERE I SLEEP, FOR EVERY FAVOUR

7 st. 8.33.6

J. Cennick (69), *Hymns for the Children of God*, 1741.

US & CAN: P511/-/- ● ENG: An48: B690: CH294/648: CP619: M947

169. ETERNAL FATHER, STRONG TO SAVE

4 st. 88.88.88   **PCH 220**

W. Whiting, 1860, rev. in *Hymns A & M*, 1861, to text now familiar. This has always been the 'Navy Hymn' in Britain & U.S. Some U.S. books either adapt or replace it by a new text, for intercession for travelers otherwise than by sea. *H* (U.S.) and *P²* (U.S.), *CLB* and *W*, use Whiting for sts. 1 & 4 and interpolate 2 st. by R. N. Spencer; placing this alongside the older vn. *Worshipbook* has only this adapted vn. The *Armed Forces Hymnal* (1975) has Whiting for sts. 1-3 followed by 12 optional sts. by different hands and ending with Whiting st. 4. Inseparable now from the tune MELITA which *Hymns A & M* placed with it in 1861, that tune being named for Malta, in Latin form, Acts 27. Sung at signing of Atlantic Charter, 1942.

US & CAN: BP435: Can221: CW610/370: H512: L338: M538: P492/521/356‡: Pm429: CLB508‡: W71‡ • ENG: AM370/487: An408: B665: BB384: CH626/527: CP680: E540: M917: NC55

WILLIAM WHITING, b. Kensington, London, 1 xi 1825; Sch. Clapham and King Alfred's Coll., Winchester; Master of Choristers' School, Winchester, 1842-†, there 3 v 1878 (52).

170. ETERNAL GOD, WHOSE POWER UPHOLDS

5 st. CMD   **PCH 544**

H. H. Tweedy, winning entry in first contest org. by the Hymn Society of America, 1928/9, for 'modern missionary hymns.' First in a hymnal, *M* (U.S.) 1933, first in a British Hymnal, *BBC Hymn Book*, 1951; first sung 30 v 30 in Riverdale Presbyterian Ch., New York.

US & CAN: Can236: B535: L322: M476: P -/485/357: Pm294: CLB477: W72 • ENG: BB23: CH -/499

HENRY HALLAM TWEEDY, b. Binghamton, N.Y., 5 viii 1868; Sch. Phillips Andover Academy, Yale, Union Theol. Sem.; Ord. Congl., Utica, N.Y., 1898; South Ch., Bridgeport, 1902; Prof. practical theology, Yale Divinity Sch., '09-'37. Author of many books chiefly on pastoral concerns, and several successful hymns. † Brattleboro, Vt., 11 iv, 1953 (84).

171. ETERNAL LIGHT! ETERNAL LIGHT!

5 st. 8.6.88.6   **PCH 130**

T. Binney, wrtn. about 1826 at Newport, Isle of Wight (in 1866 he wrote 'about forty years ago'); pub. in *New Congregational Hymn Book*, 1855.

US & CAN: BP529: H478 • ENG: An4: B51: CH36/357: CP21: M544

THOMAS BINNEY, b. Newcastle upon Tyne, 30 iv 1798; Sch. Coward Theol. Sem., Wymondley, Herefs; Ord. Congl., St. James', Newport, Isle of Wight; King's Welsh House Chapel, London, 1829-69, which in his time became a center of nonconformist liturgical life & thought. He was a noted advocate of reason and dignity in liturgy, and brought to England the American scholar Charles Baird's *A Chapter on Liturgies*, writing a preface and epilogue for it; this was the first important American liturgical manual of the time. Chairman of the Congl. Union of England & Wales, '45. See 163 for his intervention in *Rivulet* Controversy, '56-'57. Prof. homiletics, New Coll. (Theol. Sem.) London, from '69. † London, 24 ii 1874 (75).

ETERNAL LOVING LORD OF ALL: see 854.

ETERNAL MONARCH, KING MOST HIGH: see 834.

172. ETERNAL RULER OF THE CEASELESS ROUND

4 st. 10.10.10.10.10 10   **PCH 382**

J. W. Chadwick, wrtn. for graduation service at Harvard Divinity Sch., 19 vi 1864, when American Civil War was at its height & a matter of student concern. Pub. in *A Book of Poems*, 1876 but prob. used as a hymn for the first time when W. G. Horder included it in *Congregational Hymns*, 1884; became well known after *EH* set it to Gibbons' tune.

US & CAN: BP473: Can252: B506: L350: P406/-/358: Pm275: CLB522: W73 • ENG: AM*20: An419: B358: BB321: CH489/514: CP554: M892

JOHN WHITE CHADWICK, b. Marblehead, Mass., 1840; Sch. Harvard; Ord. Unit., 1864, and spent all his working life at Second Unit, Ch., Brooklyn, N.Y., where † 1904.

173. EVERY STAR SHALL SING A CAROL

6 st. 8.7.8.7.6.7   **PCH 522**

S. Carter, *9 Ballads or Carols*, 1964; later in several collections of his songs pub. by Galliard (Stainer & Bell), 1968 onwards.

US & CAN: Can428: H*53: P -/-/359: W74 • ENG: AM*21: B*13: CP*20: E*39: M*77: PL154

SYDNEY CARTER, b. Camden, London, 6 v 1915, spent his earlier years in journalism and served in World War II with the Friends' Ambulance Unit. Became celebrated in the mid-1960's after working among folk groups in the English 'underground,' and adapting their technique to Christian song. Very well known after about 1965 in England as Christian folk singer and broadcaster. Most complete colln. of his work to date is *Green Print for Song* (1974), wh. contains comments and explanations as well as the songs. Also pub. *Nothing Fixed or Final*, 1972, a book of poems. His *Lord of the Dance* (308) has been trsld. into many foreign languages.

174. FAIR WAVED THE GOLDEN CORN

6 st. SM

J. H. Gurney, *Psalms and Hymns for Public Worship*, 1851; st. 3 always om.

US & CAN: • ENG: AM339/338: An649: B725: BB436: CH494/629: CP647: E290

JOHN HAMPDEN GURNEY, b. London, 15 viii 1802; Sch. Trinity Camb.; Ord. C/E 1827; curate of Lutterworth, '27; Rector of St. Mary's, Marylebone (London), '47; prebendary of St. Paul's Cathl., '57. † London, 8 iii 1862 (59).

FAIREST LORD JESUS: see 873.

175. FAITH OF OUR FATHERS! LIVING STILL

4 st. 8.8.8.8.88   **PCH 209**

F. W. Faber, *Jesus & Mary*, 1849. In st. 3 lines 1-2 contained the phrase 'Mary's prayers/ shall bring . . .'; this altd. to "Good men's prayers' in Unitarian *Hymns for the Church of Christ*, 1853, so that within 4 years RCs and Unitarians were singing the same words about their history, aspirations and conflicts. In modern books this usually reads 'God's great power . . . ,' and in st. 3 later, 'England shall . . . be free' reads 'Mankind . . .' This hymn is now much more popular in U.S. than in G.B. F. W. F. wrote a parallel hymn in the same book for the conversion of all Ireland: this required 7 st. to handle the issues involved.

US & CAN: Can187: B143: CW348/253: H393: L516: M151: P267/348/361: Pm365: CLB474: W75 • ENG: B466: M402: NC297

FREDERICK WILLIAM FABER, b. Calverley, Yorks, 28 vi 1814, son of an Anglican vicar; Sch. Balliol, Oxf. & Univ. Coll. Oxf.; Ord. C/E, Rector of Elton, Hunts., 1843; joined R.C. church, '46, Ord. R.C., established in London 'Priests of the Congregation of St. Philip Neri.' Wrote some 150 hymns, many of wh. are popular still; he expressed his hope that he could do for the R.C. church in Britain (emancipated 1833, hierarchy re-established 1850) what Cowper (235) had done for Anglicans in *Olney Hymns*. † London 26 ix 1863 (49).

176. FAR ROUND THE WORLD THY CHILDREN SING THEIR SONG

6 st. 10 10. 10 10

B. Mathews, orig. wrtn. for a Sunday School Anniversary in Bowes Park, London, 1909. Two st. and a third not now used pub. in *The Fascinated Child* (no date), as 'A Song to the Hero.' Full text in 6 st. pub. *School Worship*, 1926. (The earliest tune is preserved at CP345).

US & CAN: BP383 ● ENG: CH373/501: CP345: M798

BASIL JOSEPH MATTHEWS, b. Oxford, 28 viii 1879, Sch. Oxford High Sch. and Univ.; private sec. to Dr. Fairbairn, Principal of Mansfield Coll., Oxf., 1899; journalist on the *Christian World*, 1904-10; Editor, London Missionary Society, '10-19; Chairman & Sec. of Literary Cttee. of the Ministry of Information, '17-'19; Director, Press Bureau, Conference of Missionary Societies, '20-4; Prof. of World Relations, Univ. Boston, Mass., '24-'44. † Boars Hill, Oxford, 29 iii 1951 (71).

177. FATHER ETERNAL, RULER OF CREATION

5 st. 11.10.11.10.10   PCH 454

L. Housman, wrtn. 1919 at request of H. R. L. Sheppard, Vicar of St. Martin in the Fields, London, for the Life & Liberty Movement (to promote peace after World War I); first pub. in *Songs of Praise*, 1925, with tune now very widely used in U.S.A., where the hymn is in much more general use than in Britain.

US & CAN: Can279: CW -/265: H532: L*1-6: M469: P -/486/362: Pm 445: W76 ● ENG: CH645/507

LAURENCE HOUSMAN, b. 18 vii 1865, Bromsgrove, Worcs.; worked first as an illustrator but later more distinguished as poet & dramatist; wrote *Little Plays of St. Francis* and famous feature *Victoria Regina* (1937) was made out of material wrtn. many years before but refused licence. Worked with P. Dearmer (88) on English Hymnal, 1904-6 and wrote hymns and translations for it. Later had affinity with the Society of Friends. † Glastonbury, Som., 20 ii 1959 (93).

178. FATHER, HEAR THE PRAYER WE OFFER

5 st. 8.7.8.7

L. M. Willis—orig. as FATHER, HEAR THE PRAYER I OFFER, in *Psalms of Life* (U.S.A.), 1857, then in altd. form more like the present in *Hymns of the Spirit* (1864), S. Longfellow (7) probably being the reviser. In this 5 st. form, brought to England in W. G. Horder's *Congregational Hymns*, 1884; in a new 4 st. form, dropping last st. and slightly revising the rest, in *EH* (1906), Dearmer (88) no doubt being responsible. Perhaps the only hymn to win wide currency despite a flat contradiction of the Psalmist.

US & CAN: Can260: CW -/226: Pm368 ● ENG: AM -/182: An579: B467: BB352: CP523: E385: NC56

LOVE MARIA WILLIS, b. 1824, was married to Dr. Willis, a physician who worked in Rochester, N.Y. Later they moved to Glencora, Seneca Lake. † 1908.

FATHER IN HEAVEN WHO LOVEST ALL: see 383.

179. FATHER IN HIGH HEAVEN DWELLING

4 st. 88.7.88.7

G. Rawson (99), *Leeds Hymn Book*, 1853; Luke 11:3-4.

US & CAN: ● ENG: An50: B692: CH283/-: CP624: M938

180. FATHER, IN THY MYSTERIOUS PRESENCE KNEELING

3 st. 11.10.11.10

S. Johnson (121), *A Book of Hymns for Public & Private Devotion*, 1846.

US & CAN: CW345/225: P256/384/363: Pm334

181. FATHER, LEAD ME DAY BY DAY

7 st. 77.77

J. P. Hopps, *Hymns, Chants & Anthems for Public Worship*, 1877; st. 5 always, st. 6 sometimes, om.

US & CAN: CW -/36: P445/458/- ● ENG: B469: CH565/97: CP526: M849

JOHN PAGE HOPPS, b. London, 6 xi 1834; Sch. Baptist Coll., Leicester; Ord. Bapt., Ibstock, Leics, but after 2 years Ord. Unit., and between 1860 and '76 ministered at Sheffield, Dukinfield (Lancs) & Glasgow; thereafter in Leicester & London. † Shepperton, Middx., 6 iv 1911 (76).

182. FATHER, LET ME (HERE WE) DEDICATE

4 st. 7.5.7.5 D

L. Tuttiett, *Gems of Thought . . .*, 1864; made popular by *Hymns A & M*, which printed it from 1875 & still preserves orig. text. Elsewhere altd. as above to 1st person plural. *CP* reverses order of sts. 4-3 prob. with improved effect.

US & CAN: CW -/357 ● ENG: AM74/72: An657: B713: CH606/- : CP 640: M957

LAWRENCE TUTTIETT, b. Colyton, Devon, 1825; Sch. Christ's Hospital & King's Coll., London; Ord. C/E 1848; Vicar of Lea Marston, Warks, '54; Rector of St. Andrew's Fife, '70; Canon of St. Ninian's Cathedral, Perth, '80. Retired to St. Andrews and † there 21 v 1897 (71).

FATHER MOST HOLY, GRACIOUS AND FORGIVING
FATHER MOST HOLY, MERCIFUL AND LOVING
FATHER MOST HOLY, MERCIFUL AND TENDER
see 866.

183. FATHER OF HEAVEN, WHOSE LOVE PROFOUND

4 st. LM-coup

E. Cooper, *Selection of Psalms & Hymns . . .* (Uttoxeter, Staffs), 1805; doxology in *Hymns A & M* (1861) added by compilers. Based on the Prayer Book Litany.

US & CAN: BP275: Can66: CW -/235: M140 ● ENG: AM164: An483: B39: BB290: CH5/77: E387: M38: PL101

EDWARD COOPER, b. London, 1770, Sch. Queen's Coll., Oxf.; Fellow of All Souls, Oxf.; Ord. C/E 1793; Rector of Hamstall-Ridware, Derbs, '99; Yoxall, Staffs, 1808, holding both livings until † Yoxall, 26 ii 1833 (62).

184. FATHER OF MEN, IN WHOM ARE ONE

8 st. 888

H. C. Shuttleworth, *St. Nicolas Cole Abbey Supplement*, 1897; then, with a tune by author, in *Church Monthly*, 1898. 888D form made popular by *EH*, 1906.

US & CAN: P489/-/- ● ENG: B359: CH493/- : CP555: E528: M982

HENRY CARY SHUTTLEWORTH, b. Egloshayle, Cornwall, 20 x 1850; Sch. Walthamstow, Essex, then St. Mary Hall & Christ Church, Oxf.; Ord. C/E 1873; curate at St. Barnabas, Oxford, then minor canon at St. Paul's, London '76-84, and from '83 Rector of St. Nicolas, Cole Abbey, London. Prof. of Pastoral Theology & Liturgies, King's Coll., London; leader of Christian Socialist mvt. Author of *The Place of Music in Public Worship*, 1892. His hymn book above designed as a supplement to *Church Hymns*, 1871. † Westminster, London, 24 x 1900 (50).

185. FATHER OF MERCIES, IN THY WORD

12 st. CM   PCH 271

A. Steele, *Poems on Subjects Chiefly Devotional*, 1760. The 6 st. vn. in Ash & Evans, *Collection* (Bristol, 1769) is basis of current selns., which are usually in 5 st. This is the earliest hymn by an English woman hymnwriter in current use.

US & CAN: BP292: CW440/-: L256: M367: P218/249/- • ENG: AM531/251: An300: B245: BB189: CP227: M302

ANNE STEELE, b. Broughton, Hants, 1717, where her father William Steele was Bapt. minister; suffered much ill-health in consequence of shock induced by death of her fiancé on day appointed for the marriage. Pub. her *Poems . . .* 1760 under pen-name 'Theodosia.' † 11 xi 1778 (61).

186. FATHER OF PEACE AND GOD OF LOVE

4 st. CM   **PCH 101**

Scottish Paraphrases, 1781 (76) based on a 4 st. hymn by P. Doddridge (64) of which this keeps st. 1 intact, rewrites sts. 2-3 and substitutes a new 4th st. by W. Cameron (76). In Scotland, Paraphrase 60.

US & CAN: BP419: Can111: P -/328/- • ENG: An619: B593: BB488: CH481/395: CP394

FATHER, WE PRAISE THEE, NOW THE NIGHT IS OVER: see 862.

187. FATHER, WE THANK THEE FOR THE NIGHT

2 st. LM-coup.

Attributed to Rebecca Weston, a person of whom nothing is known and even of whose name editors are now uncertain. Appeared in Batchellor & Charmbury, *Manual for Teachers* (Boston, Mass.), 1884, which was a course in tonic sol-fa music reading; the tune by Batchellor still popular in U.S. appeared there with it. Introduced to Britain in *Sunday School Hymnary*, 1905.

US & CAN: BP551: H240: P -/467/-: Pm479 • ENG: B736: CH -/99: CP702

188. FATHER, WE THANK THEE, WHO HAST PLANTED

4 st. 9.8.9.8   **PCH 552**

F. Bland Tucker (22), *The Hymnal, 1940* (U.S.), based on the prayers in the *Didache*, the oldest manual of Church Order, Greek, possibly 2nd cent., alternatively called *The Teaching of the Twelve Apostles*; the prayer here paraphrased is a pattern of prayer to be used after the Eucharist. In *CLB*, FATHER, ALL THANKS FOR HAVING PLANTED . . . .

US & CAN: CAN225: CW -/322: H195: M307: P -/-/366: Pm289: CLB 376‡: W79 • ENG: AM*24: B315: BB201: CH -/586: E*62: M*16: PL69

189. FATHER, WHO ON MAN DOST SHOWER

6 st. 888.7

P. Dearmer (88), *English Hymnal*, 1906.

US & CAN: • ENG: BB389: CH349/- : E531: M894

190. FATHER WHOSE WILL IS LIFE AND GOOD

5 st. CM

H. D. Rawnsley, *Missionary Hymn Book*, 1922; in some books, O GOD, WHOSE WILL . . . . For Medical Missions.

US & CAN: Can231: H516: M411‡: P -/309/367: CLB511 • ENG: AM 875‡: B38;‡: CH353/526

HARDWICKE DRUMMOND RAWNSLEY, b. Shiplake, 28 ix 1851; Sch. Uppingham Sch. & Balliol, Oxf.; Ord. C/E '75; curate, St. Barnabas, Bristol; Vicar of Low Wray, Lancs, '78, then of Crosthwaite, Cumberland, 1883-1917 & Hon. Canon of Carlisle from '93; poet and naturalist, founder of the National Trust (English institution for preservation of historic buildings and sites of natural beauty). † Grasmere, Cumb., 28 v 1920 (68).

191. FIERCE RAGED THE TEMPEST O'ER THE DEEP

4 st. 888.3   **PCH 225**

G. Thring, *Congregational Hymn & Tune Book*, 1862 (no denominational significance in title); then *Hymns A & M*, 1868; Mark 4:39.

US & CAN: • ENG: AM285/313: An553: B117: CH83/- : CP108: E541: M167

GODFREY THRING, b. Alford, Som., 25 iii 1823; Sch. Shrewsbury & Balliol, Oxf.; Ord. C/E '46; after several curacies succeeded father as Rector of Alford, '58, where he stayed till '93. Ed. *Church of England Hymn Book*, 1880, and revision of '82. † Ploncks Hill, Shamley Green, Guildford, 13 ix 1903 (80).

192. FIERCE WAS THE WILD BILLOW

3 st. 6.4.6.4 D, dact.

J. M. Neale (2), *Hymns of the Eastern Church*, 1862; suggested by, but only remoted connected with, a Greek poem beginning ζοφερᾶς τρικυμίας. Matt. 14:31.

US & CAN: • ENG: AM -/312: CH84/-: CP103: E388

193. FIGHT THE GOOD FIGHT WITH ALL THY MIGHT

4 st. LM-coup.   **PCH 226**

J. S. B. Monsell, *Hymns of Love & Praise*, 1863; 2 Tim. 4:7. It is likely that this very famous hymn was suggested by a hymn of J. Montgomery (6) wrtn. 14 ii 1834 and appearing in Montgomery's *Hymns*, 1853, in 5 st. 6.6.6.6.88, entitled 'Valiant for the Truth.' Sts. 1 and 4 of this are:

> Fight the good fight: lay hold
>   upon eternal life;
> Keep but thy shield, be bold,
>   stand through the bitterest strife;
> invincible while in the field,
> thou canst not fail unless thou yield. . . .
>
> Trust in thy Saviour's might;
>   yea, till thy latest breath,
> fight, and like him in fight,
>   by dying conquer death;
> and, all-victorious in the field,
> then, with thy sword, thy spirit yield.

Monsell's orig. st. 3 is as in *EH*; some books follow the alteration in *Hymns A & M*, 1868. Orig. is '. . . and on thy Guide/lean . . ./Lean, and the trusting . . . .' Tune PENTECOST with wh. the text is still often associated, was intended for COME, HOLY GHOST (880); the association was first suggested by Sir Arthur Sullivan.

US & CAN: BP487: Can175: B394: CW376/256: H560: L557: M240: P270/359/- : Pm367 • ENG: AM540/304: An577: B289: BB302: CH517/442: CP512: E389: M490

JOHN SAMUEL BEWLEY MONSELL, b. Derry (Ireland), 2 iii 1811; Sch. Trinity Coll., Dublin; Ord. C/E 1834; Chaplain to Bp. Mant (95); Vicar of Egham, Surray, '53; Rector of St. Nicholas, Guildford, '70. Poet and hymn writer; † as a result of an accident in his church while it was being rebuilt, Guildford, 9 iv 1875 (64).

194. FILL THOU MY LIFE, O LORD MY GOD

6 st. CMD   **PCH 337**

H. Bonar (81), *Hymns of Faith & Hope* III, 1866; 'Life's Praise.' Now always abr., in CM, to 6 st. or fewer; various selns. are used; typical (*CP*) is lines 1-12, 33-6, 40-8 of orig.

US & CAN: BP462: B460: Pm396 • ENG: AM705/373: An621: B628: BB271: CH -/457: CP22: E*304: M604

195. FILLED WITH THE SPIRIT'S POWER

3 st. 10.10.10.10

J. R. Peacey, *100 Hymns for To-day*, 1969.

US & CAN: Can226 ● ENG: AM*26: B*14: PL267

JOHN RAPHAEL PEACEY, b. All Saints Vicarage, Hove, Sussex, 16 vii 1896; Sch. St. Edmund's Sch., Canterbury; Selwyn, Camb.; served in World War I & gained M.C.; Dean & Fellow, Selwyn Coll., 1924-7; Head Master, Bishop Cotton Sch., Silma, India, '27-'36; Principal, Bishop's Coll., Calcutta, '36-'45; Residentiary Canon, Bristol Cathedral, '45-'66; Rural Dean of Hurstpierpoint, Sussex, '68-'71. † Hurstpierpoint 31 x 1971 (75).

196. FIRMLY I BELIEVE AND TRULY

5 st. 8.7.8.7   **PCH 441**

J. H. Newman, in *The Dream of Gerontius*, a dramatic poem (Jan. 1865), canto 1; there it is a continuous poem of 36 lines of which the first, 5th and 9th quatrains are a Latin refrain,

> Sanctus fortis, Sanctus Deus,
> de profundis oro te:
> miserere ludex meus
> mortis in discrimine.

St. 3 of norm. vn., at 'Him the holy, him the strong' reflects the opening words of this refrain. The poem is spoken by Gerontius (the dying Christian, in old age) in contemplation of the Judgment. First as a hymn in *EH*, 1906, omitting the 3 refrains and one other quatrain, using lines 5-16, 21-4, 29-32: sometimes lines 21-4 om. in other versions.

US & CAN: ● ENG: AM-/186: BB168: CH -/400: E390: M*17: NC57: PL219

JOHN HENRY NEWMAN, b. London, 21 ii 1801; Sch. Ealing and Trinity, Oxf.; Fellow of Oriel, '22; Ord. C/E, '24; Vicar of St. Mary's, Oxford (University Church), '28-32; travelled in S. Europe (see 384), '32-'37; became the most powerful mind in the Oxford Movement (83); wrote many of the Tracts associated with its inception including the famous Tract 90, 1841, demonstrating that the 39 Articles of the C/E were not opposed to Catholic teaching though they were opposed to Catholic error; after 3 years of prayer & meditation at Littlemore, near Oxford, received into R.C. Church, '45; Ord. R.C. in Rome, '46; established the Oratory (House of Prayer) at Birmingham, '47, and also that in London (Brompton Oratory), '50. Created Cardinal, '79. Author of many theological and philosophical works including *Essay on the Development of Christian Doctrine*, '45, *The Idea of a University*, '52, *Apologia pro Vita Sua*, '64, *The Grammar of Assent*, '70. By far the outstanding intellect in the 19 c. English R.C. church, and as some believe the leading English theologian and preacher of the 19 c.; his wide friendships included many eminent divines of all denominations. † Edgbaston, Birmingham, 11 viii 1890 (89).

197. FLING OUT THE BANNER! LET IT FLOAT

6 st. LM-alt.

G. W. Doane, for 2nd Sunday in Advent, 1848, for St. Mary's Sch., Burlington, N.J., of which he was founder. Pub. in *Verses for 1851 in Commemoration of the 3rd Jubilee of the S.P.G.* (Society for the Propagation of the Gospel—Anglican organization), and thus introduced to Britain. Incl. in W. G. Horder's *Congregational Hymns*, 1884. Full text in *EH*; elsewhere abr.

US & CAN: CW540/- : H259: L315: P384/506/- : Pm296 ● ENG: AM -/ 268: CH383/ -: CP331: E546: M817

GEORGE WASHINGTON DOANE, b. Trenton, N.J., 27 v 1799; Sch. Union Coll., Schenectady, N.Y., Ord. Episc., '23; Prof. of Rhetoric, Trinity Coll., Hartford, '24; Rector of Trinity Ch., Boston, Mass., '28; Bp. New Jersey, '32. † Burlington, N.J., 27 iv 1859 (59).

198. FOR ALL THE SAINTS, WHO FROM THEIR LABOURS REST

11 st. 10.10.10.4   **PCH 230**

W. W. How (75), in *Hymn for a Saint's Day and Other Hymns by a Layman*, 1864 (the 'other hymns' being by Earl Nelson [54]). Orig. sts. 3-5 reflected the threefold formula 'Apostles, prophets, martyrs' as in the *Te Deum*, and How's orig. beginning was FOR ALL THY SAINTS. Julian notes that it was U.S. hymnals which first used author's revised reading, 'the saints.' Now known norm. in 8 st. vn. in Britain, 6 st. in U.S., the 8 st. vn. being made popular by *Hymns A & M*, 1875.

US & CAN: BP310: Can501: B144: CW577/279: H126: L144: M536: P429/425/369: Pm306: CLB303: W80 ● ENG: AM437/527: An460: B403: BB227: CH220/534: CP363: E641: M832: NC58: PL242

199. FOR ALL THY SAINTS, O LORD (FOR THY DEAR SAINT . . .)

6 st. SM.

R. Mant, (75), *Ancient Hymns* . . . 1837; (but this is not a translation). Altd. in *Hymns A & M*, 1861, in wh. it was the last hymn, to 'For thy dear Saint,' and a different doxology substituted. Orig. text, om. one st., in *EH*.

US & CAN: Can502: H124: L141 ● ENG: AM448/531: An445: BB228: E196

200. FOR EVER WITH THE LORD

2 parts, 9 st. and 13 st., SM

J. Montgomery (6), *A Poet's Portfolio*, 1835; 1 Thess. 4:17. Various centos appeared in hymnals in mid-19 c., but the 4 st. (SMD) vn. in *Hymns A & M*, 1875, is now more or less standard.

US & CAN: BP532: L590 ● ENG: AM231/346: An428: B609: CH583/- : E391: M658

201. FOR THE BEAUTY OF THE EARTH

8 st. 7.7.7.7.77   **PCH 234**

F. S. Pierpoint, in Orby Shipley's *Lyra Eucharistica*, 1864; orig. designed as a hymn of thanksgiving at the Eucharist, 'sacrifice of praise' in refrain echoing that phrase in the post-communion prayer in Anglican prayer-book (1662). Refrain orig. began, 'Christ our God, to thee we raise.' In abr. vn., wh. drops last 2, or more often, 3 stanzas, the refrain altd. to 'Father, unto thee . . . ,' and in that form it has become one of the most popular nature hymns. St. 6, when used, norm. now reads 'For thy Church . . .' but author wrote, 'For thy Bride . . .' Full orig. text in *EH* which alone places it in Eucharistic section.

US & CAN: BP98: Can109: B54: CW167/7: H296: L444: M35: P71/2/372: Pm66: W81 ● ENG: AM663/171: An18: B8: BB272: CH17/367: CP37: E309: M35: PL263

FOLLIOTT SANDFORD PIERPOINT, b. Bath, 7 x 1835, Sch. Grammar Sch. Bath, and Queen's, Camb.; lived as a man of letters, poet & hymn writer; † Newport, Monmouth, 10 iii 1917 (61).

202. FOR THE HEALING OF THE NATIONS

4 st. 8.7.8.7.8.7

F. Kaan, *Pilgrim Praise*, 1968.

US & CAN: BP595: Can210: W82 ● ENG: AM*28: B*20: PL294

FREDERIK HERMAN KAAN (always known as Fred), b. Haarlem, Netherlands, 1929; Sch. in Netherlands and Univ. Utrecht, then Western College (Theol.), Bristol. Ord. Congl. (Brit.), '55; served at Barry, S. Wales, '55-63, Pilgrim Church, Plymouth, '63-8. Gen. Sec. International Congregational Council, Geneva, '68; Exec. Sec. World Alliance of Reformed Churches, '70; member of Ed. Cttee., *Cantate Domino* (WCC), '68-'75. Now the most sought-after of contemporary hymn writers, 25 of his pieces being in *Can* (1971). He has wrtn. no hymns in his native language, but nearly 100 in English. His *Pilgrim Praise* appeared first in mimeographed form, '67; printed (texts only), '68; full music edn., '71. Since then he has wrtn. many more, inc. many translations for *Cantate Domino*, and some of his later work is in *Break Not the Circle* (1976). He writes, 'very often I would write a hymn as late as Saturday night, after sermon preparation; I then mimeographed it and used it in the worship service the next morning.' This refers to his ministry at Pilgrim, Plymouth. All his hymns are in familiar meters so that they can be sung to well known tunes, but they have inspired many contemporary musicians to write tunes for them, and no writer has made bolder gestures in expression of late 20th century needs, attitudes, and theology.

203. FOR THE MIGHT OF THINE ARM WE BLESS THEE, OUR GOD, OUR FATHERS' GOD

4 st. 13 13 13 13 (7.6.7.6 D) Irreg.

C. S. Horne, wrtn. for Whitefield's Tabernacle (Congl.), London; pub. in *Fellowship Hymn Book*, 1909; suggested by a poem of Felicia Hemans called 'Hymn of the Vaudois Mountaineers in Time of Persecution,' of wh. indeed it is a paraphrase, even quoting certain lines directly. The Vaudois were the Waldensians, Italian Protestants in the Savoy-Piedmont area who were brutally massacred in 1654, an incident celebrated in Milton's poem 'On the Late Massacre in Piedmont.' The community still exists vigorously in this region.

US & CAN: M534 ● ENG: B256: BB242: CH212/365: CP666: M715

CHARLES SYLVESTER HORNE, b. Cuckfield, Sussex, 15 iv 1865; Sch. Newport School and Univ. Glasgow; then Mansfield Coll., Oxf., wh. he entered when it opened, 1886; Ord. Congl., 1889, Allen Street Church, Kensington (London); then Whitefield's Tabernacle, 1903-†. Chairman, Congl. Union of England & Wales, 1910-1. Member of Parliament, 1910. Delivered Lyman Beecher Lecture on preaching at Niagara Falls, 1914, and on the way back from there to Toronto, † 2 (or 4) v 1914 (49).

FOR THEE, O DEAR, DEAR COUNTRY: see 851.

204. FOR THOSE WE LOVE WITHIN THE VEIL

7 st. 8.8.8.4   **PCH 459**

W. Charter Piggott, wrtn. for a Commemoration service, 1915, during World War I at Whitefield's Tabernacle (mentioned in preceding note), London. First pub., *Songs of Praise*, 1925.

US & CAN: H222: L598 ● ENG: B610: BB243: CH218/538: CP364: M657

WILLIAM CHARTER PIGGOTT, b. 6 viii 1872, Leighton Buzzard, Beds; Sch. Huddersfield Coll. and Headingley (Methodist) Coll., Leeds; but never Ord. in Methodism; founded the Brotherhood Church in Harrow Road, London, 1896 (C. S. Horne, 203, was chairman of Brotherhood Movement c. 1910). Ord. Congl., 1900, and after charges in London & Bedford, succeeded Horne as Minister at Whitefield's, 1914, then was at Streatham (London), '17-'37. Chairman, Congl. Union of England & Wales, 1931/2, † Epsom, Surrey, 5 xi 1943 (71).

205. FOR THY MERCY AND THY GRACE

7 st. 7.7.7.7

H. Downton, wrtn. 1841, pub. *Church of England Magazine*, 1843; orig. text, om. one st., in *EH*; altd. text, as in *Hymns A & M*, 1861, better known.

US & CAN: BP573: Can377 ● ENG: AM73: An656: B714: BB429: CH 604/612: E286

HENRY DOWNTON, b. 12 ii 1818, Pulverbatch, Salop; Sch. Trinity, Camb.; Ord. C/E, 1843; curacies in Isle of Wight and Cambridge; perpetual curate, St. John's, Chatham, '49; British Chaplain to Geneva, '57; Rector of Hopton, Sfk., '73; † there 8 vi 1885 (67).

206. FORGIVE, O LORD, OUR SEVERING WAYS

4 st. 888

Composite. Sts. 2-4 are from J. G. Whittier's (11) poem, 'Amidst these glorious works of thine,' wrtn. 1864 for dedication of the Unitarian House of Worship, San Francisco. St. 1 is anon. It may have appeared first in this form in Presbyterian *Hymnal* (P¹), 1933.

US & CAN: CW484/- : H*8: P344/476: Pm262: W83 ● ENG:

207. 'FORGIVE OUR SINS AS WE FORGIVE'

4 st. CM   **PCH 508**

R. Herklots, first printed in Parish Magazine of St. Mary's Church, Bromley, Kent, 1966; then in *100 Hymns for To-day* and *Hymns & Songs* (both 1969).

US & CAN: Can74: H*9: CLB497: W84 ● ENG: AM*29: B*22: M*17: CP*25: E*24: NC60

ROSAMUND HERKLOTS, b. 1905 in India of missionary parents; Sch. Leeds Girls' High Sch. and Univ.; trained as teacher but left the profession for secretarial work, and was over 20 years sec. to an eminent neurologist. Later, in the Head office of the Association for Spina Bifida and Hydrocephalus. Has written 60 hymns, of which at present (1977) only the above has gained wide acceptance, though others have been used in Sunday Schools.

FORTH FROM ON HIGH THE FATHER SENDS: see 867.

208. FORTH IN THY NAME, O LORD, I GO

6 st. LM-alt.   **PCH 67**

C. Wesley (1), *Hymns & Sacred Poems*, 1749; 'Before Work'—perhaps the first and greatest of weekday hymns. St. 3, 'Preserve me from my calling's snare' often om.; but full text, including orig. reading of st. 2, in *EH*.

US & CAN: BP456: Can306: H150: L214: M152: Pm406 ● ENG: AM8/336: An604: B629: BB406: CH651/463: CP593: E259: M590: NC61: PL87

209. FORTY DAYS AND FORTY NIGHTS

9 st. 7.7.7.7

G. H. Smyttan, *Penny Post*, March 1856; 'Poetry for Lent, as Sorrowful but always Rejoicing.' In *Hymns A & M*, 1861, text drastically revised by F. Pott (45) in 6 st., and now norm. found in this form.

US & CAN: Can438: H55: Pm148: CLB243: W85 ● ENG: AM92: An141: B118: BB341: CH79/210: E73: M165: NC62

GEORGE HUNT SMYTTAN, b. Bombay, 1822, Sch. Corp. Christi, Camb.; Ord. C/E '48; Rector of Hawksworth, Notts, '50-9; † Frankfurt/Main, 21 ii 1870 (48).

FOUNTAIN OF GOOD, TO OWN THY LOVE: see 361.

210. FROM ALL THAT DWELL BELOW THE SKIES

2 st. LM-coup.

I. Watts (10), *Psalms of David* . . . 1719; Ps. 117. In many books now 'Alleluias' are added to carry the tune LASST UNS ERFREUEN first set to it in *Church Hymnary*, 1927, and in some books in U.S. extra sts. are added. *H* (U.S.) adds Ken's 'Praise God from whom all blessings flow' (63) as st. 3; and P¹,²,³ add as st. 2, 'In every land begin the song,' which is anon. in Robert Spence's *Pocket Hymn Book* (York, no date), designed for classes in J. Wesley's time. *M* (U.S.) has this as st. 4; and as st. 3, 'Your lofty themes, ye mortals, bring,' from the same source. Both these extra sts. were in John Wesley's own *Pocket Hymn Book*, 1787. Extended vns. ‡ below.

US & CAN: BP51: Can3: CW104/- : H277‡: L429: M14‡: P388‡/33‡/373‡: Pm11: CLB417: W86 ● ENG: AM -/630: An31: B760: BB5: CH 228/362: CP746: E*63: M4: PL91

FROM DEPTHS OF WOE TO THEE I RAISE: see 838.

211. FROM EAST TO WEST, FROM SHORE TO SHORE

Latin: A SOLUS ORTUS CARDINE, 23 st. acrostic LM, C. Sedulius; in ms. of 8th cent. in British Museum.

Tr. J. Ellerton (80) in CM, 5 st., *Church Hymns*, 1871; later expanded to 7 st. LM (sts. 1-7 of orig.) in *Hymns A & M*, 1889. *M** has CM vn. of sts. 1, 4, 5, 6, its st. 3 being the LM st. 3 minus 2 adjectives.

US & CAN: Can403: L20 ● ENG: AM483/57: B94: BB47: CH -/189: E18: M*19‡: NC64

CAELIUS SEDULIUS, born and died prob. in Rome during 5th cent., was a Christian Latin poet who wrote a long poem in hexameters on parts of O. T. history and on the life of Jesus; also the 23 st. acrostic poem referred to above, wh. was called *Hymnus de Christo* and of which each stanza began with a successive letter of the Latin alphabet. HOSTIS HERODES IMPIE (*AMR74, EH38*) is another cento from this.

212. FROM GLORY TO GLORY ADVANCING, WE PRAISE THEE, O LORD

2 st. 14 14. 14 15 anap.   PCH 182

C. W. Humphreys, *English Hymnal*, 1906, based on opening words of the Prayer of Dismissal in the Liturgy of St. James (Greek, 4th cent.).

US & CAN: Can307: H492: CLB381: W88 ● ENG: AM -/417: BB244: CH -/325: CP315: E310: M30

CHARLES WILLIAM HUMPHREYS, b. 1840 Oswestry, Shropshire, † Hastings, Sussex, 1:1921 (80). Lived in S. America in early 20th cent., but nothing else is known of him.

213. FROM GREENLAND'S ICY MOUNTAINS

4 st. 7.6.7.6 D

R. Heber (90), Hymns, posth., 1827; wrtn. the day before Pentecost, 1819. His father-in-law, the Dean of St. Asaph (N. Wales), was preaching at Pentecost in Wrexham (on the border of Wales & England, not far from Heber's rectory) in support of an appeal for the Eastern operations of the Society for the Propagation of the Gospel. On the Saturday he asked R. H. to write 'something for us to sing in the morning,' R. H. wrote the first 3 st. of this, and they were approved; later the same day he wrote st. 4. In the first print, 1827, 'Ceylon's isle' was altd. to 'Java's isle,' no doubt for metrical reasons, and in the ms. he first wrote 'savage' before substituting 'heathen.' Often now abr. to 3 st. by om. st. 2 in which that phrase occurs. Probably the tune used at that first singing was the one preserved at *EH547*.

US & CAN: H254: L310: P385/-/- ● ENG: AM358/265: CH371/- : CP 329: E547: M801

FROM HEAVEN ABOVE TO EARTH I COME
FROM HEAVEN HIGH I COME TO YOU   see 884.

214. FROM THE EASTERN MOUNTAINS

6 st. 6.5.6.5 D

G. Thring (191), *Sacred Lyrics*, 1874; Matt. 2:2.

US & CAN: BP155: H49: P380/-/- ● ENG: AM -/595: An128: B95: BB65: CH66/- : E615: M133

215. FROM THEE ALL SKILL AND SCIENCE FLOW

CM   PCH 245

C. Kingsley; this is sts. 3-6 of a 6 st. hymn beginning 'Accept this building. . . .' Two accounts of its origin exist. (i) Mrs. Kingsley's *Life & Letters of C. K.*, 1876, says it was wrtn. for the laying of the foundation stone

of a new working men's block at Queen's Hospital, Birmingham, 4 xii 1871; (ii) C. K.'s (posth.) *Collected Poems* (1880) has a note against the hymn, 'written Eversley 1870; sung by 1,000 school children at opening of New Wing of the Children's Hospital, Birmingham.' Possibly both are true. Julian's note suggests that the 4 st. now current was found in America before British editors took it. Popular in Britain after W. G. Horder's inclusion of it in *Worship Song*, 1896, Supplement, 1898, and in *EH*, 1906.

US & CAN: BP497: Can230: CW -/270: H515: L216: M485: P -/315-/-: CLB512 ● ENG: AM -/479: An398: B635: CH351/535: CP671: E525

CHARLES KINGSLEY, b. 12 vi 1819, Holne Vicarage, Devon; Sch. privately in Devon & Cornwall, then King's Coll., London and Magdalene, Camb.; Ord. C/E, Eversley, Hants, where became Rector, 1844, and stayed till †. Canon of Chester, 1869; of Westminster, '73. Celebrated for *The Heroes, The Water Babies* and a sometimes violent public controversy with J. H. Newman (196); champion of Christian Socialism. † Eversley, 23 i 1875 (55).

216. GENTLE JESUS, MEEK AND MILD LAMB OF GOD, I LOOK TO THEE

Each 7 st. 77/77   PCH 297

Two consecutive hymns by C. Wesley (1) in *Hymns & Sacred Poems*, 1742, & in *Hymns for Children*, 1763. Modern hymnals make centos from both; longest in *EH* and *M (Brit.)*. Sometimes a cento beginning LAMB OF GOD . . . is used, even if it contains stanzas from GENTLE JESUS . . . .

US & CAN: BP452: H251 ● ENG: AM568/451: B739: CH662/- : CP700: E591: M842

217. GENTLE MARY LAID HER CHILD

3 st. 7.6.7.6 troch.

J. S. Cook, *Hymnary* of the United Church of Canada, 1930.

US & CAN: Can420: H37: M395: P453/167/375 ● ENG:

JOSEPH SIMPSON COOK, b. in Durham County, England, 4 xii 1859; Sch. Wesleyan Coll., McGill Univ., Montreal; Ord. Meth. in Canada, & later became minister in United Ch. of Canada. † Toronto, 27 v 1933 (73).

GIVE HEED, MY HEART! LIFT UP THY VOICE: see 884.

218. GIVE ME (US) THE WINGS OF FAITH, TO RISE

5 st. CM   PCH 37

I. Watts, (10), *Hymns . . . ,* 1707, Bk. II; 'The Examples of Christ and the Saints.' 'GIVE US' in *AM*.

US & CAN: BP317: Can503: B498: L594: M533 ● ENG: AM623/571: An462: B404: BB229: CP358: E197: M831

219. GIVE TO OUR GOD IMMORTAL PRAISE

8 st. LM-coup.

I. Watts (10), *Psalms of David . . . ,* 1719; Ps. 136; 'God's wonders of Creation, Providence, Redemption and Salvation.' All mod. hymnals om. sts. 5-6 and some others as well. In orig. vn. there is an alternating refrain wh. is obscured in those vns. wh. include an odd number of sts. (as *Worshipbook*).

US & CAN: BP61: L441: P -/-/376 ● ENG: An235: B9: BB6: CP9: NC69

220. GLORIOUS THINGS OF THEE ARE SPOKEN

5 st. 8.7.8.7 D   PCH 86

J. Newton (37), *Olney Hymns*, 1779; Zion, or the City of God: Is. 33: 20-1; but containing also refs. to Ps. 87, 1 Pet. 2, Rev. 1. Always abr. in modern use. In Brit., st. 3 norm. om.; in U.S. often sts. 4-5 om. *CP* has orig. vn. om. st. 3.

US & CAN: BP297: Can144: CW431/354: H385: L152: M293: P339/434/379: Pm267: CLB471: W92 ● ENG: AM545/257: An424: B257: BB176: CH206/421: CP243: E393: M706

221. GLORY BE TO JESUS

9 st. 6.5.6.5

The Italian original of this appeared (anon.) in Galli's *Raccolta di Orazione e pie Opera colla Indulgenze* (1837), with a notice that 100 days' Indulgence would be granted to all who repeated this prayer, 'which Indulgence is also applicable to the faithful departed.' The Indulgence is dated 18 Oct., 1815, so despite the later date of the printed source the song probably dates from early 19 c. It is in 9 st. 6.6.6.6 troch. Tr. E. Caswall (26), *Hymns for the Birmingham Oratory* (196), 1857 in 9 st. 6.5.6.5: sts. 4-5 always om. now, sometimes others as well.

US & CAN: H335: L76: CLB451 ● ENG: AM107: An154: E99: NC71

GLORY TO THEE, MY GOD, THIS NIGHT
GLORY TO THEE, WHO SAFE HAST KEPT   see 63.

222. GO, LABOUR ON, SPEND AND BE SPENT

8 st. LM-alt.

H. Bonar (81), leaflet, 1843, then *Hymns of Faith & Hope*, I, 1857; *Leeds Hymn Book*, 1853; *New Congl. Hymn Book, Supplement*, 1859, printed it in full with Pt. II beginning at st. 5. Mod. hymnals always abr., norm. using sts. 1, 2, 7, 8 (*EH*) or 1, 3, 5, 7, 8 (*H-U.S.*). Author's title (1857) was 'The Useful Life' with added Greek quotation (origin unknown): Ψυχή μου . . . μου . . . ἀνάστα, τί καθεύδεις.

US & CAN: BP488: CW473/- : H573: P376/283/- : W93 ● ENG: AN595: B513: CH356/483: CP540: E556: M589

223. GO, TELL IT ON THE MOUNTAIN

Negro Spiritual, text in U.S. hymnals always taken from *American Negro Songs & Spirituals*, by John W. Work, who attributes the words to F. J. Work.

US & CAN: Can404: B82: H*54: M404: P -/-/380: Pm488: W95 ● ENG: NEGRO SPIRITUALS: their origin is thus described in T. F. Seward's Preface to the 1872 edition of *The Story of the Jubilee Singers of Fisk University*: "They are never 'composed' after the manner of ordinary music, but spring into life, ready made, from the white heat of religious fervor during some protracted meeting in church or camp. They come from no musical cultivation whatever, but are the simple, ecstatic utterances of wholly untutored minds." These 'camp meetings'— open-air services, often of prodigious length & fervor—date probably from the Kentucky Revivals of c. 1797. The popularity of the Spirituals outside the communities which invented them probably dates from the foundation, 1866, of Fish University, Nashville, Tenn., a school primarily for black students, and the inception at once of the Jubilee Singers, who within a year or two were a celebrated travelling choir, first visiting London in 1871. During the past 100 years Negro Spirituals have been familiar to all, but it is only recently that in the U.S.A., owing to the strenuous campaign for mutual recognition of the black and white races, that they have appeared in hymnals—as the above index testifies. When they so appear the harmony is always editorial, and the songs are always anonymous. For the best brief account of these songs, see A. Sandilands, *120 Negro Spirituals* (Morija, Lesotho, S.A., 1951); and for the history of their original promotion, see Marsh and Loudin, *The Story of the Jubilee Singers* (ed. of 1899).

224. GO TO DARK GETHSEMANE

4 st. 7.7.7.7.77

J. Montgomery (6), Cotterill's *Selection*, 1820, altd. by him in *Christian Psalmist*, 1825. Only *EH* has 1820 text, sts. 1-3; others either use 1825 text or modify it by using a line or two from 1820. Some U.S. Hymnals omit st. 4 which leads to the Resurrection. (Mixed texts ‡ below).

US & CAN: Can451‡: B112: CW227/170‡: H70‡: L78: M434: P -/193/- : Pm158‡ ● ENG: AM110: E100: M194

225. GOD BE IN MY HEAD   PCH 409

English version (old spelling) first found in *Hore Beatae Marie Virginia* (1514) beginning GOD BE IN MY HEAD AND IN MYN UNDERSTANDYNGE, and with final line 'God be at myn ende and my departynge.' In *Sarum Primer* it is in the spelling and version more familiar. It is a trsln. of a French poem beginning 'Jésus soit en ma teste et mon entendement,' for origin of wh. see *Bulletin* of the Hymn Society of Gt. Britain & Ireland, Sept. 1951, pp. 262-3. The early English sources are books of private devotion. First as a hymn in *Oxford Hymn Book*, 1908. Authorship of both English and French is unknown.

US & CAN: Can69: CW -/432: H466: P -/395/- : Pm393 ● ENG: AM 695/332: An623: B471: BB512: CH -/433: CP745: E*81: M405: NC74: PL111

226. GOD BE WITH YOU TILL WE MEET AGAIN

8 st. 9.88.9

J. E. Rankin wrote st. 1 about 1880 at First Congl. Church, Washington, D.C., and at once approved the tune, with refrain, wrtn. by W. G. Tomer in the 'Gospel Song' style. The theme of the hymn is 'Goodbye,' which is 'God be wi' ye.' Later Rankin wrote the other 7 st. which were pub. in *Gospel Bells* (U.S.), 1883. In Brit. the hymn has a double history, having been made popular with the American tune by evangelists, but having also been given in 4-line sts. without refrain by W. G. Horder in *The Treasury of Hymns*, 1896, set to a 4-line tune by A. Somervell in *Church Hymnary*, 1898, and set to another by Vaughan Williams in *EH*, 1906. In Brit. the 4-line form is now standard.

US & CAN: BP589: B261: CW129/43: H490: M540: P -/78/- : Pm61-2 ● ENG: AM740/489: B761: CH624/- : CP678: E524: M914

227. GOD BLESS OUR NATIVE LAND

66.4.666.4

This is the first line of 2 distinct hymns:

(a) by C. T. Brooks, c. 1832, wrtn. in U.S. as a translation of *Gott segne Sachsenland*, by S. A. Mahlmann (1815); this was substantially altd. by J. S. Dwight, c. 1844.

(b) by W. E. Hickson, printed in *The Dancing Master*, III, 1836, in 4 st. In Oct. 1869 Hickson wrote to D. Sedgwick in the U.S. complaining that he was author of this hymn, but accepted the reply that the U.S. composition (a) was independent of his. Brit. books use Hickson, U.S. books a composite piece: st. 1, Brooks, st. 2, Dwight, st. 3 (except *L*) Hickson. Hickson's hymn was of course an imitation of the British National Anthem & designed for the same tune. What the relation is between Brooks' hymn and MY COUNTRY 'TIS OF THEE, which first appeared in 1832 (see 458), remains obscure.

US & CAN: (composite) H146: L358: P143/514/- ● ENG: (Hickson) B 640: CH632/- : CP566: E560 pt. 2: M880

CHARLES TIMOTHY BROOKS, b. Salem, Mass., 20 vi 1833; Sch. Harvard Univ. and Divinity Sch.; Ord. Congl.; Newport, R.I., 1837-71, retiring because of failing eyesight. † Newport 14 vi 1883 (69).

SIEGFRIED AUGUST MAHLMANN, b. Leipzig, 13 v 1771; Sch. there in law; bought a bookstore in Leipzig, 1802; ed. *Zeitung fur die elegante Welt*, 1805-16, and wrote for *Leipziger Zietung* 1810-18; wrote much poetry including many popular children's songs. † Leipzig, 16 xii 1826 (55).

WILLIAM DAVID HICKSON, b. Westminster (London), 7 i 1803; in business as boot & shoe manufacturer; then in journalism, becoming ed. of *Westminster Review*, '40-52. Pioneer of state education and popular musical culture; energetic in support of social reform. † Sevenoaks, Kent, 22 iii 1870 (67).

GOD FROM ON HIGH HATH HEARD: see 853.

228. GOD HATH SPOKEN: BY HIS PROPHETS

3 st. 8.7.8.7 D

G. W. Briggs (110), *Songs of Faith*, 1945; first in hymn book, *Church Hymnal* (Church of Ireland), 1860.
US & CAN: CW -/34: M446: P -/-/382 ● ENG: An301: B247: PL257

GOD IS A STRONGHOLD AND A TOWER: see 847.

229. GOD IS ASCENDED UP ON HIGH

8 st. LM-alt.

H. More, *Divine Monologues, with Divine Hymns*, 1668. Norm. sel. in sts. 1, 6, 8; first given for congl. singing in *Oxford Book of Carols*, 1928, and *M* (Brit.) 1933.
US & CAN: ● ENG: AN201: CH -/290: CP152: M220: PL209
HENRY MORE, b. Grantham, Lincs., 12 x 1614; Sch. Eton & Cambridge; Ord. C/E, devoted his life to scholarship & philosophy and became a leading figure among the Cambridge Platonists. † Cambridge 1, ix 1687 (73).

GOD IS IN HIS TEMPLE: see 850.

230. GOD IS LOVE: HIS MERCY BRIGHTENS

5 st. 8.7.8.7

J. Bowring, *Hymns*, 1825. St. 5 identical with st. 1; now given in 4 st. omitting repetition.
US & CAN: B36: CW178/- : M63: P80/103/- ● ENG: CH33/144: CP54: M53
SIR JOHN BOWRING, b. Exeter 17 x 1792; trained for business and the first of his employers started him in world travel which later became his way of life. Ed. *Westminster Review* from 1825 (cf. Hickson, 227); M.P. for Clyde Boroughs, 1835-7, for Bolton, '41; founder of Anti-Corn-Law League, '38; obtained issue of the florin in 1840 (value two shillings) as a step towards decimal currency; this became, unchanged in size, 10p piece when decimal coinage was introduced in 1971. Knighted 1854, appointed Governor of Hong Kong. Spent much time in travel & diplomacy. † Exeter 23 xi 1872 (80).

231. GOD IS LOVE: HIS THE CARE

4 st. 666.66.55.3.9

P. Dearmer (88), *Songs of Praise*, 1925, to introduce tune THEODORIC (or PERSONENT HODIE).
US & CAN: ● ENG: B*27: CH -/416: CP*30: NC75: PL276

232. GOD IS LOVE: LET HEAVEN ADORE HIM

3 st. 8.7.8.7 D

T. Rees, posth. in *Sermons & Hymns* (ed. J. L. Rees), 1946. First in hymn book, *BBC*, 1951; in more recent books st. 2 lines 3, 7, 8 revised.
US & CAN: BP90: P -/-/386 ● ENG: AM*32: B52: BB7: M*22
TIMOTHY REES, b. Trefeglwys, Cardiganshire, 15 viii 1874; Sch. St. David's, Lampeter; Ord. C/E, Community of the Resurrection, Mirfield, Yorks; chaplain to the Forces 1915-9; remained in Community thereafter, contributing several hymns to *Mirfield Mission Hymn*

Book, 1936, until became Bp. of Llandaff (S. Wales), 1931. † Llandaff, 29 iv 1939 (64).

233. GOD IS MY STRONG SALVATION

4 st. 7.6.7.6

J. Montgomery (6), *Songs of Zion*, 1822, based on opening of Ps. 27.
US & CAN: B343: CW -/250: M211: P92/347/388: Pm373 ● ENG: B575: BB453: CH527/404: CP501

234. GOD IS WORKING HIS PURPOSE OUT

5 st. 7.6.7.6 D Troch. and iamb. Irreg.

A. C. Ainger, leaflet 1894, *Foreign Mission Chronicle* (Scotland, 1900) and in revised form, *Hymns A & M*, 1904, which vn. now is standard. Especially popular in U.S. and (in trsln.) among Latin American Protestants.
US & CAN: B509: CW -/358: H538: P -/500/389: Pm298: W99 ● ENG: AM735/271: An315: B371: BB177: CH380/303: CP340: E548: M812: PL124
ARTHUR CAMPBELL AINGER, b. 4 vii 1841; Sch. Eton & Trinity, Camb.; asst. master at Eton, 1864-1901; best known to former classical schoolboys as author of Latin Verse Dictionary, *Gradus*. † Eton, 26 x 1919 (78).

235. GOD MOVES IN A MYSTERIOUS WAY

6 st. CM   PCH 94

W. Cowper, *Olney Hymns*, 1779; John 13:9; but first pub. anonymously 1774 in John Newton's *Twenty-Six Letters on Religious Subjects*. The whole hymn except for 2 lines is quoted in 1st edn. of the *Oxford Dictionary of Quotations*, no other hymn being so fully cited there. Undoubtedly one of the great literary classics of hymnody.
US & CAN: BP101: Can159: B439: CW162/29: H310: L484: M215: P103/112/391: Pm87: CLB438 ● ENG: AM373/181: An403: B53: BB8: CH 31/147: CP56: E394: M503
WILLIAM COWPER, b. at the Rectory, Berkhamsted, Herts, 15 xi 1731; Sch. Westminster, then articled to a solicitor; called to the Bar, 1754, but after failures in that profession, especially fear of attending a public examination which was necessary before obtaining appointment as Clerk of Journals to the House of Lords, fell into serious depression, and thereafter abandoned the law; lived at Huntingdon until 1767, then at Olney, Bucks, until '86, where he formed close friendship with J. Newton (37) and assisted him in editing *Olney Hymns* (1779); indeed, he was intended to write the whole book, but collapsed mentally after completing 67 hymns, to which Newton then added 281. Moved to Weston super Mare after Newton's departure from Olney, and to Dereham, Norfolk, 1795. Became one of the major English poets, and one of the only two (R. Bridges [9] being the other) to become a significant hymn writer; but almost all his poetry was written before his mental collapse c. 1773, and his last 20 years were much clouded with mental illness, which in the end became insanity. † Dereham 25 iv 1800 (68).

236. GOD MY FATHER, LOVING ME

5 st. 77.77

G. W. Briggs (110), *Songs of Praise for Boys & Girls*, 1929; in later years he was often heard to say that he regretted writing it, describing it caustically as 'harmless'; but many editors have thought better than that of it.
US & CAN: BP359: H239 ● ENG: B742: CP689: M840

237. GOD OF CONCRETE, GOD OF STEEL

5 st. 77.77.77   PCH 490

R. G. Jones, 1962 for a Youth Group in Sheffield, to provide a hymn using modern urban images, and at the time the boldest and most picturesque of such hymns available. (In the Engl. vn. of st. 2, e.g., the word *motorway*—Americans say 'freeway'—was a very new word in 1962: only 16 miles of the motorway M1 were open in that year). Then sung by Methodist Synod in Sheffield, 1964 and printed in the *Methodist Recorder*. First in a hymn book, *Hymns & Songs*, 1969, closely followed by *100 Hymns for To-day*, 1969. Author says he wrote it 'to correct a tendency by which all the symbols of the modern world have become unrelated to our normal conception of God.'

US & CAN: Can90 ● ENG: AM*33: B*28: CP*32: M*23

RICHARD G. JONES, b. Dursley, Glos., 1926; Sch. Truro Sch., St. John's, Camb.; where studied Mechanical Sciences; read theology at Manchester; Ord. Meth., '53, serving on S.C.M. staff, '53-5; minister in Sheffield, '55-64; Birkenhead, '64-9; Lecturer in Applied Theology, Hartley-Victoria Coll., (Meth. Sem.), Manchester, from '69; Acting Principal, '73.

238. GOD OF ETERNITY, LORD OF THE AGES

5 st. 11.10.11.10 dact.   **PCH 566**

E. N. Merrington, 1912, for Jubilee of St. Andrew's Presb. Ch., Brisbane, Australia. "The main thought on my heart was of thankfulness to the Giver of all good for the splendid services rendered in the Colonies of our own blood & creed, and thankfulness for the opening of Emmanuel College (theol. sem. in Brisbane) that year." It is thus the oldest hymn in common use to come from Australia. First in England, in *Church Hymnary*, 1927.

US & CAN: Can57 ● ENG: BB390: CH642/517: CP577

ERNEST NORTHCROFT MERRINGTON, b. Newcastle, NSW, 1876; Sch. Sydney High Sch., Univ. Sydney, after 5 years in business; Univ. Edinburgh & Harvard; Ord. Presb. (Australia), served at Kiama, NSW, Haberfield, Sydney; St. Andrew's, Brisbane, 1910-23, and thereafter until retirement, First Ch. of Otago, Dunedin, N.Z. Founded Emmanuel College (mentioned above) and lectured there 1912-23 in Christian Philosophy; during World War I senior chaplain to Australian Expeditionary Force. † Wellington, N.Z., 26 iii 1953 (77).

239. GOD OF GRACE AND GOD OF GLORY

5 st. 8.7.8.7.8.7   **PCH 545**

H. E. Fosdick, 1930, first sung at opening (5 x 1930), then at dedication (8 ii 31) of Riverside Church, New York; first in hymnal, *Methodist Hymnal*, 1932; first in British hymnal, *Fellowship Hymn Book*, 1933. Now the most popular of all 20th cent. U.S. hymns. Important connection with biography below. The tune REGENT SQUARE was in the author's mind, and he wrote without approval of the decision of the Methodists to set it to CWM RHONDDA, with which at present (1977) it is very commonly associated in U.S. The last st. is often om. in American books: that st. certainly fits very badly with REGENT SQUARE, but it is a good stanza.

US & CAN: BP465: Can223: B265: CW378/245: L*1-3: M470: P -/358/ 393: Pm366 ● ENG: AM*34: B372: BB391: CH -/88: CP563: M*24

HARRY EMERSON FOSDICK, b. Buffalo, N.Y., 24 v 1878; Sch. Colgate Univ., Union Theol. Sem., New York, Columbia Univ., New York; Ord. Bapt. 1903. Minister of First Bapt. Ch., Montclair, N.J., 1903-15; Prof. homiletics, Union Theol. Sem., '08-'15; Prof. Practical Theology there, '15-'46. Minister at First Presb. Ch., New York, '19-'26. Then he was called to Park Avenue Presb. Ch., by John D. Rockefeller, who already had designs for building a massive new church. H. E. F. was at first unwilling to accept call, being alarmed by the Rockefeller wealth; but in the end accepted on the condition that the new church should be erected in a less privileged part of the city. Thus be became Minister of Riverside Church, which is situated on the edge of Harlem, and became one of the most famous of American preachers. He had in fact been obliged to resign from First Presbyterian Ch. because of what were held to be his 'heretical' views, and Rockefeller's famous reply to his doubts about accepting Park Avenue was "Do you think

more people will criticize you on account of my wealth than me on account of your heresy?" The 'heresy' was what we should now call the 'social Gospel' of liberalism. When the time came for the opening of the church, H. F. wrote the least triumphalist hymn that has ever been written for such an occasion. He wrote in his autobiography that it was "more than a hymn when we sang it that day—it was a very urgent personal prayer. For with all my hopeful enthusiasm about the new venture there was inevitably much humble and sometimes fearful apprehension." He † New York, 5 x 1969 (91).

240. GOD OF MERCY, GOD OF GRACE

3 st. 77.77.77

H. F. Lyte, *The Spirit of the Psalms*, 1834; Ps. 67.

US & CAN: BP27: B297: Can234: P465/-/- ● ENG: AM218/264: An421: B373: BB455: CH379/497: CP330: E395: M681

241. GOD OF OUR FATHERS, KNOWN OF OLD

5 st. 8.8.8.8.88   **PCH 256**

R. Kipling, in *The Times*, 17 vii 1897, and *The Five Nations*, 1903. First in hymn book in reprint (1899) of W. G. Horder's *The Treasury of Hymns*, then in *EH*, 1906. Inspired by the Procession and Naval Reivew, 26 vi 1897, which were part of the celebrations of Queen Victoria's Diamond Jubilee, it was titled 'Recessional: A Call to National Repentance & Self-Searching.' The occasion explains many refs. in text and also the title. Despite many localized associations, and one alarming phrase in st. 4, editors have been loath to let such an outstanding piece of literature disappear from hymnals.

US & CAN: CW560/- : H147: L347: Pm431 ● ENG: CH637/- : CP573: E558: M889

RUDYARD KIPLING, b. Bombay, 30 i 1865, was the son of a Methodist minister who at the time was teaching art in Bombay; Sch. United Services Coll., Westward Ho! Devon; on staff of *Civil and Military Gazette*, Lahore, India, '82-7 where be began to find success in writing short stories. Returned to England, '89, as full time poet and author; spent a short time, after marrying an American, at Brattleboro, Vt., but soon returned to England. Offer post of Poet Laureate in succession to Tennyson (620), '92, but declined it. He is often called the 'Unofficial Laureate of the British Empire at its greatest,' his work being sometimes distinguished by a now unfashionable imperialism; but that does not apply to most of what he wrote, and the poem above cited is a clear contradiction of that judgment if it is meant to imply complacency. Awarded Nobel Prize for Literature, 1907, and received many other honors, although he 3 times declined the O.M., Britain's highest civilian distinction. Prolific author of novels, stories, and poems. He † London, 2 days before the death of King George V with whom he also shared a birth year, 18 i 1936 (70).

242. GOD OF OUR FATHERS, WHOSE ALMIGHTY HAND

5 st. 10 10. 10 10   **PCH 385**

D. C. Roberts, 1876 in celebration of the first centennial of the American declaration of Independence; first in hymnal, *The Hymnal* (Episc.), 1892; tune NATIONAL HYMN composed for it 1876 for the New York City's celebration of the event.

US & CAN: B149: CW551/22: H143: L521: M552: P414/515/394: Pm 433: CLB319: W101 ● ENG:

DANIEL CRANE ROBERTS, b. Bridgehampton, L.I., 5 xi 1841; Sch. Kenyon Coll., Gambier, Ohio; served as private in 84th Ohio Volunteers in American Civil War; Ord. Episc., 1866, churches in Vt. and Mass., then became Vicar of St. Paul's, Concord, N.H., 1878-†. President of N.H. State Historical Society; active in Knights Templars at national level. † Concord, 31 x 1907 (65).

243. GOD OF OUR LIFE, THROUGH ALL OUR CIRCLING YEARS

3 st. 10.4.10.4.10 10

H. T. Kerr, 1916, for 50th anniversary celebrations of Shadyside Presb. Ch. Pittsburgh. Included in Presb. *Hymnal*, 1933. Wrtn. in meter and form of 'Lead kindly Light' (384), for tune SANDON.

US & CAN: CW583: 28: P88/108/395: Pm97 ● ENG:

HUGH THOMPSON KERR, b. Elora, Canada, 11 ii 1872; Sch. Univ. Toronto, Western Theol. Sem., Pittsburgh; Ord. Presb., 1897, and after charges in Kansas and Illinois, minister, Shadyside, Pittsburgh, 1913-46. Author of 22 religious books, pioneer in religious broadcasting, chairman of cttees. for the 1933 Presb. *Hymnal* and Presb. *Book of Common Worship*. † Pittsburgh, 27 vi 1950 (78).

244. GOD OF THE LIVING, IN WHOSE EYES

5 st. 8.8.8.8.88

J. Ellerton (80), *Hymns for Schools & Bible Classes, 1858*, in 3 st. LM; expanded, 6 ii 1867, to 5 st. of 6 lines, and incl. in *Words of the Supplemental Hymn & Tune Book* (Brown-Borthwick: no date) and in *Select Hymns for Church & Home, 1871*. Now always abr. to 4 st. or fewer.

US & CAN: H225: P -/-/397: Pm468: CLB406 ● ENG: B611: CH332/607: CP676: E*753: M974

245. GOD OF THE PROPHETS, BLESS THE PROPHETS' SONS

5 st. 10 10. 10 10

D. Wortman, 1884, for centenary of New Brunswick (N.J.) Theol. Sem.; 'Prayer of Young Ministers.' Included with a 6th st. in the *Hymnal* (Episc.) 1894; but this st. now always om.

US & CAN: CW472/334: H220: P481/520/398: Pm470: CLB395 ● ENG:

DANIEL WORTMAN, b. 30 iv 1835; Sch. Amherst and Reformed Seminary, New Brunswick, N.J.; Ord. Refd.; served churches in Brooklyn, N.Y., Philadelphia, Pa., Schenectady, Fort Plain and Saugerties, N.Y. President, General Synod, Reformed Church, 1901. † East Orange, N.J., 28 viii 1922 (87).

246. GOD REST YOU MERRY, GENTLEMEN

8.6.8.6.8.6 Irreg., with refrain 8 anap.

The earliest appearance of this anonymous Engl. Carol in wrtn. form is probably in the *Roxburghe Ballads*, c. 1770. *Oxford Book of Carols*, 1928, gives a 7 st. form, now very familiar in England, from Sandys' *Ancient Christmas Carols*, 1833, and an 8 st. form from an early 19 c. broadsheet. Various abrs. now appear, and in folk material of this kind, written down long after it was first sung, no authentic text can or need be established. In England carols of this sort were first found in hymnals in the *Congregational Hymnary*, 1916, wh. has this in the 7 st. form made very popular in Bramley & Stainer, *Christmas Carols New & Old*, 1871. More recently it has become usual for hymnals to include carols, and this is one of those most regularly found.

US & CAN: H40: M378: P131/166/401: Pm122: W102 ● ENG: An91: B96: CH -/184: CP707: E*9: NC76

GOD REVEALS HIS PRESENCE: see 850.

247. GOD SAVE OUR GRACIOUS KING (QUEEN)

66.4.666.4

The highly complex story of this hymn is best studied in P. A. Scholes, *God Save the Queen*, 1953. A 2 st. song beginning 'God save our Lord the King' appeared anonymously in *Harmonia Anglicana*, no date, c. 1744. (*Anglicana* means English, not Anglican). The tune is like, but not identical with, what is now known, the harmony in 2 parts. On 28

iv 1745 a song beginning 'God save our noble King' in 2 st., the 2nd being 'O Lord our God, arise . . .' as in the ?1744 text, was sung at Edinburgh on the proclamation of the Pretender (Charles, who unsuccessfully claimed the English throne for the House of Stuart, which had been ousted in 1688 with the banishment of James II). In Oct. 1745 the text as ?1744 was printed in *The Gentleman's Magazine* with added 3rd st., 'Thy choicest gifts in store,' and about that time it appeared in *Thesaurus Musicus* beginning 'God save great George our King'—thus answering the Edinburgh version in favour of the reigning House of Hanover.

Some time during the next generation the present first line came into use, and the song took its place as the British National Anthem. In later years it was altered, imitated and parodied (see *Julian*, and Scholes op. cit, and also notes on 140 and 227). After World War I, 3 stanzas were added to the two by then regarded as normal text (i.e., sts. 1 of ?1744 and 3 of 1745) celebrating the League of Nations, and these are given in *Songs of Praise*. But normally now it is confined to the two sts., 'God save . . .' and 'Thy choicest. . . .'

All speculations about author or composer have proved fruitless, though many claims and suggestions were made in 18 c. Most conjectures about the tune and curious meter are fanciful, but the meter could have been suggested by the old carol tune, 'Remember, O thou man' (*OBC*42), and there is a possible resemblance between the Anthem tune and a major-key transposition of the carol tune, especially in the second half.

Public attitudes to the Anthem have gone through various changes. Since it is centered on the Monarch, these reflect changing attitudes toward the Monarchy. In 18 c. it was merely a patriotic song. The reverential ceremoniousness which to some extent still surrounds it was at its deepest in the days of Queen Victoria and the two succeeding reigns. This has lightened somewhat; the custom of playing it at every public performance of anything whatever began to wane after about 1952, the date of the present Monarch's accession. It is now kept for large ceremonies in which Royalty is involved. The musical setting by Gordon Jacob used at the Coronation in 1953 was symbolic of the new kind of seriousness with which the piece was to be taken: less superficial pomp, but real music.

Hymnals did not include it until the last quarter of the 19 c.; it seems to have appeared first as a hymn in the Wesleyan *Collection* of 1876 (descendant of John Wesley's 1780 book) and in the *Hymnal Companion*, 1877. *Hymns A & M* did not take it until 1904; thereafter it is never absent from English and Commonwealth books, but its appearance in the *Lutheran Service Book & Hymnal* (1958) is surprising until it is realized that at that time the establishment of Lutheran congregations in England (associated with the opening of a department of Lutheran studies at Mansfield College, Oxford) was very much before the minds of the American Lutheran Church.

US & CAN: BP597: Can218: L361 ● ENG: AM707/577: An(endpaper): B641: BB392: CH631/521: CP565: B560: M879: NC298

248. GOD THAT (WHO) MADEST EARTH AND HEAVEN

8.4.8.4.888.4 troch-iamb.

St. 1, R. Heber, posth. *Hymns*, 1827, wrtn. for tune 'All through the Night' (90). In mod. hymnals always extended but in different ways:

(a) Eng. style adds 1 stanza, 'Guard us waking . . .,' by R. Whately, from Darling's *Hymns*, 1855, based on antiphon for Compline, 'Save us, Lord, waking. . . .'

(b) In Mercer's *Church Psalter & Hymn Book*, Oxford edition, 1864, st. 2 is 'And when morn again shall call us,' by Mercer; st. 3, Whately as above, and st. 4, by Mercer again, 'Holy Father, throned in heaven.' Certain U.S. books use sts. 1-3 of this form (one st. by each author).

(c) Another U.S. style is to use Heber for st. 1, and a stanza by F. L. Hosmer (483) from *The Hymn & Tune Book*, 1914.

US & CAN: CW143(a)/- : H169(a): L230(a): M490(c): P41(b)/58(c)/404(c): Pm58(c) ● ENG: [all (a)] AM26: BB415: CH293/- : CP620: E268

RICHARD WHATELY, b. St. Marylebone, London, 1 ii 1787; Sch. Oriel, Oxf.: Fellow, 1812; Ord. C/E, '11: Principal of St. Alban's Hall, Oxf., '25; Abp. Dublin, '31. Well known literary critic and early advocate of Jane Austen's works. † Dublin, 8 x 1863 (76).

WILLIAM MERCER, b. Barnard Castle, Co. Durham, 1811; Sch. Trinity Camb.; Ord. C/E, Vicar of St. George's, Sheffield, 1840-†; ed. *Church Psalter & Hymn Book*, 1857, wh. was the most popular C/E hymnal before *Hymns A & M* and one of the first to print tunes alongside hymns (though so printed that often four or more hymns would share a tune); many trslns. and adaptations of his were taken into other books. † Sheffield, 21 viii 1873 (62).

249. GOD THE ALL-TERRIBLE (OMNIPOTENT), KING WHO ORDAINEST

As now sung, a conflation of 2 hymns, both in 11.10.11.10 dact.

(a) GOD THE ALL-TERRIBLE, by H. F. Chorley, 4 st., in Hullah's *Part Music*, 1842, from wh. norm. 2 st. are taken (3 in *A & M*), viz., 'God the All-terrible . . .'; 'God the omnipotent, Mighty . . .'; and 'God the all-merciful. . . .'

(b) GOD, THE ALMIGHTY ONE, WISELY ORDAINING, by J. Ellerton (80), 4 st., wrtn. 28 viii 1870, 4 days before the battle of Sedan in the Franco-Prussian War. In *Church Hymns*, 1871, a 6 st. vn. was published, containing 3 st. from Chorley followed by 3 from Ellerton. In *Worship Song*, 1905, it is in 7 st., with all 4 of Chorley and 3 of Ellerton. Ellerton's first st. was always dropped, and the norm. seln. now seems to be sts. 1 and 3 of (a) and 2-4 of (b), 5 in all. ('So shall thy children . . .' is Ellerton, and should have been so ascribed in *A & M*). But often now begins 'God the omnipotent,' using first words of (a) st. 2 for opening.

US & CAN: BP593: Can273: CW565/33: H523: L354: M544: P420/487/- : Pm446 ● ENG: AM742/491: CH641/516: CP581: M901

HENRY FOTHERGILL CHORLEY, b. Billinge. Lancs, 15 xii 1808; went into business but soon turned to journalism. Mus. ed. for *Athenaeum*, 1830; later mus. critic for *The Times*. Published many articles, books & songs. † Westminster, London, 16 ii 1872 (63).

250. GOD WHO TOUCHEST EARTH WITH BEAUTY

5 st. 7.5.7.5

M. S. Edgar, 1926, prize hymn in a contest conducted by the American Camping Association. Thereafter in many hymnals. First in Britain, *CP* (1951).

US & CAN: BP471: Can243: CW315/- : M273: P -/102/- ● ENG: B472: CP465

MARY SUSANNAH EDGAR, b. Sundridge, Canada, 23 v 1889; Sch. Havergal Coll., and Univ. Toronto, also National Training Sch., YWCA. Founded Camp Glen Bernard for Girls in N. Ontario. Engaged much in travel & public work until retirement, 1955. Pub. poems & essays. † Toronto, 17 ix 1973 (84).

251. GOD WHOSE FARM IS ALL CREATION

3 st. 8.7.8.7   **PCH 475**

J. Arlott, *BBC Hymn Book*, 1951.

US & CAN: Can381: M514 ● ENG: AM*37: B726: BB440: M*26: CP*34: PL300

JOHN ARLOTT, b. Basingstone, Hants, 25 ii 1914, has worked as civil servant, police detective and journalist, but is best known in England for his writings & broadcast commentaries, since 1945, on cricket, on which subject he has wrtn. 30 books. He wrote 3 short 'country hymns' for *BBC*, of unusual imaginativeness and beauty, and lives in Hampshire very near Hambledon, the birthplace of cricket.

GOD WITH HIDDEN MAJESTY: see 867 IV.

252. GOLDEN HARPS ARE SOUNDING

3 st. 6.5.6.5 Ter.

F. R. Havergal, Dec. 1871. 'When visiting at Perry Barr (Birmingham) she walked into the boys' schoolroom, but feeling very tired she leaned against the playground wall while Mr. Snepp (ed. of *Songs of Grace & Glory*, 1872) went in. Returning in ten minutes he found her scribbling on an envelope.' (Havergal mss, quoted by Julian). The above hymn is what she was writing; she also wrote tune HERMAS for it, and sang it as she lay dying, 3 vi 1879, Eph. iv 8.

US & CAN: H359: L115: P456/-/- ● ENG: B166: CH133/-

FRANCES RIDLEY HAVERGAL, b. Astley Vicarage, Worcs., 14 xii 1836; early years spent in Worcester after her father became a Canon there; an accomplished linguist, she was fluent in French, German, Italian, Latin, Greek & Hebrew. Her whole life was devoted to private evangelism (see 674), and her many hymns always express this kind of fervor. † Oystermouth, Glamorgan, 3 vi 1879 (42).

253. GOOD CHRISTIAN MEN, REJOICE AND SING

4 st. 888.4

C. A. Alington, *Songs of Praise*, 1931, wrtn. for the tune GELOBT SEI GOTT.

US & CAN: BP198: Can469: B123: CW -/178: H*71: L109: M149: P -/-/ 407: Pm184: CLB273 ● ENG: AM-/603: An181: B156: BB103: CH -/270: CP149: E*31: M*29: PL194

CYRIL ARGENTINE ALINGTON, b. Ipswich, Sfk., 23 x 1872; Sch. Trinity, Oxf.; Ord. C/E 1901; Fellow of All Souls, 1896; Asst. Master, Marlborough Sch., 1896, and Eton, '99; Head Master, Shrewsbury Sch., 1908, of Eton, '17; Dean of Durham, '33-51. † St. Weonards, Herefs, 16 v 1955 (82).

254. GOOD CHRISTIAN MEN, REJOICE WITH HEART AND SOUL AND VOICE

3 st. 66.7.(2).67.5

J. M. Neale (2), *Carols for Christmas*, 1853, and Bramley & Stainer, *Christmas Carols New & Old*, 1871. It is a free rendering of the 15th cent. macaronic carol (the word means alternating Latin and vernacular lines) *In dulci Jubilo*, and was wrtn. for the same tune; the 2-syllable line in each st. was planned to fit what was later found to be a misreading of the orig. tune (see *The English Carol*, ad loc., and for a facsimile of the original score, *Piae Cantiones*, ed. G. R. Woodward, 1910); this line being easily detachable is now usually removed.

US & CAN: BP124: Can400: B90: CW193/137: H31: L39: M391: P130/ 165/406: Pm125: CLB228: W105 ● ENG: An99: B97: CH58/183: CP 716: M143

255. GRACIOUS SPIRIT, DWELL WITH ME

6 st. 77.77.77

T. T. Lynch (163), *The Rivulet*, 1855. Full text in *CP*; elsewhere norm. abr.

US & CAN: CW270/194: P214/-/-: Pm245 ● ENG: An295: CH187/-: CP213: M291

256. GRACIOUS SPIRIT, HOLY GHOST

8 st. 777.5

C. Wordsworth (27), *The Holy Year*, 1862; abr. to 6 st. in *Hymns A & M*, 1868, wh. is now standard form. In *CW†* begins 'Love is kind and suffers long,' i.e., st. 1 omitted. In *NC* mostly rewritten.

US & CAN: Can256: CW386‡/- : H379: L119: P -/-/241/- ● ENG: AM210/ 233: An543: BB153: CH484/438: CP212: E396: M290: NC150‡

257. GREAT GOD, WE SING THAT MIGHTY HAND

5 st. LM-coup.

P. Doddridge (64), *Hymns . . . .* posth., 1755; 'For New Year's Day: Acts 26:22.' Full text in *CP*.

US & CAN: BP102: CW586/364: L533: M509: P470/527/408: Pm454 •
ENG: B715: CH607/613: CP638

258. GUIDE ME, O THOU GREAT JEHOVAH (REDEEMER)

3 st. 8.7.8.7.4.7 **PCH 76**

Welsh: ARGLWYDD, ARWAIN TRWY'R ANIALWCH, W. Williams in *The Hallelujah* (Bristol), 1745, in 5 st.

Tr.: P. Williams, author's brother, *Hymns on Various Subjects* (Carmarthen, Wales), 1771, using sts. 1, 3, 5. Thus translated this is the oldest Welsh hymn in use, and the only one to achieve wide popularity. Welsh hymn-writing was abundant c. 1760-1900, but it was only certain tunes, virtually no texts, that escaped from their native country. *H* (U.S.) has an unusual and spurious version in 4 st. 8.7.8.7.

US & CAN: BP504: Can269: B202: CW393/251: H434†: L520: M271: P104/339/409: Pm93 • ENG: AM196/296: An555: B541: BB140: CH 564/89: CP500: E397: M615: NC81

WILLIAM WILLIAMS, b. Cefn-y-Coed, Wales, 11 ii 1717; studied for medicine but was moved by the preaching of the Welsh pioneer evangelist Hywel Harris to enter ministry; Ord. deacon in C/E 1740, but soon became preacher in a Welsh Calvinist-Methodist ch. It was Harris who persuaded him to become a hymn-writer at a meeting where all present were invited to write verses. † Llandovery, Carmarthen, 11 i 1791 (73).

PETER WILLIAMS, b. Llansadurnin, Carmarthenshire, 7 i 1722; Sch. Carmarthen Gram. Sch. Ord. C/E 1744, but like his brother joined Calv.-Meth. ch. 1746. He was expelled from that communion for heresy & built his own chapel in Carmarthen, where he continued to minister. Pub. Welsh Bible with commentary, 1767-70, and Welsh Concordance, '73. † Llandyfeilog, S. Wales, 8 viii 1796 (74).

HAIL, FESTAL DAY, WHOSE GLORY NEVER DIES: see 872.

HAIL, GLADDENING LIGHT: see 869.

259. HAIL THE DAY THAT SEES HIM RISE

10 st. 77.77

C. Wesley (1), *Hymns & Sacred Poems*, 1739.

Always abr.; and usually Alleluias added after each line. Longest text is in *CP, EH* (7 st.); all significant alterations from orig. are from Cotterill's *Selection*, 1819; these are now normal.

US & CAN: BP207: Can477: H104: L111: P171-/-/ : Pm205: CLB289: W108 • ENG: AM147: An203: B167: BB125: CP154: E143: M221: PL210

HAIL THEE, FESTIVAL DAY: see 872.

260. HAIL, THOU ONCE-DESPISED JESUS

8.7.8.7 D

A hymn of 2 st. beginning thus by J. Bakewell appeared in *A Collection of Hymns Addressed to the HOLY, HOLY, HOLY Triune God*, a 72 pp. pamphlet dated 1757, to be found in *Poetical Tracts*, 1757-64, in the Bodleian Library, Oxford. The hymn was expanded by M. Madan in his *Collection of Psalms & Hymns*, 1760, to 4 st., and appeared again in Toplady's (3) *Psalms & Hymns*, 1776. Nearly all hymnals now agree on a 4 st. vn. in which st. 1, 3a, 4a are Bakewell; st. 2, 'Paschal Lamb . . . ,' is Madan; st. 3b, 'There for sinners . . . ,' is Toplady; and st. 4b, 'Help, ye

bright angelic spirits,' is Madan. In *Can '71*, sts. 3a-4a are brought together again as original. Sometimes st. 2 is omitted altogether.

US & CAN: BP214: Can478: H357: L435: M454: P -/210/- • ENG: An 259: B173: CP162: M228

JOHN BAKEWELL, b. Brailsford, Derbs, 1721; began preaching in home neighborhood (N. W. Midlands of England) 1744, associated in London with Wesleyan movement from '49 and remained with them throughout working life; founded Meth. Ch. in Greenwich (E. of London). † Lewisham, Kent, 18 iii 1819, at 97/8, the longest-lived English hymn writer.

MARTIN MADAN, b. Hertingfordbury, Herts, 1726, cousin of W. Cowper (235); Sch. Westminster & Christ Ch., Oxf.; admitted to the Bar, '48; 'converted' by J. Wesley, Ord. C/E; became chaplain to the Lock Hospital (institution for 'restoration of unhappy females') and in 1780 wrote a tract, *Thelyphthora* advocating polygamy as preferable to prostitution. Obliged to retire because of this. Not a hymn writer but a very influential editor, his *Lock Hospital Collection* (1769) contained many versions and tunes which remain in common use (see e.g. 268). † Epsom, Surrey, 2 v 1790 (64).

261. HAIL TO THE LORD'S ANOINTED

8 st. 7.6.7.6 D **PCH 108**

J. Montgomery (6); first sung at Christmas 1821 at a Moravian settlement (unidentified) in England; in Jan. 1822 sent to Mr. George Bennett, then on a missionary tour to the S. Seas; printed in May issue of *Evangelical Magazine*, 1822, and in his own *Poetical Works*, 1828. Now always abr., norm. to 5 st. or fewer, but *CP* has 7. Slight variations from orig. text are mostly due to *Hymns A & M*, 1861; but final line of hymn has remained a problem and certain editors have taken their own line here. Based on Ps. 72.

US & CAN: BP113: Can154: CW257/113: H545: L328: P111/146/- : Pm105: CLB527: W110 • ENG: AM219: An129: B80: BB457: CH154/347: CP326: E45: M245: PL164

262. HAIL TO THE LORD WHO COMES

5 st. 6.6.6.6.66 **PCH 317**

J. Ellerton (80), 6 Oct. 1880, for *Children's Hymn Book* (ed. Brock), 1881; for the Feast of the Presentation.

US & CAN: H115: CLB445 • ENG: AM611/544: An441: E209: M*30: NC85: PL165

263. HAPPY ARE THEY, THEY THAT LOVE GOD

5 st. CM (1st line caesura always after 4th syll.) **PCH 174**

R. Bridges (9), *Yattendon Hymnal*, 1899 specially designed to carry the tune BINCHESTER. It is a free paraphrase of O QUAM JUVAT FRATRES DEUS by C. Coffin (52), *Paris Breviary*, 1736; this is more closely trsd. by J. Chandler (26) as O LORD, HOW JOYFUL 'TIS TO SEE (*AM-S* 273), and both more closely and also more gracefully trsd. by L. H. Bunn as CHRIST IS OUR HEAD in *French Diocesan Hymns*, by C. E. Pocknee, 1954.

US & CAN: • ENG: AM-/261: An532: B496: BB274: CH440/408: CP 418: E398: M419

LESLIE H. BUNN, b. 1901; Ord. Presb.; served at Bellingham, Northd; Crook, Co. Durham; Shrewsbury: he was in charge of the revision of Julian's *Dictionary of Hymnology* under the auspices of the British Hymn Society, but before he could complete the work, † Shrewsbury, 1971 (70).

264. HARK! A THRILLING VOICE IS SOUNDING

5 st. 8.7.8.7

Latin: VOX CLARA ECCE INTONAT, orig. perh. 5th cent., recast in *Roman Breviary*, 1632, as EN CLARA VOX REDARGUIT.

Tr. E. Caswall (26), *Lyra Catholica*, 1849, beginning HARK, AN AWFUL VOICE . . . ; this, with 'an awful' altd. to 'a herald' is in *EH*. More commonly found is the revision in *Hymns A & M*, 1861, beginning HARK A THRILLING VOICE.

US & CAN: BP220: Can392: CW -/116: H9: L1: CLB205 ● ENG: AM47: An76: E5: NC87: PL132

265. HARK, HARK, MY SOUL, ANGELIC SONGS ARE SWELLING

7 st. 11.10.11.10 with ref. 5.4.5.6

F. W. Faber (175), *Oratory Hymns*, 1854; always abr.

US & CAN: CW582/-: H472: L498: P431/426/- ● ENG: AM223/354: CH580/- : E399: M651

266. HARK, MY SOUL, IT IS THE LORD

6 st. 77.77   **PCH 92**

W. Cowper (235), *Olney Hymns*, 1779; 'Lovest Thou Me?' John 21:16.

US & CAN: BP372: H459: P224/263/- ● ENG: AM260/344: An523: B414: CH417/676: CP374: E400: M432

267. HARK, THE GLAD SOUND, THE SAVIOUR COMES

7 st. CM   **PCH 52**

P. Doddridge (64), *Hymns . . .* (posth.), 1755; 'Christ's Message: Luke 4: 18-19.' Full 7 st. vn. known in Scotland as Paraphrase 39 (76), and unlike many of his hymns, needed very little alteration in that collection; but most hymnals omit sts. 2, 4, 6, which improves the hymn.

US & CAN: BP110: Can385: H7: L6: P -/-/410 ● ENG: AM53: An82: B81: BB490: CH40/160: CP74: E6: M82

268. HARK, THE HERALD ANGELS SING

10 st. 77.77   **PCH 59**

C. Wesley (1), *Hymns & Sacred Poems*, 1739, in which it stands immediately before 'Christ the Lord is risen to-day' (114), and is in the same meter, though like it, in modern use the meter has altered. It there begins HARK, HOW ALL THE WELKIN RINGS / GLORY TO THE KING OF KINGS. 2 important changes were made in the 18 c.: (a) of the first 2 lines to the form now familiar, in G. Whitefield's *Collection*, 1753, and (b) the stanza form 77.77.77.77.77 using the 2 opening lines as a refrain, in the 1791 edition of the *New Version of the Psalms* (Tate & Brady, 53) among the 5 hymns added. This was at least 50 years before the Mendelssohn tune, now universal, was adapted for it. Original version in 8 st., using st. 1-8, at *EH* 23 with 'welkin.'

US & CAN: BP132: Can407: B83: CW189/123: H27: L25: M388: P117/163/411: Pm120: CLB225: W111 ● ENG: AM60: An112: B98: BB50: CH46/169: CP84: E23‡, 24: M117: NC86: PL150

269. HARK, THE SONG OF JUBILEE

J. Montgomery (6), on a broadsheet wh. says 'composed at the express desire of the London Missionary Society, with a special reference to the renunciation of Idolatry and acknowledgment of the Gospel in the Georgian Isles of the South Seas, and sung at Spa Fields Chapel, London, May 14, 1818.' Printed in *Evangelical Magazine*, July, 1818, and in his *Greenland and other Poems*, 1819, which gives text now used.

US & CAN: ● ENG: An317: CH389/- : CP325: E*306: M829

270. HARK, THE SOUND OF HOLY VOICES

6 st. 15 15. 15 15 (8.7.8.7 D)

C. Wordsworth (27), *The Holy Year*, 1862; 'All Saints' Day'; Heb. 11.

Often now printed as 8.7.8.7 D. In *CLB*, HEAR THE SOUND . . . .

US & CAN: H125: L143: CLB302‡ ● ENG: AM436/526: An463: CP362: E198: M830

271. HARK, WHAT A SOUND, AND TOO DIVINE FOR HEARING

4 st. 11.10.11.10   **PCH 445**

F. W. H. Myers, the last 4 st. of *St. Paul*, 1867; first as a hymn in *Congregational Hymnary*, 1916.

US & CAN: P110/150/- ● ENG: BB32: CH -/314: M254

FREDERIC WILLIAM HENRY MYERS, b. 6 ii 1843, Keswick, Cumb.; Sch. Cheltenham & Cambridge; became an inspector of schools. Poet & essayist; co-founder of the Society for Psychical Research. † 17 i 1901 (57).

272. HAST THOU NOT KNOWN, HAST THOU NOT HEARD . . . ?

CM

Scottish Paraphrases (1781); Paraphrase 22 begins WHY POUR'ST THOU FORTH THINE ANXIOUS PLAINT and runs 8 st. This, the commonest form of the hymn, uses sts. 2-7 of the Paraphrase; but the version in *CH* (1973) uses sts. 3-8 beginning ART THOU AFRAID HIS POWER SHALL FAIL . . . ? It is based on I. Watts (10), WHENCE DO OUR MOURNFUL THOUGHTS ARISE, in *Hymns . . .* , 1707, Book I, but has been substantially rewritten by the Paraphrasers.

US & CAN: BP79: Pm78 ● ENG: An250: BB491: Sc.Par.22/CH394: M*31

273. HAVE FAITH IN GOD, MY HEART

4 st. SM

B. A. Rees, *Congregational Praise*, 1951.

US & CAN: CW -/234: M141: Pm361 ● ENG: AM*39: An499: B577: CP422

BRYN AUSTIN REES, b. Chelsea, London, 21 ix 1911; Sch. Univ. London; Ord. Congl.; Sawbridgeworth, Herts, 1935; Ipswich, '40; Felixstowe, Essex, '45; Muswell Hill, London, '50; Woodford Green, Essex, '62.

274. HAVE MERCY ON US, GOD MOST HIGH

11 st. CM

F. W. Faber (175), *Jesus & Mary*, 1849. Most hymnals now begin at st. 2, MOST ANCIENT OF ALL MYSTERIES, and abr. the rest to 6 st. or fewer. Only *EH* has original opening stanza.

US & CAN: L138 ● ENG: AM162/159: E161: NC160

275. HAVE THINE OWN WAY, LORD

4 st. 5.4.5.4 D

A. A. Pollard, *Northfield Hymnal* (Stebbins), 1907; and *Hallowed Hymns New & Old* (Sankey), 1907.

US & CAN: B349: CW324/227: M154: P -/302/- ● ENG:

ADELAIDE ADDISON POLLARD, b. Bloomfield, Iowa, 27 xi 1862; Sch. Boston School of Oratory in elocution & phys. culture, then taught in girls' schools in Chicago. Assisted Alexander Dowie in healing missions, taught 8 years at Missionary Training Sch., Nyack-on-the-Hudson, N.Y.; missionary in Africa before 1914. † New York, 20 xii 1934 (72).

276. HE LEADETH ME! O BLESSED THOUGHT!

3 st. LMD-alt.

J. H. Gilmore, wrtn. after a service in First Bapt. Ch., Philadelphia, 26 iii

1862, in the home of his host; printed in Boston *Watchman and Reflector* and in *The Golden Censer* (Bradbury), 1864; made popular through the missions of Ira D. Sankey.

US & CAN: BP522: B218: CW405/45: H426: L478: M217: P106/338/-: Pm370 ● ENG:

JOSEPH HENRY GILMORE, b. Boston, Mass., 29 iv 1834; Sch. Brown Univ.; Newton Bapt. Sem.; Ord. Bapt., serving charges in N.H. and N.Y. Ed. *Daily Monitor* (Concord, N.H.), 1864-5; prof. of English, Univ. Rochester, 1868-1908. Publ. books on literature & a collection of hymns, 1877. † Rochester, N. Y., 23 vii 1918 (84).

277. HE SAT TO WATCH O'ER CUSTOMS PAID

6 st. LM-coup.   **PCH 250**

W. Bright (43), *Hymns Ancient & Modern*, 1889; St. Matthew's Day.

US & CAN: ● ENG: AM615/563: An450: E240

278. HE WANTS NOT FRIENDS THAT HATH THY LOVE

6 st. LM   **PCH 428**

R. Baxter (115), Cento, first made in *English Hymnal*, 1906, from poem dated 3 xii 1663, 'The Resolution,' beginning, 'Lord, I have cast up my account.' 'Wants not' in line 1 means 'never lacks.'

US & CAN: ● ENG: AM -/274: An430: B360: BB245: CH225/- : CP355: E401: M714

279. HELP US TO HELP EACH OTHER, LORD JESUS, UNITED BY THY GRACE

CM

C. Wesley (1) *Hymns & Sacred Poems*, 1742, 'A Prayer for Persons joined in Fellowship,' in 4 parts, orig. beginning TRY US, O LORD, AND SEARCH THE GOUND. HELP US . . . is st. 3 of pt. I, JESUS, UNITED . . . , st. 1 of pt. IV; the whole runs 29 st. If HELP US . . . is (A) and JESUS UNITED . . . . is (B) then:

    M (*Brit*) has A sts. 3-6 as #717, B, 1-6 as #721
    AM* has A3, A5, B4, B6
    BBC has A3, A5, B4 (as does *Songs of Praise*)
    CP has A3, 4, 5: B4, 5, 6
    BP and CLB have A3, A5, B4, B6
    Can has B1, A3, A5, B4
    M (*U.S.*) has B1, A3, A5, B4, B5, B6

US & CAN: BP493: Can255: M193: CLB501 ● ENG: AM*41: BB378: CP536: M717, 721

280. HERALDS OF CHRIST, WHO BEAR THE KING'S COMMANDS

4 st. 10 10. 10 10

L. S. Copenhaver, 1894, printed as part of a poem, 'The King's Highway.' First in a hymn book, *Hymns for the Living Age*, 1923.

US & CAN: CW533/- : L320: M406: P379/498/416 ● ENG:

LAURA SCHERER COPENHAVER, b. Marion, Va., 29 viii 1868; was a leader of the mission movement of the Lutheran Church in America to southern mountain settlements in U.S., and taught English 30 years at Marion College, a woman's college founded by her father in 1873. Wrote many poems & articles. † Marion, 18 xii 1940 (72).

281. HERE, LORD, WE OFFER THEE ALL THAT IS FAIREST

4 st. 11.10.11.10 dact.

A. G. W. Blunt, for a flower service, 15 vi 1879, at St. Luke's, Chelsea; in W. G. Horder's *Congregational Hymns*, 1884.

US & CAN: AM598/- : B721: CH347/; - M972 ● ENG:

ABEL GERALD WILSON BLUNT, b. Chelsea, London, 27 vii 1827; Ord.

C/E, 1851; Rector of St. Luke's, Chelsea, 1860-†. † Chelsea, 8 ii 1802 (74).

282. HERE, O MY LORD, I SEE THEE FACE TO FACE

10 st. 10.10.10.10

H. Bonar (81), October, 1855, at request of his brother, Dr. J. J. Bonar, for a communion hymn for St. Andrew's Free Church, Greenock (Scotland), where it was first sung on the first Sunday of October that year. In *Hymns of Faith and Hope*, first series, 1857. Always abr. and sts. often rearranged, as follows:

BP: 1-4, 5, 7, 10	*AM¹*: 1, 2, 5, 7
Can: 1-3	*AM²*: 1, 2, 5
CW¹: 1, 2, 4, 10	*An*: 1, 2, 5, 7, 4, 10
CW²: 1, 2, 5	*BBC*: 1, 2, 5
H: (208) 1, 2, 5, 7	*B*: 1, 2, 3 / 4, 5, 10
(206) 3, 4, 10	*CH¹*: 1, 2, 3, 4, 5, 7, 10
L: 1, 2, 3, 5, 7	*CH²*: 1, 7, 2, 3 / 4, 5, 10
M: 1, 3, 2, 4, 10	*CP*: 1, 2, 3, 4, 10
P¹P²: 1, 2, 3, 5	*E*: 1, 2, 5, 7
P³: 1, 5, 3, 4	*M*: 1, 2, 3 / 5, 7, 10
Pm: (287) 1-5	/ means division into 2 parts:
(557) 1, 2, 5	sts. 6, 8, 9 never now used

US & CAN: BP342: Can344: CW458/323: H208, 206: L275: M326: P352/442/418: Pm287, 557 ● ENG: AM715/414: An376: B316: BB202: CH 323/573: CP306: E312: M772

283. HIGH IN THE HEAVENS, ETERNAL GOD

6 st. LM-coup.

I. Watts (10), *Psalms of David . . .*, 1719; 'Ps. 36:5-9: The Perfections and Providence of God.'

US & CAN: ● ENG: An240: B56: BB9: CP51: M48

284. HILLS OF THE NORTH, REJOICE

5 st. 6.6.6.6.88

C. E. Oakley, *Hymns Adapted to the Christian Seasons* (ed. French, no date) and *Hymnal Companion*, 1870. Achieved great popularity when set, in *Public School Hymn Book*, 1919, to Martin Shaw's tune LITTLE CORNARD. Hymns of foreign mission of this kind tended to date rather quickly, and sts. 3-4 are now unacceptable to many. These have been updated in various ways, first and best in *Hymns for Church & School*, 1964, later in NC = W, and E*.

US & CAN: L321: P -/478/- : Pm106: W116 ● ENG: AM -/269: An314: B374: BB33: CH372/- : CP337: E*3: M815: NC89

CHARLES EDWARD OAKLEY, b. 9 i 1832, Brompton, nr. Chatham, Kent; Sch. Oxford; Ord. C/E, 1855; Rector of Wickwar, Glos., '56; Examiner to Univ. Oxf. in Jurisprudence & Civil Law; Rector, St. Paul's, Covent Garden (London), 1863. † Rhyl, N. Wales, 15 ix 1865 (33).

285. HIS ARE THE THOUSAND SPARKLING RILLS

6 st. 888.6

Mrs. Alexander (24), *Hymns Ancient & Modern*, 1875: for Good Friday.

US & CAN: H77 ● ENG: AM119/120: CH101/- : E117

286. HOLY FATHER, CHEER OUR WAY

4 st. 777.5

R. H. Robinson, 1869, for St. Paul's, Upper Norwood (London); *Hymns A & M*, 1875; Zech. 14:7.

US & CAN: H275 ● ENG: AM22: BB417: CH282/644: E270

RICHARD HAYES ROBINSON, b. 1842, Sch. King's, London; Ord. C/E, 1846; Incumbent of Octagon Chapel, Bath, '69-'71; Vicar of St. German's, Blackheath, Kent, '84-†. † Bournemouth, 1892.

287. HOLY FATHER, IN THY MERCY

I. Stevenson, 1869, for her brother who was departing on a trip to S. Africa for his health. It was distributed among friends on a leaflet, and became famous when it was sung on H. M. S. *Bacchante*, on which the future King George V and his brother were sailing round the world, 1881-2. They sent it back to the Royal Family who sang it at home. Included in *Hymns Ancient and Modern*, 1889.

US & CAN: BP436: H514: L337 ● ENG: AM595/488: An406: B668: BB386: CH629/529: CP679: E520: M916

ISABELLA STEPHANA STEVENSON, b. Cheltenham, Glos., 1843; invalid much of her life, but devoted parish worker in C/E. † Cheltenham, 28 iv 1890 (46).

288. HOLY GOD, WE PRAISE THY NAME

7 st. 7.8.7.8.77

German: GROSSER GOTT, WIR LOBEN DICH, I. Franz, wrtn. 1771; in *Katholische Gbch.*, 1774; paraphrase of *Te Deum Laudamus*.

Tr.: C. A. Walworth, 1853; in *Catholic Psalmist*, 1858 (Dublin). Norm. abr. to 5 st. or fewer. (U.S.) *H* has rewritten version.

US & CAN: CW -/69: H273‡: L167: M8: P -/-/420: Pm247: CLB414: W117 ● ENG: NC90: PL12

IGNAZ FRANZ, b. Protzau, Silesia, 12 x 1719; Sch. Glaz & Breslau; Ord. R.C., 1742, and spent his life as assessor at the office of the Vicar Apostolic at Breslau, Ed. *Kath. Gbch* (above). † 1790.

CLARENCE ALPHONSUS WALWORTH, b. Plattsburg, N.Y., 30 v 1820; Sch. Union Coll., Schenectady, N.Y.; admitted to the Bar, 1841. Studied for priesthood at General Theol. Sem., New York, Ord. R.C., c. 1848. Rector of St. Mary's, Albany, 1866. Assisted in founding order of Paulists (U.S.). Blind for last 10 years of his life. † Albany, N.Y., 19 ix 1900 (80).

289. HOLY, HOLY, HOLY, LORD GOD ALMIGHTY

4 st. 11.12.12.10 Irreg.   **PCH 116**

R. Heber (90), *Selection of Psalms & Hymns for the Parish Church of Banbury* (Eng.), and posth. *Hymns*, 1827. Said to be the favourite hymn of Lord Tennyson (620).

US & CAN: BP277: Can50: B1: CW107/70: H266: L131: M26: P57/11/421: Pm251: CLB409: W118 ● ENG: AM160: An227: B42: BB169: CH1/352: CP223: E162: M36: NC91: PL222

290. HOLY SPIRIT, HEAR US

7 st. 6.5.6.5

W. H. Parker, *School Hymn Book*, 1880.

US & CAN: BP263: CW -/199 ● ENG: An292: B233: CH189/124: CP 218: M286

WILLIAM HENRY PARKER, b. New Basford, Notts, 4 iii 1845; member of Bapt. Ch., New Basford, and active Sunday School teacher; became manager of an insurance company. † Basford, 2 xii 1929 (84).

HOLY SPIRIT, FONT OF LIGHT
HOLY SPIRIT, GOD OF LIGHT   see 881.
HOLY SPIRIT, LORD OF LIGHT

291. HOLY SPIRIT, TRUTH DIVINE

6 st. 77.77

S. Longfellow (7), *Hymns of the Spirit*, 1864, Num. 21:17.

US & CAN: BP265: CW274/191: H377: L130: M135: P208/240/422: Pm243: CLB297 ● ENG: AM672/- : An293: B234: BB155: CH193/106: CP214: M288

292. HOPE OF THE WORLD, O CHRIST OF GREAT COMPASSION

5 st. 11.10.11.10   **PCH 553**

G. Harkness, 1954, inspired by the General Assembly of the World Council of Churches at Evanston, Illinois, 1954, and printed in *Eleven New Ecumenical Hymns*, issued by the Hymn Society of America, 1955; it was by far the most successful of that series. First in hymnals, *Pilgrim* and Lutheran *Service Book & Hymnal*, both 1958.

US & CAN: B364: CW -/256: L581: M161: P -/291/423: Pm398 ● ENG:

GEORGIA ELMA HARKNESS, b. Harkness, N.Y., 21 iv 1891, Sch. Cornell Univ., Boston Univ., and (postdoctoral) Harvard, Yale Divinity Sch., and Union Theol. Sem. Prof. Philosophy, Elmira Coll., 1922; Ord. Meth., 1926; prof. religion, Mt. Holyoke Coll., '37; prof. applied theology, Garrett Sch. of theology, Evanston, '39; and at Pacific Sch. of Religion, Berkeley, Calif., '50-'61. Many hon. doctorates and hymn-writing awards; author of 28 books. † Claremont, Calif., 1965.

293. HOSANNA, LOUD HOSANNA

3 st. 7.6.7.6 D

J. Threlfall, *Sunshine & Shadow*, 1873.

US & CAN: BP157: Can448: M423: P147/185/424: CLB254 ● ENG: CH 93/235: M836

JEANNETTE THRELFALL, b. Blackburn, Lancs., 24 iii 1821, daughter of a Blackburn wine merchant and a lady of good family; lamed & disfigured by an accident early in life, and by another rendered a helpless invalid; but had a wide circle of friends & produced several books of poems. † Westminster (London), 30 xi 1880 (59).

294. HOSANNA TO THE LIVING LORD

5 st. LM-coup. with refrain 11

R. Heber (90), *Christian Observer*, Oct., 1811, with a letter indicating that this & other hymns were 'part of an intended series, appropriate to the Sundays and principal Holidays of the year, connected in some degree with their . . . Collects & Gospels, designed to be sung between the Nicene Creed & the Sermon.' (Indicates that at that date the Creed preceded the Sermon at Anglican Eucharist). One of the first attempts, therefore, to integrate hymnody with church seasons, rather than biblical or theological doctrines; after the Oxford Movement (83) this became much more fashionable. Marked 'Advent' and stands first in posth. *Hymns . . . 1827*. Only (U.S.) *H* has full text. Doxology in *Hymns A & M* is by compilers.

US & CAN: H381: L424: P53/-/- ● ENG: AM241: B269

295. HOW ARE THY SERVANTS BLEST, O LORD

10 st. CM

J. Addison, *The Spectator*, 20 ix 1712, norm. now abr. to 4 st.; but *EH* has 6. Between 26 vii and 18 x 1712, Addison, editor of the Spectator, printed 6 hymns; all appeared there for the first time, but the 3rd was by Watts (10), appearing as Ps. 114 in his *Psalms . . . of 1719*. This was printed on 19 viii 1712. The other five, all by Addison, were:

    (a) THE LORD MY PASTURE SHALL PREPARE (704), 26 vii;
    (b) WHEN ALL THY MERCIES, O MY GOD (799), 9 viii;
    (d) THE SPACIOUS FIRMAMENT ON HIGH (716), 23 viii;
    (e) HOW ARE THY SERVANTS BLEST (above), 20 ix;
    (f) WHEN RISING FROM THE BED OF DEATH (*EH* 92), 18 x.

All these hymns appeared after editorial essays on Saturdays; it will be seen that 4 of the 5 qualify for inclusion in our series; and of the 5 hymns added to the *Scottish Paraphrases*, 1781 (76), the first 3 are b, d, f above. Apart from authors who wrote only one hymn, Addison, having 80% of his output in common use to-day, and 100% in current hymnals, holds a record. He was a great admirer of Watts, whose example inspired his own writing.

US & CAN: M52 ● ENG: BB305: CP47: E542

JOSEPH ADDISON, b. Milston, Wilts, 1 v 1672; Sch. Charterhouse (sch.) and Magdalen, Oxf.; entered politics, became Under-Secretary of State, 1710, chief Sec. of State for Ireland, 1717. Joint founder with Richard Steele of *The Spectator*, and first editor, 1711. His inclusion (see above) of a Watts psalm in his *Spectator* series raised doubts about his authorship of the others; but these are now disposed of. † Kensington (London), 17 vi 1719 (47).

296.   HOW BEAUTEOUS ARE THEIR FEET

6 st. SM

I. Watts (10), *Hymns . . .* , 1707, Book I, 'The Blessedness of Gospel Times,' Is. 52:2, 7-10; Matt. 13:16-17. Full text is in *CP*. R. Bridges (9) rewrote the hymn for his *Yattendon Hymnal*, but his vn. found only in *Congregational Hymnary* (1916). Often abr. to 4 st.

US & CAN: ● ENG: AM755/510: CP317: M778

297.   HOW BRIGHT THOSE GLORIOUS SPIRITS SHINE

7 st. CM

I. Watts (10), *Hymns . . .* , 1707, Book I, beginning, THESE GLORIOUS MINDS, HOW BRIGHT THEY SHINE, in 6 st. Rewritten in *Scot. Paraphrases*, 1781 (76), as Paraphrase 66. Watts' title was 'The Martyrs glorified: Rev. 7:13ff.'

US & CAN: CAN499: H127 ● ENG: AM438/528: An464: B405: BB492: CH223/533: CP360: E199

HOW BRIGHTLY GLEAMS THE MORNING STAR: see 888.

298.   HOW FIRM A FOUNDATION, YE SAINTS OF THE LORD

7 st. 10 10.10 10 anap.

The author is unknown; believed by some to have been named Keen, because on its first appearance in Rippon's *Selection of Hymns . . .* , 1787, it is ascribed to 'K' and in a later edition to 'Kn.' Orig. vn., abr. to 5 st. or 4 st., much used in U.S.; but in the 2 Eng. books mentioned below the text follows the revision of *Congregational Hymnary*, 1916, in which the first-person quotes are all changed to third-person indirect speech: 'Fear not, *he is* with thee,' etc.; the last line then reads, 'He never will leave, he will never forsake.' Less fervor, maybe, but more grace. The U.S. custom of singing this to the tune of 'O come, all ye faithful' has English precedent, but this was abandoned long ago in Brit., and is now passing away in U.S.

US & CAN: BP425: Can139: B383: CW406/35: H564: L558: M48: P283/369/425: Pm372: W121 ● ENG: B579: CP503

299.   HOW GLORIOUS ZION'S COURTS APPEAR

7 st. CM

Scottish Paraphrases, 1781, #20 (76); elsewhere now in 5 st. (1-5). This is a rewritten version of I. Watts (10) HOW HONOURABLE IS THE PLACE (*Hymns*, 1707, Bk. 1, #8).

US & CAN: BP298: P340/-/- ● ENG: BB493: Sc. Par 20/CH294: CP321

300.   HOW SHALL I SING THAT MAJESTY

12 st. CMD

J. Mason, *Songs of Praise*, 1694, now abr. to 4 or 3 st., using selections from st. 1-4 of orig. With this (orig.) opening, first as a hymn in *English Hymnal*, 1906; but *Worship Song* (1905) had 5 st. CM beginning 'Thousands of thousands stand around.'

US & CAN: Can20 ● ENG: CP6: E404: M78

JOHN MASON, date of birth unknown, son of a Dissenting minister,

Sch. Strixton Hall, Northants and Clare, Camb.; Ord. C/E; curate of Isham; then 1668 Vicar of Stantonbury, Bucks; c. 1693, Rector of Water Stratford, Warks. Friend of R. Baxter (116). In 1694 he had a vision, in consequence of which he preached a sermon entitled 'The Midnight Cry' where he spoke of the imminent advent of Christ. The report that it was to take place at Water Stratford drew crowds to the neighbourhood, and strange ecstatic scenes occurred, including dancing. Before the excitement abated, J. M. suddenly died, warning Christians with his last breath to be prepared for an imminent Second Coming. None of this appears in his poems, which are mystical & often beautiful. † Water Stratford, probably aged 50-55.

301.   HOW SWEET THE NAME OF JESUS SOUNDS

7 st. CM   **PCH 85**

J. Newton (37), *Olney Hymns*, 1779; 'The Name of Jesus: Cant. 1:3.' St. 4 of orig. always omitted now.

US & CAN: BP249: Can116: B464: CW264/- : H455: L406: M81: P310/130/-: Pm221: W125 ● ENG: AM176/192: An260: B203: BB142: CH419/376: CP182: E405: M99

HUMBLY I ADORE THEE: see 867.

302.   HUSHED WAS THE EVENING HYMN

5 st. 6.6.6.6.88   **PCH 340**

J. D. Burns (60), *Evening Hymns*, 1857: 1 Sam. 3. In st. 2 there is a passage which has given rise to ribald misinterpretations:

> His watch the temple child,
>   the little Levite kept,

and some books alter this to

> Watch in the temple kept
>   the little Levite child

with the first 2 lines transposed to keep the rhyme-scheme.

US & CAN: ● ENG: AM574/- : An361: B474: CH251/123: CP455†: M848

303.   I AM NOT SKILLED TO UNDERSTAND

6 st. 888.7

D. Greenwell, *Songs of Salvation*, 1873; first as a hymn in *Sunday School Hymnary*, 1905.

US & CAN: B433: P326/-/- ● ENG: An624: B204: CH698/687: M381

DORA (originally DOROTHY) GREENWELL, b. Greenwell Ford, Co. Durham, 6 x 1821; then lived at Ovingham Rectory, Northd.; later at Golborne, Lancs, then Bristol, where † 29 iii 1882 (60).

304.   I AM NOT WORTHY, HOLY LORD

4 st. CM

H. W. Baker (101), *Hymns Ancient & Modern*, 1875; Matt. 8:8.

US & CAN: P498/-/- ● ENG: AM323/- : An377: CH316/570: M758

305.   I AM TRUSTING THEE, LORD JESUS

6 st. 8.5.8.3

F. R. Havergal (252), Sept. 1874 at Ormont-Dessous, Switzerland; printed in *Loyal Responses*, 1878; 'Trusting Jesus.' This was her favorite among her hymns.

US & CAN: BP411: P287/-/- ● ENG: An498: B432: CH695/685: M521

306.   I BIND MYSELF THIS TIDE

4 st. 67.77   **PCH 347**

L. McB. Watt, *The Tryst* (1925), a book of poems. Though an original composition it has the flavour of a Gaelic rune, and no doubt was in part suggested by *St. Patrick's Breastplate* (626). As a hymn, known only in U.S., and first in a hymnal, *New Hymnal for American Youth*, 1930.
US & CAN: CW302/219: P243/286/- • ENG:

LAUCHAN McBEAN WATT, b. Grantown on Spey, Scotland, 24 x 1867, of a Hebridean family. Sch. Univ. Edinburgh; after mission work there & in the Highlands, Ord. C/Scot., 1896; minister at Allen & Tullibody, 1901; St. Stephen's, Edinburgh, '11; Glasgow Cathedral '23-34; Moderator of Gen. Assembly, Ch. of Scotland, '33-4. Chaplain to the Forces during World War I; poet, Gaelic scholar and author of many devotional books. † Loch Carron, Ross-shire, 11 ix 1957 (89).

I BIND UNTO MYSELF TO-DAY: see 626.

307. I COULD NOT DO WITHOUT THEE

6 st. 7.6.7.6 D
F. R. Havergal (252), 7 May 1873; in *Home Words*, 1873, and *Hymns Ancient & Modern*, 1875.
US & CAN: P311/-/- • ENG: AM186/353: An485: E572: M522

308. I DANCED IN THE MORNING WHEN THE WORLD WAS BEGUN

4 st., stress 4-4-4-4- with refrain: a 5th st. added later.
S. Carter (173), *9 Ballads or Carols*, 1964; later in other collections of his. Based on 11 st. Cornish Carol, 'Tomorrow shall be my dancing day,' and tune adapted from Shaker song, 'Tis the gift to be simple' (for which see *Worshipbook*, 606). Carter writes, in *Green Print for Song* (1974), 'Scriptures and Creeds may come to seem incredible, but faith will still go dancing on. . . . I see Christ as the piper who is calling us.'
US & CAN: Can106: H863: P -/-/426: W128 • ENG: AM842: B*38: CP*41: E*39: M*82: NC99: PL92

309. I GREET THEE, WHO MY SURE REDEEMER ART

5 st. 10 10. 10 10
French: JE TE SALUE, MON CERTAIN REDEMPTEUR, which according to Douen appears in the Strasbourg Psalter (1545), and according to E. Pidoux is certainly in the edition of 1553 but not in that of 1548. It has been attributed to John Calvin, but Pidoux judges this ascription very unlikely; also attr. to J. Garnier, which Pidoux says is mere 'guesswork' (*Le Psautier Huguenot*, 1962). It must be regarded as anonymous.
Tr. in P. Schaff's *Christ in Song*, 1868, there attr. to 'Mrs. Prof. H. B. Smith,' who is otherwise known as Elizabeth Lee Smith (528). Radical revision in *Worshipbook* alters to 'we' throughout.
US & CAN: P -/144/625†: Pm207 • ENG: CH -/86

310. I HEAR THY WELCOME VOICE

6 st. SM, with refrain 5.5.7.6.
L. Hartsough, sent to Ira D. Sankey, 1873, and at once included in *Sacred Songs & Solos*, 1873, which still contains full text.
US & CAN: B175 • ENG: CH689/693: E573: M351

LEWIS HARTSOUGH, b. Ithaca, N.Y., 1828, Ord. Meth. (U.S.) at Utica, N.Y. Later retired to Utah where he established the Utah Mission and became first Superintendent of it. Edited music edition of *The Revivalist*. † 1872.

311. I HEARD THE VOICE OF JESUS SAY

3 st. CMD   **PCH 335**
H. Bonar (81), *Hymns Original and Selected*, 1846; 'The Voice from Galilee.'
US & CAN: BP369: Can115: CW288/223: H424: L499: M117: P236/280/-: W130 • ENG: AM257/351: An513: B346: BB143: CH410/212: CP376: E574: M154: NC100

312. I HUNGER AND I THIRST

J. S. B. Monsell (193), *Hymns of Love and Praise*, 1866.
US & CAN: BP526 • ENG: AM716/413: An378: B317: M462

313. I KNOW THAT MY REDEEMER LIVES

Three hymns beginning with this line are in use now, and we add a fourth to make confusion less probable.
(a) 9 st. LM-coup.
S. Medley, in G. Whitefield's *Psalms & Hymns*, 1779. Now norm. 4 st.
US & CAN: B436: L387: M445: W131 • ENG: An185: B174: M235
(b) 23 st. CM
C. Wesley (1), *Hymns & Sacred Poems*, 1742, now found in 5 st. version using sts. 1, 2, 10, 15, 19.
US & CAN: • ENG: M565
(c) 1 st. LM, with added chorus lines.
Anon., probably based on (a), in Southern U.S. folk-hymn collections.
US & CAN: • ENG: H*64
(d) 4 st. LMD-alt.
C. Wesley (1), *Hymns & Sacred Poems*, 1742, in use among Methodists in England until it was dropped from 1876 edn. of *Wesley Hymn Book*.
SAMUEL MEDLEY, b. Cheshunt, Herts, 23 vi 1738: served in Royal Navy in youth; converted on reading sermon by I. Watts (10); joined Eagle Street Bapt. Ch. (London). Ord. Bapt., Watford, 1767, ministered in Liverpool, 1772-†. Wrote many hymns which are especially used among Baptists. † Liverpool, 17 vii 1799 (61).

314. I LIFT MY HEART TO THEE

5 st. 6.4.6.4.10 10
C. E. Mudie, *Stray Leaves*, 1872.
US & CAN: • ENG: AM668/- : B438: CH427/- : CP481: M451

CHARLES EDWARD MUDIE, b. Chelsea (London), 18 x 1818; began as a bookseller but in 1842, aged 24, began Mudie's circulating Library. A Congregationalist, he was for many years a director of the London Missionary Society; conducted a mission in the neighborhood of Vauxhall Bridge Road, London. † Hampstead (London), 28 ix 1890 (72).

315. I LOOK TO THEE IN EVERY NEED

4 st. 8.6.8.6.88   **PCH 377**
S. Longfellow (7), *Hymns of the Spirit*, 1864; introduced to Britain in W. G. Horder's *Worship Song*, 1896.
US & CAN: CW -/239: M219: P79/114/- : Pm92 • ENG: E406

316. I LOVE THY KINGDOM, LORD

8 st. SM   **PCH 350**
T. Dwight, in his revision of Watts' *Psalms . . .*, 1800, as Psalm 137: in fact a meditation on Ps. 137:5-6. Sometimes nowadays 'We' for 'I.'
US & CAN: BP305: B240: CW -/348: H388: L158: M294: P337/435/626†: Pm269 • ENG: CH210/- : CP246: M708‡

TIMOTHY DWIGHT, b. Northampton, Mass., 14 v 1752, grandson of Jonathan Edwards; Sch. Yale, where he was tutor, 1771-7; Ord. Congl.; chaplain during Revolutionary War (much admired by George Washington); minister at Fairfield, Conn., '83-'95, where he also ran a divinity school; President of Yale, '95, which office he combined with that of chaplain, becoming one of the first famous campus-preachers. † Philadelphia, 11 i 1817 (65).

317. I LOVE TO HEAR THE STORY

3 st. 7.6.7.6 D, sometimes with 4-line refrain in same meter.   **PCH 311**
E. Miller, *The Little Corporal*, 1867; *Hymns Ancient & Modern*, 1875.

US & CAN: BP167: B461: CW428/- : P447/-/- ● ENG: AM330/445: An 347: B119: CH71/227: E594: M856

EMILY MILLER, b. Brooklyn, Conn., 22 x 1833; Sch. Oberlin; m. (1860) Prof. J. E. Miller, For many years joint-editor of *The Little Corporal* (a journal published in Chicago). † Northfield, Minn., 1913 (80).

318.   I NEED THEE EVERY HOUR
5 st. 6.5.6.5 with refrain 7.6.7.4 added later.

A. S. Hawks, April, 1872, for Convention of National Baptist Sunday School Association, Cincinnati, Ohio, Nov., 1872; published in *Royal Diadem*, 1872, ed. by R. Lowry, who added refrain.

US & CAN: B379: CW341/240: L479: M265: P332/324/- : Pm342 ● ENG: B475: CH700/688: CP416: M475

ANNIE SHERWOOD HAWKS, b. Hoosick, N.Y., 28 v 1835, lived most of her life in Brooklyn, N.Y., member of Hanson Place Bapt. Ch. Wrote over 400 hymns. † Bennington, Vt., 3 i 1918 (82).

ROBERT LOWRY, b. Philadelphia, 12 iii 1826; Sch. Bucknell Univ. Ord. Bapt., served in Pennsylvania, New York, and Brooklyn, N.Y.; taught for a time at Bucknell, '69-75; later at Park Avenue Baptist Ch., Plainfield, N.J.; well known writer and composer of Gospel Songs. † Plainfield, 25 xi 1899 (73).

I SHALL PRAISE MY SAVIOUR'S GLORY: see 867 I.

319.   I SING A SONG OF THE SAINTS OF GOD
3 st. stress 4-3-4-3-4-4-4-3.   **PCH 485**

L. Scott, *Everyday Hymns for Children*, 1929 (U.S.A.); first in general hymnal, *Hymnal 1940* (U.S.A.); first in Britain, *BBC*, 1951.

US & CAN: H243: Pm481 ● ENG: B259: BB353

LESBIA SCOTT, b. Willesden (London), 2 viii 1898; Sch. Raven's Croft, Sussex. M. (1917) J. Mortimer Scott, naval officer. Her *Everyday Hymns* were written for her own 3 children; though this was published in U.S.A., she has lived all her life in England, latterly in Devonshire. Has written several plays and has had a long association with amateur drama.

I SING AS I ARISE TO-DAY: see 626.

320.   I (WE) SING THE ALMIGHTY POWER OF GOD
8 st. CM   **PCH 296**

I. Watts (10), #2 in *Divine Songs for Children*, 1715. In British books normally sts. 4 and 7 omitted. In U.S. books as 'I (or We) sing the mighty power . . . ,' using sts. 1-5 and an altd. version of st. 6, always CMD. (Neither U.S. editors nor Companions ever admit the alteration.)

US & CAN: Can81: B154: CW -/4: M37: P65/84/628: Pm68: W133 ● ENG: An241: B58: CP33: M46

321.   I SOUGHT THE LORD, AND AFTERWARD I KNEW
3 st. 10. 10. 10. 6

Anon., *Holy Songs, Carols and Sacred Ballads*, Boston, 1889; sometimes attrib. to Jean Ingelow (41), and in a meter she used, but not found in her collected Works.

US & CAN: CW403/11: H405: L473: M96: P324/402/- : Pm408 ● ENG:

322.   I THINK WHEN I READ THAT SWEET
STORY OF OLD
3 st. 11.8.11.8 D anap.   **PCH 301**

J. Luke, *Sunday School Teachers' Magazine*, March 1841, first sung at a Sunday School in Blagdon, Som., where her father was rector. When her father first heard it he asked who had written it, and learning with surprise that the writer was his daughter he sent it at once to the Magazine. It had been written in a 2-horse carriage on the way to Wellington (Som.). The so-called 'Greek Air' with which it is still often associated (about which there is probably nothing Greek at all) was with it in the original printed source, and at later stages has been variously arranged.

US & CAN: CW213/- : H246: L497: P442/460/- : Pm483 ● ENG: An346: B120: CH82/- : CP104: E595: M865

JEMIMA LUKE, b. Islington (London), 19 viii 1813; her father was a pioneer of the Bible Society and the Sunday School Union. M (1843) Rev. Samuel Luke (Congregationalist). Published (1900) a memoir, *The Early Years of my Life*, from which the above information is taken. † Newport, I. o. W., 2 ii 1906 (82).

323.   I TO THE HILLS WILL LIFT MINE EYES

Psalm 121 in *Scottish Psalter*, 1650. This and Ps. 23 are the only two original Scottish Psalms which are both widely sung outside Scotland and also sung in their entirety. See below.

US & CAN: Can128: P -/377/430: Pm85 ● ENG: B59: BB459: ScPs121/ CH139: CP741: M625

SCOTTISH PSALTERS. The first complete metrical psalter for Scottish use was published by order of Assembly in 1564. Between that date and 1650, when the last authorized metrical psalter was published, many attempts were made at revision and improvement, but none was authorized. The most important of these was that of 1595, which first added doxologies to each psalm, and the most unusual was that of King James VI (of Scotland: James I of England), which was printed six years after the King's death, 1631, but again not authorized. The final edition, which is still in use in Scotland, was assembled with many previous unofficial versions, as well as the Sternhold and Hopkins version, in view, but the largest influence in it was that of an Englishman, Francis Rous (705). It was Rous' version of 1643 which was most often turned to, although those of Wm. Barton (1644) and Zachary Boyd (1648) were also under review. The resulting Psalter of 1650, it should be noted, was authorized by the Westminster Assembly, and therefore, although it is always referred to as the *Scottish Psalter* because it is in official use in that country, it was designed as a Psalter for all Presbyterians, including the English, in competition with Sternhold & Hopkins, which was in use by the Episcopal Church. It was in fact never adopted in England, but until quite recently the Scottish Psalter has been in Scotland the central manual of praise, and in some communions it is the only such manual still, even the Paraphrases (q.v., 76) being disallowed. In the Church of Scotland until 1973 it was a separate book from the hymnal (even if often bound in with it); only in 1973 did that Church authorize an edition of the hymnal in which selected metrical psalms were distributed through the book and referred to not by their traditional psalm numbers but by hymn numbers. All efforts at revising the Psalter have so far met with failure, and two or three of the psalms have now become part of universal hymnody, especially Ps. 23, which before 1945 was never included in Anglican hymnals. Psalm 100, 2nd version, 'All people that on earth do dwell' (20), it may be noted, was the work of an Englishman and the 1564 Scottish Psalter was not the first to print it.

324.   I VOW TO THEE, MY COUNTRY
2 st. 13 13. 13 13. 13 13 (or 7.6.7.6 Ter)

C. Spring-Rice, 'Written 12 i 1918 on the eve of his final departure from Washington (D.C.). The vow recorded in it had been kept before he ever put it into words; . . . though he knew it not he was already a dying man.' (V. Chirol, *Memoir* of C. S. R.). The author died on the night of 13/14 i 1918. First as a hymn in *Songs of Praise*, 1925.

US & CAN: ● ENG: AM -/579: B642: CP756: M900: NC110

CECIL ARTHUR SPRING-RICE, b. Westminster (London), 27 ii 1859; Sch. Eton & Balliol, Oxf.; politician and diplomat; Charge d'Affaires, Tehran, 1900; British Commissioner of Public Debt, Cairo, '01; Embassies of St. Petersburg, '03; Persia, '06; Sweden, '08; British Ambassador to the U.S.A., '12-18. † Ottawa, Canada, 13/14 i 1918 (58).

325. I WAITED FOR THE LORD MY GOD
CM
Ps. 40 in *Scottish Psalter*, 1650 (323); 22 verses, 19 st.; authorized selection is vv. 1-5 (6 st.), but hymnals sometimes use other selections.
US & CAN: BP17: B402: P -/413/- ● ENG: B501: ScPs40/CH73: CP731

326. I WILL SING THE WONDROUS STORY
5 st. 8.7.8.7 D (last 4 lines refrain)
F. H. Rowley, written about 1886 for Gospel Singer Peter Bilhorn who had suggested during a religious revival meeting at First Bapt. Ch., North Adams, Mass., that he (F. H. R.) should write a hymn. P. B. at once set it to music. Later included in I. D. Sankey's *Sacred Songs & Solos.*
US & CAN: B53 ● ENG: An261: B502: CH683/381: M380
FRANCIS HAROLD ROWLEY, b. Hilton, N.Y., 1854; Sch. Rochester Univ. & Theol. Sem.; Ord. Bapt., Titusville, Pa.; then served at N. Adams, Mass., Oak Park, Ill., Fall River, Mass., and First Bapt. Ch., Boston, Mass. Became President of Massachusetts Society for Prevention of Cruelty to Animals, and of American Humane Education Society. † Boston, 1952 (98).

IF THERE BE THAT SKILLS TO RECKON: see 402.

IF THOU BUT SUFFER GOD TO GUIDE THEE: see 886.

327. I'LL PRAISE MY MAKER WHILE I'VE BREATH
6 st. 88.8.88.8
I. Watts (10), Ps. 146, 2nd vn. in *Psalms of David . . .*, 1719; 'Praise to God for his goodness and truth.' Norm. seln., now is sts. 1, 3, 4, 6. This hymn was sung by J. Wesley as he lay dying. *Worshipbook* rewrites as PRAISE WE OUR MAKER. . . .
US & CAN: Can51: CW -/74: M9: P -/-/558‡ ● ENG: B60: CP8: M428

328. I'M NOT ASHAMED TO OWN MY LORD
4 st. CM
I. Watts (10), *Hymns . . .*, 1707, bk. I; 'Not ashamed of the Gospel: 2 Tim. 1:12'; with small alts., incl. in *Scot. Paraphrases*, 1781 (76) as #54.
US & CAN: BP484: Can188: P -/292/- ● ENG: An501: B292: BB494: CH507/591: CP467: M485

329. IMMORTAL, INVISIBLE, GOD ONLY WISE
6 st. 11 11. 11 11 anap.   **PCH 342**
W. C. Smith, *Hymns of Christ and the Christian Life*, 1867; 1 Tim. 1:17. Always now in 4 st., omitting orig. st. 4 and 5b, 6b. The theological set of the whole poem is so radically altered by this that we here quote the last 2 st. (5-6) of the original, which are printed in full now only in the British *Baptist Hymn Book* (1962) and *Australian Hymnal* (1977):

> Great Father of glory, pure Father of light,
> thine angels adore thee, all veiling their sight;
> but of all thy rich graces this grace, Lord, impart—
> take the veil from our faces, the veil from our heart.
>
> All laud we would render, O help us to see
> 'tis only the splendour of light hideth thee.
> And so let thy glory, Almighty, impart,
> through Christ in the story, thy Christ to the heart.

The abridgment now familiar is due to P. Dearmer, *English Hymnal*, 1906.

US & CAN: BP70: Can26: B32: CW159/75: H301: L172: M27: P66/85/433: Pm7: CLB431: W135 ● ENG: AM -/372: An242: B61: BB10: CH12/32: CP28: E407: M34: NC102
WALTER CHALMERS SMITH, b. Aberdeen, 5 xii 1824; Sch. Aberdeen Gram. Sch., and Univ. & New Coll., Edinburgh; Ord. C/Scot.; served at Chadwell St., Islington (London); Free Ch., Milnathort, Fife; Free Tron Ch., Glasgow; Free High Kirk, Edinburgh '76; Moderator Free Kirk of Scotland, '93; retired '94. † Kinbuck, Perthshire, 20 ix 1908 (83).

330. IMMORTAL LOVE, FOR EVER FULL   PCH 363
O LORD AND MASTER OF US ALL   PCH 364
C.M.
J. G. Whittier (11), *The Panorama and Other Poems*, 1856. The poem, 'Our Master' orig. in 38 st., generated many centos since it was first used for this purpose in W. G. Horder's *Congregational Hymns*, 1884. There it appeared in 17 st., divided in 2 parts, the first beginning 'Immortal love . . .' the second, 'Our Friend, our brother and our Lord.' In 1887 the *Congregational Church Hymnal* used 19 st. in 3 parts, beginning 'Immortal love . . .' 'Our Lord and Master,' and 'We faintly hear. . .' In 1890 the Anglican *Hymnal Companion* used 10 st. as one hymn, beginning 'Immortal love . . .' and using 'O Lord and Master . . .' as st. 6. In more modern books the opening lines as given in our lead-line. P. Dearmer included it thus in the *English Hymnal*, 1906, after which it became universally popular. In most centos the stanzas in normal use can be thus identified from the original poem:
(Usually in IMMORTAL LOVE . . .): 1, 'Immortal . . .'; 2, 'Our outward . . .'; 5, 'We may not . . .'; 13, 'But warm . . .'; 14, 'The healing . . .'; 15, 'Through him . . .'; 31, 'Alone, O love. . . .' (Usually in O LORD & MASTER . . .): 16, 'O Lord . . .'; 17, 'Thou judgest . . .'; 18, 'Our thoughts . . .'; 20, 'Yet weak . . .'; 21, 'To thee our full . . .'; 30, 'Apart from thee . . .'; 24, 'Our Friend, our Brother . . .'; 26, 'We faintly hear. . . .' But sometimes sts. are taken from one section to the other.
IMMORTAL LOVE
US & CAN: BP160: B329: CW254/12: H360: L476: M157: P178/229/434: Pm230 ● ENG: AM -/208: An537: B121: CH141/306: CP186 i: E408: M102
O LORD & MASTER
US & CAN: BP481: Can287: H501: Pm224 ● ENG: An272: B125: CH 513/439: CP186 ii: E456: M103

331. IN CHRIST THERE IS NO EAST NOR WEST
4 st. CM
John Oxenham, 1908, for 'The Pageant of Darkness and Light,' an exhibition run by the London Missionary Society (founded 1795, merged with Council for World Mission, 1966) in London. Published in *Bees in Amber*, 1913; first as a hymn in Supplement (1920) to *Fellowship Hymn Book.*
US & CAN: BP389: Can149: B258: CW480/269: H263: L342: M192: P 341/479/435: Pm415: CLB479: W137 ● ENG: AM*43: An420: B661: CH -/425: CP346: E*95: M*34: NC104: PL268
'JOHN OXENHAM' was the pen-name of William Arthur Dunkerley, b. Cheetham, Manchester, 12 vi 1852; Sch. Old Trafford School, Manchester and Victoria Univ. (later Univ. Manchester); in business with his father, a wholesale merchant, 1872-81; then in full time literary work. Wrote 41 novels and 11 vols. of religious work besides poetry. Was a Congregationalist; edited *Christian News-Letter* during World War I; taught a Bible class in Ealing Congl. Ch., London. † High Salvington, Sussex, 23 i 1941 (88).

332. IN HEAVENLY LOVE ABIDING
3 st. 7.6.7.6 D   **PCH 279**
A. L. Waring, *Hymns & Meditations*, 1850.
US & CAN: BP505: B204: CW384/- : H431: L574: M230: P284/417/- : Pm343: CLB487: W138 ● ENG: An524: B581: CH442/681: CP412: M528

ANNA LETITIA WARING, b. Plas y Velim, Neath, Glamorgan, 19 iv 1823; Sch. as member of Society of Friends, but joined C/E 1842; lived in Bristol, much engaged in social work especially among discharged prisoners. † Clifton, Bristol, 10 v 1910 (87).

333. IN MEMORY OF THE SAVIOUR'S LOVE

3 st. CM

T. Cotterill, in Stubbs' Selection of *Psalms & Hymns* (Uttoxeter, 1805) as a 6 st. hymn beginning 'Blest with the presence of their God.' First line as now sung is altd. from 'In memory of his dying love.' *M* (U.S.) adds one anonymous st. Where still in use, always much altd. from orig.

US & CAN: Can334: B249: CW462/- : M319 ● ENG: M762

THOMAS COTTERILL, b. Cannock, Staffs, 1 (or 4) xii 1779; Sch. Free School, Birmingham, St. John's, Camb.; Fellow of St. John's, 1801. Ord. C/E and after 2 curacies in Staffs, Vicar of St. Paul's, Sheffield, 1817-23. Became an historic figure in hymnology through his *Psalms & Hymns for Public & Private use*, first edition, 1810. Successive revisions appeared until the 8th ed., 1819, in which he was assisted by J. Montgomery (6). This contained the 150 Psalms in meter and 367 hymns; members of his congregation objected and the case was taken to the Diocesan Court at York, since hymns were still technically illegal in the C/E, even though in many places they were being sung quite freely. The Abp. of York, Vernon Harcourt, was obliged to order withdrawal of the edition, but suggested that it be revised and submitted for his approval. The revised edition, dedicated to him and approved, contained 146 hymns, and with it hymn-singing finally became fully legal in the C/E. Cotterill † 29 xii 1823 (44), and in memory of him Montgomery wrote the hymn 'Friend after friend departs.'

334. IN STATURE GROWS THE HEAVENLY CHILD (a) THE HEAVENLY CHILD IN STATURE GROWS (b) THE SON OF GOD HIS GLORY HIDES (c)

CM   PCH 171

All three are variants of tr. by J. Chandler (26) in *Hymns of the Primitive Church* (1837) of Latin DIVINE CRESCEBAS PUER (5 st. LM) by J. B. de Santeuil in *Hymni Sacri et Novi*, 1689. (a) is orig., (b) his revision in *Hymns A & M*, 1861, (c) is orig. beginning at st. 2. Doxology is not orig. A new translation by G. B. Timms is in *English Praise*, 1976, LM.

US & CAN: ● ENG: AM78: BB68: E46: E*22

335. IN THE BLEAK MIDWINTER

5 st. 6.5.6.5 D Irreg.   PCH 290

C. Rossetti, c. 1872; first as hymn in *English Hymnal*, 1906, at once made popular by Holst's tune. *EH* has full text, but often st. 3 is om. Like many Christmas songs written at that period, it assumes English surroundings (including weather) for the Nativity.

US & CAN: BP121: Can418: CW -/135: H44: L36: M376: Pm128 ● ENG: AM -/67: An100: B99: BB51: CH50/178: CP90: E25: M137: NC107

CHRISTINA GEORGINA ROSSETTI, b. St. Pancras (London), 5 xii 1830, sister of Dante Gabriel Rossetti and William Michael Rossetti, the family of Prof. Gabriele Rossetti, an Italian refugee who was Prof. of Italian at Univ. London. Became a distinguished minor poetess after her first poems were published in *The Germ*, a pre-Raphaelite magazine, 1850. † London, 29 xii 1894 (64).

336. IN THE CROSS OF CHRIST I GLORY

5 st. (5 the same as 1) 8.7.8.7   PCH 114

J. Bowring (230), *Hymns*, 1825; 'Glorying in the Cross: Gal. 6:14.' 'The first thing you see as you approach Macao (Island near Hong Kong) is the great white church of Our Lady of Fatima, perched on the island's highest hill. In a revolution the church was destroyed, save for the great west front. The west wall still stands, and crowning the topmost point is a great metal cross, which (in repeated attacks) has survived destruction. It was this cross, blackened with smoke, that inspired John Bowring's hymn'—(the late A. M. Chirgwin, quoted in *Companion to Congregational Praise*, 1953; he had been told this by the London Missionary Society's Secretary in China, A. Baxter).

BP174: Can113: B70: CW237/208: H336: L64: M416: P154/195/437: Pm157: CLB457 ● ENG: An556: B141: CH113/259: CP134: E409: M183

337. IN TOKEN THAT THOU SHALT NOT FEAR

5 st. CM

H. Alford (150), staying at Heale, Devon, 1832; printed in *British Magazine* 1832, therefore written at age 22; inspired by a passage in Hooker's *Ecclesiastical Polity*, Bk. 5, sec. 65. In *Hymns A & M*, 1861.

US & CAN: Can315 ● ENG: AM328/424: An339: BB193: E337

338. INFANT HOLY

2 st. 44.7.44.7.4444.7

Polish, W ZLOBIE LEZY, Anon.

Tr. E. M. G. Reed in *Music & Youth*, 1924; *School Worship*, 1926. A classic 'howler' in hymnology was perpetrated when eds. of *Congregational Praise*, misled by *School Worship*, indicated in early editions that they thought 'w zlobie lezy,' Polish for 'He lies in the cradle,' was the author's name.

US & CAN: BP123: B94: CW -/136: M396: P -/164/-: W141 ● ENG: An 103: B100: CH -/186: CP696: PL153

EDITH MARGARET GELLIBRAND REED, b. Islington (London), 1885, † Barnet, Herts, 4 vi 1933.

INSPIRER AND HEARER OF PRAYER: see 3.

339. IT CAME UPON THE MIDNIGHT CLEAR

5 st. CMD   PCH 373

E. H. Sears, in *The Christian Register*, Boston, Mass., 1850, thus narrowly predating 'Good King Wenceslas' as the first Christmas hymn in English with a social message. First in Britain in W. G. Horder's *Treasury of Hymns*, 1884.

US & CAN: BP144: Can427: B86: CW191/119: H19: L23: M390: P127/160/438: Pm129: CLB220: W142 ● ENG: AM -/66: An104: B101: BB52: CH47/170: CP88: E26: M130: PL138

EDMUND HAMILTON SEARS, b. 6 iv 1810, Sandsfield, Mass.; Sch. Union Coll., Schenectady, N.Y.; Ord. Unit.; Wayland, Mass., 1838; Lancaster, Mass., '40; Wayland again, '47: Weston '63. † January 1876, (65).

340. IT FELL UPON A SUMMER DAY

12 st. 8.8.8.6

S. Brooke, *Christian Hymns*, 1881; slow to take its place among popular hymns, but incl. in *A Students' Hymnal*, 1923, then in *Church Hymnary*, 1927. Always abr. to 8 st. or fewer—but S. Brooke often expressed his special pleasure in long hymns.

US & CAN: P444/461/- ● ENG: B122: BB71: CH80/213: CP111: M166

STOPFORD AUGUSTUS BROOKE, b. 14 xi 1832, Letterkenny, Co. Donegal (Ireland); Sch. Trinity, Dublin. Ord. C/E 1857; London curacies, then Minister of the proprietary chapel of St. James', London '66, Bedford Chapel, Bloomsbury, '75-'93; seceded from C/E 1880 to join Unitarians. Poet, critic, essayist. † London 18 iii 1913 (80).

341. IT IS A THING MOST WONDERFUL

7 st. LM-alt.   PCH 315

W. W. How (75), *Children's Hymns*, 1872; *EH* has full text, but norm. abr. to 5 st. or fewer; 'Herein is love: 1 John 4:10.'

US & CAN: • ENG: AM -/435: An350: B142: BB81: CH436/385: CP137: E597: M854: NC109

342A. 'IT IS FINISHED!,' BLESSED JESUS

10 st. 8.7.8.7   **PCH 251**

W. D. Maclagan, for *Hymns Ancient & Modern*, 1875; alt. and abr. by author for 1904 ed., and now always in that form. For Holy Saturday.

US & CAN: • ENG: AM122/124: EH120

WILLIAM DALRYMPLE MACLAGAN, b. Edinburgh, 18 vi 1826; served with army in India, then Sch. St. Peter's Coll. Cambridge (Peterhouse); Ord. C/E; after curacies, Rector of Newington '69; Vicar of Kensington, '75; Bp. of Lichfield, '78; Abp. York '91. Composed many hymns and also some tunes. † Kensington, 19 ix 1910 (84).

342B. 'IT IS FINISHED!' CHRIST HATH KNOWN

3 st. 7.88.7.8.7.8.7   **PCH 268**

G. Gillett, for *English Hymnal*, 1906, for Good Friday (the Sixth Word from the Cross); a very sensitive and beautiful text.

US & CAN: H78 • ENG: EH118

GEORGE GABRIEL SCOTT GILLETT, b. Hawley, Hants, 1 xii 1873; Sch. Westminster and Keble, Oxf.; curacies in London & Brighton; domestic chaplain to Earl Beauchamp and Viscount Halifax; in S. Africa 1913-25; then editor, Society for Propagation of the Gospel, '26-'33; then chaplain to Community of St. Peter, St. Leonard's on Sea, Sussex. † there, 12 viii 1948 (74).

343. I'VE FOUND A FRIEND, O SUCH A FRIEND

3 st. 8.7.8.7 D Iamb

J. G. Small, *The Revised Hymn Book*, 2nd series, 1863; 'Jesus the Friend.'

US & CAN: BP421: B423: CW290/- : M163: P -/220/- • ENG: An626: B440: CH705/- : CP377: M423

JAMES GRINDLAY SMALL, b. Edinburgh 1817; Sch. Royal High Sch., Edinburgh & Univ. Edinburgh; Ord. Free Ch/Scot.; minister, Vervie (Montrose) 1847-† Renfrew, 11 ii 1888.

344. JERUSALEM, MY HAPPY HOME   PCH 410

Five texts on this theme, 4 beginning with the same first line, and one beginning O MOTHER DEAR, JERUSALEM, concern us here.

(a) by W. Prid. *The Glasse of Vain-Glorie*, 1585 (2nd ed. 1593), 176 lines (22 st. CMD); this does not survive in a hymnal except (altd. and abr.) at *Songs of Praise* (1931) 393, but it may be the original on which the most famous variant is based, though that would depend on the dating of the next entry.

(b) by 'F. B. P.,' 104 lines (26 st. CM), in a British Museum ms., and abr. to 19 st. in *The Song of Mary*, 1601. Full text is at *EH638* and *CP762*. Both the above seem to be based on the passage in the *Meditations* of St. Augustine beginning *Mater Hierusalem, Civitas Sancta Dei*, and we tentatively conjecture that (b) is later because briefer and in some ways more exquisite. Many lines, however, are common to both, and modern hymnals make centos from (b) of 6 to 10 stanzas. The identity of the author remains obscure but it is thought he may have been a R.C. priest, possibly under sentence of death. If both those conjectures are true the date could be about 1593, when there was an explosion of persecution both of the R.C.s and of extreme protestants in London. What the relation between this (if true) and the 2nd appearance of (a) in the same year may be is still unknown.

(c) O MOTHER DEAR, JERUSALEM, a poem of 248 lines (31 st. CMD), made up of lines from (a) and (b) together with 12 lines of his own, by David Dickson, minister of the Church of Scotland, and first brought to light in *The New Jerusalem: A Hymn of the Olden Time*, ed. H. Bonar (81), 1852. No earlier source for this is now known. Certain U.S. books make centos from this.

(d) Anon., in *Psalms and Hymns* (1729), by 'W. S.,' London: 40 st. CM,

detectable by the verse, 'There David stands with harp in hand....'

(e) the 'Bromehead' version in *Psalms & Hymns for Public & Private Devotion*, 1795, ed. J. Bromehead—the text being therefore insecurely attrib. to the editor. This is in 7 st. CM and has evangelical overtones not found in the others. With st. 3 om., it is at *CP354*; with sts. 1, 2, 6, 7 and a spurious 5th, it is in *A & M* (both) and *An*.

The ms. of (b) mentions tune DIANA which is at *M*(Brit.)655 and *H*(U.S.) 585.

US & CAN: B488 (d, 4 st.): CW572 (c, 6 st.)/-: H584 (c, 8 st.), 585 (b, 6 st.): L587 (b, 6 st.): P436 (c, 6 st.)/-/- : Pm312 (d, 6 st.): W143 (e, 5 st.) • ENG: AM236/282 (e‡), -/623 (b, 16 st.): BB247 (b, 7 st.): CH595 (b, 8 st.)/- : An429 (e‡) CP353 (e), 354 (b, 10 st.) 762 (b, 26 st.): E638 (b, 26 st.): M655 (d, 11 st.)

W. PRID. Nothing is known of him but the partly revealing title of his only publication: *The Glasse of Vain-Glorie: Faithfully translated (out of S. Augustine his booke, intituled* Speculum Peccatoris*) into English by W. P., Doctor of the Lawes . . .* , 1585.

F. B. P. The only plausible guess—it is no more— is that these initials stand for FRANCIS BAKER, Priest, who was a R.C. priest imprisoned in the Tower of London c. 1593. (About that time the Fleet Prison contained Blessed Robert Southwell, R.C. Priest, and Henry Barrow and John Greenwood, Brownists, all of whom perished at Tyburn). A wave of panic-persecution broke out at that time because of Britain's strained relations with Spain, in which those who deviated from the Anglican Church as by Law Established in 1570 were subjected to imprisonment and sometimes death, R.C.s because they were suspected of dangerous loyalties, and extreme protestants as being in treason to the Crown.

DAVID DICKSON, c. 1583-1663, Scottish divine, was Prof. of Philosophy at Univ. Glasgow, minister at Irvine, Ayrshire, 1618; deprived of offices for a year, 1621/2, over a dispute about the Five Articles of Perth; Prof. of Divinity, Glasgow, '40-'50, and of Divinity, Univ. Edinburgh, '50-'60. Ejected 1660 for refusing the Oath of Supremacy. Wrote commentaries on Scripture.

JOSEPH BROMEHEAD, b. November 1747; Sch. Queen's, Oxf.; Ord. C/E, curate of Eckington, Derbs till †. In his 1795 hymnal, mentioned above, 'Jerusalem, my happy home' is signed 'B.' † Eckington, 30 i 1826.

345. JERUSALEM ON HIGH

14 st. 6.6.6.6.6.4.44.4

S. Crossman, *The Young Man's Meditations*, 1664; first as a hymn in *Hymns A & M*, 1868; now abr. to 6 st. or fewer. *M*(Brit.) begins at st. 2, SWEET PLACE, SWEET PLACE ALONE.

US & CAN: • ENG: AM233/280: An431: CP357: E411: M653‡

SAMUEL CROSSMAN, b. Bradfield Monachorum, Sfk., c. 1624; Sch. Pembroke, Camb.; Ord. C/E but gathered a Congregational church in Sudbury, Sfk. Ejected 1662, returned to C/E '65, Prebendary of Bristol, '67, and Vicar of St. Nicholas, Bristol; Dean of Bristol, late 1683, a few weeks before † there 4 ii 1684.

JERUSALEM THE GOLDEN: see 851.

JESUS, ALL MY GLADNESS: see 859.

346. JESUS CALLS US: O'ER THE TUMULT

5 st. 8.7.8.7   **PCH 280**

C. F. Alexander (24), *Hymns* (SPCK), 1852. Text as norm. used was rev. by author in *Church Hymns*, 1881, but *A & M* has 1852 text with one alt.

US & CAN: BP374: Can166: B367: CW281/204: H566: L553: M107: B223/269/'439: Pm322 • ENG: AM403/533: An442: B416: BB354: CH 500/211: CP451: E205: M157

347. JESUS CHRIST IS RISEN TO-DAY

3 st. 77.77 with interpolated Alleluias.   **PCH 78**

Anon. A hymn beginning with the first 3 lines of the now familiar vn. was in *Lyra Davidica*, 1708, as a trsn. of Latin SURREXIT CHRISTUS HODIE (Munich ms., 14 c.). A radical revision appeared in Arnold's *Complete Psalmodist*, 1741, but the form now used is owed to the *Supplement* (1816) to Tate & Brady's *New Version* (see 53). In the U.S., a st. from C. Wesley's 'Hymn to the Trinity' (1740) is often added as st. 4. The tune EASTER HYMN was associated with orig. text in 1708 source in orig. vn.; and in its now well known florid version, was in the 1741 source.

US & CAN: BP190: Can465: B115: CW -/174: H85: L92: M443: P163/ 204/440: Pm187: CLB272: W145 • ENG: AM134: An194: B157: BB105: CH119/264: E133: M205: NC114: PL195

348. JESUS, FRIEND OF LITTLE CHILDREN

7 st. 8.5.8.3   **PCH 318**

W. J. Mathams, *Psalms & Hymns for School & Home*, 1882, written at request of the editors.

US & CAN: BP507: Can266 • ENG: An357: B747: CH667/100: CP701: M841

WALTER JOHN MATHAMS, b. Bermondsey (London), 30 x 1853, spent early life at sea; then Sch. Regent's Park (Bapt.) Seminary, London, and Ord. Bapt. Served at Preston, Lancs; Falkirk, Scotland; Birmingham; chaplain to the forces in Egypt, 1902-5; then Ord. C/Scot., Minister at Stronsay, Orkney, then at Mallaig Mission Ch., 1909-19. Published many religious books. † Swanage, Dorset, 29 i 1931 (77).

349. JESUS, GENTLEST SAVIOUR

12 st. 6.5.6.5

F. W. Faber (175), *Oratory Hymns*, 1854; 'Thanksgiving after Communion.' *Hymns A & M* has sts. 6. 8, 2, 4, 9: *EH* has 1, 2, 3, 4, 6, 8. *H*(U.S.) has 1, 2, 3, 4, 6, 8, 9.

US & CAN: H348 • ENG: AM324/418: E315

350. JESUS, GOOD ABOVE ALL OTHER

5 st. 888.7   **PCH 267**

P. Dearmer (88), *English Hymnal*, 1906; it uses several lines from, and same meter as, JESUS, KIND ABOVE ALL OTHER, by J. M. Neale (2), which is the last (double) st. of 'Gabriel from heaven descending,' his tr. of the Sequence of Adam of St. Victor, for the Incarnation, in *Medieval Hymns*, 2nd ed., 1863. This fragment is preserved at AM456, but *AM** has Dearmer's vn. Orig. in st. 2, 'keep us by thine altar near,' altd. by author later to 'keep us to thy presence near.'

US & CAN: BP164: H322 • ENG: AM*45: An263: BB72: CH -/111: CP464: E598: NC115

351. JESU, GRANT ME THIS, I PRAY

4 st. 77.77

Latin: DIGNARE ME, O JESU, ROGO TE, 4 st. 10 10.8 10, anon., in *Symphonia Sacra Sirenum Selectarum* (Cologne), 1695.

Tr. H. W. Baker (101) for *Hymns A & M*, 1861.

US & CAN: • ENG: AM182/211: BB517: E413: PL280

352. JESUS LIVES!

5 st. 7.8.7.8.4

German: JESUS LEBT, C. G. Gellert, *Geistliche Oden und Lieder*, Leipzig, 1757, in 6 st., 7.8.7.8.77.

Tr. F. E. Cox, *Sacred Hymns from the German*, 1841 in orig. meter, beginning JESUS LIVES! NO LONGER NOW CAN THY TERRORS, DEATH,

APPALL US. In Rorison's *Hymns & Anthems* (1851) it appeared first in 6 st., 7.8.7.8.4, with last 2 lines of each st. replaced by 'Alleluia.' Murray's *Hymnal*, 1852, made further alts., which were taken into *Hymns A & M*, 1861, but with the unfortunate first line still unchanged; but author approved the change, first made in *Church Hymns*, 1871, to JESUS LIVES! THY TERRORS NOW CAN NO LONGER . . . and this is now standard. In this vn. of 1871, which is in 5 st., all but *M*(Brit.) follow *A & M* in order of stanzas, *M*(Brit.) having 1, 5, 3, 4, 2—which is the order of the original (longer) text. The last hymnal in common use to include the orig. vn. was *Congregational Hymnary*, 1916. The 1852 revision was fortunate in generating what may be the finest of all 19 c. English tunes.

US & CAN: Can179: H88 • ENG: AM140: An187: B158: BB106: CH121/ 605: CP147: E134: M216‡

CHRISTIAN FURCHTEGOTT GELLERT, b. Hainichen, Germany, 4 vii 1715; Sch. Univ. Leipzig where became Prof. of Philosophy, and had Goethe and Lessing among his pupils. Pub. 54 of his own hymns at Leipzig, 1757, and † there 13 xii 1769 (54).

FRANCES ELIZABETH COX, b. Oxford, 10 v 1812; friend of Baron Bunsen, German Ambassador to Britain, who gave her much advice on selection of hymns for translation; she was one of the first of a group of distinguished translators of German hymns. † Headington, Oxford, 23 ix 1897 (85).

353. JESUS, I MY CROSS HAVE TAKEN

6 st. 8.7.8.7 D

H. F. Lyte (5), *Sacred Poetry*, 1824; Mk. 10:28. There anonymous. Now abr. to 4 st.

US & CAN: CW375/- : L512: M251: P274/279 • ENG: CH353/-

354. JESUS, KEEP ME NEAR THE CROSS

4 st. 7.6.7.6 with refrain 3.3.6.7.6

Fanny Crosby (84), with tune, in *Bright Jewels*, 1869.

US & CAN: B351: CW339/- : M433: P -/376-/- • ENG:

355. JESUS IS TENDERLY CALLING

4 st. 10.4-4.10-7 with refrain 4-4.10

Fanny Crosby (84), *Gospel Hymns*, 1883.

US & CAN: B188: CW280/- : M110: P -/267/- • ENG: B417

JESUS, LEAD THE WAY: see 858.

356. JESUS, LORD OF LIFE AND GLORY

7 st. 8.7.8.7.4.7

J. J. Cummins, *Poetical Meditations . . .* , 1839. Full text in *EH*; elsewhere abr.

US & CAN: • ENG: AM287/321: An488: BB291: CH524/- : E75: M724: PL102

JOHN JAMES CUMMINS, b. Cork, Ireland, 5 v 1795. Went to London 1834 & became a director of the Union Bank of Australia. † Buckland, Surrey, 23 xi 1867 (72).

357. JESUS, LORD, WE LOOK TO THEE

77.77

C. Wesley (1), and see 107. The text varies. It always begins with, and sometimes confines itself to, lines from a hymn with this opening in *Hymns & Sacred Poems*, 1749, orig. in 32 lines of which *M*(U.S.) has 24, *M** has 20, and all others but *CP* have 16. *CP*, however, following *Congregational Hymnary*, 1916, has 4 st. from this followed by 2 from the 39 st. hymn noted at 107 (a substantial part of which can be read in the 1876 *Wesley Hymn Book*). If it ends, 'all the heights of holiness,' or

'show how true believers die,' it is 1749 throughout.
US & CAN: M309 ● ENG: AM*47: An423: BB374: CP240†: E*97: M*35

358. JESUS, LOVER OF MY SOUL

5 st. 7.7.7.7 D

C. Wesley (1), *Hymns & Sacred Poems*, 1740; 'In Temptation; Wisdom 11:26'. J. Wesley omitted it from his 1780 collection because of what he judged the excessive intimacy of the opening lines. St. 3, 'Wilt thou not regard my call?' always om., and sometimes also st. 4, 'Thou, O Christ, art all I want.'

US & CAN: BP399: Can77: B172: CW414/205: H415: L393: M125: P216/211/-: ● ENG: AM193: An506: B441: BB145: CH414/78: CP473: E414: M110: NC116

359. JESUS LOVES ME, THIS I KNOW

3 st. 77.77 with ref. 5-5-5.6

A. B. Warner, *Say and Seal*, 1859.

US & CAN: BP378: Can123: B336: P -/465/- ● ENG: B749: CH660/418

ANNA BARTLETT WARNER, b. New York, 1820, collaborated with her sister Susan (authoress of 'Jesus bids us shine') in several novels, of which the source of the above is one; under pseudonym 'Amy Lathrop' wrote several stories, including *Dollars and Cents*, 1852, for which see 789. † 1915 Highland Falls, N.Y. (95).

360. JESUS, MEEK AND GENTLE

5 st. 6.5.6.5

G. R. Prynne, *Hymnal Suited for the Services of the Church*, 1858.

US & CAN: H358 ● ENG: AM194: An554: CH462/- : E415: M734

GEORGE RUNDLE PRYNNE, b. West Looe, Cornwall, 23 viii 1818; Sch. St. Catherine's, Camb.; Ord. C/E; Vicar of St. Peter's, Plymouth, 1848-1903, when he † there 25 iii 1903 (84).

361. JESUS, MY LORD, HOW RICH THY GRACE

5 st. CM　　　　　　　　　　　　**PCH 51**

P. Doddridge, *Hymns* . . . (posth.), 1755; 'Relieving Christ in his poor saints: Matt. 25:40.' This text has until recently (since being revived in *CP*, 1951) been known in an altered form beginning FOUNTAIN OF GOOD, TO OWN THY LOVE, which is a rewritten version in 4 st. by E. Osler from the *Mitre Hymn Book*, 1836. There sts. 2-4 are mostly Doddridge's 3-5 and st. 1 uses phrases from his st. 2. Revision is so extensive that the ascription to Doddridge in *CH³* must be judged wrong. The original text is now returning to favour, and in this form is the oldest English hymn on the social applications of the Gospel.

US & CAN: BP494: L565‡ ● ENG: AM*45: BB379: CH345‡/459†: CP669

EDWARD OSLER, b. Falmouth, Cornwall, 30 i 1798; Sch. Falmouth & Guy's Hosp., London in medicine; worked for SPCK, 1836-41; edited *Royal Cornwall Gazette* at Truro 1841-†. Collaborated with W. J. Hall in editing *Mitre Hymn Book*, '36. † Truro, 7 iii 1863 (65).

362. JESUS, MY LORD, MY GOD, MY ALL

4 st. 88.88.88

H. Collins, *Hymns for Missions*, 1854, but clearly based on a 9 st. hymn by F. W. Faber (175) with the same first line, the same last line of refrain, and 5th line, 'Sweet Sacrament, we thee adore,' (*Jesus and Mary*, 1849).

US & CAN: CW389/238: H460: L504 ● ENG: AM191/202: An535: CH 430/- : CP429: E417: M438

HENRY COLLINS, b. Barningham, Co. Durham, 1827; Sch. Oxford; Ord. C/E 1853; joined R.C. Church '57 and admitted to Cistercian Order '60, after which known as Father Augustine. † Coalville, Warks, 29 i 1919 (91).

363. JESUS, MY STRENGTH, MY HOPE

8 st. SMD

C. Wesley (1), *Hymns & Sacred Poems*, 1742; 'A Poor Sinner'; now always abr.

US & CAN: BP443: H452 ● ENG: An522: CP474: M542

364. JESUS, NAME ALL NAMES ABOVE

6 st. 7.6.7.6.88.77

J. M. Neale (2), *Hymns of the Greek Church*, 1862, founded on the *Suppliant Canon* of Theoktistos, 9th cent. Explanatory alteration of one line in *A & M* makes clearer a reference to the Penitent Thief. Norm. sel. is now sts. 1, 2, 5, 6, but *Westminster Praise*, 1976, has sts. 1, 3, 2.

US & CAN: H342: L67 ● ENG: AM775/- : E418

365. JESUS! NAME OF WONDROUS LOVE

5 st. 77.77

W. W. How (75), *Psalms & Hymns*, 1854: Matt. 1:21.

US & CAN: Can491: B74: H323: L50 ● ENG: CH62/205

JESUS, OUR HOPE, OUR HEARTS' DESIRE: see 498.

JESUS, PRICELESS TREASURE: see 859.

366. JESUS, SAVIOUR, PILOT ME

6 st. 77.77.77

E. Hopper, *Sailor's Magazine*, 1871, there anon., and *Spiritual Songs*, 1875. Now abr. to 4 st. or fewer.

US & CAN: Can267: CW409/- : L531: M247: P286/336/- : Pm213 ● ENG: CH706/-

EDWARD HOPPER, b. New York, 17 ii 1816 (or 1818), Sch. Univ. N.Y., and Union Theol. Sem., N.Y.; Ord. Presb., served at Greenville, N.Y., Sag Harbour, Long Island, and Church of Sea and Land, New York. † New York, 23 iv 1888.

367. JESUS SHALL REIGN WHERE'ER THE SUN

8 st. LM-coup.　　　　　　　　**PCH 43**

I. Watts (10), *Psalms of David* . . . , 1719; Ps. 72, part II: 'Christ's Kingdom among the Gentiles.' Norm. sel. of sts. is 1, 5, 6, 8; some add 4, and *M (Brit.)* adds 7 as well.

US & CAN: BP385: Can164: B282: CW527/288: Hy542: L307: M472: P377/496/443: Pm202: W147 ● ENG: AM220: An320: B184: BB460: CH388/413: CP158: E420: M272

368. JESUS, STAND AMONG US

3 st. 6.5.6.5

W. Pennefather, *Original Hymns*, posth., 1873.

US & CAN: BP323: CW -/391: P -/222/- ● ENG: An7: B336: BB262: CH248/11: CP274: M684: NC120

WILLIAM PENNEFATHER, b. Dublin, 5 ii 1816; Sch. Westbury, Bristol and Trinity, Dublin; Ord. Episc. (Ireland), '41; Vicar of Mellifont, nr. Drogheda, then in England, of Trinity Ch., Walton, Aylesbury; Christ Ch., Barnet; St. Jude's, Mildmay Park, London. Founder of Mildmay Conference (first at Barnet) and Mildmay Trust, for religious & benevolent purposes, and introduced to England the Anglican order of deaconesses. † Muswell Hill (London), 30 iv 1873 (57).

JESUS, STILL LEAD ON: see 858.

369. JESUS, TENDER SHEPHERD, HEAR ME

3 st. 8.7.8.7   PCH 300

M. Duncan, written for her own children, 1839; pub. in posth. *Memoir,* 1841.

US & CAN: BP562: H241: L235: P449/-/- • ENG: An348: B750: CH654/656: CP703: E599: M844

MARY DUNCAN, nee Lundie, b. Kelso, Scotland, 26 iv 1814, d. of Rev. Robert Lundie, parish minister there; her younger sister married H. Bonar (81); m. (1836) Rev. William Wallace Duncan, minister of Cleish, Kinross-shire. Her hymns were published in the *Memoir* (above) and in (posth.) *Rhymes for my Children,* 1842. † Cleish, 5 i 1840 (25).

JESUS, THE VERY THOUGHT IS SWEET   see 857.
JESUS, THE VERY THOUGHT OF THEE

370. JESUS, THESE EYES HAVE NEVER SEEN

5 st. CM   PCH 356

R. Palmer, *Sabbath Hymn Book,* 1858; 1 Peter 1:8. St. 3 sometimes om.

US & CAN: L469: P319/-/- • ENG: AM -/347: An354: B206: CH418/674: CP188: E421: M111

RAY PALMER, b. Little Compton, Rhode Island, 12 xi 1808; after a short time in business, Sch. Phillips Academy, Andover and Yale; Ord. Congl.: served at Bath, Maine, 1835; First Congl. Ch., Albany, N.Y., '50; Corresponding Secretary of American Congl. Union, '65-'78; retired to Newark, N.J., where † 29 iii 1887 (78).

JESUS, THOU JOY OF LOVING HEARTS: see 857.

371. JESUS, THY BLOOD AND (ROBE OF) RIGHTEOUSNESS

24 st. LM   PCH 56

German: CHRISTI BLUT UND GERECHTIGKEIT, N.L. von Zinzendorf, 33 st. LM, in *Appendix,* 1739, to *Herrnhut Gbch* (1735).

Tr.: J. Wesley (1), 24 st. LM, *Hymns & Sacred Poems,* 1740. Longest seln. now 10 st. in *M(Brit.)* but norm. 5 st. or fewer. 'Robe' version was in *Congregational Hymn Book,* 1836, and its successors.

US & CAN: BP405: Can118: L376: M127 • ENG: An504: B208: CP470: M370

NIKOLAUS LUDWIG von ZINZENDORF, b. 26 v 1700, Dresden, Germany; Sch. Halle and Wittemberg in law; court poet at Dresden, 1721; owned large estate at Herrnhut which became a settlement for Moravians, some of whom J. Wesley met in his journey to Georgia, 1735, with decisive effects on his theology and mission; retired from court business 1727 to devote himself to leadership of Moravian pietists, and made bishop of Moravians by D. E. Jablonski, 1737. Banished from Saxony for his unorthodoxy, but founded Moravian settlements elsewhere in Germany, and in England, Holland and N. America. Returned to Herrnhut, 1748. Wrote over 2,000 hymns between 1712 and 1760. † Herrnhut, 4 v 1760 (59).

JESUS, THY MERCIES ARE UNTOLD: see 857.

JESUS, UNITED BY THY GRACE: see 279.

372. JESUS, WE THUS OBEY

4 st. SMD

C. Wesley (1) *Hymns for the Lord's Supper,* 1745; now norm. abr. in SM.

US & CAN: • ENG: An381: B320: CP300: M761

373. JESUS, WHERE'ER THY PEOPLE MEET

6 st. LM-coup.

W. Cowper (235), *Olney Hymns,* 1779; one st., 'Behold, at thy commanding word,' always om. Written, like 161, for the removal of the weekday prayer meting from a small room to 'the great room in the Great House,' of which Newton (37) wrote, 'It is a noble place . . . and holds 130 people conveniently.' 'Bring all heaven before our eyes' is a quotation from Milton's *Il Penseroso,* line 167, and the author is here contrasting the simplicity of the village meeting with the cathedral imagined by Milton.

US & CAN: BP331: Can65: CW115/- : M98: Pm402 • ENG: AM529/245: An8: B338: BB263: CH247/- : CP266: E422: M675

374. JESUS, WITH THY CHURCH ABIDE

20 st. 777.6

T. B. Pollock, *Metrical Litanies . . .,* 1870. A series of these was published in *Hymns A & M,* 1875, all beginning 'God the Father, God the Son'; they became extremely popular. This is among them, 'Litany of the Church.' It alone has found wide acceptance outside the C/E, and in non-Anglican books is always abr. to 8 st. or fewer. Full text is in *A & M* and *EH.*

US & CAN: BP308: B241: CW -/148: H233: M311: Pm301 • ENG: AM 471/- : B260: CH208/490: CP286: E651: M727

THOMAS BENSON POLLOCK, b. Strathallan, Isle of Man, 28 v 1836; Sch. Trinity, Dublin, where he won a prize for English Verse (1855); Ord. C/E '61; curate of Leek, Staffs, then at St. Thomas', Stanford Hill, Middx.; with his brother, Rev. J. S. Pollock, on staff of St. Alban's Mission, Birmingham, '65-'95. † Bordesley (Birmingham), 15 xii 1896 (60).

375. JOIN ALL THE GLORIOUS NAMES

12 st. 6.6.6.6.88   PCH 34

I. Watts (10), standing last in Book I of *Hymns . . .,* 1707; 'The Offices of Christ: from several Scriptures,' in which each st. is built round one or more of the scriptural names of Christ. *CP* has 11 st. in 2 parts, *M (Brit.)* 10; elsewhere abr. to 5 st. or fewer.

US & CAN: BP248: L412: Pm229 • ENG: An266: B175: CH165/304: CP176: M96

JOY, BECAUSE THE CIRCLING YEAR: see 839.

JOY DAWNED AGAIN ON EASTER DAY: see 837.

376. JOY TO THE WORLD! THE LORD IS COME

4 st. CM

I. Watts (10), Psalm 98 Part 2 in *Psalms of David . . .,* 1719; 'The Messiah's Coming & Kingdom.' Unknown in Britain since the mid-19th century, it is universally accepted in the U.S.A. and Canada as an advent or Christmas hymn.

US & CAN: BP134: Can401: B88: CW190/122: H319: L15: M392: P122/161/444: Pm130: CLB217: W153

377. JOYFUL, JOYFUL WE ADORE THEE

4 st. 8.7.8.7 D

H. van Dyke, *Poems,* 1911. During a vacation to Williams College in 1907 he wrote this and placed it before the President at breakfast saying, 'Here is a hymn for you. Your mountains (the Berkshires) were my inspiration. It must be sung to the tune of Beethoven's "Hymn to Joy."' It always is so set (except in *H,* which capitulated in *H**) to an approximate version of the famous melody in Beethoven's Ninth Symphony.

US & CAN: BP569: Can19: CW95/1: H281: L438: M38: P5/21/446: Om8: CLB426: W154

HENRY van DYKE, b. Germantown, Pa., 10 xi 1852; Sch. Brooklyn Polytechnic, then Princeton Univ. & Theol. Sem.; Ord. Congl., Newport, R.I., 1879; served at Brick Presbyterian Ch., New York, '83-'99 and 1902-11; Murray Prof. of Eng. Lit. at Univ. Princeton, 1899, and lived at Avalon, Princeton till †. President, National Institute of Arts & Letters, 1912. Served as diplomat, being Minister to Netherlands & Luxembourg, 1913-16; Lt./Commander in U.S. Corps (Navy) of Chaplains, 1917. Retired 1923, and † Princeton, N.J., 10 iv 1933 (80).

378. JUDGE ETERNAL, THRONED IN SPLENDOUR

3 st. 8.7.8.7.8.7   PCH 265

H. Scott Holland, *The Commonwealth*, July 1902 and *EH*, 1906, this being the only hymn he wrote. In line 17 orig. 'empire' now usually altd. to 'nation.'

US & CAN: BP592: Can213: CW515/- : H518: L343: M546: P417/417/447: Pm435: W155 ● ENG: An662: B643: BB393: CH636/519: CP572: E423: M883

HENRY SCOTT HOLLAND, b. Ledbury, Herefs., 27 i 1847; Sch. Eton & Balliol, Oxf.; Ord. C/E 1874; Fellow Student - Christ Church, Oxf., '70-'84; Canon of St. Paul's, London and precentor, 1886. Regius Prof. Divinity at Oxford, 1911. Author of essay on Faith in *Lux Mundi*, 1889, one of the literary landmarks of English liberal movement in theology; founder and supporter of Christian Social Union; editor of *The Commonwealth*, 1895-1912; assisted in editing *English Hymnal* and *New Cathedral Psalter*; wrote a biography of Jenny Lind, 1891. † 17 iii 1918, Oxford (71).

379. JUST AS I AM, THINE OWN TO BE

6 st. 888.6

M. Farningham, *The Voice of Praise*, 1887, modelled on the following hymn: now always abr. to 4 st.

US & CAN: BP408: CW297/217: M169: P -/472/- ● ENG: An630: B442: CH497/448: CP457: M394

MARIANNE FARNINGHAM was the pen-name of MARIANNE HEARN, b. Farningham, Kent, 17 xii 1834, and early orphaned; taught at a private school in Gravesend, Kent, later at Northampton (1865). Much encouraged in youth to write by minister of the neighbouring Kent village, Eynsford; on staff of the *Christian World* from its foundation; ed. *Sunday School Times*; pub. many books of poems including hymns. † Barmouth, N. Wales, 16 iii 1909 (74).

380. JUST AS I AM, WITHOUT ONE PLEA

7 st. 888.6   PCH 275

C. Elliott (119), *The Invalid's Hymn Book*, 1838, in 6 st.; the last st. (as in *A & M* and *CP*) added in *Hours of Sorrow Cheered and Comforted*, 1838. Only *CP* has full text; elsewhere abr. to 6 st. or fewer, and in U.S.A. nor. 4 st. Edward Quillian, husband of Dora Wordsworth (daughter of the poet) wrote to the author 28 July 1847 that on her death bed Dorothy had said, 'This is the very thing for me,' and added, 'I do not think Mr. Wordsworth could bear to have it repeated in his presence, but he is not the less sensible of the solace it gave his one and matchless daughter.' (The poet Wordsworth outlived his daughter by three years).

US & CAN: BP394: Can284: B187: CW295/216: H409: L370: M119: P230/272/- : Pm320 ● ENG: AM255/349: An472: B443: BB292: CH411/79: CP385: E396: M353

381. KING OF GLORY, KING OF PEACE

3 st. 7.4.7.4 D   PCH 416

G. Herbert (137), *The Temple* (posth.), 1633, in 7 st. 7.4.7.4. Used in a much altd. form, 77.77, by J. Wesley in his Charleston Hymn Book (1737), but modern form in 8-line sts. with one quatrain omitted is first found in *English Hymnal*, 1906. Its original title was 'Praise.' Its irresist-

ible opening, and the Welsh tune GWALCHMAI, have ensured it very wide popularity in Britain, despite the characteristically condensed thought and elusive language of some later lines.

US & CAN: BP476: Can195 ● ENG: AM665/367: An539: B12: BB325: CH -/364: CP426: E424: M23: NC123: PL295

LAMB OF GOD, I LOOK TO THEE: see 216.

382. LAMP OF OUR FEET, WHEREBY WE TRACE

11 st. CM   PCH 132

B. Barton, *The Reliquary*, 1836; Psalm 119:105. The 5 st. vn. now in use first in *Congregational Hymn Book*, 1855.

US & CAN: BP283: CW436/- : H400: M368: P -/254/- : Pm256 ● ENG: An302: B248: CP229: CH201/-

BERNARD BARTON, b. Carlisle, 31 i 1784; Sch. Quaker School in Ipswich, Sfk. In business at Woodbridge, Sfk. Pub. some poetry, and was a friend of Byron, Charles Lamb, Robert Southey and Sir Walter Scott. † Woodbridge, 19 ii 1849 (75).

383. LAND OF OUR BIRTH, WE PLEDGE TO THEE

8 st. LM-coup.

R. Kipling (241) in *Puck of Pook's Hill*, 1906; first as a hymn in *Methodist School Hymnal*, 1911. Norm. now appears in hymnals with first & last sts. italicized, indicating that sts. 2-7 (beginning FATHER IN HEAVEN, WHO LOVEST ALL) are for normal use. Executors of the Kipling estate normally decline to allow it to be printed in any abridged form, though Supplement (1920) to *Fellowship Hymn Book* did so print it, as do *Can.* and *Pm*.

US & CAN: Can250: H506: Pm392 ● ENG: An575: CH647/446: CP463: M899

LAUD, O SION, THY SALVATION: see 867 III.

384. LEAD, KINDLY LIGHT, AMID THE ENCIRCLING GLOOM

3 st. 10.4.10.4.10 10   PCH 440

J. H. Newman (196), *British Magazine*, 1834, and *Lyra Apostolica*, 1836. First as a hymn in *Hymns Ancient & Modern*, 1861 with tune which, as author always admitted, made it famous. In the winter of 1832/3 Newman, then 31, went on a Mediterranean voyage with his friends J. A. and H. Froude. When they left him he was ill, alone and homesick. A servant said he would die, and he replied, 'I shall not die, for I have not sinned against the light.' When at last he found a passage home he wrote the poem while becalmed in the Straits of Bonifacio. At this time he was still a priest of the Church of England. See biography at 196 and note at 83.

US & CAN: BP576: Can270: CW578/46: H430: L523: M272: P289/331/- : Pm215 ● ENG: AM266/298: B545: BB306: CH568/682: CP509: E425: M612: NC125

385. LEAD ON, O KING ETERNAL

3 st. 7.6.7.6 D

E. W. Shurtleff, *Hymns of the Faith*, 1888, written in that year at request of his classmates for graduation hymn at Andover Theol. Sem.

US & CAN: BP509: Can173: B420: CW363/246: H554: L550: M478: P371/332/448: Pm375: CLB529 ● ENG: B375

ERNEST WARBURTON SHURTLEFF, b. Boston, Mass., 4 iv 1862; Sch. Boston Latin Sch., Harvard and Andover Th. Sem.; Ord. Congl., served at Palmer, Plymouth, Mass., and First Church, Minneapolis. Organized the American Church in Frankfurt, Germany, 1905. On relief work in World War I until † in France, 24 viii 1917 (55).

386. LEAD US, HEAVENLY FATHER, LEAD US

3 st. 8.7.8.7.8.7

J. Edmeston, *Sacred Lyrics*, 1821.

US & CAN: BP513: Can268: H567: P304/343/- : Pm344 ● ENG: AM281/
311: An583: B43: BB307: CH563/90: CP507: E426: M611: NC127: PL112

JAMES EDMESTON, b. Wapping (London), 10 ix 1791; Sch. and practised as architect and surveyor, one of his pupils being Sir Gilbert Scott,
designed of the Albert Memorial in London, St. Pancras Station and the
buildings of Glasgow University (himself the grandfather of Sir Giles
Gilbert-Scott, designer of Liverpool Anglican Cathedral, England).
Wrote many hymns (some say, over 2,000), esp. for children. † Homer-
ton, London, 7 i 1867 (75).

387. LEAD US, O FATHER, IN THE PATHS OF PEACE

4 st. 10.10.10.10   **PCH 382**

W. H. Burleigh, *New Congregational Hymn Book*, Supplement, 1859;
first in a U.S. hymnal, *Lyra Sacra Americana*, 1868.

US & CAN: CW566/- : H433: L462: M269: P262/341/- : Pm376 ● ENG:
B546: BB308: CH566/- : CP514: M613

WILLIAM HENRY BURLEIGH, b. Woodstock, Conn., 2 ii 1812; Sch. pub.
sch. Plainfield, Conn.; journeyman printer '30-7 and journalist; lecturer for Anti-Slavery Society, '36. Publisher of *Christian Witness* and
Temperance Banner, Pittsburgh, '37; of *Christian Freeman* (anti-
slavery journal), Hartford, Conn., '43; agent of New York Temperance
Society in Syracuse and Albany, '49-'55; harbor-master, New York City,
'55-'70. † Brooklyn, N.Y., 18 iii 1871 (59).

LEAVE GOD TO ORDER ALL THY WAYS: see 886.

388. LET ALL MORTAL FLESH KEEP SILENCE

4 st. 15 15 15 (or 8.7.8.7.8.7)   **PCH 180**

G. Moultrie, *Lyra Eucharistica*, 1864, being a close paraphrase of the
ancient prayer at opening of Eucharist in the Liturgy of St. James. A
popular hymn after being set to tune PICARDY in *English Hymnal*,
1906.

US & CAN: BP354: Can332: CW -/114: H197: L281: M324: P112/148/
449: Pm376: CLB360: W157 ● ENG: AM-/ 390: B102: BB204: CH -/577:
E318: M*38: NC128: PL171

LITURGY OF ST. JAMES: one of the earliest extant liturgies of the
Christian Church; traditionally ascribed to St. James, our Lord's Brother, but probably reached its first written form in mid-4th century; exists
in Greek & Syriac, and is still in use among Orthodox Christians, who
use it in Jerusalem on the Sunday after Christmas. Therefore, though
properly a Eucharistic hymn, appears often in the Incarnation section
of hymnals.

GERARD MOULTRIE, b. The Rectory, Rugby, Warks, 16 ix 1829; Sch.
Rugby & Exeter, Oxf.; Ord. C/E; Vicar of Southleigh '69, Warden of St.
James' Coll., Southleigh, '73, holding both appointments till † South-
leigh 24 iv 1885 (55).

389. LET ALL THE WORLD IN EVERY CORNER SING

       PCH 414

G. Herbert (137), *The Temple* (Posth.) 1633; 'Antiphon.' First as a hymn
in *Hymns Ancient & Modern*, 1889, but there set out as 2 st. 10.4.66.66.
10 4. This, though almost universally followed, does violence to the
intentions of the author, who wrote it as a single poem 10 4. 66.66.10 4.
66.66.10 4 (refrain three times, not four). The first hymn setting in this
form was by A. Brent Smith, privately printed for use at Lancing College, c. 1919. (Cf 137). Another setting in that form is in *Hymns for
Church & School* (1964) and in *Westminster Praise* (1976), and a third,
by John Worst, is in *Psalter-Hymnal Supplement* (1974). All refs. below
have 2 st. form.

US & CAN: BP71: Can2: B24: CW -/83: H290: L418: M10: P9/22/- :
W159 ● ENG: AM548/375: An243: B13: BB275: CH15/361: CP3: E427:
M5: NC129

LET HEARTS AWAKEN, NOW THE NIGHT IS ENDED: see 862.

390. LET OUR CHOIR (US NOW) NEW ANTHEMS RAISE

4 st. 7.6.7.6 D, troch.

J. M. Neale (2), *Hymns of the Eastern Church*, 1862, paraphrasing the
Canon of Timothy and Maura, martyrs commemorated in the Greek
Church on 3 May. St. 3 now omitted; in U.S., 'Let us now . . .'

US & CAN: H136: L546 ● ENG: AM441/518: E187

LET SAINTS ON EARTH IN CONCERT SING: see 132.

LET SIGHING CEASE AND WOE: see 853.

391. LET THE SONG GO ROUND THE EARTH

5 st. 7.5.7.5.77

S. G. Stock, *Church Missionary Hymn Book*, 1899; 'Praise for Salvation.'

US & CAN: B306: CW531/- ● ENG: AM736/- : An321: B376: M806

SARAH GERALDINE STOCK, b. Islington (London), 27 xii 1838, sister
of Eugene Stock (ed. of London Missionary Society); pub. *Lessons on
Israel in Egypt* and *The Child's Life of our Lord*: ed. hymnal named
above but, before it was published, † Penmaenmawr, N. Wales, 29 viii
1898 (59).

392. LET THERE BE LIGHT, LORD GOD OF HOSTS

4 st. 8.88.8   **PCH 541**

W. M. Vories, *Advocate of Peace*, Feb. 1909, written in response to
increasing threat of German militarism before World War I.

US & CAN: CW513/331: P402/480/451: Pm449: W161 ● ENG:

WILLIAM MERRILL VORIES, b. Leavenworth, Kansas, 28 x 1880, is
known as one of the greatest lay missionaries of history; his work was
in Japan, where he went under the auspices of the American Y.M.C.A.
in 1905 to found the Omi Mission in the province of Omi-Hachiman. In
early years he suffered much persecution from those he tried to evangelize but lived to hear Kagawa say of him, 'while the majority of
Americans seem to me to love their country first and the Kingdom of
God second, this is certainly not true of my friend W. M. Vories.' The
story of the Omi Mission is in his *A Mustard Seed in Japan*, 1911. For a
fuller account, see A. Haeussler, *The Story of our Hymns*, 1952. † 1964.

393. LET US BREAK BREAD TOGETHER ON OUR KNEES

Negro Spiritual, probably first printed in J. Weldon Johnson's *Negro
Spirituals*, Book II, 1927. One of the very few Spirituals to have a Eucharistic reference, it has become very popular since about 1955. See 223.

US & CAN: Can325: B252: CW -/315: H*48: L*IV-28: M330: P -/447/
452: Pm288: CLB368: W162 ● ENG: B*46: M*84

394. LET US WITH A GLADSOME MIND

77.77 irreg.   **PCH 417**

J. Milton, written 1623 while still at school, aged 15; printed in his
Poems . . ., 1645 in 24 st., broadly but not precisely 77.77, as a version of
Ps. 136. Hymnals always abr., and usually adjust text to fit 77.77 and
sometimes also to remove archaisms; one of the first to do this was
Congregational Church Hymnal, 1855; and its descendant, *CP*, still has

longest selection, 9 st. (1, 2, 7, 8, 9, 15, 20, 22, 23). But *EH* keeps closer to Milton's text. *Hymns A & M* did not use it until 1950 (but see 598).

US & CAN: BP60: Can28: B27: CW -/3: H308: L405: M61: P64/28/453: Pm71 ● ENG: AM -/377: An20: B15: BB461: CH11/33: CP44: E532: M18: NC132: PL259

JOHN MILTON, b. 9 xii 1608, London, usually regarded as England's greatest poet; Sch. St. Paul's Sch. and Christ's, Camb.; lived with family at Horton, Bucks, '32-8; then from '39, after European travel, in London. Latin Secretary to the Council of State under Cromwell, '49-'59; went blind, '52; supporter of Dissenting Interest (Congregationalist); lived latterly at Chalfont St. Giles, Bucks, where his house is still preserved. Most important works: *Ode on the Morning of Christ's Nativity*, 1629, *L'Allegro* and *Il Penseroso*, '32; *Lycidas*, '37; *Paradise Lost*, '67; *Samson Agonistes* and *Paradise Regained*, '71. In middle years wrote much prose, especially political and religious polemic. His sonnets (var. dates) are probably his most familiar writings. (N.B.: in note 235 Cowper & Bridges are said to be the only major Engl. poets who were also hymn writers. This remains true, since Milton's work sung as hymnody was not so designed). † London, 8 xi 1674 (65).

395. LIFE OF AGES, RICHLY POURED

10 st. 7.7.7.7   **PCH 378**

S. Johnson (120), *Hymns of the Spirit*, 1864; 'Inspiration.' First in Britain in W. G. Horder's *Worship Song*, 1896. Always, as there, abr. to 6 st. or fewer.

US & CAN: CW177/- : H373: P95/-/- : Pm236 ● ENG: B630: CP580: M908

396. LIFT HIGH THE CROSS, THE LOVE OF CHRIST PROCLAIM

12 st. 10.10 with refrain 10.10 (st. 1 as refrain).

G. W. Kitchin, *Hymns Ancient & Modern*, Supplement, 1916, altd. by M. R. Newbolt. Elsewhere norm. abr.

US & CAN: Can321 ● ENG: AM745/633: CH -/550: M*40

GEORGE WILLIAM KITCHIN, b. Naughton Rectory, Sfk., 7 xii 1827; Sch. Ipswich Gram. Sch., King's, Camb., Christ Church, Oxf. (Fellow: 1846). Censor & Tutor of Ch. Ch., '63; Dean of Winchester '83; Dean of Durham '94; Chancellor, Univ. Durham, 1909. † 13 x 1912 (84).

MICHAEL ROBERT NEWBOLT, b. Dimock, Glos., 1874; Sch. St. John's, Oxf., Ord. C/E, curate, Wantage, 1899; Vicar, Iffley, 1905; Principal, Missionary Coll., Dorchester (Oxon.) 1910; Perpetual Curate, St. Michael's, Brighton, 1916; Canon of Chester '27-'46. † Bierton, Bucks, 7 ii 1956 (81).

397. LIFT UP YOUR HEADS, YE GATES OF BRASS

19 st. CM

J. Montgomery (6), *Evangelical Magazine*, 1843; 'China Evangelized.' Always abr. to 8 st. or fewer. *Hymns A & M* has longest text: sts. 1, 2, 3, 7, 13, 15, 18, 19.

US & CAN: BP390: L308 ● ENG: AM586/306: An319: B378: BB178: CH 385/471: CP324: E549: M265

398. LIFT UP YOUR HEADS, YE MIGHTY GATES

5 st. 88.88.88.66

German: MACHT HOCH DIE THUR, by G. Weissel, *Preussische Fest-Lieder*, 1642.

Tr. C. Winkworth (14). *Chorale-Book for England*, 1863, full text in original meter. In U.S. books this superb hymn of praise and hope from the depths of the Thirty Years' War always appears in LM, usually abr. to 4 st. In British books many recensions appear, and the full text with original tune is very rarely found (but 4 st. with orig. tune are in Lutheran *Service Book & Hymnal*, 1958, as 2nd version). Versions current are:

   (a) Full original text;
   (b) LM abridgement;
   (c) LM with interpolated Alleluias;
   (d) LMD, full text slightly altd.;
   (e) 5 st. 88.88.88;
   (f) LM, 3 st., revised by editors of *English Praise*.

All U.S. and Canadian entries are (b).

US & CAN: BP119: CW224/105: H464: L8‡: M363: P114/152/454: Pm 114: CLB207: W163 ● ENG: An80 (c): B82 (e): BB34 (c): CH -/12 (c): CP77 (d): E*4 (f): M890 (a)

GEORG WEISSEL, b. Domnau, Prussia, 1590; Rector of School at Friedland, 1614; went to theol. sch. at Konigsberg, 1623 and Ord. Luth., becoming pastor there. † Konigsberg 1635 (45).

399. 'LIFT UP YOUR HEARTS!': WE LIFT THEM TO THE LORD

8 st. 10 10. 10 10

H. M. Butler, *Harrow School Hymn Book*, 1881, written for the school, to which specific allusion is made in orig. at st. 5. (*Congregational Hymnary*, 1916, preserves full text). Now always abr. to 5 st., om. 4-6.

US & CAN: BP461: CW372/- : H482: P258/-/- : Pm352 ● ENG: AM -/ 341: An474: B444: BB426: CH -/440: CP661: E429: M686: PL54

HENRY MONTAGU BUTLER, b. Gayton, Northants, 2 vii 1833; Sch. Harrow and Trinity, Camb.; Ord. C/E; Fellow of Trinity, '55. Head Master, Harrow, '59-'85; Dean of Gloucester, '85-6; Master of Trinity, Camb., '86. Vice-Chancellor, Univ. Camb., '89. Eminent classical scholar and translator. † Cambridge 14 i 1918 (84).

400. LIGHT OF LIGHT, ENLIGHTEN ME

6 st. 7.8.7.8.77

German: LICHT VON LICHT, ERLEUCHTEN MICH, B. Schmolck, *Andachtige Hertze*, 1714.

Tr.: C. Winkworth (14), *Lyra Germanica* II, 1858, full text, orig. met.; 'For the Sabbath Morning.' Norm. abr. now.

US & CAN: BP336: CW445/- : L186: P21/73/- ● ENG: M663

BENJAMIN SCHMOLCK, b. 21 xii 1672, Brauchitschdorf, Leignitz; Sch. Univ. Leipzig, of wh. he was crowned poet laureate; Ord. Luth., asst. to his father in home town, 1701; deacon at Schweidnitz, 1702, later archdeacon. Wrote 1188 hymns in 16 collections. † Schweidnitz, 12 ii 1737 (64).

401. LIGHT OF THE WORLD, FOR EVER, EVER SHINING

7 st. 11.6.11.6

H. Bonar (81), *Hymns of Faith & Hope*, 2nd series, 1861, orig. beginning 'Why walk in darkness? Has the dear light vanished?' Norm. sel. now is sts. 2, 3, 4, 7.

US & CAN: ● ENG: B209: CH171/131: CP189

402. LIGHT'S ABODE, CELESTIAL SALEM

12 st. 8.7.8.7.8.7

A trio of Latin Hymns is preserved in a 15 c. Karlsruhe ms., which are credibly attributed to St. Thomas à Kempis. J. M. Neale (2) tr. all three in *Hymns Chiefly Medieval, on the Joys and Glories of Paradise* (1865). In order of appearance these are:

   (a) QUISQUIS VALET NUMERARI (IF THERE BE THAT SKILLS TO RECKON): EH250 has sts. 1, 2, 4, 7, 8, 9 of Neale's 9-st. trsln.

   (b) this one—JERUSALEM LUMINOSA, tr. in 12 st. of which norm. sel. (as *EH*) is sts. 1, 3, 4, 11, 12, plus the standard Neale doxology.

   (c) NEC QUISQUAM OCULIS VIDIT (EYE HATH NEVER SEEN THE GLORY), 7 st., not now in use.

Immediately before these in the same ms. is IN DOMO PATRIS (11.11.

11.5 in orig.) wh. was trsld. by Neale as MY (OUR) FATHER'S HOME ETERNAL (*EH*252, *AM*621/625), and may be by the same author.
Light's abode:
US & CAN: BP537: H587: L591 ● ENG: AM232/279: An434: BB250: E431

THOMAS À KEMPIS, St., b. Thomas Hemerken at Kempen, nr. Cologne, c. 1380; Sch. Deventer, then entered House of the Canons Regular of Agnietenberg (a monastic foundation), founded by his elder brother John; took the habit, 1406; lived there the rest of his life writing, copying mss. and preaching. Author of much poetry and of the celebrated *Imitation of Christ* as well as much other devotional literature. † there 1471 (about 90).

LIGHT'S GLITTERING MORN BEDECKS THE SKY: see 838.

LO, GOD IS HERE: LET US ADORE: see 850.

403. LO, HE COMES WITH CLOUDS DESCENDING
6 st. 8.7.8.7.4.7
C. Wesley (1), *Hymns of Intercession for all Mankind*, 1758, founded on a 6 st. hymn with the same opening line by J. Cennick (68) which was first sung 20 April 1750 in Dublin & published in 5th edn., 1752, of Cennick's *Collection of Sacred Hymns*: thus Wesley's version was made after Cennick's death. Text has undergone much revision and selection from the 2 hymns, but it has now settled down to the Wesley text, 4 st., with only these alterations: in our st. 3, 'Those dear tokens' for 'The dear . . .' and in st. 4 C. W.'s last 2 lines replaced by Cennick's last 2—'O come quickly . . .' which, apart from the opening line, are the only Cennick words in original now sung. But much revised vn. in *NC*.
US & CAN: BP228: Can393: CW -/187: H5: L13: P184/234/- ● ENG: AM51: An81: B185: BB35: CH160/316: CP160: E7: M264: NC169‡

LO, HOW A ROSE IS BLOOMING: see 848.

404. LO, ROUND THE THRONE A GLORIOUS BAND
9 st. LM-coup.
R. Hill, *Collection of Psalms & Hymns . . .*, 1783, Rev. 7:13ff. Orig. began 'Exalted high at God's right hand.' First line altd. and text rev. and abr. to 5 st. in Cotterill's *Selection*, 1810 (see 333); this vn. now standard.
US & CAN: Can505 ● ENG: AM435/535: BB230

ROWLAND HILL (Rev. Sir), b. Hawkstone, nr. Shrewsbury, 23 viii 1744; Sch. Eton & St. John's, Camb.; Ord. C/E, curate of Kingston, nr. Taunton (Som.), and afterwards an itinerant preacher in W. England; opened Surrey Chapel, London, 1783, one of the first really large preaching-houses in the evangelical tradition (in which it is said the first organ recitals in Britain were given); remained there 40 years; a founder of the London Missionary Society (1795); compiled 3 hymnals. † London 11 iv 1833 (88).

405. LONG DID I TOIL, AND KNEW NO EARTHLY REST
6 st. 10.10.10.10.10 10   **PCH 127**
H. F. Lyte (5), *Poems, Chiefly Religious*, 1833; 'My beloved is mine and I am his: Imitated from Quarles.' Ref. is to a poem with title 'My beloved . . .' as above by Francis Quarles, 1592-1644, beginning 'Ev'n like two little bank-dividing brooks,' 6 st. 10.10.10.10.10 12. The last line of each stanza in that poem is 'So I my best beloved's am: so he is mine,' or variant of that phrase. Apart from imitating this, Lyte takes nothing else from Quarles (see *Oxford Book of Mystical Verse*, p. 22).
US & CAN: ● ENG: CH544/- : CP767: E432: M458

LOOK UPON US, BLESSED LORD: see 860.

406. LOOK, YE SAINTS, THE SIGHT IS GLORIOUS
4 st. 8.7.8.7.4.7
T. Kelly, *Hymns*, 3rd ed., 1809; 'The Second Advent: "and he shall reign for ever and ever." '
US & CAN: BP205: B121: CW256/186: H105: L114: M453: P201/133/- : Pm203 ● ENG: An206: B169: BB127: CH134/289: CP165: M226

THOMAS KELLY, son of an Irish judge, b. Stradbally, Queen's Co., Ireland, 13 vii 1769; Sch. Trinity, Dublin for the bar. Ord. Ch. of Ireland (Episc.) 1792; but inhibited, with his friend Rowland Hill (404) by the Abp. of Dublin from preaching, so became minister among Independents (Congl.). Remained in or near Dublin throughout his life, greatly loved by the poor. He wrote 765 hymns, of which a few excellent ones survive, and some tunes which are now forgotten—he wrote a tune for every metre in his hymnal. Hymns of his not known elsewhere are preserved among the Brethren in England & Ireland. † Dublin 14 v 1855 (85).

407. LOOKING UPWARD EVERY DAY
5 st. 7.6.7.6 troch.
M. Butler, *The Children's Hymn Book*, 1881, written for the confirmation of her niece & daughter.
US & CAN: ● ENG: B477: CH674/449: CP529: M850

MARY BUTLER, b. Langar, Notts, 1841; sister of Samuel Butler (author of *Erewhon* and *The Way of All Flesh*); lived at home with her father, Rector of Langar, until he retired to Shrewsbury, where she became an active social worker & founded St. Saviour's Home for Girls. Many of her hymns were written for that institution. † Shrewsbury 6 i 1916 (74).

408. LORD, AS TO THY DEAR CROSS WE FLEE
6 st. CM
J. H. Gurney (174), *Lutterworth Collection of Hymns*, 1838.
US & CAN: CW356/258: H413: L455: P145/-/- : Pm347: CLB388 ● ENG: AM267/334: An487: BB293: CH90/- : M512

409. LORD, AS WE RISE TO LEAVE THIS SHELL OF WORSHIP
4 st. 11.11.11.5 Sapphic unrhymed   **PCH 495**
F. H. Kaan (202), *Pilgrim Praise*, 1965, 1971.
US & CAN: BP320: Can305: H*18: CLB382 ● ENG: AM*56: B*49: CP*53

410. LORD, BE THY WORD MY RULE
2 st. 6.6.6.6   **PCH 224**
C. Wordsworth (29), *The Holy Year*, 6th ed., 1872; 'At Confirmation'; based on a prayer of King Charles I, 'O Lord, make thy way plain before me. Let thy glory be my end, thy word my rule; and then, thy will be done.' (Conjecture of the Rev. D. M. Sale). One of the shortest hymns in common use, and one of the most perfect.
US & CAN: Can98 ● ENG: AM701/327: An299: E*751: PL279

411A. LORD, BEHOLD US WITH THY BLESSING (Buckoll)
4 st. 8.7.8.7.4.7
H. Buckoll (135), *Psalms & Hymns for . . . Rugby School Chapel*, 1850; hymn for the first Sunday of the Half-Year (i.e. school term). 2 st. only in *EH*, 3 in *M*.
US & CAN: ● ENG: AM576/457: CH677/- : E523 pt I: M870 pt. I

411B. LORD, DISMISS US WITH THY BLESSING (Buckoll)

4 st. 8.7.8.7.4.7

H. Buckoll, the companion hymn to the above; for the last Sunday of the Half-Year; similarly abr. in *EH* and *M (Brit.)*. Clearly imitating 412.

US & CAN: ● ENG: AM577/458: CH678/- : E523 pt. II: M870 pt. II

412. LORD, DISMISS US WITH THY BLESSING (Fawcett)

3 st. 8.7.8.7.4.7

J. Fawcett (87)—almost certainly; *Supplement* (1773) to the *Shawbury Hymn Book* (Shrewsbury, England). See *Julian* for detailed discussion of authorship. Only *An* and *B (Brit.)* have full text of orig.; all other British books below have sts. 1 and 2; U.S. books use for st. 3 the rewritten vn. by G. Thring (191) in *Church of England Hymn Book*, 1880.

US & CAN: B319: Can308: CW127/- : H489: L191: M165: P54/79/458: Pm63 ● ENG: An56: B762: CH299/638: CP282: M693: NC137

413. LORD CHRIST, THE FATHER'S MIGHTY SON

4 st. 88.5.8.6 iamb. and anap.　　　　　　　　**PCH 497**

B. Wren, written c. 1965; *Dunblane Praises II*, 1967; *100 Hymns for Today*, 1969.

US & CAN: CW -/347: H*19: W165 ● ENG: AM*53: B*51: CP*55: E*96: NC136

BRIAN WREN, b. Romford, Essex, 3 vi 1936; Sch. Mansfield Coll., Oxf.; Ord. Congl.; minister at Hockley, Essex, 1964-70; with Council for World Development, London, '70-　. The above was his first hymn to win wide acceptance, but many more can be found in *New Church Praise*, 1975. With Pratt Green (109) and F. H. Kaan (202) one of the leaders of modern British hymn writing.

414. LORD CHRIST, WHEN FIRST THOU CAM'ST TO MEN

4 st. 8.7.8.7.88.7　　　　　　　　**PCH 543**

W. R. Bowie, written 1928 at request of F. W. Dwelly, first Dean of Liverpool (Eng.), who asked for 'a modern version of the *Dies Irae*'; author said, 'written to express both the solemnity and inspiration of the thought of Christ coming into our modern world in judgment.' First pub. in *Songs of Praise*, 1931, and not widely used in U.S. until after *Hymnal-1940*.

US & CAN: CW -/222: H522: M355: Pm325: CLB514 ● ENG: AM*54: CH -/235: CP172: M906

WALTER RUSSELL BOWIE, b. Richmond, Va., 8 x 1882; Sch. Harvard (Phi Beta Kappa) and Virginia Theol. Sem.; Ord. Episc., 1909. Rector, Emmanuel Ch., Greenwood, Va., '09; St. Paul's, Richmond, Va., '11; Grace Ch., New York City, '23-'39; prof. practical theol., Union Theol. Sem., New York and dean of students, '39-'53. Ed. for some years *The Modern Churchman*; wrote many religious books and two of the finest 20th century American hymns. † Alexandria, Va., 23 iv 1969 (86).

LORD CHRIST, WHO IN THY HEART DIDST BEAR: see 98.

415. LORD, ENTHRONED IN HEAVENLY SPLENDOUR

5 st. 8.7.8.7.4.7

G. H. Bourne, *Seven Post-Communion Hymns* (1874) for St. Edmund's College, Salisbury (England); first in a hymnal; *Hymns A & M*, 1889. A rewritten version by P. Dearmer (88) appeared in *Songs of Praise*, 1931, using Bourne's sts. 1-2 and then, as Part II, 3 st. by Dearmer beginning DRAW US IN THE SPIRIT'S TETHER; this Part by itself appears in *CW²* and *W*.

US & CAN: Can324: CW -/58‡: L*764: Pm291: W67‡ ● ENG: AM555/ 400: An382: BB206: CH -/583: E319: PL72

GEORGE HUGH BOURNE, b. 8 xi 1840 St. Paul's Cray, Kent; Sch. Eton & Corpus Christi, Oxf.; Ord. C/E, 1864: asst. curate, Sandford on Thames (Oxon), '63; Head Master, St. Andrew's School, Chardstock, '66; Warden. St. Edmund's Coll., Salisbury, '74; Chaplain to Bp. of Bloemfontein, S.A., '79-'98; sub-dean, treasurer, prebendary, Salisbury Cathedral, '87 onwards. † Salisbury, 1 xii 1925 (85).

416. LORD GOD OF HOSTS, WHOSE PURPOSE, NEVER SWERVING

4 st. 11.10.11.10　　　　　　　　**PCH 538**

S. Knapp, 1907, for the Men's Association at Brick Presbyterian Church, New York, where he was at the time asst. pastor. Presbyterian *Hymnal*, 1912.

US & CAN: P368/288/460: Pm411 ● ENG:

SHEPHERD KNAPP, b. 1873, Ord. Congl., asst. pastor, Brick Presb. Ch., New York; later for 28 years minister at Central Congl. Ch., Worcester, Mass. Author of several theol. books, including *The Liberated Bible*, 1941. (Brick Presby. Church, New York, has special associations with hymnody in that H. Van Dyke (377) and W. P. Merrill (482) were pastors there; and Clarence Dickinson, editor of 1933 Presb. *Hymnal*, was organist there.) See also 783. † 1946.

417. LORD GOD THE HOLY GHOST

3 st. SMD

J. Montgomery (6), in Cotterill's *Selection* (333), 8th ed., 1819; text altd. by author in *Christian Psalmist*, 1825, to form now in use. Always now appears in SM.

US & CAN: BP270: Can482: CW -/198 ● ENG: AM525/615: An219: B235: CH -/332: CP208: M298

418. LORD, HER WATCH THY CHURCH IS KEEPING

3 st. 8.7.8.7 D

H. Downton (205), written in Geneva 1866 and sung there that year at the annual conference of the Church Missionary Society. Pub. in Berry's *Psalms and Hymns*, 1867.

US & CAN: ● ENG: AM362/267: B379: CH378/- : M267

419. LORD, I WAS BLIND: I COULD NOT SEE

5 st. 8.88.8

W. T. Matson, in H. Allon's *Supplemental Hymns*, 1868; taken from a longer poem, 'The Inner Life,' 1866. Another hymn, O BLESSED LIFE (*CP415*) comes from the same poem.

US & CAN: ● ENG: An486: B445: CP378: M373

WILLIAM TIDD MATSON, b. West Hackney (London) 17 viii 1833, son of a politician & reformer; Sch. privately; joined Methodist, but later trained for Congl. ministry and Ord. Congl., 1860. Served at Havant, Gosport, Stratford (London), Rothwell, Portsmouth and Salisbury Green: retired 1897. † Portsea, Hants, 23 xii 1899 (66).

420. LORD, I WOULD OWN THY TENDER CARE

5 st. CM　　　　　　　　**PCH 298**

Jane Taylor, *Hymns for Infant Minds*, 1809.

US & CAN: ● ENG: AM572/443: An538: CH655/419: E601

JANE TAYLOR, b. 23 ix 1783, London, d. of an engraver who later became a Congl. minister; collaborated with her sister Ann (Mrs. Ann Gilbert) in producing some of the earliest fashionable hymns for children. Source above, containing work by both, reached 52 editions by 1877. † Ongar, Essex, 13 iv 1824 (40).

421. LORD, IN THE FULNESS OF MY MIGHT

8 st. CM

T. H. Gill, written 1855, pub. in *The Golden Chain of Praise*, 1869, orig. in 8 st. beginning 'With sin I would not make abode,' and headed 'Early Love: "How good it is to close with Christ betimes."—Oliver Cromwell.' Normal selection is sts. 6, 2, 3, 5, 7, but one of its earliest appearances, in *Baptist Church Hymnal*, 1900 (Britain), adds st. 8:

> I cannot, Lord, too early take
> the covenant divine;
> Oh, ne'er the happy heart may break
> whose earliest love was Thine

which especially links it with title & quotation.

US & CAN: BP449 ● ENG: B446: CH498/435: M396

THOMAS HORNBLOWER GILL, b. Birmingham 10 ii 1819; Sch. K. Edward's Sch. Sympathy with Unitarians & scruples against signing the Anglican Articles debarred him from going to Oxford; remained all his life a student, historian and writer of independent means; influenced towards orthodoxy by hymns of I. Watts (10), and finally joined evangelical wing of C/E. Regarded by W. G. Horder as the best hymn writer alive in the 1880s—perhaps an overstatement. At the beginning of his collection, *The Golden Chain . . .* he wrote, 'Hymns are not meant to be theological statements, expositions of doctrine or enunciations of precepts; they are utterances of a soul in its manifold moods of hope and fear, joy and sorrow, love, wonder and aspiration. . . . The best and most glorious hymns cannot be more exactly defined than as divine love songs.' † Grove Park, Kent, 4 iii 1906 (87).

422. LORD, IN THIS THY MERCY'S DAY

6 st. 888

I. Williams (71), being sts. 99-104 of a 105-st. poem in *The Baptistery*, 1842. 6 st. version first in Cooke & Denton, *Hymnal*, 1853.

US & CAN: ● ENG: AM94: CH405/- : E76: M725

423. LORD, IN THY NAME THY SERVANTS PLEAD

5 st. CM

J. Keble (83), not in the famous colln., *The Christian Year* but written much later, dated Malvern 4 viii 1853; pub. posth. in *Poems*, 1869 but earlier, anonymously, *Salisbury Hymn Book*, 1857; for Rogationtide.

US & CAN: L362: CLB287 ● ENG: AM143/144: An646: CH611/- : E140

424. LORD, IT BELONGS NOT TO MY CARE

6 st. CM   **PCH 429**

R. Baxter (115), *Poetical Fragments*, 1681, part of a poem in 8 st. beginning 'My whole, though broken heart, O Lord,' and superscribed 'London, at the Door of Eternity, Aug. 7, 1681: Heart-Employment with God and itself: the concordant discord of a broken-hearted heart.' A later ed. says, 'The Covenant & Confidence of Faith: this Covenant my dear wife in her former sickness subscribed with a cheerful will.' (His wife died 1681). A 3 st. version was in Mercer's *Ch. Psalter & Hymn Book*, 1853, but the 6 st. vn. now familiar was first in *Congregational Hymn Book*, 1855.

US & CAN: Can190: H445: L308: M218 ● ENG: AM535/342: B612: BB355: CH549/- : CP435: E433: M647: NC139

425. LORD JESUS CHRIST, OUR LORD MOST DEAR

3 st. 88.88.88

German: ACH LIEBE HERRE, JESUS CHRIST, H. von Laufenberg, ms. of 1429—a Cradle Song addressed to Christ.

Tr.: C. Winkworth (14), *Christian Singers of Germany*, 1870.

US & CAN: P351/-/461: Pm278 ● ENG: AM -/425: CH304/- : E338: M755

HEINRICH von LAUFENBERG, b. about 1385 Laufenberg, Switzerland; mentioned as deacon of Collegiate Ch. of St. Maurice, Zofingen, and later member of choir at Freiburg in Baden. Became a monk, 1445, in Monastery of the Knights of St. John, Strassburg. † there 31 iii 1460.

LORD JESUS, GOD OF HEAVENLY GRACE: see 875.

426. LORD JESUS, THINK ON ME

SM   **PCH 183**

A. W. Chatfield, *Hymns Ancient & Modern*, 1875, 5 st., expanded to 9 st. in his *Songs & Hymns from Earliest Greek Poets*, 1876. It is a paraphrase of a Greek prayer in 20 lines of 5 or 6 syllables, dactylic rhythm, by Synesius of Cyrene. From the 1876 text *EH* takes sts. 2-7 in the longest vn. in use now. *AMR* has sts. 2, 3, 5, 7. Benjamin Britten's *Noye's Fludde* uses sts. 2, 3, 6, 7.

US & CAN: CW -/255: H417: L365: M284: P239/270/- : Pm314: CLB390: W167 ● ENG: AM185/200: An138: B565: CH403/80: CP380: E77: M239: NC142: PL104

SYNESIUS, b. Cyrene (N. Africa) of aristocratic family, c. 365; Sch. Alexandria under neoplatonist philosopher Hypatia (celebrated in Kingsley's novel); went to Constantinople 397 on a mission to warn Emperor Arcadius (in charge of eastern half of Roman Empire) of the serious threat presented by the Goths who eventually overran Rome (410). Converted to Christianity c. 400, and became Bp. of Ptolemais (Egypt), 410. † about 414.

ALLEN WILLIAM CHATFIELD, b. the Vicarage, Chatteris, Cambs.; 2 x 1808; Sch. Charterhouse and Trinity, Camb.; Ord. C/E, 1832; Vicar of Stotfold, Beds., '33-'47, and Much Marcle, Herefs., '47- † there 10 i 1896 (87).

427. LORD OF ALL BEING, THRONED AFAR

5 st. LM-coup.   **PCH 375**

O. W. Holmes, at the end of *The Professor at the Breakfast Table*, 1859, which was originally essays in the *Atlantic Monthly*; the poem is prefaced by the words, 'Peace be to all such as may have been vexed in spirit by any utterance these page may have repeated! They will doubtless forget for a moment the difference in the hues of truth we look at through our human prisms, and join in singing (inwardly) this hymn to the source of light we all need to lead us, and the warmth which alone can make us brothers.' See in the light of this the ref. to John 8:32 in st. 3. Introduced to England by W. G. Horder in *Congregational Hymns*, 1884.

US & CAN: BP93: CW151/- : H291: L170: M64: P87/87/463: Pm89 ● ENG: An245: B63: BB11: CH24/34: CP23: E434: M32: NC143

OLIVER WENDELL HOLMES, b. Cambridge, Mass., 29 viii 1809; Sch. Harvard, then entered medicine, and taught anatomy & physiology at Dartmouth, '39-'47, and at Harvard, '47-'82. Man of letters and liberal lay theologian, in revolt against traditional New England Calvinism. † Cambridge, Mass., 7 x 1894 (85).

428. LORD OF ALL HOPEFULNESS, LORD OF ALL JOY

4 st. 10 11. 11 11 dact.

Jan Struther, *Songs of Praise*, 1931. Her hymns, first pub. in this source, are among the first to address God with the pronoun 'You,' although the first poem in hymnic use (which was not designed as a hymn) is Hankey's 'Lord of the strong,' *SP*568 (*Worshipbook* 466) which was written before 1916.

US & CAN: BP420: Can262: H363: Pm217: CLB466: W169 ● ENG: AM*61: B631: BB309: CH -/92: CP534: NC144: PL288

JAN STRUTHER is the pen-name of Joyce Anstruther, b. Westminster (London), 6 vi 1901; Sch. privately; m. (1) A. M. Graham 1923, (2) A. K. Placzek, 1948. Wrote much poetry and a celebrated novel (later filmed), *Mrs. Miniver*; was in much demand as a lecturer in U.S.A. Contributed

11 hymns to *Songs of Praise* in unusual meters and freshly contemporary style. † New York, N.Y., 20 vii 1953 (52).

429. LORD OF LIFE AND KING OF GLORY

5 st. 8.7.8.7.8.7

C. Burke, December 1904, printed Feb. 1905 in *The Treasury* as a prize hymn for a Mothers' Union service, and pub. *EH*, 1906.

US & CAN: M517 ● ENG: AM -/498: B618: CH652/- : E530: M397

CHRISTIAN CAROLINE ANNA BURKE, b. Camberwell (London) 18 ix 1857; pub. collected verse 1896 in *The Flowering of the Almond Tree*. † Saffron Walden, Essex, 6 iii 1944 (86).

430. LORD OF LIGHT, WHOSE NAME OUTSHINETH

4 st. 8.7.8.7 D   **PCH 451**

H. Elvet Lewis, *Congregational Hymnary*, 1916. The author wrote of it: 'This hymn was written to declare that in doing God's will, active co-operation is as much needed as humble resignation. Charlotte Elliott in her hymn, "My God and Father," has expressed the latter thought beautifully. My thought was to supplement her hymn as best I could.' (See 462).

US & CAN: BP489: Can280: CW504/- ● ENG: B380: CH337/510: CP560

HOWELL ELVET LEWIS (Hywel Elfed), b. 14 iv 1860, Cynwil Elfed, near Blaenycoed, Carmarthenshire (S. Wales), eldest of 11 children of humble parents; Sch. Gram. Sch. Newcastle Emlyn, Carms; then Carmarthen Presb. Coll., and Aberystwyth Coll. (later part of Univ. of Wales); Ord. at age 20 at St. John's Congl. Ch., Buckley, Flintshire; Fish St. Congl. Ch., Hull, '84; Llanelli, '90; Harcourt, London, '98; King's Cross Welsh Church, London, 1904-40. Chairman, Congl. Union of England & Wales, '33-4; President, Free Ch. Council in Britain '26; Hon. D.D., Univ. Wales, '33; Companion of Honour, '49. Crowned as bard at Welsh Eisteddfod, 1888; Chairman of Eisteddfod, 1894; became known as one of the leading Welsh poets of his generation, did much to revive the Welsh language; wrote many hymns in Welsh and English. His sermon, 1 viii 1953, on his last visit to Buckley (73 years after ordination there) is preserved in E. Wyn Parry's memorial booklet, *Howell Elfed Lewis* (London, 1954); in the course of the sermon, which was broadcast, he quoted a hymn he had written at Buckley 70 years earlier:

> We tarry, Lord, thy leisure still,
>   thy best is yet to be;
> nought ever comes too late for man
>   that is in time for thee.   (see PCH 450)

He † Penarth, Glamorgan, 10 xii 1953 (93).

431. LORD OF OUR LIFE AND GOD OF OUR SALVATION   **both trs. at PCH 190**

5 st. 11 11. 11 5: long lines 4 plus 7 so in English not strictly Sapphic.

P. Pusey in *Psalm and Hymn Tunes* (Reinagle), 1834, but popularized as a hymn by *Hymns Ancient & Modern*, 1868. It is a free paraphrase of M. von Lowenstern's CHRISTE DU BEISTAND, which was written during the Thirty Years' War, entitled 'Sapphic Ode: for Spiritual and Temporal Peace' (1644). This was trsd., faithfully but not quite in orig. meter, by C. Winkworth (14) in her *Lyra Germanica*, 1855. Pusey, in a letter to his brother, E. B. Pusey (a leader in the Oxford Movement, see 83) wrote, 'It refers to the state of the Church, that is to say of the Church of England in 1834, assailed from without, enfeebled and distracted within, but on the eve of a great awakening.' The 'great awakening' was the Oxford Movement, then in its earliest stages: subsequent events proved that Pusey's language was not exaggerated, but his hymn goes some distance from the thought of the German original.

US & CAN: BP295: Can272: B145: CW430/- : H395: L157: Pm378 ● ENG: AM214/253: An405: B261: BB179: CH216/491: CP508: E435: M729: PL283

MATTHAUS APELLES von LOWENSTERN, b. Neustadt, Silesia, 20 iv 1594; church and court musician under emperors Ferdinand II and III, then Councillor of State to Duke Karl Friederich of Munsterburg; wrote both texts and tunes, the tune for the above hymn being at *EH* 160 ii. † Breslau, 11 iv 1648 (53).

PHILIP PUSEY, b. Pusey, Berks, 25 vi 1799; Sch. Christ. Ch. Oxf.; inherited the country estate, 1828; devoted himself to agriculture, especially to the cause of the agricultural tenant; member of Parliament, 1830-52 (Chippenham: Cashel: Berkshire); Chairman of agricultural instrument section of the Great Exhibition of 1851; pub. articles & pamphlets on agric. subjects. † Kensington (London), 9 vii 1855 (56).

LORD OF THE DANCE: see 308.

432. LORD OF THE LIVING HARVEST

4 st. 7.6.7.6 D

J. S. B. Monsell (193), *Hymns of Love & Praise*, 1863.

US & CAN: L304: CLB398 ● ENG: An324: B381: CH335/- : M793

433. LORD OF THE WORLDS ABOVE

7 st. 6.6.6.6.4.44.4

I. Watts (10), *Psalms of David . . .*, 1719; Ps. 84, 'Longing for the House of God,' now always abr. to 4 st. or fewer.

US & CAN: L238: P50/14/- ● ENG: AM -/248: An559: B273: BB462: CP259: M678

LORD, POUR THY SPIRIT FROM ABOVE: see 596.

434. LORD, SPEAK TO ME, THAT I MAY SPEAK

7 st. LM-alt.   **PCH 284**

F. R. Havergal (252), written 28 iv 1872, at Winterdyne (England); 'A worker's prayer; None of us liveth unto himself (Rom. 14:7).' St. 5 norm. om. Pub. in *Under the Surface*, 1874, and *Hymns Ancient & Modern*, 1875.

US & CAN: BP477: Can302: B276: CW470/344: H574: L538: M195: P399/298/- : Pm397 ● ENG: AM356/- : An597: B514: CH338/485: CP552: M781

435. LORD, TEACH US HOW TO PRAY ARIGHT

4 st. CMD   **PCH 110**

J. Montgomery (6), in 4 st. on a leaflet with 3 other hymns on prayer (one of which is 608), for Nonconformist Sunday Schools in Sheffield, 1818; in 8 st. CM in Cotterill's Selection, 1819 (333). Now norm. in 7 st. or fewer and CMD only in *EH*.

US & CAN: L452: CLB485 ● ENG: AM247/317: An609: BB344: CP444: E78: M539

LORD, THY GLORY FILLS THE HEAVEN: see 95.

436. LORD, THY WORD ABIDETH

6 st. 66.66 troch.

H. W. Baker (101), *Hymns Ancient and Modern*, 1861; Ps. 119:89.

US & CAN: BP286: CW -/326: H399: P -/252/- : Pm258 ● ENG: AM243/250: An305: B250: BB190: CH199/130: CP232: E436: M308: NC146‡: PL256

437. LORD, WHEN THY KINGDOM COMES, REMEMBER ME

7 st. 10.10.10.10

W. D. Maclagan (352), *Hymns Ancient and Modern*, 1875; in later eds. and elsewhere st. 6 om. For Good Friday Three Hours Service.

US & CAN: ● ENG: AM116: CH98/245: E113

438. LORD, WHEN WE BEND BEFORE THY THRONE

6 st. CM

J. D. Carlyle, in *A Collection of Psalms & Hymns*, Carlisle, 1802, a book in use at St. Cuthbert's, Carlisle, where author regularly attended when he was Chancellor of Carlisle Cathedral. St. 3-4 norm. om. In *CLB*, LORD, WHEN WE BOW. . . .

US & CAN: H410: CLB387 ● ENG: AM244/- : An142: E79

JOSEPH DACRE CARLYLE, b. Carlisle, England (which is pronounced as his name and from which the family name is derived), 4 vi 1758; Sch. Cathedral Sch., Carlisle and Christ's, then Queens', Camb.; Fellow of Queens', 1793; Ord. C/E; prof. of Arabic at Cambridge, 1795-9; then travelled as chaplain to the Earl of Elgin (later associated with the 'Elgin Marbles,' the Parthenon frieze which he removed from Athens & sold to the British nation in 1816); this took him to Constantinople, Asia Minor and the Greek Islands. Chancellor of Carlisle Cathedral, 1799-1801; Vicar of Newcastle upon Tyne, 1801-4, where † 12 iv 1804 (45).

439. LORD, WHILE FOR ALL MANKIND WE PRAY

6 st. CM

J. R. Wreford, *Lays of Loyalty*, 1837, and J. R. Beard's *Collection of Hymns*, 1837. 'A Prayer for our Country'; prob. occasioned by the accession of Queen Victoria in that year. Now always abr. to 4 st.

US & CAN: CW544/- : M551 ● ENG: AM/-/581: B646: BB432: CH633/518: CP568: E561: M881

JOHN RUSSELL WREFORD, b. Barnstable, Devon, 12 xii 1800; Sch. Manchester Coll., York; Ord. Unit., New Meeting, Birmingham, 1826; resigned 1831 through failure of voice & opened a school in Edgbaston, Birmingham; later lived in Bristol but † Marylebone, London, 2 vii 1881 (80).

440. LORD, WHO THROUGHOUT THESE FORTY DAYS

5 st. CM

C. Hernaman, *A Child's Book of Praise*, 1873. Julian (1892) says it was in common use then; but disappeared from Eng. use in early 1920s; revived in *H(U.S.)* from which certain English books recovered it.

US & CAN: BP177: CW -/166: H59: P144/81/470: Pm153: W171 ● ENG: An144: BB83

CLAUDIA FRANCES HERNAMAN (nee Ibbotson), b. Addlestone, Surrey, 19 x 1838; m. 1858 J. W. D. Hernaman, an inspector of schools. Wrote 150 hymns for children; joint editor of *The Altar Hymnal*, 1884; and compiled several collections of her own poems. † Brussels, 10 x 1898 (59).

441. LOVE CAME DOWN AT CHRISTMAS

3 st. 6.7.6.7   PCH 292

C. Rossetti (335), in *Time Flies: A Reading Diary*, 1883; first as a hymn in *Oxford Hymn Book*, 1908.

US & CAN: BP138: Can422: CW -/134: L37: M375: P133/-/- ● ENG: An105: B103: BB53: CH52/194: CP717: M138

442. LOVE DIVINE, ALL LOVES EXCELLING

4 st. 8.7.8.7 D   PCH 66

C. Wesley (1), *Redemption Hymns*, 1747; 2 Cor. 3:18. St. 2, 'Breathe, O

breathe thy loving Spirit' always now om. in Britain, but norm. included in U.S. Its final line is taken verbatim from line 4 of 799, q.v.

US & CAN: BP233: Can241: B58: CW379/297: H479: L397: M283: P308/399/471: Pm228: W172 ● ENG: AM520/205: An625: B595: BB328: CH479/437: CP179: E437: M431: NC147: PL113

443. LOVE OF THE FATHER: LOVE OF GOD THE SON

5 st. 10.10.10 10   PCH 257

R. Bridges (9), *Yattendon Hymnal*, 1899; suggested by, but hardly even a paraphrase of, a Latin poem in a 14th century ms., AMOR PATRIS ET FILII. The *caesura* after the 5th syllable in line 1 of each stanza is devised to accommodate the rhythm of O. Gibbons' tune, SONG 22, almost always set to it.

US & CAN: BP441: L125 ● ENG: AM -/238: BB522: CH -/335: CP217: E438

444. LOVING SHEPHERD OF THY SHEEP

3 st. 77.77 D   PCH 304

J. E. Leeson, *Hymns & Songs of Childhood*, 1842; John 10:27. *Hymns A & M*, 1875, brought it into currency by altering the text and setting it out in 5 st. 77.77 (omitting 2nd half of st. 1) and this form is now in normal use.

US & CAN: ● ENG: AM334/444: An337: B287: BB146: CH668/93: E602: NC149

JANE ELIZABETH LEESON, b. London, 1809, was for many years a well known figure in the Catholic Apostolic Church (Irvingite), a group founded 1832 out of an evangelical circle gathered round the Scottish politician and evangelist, Henry Drummond (1786-1860) and the Scottish minister Edward Irving (1792-1834). It had considerable influence up to the early years of the 20th century. After the dissolution of the group, its metropolitan church became the Chapel of the University of London. Miss Leeson, after writing a number of hymns for this body, became later in life a Roman Catholic (see 883). † Leamington, Warks., 18 xi 1881 (72).

445. MAJESTIC SWEETNESS SITS ENTHRONED

CM

S. Stennett, 9 st. in Rippon's *Selection*, 1787, beginning 'To Christ the Lord let every tongue'; based on Cant. 5:10-16. Now always found in the abridged form beginning as above with st. 3.

US & CAN: CW381/- : H553: L570: M83: P197/142/- ● ENG:

SAMUEL STENNETT, b. Exeter, 1727; at age 20 became assistant to his father, a Baptist minister, at Little Wild Street, London, and in 1758 succeeded him. Remained there until †. The prominent prison reformer John Howard was a member of his congregation. His hymns are still sung by English Baptists—he contributed 38 to Rippons Collection; but the only one qualifying for inclusion here is now known only in U.S.A. † Muswell Hill (London), 25 viii 1795.

446. MAKE ME A CAPTIVE, LORD

3 st. SMD

G. Matheson, *Sacred Songs*, 1890; 'Christian Freedom: Paul the Prisoner of Jesus Christ; Eph. 3:1.'

US & CAN: Can242: CW -/2;5: L508: M184: P247/-/-: Pm356 ● ENG: An633: B478: CH464/445: CP460: M596

GEORGE MATHESON, b. Glasgow, 27 iii 1842; Sch. Glasgow Academy & University; Ord. C/Scot., 1866 & after 2 years in Glasgow became minister at Innellan, Argyllshire; St. Bernard's, Edinburgh, 1886-99. Fellow of the Royal Society of Edinburgh, 1890. One of the most brilliant students and preachers of his time, his sight was defective from birth and from age 18 he was virtually blind; author of many books of theology, he is best known for having written 547, q.v. † North Berwick, E. Lothian, 28 viii 1906 (64).

447. MAN OF SORROWS! WHAT A NAME

5 st. 777.8

P. P. Bliss, *International Lessons Monthly*, 1875; Is. 53.

US & CAN: BP172: B56 • ENG: An159: B186: CH693/380: M176

PHILIPP BLISS (who at an early stage disguised the eccentric spelling of his first name by always signing himself 'P. P.'), b. Clearfield County, Pa., 1838; entered on a musical career at Chicago, 1864, composing Sunday School songs; joined the evangelist, D. W. Whittle, 1874, as song-leader in his campaigns; when Moody & Sankey returned from their first British tour, they combined their collection of hymns with that of Bliss in *Gospel Hymns and Sacred Melodies*, which is generally regarded as the birth of the American-style 'Gospel Song.' (Undated: c. 1873). Bliss died in a railway accident on the way to Chicago, attempting to save his wife from a blazing carriage, 1876 (38).

448. MARCH ON, MY SOUL, WITH STRENGTH

4 st. 6.6.6.6.88

W. Wright, in *YMCA Hymnal*, 1st edition (n.d.): not in revised ed. of 1927, but in *Church Hymnary*, 1927.

US & CAN: • ENG: B716: CH537/614: CP531

WILLIAM WRIGHT, b. Lockerbie, Dumfries-shire, 4 viii 1859, brought up in Free Ch. of Scotland, became elder 1883 (age 24); went into business as a pharmacist in Lockerbie after apprenticeships in Worthing (Sussex) and Glasgow, then joined Secretariat of YMCA (Scotland), and in 1900 became National Secretary of YMCA in Ireland. During World War I was responsible for 'Red Triangle' work in YMCA service. † Belfast, 9 ix 1924 (65).

449. MARCH ON, O SOUL, WITH STRENGTH

4 st. 6.6.6.6.88

G. T. Coster, written at Bedford Park, London, 3 viii 1897, printed in *Evangelical Magazine*, Feb. 1898 and *Hessle Hymns* (Hull, Yorks), 1901; Judges 5:21. Orig. meter was 6.6.6.6.86, but in U.S., where alone it survives, always appears abridged from orig. 6 st. and in 6.6.6.6.88; sts. 3-4 of original are omitted.

US & CAN: CW359/- : M243: P273/351/- : Pm180 • ENG:

GEORGE THOMAS COSTER, b. Chatham Kent, 3 x 1835; Sch. New Coll., London and Ord. Congl., 1859; served both Congl. and Meth. churches till retirement, 1902; assisted in founding Victoria Hospital, Hull; was one of 13 children all of whom went into religious or social work. † Rotherham, Yorks, 29 viii 1912 (77).

450. MASTER, SPEAK! THY SERVANT HEARETH

9 st. 8.7.8.7.77

F. R. Havergal (252), 19 v 1867, written at Weston super Mare (England); *The Ministry of Song*, 1869. Normal vn. now uses sts. 1, 5, 8, 9.

US & CAN: BP433: M274 • ENG: An475: B479: M780

451. MAY THE GRACE OF CHRIST OUR SAVIOUR

1 st. 8.7.8.7 D

J. Newton (37), *Olney Hymns*, 1779; 'After Sermon: 2 Cor. 13:14'; now normally in 2 4-line sts.

US & CAN: Can209: CW126/436: H216: M334: P495/76/- : Pm539: CLB402: W176 • ENG: AM551/636: An21: B763: BB375: CH -/634: CP751: E*67: M*45: NC157

452. MEN AND CHILDREN EVERYWHERE

3 st. 77.77.5.7.4.7

J. J. Moment, *The Hymnal* (P¹, 1933).

US & CAN: CW96/8: M11: P4/-/- • ENG:

JOHN JAMES MOMENT, b. Orono, Ontario, 1 ii 1875; Sch. Princeton Univ., Hartford Theol. Sem.; taught at Lawrenceville School, N.J., 1898-1904; Ord. Presb., served in New Jersey at E. Orange, Jersey City, Newark and Plainfield; member of ed. cttee. Presbyterian *Hymnal* (1933). † Plainfield, N.J., 11 v 1959 (84).

453. MIGHTY GOD, WHILE ANGELS BLESS THEE

9 st. 8.7.8.7 with ref. 4.6   **PCH 83**

R. Robinson (141), *Hymns* (ed. J. Middleton), 1793, and his own *Misc. Works*, 1807. In orig. form every st. ended with refrain 'Hallelujah! Hallelujah! Hallelujah! Amen!'; and in this form it appeared (7 st.) as late as W. G. Horder's *Worship Song* (1905); but it is in British *Baptist Church Hymnal*, 1900 in 8 st. 8.7.8.7, and in *Congl. Hymnary*, 1916, 4 st. 8.7.8.7 D; in both cases refrain is omitted, and the 8-line stanza in this form is now invariable—which means that 4 lines of orig. are omitted. The 4-st. form is, however, also altered in a number of details, the revision being the work of R. W. Dale in his *English Hymn Book*, 1879. See PCH.

US & CAN: CW160/- : P -/10/- • ENG: B210: CP68

454. MINE EYES HAVE SEEN THE GLORY OF THE COMING OF THE LORD

6 st. 8.6.8.6.8.6.6 irreg: with refrain 8-8-8.6   **PCH 376**

Julia Warde Howe, 1861. Behind this hymn lies the patriotic folk song, 'John Brown's Body,' with its famous tune. John Brown, a man of the old puritan tradition, believed that slavery in the U.S. should be abolished, but without violence. On 16 October 1859 he attacked the arsenal at Harper's Ferry, W.Va., with 18 men; having captured the town and the arsenal, which had been built up to attack the southern states, he was himself overpowered and taken prisoner; he was tried on a charge of treason and hanged, 2 December 1859. Emerson wrote that his death would 'make the gallows glorious like the Cross,' and H. W. Longfellow that 'this is the date of a new revolution.' The Civil War, when it began in 1861, was sung in by the abolitionists with the song which began, 'John Brown's body lies a mouldering in the grave . . . but his soul goes marching on.'

Julia Ward Howe, at that time the only woman member of the American Academy of letters and a leader in movements for peace and humanitarianism, wrote her hymn at the suggestion of J. Freeman Clarke (for one of whose hymns see PCH 372). The following is her account, taken from *The Story of the Battle Hymn of the Republic*, by her daughter, Florence Howe Hall:

> Mr. Clarke said to me, 'You ought to write some new words to that tune.' I replied that I had often wished to do so.
>
> In spite of the excitement of the day I went to bed and slept as usual, but awoke next morning in the gray of the early dawn, and to my astonishment found that the wished-for lines were arranging themselves in my brain. I lay quite still until the last verse had completed itself in my thoughts, then hastily arose, saying to myself, 'I shall lose this if I don't write it down immediately.' I searched for a sheet of paper and an old stump of a pen which I had had the night before and began to scrawl the lines almost without looking, as I had learned to do by often scratching down verses in the darkened room where my little children were sleeping. Having completed this, I lay down again and fell asleep, but not without feeling that something of importance had happened to me.

The reason for this suggestion of emergency was that she was staying in a hotel in Washington, D.C. (Willard's Hotel) for a conference. The paper on which she wrote out the verses was that of the Sanitary Commission, Washington, D.C., Treasury Building—upon which her husband was serving. She added 'Willard's Hotel,' but unhappily only the date of the year, 1861.

Florence Hall, relying on the Reminiscences of Julia Ward Howe (1899) says a little later on:

> We find from her letters that she hesitated to allow the publication of the original draft of the 'Battle Hymn,' because it contained this

final verse. She did not consider it equal to the rest of the poem. This probably explains why a poem designed for singing and written at such speed, with such evident internal coherence, appears subsequently in so many different stanza-selections.

Naturally the hymn has special significance in the U.S.A., where it is inseparable from the 'John Brown' tune. But it was brought to Britain by that indefatigable Americophile W. Garrett Horder, who included sts. 1, 4 and 5 in *The Treasury of Hymns*, 1896. Walford Davies, in a small hymn-collection for wartime, *In Hoc Signo*, 1915 (mentioned again under 585), included sts. 1-5 with a new tune of his own, and thereafter, especially with this music, it achieved some popularity in Britain as a hymn of social aspiration, or as an Advent song. Another tune, suitable for schools or social meetings, was composed by Martin Shaw, who included it in his *Songs of Praise*, 1925, and there the poem appeared complete for the first time in Britain.

The stanzas, for purposes of identification, are these: (1) Mine eyes ... (2) I have seen him ... (3) I have read a fiery gospel ... (4) He has sounded ... (5) In the beauty ... (6) He is coming ... The distribution in listed hymnals is: 1-5, NC: 1, 2, 4: H*: 1, 2, 4, 5, P³, Pm: 1, 2, 4, 5, 6, B (U.S.), M (Brit.): 1, 4, 5: M (U.S.), L: 1, 4, 5, 6: CH, CP, Can.

US & CAN: BP225: Can156: B510: H*28: L356: M545: P -/-/474: Pm443: W178 ● ENG: CH155/318: CP170: M255: NC158

JULIA WARD HOWE, b. New York, 27 v 1819, was a lifelong social worker and pacifist; she assisted her husband in work among the blind and in other humane projects, and in 1870 attempted to organize a movement among women to end war. A learned woman and an accomplished speaker she often preached from the pulpits of Unitarian churches, especially in the abolitionist cause. Three volumes of her poetry were published. † Newport, R.I., 17 x 1910 (91).

455. MORE LOVE TO THEE, O CHRIST

4 st. 6.4.6.4.66.4-4

E. P. Prentiss, written c. 1856, printed on a leaflet 1869, then in *Songs of Devotion for Christian Associations*, 1870. St. 2 sometimes omitted.

US & CAN: B484: CW390/- : H461: L392: M185: P315/397/- : Pm400 ● ENG:

ELIZABETH PAYSON PRENTISS, b. Portland, Maine, 26 x 1818; Sch. in public schools of Portland; taught there and in Ipswich, Mass., and Richmond, Vt.; then m. Dr. G. L. Prentiss, a Congl. minister who later became Prof. of homiletics & polity at Union Theol. Sem., New York. † Dorset, Vt., 13 viii 1878 (59).

456. MORNING HAS BROKEN

3 st. 5.5.5.4 D

E. Farjeon, *Songs of Praise*, 1931, written for the tune BUNESSAN, whose older association was with 102. Since it achieved prominence in the late 1960's in the world of secular and popular music, it has lately become a favourite with many who have no Christian associations.

US & CAN: BP550: B157: P -/464/- : Pm38: CLB323: W179 ● ENG: CP601: NC159

ELEANOR FARJEON, b. Westminster (London), 13 ii 1881; a member of a family distinguished in the arts. Her brothers Harry (b. 1878, musician & poet) and Herbert (b. 1887, poet & literary critic) were both born in New Jersey. She too was a poet and critic. † Hampstead (London) 5 vi 1965 (84).

MOST ANCIENT OF ALL MYSTERIES: see 274.

457. MOST GLORIOUS LORD OF LIFE, THAT ON THIS DAY

Sonnet **PCH 411**

E. Spenser, *Amoretti & Epithalamion*, 1595. First as a hymn in *English Hymnal*, 1906. The idea of setting an English Sonnet to three runs of a

hymn tune in 10 10 10 10 plus a repetition of its second half originated with its editor, P. Dearmer (88); with greater daring he extended the principle to a Shakespeare sonnet in *Songs of Praise* (# 622).

US & CAN: ● ENG: An73: BB398: CH -/44: CP602: E283

EDMUND SPENSER, b. about 1552 in London; Sch. Merchant Taylors' School, London and Pembroke Hall, Camb.; became secretary to Lord Gray of Wilton, 1580, with whom he went to live in Ireland for 10 years; briefly returned to England 1590, but soon returned to Ireland and became Sheriff of Cork, 1598. In the rebellion of Tyrone, 1599, his castle at Kilcolman, Co. Cork, was burned and his youngest child perished; from this he never recovered; he returned for the last time to London. He is one of England's foremost poets, chiefly remembered for *The Faerie Queene*. The two works mentioned above, published as a single volume, were inspired by his marriage to Elizabeth Boyle, who was also the inspiration for *The Faerie Queene*. The wide success of the above sonnet during the 20th century as a hymn, even more as a text for choral works, attests that lyric gift which he combined with his outstanding talent in the larger poetic forms. † London 1599 (about 47).

458. MY COUNTRY, 'TIS OF THEE

4 st. 66.4.666.4

S. F. Smith, *Union Collection of Church Music*, 1832. Author's account taken from later recollections is much confused; it seems that Lowell Mason, the most influential U.S. musician of his time and founder of the Boston Haydn and Handel Society, handed him several books of German songs inviting him to translate them—which Mason himself was not equipped to do—or to provide new texts; this was one of the texts produced for this project. Smith was at the time 24, and a student at Andover Theol. Sem. If this account is true, the books contained not only German songs, for no German piece in this meter is known. But the English national anthem had appeared in U.S. in the *Christian Lyre*, vol. I, 1830, and of course COME THOU ALMIGHTY KING (140) was well known. It is not therefore certain that these words were written for the National Anthem tune, though it must be regarded as highly probable. (See also 247)

US & CAN: B511: CW548/371: H141: L360: M547: P412/513/476: Pm 437: CLB322: W181 ● ENG:

SAMUEL FRANCIS SMITH, b. Boston, Mass., 21 x 1808, Sch. Eliot Sch., Boston Latin Sch., Harvard and Andover Th. Sem.; Ord. Bapt., served at Waterville, Maine, '34-42, Newton Center Bapt. Ch., Boston, '42-'54; then editorial Sec. to American Bapt. Missionary Union; ed. *The Psalmist*, 1843, with Baron Stowe, this being the most popular of American Bapt. Hymnals. Wrote about 100 hymns. † Boston 16 xi 1895 (87).

459. MY FAITH LOOKS UP TO THEE

6 st. 66.4.666.4 **PCH 355**

R. Palmer (370), written late 1830 or early 1831 (age 22-3), at a school for young ladies where he taught for a year after graduating from Yale & before ordination. In 1831 he met L. Mason (see preceding note) who was looking for hymns for a new hymnal; there this was pub. with its famous tune by L. M., in *Spiritual Songs for Social Worship*, 1831. Then, and always thereafter, in 4 st.

US & CAN: BP398: Can285: B382: CW355/244: H449: L375: M143: P285/378/- : Pm348 ● ENG: An507: B549: CH415/81: CP479: E439: M238

460. MY FATHER, FOR ANOTHER NIGHT

4 st. CM

H. W. Baker (101), *Hymns Ancient & Modern*, 1875, with his own tune.

US & CAN: ● ENG: AM5: An41: BB407: M926

461. MY GOD, ACCEPT MY HEART THIS DAY

5 st. CM

M. Bridges (78), *Hymns of the Heart*, 1848; norm. now in 4 st. but *AM* adds doxology not by author, *CLB* begins O GOD, ACCEPT. . . .

US & CAN: H404: P232/-/-: Pm321: CLB343 • ENG: AM349/459: An363: BB356: CH -/429: E341: PL10

462. MY GOD AND FATHER, WHILE I STRAY

888.4

C. Elliott (119), 8 st. in Appendix to first ed. of *The Invalid's Hymn Book*, 1834, 7 st. in H. V. Elliott's *Psalms & Hymns*, 1835, beginning MY GOD, MY FATHER, 6 st. in her own *Hours of Sorrow*, 1836. Modern hymnals mostly use 6 st. or fewer from the 1834 text with alterations of details from later vns. The fact that this hymn inspired, by reaction, two others so different as 430 and 467 shows how well it was known in the opening years of the present century.

US & CAN: H420: L465 • ENG: AM264/357: CH539/- : E440

463. MY GOD, AND IS THY TABLE SPREAD

6 st. LM-alt.

P. Doddridge (64), *Hymns* (posth.) 1755; 'God's Name Profan'd when his Table is treated with Contempt: Mal. 1:12. Applied to the Lord's Supper.' Full text in *CP*, elsewhere abr. to 4 st. or fewer.

US & CAN: BP355: Can327: H203 • ENG: AM317/396: An396: BB207: CH311/- : CP297: E320: M*46

464. MY GOD, HOW WONDERFUL THOU ART

9 st. CM   **PCH 208**

F. W. Faber (175), *Jesus & Mary*, 1849; 'Our Heavenly Father.' Vn. made familiar in *Hymns A & M* from 1861 has 7 st., being 1-5, 7, 9; but *CP* uses 1-6 and others make other selections.

US & CAN: H284: L181 • ENG: AM169: An10: B64: BB12: CH23/356: CP24: E441: M73: NC162

465. MY GOD, I LOVE THEE: NOT BECAUSE I HOPE FOR HEAVEN THEREBY

6 st. CM

Spanish: NO ME NUEVE, MI DIOS, PARA QUERERTE, in 14 12-syllable lines rhymed like a sonnet *abba cddc eee eee*: text in *Hymnal 1940 Companion* p. 282. It is ascribed, not with complete certainty, to St. Francis Xavier, and is first printed (as far as is known) in *Epitome de la vida y muerte de San Ignacio de Loyola*, 1662, without ascription; but in *Conceptus Evangelici*, also 1662, it is ascribed to F. X. It had already been published in Latin, tr. by Johannes Nadasi in *Pretiosae Occupationes Morientium*, 1657; the distinguished degree of doggerel achieved by the Latin precludes any thought of its being the original. This is mostly, but not consistently, in LM, runs 21 lines, and begins:

> O deus ego amo te
> nec amo te ut salves me
> aut quia non amantem te
> aeterno punes igne.

We can take it as certain that the Spanish poem has a Jesuit origin, and there is no strong reason to doubt that it was written, as tradition holds, c. 1546 by F. X.

Tr. E. Caswall (26), *Lyra Catholica*, 1849—but the trsn. is from the Latin version.

US & CAN: B57: CW -/84: H456: P313/-/-: Pm313: CLB492 • ENG: AM106: B211: BB276: CH435/379: CP425: E80: M446

ST. FRANCIS XAVIER, b. 7 iv 1506, Xavier Castle, nr. Sanguese, Spain: Sch. Univ. Paris, where he was appointed lecturer in Aristotelian philosophy, 1528; one of the seven who took original Jesuit vows with St. Ignatius Loyola, the movement's founder, in 1534; Ord. R.C., 1537; after mission work in Italy, went on missions to Goa and Malaysia; in 1549, to Japan where stayed 2 years; then Singapore and finally to China. † on Island of St. John, off coast of Kwang-tung, 2 xii 1552 (46). Canonized March, 1622, commemorated 3 December.

466. MY GOD, I THANK THEE, WHO HAST MADE

6 st. 8.4.8.4.8.4

A. A. Proctor, *Legends and Lyrics*, 1858; originally began, 'I thank thee, O my God, who made,' but altd. as here in *Hymnal Companion*, 1877. Often abr. now to 3 st., om. sts. 3, 4, 5.

US & CAN: BP107: CW109/- : L447: M50: P73/409/- • ENG: An581: B502: CH441/146: CP62: M524

ADELAIDE ANNE PROCTOR, b. Bloomsbury (London), 30 x 1825, d. of B. W. Proctor, who was a writer under pen-name Barry Cornwall, and friend of Charles Lamb & Charles Dickens; first poems by A. A. P. pubd. by Dickens in *Household Words*; her most famous lyric is 'The Lost Chord.' Became R.C., 1852; worked much among the poor of London. † London 2 ii 1864 (38).

467. MY GOD, MY FATHER, MAKE ME STRONG

6 st. 888.4

F. Mann, sung in St. Martin-in-the-Fields, London, before 1928, since it is then referred to by the then Vicar (Rev. Pat McCormick) in an obituary appreciation; first published in *Songs of Praise*, 1931. Based on 462, but designed, like 430, to replace resignation by resolution.

US & CAN: • ENG: An574: B480: BB357: CP530

FREDERICK MANN, b. in Devonshire, 1846, is known to have begun his working life as a Free Church minister; later Ord. C/E, Vicar of Ewell, Surrey, Chaplain of Claybury Asylum. He was Chairman of the Croydon branch of the Guild of Health, and had a special interest in psychical research. The fact that no biography of him appears in *Songs of Praise Discussed*, the companion book to the hymnal that first published his hymn, itself published soon after his death, suggests that he wished to keep biographical details private. He was written of by the late Canon Harold Anson, Master of the Temple, with high appreciation; Anson's article in the Guild of Health Quarterly is the only source of information now available. † Croydon, Surrey, 20 vii 1928.

468. MY GOD, MY KING, THY VARIOUS PRAISE

6 st. LM

I. Watts (10), Ps. 145, first version, in *Psalms of David* . . . , 1719; 'The greatness of God.' Not strictly a qualifier, but long neglected in standard hymn books it has recently begun to return to favor through English school hymn books, being included in *Public School H. Bk.*, 1919, 1941, *Clarendon H. Bk.*, 1936, *Wellington College H. Bk.*, 1937, *Winchester Coll. H. Bk.*, 1962, and *Hymns for Church & School*, 1964. Also in Irish *Ch. Hymnal*, 1960, *Hymns for Celebration*, 1974 and *Westminster Praise*, 1976. All omit st. 4, some st. 5 also, and all agree on tune ST. BARTHOLOMEW.

US & CAN: • ENG: BB13: CP*65: NC161

469. MY HOPE IS BUILT ON NOTHING LESS

6 st. 88.88.88

E. Mote, *Hymns of Praise* . . . , 1836; *CH* has 3 st., others 4. The refrain came into his mind while walking to work in Holborn (London), before he was ordained; during the day he completed 4 st. A friend, asking him the following Sunday to visit his sick wife, and being unable to find his hymnal, agreed that they should sing these verses, which cheered her so much that the friend asked for a copy; when sending the copy, Mote added the last 2 sts.

US & CAN: BP404: B333: L385: M222: P -/368/- • ENG: An527: CH 697/411

EDWARD MOTE, b. London, 21 i 1797, after some years of professional life was Ord. Baptist and ministered 26 years at Horsham, Sussex. Wrote about 100 original hymns which were published in the 1836 book above and in *A New Selection of Gospel Hymns* . . . (no date). † Horsham, 13 xi 1874 (77).

470. MY JESUS, AS THOU WILT

3 st. 6.6.6.6 D

German: B. Schmolck (400), MEIN JESU, WIE DU WILLT, 11 st. in *Heilige Flamme*, 1704.

Tr. in 7 st. by J. Borthwick in *Hymns from the Land of Luther* (70); now norm. 3 st. using sts. 1, 4, 7 (1, 5, 11 of original).

US & CAN: CW408/- : L580: M167: P280/367/- • ENG:

471. MY MASTER WAS SO VERY POOR

3 st. LM-alt.

H. Lee, *Junior School Hymnal*, 1927.

US & CAN: B103: CW216/152: H*58: P497/-/- • ENG:

HARRY LEE, b. Canton, Ohio, 17 xii 1875; Sch. and taught in country schools in Ohio and W. Virginia; later, after marriage, bookkeeper in Canton and assistant to the Rector of an Episcopal Church. Helped to found Briar Brae social settlement in Canton, and founded a similar settlement later in New York City; served with Red Cross in World War I. Best known literary work was *The Little Poor Man*, prize-winning poetic drama on St. Francis of Assisi. † New York, 19 xii 1942 (67).

472. MY SHEPHERD SHALL SUPPLY MY NEED

6 st. SM   **PCH 42**

I. Watts (10), Ps. 23 in *Psalms of David . . .* , 1719; 'God our Shepherd'; the psalm really ends at st. 5, st. 6 being an addition to it, and perhaps the most inspired such addition ever made. Like 468 and 477, returning to favor after long neglect, largely through American enterprise and its association with the now famous tune from *Southern Harmony*.

US & CAN: CW -/10: H*29: P -/-/477: W182 • ENG: CP50

473. MY SONG IS LOVE UNKNOWN

7 st. 6.6.6.6.4.44.4   **PCH 431**

S. Crossman (345), *A Young Man's Meditation*, 1664. First as a hymn in *Anglican Hymn Book*, 1868, but ignored by all mainstream Anglican books until *Hymns A & M*, 1950. Full text norm. in Britain; abr. in U.S.

US & CAN: BP171: Can442: B486: H*27: L65: Pm169: W183 • ENG: AM -/102: An155: B143: BB84: CH -/224: CP128: E*27: M144: NC166: PL178

474. MY SOUL, BE ON THY GUARD

4 st. SM

G. Heath, *Hymns & Poetic Essays . . .* , Bristol, 1781; text altd. to present form in early 19 c. British hymnals, but not now found at all in Britain.

US & CAN: CW370/- : H555: L559: M246: P -/363/- • ENG:

GEORGE HEATH, b. about 1745, Sch. Dissenting Academy, Exeter (England); Ord. Presb., and served for a time as minister at Honiton, Devon, but dismissed for misbehavior. Later Unit. minister. Published the above book of poems and a *History of Bristol*. † 1822.

475. MY SOUL, THERE IS A COUNTRY

            PCH 426

H. Vaughan, *Silex Scintillans*, II, 1655. First as a hymn in *Worship Song*, 1896, where text is discreetly altd. to 7.6.7.6 from its orig. irregular meter. Tune set in 1905 edn. of that book is that mostly used now. First in orig. text, 5 st., same tune, *Oxford Hymn Book*, 1908, but popularity really began with its inclusion in *Songs of Praise*, 1925.

US & CAN: Can181 • ENG: AM -/286: BB526: CH463/693: CP356: E*82: M466

HENRY VAUGHAN, b. Llansaintffraed, Brecon (Wales), 17 iv 1622; Sch. Jesus Coll., Oxf., and studied law in London. Imprisoned with twin brother as royalist in Civil War. Later practised medicine in home town. Ascribed his Christian conviction to George Herbert (137). A

notable religious poet, he signed himself 'Henry Vaughan the Silurist,' taking the cognomen from the Silures, ancient inhabitants of S. Wales; this probably also suggested the title of his collections of poems above, which is Latin for 'Flint giving sparks.' † Skethiog, Brecon, 23 iv 1695 (73).

476. MY SPIRIT LONGS FOR THEE

4 st. 6.6.6.6

J. Byrom (119), posth., *Miscellaneous Poems*, 1773; originally a pair of poems, the first beginning 'My Spirit longeth for thee,' and called 'The Wish'; the second, 'Cheer up, desponding soul,' 'The Answer'; both in 4 st. The *Oxford Hymn Book*, 1908, gives both parts. Pt. 1 as above is the form in common use. Throughout the poem (but not between pts. 1 and 2) the last line of each st. is the first of the next. First as a hymn in *English Hymnal*, 1906.

US & CAN: M508: P -/321/- • ENG: AM -/89: B181: BB531: CH456/- : CP296: E443: M467

477. NATURE WITH OPEN VOLUME STANDS

6 st. LM   **PCH 39**

I. Watts (10), *Hymns . . .* , 1707, Book III: 'Christ Crucified, the Wisdom and Power of God.' This did not appear in any hymnal in Britain or America between 1900 (*Baptist Hymnal*, British) and 1951 (*Congregational Praise*); but, like 468 and 472, is now returning to favor, being found in certain supplemental hymnals, in addition to those below, such as *Ecumenical Praise* (1977) and *Westminster Praise* (1976) in the U.S., and *Hymns for Celebration* (1974) in Britain. Its revival among the people of Watts' own communion is attributable to its appearance in a private supplemental hymnal used at Mansfield College, Oxford, compiled about 1934 for college services by the then Principal, Nathaniel Micklem (724). St. 4 of the original is now always omitted in st. 5 'Christ my Saviour' is normally read for 'God the Saviour.'

US & CAN: • ENG: An156: CP129: E*28: M*48

NEAR THE CROSS HER VIGIL KEEPING: see 876.

478. NEARER, MY GOD, TO THEE

5 st. 6.4.6.4.66.4   **PCH 277**

S. F. Adams, written 1840, published in *Hymns & Anthems* (ed. Fox), 1841; based on the story of Jacob at Bethel (Gen. 28). Two associations, both now beginning to fade, projected this fine text into top-popularity. The first was the tune of J. B. Dykes to which it was set in *Hymns Ancient & Modern* 1861, the hymn being there given in 3 st. The other was the story of its being sung when the *Titanic* was sinking in 1912.

The truth about the tune played by the ship's band on that occasion will probably never be known in full. The confusion arises quite naturally because the report was that the band played the hymn, 'Nearer, my God, to thee,' which of course they cannot possibly have done. They must have played the tune associated with 'Nearer, my God, to thee,' and everything depends on which tune it occurred to them to play. If they were Americans, the tune was certainly that of Lowell Mason. If they were English, it will probably have been either that of J. B. Dykes or the equally well known one (but known in different circles) by Sir Arthur Sullivan. The story is engagingly complicated by a parallel report that the band played 'The Episcopal tune AUTUMN.' This is commented on by Sir Ronald Johnson in the Bulletin of the Hymn Society (Gt. Britain) #129, February, 1974. No tune of the name of AUTUMN is known to Episcopals or anybody else, but Sir Ronald ingeniously suggested that the tune referred to was AUGHTON (*H* 426), which goes with 'He leadeth me' (276). This does not seem to help with the mystery about 'Nearer, my God, to Thee'; but it really seems probable that the band played more than one hymn, if they played at all. It is likely, then, that they played what they could play easily, and play without scores. If 'He leadeth me' occurred to them, that is a hymn of American origin which the English had come to know through the missions of American evangelists. The tune to 'Nearer, my God, to thee' which is nearest to that in association is the American tune by Lowell Mason. Therefore possibly the band's knowledge of hymnody was derived either from American practice or from the field of British hymn-singing which had been influenced by America. No doubt they played several hymns, including some that are now un-remembered.

US & CAN: BP519: Can254: B333: CW329/- : H465: L577: M263: P261/326/- : Pm351 ● ENG: AM277/352: B598: BB332: CH475/689: CP480: E444: M468

SARAH FULLER ADAMS (nee FLOWER), b. Harlow, Essex, 22 ii 1805; her father was editor of the *Cambridge Intelligencer and Political Review*; m. 1843 William Bridges Adams, civil engineer and inventor (of, among other devices, the 'fishplate' for joining railway metals). The book containing her 13 hymns, including that above, was a Unitarian publication; she also wrote a catechism for children, 'The Flock at the Fountain' and a dramatic religious poem, *Vivia Perpetua*. † London, 14 viii 1848 (43).

479. NEVER FURTHER THAN THY CROSS

6 st. 7.7.7.7   **PCH 285**

Elisabeth Rundle Charles, *The Family Treasury*, February 1860; first in a hymnal, *Congregational Psalmist*, 2nd ed., 1886; an unusual and distinguished combination of evangelical fervour and poetic discipline.

US & CAN: M430 ● ENG: An560: CP453: M198

ELISABETH RUNDLE CHARLES, b. Tavistock, Devon, 2 i 1828 (nee Rundle); painter, musician, poet and author; Sch. privately, first literary work was a translation of a hymn by Neander (9) made at age 22 in 1850, which has not survived. Wrote much to spread knowledge of history in popular form, including works on Luther and the Wesleys. m. Andrew Paton Charles, Barrister. † Hampstead (London), 28 iii (or 1 iv) 1896 (68).

480. NEW EVERY MORNING IS THE LOVE

LM-coup.   **PCH 121**

J. Keble (83), *The Christian Year*, 1827. The first poem in this collection is one beginning 'Hues of the rich unfolding morn,' from which this hymn is taken. Of its 16 st., all current hymnals select sts. beginning at st. 6, following the fashion set by *Hymns A & M* in 1861, though formerly some began at st. 5, 'O timely happy, timely wise.' Selections differ. *EH* has longest, 7 st. (6-9, 13, 14, 16) but norm. vn. is 5 st. (6-8, 14, 16). Note references to Lam. 3:26 and Gen. 22:8.

US & CAN: BP548: Can360: H155: L201: M499: P31/45/- : Pm36 ● ENG: AM4: An43: B678: BB408: CH259/47: CP596: E260: M927

481. NONE OTHER LAMB

3 st. 8.10 10. 4   **PCH 293**

C. Rossetti (335), *The Face of the Deep: A Devotional Commentary on the Apocalypse*; Rev. 5:6, 1892. First as a hymn in *Methodist H. Book* (Brit.) 1904.

US & CAN: BP410: P504/-/- ● ENG: An617: B169: CP308: M94

482. NOT ALONE FOR MIGHTY EMPIRE

4 st. 8.7.8.7 D   **PCH 539**

W. P. Merrill, 1909; printed in *The Continent*, 1911. 'It came out of a Thanksgiving Service in Chicago at which Jenkin Lloyd Jones offered a prayer which impressed me greatly by its emphasis on the spiritual national blessings and assets.'

US & CAN: CW597/- : H145: L345: M548: P416/512/479: CLB318 ● ENG:

WILLIAM PIERSON MERRILL, b. East Orange, N.J., 10 i 1867; Sch. Rutgers Univ., N.J. & Union Th. Sem., New York; Ord. Presb., 1890; served at Chestnut Hill, Pa., 1890, Chicago, '95; Brick Presbyterian, New

York, 1895-1938. President, Trustees of the Peace Union from 1915. Author of many popular theological books. † New York, 29 vi 1954 (87).

483. NOT ALWAYS ON THE MOUNT MAY WE

5 st. LM-coup.

F. L. Hosmer, sts. 1-3 and 5 in Chicago *Unity*, XIII, 1884; st. 4 added in *Thought of God*, 1885. Brought to England by W. G. Horder in *The Treasury of Hymns*, 1896.

US & CAN: Can493: CW -/333: H571: L535 ● ENG: AM -/561: An283

FREDERICK LUCIAN HOSMER, b. Framingham, Mass., 16 x 1840; Sch. Harvard Univ. and Div. Sch.; Ord. Unit., 1869; served at First Congl. Ch., Northboro, Mass., '69-'72; Second Congl. Ch., Quincy, Ill., '72-7; after a year and a half of study and travel, Church of Unity, Cleveland, Ohio, '78-'92; St. Louis, Mo., '92-9; First Unit. Ch., Berkeley, California, 1900-4. Wrote at least 50 hymns, mostly in the 1885 book above, and ed. with W. C. Gannett and J. V. Blake, *Unity Hymns & Carols*, 1911. † Berkeley, 7 vi 1929 (88).

484. NOT FAR BEYOND THE SEA, NOR HIGH

4 st. 88.6.88.6   **PCH 479**

G. B. Caird (33), written 1947, printed in *New Songs* (Redhill, ed. Massey), 1962; first in a hymnal in the two 1969 Supplements below, *AM** and *M**. Deut. 30:15.

US & CAN: Can96 ● ENG: AM*68: CP*67: M*49

485. NOT FOR OUR SINS ALONE

5 st. 6.6.6.6.6.6   **PCH 242**

H. Twells (57), *Hymns Ancient & Modern*, 1889.

US & CAN: ● ENG: AM528/324: An490: B449: BB345: M743

486. NOT WHAT THESE HANDS HAVE DONE

12 st. SM

H. Bonar (81), *Hymns of Faith & Life*, 2nd series, 1861; 'Salvation in Christ alone.' Norm. sel. is sts. 1-5 and 7.

US & CAN: ● ENG: An491: B450: CH -/410: M81

NOW ALL THE WOODS ARE SLEEPING: see 863.

487. NOW CHEER OUR HEARTS THIS EVENTIDE

2 st. LM-coup.

R. Bridges (9), *Yattendon Hymnal*, 1899, based on the German hymn ACH BLEIB' BEI UNS, HERR JESU CHRIST, usually attributed to N. Selnecker. A hymn beginning thus is in *Geistliche Psalmen*, Nurnberg, 1611, in 9 st., some of which are by Selnecker. But st. 1 is actually from Melanchthon's *Vespera iam venit*, c. 1530; and st. 9 forms part of a hymn in Selnecker's *Der Psalter*, 1572. Bridges paraphrased Melanchthon in st. 1 and Selnecker in his st. 2.

US & CAN: Can368 ● ENG: BB527: CH278/642

PHILIP MELANCHTHON (born Schwarzerd), b. 1497, Sch. Heidelberg & Tubingen; prof. Greek at Wittemberg, 1518; became friend and popularizer of Luther, and accompanied him in several famous disputations and colloquies; a leading figure on the Reformed side in the Diet of Augsburg, and mostly responsible for the wording of the Augsburg Confession, 1530; more in the tradition of the humanistic Renaissance than most German Reformers, and more conciliatory with the Catholic Establishment. Assisted in first German trsln. of the Bible and in writing commentaries on it. Tutor of Selnecker below. † Wittemberg, 1560.

NICOLAUS SELNECKER, b. Hersbruck, nr. Nurnberg, 6 xii 1528, and at age 12 organist of the City Chapel there. Sch. Wittemberg, and favorite pupil of Melanchthon. Ord. Luth., court preacher at Dresden, 1557; prof. theol., Jena, '65, Leipzig, '68, also pastor of St. Thomas' Church there (later famous as the working place of J. S. Bach 1723-50); court preacher, Wolfenbuttel, '70-4; returned to Leipzig, '74; collaborator on Formula of Concord, an important confessional document, 1577; but in 1588 deprived of offices in Leipzig and became superintendent minister at Hildesheim; once again returned to Leipzig and † there 24 v 1592 (63).

NOW GOD BE WITH US, FOR THE NIGHT IS FALLING: see 845.

488. NOW I HAVE FOUND THE GROUND WHEREIN

6 st. 8.8.8.8.88

German: J. A. Rothe, ICH HABE NUN DEN GRUND GEFUNDEN, 10 st. 9.8.9.8.88, in Zinzendorf's *Christ-Catholisches Singe- und Bet-Buchlein* ('Universal Hymn and Prayer Book for Christians'), 1727 (see 371).

US & CAN: ● ENG: An528: B451: CP468: M375

Tr. J. Wesley (1), *Hymns & Sacred Poems*, 1740, using sts. 1, 2, 4, 5, 6, 10; full text is in *M(Brit.)* and *CP*.

JOHANN ANDREAS ROTHE, b. Lissa, Silesia, 12 v 1688; Sch. Univ. Leipzig; Ord. Luth. 1712, Gorlitz; tutor to family Schweinitz at Leube nearby, 1718; presented to living of Berthelsdorf by Zinzendorf, '22; here the Moravian community at Herrnhut (which so greatly influenced J. Wesley) was part of his parish; later fell out with Zinzendorf & moved '37 to nearby Hermsdorf; appointed pastor at Thommendorf (asst. '39, senior pastor '42) and † there 6 vii 1758 (70).

NOW IT IS EVENING: TIME TO REST FROM LABOR: see 845.

489. NOW JOIN WE TO PRAISE THE CREATOR

6 st. 9.8.9.8 anap.

F. Kaan (202), *Pilgrim Praise*, 1966, 1971.

US & CAN: BP568: Can387: W187 ● ENG: AM*60: CP*71: NC170

NOW, MY TONGUE, THE MYSTERY TELLING: see 867.

490. NOW ON LAND AND SEA DESCENDING

2 st. 8.7.8.7

S. Longfellow (7) *Vespers*, 1859; associated with a 'Russian air' first pub. 1818 by J. A. Stevenson, which requires a 2-line refrain plus repetition of lines 3-4 of each quatrain, leaving an impression of 8.7.8.7 D.

US & CAN: CW141/- : M505: P -/67/480: Pm52: W188 ● ENG:

491. NOW PRAISE WE GREAT AND FAMOUS MEN

7 st. 8.7.8.7 iamb.

W. G. Tarrant, *Songs of the Devout*, 1912; full text in Britain; abr. in U.S. Ecclus. 44.

US & CAN: CW603/- : M532: P491/-/- : Pm476 ● ENG: B648: CP667: M896

WILLIAM GEORGE TARRANT, b. Pembroke Dock, S. Wales, 2 vii 1853; Sch. at an orphanage in Birmingham, both parents being dead when he was 6; apprenticed to a silversmith, but entered Unitarian Home Missionary College, Manchester, '79; Ord. Unit., '83; served Unit. Ch. Wandsworth, London till 1920. Ed. *The Inquirer*, 1887-97 and 1918-27, and co-editor of *Essex Hall Hymnal*, 1890. † Wandsworth, London, 15 i 1928 (74).

492. NOW THANK WE ALL OUR GOD

3 st. 6.7.6.7.6.6.6.6
PCH 191

German: M. Rinkart, NUN DANKET ALLE GOTT; earliest surviving text is in *Praxis Pietatis Melica*, 1647, but it is assumed to have been also in the (lost) first ed. of 1636, thus being a hymn of praise, originally designed as a grace at table, written in the darkest days of the Thirty Years' War (1618-48).

Tr. C. Winkworth (14), *Chorale-Book for England*, 1863. Now tr. into a great number of languages, and never absent from English & German-speaking hymnals: it may be the most famous hymn in the world.

US & CAN: BP103: Can197: B234: CW598/99: H276: L443: M49: P459/9/481: Pm29: CLB429: W189 ● ENG: AM379: An22: B18: BB277: CH29/368: CP42: E533: M10: NC171: PL93

MARTIN RINKART, b. Eilenburg, Saxony, 23 iv 1586; Sch. Latin Sch., Eilenburg and St. Thomas, Leipzig, where he was a chorister; and Univ. Leipzig; Ord. Luth., cantor, later deacon, at Eisleben, pastor at Ardeborn, and 1617 archdeacon of Eilenburg; ministered there throughout the Thirty Years' War and is said to have buried 5,000 people, including his own wife, in the plague of 1637. Wrote a cycle of seven plays to celebrate the first centennial of the Reformation, 1617. † Eilenburg, 8 xii 1649 (63).

NOW THAT THE DAYLIGHT FILLS THE SKY   see 854.
NOW THAT THE DAYSTAR GLIMMERS BRIGHT

493. NOW THE DAY IS OVER

8 st. 6.5.6.5
PCH 312

S. Baring-Gould, for the children of his parish (see below); *Church Times*, 16 ii 1867; *Hymns Ancient & Modern*, 1868; tune EUDOXIA always associated with it in Britain, is his own, said to be arranged from a German song.

US & CAN: CW 149/- : H172: L231: M495: P35/51/- : Pm51: CLB330 ● ENG: AM346/431: An59: B698: BB420: CH288/653: CP627: E603: M944

SABINE BARING-GOULD, b. Exeter, 28 i 1834; Sch. Clare, Camb.; asstmaster at St. Barnabas Choir Sch., Pimlico, '57; similar appt. at Hurstpierpoint College, Sussex, to '64; Ord. C/E '65; curate at Horbury Bridge, Yorks, Dalton, Yorks, Thirsk, Yorks, '65-71; Rector, East Mersea, Essex, '71; and of Lew Trenchard, Som., where he inherited the family estates, '81. Very prolific writer of wide interests. Wrote 15-vol. *Lives of the Saints*; pioneer collector of folk songs & carols a generation before C. Sharp and Vaughan Williams. † Lew Trenchard, 2 i 1924 (89).

494. NOW THE GREEN BLADE RISETH

4 st. 6.5.6.5 with refrain 4.6.6.5

J. M. C. Crum, *Oxford Book of Carols*, 1928, for the French Carol tune *Noel Nouvelet*.

US & CAN: BP195: M441: CLB285 ● ENG: BB109: CH -/278: NC172: PL201

JOHN MACLEOD CAMPBELL CRUM, b. More Old Hall, Cheshire, 12 x 1872; Sch. Eton and New Coll., Oxf.; Ord. C/E; Chaplain to Bp. Francis Paget of Oxford, then Vicar of Mentmore, Bucks; Rector of Farnham, 1913; Canon of Canterbury, '28-'43. Published works on Scripture and books for children; especially known for his children's hymns, most of which appeared in *Church & School Hymnal*, 1926, and the most remarkable of which is quoted at PCH 483. † Farnham, Surrey, 19 xii 1958 (86).

495. NOW THE LABOURER'S TASK IS O'ER

6 st. 7.7.7.7.88

J. Ellerton (80), *Church Hymns*, 1871. Full text only in *A & M (S)*; elsewhere abr. to 5 st. or fewer. *M(Brit.)* has a st. beginning 'There the Shepherd . . .' wh. comes from a revised vn. in *Select Hymns for Church*

& *Home* (1885). Author said that the hymn was inspired by one by G. Moultrie (388), beginning 'Brother, now thy toils are o'er,' in *People's Hymnal*, 1867; this was in 7.7.7.7.77, and is used, but with Ellerton's opening line, in *EH*.

US & CAN: H224: L296: P440/-/- ● ENG: AM401/467: BB448: E358†: M976

NOW WOODS AND WOLDS ARE SLEEPING: see 863.

496. O BEAUTIFUL FOR SPACIOUS SKIES

4 st. CMD

K. L. Bates, written 1893 in Colorado Springs after an expedition to Pike's Peak, where the opening lines came to her after 'one ecstatic gaze' from the summit which, in the rarefied air, was all the party found possible. Printed in *The Congregationalist*, 1895, and an altd. vn. in the *Boston Transcript*, 19 xi 1904. The final form, as now used, was written by her when she wrote the history of the hymn for the Boston Athenaeum Library. The 'alabaster cities' in st. 4 refers to the Columbian World's Exposition at Chicago, 1893, which the authoress had seen on her way to Colorado. This has more recently been adopted as a very popular patriotic hymn. The tune now inseparable from it was originally written for 'O Mother dear, Jerusalem' (see 344), but was given this new association about 1915.

US & CAN: B508: CW550/374: L346: M543: P411/510/483: Pm440: CLB321: W191 ● ENG:

KATHARINE LEE BATES, b. Falmouth, Mass., 12 viii 1859, d. of a Congl. minister; Sch. Wellesley; taught at Natick School and Dana Hall, both in Mass. Instructor in English, Wellesley, 1886; later head of dept., until retirement, 1925. Honorary doctor of Oberlin, Wellesley and Middlebury. † Wellesley, Mass., 28 iii 1929 (69).

O BLESSED LIFE! THE HEART AT REST: see 419.

O BLEST CREATOR OF THE LIGHT: see 861.

O BREAD TO PILGRIMS GIVEN: see 864.

497. O BROTHER MAN, FOLD TO THY HEART THY BROTHER

11.10.11.10

J. G. Whittier (11), *Labor and Other Poems*, 1850: James 1:27, beginning 'The Pagan's Myths through marble lips are spoken,' written in 15 st. in 1848 as an expression of contempt for pagan worship. First as a hymn in *Fellowship Hymn Book* (Britain), 1909, using sts. 13, 11, 14; in some later selections st. 15 was added (as st. 4).

US & CAN: Can299: CW515/264: H493: L539: M199: P403/474/484: Pm410 ● ENG: B662: BB376: CH485/460: CP541: M911

498. O CHRIST (JESUS) OUR HOPE, OUR HEARTS' DESIRE

6 st. CM					**PCH 139**

Latin: JESU NOSTRA REDEMPTIO, 6 st. LM, probably 8th cent.

Tr. J. Chandler (52), *Hymns of the Primitive Church*, 1837; in *A & M* and others, JESUS, OUR HOPE. . . .

US & CAN: L400 ● ENG: AM150/146: An200: BB126: CH -/302: E144

499. O CHRIST WHO ART THE LIGHT AND DAY

6 st. LM

Latin: CHRISTE QUI LUX ES ET DIES, before 8th cent., Office Hymn for Sunday Compline; one of the most widely used of all Latin hymns in

medieval liturgies.

Tr. now exists in 2 versions with same opening line, one in *A & M*, the other in other sources, both based on tr. of W. J. Copeland in *Hymns of the Week*, 1848, beginning O CHRIST THAT ART. . . . (The ascription of tr. to R. R. Terry in *CH³* is an error.)

US & CAN: H163 ● ENG: AM95: BB421: CH -/652: E81

WILLIAM JOHN COPELAND, b. Chigwell, Essex, 1 ix 1804; Sch. St. Paul's Sch. & Trinity, Oxf.; Fellow of Trinity; Ord. C/E 1827; curate of Littlemore, Oxford (where for a time J. H. Newman lived—see 196); rector of Farnham, Essex, 1849 to † there 25 viii 1885 (80).

500. O COME, ALL YE FAITHFUL

Stress 2-2-4 D					**PCH 175**

Latin: ADESTE FIDELES. Despite many fanciful ascriptions in older books, the earliest source of one of the world's most celebrated hymns (with its tune) is dated c. 1744, the work of J. F. Wade, to whom the tune is ascribed with some certainty, the text with less. The text there is in 4 st. (1, 2, 7, 8 below), with 'Venite adorate in the refrain, and these correspond with the 4 st. most often found in modern books. But the hymn now appears in a longer form, and the only accessible version of the full Latin text, with all later accretions, in 8 st., is the *Westminster Hymnal*, 1940. In Latin the sts. begin as follows:

1. Adeste fideles
2. Deum de Deo
3. En grege relicto
4. Stella duce Magi
5. Aeterni Parentis
6. Pro nobis egeno
7. Cantet nunc 'io'
8. Ergo qui natus.

Of the interpolated sts., 3 and 6 are by Abbé E. J. F. Borderies (tr. 'See how the Shepherds' and 'Child for us sinners') written 1793, as given in the *Office de St. Omer*, 1822; st. 5 above (tr. only by Ronald Knox in the *Westminster Hymnal*) is also by Borderies and stands as st. 4 in the 1822 text. St. 4 above, (tr. 'Lo, star-led chieftains') is anonymous in *Paroissien Romain* (Paris) 1868. So the longest text available in English (except that just mentioned), namely that in the *English Hymnal* (#614) has 7 st. of which 1, 2, 6, 7, (1, 2, 7, 8 above) are from the Wade ms. of 1744, sts. 3, 5 (3, 6 above) are by Borderies, and 4 (4) is anonymous 1868. The Latin text in part is found in the U.S.A. in *Pm*, *CLB* and *W*. (Occasionally the cheerful line 'Cantet nunc io' appears as 'Cantet nunc hymnos'—a 19 c. corruption of the original.)

Tr. O COME, ALL YE FAITHFUL, is the second version, much altered, of an original in 4 st. made by F. Oakeley in 1841 for the Margaret Chapel, London (now All Saints', Margaret Street). It first appeared in Murray's *Hymnal*, 1852. Originally it began YE FAITHFUL, APPROACH YE. But the vn. of sts. 1, 2, 7, 8 now best known is the alteration of this made for *Hymns Ancient & Modern*, 1861. St. 6, *pro nobis egeno*, was first tr. by W. T. Brooks in *The Altar Hymnal*, 1884; sts. 3 and 4 were tr. by P. Dearmer (88) for the *English Hymnal*, 1906.

The irregularity of the meter and consequent difficulty of fitting syllables to the tune (never noticed now) caused W. Mercer (248) in his *Church Psalter & Hymn Book*, 1854, to modify Oakeley's version, using much of the 1852 text but filling in syllables to ensure uniformity of meter. This is now recognizable by the 2nd st., 'True God of true God,' as still found in certain Eng. hymn books (The whole version is at #55, second style, in the *Church Hymnary*, 1927).

While Eng. books now always use the 1861 text as expanded in 1884 and 1906, certain variations appear in Canada and the U.S. The trsln. is sometimes modified, (e.g. *Worshipbook*, 1972) with the same purpose as Mercer's, and the stanza-selection is more variable. Thus in *P(55)* and *UCC Hymnal* we have sts. 1, 7, 8 only; in *P(33)*, *Worshipbook*, *M*, *L* and *Worship II*, 1, 2, 7, 8 (as most Eng. books); in Pilgrim and *CW* (1970), 1, 7, 2, 8; in *CLB*, 1, 7, 6, 8; in *Can* 1971, 1, 2, 7, 6, 8; in *BP*, 1, 2, 3, 7, 8, and in *Hymnal-1940*, 1, 2, 7, 3, 6, 8. Only in the U.S. and Canada is the order of stanzas altered, but this brings out the important formal point that in the 7 st. version of *EH* the hymn makes the original 4 st. dogmatic and theological statement a framework for the legendary material about the shepherds and the Magi and the perhaps slightly incongruous moralistic verse *pro nobis egeno*, while editors on the other side of the Atlantic thought it right to place the angelic choir before the shepherds and the Magi because that is how the story is told in Luke 2. Certainly for ordinary use sts. 1, 2, 7, 8 make a wholly satisfactory hymn (i.e. the original 1744 sts.); if the full version were ever used the most logical order would be 1, 2, 5, 3, 4, 6, 7, 8, since 5, the least familiar, properly follows the thought of 3 and forms part of the dogmatic framework. We quote it here in Knox's translation:

> The splendour eternal of eternal Godhead
> veiled with infirmities of flesh we see;
> hiding his glory swaddling clothes he weareth:
> O come . . . . &c.

The TUNE inseparable from the text—the only 20th century hymnal known to the writer that contains an alternative is *Arundel Hymns*, 1901—was known to Eng. protestants long before the Latin was translated; having been in use in the Chapel of the Portuguese Embassy in London, since at latest 1780. This was one of the very few places where R. C. worship was permitted in Britain before 1833, and was a considerable musical center. The tune was overheard by Prot. musicians and soon appeared in their hymnals to such hymns as 'Begone, unbelief' (74) and 'How firm a foundation' (298—a practice that still survives in the U.S.A.). Since Catholic and Protestant cultures did not meet at that time no incongruity seemed to be involved. Oakeley's translation, however, was made under the influence of the Oxford Movement (83), of which his church was a leading example, and the hymn is therefore symbolic of the meeting of cultures which that Movement fostered and which hymnody has always promoted.

All the research into the origins of this hymn was conducted by Dom John Stéphan and embodied in his book, *Adeste Fideles*, 1947. For further details see Frost, *Historical Companion to Hymns Ancient & Modern*, 1961, at #593.

US & CAN: BP120: Can415: CW205/121: H12: L42: M386: P116/170/486: Pm123: CLB227: W193 ● ENG: AM59/59,593: An106: B104: BB55: CH55 (2vns.)/191: CP85: E28, 614: M118: NC173: PL139

WILLIAM THOMAS BROOKE, b. London, 9 i 1848, Sch. City of London School, brought up Baptist; later joined C/E and edited 2 collections of hymns. † Stratford, Essex, 23 ii 1917 (69).

FREDERICK OAKELEY, b. Shrewsbury, 5 ix 1802; Sch. Christ Ch. Oxf.; Fellow of Balliol, '27; Ord. C/E; prebendary of Lichfield, Vicar of Margaret Chapel, London; a leader in Oxford Movement (83) and friend of J. H. Newman (196). Became R.C., 1845, after wh. time he spent his life working among the London poor. Canon of Westminster pro-Cathedral (as then known), '52. Author & liturgist. † London, 21 i 1880 (77).

JOHN FRANCIS WADE, whose name was dredged out of obscurity by Dom John Stéphan (above), was a music copyist in the Catholic centre at Douay, France. All we know of him comes from an entry in the Catholic Directory for 1787 which records that he † 16 viii 1786 aged 75, and recalls with pride his skill as a writer of manuscripts.

501. O COME AND MOURN WITH ME AWHILE

12 st. LM-alt. PCH 212

F. W. Faber (175), *Jesus and Mary*, 1849. Longest selection is now in *EH*, of 8 st. (om. 6, 7, 8, 11); elsewhere 6 st. or fewer.

US & CAN: BP187: CW233/168: H74: L86: P159/193/- : Pm114 ● ENG: AM114/113: An173: B144: CH96/243: CP135: E111: M187: NC175

502. O COME, O COME, IMMANUEL

88.88.88 PCH 172

Latin: VENI VENI IMMANUEL, *Psalteriolum Cantionum Catholicarum* (Cologne) 1710, Appendix. It is a metrical version in 5 st. of five of the seven 'Great O's of Advent.' These are a series of 7 antiphons (in post-Counter Reformation Catholic use, 8) appointed to be sung successively December 16-22 (or 23). In old mss. the order varies but it settled down to this:

(1)	*O Sapientia*	O Wisdom . . .
(2)	*O Adonai*	O Lord . . .
(3)	*O Radix Jesse*	O Root of Jesse . . .
(4)	*O Clavis David*	O Key of David
(5)	*O Oriens*	O Dayspring . . .
(6)	*O Rex Gentium*	O King of the Nations . . .
(7)	*O Emmanuel*	

The initials of each cue-word, read backwards, in the Latin form the phrase ERO CRAS, (Tomorrow I shall be there), which no doubt determined the accepted order. The Latin text versifies ## 7, 3, 5, 4, 2 in that order.

The biblical background of the antiphons is: (1) (probably) Prov. 8: 22ff; (2) Ex. 20:1ff; (3) Is. 11:1; (4) Rev. 3:7; (5) Lk. 1:78; (6) (whose opening is more fully *O Rex gentium et desideratus earum*), Hag. 2:7; (7) Is. 7:14. Antiphon 8, O VIRGO VIRGINUM, is not used in the hymn.

Tr.: All trs. in use now begin, O COME, O COME, IMMANUEL, a line not directly attributable to any author, the story being as follows:

(a) J. M. Neale (2) in the *Hymnal Noted*, 1852, made a version in 5 st., following the Latin (7, 3, 5, 4, 2), beginning 'Draw nigh, draw nigh, Immanuel'; this was considerably altered by compilers of *Hymns Ancient & Modern*, 1861 into the 5 st. trsln. which is still the most familiar. This is used in *CP*, but there the order is altered to 7, 3, 5, 2, 4, bringing *O Adonai* (Exodus) earlier than *O Clavis* (Revelation).

(b) T. A. Lacey made a new trsln. for the *English Hymnal* (1906), using Neale's selection and order.

(c) The only version which goes beyond the Latin in paraphrasing all seven clauses is that of the Compilers of the *Hymnal-1940*, who use the order 7, 1, 2, 3, 4, 5, 6, thus deviating from the Latin only in placing 7 at the beginning (for good lyric reasons established by Neale) and in abandoning the argument of the latter part of #6 in their st. 7.

All these versions are associated with the tune used in Neale's *Hymnal Noted*, but not in the Latin source.

US & CAN: BP116: Can390: B78: CW182/108: H2 (c): L2: M354: P109/147/489 (a), 490 (b): Pm110: CLB210: W195 ● ENG: AM49: An83: B83: BB36: CH149/165: CP72: E8 (b): M257: NC176: PL131
(all (a) except where noted)

THOMAS ALEXANDER LACEY, b. Nottingham 20 xii 1853; Sch. Balliol, Oxf.; Ord. C/E 1876; asst. master, Wakefield Gram. Sch., and Denstone College; Vicar of Madingley, Cambridge, '94; Warden & Chaplain, London Diocesan Penitentiary, Highgate (London), 1903-19; Canon of Worcester, '18; member of ed. cttee., *English Hymnal* (1906). † Worcester, 6 xii 1931 (77).

503. O DAY OF GOD, DRAW NIGH

5 st. SM PCH 562

R. B. Y. Scott, leaflet of Fellowship for a Christian Social Order, 1937; *Hymns for Worship* (U.S.), 1939. St. 5 now always given as altd. in *Hymnal-1940*. Zeph. 1:14-18.

US & CAN: BP598: Can275: CW -/266: H525: M477: P -/-/492: Pm444: CLB520 ● ENG: AM*72: B187: BB24: CH -/511: M*52

ROBERT BALGARNIE YOUNG SCOTT, b. Toronto, 18 vii 1899; Sch. Univ. and Knox Coll., Toronto; Ord. Utd. Ch. Canada 1926; pastor at Long Branch, Ontario, then prof. O. T., Union Coll., Vancouver, '28; prof. O. T., United Coll., McGill Univ., Montreal, '31-55; prof. Religion, Univ. Princeton, '55-'68. Always active as worker and writer in field of social reform.

504. O DAY OF REST AND GLADNESS

6 st. 7.6.7.6 D

C. Wordsworth (27), *The Holy Year*, 1862. Norm. vn. altd. with omission of sts. 3-4 as in *Hymns A & M*, 1868, but *EH* subst. st. 3 for st. 5.

US & CAN: CW443/- : H474: L182: M488: P18/70/- ● ENG: AM36/41: An72: B275: CH268/- : CP609: E284: M659

505. O DEAREST LORD, THY SACRED HEAD

4 st. CM

H. E. Hardy, *The Divine Compassion*, 1930, with 'brow' for 'head.' 'The Sacred Wounds.' Orig. vn. in *Mirfield Mission H. Bk.*, 1936.

US & CAN: Can453 • ENG: AM -/436: An153: B516: CH -/252: M*53

HENRY ERNEST HARDY, also known as Brother Andrew of the Order of the Divine Compassion, b. Kaskuli, India, 7 i 1869; Sch. Keble, Oxf.; Ord. C/E 1895; asst. curate of St. Andrew's, Plaistow (London), then devoted himself to the work of his Order. † Watford, Herts, 31 iii 1946 (76).

506. O FATHER, ALL CREATING

4 st. 7.6.7.6 D

J. Ellerton (80), 29 i 1876, for wedding of Lady Elizabeth Grosvenor (d. of the Duke of Westminster), 2 Feb. *Church of England Hymnal*, 1880, and *Hymns A & M* 1889.

US & CAN: BP578: Can350: CW -/381: CLB399 • ENG: AM579/- : An 391: B622: BB221: CH326/600: E345: M776

O FOOD OF MEN WAYFARING
O FOOD THAT WEARY PILGRIMS LOVE   see 864.
O FOOD THAT WEARY TRAVELLERS LOVE

507. O FOR A CLOSER WALK WITH GOD

6 st. CM   **PCH 90**

W. Cowper (235), *Olney Hymns*, 1779; 'Walking with God: Gen. 5:24.' Sts. 3-4 sometimes omitted.

US & CAN: BP145: CW310: H416: L466: M268: P259/319/- : Pm349 • ENG: AM630/326: An147: B599: BB333: CH457/663: CP476: E445: M461

508. O FOR A FAITH THAT WILL NOT SHRINK

6 st. CM

W. H. Bathurst, *Hymns for Public and Private Use*, 1831; st. 4 norm. om.

US & CAN: BP444: B390: L395: M142: CLB491 • ENG: AM278/- : An 502: BB310: CH474/664

WILLIAM HILEY BATHURST, b. Clevedon, Bristol, 28 viii 1796; Sch. Winchester Coll. & Christ Ch. Oxf.; Ord. C/E 1810; Rector of Barwick, a living in the gift of his uncle; at this time he changed his name to Bathurst from Bragg, using the uncle's name; remained there until 1852 when retired to family estate at Lydney Park, Glos., where † 25 xi 1877 (81).

509. O FOR A HEART TO PRAISE MY GOD

8 st. CM

C. Wesley (1), *Hymns & Sacred Poems*, 1742; Ps. 51:10. Sts. 5 & 7 norm. om., sometimes also st. 6.

US & CAN: BP422: H414: L389: M282: P260/325/- : CLB389: W196 • ENG: AM549/325: An544: B600: BB334: CH459/85: CP439: E82: M550

510. O FOR A THOUSAND TONGUES TO SING

18 st. CM   **PCH 60**

C. Wesley (1), 21 May 1739: *Hymns & Sacred Poems*, 1740; 'For the Anniversary Day of one's Conversion,' beginning 'Glory to God, and praise, and love.' Beginning at st. 7 as above it has stood first in all Eng. Meth. hymnals since first edition, 1780, John Wesley being responsible for selection of sts. in that 1780 book. His choice was (9 st.) 7, 8, 9, 10, 11, 13, 14, 17, 18. Versions now vary so widely as to alter the impact of the hymn from book to book, reducing it sometimes from a celebration of conversion to a hymn of general praise. The selections are: (7 st.)

7-12, 1 (*CH²*, *L*); (6 st.) 7-12 (*M-U.S.*): 7, 8, 9, 11, 10, 14 and (*M-Brit.*); 7, 9, 10, 11, 12, 8 (*An*, *B*, *CH³*, *CP*, *E*); (5 st.) 7, 9, 10, 14, 8 (*BP*), 7, 9, 10, 8, 1 (*P³³*) and 7, 9, 11, 12, 8 (*AM*, *BB*, *Can*, *H-U.S.*); (4 st.) 7-10 (*B-U.S.*); 7, 8, 9, 11 (*CW²*), 7, 9, 8, 1 (*Wbk.*) and 7, 9, 10, 8 (*P⁵⁵*); (3 st.) 7, 8, 1 (*CW¹*, *Pm*).

US & CAN: BP247: Can48: B69: CW262/72: H325: L428: M1: P119/141/193: Pm223 • ENG: AM522/196: An270: B212: BB278: CH166/371: E446: CP180: M1

O GLADSOME LIGHT: see 869.

O GOD, CREATION'S SECRET FORCE
O GOD, CREATION'S STRENGTH AND STAY   see 854.

511. O GOD, BENEATH THY GUIDING HAND

6 st. LM-coup.

L. Bacon, 21 iv 1838, for a service in Center Congl. Ch., New Haven, Conn., combining bicentennials of church and city; it began 'The Sabbath morn was bright and calm.' Revised when included in the author's *Psalms & Hymns for Christian Use & Worship*, 1845, to 5 st. beginning as above; now further abr. to 4 st.

US & CAN: CW543/- : H148: M550: P462/523/495: Pm49 • ENG:

LEONARD BACON, b. 19 ii 1802, Detroit; Sch. Yale & Andover Theol. Sem.; Ord. Cong., 1824, First Ch., New Haven, where he stayed 41 years. Ed. *Independent* from inception, 1848-61; acting prof. of Theology, Yale Div. Sch., '66-71; then lecturer there in American ch. history. Wrote *The Genesis of the New England Churches*, 1874. † 2 ii 1881 New Haven (79).

512. O GOD OF BETHEL, BY WHOSE HAND

5 st. CM   **PCH 96**

Scottish Paraphrases, 1781 (76), #2, based on, but extensively revising, a hymn by P. Doddridge (64) beginning with the same line, but appearing in his *Hymns* (posth. 1755) as 'O God of Jacob . . .' being thus altd. by Job Orton, who edited that collection. 'Bethel' is orig. Paraphrases Gen. 28:20-2.

US & CAN: BP510: Can263: CW174/- : H497: L519: P98/342/496: Pm 389 • ENG: AM512/299: An561: B550: BB495: CH562/72: CP55: E447: M607

513. O GOD OF EARTH AND ALTAR

3 st. 7.6.7.6 D   **PCH 269**

G. K. Chesterton, for *English Hymnal*, 1906, printed earlier that year in *The Commonwealth*. Author told P. Dearmer (88) that 'not knowing one tune from another, he had written this with the idea that "The church's one foundation" (AURELIA) was the typical tune for hymns, and had therefore used that meter.' This should not be interpreted as saying that that is the appropriate tune for this text, which is its author's only contribution to hymnody.

US & CAN: BP594: Can214: CW546/373: H521: L344: P419/511/497: Pm436: CLB515 • ENG: BB394: CH638/520: CP578: E562: NC177: PL105

GILBERT KEITH CHESTERTON, b. Kensington, London, 29 v 1874; Sch. St. Paul's Sch. and Slade Sch. of Art; entered journalism and became one of the great characters in early 20 c. English life and literature, writing over 100 books, many of which were collections of occasional articles but which also included theology, history, criticism, biography and the famous series of 'Father Brown' detective stories. Coming from a nonconformist family background he early became an apologist for the R.C. Church at a time when that communion was still suspect in England; he was received into that Church in 1925 and after his death was described by the Pope as 'Defender of the Faith,' a phrase only used once before by the Holy Office—of King Henry VIII. † Beaconsfield, Bucks, 14 vi 1936 (62).

514. O GOD OF LOVE, O KING OF PEACE

4 st. LM-Coup.

H. W. Baker (101), for *Hymns Ancient & Modern*, 1861; Ps. 46:8.

US & CAN: BP600: Can271: CW557/- : H528: L352: P421,483/- : Pm 447: CLB521: W201 ● ENG: AM376/490: B663: CH -/504: CP579: M903

515. O GOD OF MERCY, GOD OF MIGHT

6 st. 888.6

G. Thring (191), 1877: *Collection of Hymns*, 1880; Lk. 10:36-7.

US & CAN: L316 ● ENG: CH487/461: CP549: E448: M728

O GOD OF TRUTH AND LORD OF POWER
O GOD OF TRUTH, O LORD OF MIGHT   see 854.

516. O GOD OF TRUTH, WHOSE LIVING WORD

9 st. CM   **PCH 219**

T. Hughes, given to the Hon. Mrs. Norton for *Lays of the Sanctuary*, 1859; first as a hymn in *Church Hymns*, 1871, but with altd. text in 6 st. True text restored in 7 st. in W. G. Horder's *Congregational Hymns*, 1884; most hymnals now have 6 st. (*CP* has 7.) *CH²* has 6 st. with text altd., but less radically than the 1871 book. This is the only hymn written by this famous author (like 513 above.).

US & CAN: Can209: CW365/- : H547 ● ENG: AM513/309: B517: BB 359: CH531/- : CP522: E449

THOMAS HUGHES, b. in Berkshire 20 x 1822; Sch. Rugby Sch., and Oriel, Oxf.; called to the bar, '48; member of Parliament, '65-'74; appointed Q.C., 1874; a member of the group of social & political reformers wh. included F. D. Maurice and C. Kingsley; founded the London Working Men's College, and was Principal '72-'83; on a visit to U.S. became a friend of J. R. Lowell (585), and in 1879 established a model community in Tennessee called Rugby. Most famous as author of novel, *Tom Brown's Schooldays* (1856), based on his experiences at school. † Brighton, 22 iii 1896 (73).

O GOD, OUR HELP IN AGES PAST: see 592.

517. O GOD, THE ROCK OF AGES

4 st. 7.6.7.6 D

E. H. Bickersteth, written 1860 or 1862 (conflicting notes by author); *Psalms & Hymns* (Presb. Ch. of England), 1867; 'For the last Sunday of the Year.'

US & CAN: CW154/- : L176: P62/92 ● ENG: B67: M958

EDWARD HENRY BICKERSTETH, b. 25 i 1825; Sch. Trinity, Camb.; Ord. C/E, '49; after curacies, Vicar of Christ Church Hampstead, '55-'85; Dean of Gloucester, '85, but the same year made Bishop of Exeter, where remained until 1900. Ed. first edn. of *Hymnal Companion*, 1858, which remained for several generations an important competitor (for evangelicals) of *Hymns A & M*, being revised 1877 and 1900. † London, 16 v 1906 (81).

518. O GOD, THOU ART MY GOD ALONE

6 st. LM-alt.   **PCH 112**

J. Montgomery (6), *Songs of Zion*, 1822; based on Ps. 63.

US & CAN: ● ENG: BB468: CH473/665: CP403

O GOD, THOU ART THE FATHER: see 855.

O GOD, THY SOLDIERS' CROWN
AND GUARD (GREAT REWARD): see 834.

519. O GOD, UNSEEN, THOUGH EVER NEAR

4 st. CM

E. Osler (361), *Church and King*, 1837; 'Spiritual Food.'

US & CAN: Can322: CW452/- : H198: L263 ● ENG: AM320/412: An 384: BB210: E*752

520. O HAPPY BAND OF PILGRIMS

8 st. 7.6.7.6   **PCH 187**

J. M. Neale (2), *Hymns of the Eastern Church*, 1862; said by him to be suggested by the Canon of SS. Chrissanthus & Damian (Greek), but note at (51) applies. Full orig. text only in *EH*. Elsewhere abr. and altd. as *AM* 1868; but omission of st. 5 upsets the shape of the whole, which should run (through sts. 4-5): 'The Faith by which ye see him . . . the Hope . . . the Love . . .'

> What are they but vaunt-couriers
> to lead you to his sight?
> What are they but the effluence
> of uncreated light?

and (through sts. 6-7): 'The trials . . . the sorrows . . . the temptations . . .'

> What are they but his jewels. . . .

US & CAN: ● ENG: AM224/289: An582: B551: CH577/- : CP517: E452: M618

521. O HAPPY DAY THAT FIXED MY CHOICE

5 st. LM-alt.

P. Doddridge (64), posth. *Hymns*, 1755; 'Rejoicing at our covenant Engagements with God: 1 Chr. 15:15.'

St. 4 om. in *B(Brit.)*, present textual problems. Earliest surviving form is as *CP* reading in line 3 'with ashes who would grudge to part,' but Doddridge's great-grandson, J. Doddridge Humphreys, republishing the *Hymns* in 1839, claimed that the authentic form was 'O who with earth would grudge to part.' Since Orton did alter texts (cf. 512) in the 1755 edn., it is possible that the 1755 reading, picturesque though it is, is not author's original: though it is perhaps odd that Orton should have replaced in 512 the evocative *Bethel* by the more commonplace *Israel* and then here replaced a less evocative reading by a more arresting one. However, other alts. in other books have no claim to authenticity, least of all the refrain added in some evangelical books.

US & CAN: BP464: B457: M128 ● ENG: B297: CH499/- : CP373: M744

522. O HAPPY HOME, WHERE THOU ART
LOVED THE DEAREST

5 st. 11.10.11.10

German: O SELIG HAUS, WO MAN DICH AUFGENOMMEN, C. J. P. Spitta, in *Psalter und Harfe*, 1833; Luke 19:9.

Tr. S. Findlater in *Hymns from the Land of Luther*, 3rd series, 1858, in orig. sts. and meter.

US & CAN: CW601/278: L336: P -/455/- ● ENG: An394: B621: CH648/523: M875

CARL JOHANN PHILIPP SPITTA, b. Hanover, 1801; after apprenticeship to a watchmaker, Sch. Gottingen Univ. and Ord. Luth., 1828; asst. pastor at Sudwalde, Germany. From early youth a song writer, took to hymn writing from 1824; chaplain to garrison & prison at Hamelin, 1830; then pastor at Wechold, and finally, just before death, superintendent at Burgdorf. He was the father of J. S. Bach's biographer, J. A. P. Spitta. † Burgdorf, 1859.

SARAH LAURIE FINDLATER, nee Borthwick, sister of J. L. Borthwick (70), b. Edinburgh 26 xi 1823; m. E. J. Findlater, minister of Free Ch. of Scotland and lived at Lochearnhead, Perthshire. Collaborated with her sister in *Hymns from the Land of Luther*, writing 53 of the 122 trslns. in that book. † Torquay, Devon, 25 xii 1907 (84).

523. O HEAVENLY JERUSALEM

6 st. 7.6.7.6

Latin CAELESTIS O JERUSALEM, 6 st. LM, in *Toulouse Breviary*, 1777. Tr. I. Williams (71) in *Hymns from the Paris Breviary*, 1839. *EH* alone has true text of st. 5. *BBC* begins O DEAR AND HEAVENLY CITY.

US & CAN: H592 • ENG: AM429/569: BB251‡: E251

524. O HELP US, LORD, EACH HOUR OF NEED

6 st. CM

H. H. Milman, in Heber's *Hymns*, 1827; Matt. 15:21. In his own *Selection of Psalms & Hymns*, 1837, Milman rewrote it in the 4 st. vn. now in common use. (See 619 for a much more famous hymn by this author).

US & CAN: • ENG: AM279/320: BB336: CH455/- : E83

HENRY HART MILMAN, b. London 10 ii, 1791, son of the physician to King George III; Sch. Eton & Brasenose, Oxf.; Ord. C/E, 1816; Vicar of St. Mary's, Reading, 1818; Prof. of Poetry, Oxf. Univ., 1821; Bampton Lecturer, '27; Rector of St. Margaret's, Westminster and Canon of Westminster, '35; Dean of St. Paul's, London, '49. Distinguished writer of religious verse; Newdigate prizewinner; friend of R. Heber (93). † London, 24 ix 1868 (77).

525. O HOLY CITY, SEEN OF GOD

5 st. 8.6.8.6.8.6   **PCH 542**

W. R. Bowie (415), 1909, at request of Dr. Henry Sloane Coffin, who was collecting material for *Hymns of the Kingdom of God*, where it was first pubd., 1910; editor 'wanted hymns that would express the conviction that our hope of the Kingdom ... may be prepared for here on our actual earth.' St. 2 now norm. om. Introduced to Britain in *Hymns for Church & School*, 1964.

US & CAN: Can160: H494: L332: M481: P409/508/505: Pm420: CLB496: W204 • ENG: AM*76: CH -/509

526. O HOLY GHOST, THY PEOPLE BLESS

6 st. CM

H. W. Baker (101), 3 vi 1873, *Monkland Parish Magazine*; then in *Hymns for the London Mission*, 1874 and *Hymns A & M*, 1875, sharing his tune for (481).

US & CAN: • ENG: AM211/234: An221: BB156: CP215

O HOLY SPIRIT, BY WHOSE BREATH: see 880.

527. O HOLY SPIRIT, LORD OF GRACE

3 st. CM

Latin: O FONS AMORIS, C. Coffin, in 3 st. LM, *Paris Breviary*, 1736 (see 52).

Tr.: J. Chandler (52), *Hymns of the Primitive Church*, 1837; perhaps this and 658, on closely related subjects, are among the best examples in well-known hymnody of the art of writing very short texts. (See also 410).

US & CAN: Can71 • ENG: AM208/231: An291: BB157: H453

528. O JESUS CHRIST, GROW THOU IN ME

10 st. CM

German: O JESUS CHRISTUS, WACHS IN MIR, J. C. Lavater, *Christliche Lieder*, 1780: John 3:30.

Tr. E. L. Smith, *Christ in Song* (P. Schaff), 1870. Norm abr. to 6 st. or fewer.

US & CAN: BP485 • ENG: An636: B601: CP443: M463

JOHANNES CASPAR LAVATER, b. Zurich, Switzerland, 15 xi 1741, son

of a local physician; Sch. Univ. and Theol., Sem., Zurich; Ord. Luth., 1762, but did not begin regular work until '69 as diaconus of Orphanage Church there; pastor, '75; diaconus of St. Peter's, Zurich, '78, pastor, '86. During French Revolution, when Swiss Cantons were made to pay special taxes, he protested in writing & preaching; for this, imprisoned 3 months in Basel, '99. Shot by a French soldier 25 ix 1799 and never recovered from the wound; resigned charge and † 2 i 1800 (58).

ELIZABETH LEE SMITH, nee Allen, b. 1817, d. of President of Dartmouth Univ., U.S.; m. 1843 H. B. Smith, prof. in Union Theol. Sem., New York. Her hymns, all trs. from German, are in Schaff's *Christ in Song*, 1869, 1870. (Schaff, Swiss-born historian, was prof. of Sacred Literature at Union Th. Sem., 1870, and an eminent hymnologist). Mrs. Smith † New York 1877.

529. O JESUS, I HAVE PROMISED

6 st. 7.6.7.6 D

J. E. Bode, leaflet (SPCK), 1868; 'A hymn for the newly confirmed.' Then in Appendix (1869) to *Psalms & Hymns* (SPCK); written c. 1866 as a confirmation hymn for his daughter & 2 sons. St. 4 now always om., st. 6 sometimes.

US & CAN: BP478: Can304: B365: CW308/213: H570: L515: M164: P268/307/- : Pm218 • ENG: AM271/331: An365: B298: BB360: CH508/434: CP447: E577: M526

JOHN ERNEST BODE, b. London 23 ii 1816; Sch. Eton, Charterhouse, Christ Ch., Oxf.; Ord. C/E '43; tutor at Ch. Ch., Oxf., '40-7: Rector of Westwell, Beds, '47; of Castle Camps, Cambs., '60 where † 6 x 1874 (58).

O JESUS, KING MOST WONDERFUL: see 857.

530. O JESUS, THOU ART STANDING

6 st. 7.6.7.6 D   **PCH 231**

W. W. How (75), *Psalms & Hymns* (Morrell & How), 1867; Rev. 3:20. Often supposed to have been inspired by Holman Hunt's famous picture, 'The Light of the World' (1854); but author wrote that it came to him after reading a poem by Jean Ingelow (41), 'Brothers, and a Sermon,' wh. has the lines

> Open the door, if ye have sinned,
> if ye be sorry, open it with sighs.

Now usually abr. to 3 st.

US & CAN: CW279/- : L386: M108: P228/266/- : Pm329 • ENG: AM 198/355: An416: B418: CH397/- : E578: M330

O JESUS, THOU THE BEAUTY ART: see 857.

O JOY BECAUSE THE CIRCLING YEAR: see 839.

531. O KING ENTHRONED ON HIGH

4 st. 6.6.8.4

Greek: Βασιλεῦ οὐράνιε, *Pentecostarion*, 8th cent.

Tr. J. Brownlie, *Hymns of the Early Church*, 1900. St. 2 of tr. always omitted, as in *EH*, 1906, wh. first introduced it as a hymn. *An* begins O SPIRIT FROM ON HIGH. Another version of this Greek hymn, in Russian with other trslns. and with the traditional chant, is at *Cantate Domino* (1974) #174.

US & CAN: H374 • ENG: AM -/237: An218‡: BB158: CP199: E454

JOHN BROWNLIE, b. Glasgow, 6 viii 1859, Sch. Glasgow Univ. and Free Ch. College; Ord. C/Scot. (free Ch.) 1884; junior minister, Free Ch. Portpatrick, '85, full charge '90; chairman of governors, Stranraer High School, 1901. † Crieff, Scotland, 18 xi 1925 (66).

532. O LET HIM WHOSE SORROW

7 st. 6.5.6.5

German: WEM IN LEIDENSTAGEN, H. S. Oswald, 14 st. 6.5.6.5, in *Letzte Mittheilungen*, 1826, 'An Exhortation to Tranquility'; Ps. 50:15. In Baron Bunsen's *Versuch*, 1833, sts. 1-3, 10, 12-14 were selected, and the famous trsln. was made from these.

Tr. F. E. Cox (352), *Sacred Poems from the German*, 1841; present text as slightly altd. in *Hymns Ancient & Modern*, 1861.

US & CAN: ● ENG: AM286/- : B771: CH525/671: E455

HEINRICH SIEGMUND OSWALD, b. Mimmersatt, Silesia, 30 vi 1751; clerk in civil service, Breslau; secretary to Landrath von Prittwitz at Glatz, '73; in business at Hamburg and Breslau from '75; Reader to the King of Prussia, Potsdam, '91; on king's death became a royal pensioner & retired to Hirchberg, then to Breslau where † 8 ix 1834 (83).

O LET US ALL BE GLAD TO-DAY: see 884.

533. O LIGHT THAT KNEW NO DAWN

5 st. 6.6.6.6.88   PCH 184

Greek: ἄτερ ἀρχῆς τὸν ἀπέραντον,
St. Gregory Nazianzen.

Tr. J. Brownlie (531), *Hymns of the Early Church*, 1900, 5 st.

US & CAN: Pm407 ● ENG: CH458/95: CP431

ST. GREGORY NAZIANZEN, b. 329, was one of the group of three theologians known as the Cappadocian Fathers, the other two being St. Basil of Caesarea (c. 329-379) and his younger brother, St. Gregory of Nyssa (c. 330-395); these were responsible for two vital developments in early Christian learning & life, the reconciling of neoplatonic philosophy with Christian doctrine and the foundation (indeed, the rescuing from much disorder) of the monastic system which preserved Christian culture during the Dark Ages. Greg. Naz., so called because he was the son of the Bp. of Nazianzus in Cappadocia (N. Turkey) was himself (unwillingly) Ord. priest c. 362; made Bp. of Sasima c. 372 but never went there; assisted his father as suffragan until 374, then retired to a life of contemplation, much influenced by Basil's rule of life established c. 360 in his monastery on the Black Sea Coast. Of the three he was the poet, and the above hymn well illustrates his talent. † 395.

534. O LIGHT WHOSE BEAMS ILLUMINE ALL

5 st. 8.8.8.8.88

E. H. Plumptre, *Lazarus and Other Poems*, 1864; 'The Way, the Truth and the Life.' *Hymns Ancient & Modern*, 1875.

US & CAN: P180/145 ● ENG: AM345/- : CH172/- : CP195

EDWARD HAYES PLUMPTRE, b. London, 6 viii 1821; Sch. Kings, London and Univ. Coll., Oxf.; Ord. C/E: Fellow of Brasenose, Oxf.; Chaplain, King's, London, '47-'68; Prof. Pastoral Theol. there '53-'63, and of exegesis, '64-'81. Served on cttee. for Revised Version of the Bible, '64-'81; Dean of Wells till † there 1 ii 1891 (69).

535. O LITTLE TOWN OF BETHLEHEM

5 st. 7.6.7.6 D, slightly irreg.   PCH 383

P. Brooks, after a visit to Bethlehem, 1866, for his Sunday School at Philadelphia, 1868, and incl. in *The Church Porch* (New York), 1874. Introduced to England by W. G. Horder in *The Treasury of Hymns*, 1896, and after being included in *EH* became a favorite Christmas hymn there as in U.S. *EH* has full text, but most hymnals omit st. 4, 'Where children pure and holy . . .'; and in most the 2 quatrains forming st. 2 are transposed from orig., so that it begins, 'For Christ is born of Mary . . .' instead of 'O morning stars together. . . .'

US & CAN: BP130: Can421: B85: CW184/120: H21: L27: M381: P121/171/521: Pm134: CLB216: W207 ● ENG: AM642/65: An122: B105:

BB56: CH48/172: CP718: E15: M125: NC181: PL142

PHILLIPS BROOKS, b. Boston, Mass., 13 xii 1835; Sch. Boston Latin Sch. & Harvard; Ord. Episc., '59; Ch. of the Advent, Philadelphia; Rector of Holy Trinity, Philadelphia, '62; of Trinity Ch., Boston, '68; Bp. Massachusetts '91. From an early stage he was well known as a preacher and public figure, and some thought him the greatest American preacher of his time. † Boston, 23 i 1893 (57).

O LORD AND MASTER OF US ALL: see 330.

536. O LORD, HOW HAPPY SHOULD WE BE

5 st. 88.6.88.6

J. Anstice, posth. *Hymns*, 1836 and C. M. Yonge's *Child's Christian Year*, 1841; Matt. 6:24. Full text in *A & M (S)*; elsewhere norm. abr. to 3 st.

US & CAN: ● ENG: AM276/- : An510: B482: BB311: CH543/- : CP 409: E457: M551

JOSEPH ANSTICE, b. Madeley Wood, Salop, 21 xii 1808; Sch. private and Christ Ch., Oxf. After gaining Newdigate poetry prize, appointed at age 22 Prof. of Classical Literature at King's, London. † Torquay, Devon, 29 ii 1836 (27).

537. O LORD OF EVERY SHINING CONSTELLATION

5 st. 11.10.11.10   PCH 469

A. F. Bayly, 1946; *Rejoice, O People*, 1950; text slightly altd. with author's approval in *100 Hymns for To-day*, 1969. Author wrote—'one attempt to write a hymn which would express a Christian response to life in the 20th century world, which science and technology have influenced so greatly.' Though written before the 'space age,' later events have proved it prophetic, and it has become much sought-after. The author is virtually a pioneer in this field; although he now has many followers, about the only predecessor was G. A. Studdert-Kennedy (62) in one or two poems not designed as hymns but now in hymnals, such as 'When through the whirl of wheels' (*Pm 422, SP 698*).

US & CAN: Can83: P -/-/512 ● ENG: AM*78: B*64: CH -/141: M*56: NC182: PL266

ALBERT FREDERICK BAYLY, b. Bexhill, Sussex, 6 ix 1901; Sch. Mansfield Coll., Oxf. and Ord. Congl., '29; served at Whitley Bay, Northd., '29; Morpeth, Northd., '38; Burnley, Lancs, '46; Swanland, Yorks, '50; St. Helens, Lancs, '56; Thaxted, Essex, '62-8; retired to Chelmsford. Published 3 books of original poems & hymns, mostly written 1935-60, at a time when English hymn writing was producing very little that was significant apart from the later work of G. W. Briggs (110).

538. O LORD OF HEAVEN AND EARTH AND SEA

9 st. 888.4

C. Wordsworth (27), *The Holy Year*, 1862; *Hymns Ancient & Modern*, 1868 included 7 st. (om. 4, 5); other hyls. retain 4 & 5 (which mention the Son and the Holy Spirit) and omit others, but norm. abr. to 6 st. Based on the General Thanksgiving in the Book of Common Prayer. One st. in *A & M*, omitted from latest edn. and all other books, shows the author below his usual perceptiveness, a quality tactlessly brought out by editors of the earlier editions:

mf	Whatever, Lord, we lend to thee
f	repaid a thousandfold will be;
ff	then gladly, Lord, we lend to thee
	who givest all.

The expression marks are transcribed from *AM(S)*.

US & CAN: BP565: Can206: H305: L448: M523: P398/-/- ● ENG: AM 365/480: An599: B68: BB14: CH19/145: CP670: E521: M969

539. O LORD OF LIFE, THY QUICKENING VOICE

5 st. CM

G. Macdonald, *The Disciple, and other Poems*, 1860: *Congl. Ch. Hymnal*, 1887.

US & CAN: BP552: CW132/- ● ENG: B681: CH264/48: CP599: M930

GEORGE MACDONALD, b. 10 xii 1824, Huntly, Aberdeenshire; Sch. Univ. Aberdeen and Highbury Theol. Sem., London; Ord. Congl., served at Arundel, Sussex, but after a few years left ministry for reasons of health and theological doubt; became a man of letters, poet & novelist (*David Elginbrod*, '62; *Robert Falconer*, '68, and many others). Later years spent at Bordighere, Italy. The late C. S. Lewis often acknowledged his great debt to G. Macdonald. † Ashtead, Surrey, 18 ix 1905 (80).

540. O LORD OF LIFE, WHERE'ER THEY BE

4 st. 888 (4)

F. L. Hosmer (483), for Easter service 1888 at his church in Cleveland, Ohio; first printed in Chicago *Unity*, and later in *Thoughts of God*, 1894. Apparently not first designed as a funeral or commemoration hymn, though always so used now. The 'Alleluias' seem first to have been added in the first British hymnal to use it, which was the *Congregational Hymnary*, 1916.

US & CAN: Can183: CW575/- : L600: P -/-/513: Pm469 ● ENG: B613: CH331/606: CP677

541. O LORD OUR GOD, ARISE

4 st. SM   **PCH 329**

R. Wardlaw, *A Collection of Hymns for the Use of the Tabernacles in Scotland*, 1803; this was the first hymn book for the use of Scottish Congregationalists.

US & CAN: BP380 ● ENG: An331: B385: BB25: CH376/495: CP327: E*103

RALPH WARDLAW, b. Dalkeith, Midlothian, 22 xii 1779; Sch. Univ. Glasgow; Ord. Congl., served at Albion Ch., Glasgow, which he founded; then Prof. Divinity in Congl. Theol. Hall., Glasgow, 1811-51; offered principalship of 3 seminaries but declined them all. One of the founder-theologians of Scot. Conglsm. † Easterhouse, Glasgow, 17 xii 1853 (almost 74).

542. O LORD, THOU ART MY GOD AND KING

5 st. LM-coup.

Scottish Psalter, 1650 (323), Ps. 145:1-7, this being the customary selection. In U.S. given as revised in *The Psalter* (U.S.) 1912.

US & CAN: BP64: Can34: P -/5/517 ● ENG: B277: BB470: ScPs 145/346: CP743

543. O LORD, TURN NOT THY FACE AWAY

CM   **PCH 17**

This is the oldest post-Reformation English hymn still in use, being, in orig. vn. (as above) one of the five songs appended, with the metrical Creed and Canticle, to Sternhold & Hopkins, *Old Version* of the metrical Psalter, 1560. It is there in 11 st. CM, with initial 'M' following; in ed. of 1565 it is ascribed to J(ohn) Marckant, whose name in later edns. is variously spelt. Sts. 1, 2, 3, 9, 11 of this, slightly altd. are in *EH* and *CH*; the song was revised in Playford's *Psalter*, 1677, and again in Tate & Brady. *Supplement to the New Version*, 1708. A & M uses the 1708 text (sts. 1, 2, 3, 11); *Pilgrim* has st. 1, 2, 11 of a composite version, 1677 and 1708. O LORD, TURN NOT AWAY THY FACE is the opening line in 1677 and often used now.

US & CAN: P503 (st. 1-2 of 1560)/-/-: Pm580 ● ENG: AM93: CH401: E84

JOHN MARCKANT: Ord. C/E, at Clacton Magna, Essex, 1539, and

Shopland, 1563. Apart from a handful of minor literary works, that is all that is known of him.

544. O LOVE DIVINE, HOW SWEET THOU ART

7 st. 88.6.88.6   **PCH 65**

C. Wesley (1) *Festival Hymns*, 1746; 'Desiring to love.' Norm. sel. now is sts. 1-4 or 1-3.

US & CAN: M285 ● ENG: AM195: An531: B772: CH428/- : CP428: M434

545. O LOVE, HOW DEEP, HOW BROAD, HOW HIGH

23 st. LM-coup.   **PCH 167**

Latin: APPARUIT BENIGNITAS, 15 c. ms. at Karlsruhe, credibly attributed to St. Thomas a Kempis (402).

Tr.: B. Webb in *Hymnal Noted* (ed. J. M. Neale), 1852: since it is not there acknowledged it has been mistakenly attr. to Neale himself. The tr. in 8 st. begins at st. 2 of original and compiles a cento from the rest; now in 7 st. (*CP*) or fewer.

US & CAN: Can100: CW -/146: H344: L*750: P139/-/518: Pm150 ● ENG: AM173/187: B126: BB73: CH -/223: CP63: E459: M62

BENJAMIN WEBB, b. London, 28 xi 1819, Sch. St. Paul's Sch. & Trinity, Camb.; Ord. C/E, '45; Vicar of Sheen, Staffs, '51; of St. Andrew's, Wells St., London, '62-†; one of the editors of the *Hymnal Noted*. † London, 27 xi 1885 (66 less one day).

546. O LOVE OF GOD, HOW STRONG AND TRUE

10 st. LM-coup.   **PCH 336**

H. Bonar (81), *Hymns of Faith & Hope*, 2nd series, 1861; 'The Love of God.' Now abr. to 7 st. or fewer.

US & CAN: CW -/16: Pm99 ● ENG: B69: CP69: M52: PL274

547. O LOVE THAT WILT NOT LET ME GO

4 st. 8.8.8.8.6   **PCH 344**

G. Matheson (446), 6 vi 1882 at the manse of Innellan, Scotland; 'It was written with extreme rapidity; it seemed to me that its composition occupied only a few minutes, and I felt myself rather in the position of one who was being dictated to than of an original artist. I was suffering from extreme mental distress and the hymn was the fruit of that pain.' Pubd. in *Scottish Hymnal* 1885 with change of one word—trace—for —climb—in st. 4. There was a 5th st. added later, which has never been used in hymn books.

The above remark of the author is interesting when one recalls that the composer of the famous tune ST. MARGARET, its oldest and still inseparable partner, said, 'After reading it very carefully, I wrote the tune straight off, and may say that the ink of the first note was hardly dry when I had finished the tune.'

US & CAN: BP449: Can192: B368: CW388/17: H458: L402: M234/307/519: Pm399 ● ENG: AM699/359: B20: CH424/677: CP774: M448

548. O LOVE WHO FORMEDST ME TO WEAR

6 st. (1657) 7 st. (1697) 8.7.8.7.77   **PCH 197**

German: LIEBE DIE DU MICH ZUM BILDE, J. Scheffler, *Heilige Seelenlust*, 1657; another st. (4) added in posth. *Geistreiches Gbch*, Halle, 1697.

Tr. C. Winkworth (14) in *Lyra Germanica*, 2nd ser., 1858; all 7 st. in 8.8.8.8.88; norm. now abr. to sts. 1, 2, 3, 7.

US & CAN: ● ENG: AM192/203: BB361: CH496/- : CP436: E460: M447

JOHANN SCHEFFLER, b. 1624 Breslau; Sch. there and Univ. Strassburg, where studied medicine, completing courses at Leyden and Padua; private physician at Oels, Silesia, to Duke Sylvius Nimrod of Wurttemberg-Oels; brought up Luth., but became R.C. 1653, taking name 'Angelus Silesius'; Imperial Court physician to Emperor Ferdinand III, 1654; became a Franciscan, '61 and Ord. R.C.; received into monastery of St. Matthias, Breslau, '71, where † 9 vii 1677 (53).

O MARTYRS YOUNG AND FRESH AS FLOWERS: see 870.

549.   O MASTER, LET ME WALK WITH THEE

3 st. LMD-coup.

W. Gladden, *Sunday Afternoon*, III, 1879, without thought of its being used as a hymn. Pub., without st. 2, in Richards' *Songs of Christian Praise*, 1880. Introduced to England in W. G. Horder's *Congl. Hymns.*, 1884; now always 4 st. LM.

US & CAN: BP469: Can301: B369: CW306/218: H572: L537: M170: P364/304/520: Pm418 ● ENG: B518: CH339/436: CP553: M600

WASHINGTON GLADDEN, b. Pottsgrove, Pa., 11 ii 1836; Sch. Oswego Academy & Williams Coll.; Ord. Congl., 1860; served in Brooklyn, N.Y.; N. Adams and Springfield, Mass.; and 1883-1918, Columbus, Ohio (First Congl. Ch.). Moderator of National Council of Congl. Chs., 1904-7. † 2 vii 1918 (82).

550.   O MASTER WORKMAN OF THE RACE

4 st. CMD

J. T. Stocking, Spring 1912, asked for a hymn for *Pilgrim Hymnal* in which it was published 1913; written on vacation after watching carpenters at work near his summer camp in the Adirondacks. 'The figure of Jesus the carpenter flashed upon me as never before, and I sat down and wrote the hymn almost . . . in the form in which it now appears.'

US & CAN: CW210/- : M171: P171/140/- : Pm412 ● ENG:

JAY THOMAS STOCKING, b. Lisbon, N.Y., 19 iv 1870; Sch. Amherst, Yale Div. Sch., and Univ. Berlin; Ord. Congl., 1901; served in New England, N.J., Missouri and Washington D.C. Moderator of General Council of Congl. Chs., '34-5; member of Commission on International Justice & Goodwill of the Federal Council of Churches in America. † Newton Center, Mass., 27 i 1936 (65).

O MORNING STAR, HOW FAIR AND BRIGHT: see 888.

551.   O MY SAVIOUR, LIFTED FROM
     THE EARTH FOR ME

6 st. 6.5.6.5

W. W. How (75), *Hymns for Mission Services*, 1876: John 12:32. St. 2 norm. om.

US & CAN: BP400: P161-/-/ ● ENG: AM773/360: An477: B453

552.   O MY SOUL, BLESS GOD THE FATHER

16 st. 8.7.8.7

Anon. version of Ps. 103 in *United Presbyterian Book of Psalms* (U.S.), 1871; now abr. to 6 st. or fewer.

US & CAN: B34: M65: P -/-/523: Pm100

553.   O PERFECT GOD, THY LOVE

1 st. SM

A. R. Greenaway, Lent 1902; *Hymns Ancient & Modern*, 1904; on the Seventh Word from the Cross.

US & CAN: ● ENG: AM649/121: An174: CH -/248

ADA RUNDALL GREENAWAY, b. Trivandrum, India, 12 x 1861, d. of General Thomas Greenaway of Indian Army; wrote verses for many years for Mowbray's Christmas and Easter Greeting cards; † Woking, Surrey, 15 v 1937 (75).

554.   O PERFECT LIFE OF LOVE

7 st. SM

H. W. Baker (101), *Hymns Ancient & Modern*, 1875; on the Sixth Word from the Cross.

US & CAN: L89 ● ENG: AM120/122: An175: CH103/249: M190

555.   O PERFECT LOVE, ALL HUMAN
     THOUGHT TRANSCENDING

3 st. 11.10.11.10

D. F. Gurney, 1884, asked by her sister for a hymn to be sung at her wedding, to be sung to her favorite tune, STRENGTH AND STAY, by J. B. Dykes; this tune has largely been replaced by an inferior one. Printed in *Hymns Ancient & Modern*, 1889; since then perhaps the most popular of wedding hymns.

US & CAN: BP579: Can351: B395: CW -/378: H214: L300: M333: P484/453/- : Pm465: CLB401 ● ENG: AM578/463: An393: B624: CH327/- : CP675: E346: M777: NC187: PL116

DOROTHY FRANCES GURNEY, b. London 4 x 1858, d. of the Rector of St. Andrew Undershaft, the Rev. F. G. Blomfield; m. 1897 Gerald Gurney. † Kensington, London, 15 vi 1932 (73).

556.   O PRAISE YE THE LORD, PRAISE HIM
     IN THE HEIGHT

4 st. 5.5.5.5.6.5.6.5

H. W. Baker (101), *Hymns Ancient & Modern*, 1875; paraphrase of Ps. 150.

US & CAN: Can9: W210 ● ENG: AM308/376: An23: BB279: CP25: E*88: PL4

557.   O QUICKLY COME, DREAD JUDGE OF ALL

4 st. 8.8.8.8.88

L. Tuttiett (182), *Hymns for Churchmen*, 1854.

US & CAN: ● ENG: AM204/227: E462: PL128

O SACRED HEAD, SORE
WOUNDED (SURROUNDED): see 871.

558.   O SAVIOUR, PRECIOUS SAVIOUR

4 st. 7.6.7.6 D

F. R. Havergal (252), 1870; in *Under the Surface*, 1874, and *Hymns Ancient & Modern*, 1875.

US & CAN: H349: L419: P200/-/- ● ENG: AM307/- : An273

559.   O SING A SONG OF BETHLEHEM

4 st. CMD   PCH 536

L. F. Benson, *School Hymnal* (Philadelphia), 1899; introduced to Britain in *Church Hymnary*, 1927.

US & CAN: B99: P138/177/526 ● ENG: AM*80: CH74/220

LOUIS FITZGERALD BENSON, b. 22 vii 1855, Philadelphia; Sch. Univ. Pennsylvania and practised law for 7 years before entering Princeton Theol. Sem. Ord. Presb., 1886; minister of the Church of the Redeemer, Germantown, Pa. Resigned 1892 to edit a series of hymnals for Presb. Ch. and to become lecturer in liturgics at Auburn Theol. Sem. and in hymnology, Princeton Th. Sem. Edited the *Hymnal* (1892), *The Chapel Hymnal*, *The School Hymnal*, and the *Hymnal for Congregational Churches*, and with H. van Dyke (377) ed. *The Book of Common Worship* (Presb., U.S.A.). An unusually good hymn writer, he is best known as America's leading hymnologist of all time to the present; his *The English Hymn* (1915) remains a classic, and the Benson library of hymnology, some 8,000 volumes, now housed in the Speer Library of

Princeton Seminary, is the finest such library in the world. † 10 x 1930 (75).

560. O SON OF GOD, OUR CAPTAIN OF SALVATION

6 st. 11.10.11.10   **PCH 246**

J. Ellerton (80), *Church Hymns*, 1871, for St. Barnabas' Day; full text in *A & M(S)*; elsewhere abr.

US & CAN: P386/-/- ● ENG: AM413/550: CH360/-

561. O SON OF MAN, OUR HERO STRONG AND TENDER

4 st. 11.10.11.10

F. Fletcher, 1924, for Charterhouse School; *Songs of Praise*, 1925.

US & CAN: CW220/147: H364: P177/217/- ● ENG: B127: CH146/309: CP116: M241

SIR FRANK FLETCHER, b. Atherton, Lancs, 3 v 1870; Sch. Rossall Sch. & Balliol, Oxf.; schoolmaster at Rugby, 1894; Master of Marlborough Sch., 1903-11; Head Master of Charterhouse, 1911-35. Knighted 1937. † Hindhead, Surrey, 17 xi 1954 (84).

562. O SONS AND DAUGHTERS, LET US SING

12 st. 888.4, introduced by 3 Alleluias   **PCH 168**

Latin: O FILII ET FILIAE, J. Tisserand, found in an untitled book dated between 1518 and 1536, probably published in Paris.

Tr. J. M. Neale (2), beg. YE SONS AND DAUGHTERS, 10 st. in *Medieval Hymns*, 1851; this text preserved exactly in *EH*; 2 st. added in *Hymnal Noted*, 1854. Present vn., norm. 9 st. but sometimes abr., is now always found outside *EH* and is taken from revision by compilers of *Hymns Ancient & Modern*, 1861.

US & CAN: BP194: Can467: CW -/179: H99: L96: M451: P167/206/527: Pm191: CLB279: W312 ● ENG: AM130: BB110: CH124/277: CP724: E626

O SPIRIT FROM ON HIGH: see 531.

563. O SPIRIT OF THE LIVING GOD

6 st. LM-alt.   **PCH 109**

J. Montgomery (6), 1823, 'to be sung at the Public Meeting of the Auxiliary Missionary Society for the West Riding of Yorkshire . . . in Salem Chapel, Leeds, 4 June 1823.' The 'auxiliaries' were local chapters of the London Missionary Society, 1795-1966, and from an early stage this Society was chiefly administered by Congregationalists. Appeared in *Evangelical Magazine*, Aug. 1823; revised vn., now always used, *The Christian Psalmist*, 1825; 'The Spirit Accompanying the Word of God.' *CP* has full text; all others omit st. 6, but the omission importantly alters the sense of the whole.

US & CAN: BP387: Can233: B264: H256: L306: M136: P207/242/528: Pm279 ● ENG: AM585/- : An328: B387: BB159: CH386/496: CP323

O SPLENDOUR OF GOD'S GLORY BRIGHT: see 875.

O STRENGTH AND STAY, UPHOLDING ALL CREATION: see 854.

O THOU ETERNAL KING MOST HIGH: see 834.

564. O THOU FROM WHOM ALL GOODNESS FLOWS

6 st. CM   **PCH 103**

T. Haweis, in a tract, *The Reality and Power of the Religion of Jesus*

Christ (Bristol), 1791; this was an obituary tribute to a Mr. William Browne who had expressly chosen the hymn to be sung at his funeral. Text as there given is in *CP*. Other books print variations of the text based on the version, 7 st., in Cotterill's *Selection*, 1819 (333), which has a uniform final line for each st., 'Good Lord, remember me.' *AM* has sts. 1, 2, 3, 5, 6 of this vn. *EH* returns nearer original but ends each st. 'Dear Lord, remember me,' which is line 4 of st. 1 in original. The tune very well known in England as RICHMOND ('City of God') was composed by the author for this text. See note in *Hymnal (1940) Companion*, #319, or *Companion to Congregational Praise*, #253, for the form in which he wrote the tune.

US & CAN: ● ENG: AM283/117: CP766: E85

THOMAS HAWEIS, b. 1 i 1734, Redruth, Cornwall; Sch. Truro Gram. Sch., then apprenticed to a surgeon & apothecary. After brief period at Oxford, Ord. C/E, 1757; chaplain to the Earl of Peterborough; later curate of St. Mary Magdalen, Oxford, but removed for evangelical sympathies & became assistant to M. Madan (260) at Lock Hospital, London. Rector of Aldwinkle, Northants, 1764-1820; for some years after 1768 was also chaplain to the Countess of Huntingdon and manager of her Theol. Sem. at Trevecca, S. Wales (a foundation which survives in Westminster-Cheshunt, Cambridge). He was one of the founders of the London Missionary Society, 1795 (see preceding note). † Bath, 11 ii 1820 (86).

565. O THOU GREAT FRIEND TO ALL THE SONS OF MEN

3 st. 10.10.10.10

T. Parker: originally a sonnet; recast as a hymn and incl. in *Singers and Songs of the Liberal Faith* (Boston) 1875 and introduced to Britain in W. G. Horder's *Congregational Hymns*, 1884.

US & CAN: CW347/- : P174/-/-: Pm219 ● ENG: CP105

THEODORE PARKER, b. Lexington, Mass., 1810; Sch. Harvard; Ord. Unit., but as early as age 30 was denounced by fellow-Unitarians as unorthodox; lived thereafter in Boston area as free-lance lecturer and preacher, supporter of anti-slavery movements, and writer. In one of his political lectures he said: 'Democracy is direct self-government, over all the people, by all the people, and for all the people,' and this is said to have suggested the phraseology of the most famous section of Abraham Lincoln's Gettysburg Address. †, while travelling for his health, Florence, Italy, 1870.

566. O THOU IN ALL THY MIGHT SO FAR

4 st. CM

F. L. Hosmer (483), *New York Inquirer*, 1876; *The Thought of God . . .*, 1885. Introduced to Britain by P. Dearmer in *English Hymnal*, 1906.

US & CAN: H444: L480: M12: P176/219/- ● ENG: E463

567. O THOU NOT MADE WITH HANDS

5 st. 6.6.6.6.66   **PCH 237**

F. T. Palgrave, *Hymns*, 1867; 'The Kingdom of God within.' Also in Horder's *Congregational Hymns*, 1884. In *Hymnal-1940* begins CITY, NOT MADE. . . .

US & CAN: CW478/- : H491‡ ● ENG: AM -/259: BB180: CP550: E464: M707

FRANCIS TURNER PALGRAVE, b. 28 ix 1824, Great Yarmouth, Nfk., but from early childhood lived in Hampstead (London); Sch. Charterhouse and Balliol, Oxf.; Fellow of Exeter Coll. Oxf.; asst. Sec. to W. E. Gladstone (later Prime Minister of England) for a short time, then Vice-Principal of Kneller Hall Training Coll., London, 1850-5. Thereafter in Ministry of Education, where he was finally Asst-Secretary. Eminent man of letters, best known for editing *The Golden Treasury*, most famous anthology of poetry in 19th cent. (1861). Wrote 3 vols. of original poems. Prof. Poetry, Oxford, 1885-95. † Kensington, London, 24 x 1897 (73).

O THOU TO WHOSE ALL-SEARCHING SIGHT: see 858.

568. O THOU WHO AT THY EUCHARIST DIDST PRAY (THOU WHO AT THY FIRST . . .)

4 st. 10.10.10.10.10 10

W. H. Turton, 22 vi 1881, at St. Mary Magdalen, Munster Square (London) for English Church Union; *Altar Hymnal*, 1884, and *Hymns Ancient & Modern*, 1889, where opening line was altered to 'Thou who . . .' But orig. vn. is more often used now. Altered again in *CLB*: 'At that first Eucharist . . .'

US & CAN: Can345‡: H191: CLB359‡ • ENG: AM553‡/402‡: BB213: CH -/492: E324: PL79

WILLIAM HARRY TURTON, b. Peshawar, India, 30 xii 1856, son of an English army officer; Sch. Clifton Coll. and Royal Military Academy, Woolwich; comissioned 1876 Royal Engineers; Lt/Colonel, 1902: received DSO. Author & historian, including *The Truth of Christianity* (12 edns.). † Bristol, 16 vi 1938 (81).

569. O THOU WHO CAMEST FROM ABOVE

2 st. LMD-alt.

C. Wesley (1), *Short Hymns . . .* , 1762; Lev. 6:13, based on Matthew Henry's Commentary on that passage (cf. 1). *EH* has original text, in LM as all hymnals now; some alter st. 2 line 2 to avoid difficulty of singing the word 'inextinguishable.'

US & CAN: BP460: Can239: H463: M172 • ENG: AM698/329: An366: B519: BB362: CH471/110: CP438: E343: M386

570. O THOU WHO MAKEST SOULS TO SHINE

3 st. LMD-alt.

J. Armstrong, *The Pastor in his Closet*, 1847; *Hymns Ancient & Modern*, 1868, in LM.

US & CAN: Can232: P480/305/- • ENG: AM353/471: An412: BB225: CH334/-

JOHN ARMSTRONG, b. Wearmouth, Co. Durham, 22 viii 1813; Sch. Charterhouse & Lincoln, Oxf.; Ord. C/E; curate at Alford, 1837; Bp. Grahamstown, S. Africa, 1853, where † 16 v 1856 (42).

O TRINITY, O (OF) BLESSED LIGHT: see 865.

571. O WHAT THEIR JOY AND THEIR GLORY MUST BE

7 st. 12 12. 12 12 dact.   **PCH 161**

Latin: O QUANTA QUALIA SUNT ILLA SABBATA, P. Abélard (34) in St. Gall ms., 14 cent.

Tr. J. M. Neale (2), *Hymnal Noted*, 1854, in 10 10. 10 10 dact. (A tr. by R. A. Knox, 866, in 11-syllable lines, nearer orig. meter, can be read in *PCH*, or *Westminster Hymnal*, 1941, #205).

Orig. Latin vn. written for Abbey of the Paraclete (see 34). *EH* has full text of Neale's tr.

US & CAN: Can186: H589: L596: P430/424/- : Pm310 • ENG: AM235/ 281: BB252: CH224/535: CP349: E465: NC191

572. O WHERE ARE KINGS AND EMPIRE NOW?

4 st. CM

A. C. Coxe, at age 21: from a ballad, 'Chelsea' in 8 st. CMD beginning 'When old Canute the Dane was merry England's King.' The hymn was made out of sts. 6a, 8b and 7, split into CM, with alterations in text. In this form it was well known in 1873 when quoted on a famous occasion by Theo. D. Woosley, President of Yale 1846-71, at a meeting of the Evangelical Alliance in New York; since then achieved popularity as a hymn.

US & CAN: CW427/- : H382: L154: M308: P334/431/530: Pm264 • ENG: **ARTHUR CLEVELAND COXE**, b. 10 v 1818, Mendham, N.J.; surname at birth was Cox; Sch. Univ. of City of New York, General Theol. Sem., N.J.; Ord. Episc., 1842; Rector, St. John's, Hartford, Conn.; Grace Ch., Baltimore, Md.; Calvary Ch., N.Y.C.; then bp-coadjutor of Western New York, '65, later diocesan. Highly conservative in outlook, opposed consecration of Phillips Brooks (535) and revision of Bible translation. Contributed notes to the *Ante-Nicene Fathers* which brought attacks from R.C. clergy. His attachment to text of King James Bible appears strongly in many of his hymns (e.g. 631, and *PCH* 371). † Buffalo, N.Y., 20 vii 1896 (78).

O WONDROUS TYPE, O VISION FAIR: see 841.

573. O WORD OF GOD INCARNATE

4 st. 7.6.7.6 D

W. W. How (75), *Supplement* (1867) to Morrell & How, *Psalms & Hymns*.

US & CAN: BP287: B140: CW434/328: H402: L252: M372: P215/251/ 532: Pm252 • ENG: An301: B251: BB291: CH198/- : CP231: M303

574. O WORD OF PITY, FOR OUR PARDON PLEADING

4 st. 11.10.11.10   **PCH 295**

A. R. Greenaway (553) for *Hymns Ancient & Modern*, 1904, on the First Word from the Cross.

US & CAN: • ENG: AM648/115: B176: CH97/244: CP138: M240

575. O WORSHIP THE KING

6 st. 5.5.5.5.6.5.6.5   **PCH 125**

R. Grant, in Bickersteth's *Church Psalmody*, 1833. It is a vn. of part of Ps. 104, whose meter is copied from that W. Kethe in the *Old Version*, 1560. (Kethe's vn. was sensitively revised in R. Bridges [9] in *Yattendon Hymnal*, 1899, and survives at #45 in *M[Brit.]*). Virtually unaltered in all Eng. hymnals, except those which read 'sing' for 'lisp' in st. 6, line 8, and those which, oddly, omit st. 6 altogether (as mostly in U.S.). A good example of the impact on hymnody of the new search for poetic standards which Heber (93) so strongly promoted.

US & CAN: BP76: Can 127: B30: CW94/67: H288: L163: M473: P2/26/ 533: Pm6 • ENG: AM167: An248: B22: BB471: CH9/35: CP17: E466: M8: NC192: PL226

SIR ROBERT GRANT, b. Bengal, 1779; Sch. Magdalene, Camb.; called to the Bar, 1807; enter Parliament 1818 representing Elgin; rep. Inverness, '28; Norwich, '30; Finsbury (London), '34; carried Jewish Emancipation Bill in House of Commons, '33; Judge Advocate General, '32; Governor of Bombay (and knighted) '34. † Dalpoorlie, India, 9 vii 1838 (58).

576. O WORSHIP THE LORD IN THE BEAUTY OF HOLINESS

5 st. 12.10.12.10 dact. (st. 1, 13.10.13.10). St. 5 the same as st. 1.   PCH 227

J. S. B. Monsell (193), *Hymns of Love & Praise*, 1863. In some books st. 5 om., and occasionally initial 'O' omitted for metrical uniformity.

US & CAN: BP148: Can33: CW106/-/-: P7/-/-: Pm31 • ENG: AM -/77: An11: B35: BB267: CH232/40: CP275: E42: M9: PL162

577. O ZION, HASTE, THY MISSION HIGH FULFILLING

4 st. 11.10.11.10 with refrain 9.11

M. A. Thomson, 1868: in *Church Hymns* (U.S.), 1894. "I wrote the greater part of it in 1868 . . . while I was sitting up with one of my children who was ill with typhoid fever. I thought I should like to write a missionary hymn to the tune of . . . 'Hark, hark, my soul;' but as I could

not get a refrain I liked, I left the hymn unfinished, and about 3 years later I finished it by adding the refrain.''
US & CAN: BP388: B295: CW529/330: H261: L314: M299: P382/491/- : Pm302 ● ENG:
MARY ANN THOMSON, b. London, 5 xii 1834, became the wife of John Thomson, librarian of the Free Library in Philadelphia; wrote much religious poetry. Lived from marriage till † in Philadelphia 2 iii 1923 (88).

578. OFT IN DANGER, OFT IN WOE

5 st. 77.77
H. Kirke White and S. Fuller-Maitland: *Hymns for Private Devotion*, 1827, and *Mitre Hymn Book*, 1836.

Few popular hymns have a more remarkable story than this. Ten lines of an incomplete hymn were found, written by White (who died aged 21) on the back of a mathematical paper, by W. Collyer, who added 6 lines and published the whole in his *Hymns . . .* , 1812, with a note about its origin. This began with White's original first line, MUCH IN SORROW, OFT IN WOE. In the 1827 source it appears as a 6 st. hymn with the last 14 lines by S. Fuller-Maitland, who was 14 years old when she wrote them: so that in this form it is a hymn by two teenagers. The 1836 book altered st. 1 as we now have it, and reduced the hymn to 4 st. The accepted text is now 5 st. as in *EH*, in which lines 1-6 are by White (altd. 1836) and lines 7-20 by S. F-M. *Hymns A & M* transposes sts. 4 and 3; *M(Brit.)* has a slightly different selection of lines but same proportion of authorship.
US & CAN: H558 ● ENG: AM291: An584: BB363: CP506: E467: M488
HENRY KIRKE WHITE, b. Nottingham, 21 iii 1785; at 14 became assistant to a hosiery maker but later went into an attorney's office to study law; intended in the end to study for the ministry. Pub. a collection of poems, *Clifton Grove*, 1803; went to St. John's, Camb., but † there in his rooms, 19 x 1806 (21).
FRANCES SARA FULLER-MAITLAND, b. 20 vi 1809, Shinfield Park, Reading, Berks; *Hymns for Private Devotion* (above) was compiled by her mother. M. 1834 John Colquhoun, sports journalist. † Edinburgh, 27 v 1877 (68).

579. ON CHRISTMAS NIGHT ALL CHRISTIANS SING

4 st. LM-coup. (music requires repetition of last couplet & makes it 88.88.88).
Carol collected from Mrs. Verrall, Monks Gate, Sussex, by R. Vaughan Williams: see *Journal of the Folk Dance & Song Society* II (1904), p. 127. Pub. in this form *Oxford Book of Carols*, 1928.
US & CAN: ● ENG: An114: CH -/181: CP706: NC185: PL145
RALPH VAUGHAN WILLIAMS would not normally appear in a lexicon of text writers, but the number of carol and folk song texts he collected and edited excuses his appearance here, and we have at least the opportunity of reminding American readers that he should not be referred to, or indexed, as Williams (perhaps the only solecism in all the distinguished pages of the *Hymnal-1940 Companion*). Vaughan Williams is the name, and Rayph the pronunciation of what precedes. He was b. 12 x 1872 at Down Ampney, Glos.; Sch. Charterhouse and Royal Coll. of Music, then Trinity, Camb.; before he became internationally famous as a symphonist he was an ardent folk song collector, the results of his researches appearing in the journal mentioned above, the *English Hymnal*, 1906 and 1933, and the *Oxford Book of Carols*. For his collaboration on *EH*, see 88. He lived all his long life as an independent musician, producing 9 symphonies, many choral works, smaller orchestral works sometimes based on folk songs, solo songs, chamber music, a Masque (*Job*) and operas. He also lectured in composition at the Royal College of Music, and was the central figure in the early 20th century renaissance of English music. † Dorking, 26 viii 1958 (85).

580. ON JORDAN'S BANK THE BAPTIST'S CRY

5 st. LM-coup.
Latin: JORDANIS ORAS PRAEVIA, C. Coffin (52), *Paris Breviary*, 1736 and *Hymni Sacri*, 1736.
Tr. J. Chandler (52), *Hymns of the Primitive Church*, 1837. *EH* stays near original text but norm. vn. is that of *Hymns A & M*, 1861. (*M* * takes two from *EH* version)
US & CAN: BP115: Can391: CW -/115: H10: L4: Pm115: CLB206: W218
● ENG: AM50: An79: B86: BB38: CH78/208: CP73: EH9: M*57: PL133

581. ON OUR WAY REJOICING

4 st. 6.5.6.5 D
J. S. B. Monsell (193), *Hymns of Love & Praise*, 1863; rearranged in *Parish Hymnal*, 1873, using first 4 lines as refrain after each st., which is the form used in U.S. hymnals. *H(U.S.)* and *L* use sts. 3, 2, 4 only.
US & CAN: CW417/- : H568: L195: P56/80/- ● ENG:

582. ON THIS DAY, THE FIRST OF DAYS

7 st. 77.77
Latin: DIE PARENTE TEMPORUM, LM, *Carcassonne Breviary*, 1745.
Tr. H. W. Baker (101), *Hymns Ancient & Modern*, 1861; elsewhere than in *A & M* always abr. Variant texts in *NC* and *PL*.
US & CAN: Can373: CW -/191: CLB416: W219 ● ENG: AM34/39: An 70: NC186: PL21

583. ONCE IN ROYAL DAVID'S CITY

6 st. 8.7.8.7.77 (88)   PCH 307
Mrs. Alexander (24), *Hymns for Little Children*, 1848; on the clause in the Creed, 'who was conceived of the Holy Ghost, born of the Virgin Mary.'
US & CAN: BP129: Can112: CW -/125: H236: L41: P454/462/539: CLB 226: W220 ● ENG: AM329/432: An107: B106: BB58: CH69/193: CP89: E605: M859: NC184

584. ONCE, ONLY ONCE, AND ONCE FOR ALL

6 st. CM (plus doxology).
W. Bright (43), *Hymns & Other Poems*, 1866; small alts. in *A & M* 1868 accepted by author and now standard: but doxology there added not always used.
US & CAN: Can350 ● ENG: AM315/398: BB214: E327

585. ONCE TO EVERY MAN AND NATION

4 st. 8.7.8.7 D   PCH 372
This hymn, at present very popular in the U.S., is made out of lines from a poem by J. R. Lowell entitled 'The Present Crisis' in his *Poems*, 1849, written in protest against the War with Mexico, 1845. The poem is in 18 5-line stanzas and is set out in full at *PCH 372*. The opening stanza is:

> When a deed is done for freedom, through the broad earth's aching breast
> runs a thrill of joy prophetic, trembling on from east to west,
> and the slave, where'er he cowers, feels the soul within him climb
> to the awful verge of manhood, as the energy sublime
> of a century bursts full-blossomed on the thorny stem of time.

The most popular version, despite its fame in the U.S., is owed to the English hymnologist W. G. Horder who selected 16 of these lines, arranging them in 8.7.8.7 D, and included the result in his *Hymns, Supplemental to existing Collections*, 1894. To show how radical his work was we give here his selection of lines:

| (st. 1) 21, 22, 23, 25 | (st. 3) 61, 62, 86, 87 |
| (st. 2) 51, 52, 53, 55 | (st. 4) 28, 38, 39, 40 |

He altered line 61 (st. 3 lines 1-2) from 'By the light of burning heretics Christ's bleeding feet we track,' and in line 38 for the original 'Truth for ever on the scaffold, wrong for ever on the throne' wrote, to follow the new rhyme-scheme, 'Though her portion be the scaffold and upon the throne be wrong.' This altered text became normal, although *Pilgrim* boldly restored the original line 38, defying the rhyme scheme but preserving the original well-balanced line. (It also omits Horder's st. 3 altogether).

Sir Walford Davies, however, when editing *In Hoc Signo* (1915: see 454), returned to Lowell's original stanza-form and included, without alteration, lines 21-5, 51-5 and 36-40, providing a tune of his own for the unusual meter. *Hymns Ancient & Modern*, in its 1916 Supplement, took over this tune, and the 5-line stanza, but included only 2 st., these being lines 21-5 and 41-5. It also made two alterations: (1) in line 23, 'Like Christ in Jewry' for 'God's new Messiah,' and in line 43 for the original:

> But the soul is still oracular; amid the market's din,
> list the ominous stern whisper from the Delphic cave within,

offered the more euphonious:

> But the soul is still prophetic: list amid the market's din
> to the ominous stern whisper of the oracle within.

Horder's version, though rather stridently moralistic, is certainly the more singable. It was taken into the *English Hymnal*, 1906, and later into *Songs of Praise*, 1925 and 1931; it was given in the *Oxford American Hymnal*, 1930, with the tune EBENEZER (as *Songs of Praise*) and from there passed quickly into general use.

US & CAN: Can167: B385: CW558/247: H519: L547: M242: P373/361/540: Pm441: CLB513 ● ENG: AM689‡/- : E563: M898

JAMES RUSSELL LOWELL, b. Cambridge, Mass., 22 ii 1819; Sch. Harvard; practised law to '55; became Smith Prof. of Modern Languages at Harvard. U.S. Minister to Spain, '77 and Ambassador to England, '81. Ed. *Atlantic Monthly*, '57-'62, *North American Review*, '63-'72; wrote much poetry of religious and political tone. † Cambridge, Mass., 12 viii 1891 (72).

586. ONE WHO IS ALL UNFIT TO COUNT

7 st. CM   **PCH 348**

Marathi: N. V. Tilak

Tr. N. Macnicol in *The Life of Tilak*, by J. C. Winslow, 1920, having earlier appeared in *The Indian Interpreter* (n.d.). Included in *A Missionary Hymn Book*, 1922, and *Church Hymnary*, 1927.

US & CAN: L384: P234/-/-: Pm330 ● ENG: B456: CH406/82: CP388: M159

NARAYAN VAMAN TILAK, b. Karazgaon, India, 1862, to an aristocratic Hindu family; after working as a schoolmaster became a Christian, 1894, and worked until 1915 with American Marathi Mission at Ahmednagar. In 1917 abandoned all means of lifelihood to form a community, 'God's Durbar,' to promote Christian doctrine and ethics in association with Indian patriotism, hoping thus to evangelize India. Wrote many poems & spiritual songs, a few of which, the above being the most famous, have become Christian hymns. † Ahmednagar 1918 (56).

NICOL MACNICOL, b. Lochranza, Isle of Arran, 26 ii 1870, Sch. Glasgow Univ. and Free Ch. Coll.; Ord. Free CH/Scot., and from 1895 to 1927 missionary of the Free Ch. in Poona, India; became outstanding Indian language scholar. Retired to Edinburgh and † there 13 ii 1952 (81).

587. ONWARD, CHRISTIAN SOLDIERS

6 st. 6.5.6.5 D, with refrain 6.5.6.5. using first 4 lines   **PCH 232**

S. Baring-Gould (493), June 1864 for a children's festival at Horbury Bridge, Torks, his parish; sung there Whit Sunday 1864 in an outdoor procession; pub. *Church Times*, 1864, and, dropping st. 4, in *Hymns A & M*, 1868; norm. found now in this form. The 'cross of Jesus' refers to

the processional cross. He had in mind the tune from the 2nd movement of Haydn's 53rd Symphony (found as 2nd tune in *EH*). The tune now famous supplanted this in 1872.

US & CAN: BP301: Can178: B393: CW482/- : H557: L560: M305: P365/350/542: Pm382 ● ENG: AM391/629: An562: B520: CH535/480: CP 527: E643: M822

588. OPEN NOW THY GATES OF BEAUTY

5 st. 8.7.8.7.77   **PCH 193**

German: THUT MIR AUF DIE SCHONE PFORTE, B. Schmolck (400), *Kirchen-Gefahrte*, 1732, in 7 st., 'Appearing before God.'

Tr. C. Winkworth (14), *Chorale-Book for England*, 1863, in 5 st.

US & CAN: BP427: CW121/392: L177: P -/40/544: Pm503: CLB345: W222 ● ENG: CP258

589. OUR BLEST REDEEMER, ERE HE BREATHED

7 st. 8.6.8.4   **PCH 274**

H. Auber, *Spirit of the Psalms*, 1829, 'Whitsunday'; *CP* has full text, elsewhere abr. to 6 st. or fewer.

US & CAN: BP260: H368: P205/-/- ● ENG: AM207/230: An233: B236: BB160: CH180/336: CP209: E157: M283

HARRIET AUBER, b. London, 4 x 1773, great-granddaughter of a Huguenot refugee; now principally known for this one hymn, which is not characteristic of the collection from which it comes, a book of poems designed to put flesh on the dry bones of metrical psalmody; at several points it did it very well. (See *PCH 273* and *EH* 461 for an example). She † Hoddesdon, Herts, 20 i 1862 (88).

590. OUR DAY OF PRAISE IS DONE

6 st. SM

J. Ellerton (80), *Church Hymns*, 1871; originally written for Nantwich Festival of Choirs, 1868, using 4 st. from a hymn by W. J. Blew followed by 3 of his own. Revised form in 1871 source, almost all his own, is now standard.

US & CAN: H175 ● ENG: AM30/38: CH290/- : M690: NC188‡

591. OUR FATHERS BY WHOSE SERVANTS

4 st. 7.6.7.6 D

G. W. Briggs (110), 1920, for Loughborough School; *Songs of Praise*, 1925; one of the earliest hymns by this later illustrious author.

US & CAN: H505: L248 ● ENG: B279: CP665: M979

OUR FATHER'S HOME ETERNAL: see 402.

592. OUR GOD, OUR HELP IN AGES PAST

9 st. CM   **PCH 44**

I. Watts (10), Psalm 90, 2nd vn., pt. I, in *Psalms* . . . 1719; 'Man Frail and God Eternal.' Sts. 4, 6, 8, norm. omitted—in U.S. often st. 2 as well. It rose to the standing of an internationally famous hymn through its marriage with the tune ST. ANNE; though the tune is 11 years older than the text they did not meet until *Hymns Ancient & Modern*, 1861. 'O God' for 'Our God . . .' substituted by J. Wesley in his first *Collection* of 1780, but orig. reading is now returning to favor. In st. 7 (st. 5 of version now known) the 'sons of time' are probably hours and minutes rather than human beings, but whichever way that is taken the sense remains the same.

US & CAN: BP87: Can133: B223: CW585/23: H289: L168: M28: P77/111/549: Pm1: CLB421: W203 ● ENG: AM165: An244: B71: BB467: CH601/611: CP52: E450: M878: NC179: PL286

593. OUR LORD, HIS PASSION ENDED

4 st. 77.77 iamb. 77.77 troch.

F. C. Burkitt, *Three Hymns for Whitsuntide* (SPCK, 1920); *Church & School Hymnal*, 1926.

US & CAN: ● ENG: AM -/155: An224: B237: BB161: CP*76: PL215

FRANCIS CRAWFORD BURKITT, b. London 3 ix 1864; Sch. Harrow & Trinity, Camb.; Ord. C/E; from 1905-†, Norrisian Professor of Divinity, Univ. Cambridge (in wh. chair he was succeeded by C. H. Dodd). Distinguished N.T., Semitic and Patristic scholar; one of the first to make known in England the work, both in theology and music, of Albert Schweitzer. Numerous scholarly publications. † Cambridge 11 v 1935 (70).

OUT OF THE DEPTHS I CRY TO THEE: see 838.

594. PEACE, PERFECT PEACE, IN THIS DARK WORLD OF SIN

7 st. 10 10

E. H. Bickersteth (517), *Songs in the House of Pilgrimage*, c. 1875 (a leaflet of 5 hymns) and *Hymnal Companion*, 1876, written after hearing a sermon on Is. 26:3. The famous tune, PAX TECUM, long associated with it, was the subject of a strange story. Its composer, George Thomas Caldbeck (b. 1852), after being a theol. student at Islington and music director at the college, prevented by ill-health from becoming a missionary, became an itinerant evangelist; he was arrested in London in 1908 for peddling tracts without a license, having by that time descended to extreme poverty and being accommodated in a common lodging house; when the magistrate learned that he had composed this tune, which, harmonized by a professional musician, had by that time become very well known, he dismissed the case. Despite the story, the tune has now exhausted its usefulness.

US & CAN: H436: L571: M229: P301/420/- ● ENG: AM537/358: An 422: B584: CH444/- : CP414: E468: M501

595. PLEASANT ARE THY COURTS ABOVE

4 st. 77.77 D

H. F. Lyte (5), *Spirit of the Psalms*, 1834; 2nd version of Ps. 84.

US & CAN: BP324: H392: L184: P -/441/- ● ENG: AM240: An563: B280: CH235/- : E469: M679

596. POUR OUT THY SPIRIT FROM ON HIGH (LORD POUR . . .)

5 st. LM-alt.

J. Montgomery (6), 23 i 1833, for Rev. J. Birchall, who published it in *Christian Psalmody*, 1833. Some hymnals, following *Hymns A & M*, read 'Lord, pour . . .'

US & CAN: BP366: Can353: H219: L402: M337 ● ENG: AM355/473: An413: B351: BB224: CH333/597: CP656: E167

PRAISE GOD, FROM WHOM ALL BLESSINGS FLOW: see 63.

597. PRAISE, MY SOUL, THE KING OF HEAVEN

5 st. 8.7.8.7.4.7   **PCH 126**

H. F. Lyte (5), *Spirit of the Psalms*, 1834; Ps. 103. In original source st. 4, often omitted in modern hymnals, is marked for permissive omission; available tunes now insist on its being sung as 8.7.8.7.8.7. In *Hymns A & M*, and often in U.S., 'Alleluia! Alleluia!' for 'Praise him! praise him!' Noted in 1952 (*Hymns & Human Life*) as the most used of all English hymns at that time.

US & CAN: BP250: Can30: B8: CW259/73: H282: L160: M66: P14/31/

551: Pm16: CLB425: W228 ● ENG: AM298/365: An247: B23: BB15: CH21/360: CP18: E470: M12: NC193: PL95

598. PRAISE, O PRAISE OUR GOD AND KING

8 st. 77.77

H. W. Baker (101), *Hymns Ancient & Modern*, 1861, a harvest hymn in imitation of Milton's 'Let us with a gladsome mind' (394), to provide a simple hymn on the same theme and using, with one word altered, the same refrain, avoiding the metrical irregularities of the original.

US & CAN: CLB313 ● ENG: AM381/481: An650: BB441: M19

PRAISE, O SION, PRAISE THY MASTER: see 867.

599. PRAISE THE LORD, HIS GLORIES SHOW

2 st. 77.77 D

H. F. Lyte (5), *The Spirit of the Psalms*, 1834: Ps. 150; now norm. found as 77.77 or as 77.77 with interpolated alleluias. *AM(S)* has original form.

US & CAN: BP68: Can11: CW112/56: P12/4/552: Pm19 ● ENG: AM 544/- : CH16/359: CP20

600. PRAISE THE LORD OF HEAVEN, PRAISE HIM IN THE HEIGHT

3 st. 11 11.11 11 (or 6.5.6.5 D)

T. B. Browne, *The National Bankruptcy and Other Poems*, 1844; Ps. 148.

US & CAN: L427: CLB424 ● ENG: AM -/381: E534

T. B. BROWNE, b. Welshpool, Montgomeryshire, 25 xii 1805, is listed in *Julian* as THOMAS BRIERLEY BROWNE of Wellington, and in the early editions of *EH* as THOMAS BROWNE BROWNE of Wellington; which confusion is explained by the note in Frost's *Historical Companion to Hymns A & M* (1961) that in middle life he changed his name from Brown to Browne, starting out as T. Brierley Brown and later known as T. Browne Browne. Sch. Harrow Sch. and Brasenose, Oxf.; Barrister at Lincoln's Inn, '27; H. M. Inspector of Schools, '47-'74. Author of several pamphlets, including some against the Oxford Movement (83), and prominent evangelical Anglican churchman. Latterly lived at Mellington Hall, Montgomeryshire, and † there 16 ii 1874 (68).

601. PRAISE THE LORD! YE HEAVENS, ADORE HIM

2 st. 8.7.8.7 D   **PCH 82**

Anonymous, on a 4-page leaflet pasted into certain editions of the *Foundling Hospital Collection*, the earliest found being 1797. The tract is headed, 'Hymns' (in some, 'Hymn') *for Foundling Apprentices, attending Divine Service, to return Thanks,'* and in some this hymn is headed, 'Hymn from Ps. 148: Hayden,' which (since tune-indications are given with some others) indicates that the recently composed tune AUSTRIA, by F. J. Haydn, was intended (that tune was first sung 12 ii 1797 on the birthday of the Emperor of Austria). Sometimes this hymn appears with a 3rd st., WORSHIP, HONOUR, GLORY, BLESSING, which is a separate 1-st. hymn in the *Mitre Hymn Book*, 1836 by E. Osler (519) and stands as a separate hymn at CP750.

US & CAN: BP67: Can10: B11: CW110/79: L407: M42: P10/3/554: Pm 13: CLB440: W229 ● ENG: AM292/368: An29: B24: BB16: CH35/37: CP13: E535: M13: NC194: PL196

602. PRAISE TO GOD, IMMORTAL PRAISE

9 st. 77.77   **PCH 272**

A. L. Barbauld, *Hymns for Public Worship*, 1772: 'Praise to God in Prosperity and Adversity.' In modern abridgments the 'adversity' stanzas are omitted. *Pilgrim* uses it twice: once (464) rearranged in 6-line sts., adding a few non-original lines, and once (462) conflating 3 stanzas, slightly altered, with 12 lines of 'Come ye thankful people, come' (150) as an alternative—and a most intelligent one—to the normal version of that hymn for harvest.

US & CAN: Can386: CW595/95: P -/-/556: Pm464‡(462) • ENG: AM -/485

ANNA LAETITIA BARBAULD, b. Kibworth-Harcourt, Leics, 20 vi 1743, d. of a Dissenting minister, Rev. J. Aikin; received teaching from P. Doddridge (64) in her earliest youth, not far away at Northampton; m. a French Prot. minister, Rochemont Barbauld, '74; together they opened a boarding school at Palgrave, Sfk. † Newington Green (London), 9 iii 1825 (81).

603. PRAISE TO THE HOLIEST IN THE HEIGHT

CM   **PCH 442**

J. H. Newman (196), from *The Dream of Gerontius*, 1865, his long dramatic poem centred on death, resurrection and the Beatific Vision. In Pt. 5 of this it appears as 5 hymns, all beginning with the same stanza, sung by Choirs of Angelicals, and totalling (excluding the repeats of st. 1), 30 st. *Hymns Ancient & Modern*, 1868, brought the 5th section into use as a hymn by repeating st. 1 (the refrain stanza) at the end; and, with a very successful tune by J. B. Dykes, it at once established itself as a popular hymn in Britain; it has never done so in the U.S. This accepted vn. is in 7 st. but sometimes st. 4 of it is omitted.

US & CAN: BP252: CW -/386 (st. 1 only): H343: L411: Pm597 (st. 1 only): CLB459 • ENG: AM172/185: An160: B216: BB88: CH32/238: CP71: E471: M74: NC195: PL180

604. PRAISE TO THE LIVING GOD

4 st. 6.6.8.4 D

In the 12th century Moses Maimonides summed up the Jewish Faith in 13 articles, and in the 14th century Daniel ben Judah (of whom nothing is known apart from this) versified these articles in the *Yigdal* (Doxology). The Hebrew text of part of this can be read in the *Book of Worship for U.S. Forces* (1974), #61. Chance contact with the Jewish precentor Meyer Lyon in the mid-18th century caused T. Olivers (693) to write an English hymn based on it but introducing Christian ideas, beginning THE GOD OF ABRAHAM PRAISE (693). A much more literal paraphrase was made in the 19th century jointly by the Jewish rabbi Max Landsberg and the Unitarian minister Newton Mann, and appeared in the *Union Hymnal* (for Jewish worship), 1885. This begins as above. But certain U.S. hymnals now use this version, or part of it, substituting Olivers' first line for that of the 19 c. vn., and consequently THE GOD OF ABRAHAM PRAISE in those marked below is really Mann-Landsberg, not Olivers. Norm. this vn. uses sts. 1, 3, 4 of the 19 c. text and is indexed under THE GOD OF ABRAHAM.

US & CAN: Can22: B25‡: CW124/81‡: H286: M30: P8‡/89‡/587‡: Pm14‡: W230 • ENG: M15

For Olivers, see 693.

MOSES MAIMONIDES, b. Cordova, 1130, son of a learned Jewish Talmudist; Sch. at home; during anti-Jewish persecutions, 1149, settled in Fez, Morocco; left there 1165 for Palestine and shortly Cairo, where become head of the Jewish community; wrote commentary on the Mishnah (Jewish Oral Law), 1168, and his Talmudic Code, 1180: these in Hebrew; all other works, legal and theological, were in Arabic as part of his project for promoting understanding between Israel and Islam. † Cairo, 1204.

MAX LANDSBERG, b. Berlin, Germany, 1845; Sch. privately, then Hildesheim Gymnasium, Bottingen & Breslau. Taught at Sem. for Jewish teachers, Hanover, '66-71; became rabbi, '70; ministered at Temple Berith Kodesh, Rochester, N.Y., 1871-1905. President, New York State Conference of Charities & Correction. † New York, 1928 (83).

NEWTON MANN, b. 16 i 1836, Cazenovia, N.Y.; Sch. Cazenovia Sem.; Ord. Unit., 1865. Served in Kenosha, Wis., and Troy and Rochester, N.Y. where he collaborated with Landsberg as above; finally in Omaha,

Neb. † Chicago, 25 vii 1926 (90).

605. PRAISE TO THE LORD, THE ALMIGHTY, THE KING OF CREATION

5 st. 14 14. 4 7. 8   **PCH 199**

German: LOBE DEN HERREN, DEN MACHTIGE KONIG DER EHREN, J. Neander (19), *Glaubund Liebes-ubung*, posth. 1680; Ps. 103, 150. In using this extraordinary but highly successful meter he was imitating an earlier hymn, 'Hast du denn Liebster,' first published in 1665; the now very well known tune was first associated with that text, but was at once transferred to his.

Tr. C. Winkworth (14), 4 st., in *Chorale-Book for England*, 1863, her st. 2 including thoughts from orig. sts. 2-3. This tr., which leapt to popularity after being included in *English Hymnal*, 1906, had certain rhythmic difficulties and is never now sung in orig. form (not even in *EH*). Nearest to orig. is the 3 st. version in *Book of Worship for U.S. Forces* (1974), #18; but normally used alterations come from *EH* and from *Hymns Ancient & Modern*, 1916.

EH adds 3 st. after st. 3 which are no part of original and must be attributed to P. Dearmer (88); *M(Brit.)* uses 2 of these as its sts. 3-4. A very good tr. of all 5 orig. sts. was made by E. W. Palmer in *Hymns & Chorales* (Oxford), 1892. Two unusual versions are in *CLB*.

US & CAN: BP83: Can29: B10: CW98/57: H279: L408: M55: P6/1/557: Pm15: CLB348, 419: W231 • ENG: AM657/382: An246: B25: BB17: CH22/9: CP45: E536: M64: NC198‡: PL14

606. PRAISE WE OUR GOD THIS DAY

6 st. SM

Anon. *Hymns for the Festivals . . . ,* 1846, beginning 'Let us praise God this day'; as above in *Hymns Ancient & Modern*, 1861. In *CLB*, 'O Praise the Lord. . . .'

US & CAN: Can406: H118: CLB310‡: W232 • ENG: AM409/546: M*60: NC265‡: PL135

607. PRAY THAT JERUSALEM MAY HAVE

3 st. CM   **PCH 424**

The most usual version outside Scotland of metrical Psalm 122 in *Scot. Psalter*, 1650 (323), being vv. 6-9; in some books other sts. are added from Ps. 133 and 116. The idea of making a 3 st. hymn out of this fragment seems to have originated with C. H. Spurgeon in his first hymn book, 1866. It is one of the few Scottish Psalms which have come into wide currency outside the Presbyterian Communion (cf. 23, 121).

US & CAN: BP55 st. 3-5 • ENG: BB472: ScPs.122 vv. 6-9/CH489: CP742: E472: M*61: NC200

608. PRAYER IS THE SOUL'S SINCERE DESIRE

8 st. CM   **PCH 111**

J. Montgomery (6), 1818 for Bickersteth's *Treatise on Prayer*, 1819 (517); also in *The Christian Psalmist*, 1825. Slightly altered by author later to text now in use. In *CP*, *PM* and *BP*, the last st. is put at the beginning, O THOU BY WHOM WE COME TO GOD. Norm. abr. to 6 st. or fewer (*EH* has 7 st.).

US & CAN: BP432‡: B400: CW335/- : L458: M252: P -/391/- : Pm336‡ • ENG: An611: B340: BB347: CP445‡: E474: M533

609. PUT FORTH, O LORD, THY SPIRIT'S POWER

4 st. CM

H. C. Robbins, *New Church Hymnal*, 1937. Author's own tune at *H (U.S.)* 380.

US & CAN: H380: L243: P -/477/559 • ENG:

HOWARD CHANDLER ROBBINS, b. Philadelphia, 11 xii 1876; Sch. Yale

Univ. and Episc. Sem.; Ord. Episc., 1904; curate at St. Peter's, Morristown, Pa., 1903-5; Rector of St. Paul's, Englewood, N.J., '05; of Ch. of the Incarnation, New York, '11; Dean of Cathedral of St. John the Divine, New York, '17; Prof. Pastoral Theology, General Th. Sem., New York, '29-'41; delegate to World Conference on Faith & Order, 1937; member of ed. cttee., *Hymnal-1940*. His hymn there 'And have the bright immensities' (#354) was the first attempt in U.S. to relate the Ascension to modern scientific terminology. † 1952.

PUT THOU THY TRUST IN GOD: see 840.

610.   REJOICE, O LAND, IN GOD THY MIGHT

3 st. LM-coup.   PCH 259

R. Bridges, *Yattendon Hymnal*, 1899; Joel 2:21; written for TALLIS' CANON.

US & CAN: H520: Pm430 ● ENG: AM -/582: An663: B651: BB433: CP571: E475: M882

611.   REJOICE, O PEOPLE, IN THE MOUNTING YEARS

6 st. 10.10.10.10.10 10

A. F. Bayly (537), written 1945 for the Triple Jubilee of the London Missionary Society (founded 1795); printed in *Rejoice, O People*, 1950, *BBC Hymn Book* 1951, and *Congregational Praise*, 1951; it was the first published hymn of this later famous writer.

US & CAN: BP299: Pm304 ● ENG: B389: BB181: CP347

612.   REJOICE, THE LORD IS KING

6 st. 6.6.6.6.88

C. Wesley (1), *Hymns for our Lord's Resurrection*, 1746; 'Rejoice evermore, Phil. 4:8.' In orig. form the refrain of sts. 1-5 is changed at st. 6, but many hymnals use only sts. 1-4. Only *M(Brit.)* uses full text. The best known of the 3 hymns of C. W. which were set to music by G. F. Handel.

US & CAN: BP216: Can44: B120: CW260/188: H350: L436: M483: P193/140/562: Pm204: W235 ● ENG: AM202/216: An210: B190: BB128: CH135/296: CP161: E476: M247: NC204: PL244

REJOICE, THE YEAR UPON ITS WAY: see 839.

613.   REJOICE TO-DAY WITH ONE ACCORD

2 st. 8.7.8.7.66.66.7

H. W. Baker (101), *Hymns Ancient & Modern*, 1861; 'General Thanksgiving'; to provide a hymn for 'high church' Anglicans which would enable them to sing Luther's tune EIN FESTE BURG, without committing them to his theology.

US & CAN: ● ENG: AM378/- : An25: BB281: E537: M885: PL98

614.   REJOICE, YE PURE IN HEART

11 st. SM

E. H. Plumptre (534), for a Diocesan Festival in Peterborough Cathedral, 1865: in *Hymns Ancient & Modern*, 1868. Fullest version now in 10 st. in *AMR* (om. st. 2) and *EH* (om. 3); elsewhere abr. For some time very popular in U.S., and given extended life recently by the historic setting (1974) of Richard Dirksen (*Westminster Praise* #1).

US & CAN: BP525: B28: CW418/97: H579: L555: M233: P297/407/561: Pm345 ● ENG: AM393/635: E644

615.   REMEMBER ALL THE PEOPLE

3 st. CMD-irreg.

P. Dearmer (88), for Church Missionary Society, 1929; in *Songs of Praise for Boys and Girls*, 1930.

US & CAN: CW528/- : H262: L317: P -/495/- : Pm484 ● ENG: B390: CP344: M864

616.   REST OF THE WEARY, JOY OF THE SAD

4 st. 5.4.5.4 D dact.

J. S. B. Monsell (193), *Hymns of Love and Praise*, 1863.

US & CAN: ● ENG: B217: CH174/- : E579: M101

617.   RESCUE THE PERISHING

4 st. 11.10.11.10.11.10 dact.   PCH 402

Fanny Crosby (84), after a visit to a mission in downtown New York City; pub. in Doane's *Songs of Devotion*, 1870. The only 'Gospel Song' to be included in any edition of *Hymns Ancient & Modern*.

US & CAN: B283: M175 ● ENG: AM764/- : B522: CH681/- : M338

618.   REVIVE THY WORK, O LORD

5 st. SM (ref. added).

A. Midlane, *Evangelist's Handbook*, 1860; refrain added by Fanny Crosby (84) to give it a Gospel Song style.

US & CAN: BP269 ● ENG: AM766/362: An139: B391: CH679/- : M738: PL171

ALBERT MIDLANE, b. 23 i 1825, Carisbrooke, Isle of Wight; in business at Newport, I o W, all his life. Canon H. E. Edwards wrote to the compiler in 1953: 'When I was a boy he kept a little ironmonger's shop in St. James' Street, Newport; I remember him as a little old man with a short beard and a battered bowler on the back of his head who would sell me a pennyworth of nails across the counter. . . . On Sundays he used to lead the worship of a small group of Plymouth Brethren in the tabernacle on the outskirts of the town.' Midlane, who wrote over 700 hymns (*Gospel Hall Selection*, 1904, contains 533) said, 'Most of my hymns have been written during walks around the ancient & historic ruins of Carisbrooke Castle.' † Newport, 27 ii 1904 (79).

619.   RIDE ON, RIDE ON IN MAJESTY

5 st. LM-coup.   PCH 120

H. H. Milman (524) in Heber's posth. *Hymns*, 1827; in orig. form (as *EH, CP*) unquestionably one of the great lyrics from early 19 cent. But often altd. in form given in *Hymns A & M*, 1861: comment in note on Alford (150) certainly applies here.

US & CAN: BP176: Can449: CW223/156: H64: M425: P150/188/563: Pm175: W255 ● ENG: AM99: An167: B128: BB89: CH92/234: CP122: E620: M92: NC206: PL185

620.   RING OUT, WILD BELLS, TO THE WILD SKY

8.88.8   PCH 444

A. Tennyson, taken from canto 106 of *In Memoriam*, 1850. First as a hymn in *Fellowship Hymn Book*, 1909, which uses sts. 1, 3, 4, 6, 7, 8 of the 8 st. canto. Elsewhere other selections; *CW* (both edns.) uses 2, 4, 7, 8 beginning RING OUT THE OLD. . . .

US & CAN: CW589/363: P466/526/- : Pm453: CLB230 ● ENG: M905

ALFRED, LORD TENNYSON, b. 6 viii 1809 at the Rectory, Somersby, Lincs; Sch. Louth Gram. Sch. and Trinity, Camb.; on completion of studies went travelling with his friend Arthur Hallam (whose death, 1833, caused him to write *In Memoriam*, above); thereafter devoted himself to writing poetry, having already produced several that achieved greatness. Became the most eminent poet of his time, and in 1850 succeeded Wordsworth as Poet Laureate (these two being by far the most productive and inspired holders of that office). Among his most valued poems were *In Memoriam, Idylls of the King*, and (in smaller forms) *Ulysses* and *Ode on the Duke of Wellington*. His collected poems fill 636 double column pages in a popular edition. Created Baron, 1884; † 6 x 1892 in the Isle of Wight (83). He is buried in Westminster Abbey.

621. RISE, CROWNED WITH LIGHT, IMPERIAL SALEM, RISE

4 st. 10 10. 10 10   **PCH 45**

A. Pope, cento. In *The Spectator* for 14 v 1714 its editor T. Addison (295) published an Ode by Pope in 108 lines of heroic couplets beginning 'Ye nymphs of Solyma! begin the song; / to heavenly themes sublimer strains belong'; the poem was entitled *Messiah* and modelled on the Eclogues of Virgil (especially the 4th), being founded on thoughts from the Second Isaiah. The 16-line cento still in use has been in continuous circulation in the Episc. Ch. of the U.S.A. since being published in the first hymn book of that church, the *Hymnal of the Protestant Episcopal Church*, 1826. The cento uses (1) lines 85-6, 87-8; (2) lines 87-90; (3) lines 91-4; (4) 105-8: line 94 always altered. (See *PCH* 45 for more of the poem). It is not known who made the selection, which, as a monument of the English Augustan style, is unique in hymnody and deserves to be better known. It has never been used in the author's own country.

US & CAN: CW477/- : H389: P346/-/-: CLB475‡ ● ENG:

ALEXANDER POPE, b. London, 21 v 1688, was the son of a linen-merchant and Sch. at Catholic schools until age 12, when he had an illness which left him crippled; thereafter he was self-educated. By age 16 he was already writing verse, and becoming known in London literary circles; among the verses which first made him known were his *Pastorals*. His reputation was finally established with *The Rape of the Lock*, written at age 25. Thereafter his works, including translation of the two great works of Homer, *Essay on Criticism*, *Dunciad*, and *Essay on Man* brought him to the highest place in English letters of his time. Lived from 1718 in a villa at Twickenham, Middx, and † there 30 v 1744 (56).

622. RISE UP, O MEN OF GOD

4 st. SM

W. P. Merrill (482), on a steamer on Lake Michigan going to Chicago, after reading an article by G. S. Lee, 'The Church of the Strong Men.' It appeared in *The Continent*, 16 ii 1911, and soon became very popular. First in Britain in the *Congregational Hymnary*, 1916.

US & CAN: BP466: B268: CW374/93: H535: L541: M174: P401/352/564: Pm300 ● ENG: AM*85: B523: BB364: CH344/477: CP561: M585

623. ROCK OF AGES, CLEFT FOR ME

4 st. 77.77.77   **PCH 80**

A. M. Toplady (3); first 4 lines appeared in the *Gospel Magazine*, Oct. 1775 in an article on 'Life's Journey' followed by the words, 'Make these words of the Apostle your motto: "Perplexed but not in despair; cast down but not destroyed."' The full text came in *Gospel Magazine*, March '76, at the end of an article, 'Questions and Answers relative to the National Debt,' which is so remarkable that we reprint it in our Appendix (pp. 113-114). The story that this hymn was written in a storm in a cave in the West of England on a playing-card is without foundation; the text as it stands is orig. except that in st. 4 line 2 we do not sing orig. vn., 'When my eye-strings break in death.' Until recently this was one of the world's most famous hymns.

US & CAN: BP397: B163: CW294/- : H471: L379: M120: P237/271/- : Pm359 ● ENG: AM184/210: An492: B458: BB296: CH413/83: CP477: E477: M498

624. ROUND ME FALLS THE NIGHT

3 st. 55.88.55

W. Romanis, *Wigston Magna School Hymns*, 1878.

US & CAN: L237: P502/-/- ● ENG: AM -/35: An61: BB422: CH -/650:

E272: PL314

WILLIAM ROMANIS, b. Westminster (London), 30 iv 1824; Sch. Emmanuel, Camb.; Ord. C/E, 1847; Classical master, Cheltenham College, '46-'56; then after curacies, Vicar of Wigston Magna, Leics, '63; of Twyford, Leics, '88-'95. † Twyford, 13 xi 1899 (75).

ROUND THE LORD IN GLORY SEATED: see 95.

625. SAFELY THROUGH ANOTHER WEEK

6 st. 7.7.7.7.77

J. Newton (37), in Conyers, *A Collection of Psalms & Hymns*, 3rd ed., 1774, and *Olney Hymns*, 1779; 'Saturday evening.' 1779 text always used; st. 2 always omitted, others sometimes.

US & CAN: CW448/- : L185: M489: P -/74/- ● ENG:

626. SAINT PATRICK'S BREASTPLATE   PCH 320

Irish: ATOMRIUG INDIU NIURT TREN

This ancient Irish poem is uncertainly but affectionately attributed to St. Patrick. The history of the original is thus set out by James Moffatt in the *Handbook to the Church Hymnary* (1930).

In the year A.D. 432, when Patrick landed in Ireland to 'sow the Faith,' he made his way to Tara, the capital of Meath, where the 'High King' of Ireland, Leary, held his court among the vassal-kings of the land. It was the time of the triennial convention of those petty rulers, and the Christian Festival of Easter was also drawing near. Patrick and his company, halting at the Hill of Slane beside the Boyne Water, some ten miles from Tara, and in full view of it, celebrated the Eve of the Feast by lighting a great fire. That same night in Tara, Leary and his chieftains also kept festival, but the royal edict had gone forth that no one on pain of death should kindle a fire either in Tara or anywhere on the surrounding plains until the King himself fired the beacon which had been piled up close to the palace. As he went out to light it, far away to the north was seen the gleam of fire on the Hill of Slane. Leary summoned his Druids and demanded what this could mean. They replied, 'King: unless this fire which you see be quenched this very night, it will never be quenched, and the kindler of it will overcome all and seduce all the folk of our realm.' Greatly angered, the King replied, 'It shall not be: but we will go to see the issue of the matter, and we will put to death those who do such sin against our kingdom.' Thus saying, he gave orders for his chariots to be yoked, and wheeling them widdershins (contrary to the course of the sun), in order to counteract all spells, accompanied by two of his chief Druids he drove headlong over the plain to Boyne. They drew rein before they came within the circle of the light of Patrick's fire, lest he should cast his spell over them. But he, when he was summoned and saw this array, lifted up his voice in the 20th Psalm from the Vulgate: 'Some trust in chariots and some in horses, but we will remember the name of the Lord our God'; and then they sant the words of the *Lorica* (the 'Breastplate') in Irish. So the 'Day of Tara,' as it is called in the old Irish records, was won' (loc. cit. p. 171).

> (Note especially (i) the emphasis on magic and spells as taken up in Mrs. Alexander's translation of the hymn, and (ii) the reference to the 'High King,' which is echoed in 'Be thou my Vision' (72) whose inseparable tune is called SLANE.).

Tr. the *Lorica* is now known in 3 English translations:

> (a) I BIND UNTO MYSELF TO-DAY, by Mrs. Alexander (24) in 7½ st., DLM-irreg., with one st. 88.88 D troch. interpolated before the last. This was written for St. Patrick's Day (17 March) 1889 and printed in the Appendix to *The Writings of St. Patrick*, ed. C. H. H. Wright, 1889. It is associated with the tune ST. PATRICK'S BREASTPLATE, in C. V. Stanford's edition (1903) of Petrie's *Collection of Irish Music*, from which it was taken into *EH* in 1906. The interpolated verse, 'Christ be with me . . .' has 3 different tunes in that and in later hymnals. It is now understood to be a free translation and ex-

pansion of the original, and that its opening line rests on a mistranslation. But it is equally likely that its author who had already lived long in Ireland meant to emphasize the non-legendary aspect of the text, and to promote its main purpose, which was to be a Christian baptismal confession associated with the ancient rite of Holy Saturday baptism. Certainly this trsln. beautifully combined the dogmatic and the legendary in its choice of language, which is very different in rhythm and vocabulary from that which is found in this author's many other hymns.

(b) The *Worshipbook* (1972) has a much shorter version, I SING AS I ARISE TO-DAY, by J. W. Clokey, 1964: 2 st. LMD with 1 st. 88.88 D troch. at the end.

(c) *Church Hymnary*, 1927 and 1973, has TO-DAY I ARISE, by R. A. S. Macalister, 9 st., stress 2-4-4-4, written for the 1927 edition, adapted to Irish airs different from those used in (a) and (b), and closer to original meter and style.

Full text of (a) only in *EH*; elsewhere abr. In index below, vn. is (a) unless otherwise noted.

US & CAN: BP276: Can68: H268: L*746: P -/-/428 (b): W127 ● ENG: AM655/162: An229: B433: BB170: CH506(a), 505(c)/402(a)/401(c): CP 753: E212: M392: NC98: PL221

ST. PATRICK, b. about 389 Bannavem (unidentified: either Britain or Gaul); at age 16 captured by raiders and taken to Ireland. Made to work as a shepherd for 6 years, then escaped in a ship to Gaul, where then his family lived. But soon had a vision in which he was told to return and evangelize Ireland. In France prob. studied at monasteries of Lerins and Auxerre, and prob. Ord. c. 415. Sent to assist Palladius, bishop in Ireland, and succeeded him, 432. Thereafter by extensive travelling and preaching became the evangelist of Ireland, promoting both faith and learning. †, prob. in Ireland, about 461.

ROBERT ALEXANDER STEWART MACALISTER, b. Dublin, 8 vii 1870; Sch. Rathmines, Germany and Cambridge; became distinguished archaeologist and musician. Director of excavations to Palestine Exploration Fund, 1900-9 and '23-4, on which expeditions very important discoveries were made affecting O.T. scholarship; became Prof. of Celtic archaeology in Univ. Dublin. † Cambridge, 26 ix 1950 (79).

627. SAVIOUR, AGAIN TO THY DEAR NAME WE RAISE

4 st. 10 10. 10 10

J. Ellerton (80), 1866, for the Malpas, Middlewich and Nantwich Choral Association (cf. 589); reduced from 6 st. to 4 st. by author before going into *Hymns Ancient & Modern*, 1868.

US & CAN: BP561: Can370: B65: CW128/82: H487: L198: M236: P55/77/- : Pm60 ● ENG: AM31: An63: B702: BB423: CH301/649: CP635: E273: M691

628. SAVIOUR, BLESSED SAVIOUR

8 st. 6.5.6.5 D

G. Thring (191), *Hymns Congregational and Others*, 1862; text slightly altered in *Hymns Ancient & Modern*, 1868, and thus altd. remained standard. Norm. abr. now.

US & CAN: CW269/- : H580: L425: P202/-/- ● ENG: AM305/- : B459: E645: M672

629. SAVIOUR, BREATHE AN EVENING BLESSING

2 st. 8.7.8.7 D

J. Edmeston (386), *Sacred Lyrics*, 1st set, 1820, after reading in Salte's *Travels in Abyssinia* how the native Christians' 'short evening hymn, "Jesus forgives," stole through the camp.'

US & CAN: H178: L221: M496: P47/54/- ● ENG: CH285/-

630. SAVIOUR, LIKE A SHEPHERD LEAD US

4 st. 8.7.8.7.4.7

Authorship uncertain; anon. in Dorothy A. Thrupp's *Hymns for the Young*, 1836 therefore sometimes attributed to her; but in *The Children's Friend*, June 1838, it is followed by the name 'Lyte.' No disclaimer followed, although another hymn by Lyte was contained in a later issue, so he was known to the editor. Probability is against Mrs. Thrupp because in Mayo's *Selection of Hymns*, 1846 (another children's book), several, but not this, are credited to her. There seems to be no reason why Lyte (5) should not be the author.

US & CAN: BP527: B213: CW410/220: H247: L524: M121: P458/380/- ● ENG: CH554/- : M609

631. SAVIOUR, SPRINKLE MANY NATIONS

3 st. 8.7.8.7 D

A. C. Coxe (572), begun Good Friday, 1850—the opening line recalls the opening of the Fourth Servant Song: Is. 52:15—completed 1851 in the grounds of Magdalen College, Oxford; pub. in *Verses for 1851 in Commemoration of the 3rd Jubilee of the Society for the Propagation of the Gospel* and in *Hymns Ancient & Modern*, 1868. The first line echoes the King James version of Is. 52:15 which is now generally agreed to be a mistranslation: but (see biography) this is an objection with which the author would have been out of sympathy; sometimes now reads 'Saviour quicken. . . .'

US & CAN: L312 ● ENG: AM359/-: B392: CH382/- : CP336: E551: M800

632. SAVIOUR, TEACH ME DAY BY DAY

4 st. 77.77 D

Jane E. Leeson (444), *Hymns & Songs of Childhood*, 1842; now norm. as 77.77 and abr. by omitting sts. 1b, 2b, 3a.

US & CAN: BP479: Can288: B291: CW389/- : H428: L528: M162: P452/457/- ● ENG: An545: B484: CH437/450: CP448

633. SAVIOUR, THY DYING LOVE

4 st. 6.4.6.4.666.4

S. D. Phelps, anon. in Boston *Watchman and Reflector*, 1862, later drastically revised by author to present form in S. C. Lowry's *Pure Gold*, 1871.

US & CAN: B418: CW357/260: L463: M177: P396/311/- ● ENG: An594: B485: M579

SYLVANUS DRYDEN PHELPS, b. Suffield, Conn., 15 v 1816; Sch. Conn. Literary Institute, Brown Univ., Yale Div. Sch.; Ord. Bapt., served at First Bapt. Ch., New Haven, Conn., 1846-74, then after 2 years at Jefferson St. Bapt. Ch., Providence, R.I., became editor of *Christian Secretary*. † New Haven, 23 xi 1895 (79).

634. SAVIOUR, WHEN IN DUST TO THEE

5 st. 77.77 D

R. Grant (575), *Christian Observer*, 1815 and *Poems*, 1839.

US & CAN: H332: L72 ● ENG: AM251/86: E87: M726

635. SEE AMID THE WINTER'S SNOW (SEE IN YONDER MANGER LOW)

7 st. 77.77 with refrain 77.77

E. Caswall (26), taken from a longer poem in *The Masque of Mary*, 1858, given in 6 st. in Bramley & Stainer, *Christmas Carols New and Old*, 1871. The insular 'winter's snow' altd. in some books as above.

US & CAN: BP128: Can414 ● ENG: An119: B107: CH51/179: CP715: M124: NC208: PL144

636. SEE THE CONQUEROR MOUNTS IN TRIUMPH

10 st. 8.7.8.7 D written as 15 15. 15 15   **PCH 223**

C. Wordsworth (27), *The Holy Year*, 1862. Originally written to encompass both Ascension and Pentecost, it was divided in later editions of *H.Y.* into 2 parts, the second beginning 'Holy Ghost, Illuminator;' and appears thus in *Hymns Ancient & Modern* (1875-1922); all other books reduce it; *EH* to 7 st., others 5 or fewer, leaving a torso of what was one of the profoundest & most scriptural utterances in hymnody since the days of C. Wesley.

US & CAN: H103: L112: P173/-/- : CLB291 ● ENG: AM148: An208: B171: BB129: E145: M223: PL212

SEE THE DESTINED DAY ARISE: see 868.

637. SHEPHERD DIVINE, OUR WANTS RELIEVE

6 st. CM

C. Wesley (1), *Hymns & Sacred Poems*, 1740; 'In Temptation.' Gen. 32; Mk. 9:2-9.

US & CAN: BP521 ● ENG: AM248/318: An564: BB348: CP494: M736

SHEPHERD OF SOULS, REFRESH AND BLESS: see 68.

638. SHEPHERD OF TENDER YOUTH

5 st. 6.5.6.5.666.5

M. H. Dexter, *The Congregationalist*, Dec., 1849 and *Hymns for the Church of Christ*, paraphrasing a passage appended to the *Paidagogus* of Clement of Alexandria (c. 140-220 A.D.). Title in the original is 'Hymn of the Saviour Christ.' Another version, MASTER OF EAGER YOUTH, by F. Bland Tucker, (22) is in *H(U.S.)*. The word 'eager' is now sometimes taken from that version into the first line of the older one.

US & CAN: CW266/- : H362‡: L179: M86: P -/471/- ● ENG: B555

HENRY MARTIN DEXTER, b. Plympton, Mass., 13 viii 1821; Sch. Yale and Andover Theol. Sem.; Ord. Congl., 1844; served in Manchester, N.H. and then Berkeley St. Congl. Ch., Boston, Mass., '49-'67. Edited *The Congregationalist*, and was the leading historian of American Congregationalism. This is his only contribution to hymnody. † Boston, 13 xi 1890 (69).

SING ALLELUIA FORTH IN DUTEOUS (LOYAL) PRAISE: see 835.

SING, MY TONGUE, THE GLORIOUS BATTLE (and variants): see 868.

SING, MY TONGUE, THE SAVIOUR'S GLORY: see 867.

639. SING. O SING THIS BLESSED MORN

4 st. 77.77.77

C. Wordsworth (27), *The Holy Year*, 1862: for Christmas.

US & CAN: BP133: H26: CLB213 ● ENG: An116: BB59: CP87: PL143

640. SING PRAISE TO GOD WHO REIGNS ABOVE

8.7.8.7.88.7 (last line always refrain)   **PCH 196**

German: SEI LOB' UND EHR, 9 st., J. Schutz, *Christliches Gedankbuchlein*, 1675; Deut. 32:3.

Tr. F. E. Cox (352) sts. 1-8, orig. meter, in *Lyra Eucharistica*, 1864; now abr. to 5 st. or fewer, different selections from book to book.

US & CAN: BP75: B22: CW -/26: L422: M4: P -/15/568: Pm20: W249 ●

ENG: AM293/366: An565: B28: BB18: CL -/142: E478: M415: PL228

JOHANN JAKOB SCHUTZ, b. Frankford/Main, 7 ix 1640; Sch. Tubingen, then returned to Frankfort as a lawyer and remained there the rest of his life. † 22 v 1690 (49).

641. SING TO THE LORD A JOYFUL SONG

6 st. LM-alt.

J. S. B. Monsell (193), *Hymns of Love & Praise*, 1863; Ps. 145:2. Became especially popular in Scotland after being set to tune GONFALON ROYAL in *Church Hymnary* (1927).

US & CAN: Can198: CW -/63: W250 ● ENG: B29: BB19: CH23/366

642. SING TO THE LORD OF HARVEST

4 st. 7.6.7.6 D

J. S. B. Monsell (193), *Hymns of Love and Praise*.

US & CAN: Can382: B232: L*793: P -/-/569: CLB316 ● ENG: B730: BB442

643. SING WE A SONG OF HIGH REVOLT

4 st. LM-coup.

F. H. Kaan (202), *Pilgrim Praise*, 1966, based on the *Magnificat*; in U.S. and Canada its final line, containing the phrase 'council flat' (which in English use means subsidized limited-income apartment) normally altd.

US & CAN: A*86: B*74 ● ENG: Can177: CLB502

644. SING WE OF THE MODERN CITY

3 st. 8.7.8.7 D

F. H. Kaan (202), *Pilgrim Praise*, 1966, first line suggested by Felix Adler's 'Sing we of the golden city.'

US & CAN: Can125: H*32: W251 ● ENG: B*75

SING WE TRIUMPHANT HYMNS OF PRAISE: see 852.

645. SINNERS JESUS WILL RECEIVE

German: JESUS NIMMT DIE SUNDER AN, 8 st. 7.8.7.8.77, E. Neumeister, *Evangelische Nachklang*, 1718: Luke 15:1.

Tr. E. F. Bevan, *Songs of Eternal Life*, 1858, 8 st. 7.7.7.7.77; sts. 2, 4, 7 now always omitted, others sometimes. A 'Gospel Song' version uses 4 st. with a refrain (anon.) dating from the revivals of c. 1870, in *M322*.

US & CAN: B167‡: L377: P227/-/- ● ENG: An478: CH394/- : M322

ERDMANN NEUMEISTER, b. Uechterlitz, nr. Weissenfels, Germany, 1671; Sch. Univ. Leipzig, then lecturer there. Ord. Luth., 1697, at Bibra, then pastor & superintendent, Ekatsberg district, '98; tutor and asst. court preacher, Weissenfels, 1704; superintendent at Scrau; St. James', Hamburg, 1715. There he had an interesting association with J. S. Bach from 1720, in which year J. S. unsuccessfully applied for the position of organist at his church; Neumeister favored him & was angry at his rejection by the Church Council; subsequently N. wrote the libretti of Bach's Cantatas 18, 59, 61, 142 and 160; in so doing he invented the cantata-form which J. S. B. made so famous. † Hamburg 1756.

EMMA FRANCES BEVAN, née Shuttleworth, b. Oxford, 25 ix 1827; d. of P. N. Shuttleworth, Warden of New College and later Bp. of Chichester; m. R. C. L. Bevan, London banker, 1856; joined Plymouth Brethren but, disappointed in them, turned to study of German mystics & pietists, which led her to become a translator of their hymns. † Cannes, France, 13 ii 1909 (81).

646. SOLDIERS OF CHRIST, ARISE

16 st. SMD

C. Wesley (1), in *The Character of a Methodist*, 1742, and *Hymns & Sacred Poems*, 1749; 'The Whole Armour of God,' Eph. 6:10ff. J. Wesley in the 1780 Methodist *Collection* made it manageable by incl. sts. 1-4 only (32 lines); this selection is now used only by Engl. Methodists. *Hymns Ancient & Modern* in 1861 arranged it in SM, using sts. 1, 2a, 16a, 2b, with a spurious doxology; this (without doxology) was the pattern for most books until an attractive SMD tune appeared, called FROM STRENGTH TO STRENGTH (The tune first appeared in 1902 but became popular outside schools only when taken up by *Songs of Praise*, 1925, and *Church Hymnary*, 1927). Although in the *Public School Hymn Book*, 1919 it appears with the *A & M* selection of stanzas (and thus has to be sung 2½ times, with repeat of second half for last st.) its existence encouraged later eds. to use a more generous selection, restoring SMD: e.g. *CP*, which has 32 lines, sts. 1, 2, 4a-11a, 16. The name of the tune suggests an echo of a line always now in the hymn but not in J. W.'s selection. In U.S.A. always in SMD, 3 st., but never, so far, with the English SMD tune.

US & CAN: BP470: Can171: CW -/254: H552: L564: M250: P269/362/- : Pm384 ● ENG: AM270‡/303: An585: B508: BB366: CH534/441: CP497: E479: M484

647. SOLDIERS OF THE CROSS, ARISE

7 st. 7.7.7.7

W. W. How (75), *Psalms & Hymns*, 1854.

US & CAN: ● ENG: AM588/305: An601: B524: BB367: CH341/478: CP548

648. SOLDIERS WHO ARE CHRIST'S BELOW

5 st. 77.77

Latin: PUGNATE, CHRISTI MILITES, 5 st. LM, anon., in *Chalons-sur-Mer Breviary*, 1736.

Tr.: J. Clark, at Marston, Montgomeryshire, Palm Sunday, 1865; *Hymns Ancient & Modern*, 1868.

US & CAN: ● ENG: AM447/524: An435: BB337: E480

JOHN HALDENBY CLARK, b. Chesterfield, Derbs., 28 i 1839; Sch. Chesterfield Gram. Sch. & St. John's, Camb.; Ord. C/E; Vicar of W. Dereham, Nfk., 1870- † there 14 iv 1888 (49).

649. SOMETIMES A LIGHT SURPRISES

4 st. 7.6.7.6 D   PCH 95

W. Cowper, *Olney Hymns*, Bk. III, 1779; 'Joy and Peace in Believing.'

US & CAN: B221: CW581/- : H443: L495: M231: P296/418/- ● ENG: AM -/176: An530: B585: CH439/- : CP398: M527

650. SON OF GOD, ETERNAL SAVIOUR

5 st. 8.7.8.7 D

S. C. Lowry, *Goodwill*, Feb. 1894; *Christian Social Union Hymn Book*, 1895; *Hymns Ancient & Modern*, 1904. *EH* has full text: elsewhere st. 3 or (better) 4 omitted.

US & CAN: Can292: CW502/- : H500: L542: P393/-/573: Pm413: W254 ● ENG: AM677/207: B652: BB377: CH359/454: CP558: E529

SOMERSET CORRY LOWRY, b. Dublin, 21 iii 1855; Sch. Repton Sch. and Trinity, Camb.; Ord. C/E 1880; Vicar of St. Augustine's, Bournemouth, 1900; Rector of Wonston, 1911; Vicar of St. Bartholomew, Southsea, '14-'19. † Torquay, Devon, 29 i 1932 (76).

651. SON OF THE LORD MOST HIGH

5 st. 6.6.6.6.88   PCH 461

G. W. Briggs (110), *Prayers and Hymns for Use in Schools*, 1927.

US & CAN: ● ENG: AM*87: B129: CH -/219: CP117

652. SONGS OF PRAISE THE ANGELS SANG

6 st. 77.77

J. Montgomery (6), Cotterill's *Selection*, 8th ed. 1819 (333); 'God worthy of all Praise.' Unusual in literary form in that the phrase 'Songs of Praise' occurs 10 times in 24 lines, but in different parts of the sts. Some mus. eds., by printing it as 77.77D, or by omitting sts., miss the other formal point, which is that the hymn divides clearly into 2 groups of 3 st., not 3 of 2.

US & CAN: BP315: Can36: H292: L432: P11/-/- : CLB432 ● ENG: AM 297/369: An26: CH38/38: CP15: E481: M*64

653. SONGS OF THANKFULNESS AND PRAISE

5 st. 77.77 D

C. Wordsworth (27), *The Holy Year*, 1862; designed for 6th Sunday after Epiphany, as author wrote, 'to recapitulate all the Epiphanies' which were the subjects of previous Sundays, and to reflect Collect, Epistle and Gospel for Epiphany VI; hence the 12-fold appearance of the word 'manifest';—a point of form which by coincidence resembles that in 652 above.

US & CAN: BP147: Can433: H53: L55: CLB232: W255 ● ENG: AM81: An131: E47: PL163

654. SOULS OF MEN, WHY WILL YE SCATTER?

13 st. 8.7.8.7   PCH 211

F. W. Faber (175), *Hymns*, 1862; but in 8 st. form had appeared in *Oratory Hymns*, 1854. Longer text is now basis of selection, which is norm. 8 st. or fewer (*AMR* omits sts. 3, 6, 7, 9). Many eds. begin at st. 4, THERE'S A WIDENESS IN GOD'S MERCY, following *EH*, which has 8 st.—4, 5, 7-10, 12-13.

US & CAN: BP409: Can76: B171: CW172/13: H304: L493: M69: P93/110/601: Pm101: CLB437 ● ENG: AM634/364: An480: B419: BB20: CH395/218: CP369: E499: M318: NC215

655. SOW IN THE MORN THY SEED

7 st. SM

J. Montgomery (6), Feb. 1832; printed for Sheffield Sunday School Union that summer, and in his *Poet's Portfolio*, 1835. He wrote in a letter to his friend G. Bennett (quoted in full in *Julian*) that passing along a road between Gloucester and Tewkesbury (England) he had observed a number of women in a field engaged in an activity he could not identify. A friend explained that it was 'drilling' or 'dibbling' (planting seed in prepared holes), to which J. M. replied, 'but for my part, give me *broadcast* sowing, scattering the seed on the right and the left in liberal handfuls; this dibbling is very unpoetical and unpicturesque; there is neither grace of motion or of attitude in it.' The incident caused the writing of this hymn and is an odd gloss on the Parable of the Sower. (Modern readers may need to be reminded, by the way, that 'broadcast' was, before the invention of radio, an agricultural word used in exactly the above sense.)

US & CAN: ● ENG: An598: B526: CP538: M599

656. SPIRIT DIVINE, ATTEND OUR PRAYERS

7 st. CM   PCH 131

A. Reed, *Evangelical Magazine*, June, 1829, and *Congregational Hymn Book*, 1836. Written not for Pentecost but as an invocation for Good Friday, a day appointed in 1829 as a day of prayer in the 'Eastern district of the Metropolis' by the London Board of Congregational Ministers. The intercession was for the 'revival of religion in British Churches,' and was part of that evangelical movement in that denomination which produced in 1831 the Congregational Union of England and Wales (dissolved only when the Congl. Church in England & Wales, so called since 1966, became part of the United Reformed Church, 5 x 1972).

US & CAN: BP253: Can60: CW275/196: H370: M461: P212/243/574: Pm241: W256 ● ENG: AM -/239: An297: B239: CH183/107: CP210: M289

ANDREW REED, b. Westminster (London), 27 xi 1787; Sch. Hackney Coll., London; Ord. Congl., 1811, as first pastor of New Road Chapel, East London; in 1831 the enlarged congregation built Wycliffe Chapel, where he remained until '61, having ministered 50 years in the same community. Ardent philanthropist, assisted in founding of a series of orphanages and asylums including the London Asylum and Reedham Orphanage (Coulsdon, Surrey). Edited a hymnal in 1817 as a supplement to I. Watts' collection, and enlarged it, 1842. † Hackney, London, 25 ii 1862 (84).

657. SPIRIT OF GOD, DESCEND UPON MY HEART

5 st. 10.10.10.10

G. Croly, *Lyra Britannica*, 1867; Prime, *Songs of the Soul . . .* (New York), 1880.

US & CAN: BP258: B132: CW272/201: L129: M138: P204/236/575: Pm232 ● ENG: B240: CH195/108

GEORGE CROLY, b. Dublin, 17 viii 1780; Sch. Univ. Dublin; Ord. Ch. of Ireland, and ministered there until went to London 1810 where he combined ministry & literary activity; Rector of St. Benett's and St. Stephen's, Walbrook, 1835; well known as preacher and conservative political speaker. † London, 24 xi 1860 (80).

658. SPIRIT OF MERCY, TRUTH AND LOVE

3 st. LM-coup. PCH 81

Anon. in *Psalms, Hymns & Anthems . . . used in the Chapel of the Hospital for the Maintenance and Education of Exposed and Deserted Young Children* (commonly called the Foundling Hospital, London: cf. 601), 1774. Orig. text is in *EH*; *Hymns A & M* has altered and commoner text. No author has been discovered for this unusually shapely and chaste composition but whoever wrote it must have been a disciple of Watts.

US & CAN: BP255: Can485: H111: L118 ● ENG: AM155/153: An222: BB163: CH -/338: E631

659. SPREAD, O SPREAD, THOU MIGHTY WORD

7 st. 77.77

German: WALTE, FURDER, NACH UND FERN,' by J. F. Bahnmeier, leaflet 1827, *Kern des Deutschen Liederschatzen*, 1828.

Tr. C. Winkworth (14) 7 st., *Lyra Germanica* II, 1858.

An American tr. beginning with the same words, by A. W. Farlander and W. Douglas, is in the U.S. books listed below, but it owes too much to Winkworth to be listed separately. It is recognizable by the repeated phrase, 'Word of how. . . .' *Worshipbook* and *CLB* mix the 2 trs. & begin SPREAD, O SPREAD THE MIGHTY WORD, altering the direction of the imperative.

US & CAN: B284: H253: L323: P-/-/577‡: CLB476‡ ● ENG: An327: B394: BB182: E552: M804: PL269

JONATHAN FRIEDRICH BAHNMAIER, b. Oberstenfeld, Wurttemberg, 12 vii 1774; Sch. Tubingen, became asst. to his father, the Town Preacher, at home; Prof. education & Homiletics, Tubingen, 1815; Dean & Town Preacher, Kirchheim-unter-Teck, 1819-40. Member of editorial cttee. of *Wurttemberger Gbch.*, 1842. † 18 viii 1841 (67).

ARTHUR WILLIAM FARLANDER, b. in Germany, 21 iv 1898; Sch. Real-Gymnasium, Pforzheim; came to U.S.A., 1919; Sch. James Millikin Univ., Chicago Div. Sch. and Evang., Sem., then Chicago Div. Sch. of

the Pacific; Ord. Episc., 1927; Rector of All Saints, San Francisco, '27-'30; Dean of St. James' Cathedral, Fresno, California, '30-6; then Rector of the Ch. of the Incarnation, Santa Rosa, Calif., from '36. Member of ed. cttee., *Hymnal 1940* and Chairman of *Hymnal-1940 Companion*.

CHARLES WINFRED DOUGLAS, b. Oswego, N.Y., 15 ii 1867. See the *Hymnal-1940 Companion*, pp. 420-2, for an extended tribute, prob. written by Farlander above. As musician and priest he combined for American Episc. churches the services rendered a generation earlier by P. Dearmer (88) and R. Vaughan Williams in the *English Hymnal* (he and Dearmer were born in the same year). Ord. deacon, Episc., 1893, but ill health delayed ordination to priesthood until '99, by which time he had moved to Evergreen, Colorado and begun the services which led to the founding of the Mission of the Transfiguration. Directly associated with this Mission, 1897-1907, then Canon residentiary of St. Paul's Cathedral, Fond du Lac, Wisconsin, '07-'11; thereafter hon. canon. From 1906 to †, Director of music, Community of St. Mary, Peekskill, N.Y. His church music studies in England, France & Germany made him a special authority on plainsong, but from 1937-41 he was program-note editor for the Denver Symphony Orchestra. Chairman ed. cttee. of the *Hymnal-1940*. Author of *Church Music in History and Practice*, 1937. Made many translations of Latin Office hymns for the *Hymnal*. No other figure in the history of American hymnology so fully combined scholarship, artistry and organizing ability. † 18 i 1944 (76).

660. STAND UP AND BLESS THE LORD

6 st. SM

J. Montgomery (6), *Christian Psalmist*, 1825; slight revision from version written for a Methodist Sunday School gathering in Sheffield, Whit Monday, 1824, for whom he wrote in line 2 'ye children of his choice.'

US & CAN: BP328: Can45: B26: M16: Pm25 ● ENG: AM706/374: An27: B363: BB268: CH233/39: CP270: E*90: M685: PL16

661. STAND UP, STAND UP FOR JESUS

6 st. 7.6.7.6 D

G. Duffield, *The Psalmist* (U.S.), 1858, inspired by the words of a young dying clergyman, Dudley A. Tyng of Philadelphia, 'Tell them to stand up for Jesus.' Author added: 'Since he has been much persecuted in those pro-slavery days for his persistent . . . pleading for the oppressed, it was . . . as if he had said "Stand up for Jesus in the person of the downtrodden slave."' Luke 5:18. In the text it is rather the note of spiritual warfare (Eph. 6) that is sounded. St. 5, '. . . each soldier to his post . . .' often omitted.

US & CAN: BP472: Can174: B389: CW371/- : H562: L551: M248: P265/349/- : Pm385 ● ENG: AM542/307: An586: B556: BB368: CH532/481: CP519: E581: M821

GEORGE DUFFIELD, b. Carlisle, Pa., 12 ix 1818; Sch. Yale & Union Th. Sem., New York; Ord. Presb., 1840; served at Bloomfield, N.J.; Philadelphia; Adrian, Mich., Galesburg, Ill.; Ann Arbor and Lansing, Mich. † Bloomfield, N.J., 6 vii 1888 (69).

662. STARS OF THE MORNING, SO GLORIOUSLY BRIGHT

6 st. 10 10. 10 10 dact.

J. M. Neale (2), *Hymns of the Eastern Church*, 1862, based on an Idiomelon (seasonal song) of the Greek church, 7th-8th cent., for the celebration of angels. Almost certainly ascription to Joseph the Hymnographer is Neale's mistake. St. 4, referring to the three archangels by name, often omitted, but full text is in *EH*. In *Hymns A & M* and elsewhere slightly altd.

US & CAN: H121: L148 ● ENG: AM423/288: BB238: E245

663. STILL, STILL WITH THEE, WHEN PURPLE MORNING BREAKETH

5 st. 11.10.11.10

H. B. Stowe, written in open air, early morning, some time in 1853; pub. in *Plymouth Collection of Hymns*, 1855; Ps. 139:18. Introduced to Britain by W. G. Horder in *Congregational Hymns*, 1884.

US & CAN: CW136/- : L496: M264: P107/-/- : Pm37 ● ENG: B683: M474

HARRIET BEECHER STOWE, b. Litchfield, Conn., 14 vi 1812, d. of Lyman Beecher and sister of Henry Ward Beecher. In her childhood her father was President of Lane Seminary, Cincinnati, Ohio. M. Calvin E. Stowe, Prof. of Language & Biblical Literature at that Seminary, and later at Bowdoin Coll. & Andover Seminary. Most famous as authoress of *Uncle Tom's Cabin*, 1852, which was part of her consistent anti-slavery campaign. Published over 40 vols. of prose and one of poetry. Her brother, H. W. B., edited source above which contains 3 of her hymns. † Hartford, Conn., 1 vii 1896 (84).

STILL THE NIGHT, HOLY THE NIGHT: see 877.

664. STILL WITH THEE, O MY GOD

6 st. SM

J. D. Burns (60), *The Evening Hymn*, 1857; Ps. 139:18. In *CP* appears as WITH THEE, O LORD MY GOD.

US & CAN: P100/-/- ● ENG: B774: CP413‡: M470

665. STRENGTHEN FOR SERVICE, LORD, THE HANDS

3st. 8.7.8.7 Iamb.　　　　　　　　　　　　**PCH 181**

In present form, by P. Dearmer (88), *English Hymnal*, 1906, after passing through four stages: (i) the Liturgy of Malabar, 5th century, rite of the Nestorian Church of S. India, contained a prayer in Syriac based on a poem of Ephraim the Syrian (d. 373), which was tr. (ii) by J. M. Neale (2) in his *Liturgies of St. Mark, St. James, &c.* in prose, beginning 'Strengthen, O Lord, the hands which are stretched out to receive the Holy Thing.' (iii) This was versified in CM by C. W. Humphreys (212), but (iv) Dearmer adapted it to fit the tune he had in mind (that in *EH*), as we have it now. In *CLB* reads, MAKE STRONG FOR SERVICE. . . .

A tr. by C. S. Phillips for (young) altar-servers in 6 st. 6.5.6.5 is at reference in *AM*. (For full text of Neale's translation of the prayer, see *Hymnal-1940 Companion* at #201).

US & CAN: Can348: H201: L286: CLB378‡ ● ENG: AM*88 (AM -/494‡): An386: B328: BB215: CH -/588: CP313: E329

666. STRONG SON OF GOD, IMMORTAL LOVE

8.88.8　　　　　　　　　　　　　　　　**PCH 443**

A. Tennyson (620), from the Prologue to *In Memoriam*, 1850 (prologue dated 1849). This is in 11 st., of which various selections have been used as a hymn since the *Congregational Church Hymnal*, 1887, introduced it as such; there it is in 7 st. (1, 3-8) ending with the st. which begins 'But vaster . . . .' Horder's *Worship Song* used sts. 1, 3-7 (with full stop for the comma at end of 7); *EH*, 1906, was content with 1, 3-5. Much in demand in the earlier 20th century in Britain but orthodox theology excluded it from common use and it is now more used in U.S.A.

US & CAN: CW349/15: H365: L*I-17: M146: P175/228/578: Pm557 ● ENG: CH142/- : CP192: E483: M86

667. SUMMER SUNS ARE GLOWING

4 st. 6.5.6.5 D

W. W. How (75), *Church Hymns*, 1871.

US & CAN: ● ENG: An647: B722: CH613/624: CP644: M673

668. SUN OF MY SOUL, THOU SAVIOUR DEAR

LM-coup.　　　　　　　　　　　　　　**PCH 122**

J. Keble (83), *The Christian Year*, 1827, from a 14 st. poem beginning: ''Tis gone that bright and orbed blaze' (Cf. 480). Norm 6 st. vn. as above popularized by *Hymns Ancient & Modern*, 1861, using sts. 3, 6, 7, 12-14; but other selections sometimes found. Luke 24:49.

US & CAN: BP553: H166: L226: M502: P37/56/- : Pm50 ● ENG: AM24: An62: B703: BB424: CH292/647: CP621: E274: M942

669. SUNSET AND EVENING STAR

4 st. stress 3-3-4-3

A. Tennyson (620), 1889, 'Crossing the Bar.' His son wrote: '*Crossing the Bar* was written in my father's 81st year on a day in October when we came from Aldworth to Farringford (Isle of Wight); before reaching Farringford he had the 'moaning of the bar' in mind, and after dinner he showed me this poem written out. I said, "This is the crown of your life's work." He answered, "It came in a moment" . . . . A few days before my father's death he said, "Mind you put *Crossing the Bar* at the end of all editions of my poems." ' The 'moaning of the bar' is the sound of the sea on the rocks.

The poem was first put in a hymnal in *Methodist Hymn Book* (Brit.), 1904 and *Hymns Ancient & Modern* of the same year.

US & CAN: CW574/- : P438/- : ● ENG: AM694/- : BB537: CH588/- : M640

SWEET FLOWERETS OF THE MARTYR BAND: see 870 II.

670. SWEET HOUR OF PRAYER! SWEET HOUR OF PRAYER!

4 st. LMD-coup.

Attributed to W. W. Walford, who has never been identified with certainty though it is believed his dates were 1772-1850. The Rev. Thomas Salmon, in *New York Observer*, where the hymn was first printed, wrote that between 1838 and '42, when he was Congl. minister at Coleshill, Warwickshire, a blind preacher named W. W. Walford dictated it to him.

US & CAN: B401: CW537/- : M275: P -/398/-

671. SWEET IS THE WORK, MY GOD, MY KING

7 st. LM-coup.

I. Watts (10), Ps. 92, Part I in *Psalms . . .* , 1719; 'A Psalm for the Lord's Day.' St. 4 always omitted and in consequence st. 5 sometimes altd. from 'But I shall bear . . .' to 'Then shall I . . . ,' since 'but' makes sense only if st. 4 is included.

US & CAN: L183: P22/-/- ● ENG: An71: B281: CP603: M665

672. SWEET SAVIOUR, BLESS US ERE WE GO

7 st. 8.8.8.8.88

F. W. Faber (175), 1849; *Jesus & Mary*, 1852; 'Evening Hymn at the Oratory' (for which see 196). St. 7 always omitted: it began 'Sweet Saviour, bless us! Night is come; / Mary and Philip near us be,'—the Oratory being dedicated to St. Philip Neri. *EH* has sts. 1-6, others fewer. Sometimes begins 'O SAVIOUR, BLESS US. . . .'

US & CAN: H182: L199: Pm542 (1 st. only) ● ENG: AM28: B700: CH 302/- : CP634: E275: M692

673. SWEET THE MOMENTS, RICH IN BLESSING

8.7.8.7

In the *Kendal Hymn Book*, 1757 (Inghamite), a hymn in 6 st. 8.7.8.7 D by J. Allen appeared beginning 'While my Jesus I'm possessing.' This devastatingly pietistic piece was rewritten by W. Shirley, beginning as above, in 3 st. 8.7.8.7 D in the Countess of Huntingdon's *Collection of Hymns*, 1770. In mod. versions sts. 1-3 (in 8.7.8.7) are further revised from this. But in Cooke & Denton's *Church Hymnal*, 1854 it appeared in 8.7.8.7 with Shirley's first 12 lines and 3 st. following which are new and anon. These begin 'Lord, in ceaseless contemplation' and 'For thy sorrows we adore thee,' ending with a doxology. The first and sometimes 2nd of these complete the version now in use. (*L(U.S.)*) has an unidentifiable but good st. 3).

US & CAN: Can441: H72: L63 ● ENG: AM109/- : EH105

JAMES ALLEN, b. 24 vi 1734, Gale, Yorks, joined the Inghamites and later the Sandemanians; dissatisfied with both, built a chapel on his own estate and ministered there till † (Gale) 31 x 1804 (70).

The Inghamites were an evangelical sect formed in 2nd half of 18th century by Benjamin Ingham, a Yorkshireman; the Sandemanians, or Glasites—named after their founder Glas or their first organizer, Sandeman—were a somewhat similar Scottish evangelical sect. Both broke away from their parent bodies (Anglican, Church of Scotland) to form church polities similar to Congregationalism; and Scottish Conglsm. owes much of its early impetus to the Sandemanians, into whose movement many former Inghamites found their way.

WALTER SHIRLEY, b. Staunton Harold, Leics, 23 ix 1725; Sch. New Coll. Oxf.; Ord. C/E, Rector of Loughrea, Galway (Ireland), 1749; often preached for the Wesleys and Whitefield in their missions. † Dublin 7 iv 1786 (53).

674. TAKE MY LIFE AND LET IT BE CONSECRATED, LORD, TO THEE

12 st. 77

F. R. Havergal (252), 4 Feb. 1874; the author wrote: 'I went for a visit (at Arley House). There were ten persons in the house, some unconverted and long prayed for, some converted but not rejoicing Christians. He gave me the prayer, "Lord, give me *all* in this house!" and He just *did*! Before I left the house every one had got a blessing . . . It was nearly midnight. I was too happy to sleep . . . , and these little couplets formed themselves and chimed in my heart one after another, until they finished with "Ever, only, ALL for Thee!"' Formed into a hymn in 77.77 by her own tune, CONSECRATION; occasionally found in 77.77 D.

US & CAN: BP474: Can294: B373: CW296/94: H408: L510: M187: P242/310/- : Pm404 ● ENG: AM -/361: An641: B527: CH512/462: CP458: E582: M400

675. TAKE TIME TO BE HOLY

4 st. 11 11. 11 11 anap.

W. D. Longstaff, *Sacred Songs & Solos*, 1874; introduced to Britain in *Hymns of Consecration*, 1882. Two accounts of its origin exist: (a) from I. D. Sankey's autobiography, that W. D. L. wrote it after hearing a sermon in New Brighton (Cheshire) on 1 Peter 1:10; (b) from R. C. McCutchan, that W. D. L. wrote it immediately after hearing the phrase 'Take time to be holy' in a speech by Griffith John, missionary to China, at Keswick, England (where a famous evangelical conference was, and still is, held annually for which the 1882 source was compiled).

US & CAN: BP437: CW346/230: M266: P -/300/- ● ENG:

WILLIAM DUNN LONGSTAFF, b. Sunderland, England, 28 i 1822, son of a ship-owner. His friend, the Rev. A. A. Rees, left C/E to establish Bethesda Free Chapel in Sunderland, and he became treasurer and fabric manager. He was a close friend of Moody and Sankey, and their chapel was the second church in England to allow Moody to preach in its pulpit. † Sunderland 2 iv 1894 (72).

676. 'TAKE UP THY CROSS,' THE SAVIOUR SAID

5 st. LM-alt.   **PCH 360**

C. W. Everest, *Visions of Death*, 1833; slightly altd. in *Salisbury Hymn Book*, 1857 and in that form became one of the two American hymns admitted to *Hymns Ancient & Modern*, 1861 (the other being 738); there further altd. and a doxology added. In most books the 1857 text is followed, but *EH* (very unusually) follows *Hymns A & M*.

US & CAN: BP454: Can176: B370: CW285/151: M160: P -/293/- ● ENG: AM263/333: An589: B510: BB369: CH501/430: CP515: E484: NC218

CHARLES WILLIAM EVEREST, b. East Windsor, Conn., 27 v 1814; Sch. Trinity Coll., Hartford; Ord. Episc., 1842; Rector of Episc. Ch., Hampden, Conn., '42-'73. † Waterbury, Conn., 11 i 1877 (62).

677. TEACH ME, MY GOD AND KING

5 st. SM

G. Herbert (137), *The Temple*, 1633; 'The Elixir.' It was rewritten by J. Wesley for his First Hymn Collection (1780), but not used in orig. form until *EH* (1906). One st. of orig. there (and always) omitted because it departs from metrical pattern of the rest. One change often made in error: 'this tincture' in st. 3 should read 'his tincture' (we would now say, 'its tincture').

US & CAN: Can261: CW-/241: H476: L451: Pm401 ● ENG: AM -/337: An603: B487: CH511/692: CP433: M597: NC219

678. TELL ME THE OLD, OLD STORY

8 st. 7.6.7.6

C. Hankey, 29 Jan. 1866, 'when I was weak and weary after an illness, and especially realizing . . . that simple thoughts and simple words are all that we can bear in sickness.' Published on a leaflet, 1866, and in *Sacred Songs & Solos*, 1874: but there a refrain was added. Author always said that she particularly objected to its being so sung, and wished it always sung in the simple form in which she wrote it (So printed in *Church Hymnary*).

US & CAN: BP401: CW438/- : P -/403/- ● ENG: An481: B420: CH682/132: E583: M168

ARABELLA CATHERINE HANKEY, b. Clapham, Surrey, 1834, d. of Thomas Hankey, London banker and member of the Clapham Sect (evangelical group with high aims of social reform); ran a Bible class in London for shop-assistants in West End shops at age 18; a journey to S. Africa to bring her sick brother home, involving much adventure, inspired in her an active interest in foreign missions. † Westminster (London), 9 v 1911 (77).

679. TELL ME THE STORIES OF JESUS

6 st. 8.4.8.4.5.4.5.4 dact.

W. H. Parker (290) for Charles Street Sunday Sch. (Bapt.), Basford, Notts; on a leaflet, 1885, then in *Sunday School Hymnary*, 1905, with tune (by W. H. Challinor) that made it famous.

US & CAN: BP163: CW214/- : M88: P -/459/- ● ENG: An556: B130: CP112: M858

680. TELL OUT, MY SOUL, THE GREATNESS OF THE LORD

4 st. 10 10. 10 10   **PCH 501**

T. Dudley-Smith, *Anglican Hymn Book*, 1965; opening line founded on the New English Bible version of the *Magnificat*.

US & CAN: BP244: Can495: CLB434 ● ENG: AM*89: An439: B*77: CP*92: CH -/164: E*49

TIMOTHY DUDLEY-SMITH, b. Manchester, 26 xii 1926; Sch. Tonbridge Sch. and Pembroke, Camb.; Ord. C/E; curate at Erith, Kent; Head of Cambridge University Mission, Bermondsey, London, '53-5: Chaplain to it, '55-'60; ed. *Crusade* magazine, '55-9; Assist. Sec., Church Pastoral Aid Society '55, Sec. '59; Archdeacon of Norwich, '73. Contributed many hymns to *Youth Praise*, 1966, and *Psalm Praise*, 1974.

681. TEN THOUSAND TIMES TEN THOUSAND

4 st. 7.6.8.6 D   **PCH 235**

H. Alford (150), sts. 1-3, 1866, st. 4, 1870; sung at his funeral, 17 i 1871, printed in his *Life*, 1872, and in *Hymns Ancient & Modern*, 1875.

US & Can: CW568/- : H590: L595: P427/427/- : Pm311 ● ENG: AM222/ 284: An437: B407: BB253: CH221/- : E486: M828

682. THANKS TO GOD WHOSE WORD WAS SPOKEN

4 st. 8.7.8.7.4.7

R. T. Brooks, 1954 for Triple Jubilee of the British & Foreign Bible Society; first in hymnal, *M(U.S.)*, 1966. In *English Praise*, 'Praise to God.'

US & CAN: Can94: M18: P -/-/580 ● ENG: AM*90: B*78: E*83

REGINALD THOMAS BROOKS (always known as 'Peter'), b. 30 vi 1918, Wandsworth (London); Sch. Manfield Coll. Oxford; Ord. Congl., '42; Skipton and ('45) Horton Lane, Bradford (both Yorks); since 1950 in British Broadcasting Corporation, radio, later television, religious broadcasting dept. (see 32).

THAT EASTER DAY WITH JOY WAS BRIGHT: see 837.

THE ADVENT OF OUR GOD (KING): see 856.

683. THE BREAD OF LIFE, FOR ALL MEN BROKEN

3 st. 9.8.9.9. unrhymed

Chinese: T. T. Lew, *Hymns of Universal Praise* (China), 1936.

Tr.: W. R. O. Taylor, *BBC Hymn Book*, 1951.

US & CAN: B250: M317: P -/450/- ● ENG: BB538: CH -/569

TIMOTHY TINGFANG LEW, b. Wenchow, China, 1891; Sch. China and Columbia Univ., New York; returned to China as author and educator. Chairman of editors of 1936 ed. of *Hymns of Universal Praise* (last ed. 1948, pub. on eve of Communist take-over of China) and co-editor of *Book of Common Prayer*, used by 4 Chinese Christian denominations. Lived in U.S. 1941-7, teaching at Univ. of New Mexico, Albuquerque, where † 5 viii 1947 (66).

WALTER REGINALD OXENHAM TAYLOR, b. Portsmouth, 1 viii 1889, Sch. China Inland Mission, Chefoo, and Univ. Durham; Ord. C/E and served with Church Missionary Society in China 1924-'49; on ed. committee of *Hymns of Universal Praise* (above). Retired to Sevenoaks, Kent, where † 14 xi 1973 (84).

684. THE CHURCH OF GOD A KINGDOM IS

6 st. CM   **PCH 262**

L. B. C. L. Muirhead, *Yattendon Hymnal*, 1899; inspired by H. & J. van Eyck's painting, 'The Adoration of the Lamb' in St. Mavon's Church, Ghent, Belgium.

US & CAN: H387 ● ENG: AM67/254: BB183: E488

LIONEL BRULTON CAMPBELL LOCKHART MUIRHEAD, b. Edinburgh, 16 i 1845; Sch. Radley Sch. and Eton, then Balliol, Oxf. Man of Letters, close friend of R. Bridges (9), who dedicated to him his fourth book of *Shorter Poems* and included his hymn in *Yattendon Hymnal*. † Little Haseley, Oxfordshire, 25 i 1925 (80).

685. THE CHURCH'S ONE FOUNDATION

5 st. 7.6.7.6 D   **PCH 236**

S. J. Stone, 1866, *Lyra Fidelium*, in 7 st., being one of 12 hymns written on the 12 articles of the Apostles' Creed. It was revised and abr. to 5 st. for *Hymns Ancient & Modern*, 1868. Expanded 1885 for use as a processional in Salisbury Cathedral by insertion of 3 stanzas after st. 5 of 1866 text, and in that form used again at the first Lambeth Conference, attended by all the bishops of the Anglican Communion, where it was sung at all 3 services (Canterbury Cathedral, Westminster Abbey, St. Paul's, 1888). It settled down after this to 5 st. *A & M* text, but usually st. 3 of this version is now omitted: only sources marked ‡ below include that stanza, beginning 'Though with a scornful wonder. . . .'

But its special theological association is in being inspired (especially in that third stanza which is so often omitted & should never be) by the controversy involving Bishop Colenso of Natal.

This affair, one of the most passionate theological controversies of the 19th century, revolved round Colenso's liberal interpretations of the Bible: Colenso, a Cambridge mathematician subsequently ordained in C/E, became a missionary bishop, much loved by his people. He entirely espoused the (then) modern critical approach to the Bible in the translations he made for his people and in his preaching, making such (to the orthodox of the time) inflammatory comments as that Moses, whose death is recorded in Deuteronomy, could not have personally written the Pentateuch, or that Abraham could be thought of as a primitive sheikh. Archbishop Gray of Capetown deprived him of his see, hoping thus to safeguard orthodoxy, but Colenso never abandoned his ministry. The author of this hymn, now regarded as one of the finest examples of scriptural writing in all hymnody, was actually supporting Gray against Colenso.

US & CAN: BP307: Can146: B236: CW423/290: H396‡: L149: M297: P333/437/582: Pm260: CLB472: W261 ● ENG: AM215‡:255‡: An425‡: B263: BB184‡: CH205‡/420: E489‡: CP254: M701‡: NC222: PL271‡

SAMUEL JOHN STONE, b. Whitmore, Staffs, 25 iv 1839; Sch. Charterhouse and Pembroke, Oxf.; Ord. C/E, 1862: curate at Windsor, then at St. Paul's, Haggerston; Vicar there, '74; Rector of All Hallows on the Wall, London, '90. † Charterhouse, Godalming (Surrey), 19 xi 1900 (61).

THE COMING OF OUR GOD: see 855.

THE DAY DRAWS ON WITH GOLDEN LIGHT: see 837.

686. THE DAY IS PAST AND OVER

5 st. 7.6.7.6.88

J. M. Neale (2), *Hymns of the Eastern Church*, 1862, suggested by an old Greek metrical prayer which, he wrote, was as popular in the villages and islands of Greece as 'Glory to thee, my God, this night' in England. His first version of this, same shape, was printed in *The Ecclesiastic and Theologian*, 1853 (text, with long and informative article, in *Julian*, pp. 1139-41); but a 4 st. vn. of the 1862 text (omitting orig. st. 4) was in *Hymns Ancient & Modern*, 1868, and has since become standard. Authorship of orig. Greek is unknown; the existence of 'St. Anatolius,' sometimes said to be author, is doubtful.

US & CAN: BP554: H184: L224: M491: P44/-/- ● ENG: AM21: An65: B705: BB425: CH287/645: CP613: E276: M951

687. THE DAY OF RESURRECTION

3 st. 7.6.7.6 D   **PCH 179**

J. M. Neale (2), *Hymns of the Eastern Church*, 1862, beginning ''Tis the day of Resurrection,' and having some irreg. lines. In *Parish Hymn Book*, 1863, it begins 'The day . . .'; and alterations there & in *Hymns Ancient & Modern*, 1868, have become standard. It is a translation of Ode I in the Golden Canon of Easter (Greek, before 8th cent.).

US & CAN: BP193: Can374: CW247/183: H96: L105: M437: P166/208/ 584: Pm192: CLB280 ● ENG: AM132: An190: B162: BB112: CH123/ 267: CP141: E137: M208: NC225

688. THE DAY THOU GAVEST, LORD, IS ENDED

5 st. 9.8.9.8

J. Ellerton (80), *A Liturgy for Missionary Meetings*, 1870, and *Church Hymns*, 1874, which first carried tune now familiar, and made some alts. The text, further slightly altd., in *Hymns A & M*, 1889, is now standard.

US & CAN: BP356: Can366: CW140/38: H179: L227: M500: P45/59/- : Pm47: W263 ● ENG: AM477/33: An52: B706: BB426: CH289/646: CP626: E277: M667: NC226: PL313

THE DUTEOUS DAY NOW CLOSETH: see 863.

689. THE ETERNAL GATES LIFT UP THEIR HEADS (THE GOLDEN GATES ARE LIFTED UP)

5 st. CM   PCH 281

C. F. Alexander (24), *Hymns* (SPCK), 1853, with 'eternal . . .'; in her own *Hymns Descriptive and Devotional*, 1858, with 'golden. . . .' Sometimes abr. to 4 st., and *BBC* alters a few words.

US & CAN: ● ENG: AM -/439: An204: BB131: CH130/298: CP155: M224

690. THE ETERNAL GIFTS OF CHRIST THE KING

5 st. LM   PCH 149

Latin: AETERNA CHRISTI MUNERA, Ambrose of Milan.

Tr. always with same first line, always LM, all 5 st. except *H(U.S.)*:

  (a) J. M. Neale, *Hymnal Noted*, 1852;
  (b) Compilers of *Hymns Ancient & Modern*, 1861, based on (a) but retaining only 2 lines as there written;
  (c) Compilers of *Hymnal-1940* (U.S.), 6 st., based on (a);
  (d) Compilers of Canadian *Hymn Book*, 1971, conservative revision of (b).
        (Note: 'and others' in *CH3* is unnecessary: it is Neale's orig. text).

US & CAN: Can497 (d): H132 (c) ● ENG: AM430/503 (b): BB234 (a): CH -/540 (a): E175 (a)

AMBROSE, St., b. about 340, Trier (France), son of the Prefect of Gaul; Sch. in law and practised it; appointed, c. 370, governor of Liguria, with headquarters at Milan. In death, 374, of Auxentius, Bp. of Milan, unpopular for unorthodox (Arian) sympathies, the people demanded that Ambrose shd. succeed him. At the time he was a Christian, but only of catechumen status, not yet baptized. After much hesitation, accepted the bishopric & was baptized, but insisted on undergoing a full course of theol. instruction before taking up duties. None the less, he is the most celebrated person who went direct from lay to episcopal status (though this was not unknown in that age). Became an outstanding administrator and preacher. Was personally responsible for the conversion of St. Augustine, who writes of him at length and with great affection. Combated not only paganism and heresy, but also what he considered undue pretensions on the part of one of Rome's most spectacular emperors, Theodosius, whom he dissuaded, under threat of excommunication, from carrying out at least one notable execution and one planned massacre. Regarded with justice as the father of western (Latin) hymnody; formerly many hymns were ascribed to him, but most of those so ascribed were later imitations of the style (Latim LM) which he certainly invented; among the hymns now regarded as his with near certainty are one or two which appear only in hymnals of liturgical sympathies (such as *EH*: see ## 49 and 81) and the hymn above, which is the only one to have wider circulation in modern English-speaking circles. Wrote many theological and ascetical works, and some believe him to have been the author of the (mis-called) Athanasian Creed. He is one of the four traditional doctors of the Catholic Church, and his feast day is 7 December. † Milan, 397 (about 57).

691. THE FIRST NOWELL THE ANGEL DID SAY

9 st. stress 4-4-4-4 with refrain 4-4

Traditional English carol first printed in Sandys, *Christmas Carols . . .*, 1833, collected by him in Cornwall. Full text preserved in *Oxford Book of Carols*, 1928, #27. Normally abr. to 6 st. with verbal adjustments. First

standard hymnal to include it was *Congregational Hymnary*, 1916. For comments on the curious tune see *The English Carol*, 1958, ad loc.

US & CAN: BP131: Can410: B91: CW197/117: H30: L40: M383: P129/156/585: Pm141: CLB218 ● ENG: An117: B109: CH45/173: CP709: E*329: M131: NC228: PL149

THE FLAMING BANNERS OF OUR KING: see 882.

692. THE GOD OF ABRAHAM PRAISE

12 st. 6.6.8.4 D   PCH 73

T. Olivers, first appearing as a Tract, *A Hymn to the God of Abraham*, undated; said to have been written in the home of J. Bakewell (260), which would put the composition about 1763; 4th edn. of the tract is 1772, 6th ed., printed in London and Philadelphia, 1773. Included in J. Wesley's *Pocket Hymn Book*, 1785 omitting sts. 4 & 8. Full text is still in *M(Brit.)*. Elsewhere abr.: *Hymns A & M* omits sts. 3-4; *EH* and *L(U.S.)* om. sts. 2, 3, 4, 8; *BB* om. 2, 3, 4, 8, 11. Others reduce to 6 st. or fewer using different selns. See *Julian*, pp. 1149-51, for extended notes and orig. version of the tune. Text is based on, but soon departs from, the YIGDAL of the Jewish synagogue.

> N.B.: this note should be read in conjunction with that at 604, especially by U.S. readers. Refs. below take no account of the 19 c. vn. beginning with same first line, which is in many U.S. books.

US & CAN: BP531: H285: W230‡ ● ENG: AM601/631: An249: B30: BB283: CH571/358: CP12: E646: M21: NC249

THOMAS OLIVERS, b. Tregonan, Montgomeryshire, 1725; shoemaker's apprentice, uneducated; driven out of town for 'ungodly behavior'; wandered to Shrewsbury and Bristol, where he heard G. Whitefield preach on text, 'Is not this a brand plucked from the fire?' Converted & joined Methodist Society at Bradford on Avon. Became one of Wesley's preachers, and, 1753, an evangelist in Cornwall, then in other parts of England & Ireland. † London, March 1799 (74).

693. THE GOD OF LOVE MY SHEPHERD IS

6 st. CM   PCH 9F

G. Herbert (137), *The Temple*, 1633; Ps. 23. Used in much altered form by J. Wesley in *Charlestown Hymn Book*, 1737, but restored to orig. form, with omission of st. 5, in *EH*, 1906.

US & CAN: ● ENG: AM -/178: BB474: CP43: E93: M51: NC230

694. THE GOD WHOM EARTH AND SEA AND SKY

4 st. with doxology, LM

Latin: QUEM TERRA, PONTUS, AETHERA; anon., before 11th cent.

Tr. J. M. Neale (2), *Hymnal Noted*, 1854, *EH* has this, together with trsln. of part 2 of original hymn (##214, 215). *A & M* has altered trsln. which others mostly follow.

US & CAN: ● ENG: AM449/512: An440: BB239: E214

695. THE HEAD THAT ONCE WAS CROWNED WITH THORNS

6 st. CM   PCH 105

T. Kelly (406), *Hymns*, 1820; Heb. 2:10. One of the few hymns of that age which in English books are never altered, never separated from tune associated with it in 1861 by *Hymns A & M*, and even abridged only in the U.S. In st. 5 there is a quotation from 2 Tim. 2:12 which may itself be a reminiscence of a primitive Christian hymn.

US & CAN: BP204: Can108: B125: H106: L439: M458: P195/211/589: Pm200: CLB464: W266 ● ENG: AM301/218: An207: B192: BB132: CH131/286: CP164: E147: M244: NC231: PL213

THE HEAVENLY CHILD IN STATURE GROWS: see 334.

696. THE HEAVENS DECLARE THY GLORY, LORD

6 st. LM-alt.

I. Watts (10), Psalm 19 2nd vn., in *Psalms . . .*, 1719; 'The Books of Nature and Scripture Compared.' Full text in *CP*.

US & CAN: BP294: Can91: CW441/325: M365: P217/259: Pm257 ●
ENG: AM -/252: An308: CP318: M802

697. THE HOLLY AND THE IVY

6 st. stress 2-2-2-2 with similar refrain.

Traditional English carol collected, words & music, by Cecil Sharp from a Mrs. Clayton at Chipping Campden, Glos., and Mrs. Wyatt, East Harptree, Som. Contains much pagan imagery, as did many medieval carols, of which it is certainly one. It has been suggested (R. L. Greene) that it may have had its origin in 2 rival processions from ancient shrines in Beverley, Yorks, whose emblems were holly and ivy; others say it reflects pagan mythology in which holly is male principle and ivy female. P. Dearmer (88), on the 'merry organ' in refrain, quotes this from the Nun's Priest's Tale in Chaucer's *Canterbury Tales*:

> Chauntecleer's crown had no peer
> his voice was merrier than the mery organ
> on mass days that in the churches gon.

First in a hymnal, *Congregational Praise*, 1951, but before that in many carol collections from *Bramley & Stainer* (1871) onwards.

US & CAN: ● ENG: An108: CP711: E*330: NC232

CECIL SHARP, b. London 22 xi 1859; Sch. Uppingham and Clare Coll., Cambridge; became leader of the team of folk-song collectors whose work c. 1900 inspired the English musical renaissance; Principal of Hampstead Convervatory, 1896; Founder of English Folk Dance Society, 1911; collected songs also, 1914-18, in Massachusetts and the Applachians. † London, 23 vi 1924 (64).

698. THE KING OF LOVE MY SHEPHERD IS

6 st. 8.7.8.7 iamb.   **PCH 239**

H. W. Baker (101), *Hymns Ancient & Modern*, 1868; Ps. 23, Matt. 18, John 10. St. 3, says Ellerton (80), was on author's lips as he lay dying, 12 ii 1877. The most popular of its tunes (Dykes) appeared with it in 1868. Line 3, st. 1, is taken from G. Herbert's version (693).

US & CAN: BP80: Can132: B215: CW169/49: H345: L530: M67: P99/106/590: Pm79: CLB490: W268 ● ENG: AM197: An546: B72: BB475: CH438/388: CP61: E490: M76: NC233: PL114

699. THE KING SHALL COME WHEN MORNING DAWNS

6 st. CM   **PCH 185**

J. Brownlie (531), *Hymns from the East*, 1907 and *Hymnal* (U.S. Episc.), 1916; there is no indication of any original from which it may have been translated. Norm. abr. to 5 st. or fewer.

US & CAN: BP227: H11: L10: M353: P187/232/- : Pm201: W269 ● ENG:

700. THE LORD ASCENDETH UP ON HIGH

3 st. 88.7.88.7 iamb.

A. T. Russell (89), *Psalms & Hymns*, 1851; an altd. vn. to fit 8.7.8.7.88.7 is in *EH* (#148).

US & CAN: P172/212/- ● ENG: An211: B177: BB133: CH132/- : E148‡

701. THE LORD IS KING! LIFT UP THY VOICE

8 st. LM-coup.   **PCH 133**

J. Conder (92), *The Star in the East . . .* 1824 and *Congregational Hymn Book*, 1836. *BP* has 7 st., elsewhere always 6 st. or fewer, sts. 5, 6, 7 most often omitted.

US & CAN: BP88: Can32: P83/-/- ● ENG: AM659/175: An239: B194: BB26: CH25/36: CP58: E*312

702. THE LORD IS RICH AND MERCIFUL

3 st. CMD

T. T. Lynch (163), *The Rivulet*, 3rd ed., 1868.

US & CAN: P -/82/-: Pm328 ● ENG: B422: CH398/- : CP370

703. THE LORD IS RISEN INDEED

7 st. SM

T. Kelly (406), *Collection of Psalms & Hymns*, 1802; in 1809 ed., 8 st., but now abr. to 5 st. or fewer.

US & CAN: ● ENG: AM504/142: An188: CH120/- : E627

704. THE LORD MY PASTURE SHALL PREPARE

4 st. 88.88.88   **PCH 46**

J. Addison (295), *The Spectator*, 26 vii 1712; Ps. 23:1-4. St. 1 appeared in J. Church's *Introduction to Psalmody* (1723) with first appearance of the tune by H. Carey, but first standard hymnal to include full text was *English Hymnal*, 1906, in which the last two sts. were transposed: most other books followed this but *Hymns for Church & School*, 1964, returned to original order. The reason for the transposition may have been that in altd. form text follows Ps. 23 more closely. Composer of famous tune best known as composer of 'Sally in our Alley.'

US & CAN: ● ENG: AM -/179: BB477: C P48: E491

705. THE LORD'S MY SHEPHERD: I'LL NOT WANT

5 st. CM   **PCH 9E**

Scottish Psalter, 1650 (323); Ps: 23, being, like all the other psalms in this venerable source, a composite version made after careful study of the many psalters which had been compiled since the first Sc. Ps. of 1564. The version which is closest to this is that of Francis Rous, 1646, where st. 2 (v. 3) is as 1650 text with alteration of one word (1650 has 'within the paths . . .' where 1646 has 'on in the paths') while st. 5 (v. 6) is taken unchanged from Rous.

The history of the use of this psalm in Britain is a microcosm of the ecumenical movement. It always stood first in popularity among the Scottish Psalms, being one of the few that could be sung in its entirety, but in the earlier 20th century the only mainstream hymnals that included it were those of non-Anglican churches. The first appearance of it in an Anglican book was when the *English Hymnal Service Book*, 1962, gave it a place in its aditional hymns (it had been in the *Hymnal for Scotland*, Scottish Supplement, 1956). Thereafter it became universal. But social history also had its place, for it was the use of the Psalm at the wedding of Princess Elizabeth of England (later Queen Elizabeth II) in November 1947, with the tune CRIMOND, that gave it a sudden popularity among all English Christians. It was never in a Scottish hymn book until *CH³*, which was the first hymnal in Scotland to distribute selected metrical psalms through the hymnal instead of leaving them complete in the separate psalter.

US & CAN: BP9: Can131: B341: CW40/- : L522: M68: P97/104/592: Pm84 ● ENG: AM -/*93: An511: B73: BB480: ScPs23/387: CP729: E*80: M50: NC238: PL115

FRANCIS ROUS, b. Dittisham, Devon, 1579; Sch. Broadgates Hall (later Pembroke Coll.), Oxf., and Univ. Leyden; entered Middle Temple; M.P. for Truro 1626-48, '54-onwards. Provost of Eton, '44; member of Cromwell's Council of State, '53; author, lawyer, theologian. † Acton Middx, 7 i 1659 (80).

706. THE LORD WILL COME AND NOT BE SLOW

CM   **PCH 418**

J. Milton (394), *Nine of the Psalms Done into Metre, wherein all but what is in a different Character, are the very words of the Text, translated from the Original*, 1648. Milton is here trying his hand at metrical psalmody, within the strict rules of the game, using as much of the A.V. as possible, and (as A.V. printers formerly always did) printing in italic every word which was not in the A.V. text. He took as a sample Psalms 80-88, and this hymn is compiled from stanzas in Ps. 85, 86, 82.

It is not known who liberated these magnificent verses for congregational use, but, though the original material is somewhat uncompromising, the key to the liberation was in the construction of what has become st. 1. Ps. 85:13 in Milton runs:

> Before him righteousness shall go,
>   his royal harbinger;
> then will he come and not be slow,
>   his footsteps cannot err.

By transposing those two couplets and opening 'The Lord will come . . .' a good opening stanza was formed. Thereafter the selection was 'Truth from the earth . . .' (Ps. 85:11), 'Mercy and truth . . .' (85:10: sometimes omitted), 'Rise, God, judge thou . . .' (82:8), 'The nations all . . .' (86:9) and 'For great thou art . . .' (82:10). Thus the fine verses are disentangled from their surrounding pedantries. *Julian* is a little coy, indicating that in his time (1892) the hymn was known only to Unitarians; but the 5 st. version, exactly as in *EH*, was in the *New Congregational Hymn Book*, 1855, in the opening section of metrical psalms (# 123). The 'Mercy & Truth' st. was added in the *Congregational Church Hymnal*, 1887. P. Dearmer (88), however, probably took his 5 st. vn. from Horder's *Worship Song* when he put the hymn into *EH* and so introduced it to Anglicans. The index below will indicate how it progressed from there.

US & CAN: BP118: B128: H312: L327: M468: P185/230/- : Pm95 • ENG: AM -/52: An89: B195: BB479: CH151/321: CP156: E492: M813

707. THE MAKER OF THE SUN AND MOON

5 st. CM

L. Housman (177), in *Bethlehem*, a nativity play, 1902, and *English Hymnal*, 1906.

US & CAN: BP145 • ENG: BB60: CP93: EH16: NC136

708. THE MORNING LIGHT IS BREAKING

4 st. 7.6.7.6 D

S. F. Smith (459), 1832, while a student at Andover Theol. Sem., inspired by letters from the missionary Adoniram Judson of Burma; pub. 1833 in *Spiritual Songs for Social Worship*. St. 2 now always omitted.

US & CAN: CW524/- : H264: L313: P389/499/- : Pm305 • ENG:

THE NOBLE STEM OF JESSE: see 848.

709. THE RACE THAT LONG IN DARKNESS PINED

6 st. CM   **PCH 98**

Scottish Paraphrases (76), 1781, a new composition for that work by J. Morison. Full text in *Scot. Par.* and *CH*; elsewhere st. 3 omitted. *Hymns A & M* persists in its revised version in 7 st., THE PEOPLE THAT IN DARKNESS SAT; this is also in *M(U.S.)* and *CLB*.

US & CAN: BP154: Can430: M361‡: CLB239‡ • ENG: AM80‡: An133: B110: BB496: CH57/168: CP75: E43: M139: PL141

710. THE RADIANT MORN HATH PASSED AWAY

5 st. 8.8.8.4

G. Thring (191), *Hymns, Congregational and Others*, 1866.

US & CAN: L222: P38/-/- • ENG: AM19: B708: CH279/- : E279: M940

THE ROYAL BANNERS FORWARD GO: see 882.

711. THE SAINTS OF GOD, THEIR CONFLICT PAST

5 st. 88.88.88

W. D. Maclagan (342), *Church Bells*, 1870; *Church Hymns*, 1871.

US & CAN: H128: L145: CLB301 • ENG: AM428/572: CH219/- : M825

712. THE SANDS OF TIME ARE SINKING

7.6.7.6.7.6.7.5

Anne Ross Cousin, *The Christian Treasury*, 1857, in 19 st. The whole poem is constructed out of sayings and phrases in the *Letters and Dying Sayings* of Samuel Rutherford. Author arranged 6 st. of her poem to form a hymn in the *Baptist Church Hymnal*, 1900; from these other editors have selected 4 or 5 st.; but a different 6 st. arrangement appeared in the *Hymnal Companion*, 1877. Although it is not in Spurgeon's *Our Own Hymn Book*, 1879, it was the last hymn sung at a private service in Spurgeon's rooms at Mentone, France, which proved to be the last he conducted.

US & CAN: P434/-/- • ENG: B776: CH581/694: CP773: M637

ANNE ROSS COUSIN, b. Hull, 27 iv 1824, d. of a doctor; in childhood moved with family to Leith, Scotland; Sch. privately and became an expert pianist; m. the Rev. William Cousin, minister at Melrose. † Edinburgh, 6 xii 1906 (82).

SAMUEL RUTHERFORD, b. about 1600, Nisbet, Roxburghshire; Sch. Edinburgh Univ.; Regent of Humanity (i.e. Prof. of Latin) there, 1623; Ord. C/Scot., minister of Anwoth, Galloway, '27; banished for a time to Aberdeen for nonconformity but on re-establishment of presbytery, Prof. Divinity at St. Andrews, '38; Principal of St. Mary's College there, '51; one of Scot. Commissioners to Westminster Assembly, '44-7; at Restoration deprived of all offices, and † 1661.

713. THE SAVIOUR DIED, BUT ROSE AGAIN

CM

Scottish Paraphrases (76), 1781. The whole paraphrase begins LET CHRISTIAN FAITH AND HOPE DISPEL; and authorized selection is sts. 5-9, beginning as above. The 1745 edition paraphrased the same passage (Rom. 8:31-9); but the above version is radically re-cast, probably by J. Logan.

US & CAN: • ENG: An276: BB497: ScPar48/293

714. THE SON OF GOD GOES FORTH TO WAR

8 st. CM

R. Heber (90), posth. *Hymns*, 1827, for St. Stephen's Day. Now often in CMD.

US & CAN: CW358/- : H544: L562: M419: P271/354/- : Pm388 • ENG: AM439/529: An457: B558: BB235: CH530/541: CP502: E202: M816

715. THE SON OF GOD PROCLAIM

4 st. SM

B. Bridge, prize-winning hymn in Free Church Federal Council hymn writing competition; pub. *100 Hymns for To-day*, 1969.

US & CAN: BP345: Can323: L*IV-19 • ENG: AM*94: CP*96

BASIL ERNEST BRIDGE, b. Norwich 1927; Sch. Cheshunt Coll., Cambridge; Ord. Congl. (URC), 1951; served at Knowle, Warks and from 1955 at Leicester.

716. THE SPACIOUS FIRMAMENT ON HIGH

3 st. LMD-coup.   **PCH 48**

J. Addison (295), *The Spectator*, 23 viii 1712; words which W. M. Thackeray (in *The English Humorists*) wrote, 'shine like stars.' Much used in 19th cent., but re-married to original tune written for it 1723 only in *EH*, 1906. Final hymn in Britten's *Noye's Fludde*.

US & CAN: BP96: Can85: CW164/3: H309: L442: M43: P69/95/595: Pm72 ● ENG: AM662/170: An232: B74: BB21: CH10/143: CP30: E297: M44

717. THE SPIRIT BREATHES UPON THE WORD

5 st. CM

W. Cowper, (235), *Olney Hymns*, 1779; 'The Spirit and Glory of the Word.'

US & CAN: BP282: Can93: P -/260/- ● ENG: An310: B252: CH197/-: CP228: M307: NC243

THE STRIFE IS O'ER, THE BATTLE DONE: see 849.

THE SUN IS SINKING FAST: see 874.

718. THE VOICE OF GOD IS CALLING

3 st. 7.6.7.6 D

J. H. Holmes, Sept. 1913, at sea returning to U.S.A. from European trip; he had promised a hymn for a convention of the Young People's Religious Union (Unitarian) to take place shortly after his return: 'I tried my hand at composition several times without result . . . , then suddenly there came . . . a veritable explosion of energy; in a few days I was listening to my words sung by a chorus of voices.' Pub. in *New Hymn & Tune Book*, 1914, and *Pilgrim Hymnal*, 1931.

US & CAN: CW490/271: L*776: Pm426 ● ENG:

JOHN HAYNES HOLMES, b. 1879, Sch. Harvard; Ord. Unit., 1904, Church of the Messiah, New York; remained to 1949. In 1919 minister & church left Unit. denomination & became nonsectarian, changing name to Community Ch. of New York. Retired 1949 with reputation as eminent pacifist & social reformer. † 1964.

719. THE WISE MAY BRING THEIR LEARNING

3 st. 7.6.7.6 D

Anon., in *The Book of Praise for Children*, 1881; small alterations in modern books remove over-childish phrases & are improvements.

US & CAN: BP468: Can293: CW316/263: L545 ● ENG: An351: B528: BB370: CH363/461: CP450: E*314: NC245

THE WORD OF GOD PROCEEDING FORTH: see 867 II.

THE WORLD IS VERY EVIL: see 851.

THEE WE ADORE, O HIDDEN SAVIOUR, THEE: see 867 IV.

720. THEE WILL I LOVE, MY GOD AND KING   PCH 260

R. Bridges (9), *Yattendon Hymnal*, 1899, derived from Ps. 138 to carry tune of that Psalm in Genevan Psalter, 1551.

US & CAN: ● ENG: B75: BB314: CH -/403: CP430: M*65

721. THEE WILL I LOVE, MY STRENGTH AND TOWER

German: ICH WILL DICH LIEBEN, MEINE STARKE, 7 st. 9.8.9.8.88, J. Scheffler, (548), *Heilige Seelenlust*, 1657.

Tr. J. Wesley (1), 4 st. 8.8.8.8.88 (omitting 2, 3, 6), in *Hymns & Sacred Poems*, 1759.

US & CAN: BP445: Can286: L505 ● ENG: An547: CH431/678: M445

722. THERE IS A BLESSED HOME

4 st. 6.6.6.6 D

H. W. Baker (101), *Hymns Ancient & Modern*, 1861.

US & CAN: H591 ● ENG: AM230/-: CH594/608: E496

723. THERE IS A BOOK, WHO RUNS MAY READ

12 st. CM   **PCH 124**

J. Keble (83), *The Christian Year*, 1827; Rom. 1:20. The opening line, made less intelligible by casual punctuation (parentheses are required round the last 4 words) refers to the King James Version of Habakkuk 2:2 '. . . that he may run that readeth.'—so that 'who reads may run' would have better expressed the allusion. (It meant 'easy to read'). This has been tolerated by editors until recently, though modern books make attempts at amendment. *EH* has full text, *Hymns A & M*, 10 st. (in later eds. 5 st. CMD); others 7 st. or fewer. In *BP* '. . . that all may read.'

US & CAN: BP91‡: CW435/- ● ENG: AM168: An134: B76: CH8/- : CP35: E497: M43

724. THERE IS A FOUNTAIN FILLED WITH BLOOD

7 st. CM   **PCH 91**

W. Cowper (235), *Olney Hymns*, 1779; 'Praise for the fountain opened: Zech. 13:1.' *EH* and *CP* have full text; most others use sts. 1-5, except those which treat the text as a Gospel Song, abridge it further, substitute a spurious verse and use repeated lines from each st. as a refrain.

This hymn is the subject of one of the most felicitous revisions in the literature—which, however, is at present scarcely known. The opening stanza is Cowper's attempt to reproduce the thought and imagery of the leading text, which is in the King James version: 'In that day there shall be a fountain opened to the house of David and to the inhabitants of Jerusalem for sin and for uncleanness.' Cowper's stanza though scriptural is too vivid for comfortable singing nowadays. The amendment, by Nathaniel Micklem, which appeared in *A Gallimaufry*, a book of poems privately printed, actually is closer to Scripture and also a more vivid evocation of New Testament language:

> There springs a fountain, where for sin
>   Immanuel was slain,
> and sinners who are washed therein
>   are cleansed from every stain.

The rest of the hymn, especially in its full version, contains thoughts so fervent & precious that it is hoped that by the above amendment it might be rescued.

US & CAN: BP180: B107‡: L373: M421: P241/276‡/- ● ENG: AM633/-: An509: B148: CH692/-: CP765: E332: M201

NATHANIEL MICKLEM, b. Brondesbury, London, 10 iv 1888; Sch. Rugby and New Coll., Oxf.; then Mansfield Coll., and Ord. Congl., 1913; Prof. O.T. Selly Oak Colls., Birmingham, '21-7: Prof. N.T., Queen's Coll., Kingston, Ontario, '27-'31; Principal, Mansfield Coll., Oxf., '32-'53. Author, Poet, apologist; Chairman, Congl. Union of England & Wales, '54-5, and one of the leaders of the theological renaissance in Conglsm. during the generation 1930-60. His theological publications span a period of 50 years to 1976. † Frilford, near Oxford, 26 xii 1976 (88).

725. THERE IS A GREEN HILL FAR AWAY

5 st. CM   **PCH 306**

Mrs. Alexander (24), *Hymns for Little Children*, 1848, on the clause in the Creed, 'Suffered under Pontius Pilate; was crucified, dead and buried.'

US & CAN: BP186: Can101: CW230/- : H65: L77: M414: P157/202/- :

Pm172 ● ENG: AM332/214: An163: B149: BB92: CH105/241: CP136: E106: M180: NC240

726. THERE IS A LAND OF PURE DELIGHT

6 st. CM   **PCH 35**

I. Watts (1), *Hymns . . .* , Book II, 1707; 'A Prospect of Heaven makes death easy.' The allusion in 'sweet fields . . .' (st. 3) is variously interpreted as a view across a small river just outside Southampton (where he lived in youth), the view across Southampton Water to the Isle of Wight or possibly West Hampshire, and the view across the Humber from Hessle, Yorks. The first of these perhaps achieves probability by a narrow margin.

US & CAN: BP538: B504: H586: L583 ● ENG: AM536/285: An436: B614: BB254: CH592/536: CP359: E498: M649

727. THERE IS NO SORROW, LORD, TOO LIGHT

5 st. CM

J. Crewdson, *A Little While, and Other Poems*, n.d. (c. 1860), beginning 'There's not a grief, however slight.' Norm. vn., with alterations from B. H. Kennedy's *Hymnologia Christiana*, 1863, begins at st. 2.

US & CAN: CW342/- : P295/-/- ● ENG: An614: CH148/- : M237

JANE CREWDSON, née Fox, b. Perranaworthal, Cornwall, 22 x 1809; m. T. Crewdson, Manchester manufacturer, 1836; long an invalid, but gave much time & thought to the transformation of suffering for others' good. † Whalley Range, Lancs., 14 ix 1863 (53).

728. THERE'S A FRIEND FOR LITTLE CHILDREN

6 st. 8.6.7.6.7.6.7.6   **PCH 310**

A. Midlane (618), 7 ii 1859, printed in *Good News for Little Ones* (magazine) as final article for year 1859. Originally the first 3 sts. ran 'There's a rest . . . ,' '. . . a home . . . ,' '. . . a Friend'; rearrangement was due to *Hymns A & M*, 1875, which, with *EH*, has full text. Elsewhere abr.

US & CAN: L592 ● ENG: AM337/- : An358: B615: CH593/- : E607: M839

THERE'S A WIDENESS IN GOD'S MERCY: see 654.

729. THERE WERE NINETY AND NINE THAT SAFELY LAY

5 st. stress 4-3-4-3-4 4   **PCH 313**

E. C. Clephane (82) in *The Children's Hour*, 1868; orig. written in place of an article in this journal for children, it attracted the attention of I. D. Sankey when it appeared in The Christian Age, 1874. Asked by D. L. Moody during a revival meeting to provide a solo, Sankey placed the words on the organ stand and composed the tune as he sang. The tune has much in common with trad. carols, especially 'The Seven Joys of Mary,' and gives a clue to the cultural origin of some Gospel Songs. Thereafter very popular in revival meetings and one of the very few Gospel Songs to be included in general hymnals. Strangely absent from U.S.A.

US & CAN: BP393 ● ENG: B425: CH685/- : E584: M334

730. THESE THINGS SHALL BE! A NOBLER RACE

5 or 6 st. LM-alt.

J. Addington Symonds, *New & Old*, 1880, from a poem entitled 'A Vista' beginning, 'Sad Heart, what shall the future bring?' in 15 st.; the hymn begins at st. 3, and the selection now in hymnals is due to W. G. Horder who included the 6 st. version in *Worship Song*, 1896. During and just after World War I it had a wide acceptance, being promoted as a theme-song by the League of Nations Union. For modern taste it is

perhaps over-humanistic and later books tend to omit it. The whole poem was set as a cantata by John Ireland (1879-1962).

US & CAN: CW507/- : M198: P423/-/- : Pm150 ● ENG: B196: CH639 /- : CP583: M910

JOHN ADDINGTON SYMONDS, b. Bristol, 5 x 1840, Sch. Harrow and Oxford; lived mostly abroad as a man of letters, esp. historian of the Renaissance and biographer of English poets. His home, Clifton Hill House, Bristol, is now part of Bristol University. † Rome, 19 iv 1893 (52).

731. THINE ARM, O LORD, IN DAYS OF OLD

3 st. CMD   **PCH 229**

E. H. Plumptre (534), written 1864 for use in King's College Hospital, London; pub. in *Lazarus and Other Poems*, 2nd ed., 1865.

US & CAN: H517: L324: P -/179/- ● ENG: AM369/478: An399: B637: BB382: CH86/214: CP672: E526: M919

732. THINE BE (IS) THE GLORY, RISEN, CONQUERING SON

3 st. 5.5.6.5.6.5.6.5, iamb. and troch.

French: A TOI LA GLOIRE, E. L. Budry, *Chants Évangéliques* (Lausanne), 1885 for Handel's tune 'See the conquering hero comes' in *Judas Maccabaeus*. French text retained in Canadian *Hymn Book*, 1971.

Tr. R. B. Hoyle for the first (1924) ed. of *Cantate Domino*, became one of the first 'international' hymns.

US & CAN: BP201: CW214/181: L566: M450: P -/209/- : Pm193 ● ENG: AM*95: An193: B164: CH -/279: E*36: M213

EDMOND L. BUDRY, b. 30 viii 1854; Sch. Faculté Libre, Lausanne; Ord. Prot. in Switzerland, pastor at Cully, '89, at Vevey, '98-1923; † in Switzerland, 12 xi 1932 (78).

RICHARD BIRCH HOYLE, b. Cloughfold, Lancs, 8 iii 1875; Sch. Regents Park Coll. (Bapt. Sem.), London and Ord. Bapt. at Kingston on Thames, 1925. Edited *The Red Triangle* (YMCA magazine); later prof. at Western Theol. Sem., Pittsburgh, U.S., 1934-6. † London, 14 xii 1939 (64).

733. THINE FOR EVER! GOD OF LOVE

5 st. 77.77   **PCH 278**

Mary F. Maude, 1847, for Girls' Sunday School, St. Thomas' Church, Newport, Isle of Wight; absent from duties for 3 months she wrote a weekly letter, and these lines appear at the end of one of these. Pub. as *Twelve Letters on Confirmation*, 1848; the hymn was included in *Hymns A & M*, 1861—it is said, without author's knowledge.

US & CAN: H427: L511: P248/-/- ● ENG: AM280/- : An364: B586: CH504/- : CP252: E344: M569

MARY FAWLER MAUDE, b. London, 25 x 1819; wrote a series of books before age 20 for S.P.C.K. on Scripture customs, topography, &c. She m. Joseph Maude, Vicar of St. Thomas', Newport, I o W, '47; conducted classes throughout her life, and was still doing so (according to a letter from her, 1908) in her 90th year. † Overton, Flintshire, 30 vii 1913 (93).

734. THIS IS MY FATHER'S WORLD

3 st. SMD

M. D. Babcock, posth., Thoughts for Everyday Living, 1901, in 15 st., SM. Normal seln. is now sts. 2-5 and 15-16, arranged as SMD. Author often used to leave his home for an early morning walk up a hill overlooking Lake Ontario saying, 'I am going out to see my Father's world.' In some modern books st. 3 of familiar selection is replaced by a st. written much later by his daughter, Mary Babcock Crawford.

US & CAN: BP242: Can82: B155: CW171/5: L487: M45: P70/101/602: Pm485 ● ENG:

MALTBIE DAVENPORT BABCOCK, b. Syracuse, N.Y., 2 viii 1858; Sch. Univ. Syracuse and Auburn Theol. Sem., where he was distinguished athlete and musician. Ord. Presb., 1882, served at Lockport, N.Y., Brown Memorial, Baltimore, '87; Brick Church, New York, '99 (succeeding H. van Dyke, 377). † Naples, Italy, 18 v 1901 (42).

735. THIS IS THE DAY OF LIGHT

5 st. SM

J. Ellerton (80), *Special Services . . . in Chester Cathedral*, 1867, and *Hymns A & M*, 1868. A 6th st., 'This is the day of Bread' was added (between 4 and 5) in 1888 but never came into general use.

US & CAN: BP333: CW446/- : P20/27/- ● ENG: AM37/42: An68: B282: BB399: CH267/46: CP610: M660

736. THIS IS THE DAY THE LORD HATH MADE

5 st. CM

I. Watts (10), Ps. 118, 1st version, pt. IV, in *Psalms . . .* , 1719; 'Hosanna, the Lord's Day: or, Christ's Resurrection and our Salvation.' Altd. and abr. version in *English Praise*, 1976.

US & CAN: Can376: B68: CW -/390: P23/29/- : Pm504 (abr.) ● ENG: AM478/43: An74: BB400: CP604: E*71‡: NC247

737. THIS JOYFUL EASTERTIDE

3 st. 6.7.6.7 D

G. R. Woodward, *Carols for Easter and Ascension*, 1894, which was probably the first English carol book wholly given to a season other than Christmas. (*M** has a new hymn with the same first line and in the same meter by F. Pratt Green, 109).

US & CAN: BP200: Can471: B124: L*742 ● ENG: An197: B*86: BB115: CP726: CH -/271: E*37: M*70‡: NC248: PL205

GEORGE RATCLIFFE WOODWARD, b. Birkenhead, Ches., 27 xii 1848, Sch. Gonville and Caius, Camb.; Ord. C/E 1875; curate, St. Barnabas, Pimlico, '74; Vicar of Little Walsingham, Nfk., '82; Rector of Chelmondiston, Sfk., '88; returned to St. Barnabas, Pimlico, as curate, '94; licentiate preacher, Diocese of London, '00; curate, St. Mark's, Marylebone (London), 1903-6. Thereafter devoted himself to literary work. Edited *Cowley Carol Book*, 1902, *Songs of Syon*, '04, '10; and *Piae Cantiones* (facsimile reprint with critical notes), '10. D. Mus., Lambeth, 1924. One of the pioneers of scholarship in the literature of hymns and carols, his work ran parallel to, without greatly exchanging influences, that of Dearmer and Vaughan Williams (88); a man of pure rather than applied scholarship, his importance in hymnody was, though slower to be appreciated, hardly less. † Highgate (London), 3 iii 1934 (85).

738. THOU ART THE WAY: TO THEE ALONE

4 st. CM   **PCH 353**

G. W. Doane (197), *Songs by the Way*, 1824; 'Christ the Way.' Introduced to Britain in Bickersteth's *Christian Psalmody*, 1833. This is the first American hymn of the post-Independence age to gain acceptance in Britain, and, with 676, one of the two admitted to the 1861 edn. of *Hymns A & M*.

US & CAN: Can259: H361: L390: M75: P254/221/- : W278 ● ENG: AM199: An455: B220: BB338: CH173/121: CP102: M160

739. THOU DIDST LEAVE THY THRONE AND THY KINGLY CROWN

5 st. stress 4.3.4.3.3 3

E. E. S. Elliott, 1864, privately printed for St. Mark's, Brighton, then in Church Missionary Society's *Juvenile Instructor*, 1870 (ed. by author), and in Sankey's *Sacred Songs and Solos*, 1874.

US & CAN: BP165: CW292/150: H321: L433: P231/184: Pm326 ● ENG: AM776/363: An277: B111: CH67/- : CP92: E585: M150

EMILY ELIZABETH STEELE ELLIOTT, b. Brighton, 22 vii 1836, where her

father was Rector of St. Mark's. Pub. 2 vols. of hymns. In later years an active worker in Mildmay Park Mission (London). † London, 3 viii 1897 (60).

740. THOU GRACIOUS POWER, WHOSE MERCY LENDS

5 st. LM-coup.

O. Wendell Holmes (427), written 1869 for the class of 1829 (Harvard) at Graduation. From 1855-90 author always read a poem of his own at the Harvard Reunion. Of hymns, he wrote to J. W. Kemball, 'It would be one of the most agreeable reflections to me if I could feel that I had left a few worthy to be remembered.' First line sometimes altd. to O GRACIOUS GOD. . . .

US & CAN: BP583: CW602/- ● ENG: AM -/502: CH649/- : M873

741. THOU HIDDEN LOVE OF GOD, WHOSE HEIGHT

PCH 55

German: VERBORGNE GOTTESLIEBE DU, 10 st. 8.7.8.7.88.7, by G. Tersteegen in *Geistliches Blumengärtlein III*, 1729 and *Sammlung Geist- une liebliche Lieder* (Moravian), 1733; 'The Longing of the Soul quietly to maintain the secret drawings of the Love of God.'

Tr. J. Wesley (1), 8 st. 8.8.8.8.88 (omitting 4 & 5) in *Hymns & Sacred Poems*, 1738; written while at Savannah, under influence of the Moravian settlement there, before his conversion. Always abridged now. *M(Brit.)* has 6 st. (1-5, 8 of JW): *AM* (1889) and *An*, 5 st. (1, 3, 4, 5, 8); *CP*, 5 st. (1, 3, 4, 6, 8); others 4 st.—*CH* having 1-4; *L*, 1, 2, 4, 8; *B(Brit.)*, 1, 3, 4, 8; *H(U.S.)*, 1, 4, 5, 8; *M(U.S.)*, 1, 4, 6, 8.

US & CAN: BP377: H464: L391: M531 ● ENG: AM600/- : An494: B460: CH459/96: CP469: M433

GERHARDT TERSTEEGEN (orig. ter Steegen), b. Moers, Netherlands, 25 xi 1697; Sch. Moers Gymnasium, then worked as a silk-weaver. Had been destined for ministry but death of his father when he was 6 left family poor and deprived; after a long period of spiritual uncertainty he 'signed a new covenant with God in his own blood.' Returned to worship in Reformed Church; went to Germany and became a free-lance religious teacher, his home becoming known as The Pilgrims' Cottage. Revisited Holland, where he was never allowed to preach in public until 1750, but returned annually to hold meetings. His hymns were much used by the 18th cent. Moravians; he wrote 111, of which several were translated by J. Wesley. † Muhlheim, Germany, 3 iv 1769 (71).

742. THOU HIDDEN SOURCE OF CALM REPOSE

4 st. 8.8.8.8.88

C. Wesley (1), *Hymns & Sacred Poems*, 1749.

US & CAN: P -/423/- ● ENG: B587: CP471: M98

743. THOU, TO WHOM THE SICK AND DYING

4 st. 8.7.8.7.77

G. Thring (191), Hutton's *Supplement*, 1871; *Hymns A & M*, 1875. *CLB* begins 'LORD . . . .'

US & CAN: L464: CLB383 ● ENG: AM368/477: B638: BB383: CP668: E527: M920

744. THOU, WHOSE ALMIGHTY WORD

4 st. 66.4.666.4   **PCH 106**

J. Marriott, written c. 1813, printed as quotation in *Evangelical Magazine*, June, 1825, at end of a lecture by Rev. T. Mortimer to the London Missionary Society, with full text of lecture; from there to *The Friendly Visitor* (magazine), July, 1825, entitled 'Missionary Hymn.' Altd. to present form *Hymns A & M*, 1868, with one detail taken from Sel-

borne's *Book of Praise* 1866 (st. 4 line 1). In *CLB* begins 'GOD, WHOSE
. . . .'

US & CAN: BP95: Can235: B303: CW536/- : H272: L309: M480: P392/
-/-: CLB412‡: W279 ● ENG: AM360/266: An333: B46: BB185: CH364/
494: CP328: E553: M803: NC77: PL272

JOHN MARRIOTT, b. Cottesbach, Leics, Nov. 1780; Sch. Rugby and
Christ Ch., Oxf.; Ord. C/E, 1805; private tutor & chaplain to Duke of
Buccleuch, then Rector of Lawford, Warks, 1807-†; but lived most of
his time in Devon, taking curacies near Exeter and deputing the Lawford parish to his own curate. Friend of Sir Walter Scott who dedicated
opening lines of *Marmion* to him. † Broadclyst, nr. Exeter, 31 iii 1825
(44).

745. THREE IN ONE AND ONE IN THREE

4 st. 777.5

G. Rorison, in his *Hymns & Anthems adjusted to the Church Services*,
1851; and *Hymns A & M*, 1861.

US & CAN: ● ENG: AM163: An230: B47: E501

GILBERT RORISON, b. Glasgow, 7 ii 1821; Sch. Univ. Glasgow; Ord.
Scot. Episc., 1843; curate of St. James', Leith; later incumbent of St.
Peter's, Peterhead, Aberdeenshire. † Bridge of Allan, Perthshire, 11 x
1869 (48).

746. THRONED UPON THE AWFUL TREE

4 st. 77.77.77

J. Ellerton (80), *Hymns Ancient & Modern*, 1875.

US & CAN: Can457: CW -/167: P -/197/605: Pm174: CLB263 ● ENG:
AM118/119: An177: BB93: CH100/246: E116: M189

747. THROUGH ALL THE CHANGING SCENES OF LIFE

CM   **PCH 16**

Tate and Brady (53), *New Version of the Psalms*, 1696, Ps. 34. The Psalm
is (as in Scripture) in 22 verses, 18 st. of CM; norm. sel. is vv. 1-4, 7-9
(6 st.) with or without doxology.

US & CAN: BP15: Can137: CW -/25: L420: M56: P83/-/-: Pm81 ● ENG:
AM290: An512: B589: BB481: CP46: E502: M427: NC251

748. THROUGH THE NIGHT OF DOUBT
AND SORROW

8 st. 8.7.8.7   **PCH 233**

Danish: IGJENNEM NAT OG TRAENGSEL, 4 st. 7.6.7.6 D, by B. S. Ingemann, *Nyt Tillaeg til Evangelisk-chrestlig Psalmebog*, 1859: the only
hymn of Danish origin well known in Britain.

Tr. S. Baring-Gould (493), *The People's Hymnal*, 1867, altd. to its present
form in *Hymns A & M*, 1875. Often presented in 8.7.8.7 D.

US & CAN: BP514: CW481/- : H394: L529: P345/475/- : Pm387: CLB530
● ENG: AM274/292: An566: B559: BB186: CH214/423: CP504: E503:
M616

BERNHARDT SEVERIN INGEMANN, b. Thor Kildstrup, Island of Fal-
ster, 28 v 1789; Prof. of Danish Language & Literature, Academy of
Sorö, Sjoelland, Denmark. † 24 ii 1862 (72).

749. THY HAND, O GOD, HAS GUIDED

6 st. 7.6.7.6 D

E. H. Plumptre (534), *Hymns Ancient & Modern*, 1889. *A & M* retains
full text but elsewhere appears in 4 st., om. 3 & 5. Became very popular
under influence of ecumenical movement and of Harwood's tune
THORNBURY, in 2nd half of 20th century.

US & CAN: BP306: Can152: CW -/356: L159 ● ENG: AM604/256:
An426: B264: BB187: CH215/424: CP251: E545: M*71: PL273

750. THY KINGDOM COME, O GOD

6 st. 6.6.6.6

L. Hensley, *Hymns for the Minor Sundays*, 1867; slightly altd. in *Hymns
A & M* 1868; orig. text in *EH*; further altd. in st. 6 in some modern hymnals. Always vilified by P. Dearmer (88) but persists in popularity, not
without good reason provided st. 6 is altd. as in, *e.g.*, Canadian *Hymn
Book*, 1971.

US & CAN: BP222: Can276: CW563/- : H544: L329: P425/488/- : Pm448
● ENG: AM217/262: An334: B397: BB27: CH152/322: CP584: E554:
M811

LEWIS HENSLEY, b. Bloomsbury (London), 20 v 1824; Sch. Trinity,
Camb.; Senior Wrangler and Fellow; Ord. C/E, 1851; Vicar of Hitchin,
Herts, 1856-† Walsingham, Nfk., 1 viii 1905 (81).

751. THY KINGDOM COME! ON BENDED KNEE

5 st. CM

F. L. Hosmer (483), for Commencement at Meadville Theol. Sch.,
Pennsylvania; printed in *The Thought of God . . .* , 2nd series, 1894.
Introduced to Britain by Garrett Horder in *The Treasury of Hymns*,
1896, and made popular thereafter by *English Hymnal*, 1906.

US & CAN: BP219: Can278: CW539/- : H391: L331: P363/484/- : ●
ENG: AM -/263: B398: BB28: CH153/323: CP585: E504: M742

752. THY LIFE WAS GIVEN FOR ME

6 st. 6.6.6.6.66   **PCH 283**

F. R. Havergal (252), 10 i 1858. This, the first hymn to be written by a
prolific & celebrated writer, was inspired by the sight of a picture of
the Crucifixion while she was studying at Dusseldorf, Germany; the
picture bore the words, 'This have I done for thee. What hast thou
done for me?' It may have been the same picture that brought Zinzendorf (371) to Christian decision. She wrote, 'I scribbled it in pencil on
the back of a circular in a few minutes, and then read it over and
thought, "Well, this is not poetry . . . ," and I stretched out my hand
to put it in the fire, but a sudden impulse made me draw back, and I
put it, crumpled and singed, into my pocket. Soon after, I read the
verses to an old woman, who was so delighted that I copied them and
kept them.' Original vn. was printed on a leaflet in 1859 and in *Good
Words*, Feb. 1860, it was altd. to begin 'I gave my life for thee.' Version
now standard is as altd. with author's agreement in *Hymns A & M*, 1875.

US & CAN: CW289/- : L513: P229/262/- ● ENG: AM259/- : An643:
M391

753. THY MERCY, LORD, IS IN THE HEAVENS

4 st. CM

Scottish Psalter, 1650 (323); Psalm 36, authorized selection vv. 6-9.

US & CAN: Can87 ● ENG: BB482: ScPs36/ 6

754. THY WAY, NOT MINE, O LORD

7 st. 6.6.6.6

H. Bonar (81), *Hymns of Faith & Life*, 1st series, 1857. St. 4, 'The kingdom
that I seek' (arguably the best) normally omitted.

US & CAN: BP511 ● ENG: AM265/356: An644: CH553/- : CP449:
E505: M515

755. 'TIS GOOD, LORD, TO BE HERE

5 st. SM

J. A. Robinson, 6 August (Feast of the Transfiguration in old liturgy),
1888, at Cambridge. First pub. in *Hymns Ancient & Modern*, 1904. In
CLB archly altd. to IT'S GOOD TO BE HERE, LORD.

US & CAN: Can492: CLB456†: W281 ● ENG: AM759/560: An256:

B131: CP114: E236: PL174

JOSEPH ARMITAGE ROBINSON, b. Keynsham, Som., 9 i 1858; Sch. Christ's, Camb.; Fellow, 1881; Ord. C/E, '82; Chaplain to Bp. of Durham, '83; Dean of Christ's, Camb., '84; Norris Prof. Divinity, Camb., '93; Rector of St. Margaret's, Westminster, '99; Canon of Westminster, 1900; Dean of Westminster, '02; Dean of Wells, '11. Author of famous Commentary on *Ephesians*; originator and first editor of *Cambridge Texts & Studies* (1891). One of the leading N.T. scholars of his generation. † Upton Noble, Som., 7 v 1933 (75).

756. 'TIS MIDNIGHT, AND ON OLIVE'S BROW

4 st. LM-alt.

W. B. Tappen, *Poems*, 1822; 'Gethsemane.'

US & CAN: CW232/165: M431: P -/189/-: Pm178 ● ENG:

WILLIAM BINGHAM TAPPAN, b. Beverly, Mass., 24 x 1794; apprenticed to a Boston clockmaker at age 12; moved to Philadelphia as clock-repairer, 1815; associated with American Sunday School Union from '22. Licensed as Congl. minister, 1840, and became evangelist. Published 10 volumes of verse. † West Needham, Mass., 18 vi 1849 (53).

757. TO CHRIST THE PRINCE OF PEACE   PCH 176

Latin: SUMMI PARENTIS FILIO, 5 st. LM; anon. in *Paris Breviary*, 1736.

Tr.: E. Caswall (26), 5 st. SM, *Lyra Catholica*, 1849; altd. in *Hymns A & M* 1861, which *BBC* follows, but *NC* and *PL* have editorial revisions of their own.

US & CAN: ● ENG: AM180/198: BB94: NC252: PL182

TO-DAY I ARISE: see 626.

758. TO GOD BE THE GLORY! GREAT THINGS HE HATH DONE!

3 st. 11 11. 11 11 with refrain 12 12. 11 11 anap.

Fanny Crosby (84), *Brightest and Best*, 1875; 'Praise for Redemption.'

US & CAN: BP73: B33 ● ENG: An280: B32: CH -/374: M313

759. TO MERCY, PITY, PEACE AND LOVE

5 st. CM   PCH 437

W. Blake (40), *Songs of Innocence*, 1789-94. First as a hymn in *English Hymnal*, 1906 with full text; sometimes st. 3, 'For Mercy has a human heart,' or st. 5, 'And all must love the human form,' omitted.

US & CAN: Can138: W283 ● ENG: CP537: E506: NC253

760. TO THE NAME THAT BRINGS (OF OUR) SALVATION

Latin: GLORIOSI SALVATORIS, 6 st. 8.7.8.7.8.7 with later doxology; earliest written source, Antwerp Hymnal, 1496; then *Meissen Breviary*, c. 1510.

Tr.: (a) TO THE NAME THAT BRINGS . . . , J. M. Neale (2), *Hymni Ecclesiae*, 1851, 6 st. orig. meter without doxology. This only in *EH*.

    (b) TO THE NAME OF OUR SALVATION, same meter and length, *Hymns A & M* 1861, being revision of above.

Most hymnals have either (b) or derivatives from it. *An* has (a) with only line 1 and st. 4 from (b); *Canadian* has further revision of (b) sts. 1, 5, 4 with doxology. In many hymnals st. 3 omitted, but *M (Brit.)* has all 6 st. of (b).

US & CAN: Can37†: H326: CLB449 ● ENG: AM179/190: An282: B221: BB284: CH164/373: E507†: M93

761. TO THEE, O LORD, OUR HEARTS WE RAISE

4 st. 8.7.8.7 D iamb.

W. C. Dix (28), *Hymns for the Service of the Church* (Bristol), 1864.

US & CAN: BP564: L445: M524 ● ENG: AM384/484: An653: B731: BB443: CH616/- : CP649: E292: M964

762. TO THEE, OUR GOD, WE FLY

9 st. 6.6.6.6.88

W. W. How (75), *Church Hymns*, 1874. *EH* and *A & M* have full text; elsewhere abr. to 6 st. or fewer.

US & CAN: ● ENG: AM142/606: B653: BB434: CH635/- : CP569: E565: M886

763. TO US A CHILD OF ROYAL BIRTH

4 st. LM-alt.

C. Wesley (1), *Hymns on the Four Gospels*, ms. 1765; not included in J. W.'s 1780 *Collection*, but in its 1830 Appendix.

US & CAN: ● ENG: AM -/71: An120: M141: NC255

764. TURN BACK, O MAN, FORSWEAR THY FOOLISH WAYS

3 st. 10.10.10.10.10 in each st. line 5 is the same as line 1.

C. Bax, *Motherland Song Book*, 1919, a book of peaceable patriotic songs edited by the promoters of the League of Arts, headed by Martin & Geoffrey Shaw; written in meter of Genevan Psalm 124 which Gustav Holst used in an anthem-setting in the above collection. First as a normal hymn, *Songs of Praise*, 1925.

US & CAN: Can73: CW567/339: H536: L348: M475: P424/490/- : Pm 451: W286 ● ENG: B*89: CH -/84: CP586: M912

CLIFFORD BAX, b. Wandsworth (London), 13 vii 1886, brother of composer Arnold Bax; Sch. Slade Sch. of Art; became playwright, painter and poet; member of group (above) who sought to recover good artistic standards in the common life of England. † Westminster (London), 1 xii 1962 (76).

765. 'TWAS ON THAT NIGHT, WHEN DOOMED TO KNOW

6 st. LM-coup.

J. Morison in *Scottish Paraphrases*, 1781 (76), following the same line and using same meter as a hymn by I. Watts, but too far from it to be called a revision. Matt. 26:26-9.

US & CAN: BP343: P360/448/- : Pm558 ● ENG: B331: CH312/237: CP298

766. UNTO THE HILLS AROUND DO I LIFT UP MY LONGING EYES

4 st. 10.4.10.4.10 10   PCH 560

John Campbell, Duke of Argyll, *The Book of Psalms*, 1877: Ps. 121, using meter of 'Lead, kindly Light' (384).

US & CAN: BP54: Can129: CW166/21: L488: P96/-/- ● ENG: An567

JOHN DOUGLAS SUTHERLAND CAMPBELL, ninth Duke of Argyll, b. Westminster (London), 6 viii 1845; liberal M.P. of Argyllshire, 1868; Governor-General of Canada, 1878-83; son-in-law of Queen Victoria. When we wrote his psalm-collection from which the famous hymn comes he had title Marquis of Lorne; succeeded to Dukedom, 1900. † East Cowes, Isle of Wight, 2 v 1914 (68).

767. UNTO US A BOY IS BORN (IS BORN A SON)

Latin: PUER NOBIS NASCITUR, Trier ms., 15th cent., 5 st. 7.6.7.7.

Two trs. are in modern use:

(a) . . . IS BORN A SON, G. R. Woodward (737), *Cowley Carol Book*, 1902—English with some Latin phrases.
(b) . . . A BOY IS BORN, P. Dearmer (88), *Oxford Book of Carols*, 1928, English throughout. Both use orig. meter.

US & CAN: BP142 (b) Can 423 (b) H34 (b) Pm142 (b) W288 (b) • ENG: An121 (b) B112 (b) CH -/187 (a) CP712 (a) E*18 (b) NC256 (b) PL147 (a)

768. VICTIM DIVINE, THY GRACE WE CLAIM

5 st. 8.8.8.8.88   **PCH 64**

C. Wesley (1), *Hymns on the Lord's Supper*, 1745; often abr. to 4 or 3 st.

US & CAN: BP356: L274 • ENG: AM556/- : E333: M771

769. VIRGIN-BORN, WE BOW BEFORE THEE

4 st. 88.77

R. Heber (90), posth. *Hymns*, 1827, for Third Sunday in Lent. Sometimes 2 st. 88.77 D.

US & CAN: • ENG: AM622/514: BB240: E640

WAKE, AWAKE, FOR NIGHT IS FLYING
WAKE, O WAKE, WITH TIDINGS THRILLING   see 885.

770. WALK IN THE LIGHT, SO SHALT THOU KNOW

6 st. CM

B. Barton (382), *Devotional Verses*, 1826.

US & CAN: CW479/- : L474 • ENG: An447: B560: CH482/- : M631

771. WATCHMAN, TELL US OF THE NIGHT

3 st. 7.7.7.7 D

J. Bowring (230), *Hymns*, 1825; in dialogue form throughout; based on Is. 21:11-12 and using traveller's imagery (see biography).

US & CAN: CW183/- : H440: L525: M358: P109/149/617: Pm109: W293 • ENG:

772. WE (ALL) BELIEVE IN ONE TRUE GOD

3 st. 8.7.7.7.77

German: WIR GLAUBEN ALL IN EINEN GOTT, T. Clausnitzer, *Culmbach-Bayreuth Gbch*, 1668, being a popular replacement of Luther's lofty but difficult hymn on the Creed.

Tr.: C. Winkworth (14), *Chorale-Book for England*, 1863, in orig. meter, norm. altd. to 7.7.7.7.77 by omission of 'all' from each first line; but *Pm* has original text and melody.

US & CAN: B29: M463: P -/-/622: Pm250 • ENG: CH -/14

TOBIAS CLAUSNITZER, b. Thum, Saxony, Feb. 1619; Sch. Univ. Leipzig; Ord. Luth., chaplain to Swedish Army, '44, during Thirty Years' War; after Peace of Westphalia, pastor at Weiden, where remained until † 7 v 1684 (65).

773. WE ARE LIVING, WE ARE DWELLING

3 st. 8.7.8.7 D

A. C. Coxe (572), 1840 (age 22); *Athanasion*, 1842; 'The Present Crisis'—title and occasion the same as J. R. Lowell's 'Once to every man . . .' (585).

US & CAN: CW494/342: P374/356/618: Pm427

774. WE ARE ONE IN THE SPIRIT

4 st. stress 4-4-4 with refrain 4-3   **PCH 559**

P. Scholtes, *Hymnal for Young Christians* (F. E. L.), 1966—soon became the theme-song for radical young Christian movements in the U.S.A.; sung at open-air Mass held after the Kent State University shootings, 1970.

US & CAN: H*35: L*I-2: P -/-/619 • ENG: PL296

775. WE BEAR THE STRAIN OF EARTHLY CARE

2 st. CMD

O. S. Davis, 1909, for convention of National Congregational Brotherhood, held that year in Minneapolis.

US & CAN: M202: P179/227/621: Pm220 • ENG:

OZORA STEARNS DAVIS, b. Wheelock, Vt., 30 vii 1866; Sch. Dartmouth, Hartford Th. Sem. and Univ. Leipzig; Ord. Congl.; served in New England before becoming President of Chicago Th. Sem., 1909-20; Moderator of National Council of Congl. Chs., 1927-9. † en route from Topeka to Kansas City, 15 iii 1931 (64).

776. WE COME UNTO OUR FATHERS' GOD

7 st. 8.7.8.7.88.7   **PCH 244**

T. H. Gill (421), *The Golden Chain of Praise*, 1869; Ps. 90:1: sts. 3, 4, 5 norm. omitted.

US & CAN: BP314: H303: M58: P342/16/623: Pm271 • ENG: B265: BB255: CH211/14: CP250: M71

777. WE GATHER TOGETHER TO SEEK THE LORD'S BLESSING

3 st. 12.11.12.11 anap.

Dutch: WILT HEDED NU TREDED VOOR GOD DEN HERRE; anon., patriotic song written at end of 16 cent. to celebrate the release of the Netherlands from Spanish rule. In A. Valerius, *Neder-lantsch Gedenckslank*, 1626.

Tr. T. Baker in Boe's *Dutch Folk Songs*, 1917; now a very popular hymn for Thanksgiving Day in America.

US & CAN: B229: CW117/102: H315: M59: P -/18/624: Pm21: W294 • ENG:

THEODORE BAKER, b. New York, 3 vi 1851; trained for business but then Sch. Leipzig in music; wrote thesis on American Indian music—its first study in depth. Literary editor for G. Schirmer, Inc., 1892. Returned to Germany after retirement, 1928; compiled 3 musical dictionaries incl. *Baker's Biographical Dictionary*, 1900, many times reprinted & revised. † Dresden, Germany, 13 x 1934 (83).

778. WE GIVE THEE BUT THINE OWN

6 st. SM

W. W. How (75), *Psalms & Hymns* (Morell & How), 1864; written 1858; 2 Chron. 29:10ff.

US & CAN: BP364: Can296: CW422/261: H481: L544: M181: P394/312/- : Pm535 (1 st.) • ENG: AM366/- : An605: B530: BB438: CH346/456: CP673: E522: M923

779. WE HAVE HEARD A JOYFUL SOUND

4 st. 7.3.7.3.777.3

P. J. Owens, *Songs of Redeeming Love*, 1882; written for the tune VIVE LE ROI from Meyerbeer's *Les Huguenots*.

US & CAN: BP379: B277: CW537/- : P -/503/- • ENG: An330: B399: CH680/475: M316

780. WE LOVE THE PLACE, O GOD

7 st. 6.6.6.6

W. Bullock, 1827. Bullock was a young naval officer when he visited Newfoundland, and had been shocked by conditions there; when he returned as a missionary & built a chapel there he wrote the orig. of this for its dedication, and it was pub. long afterwards in his *Songs of the Church*, Halifax, N.S., 1854. It was substantially rewritten by H. W. Baker (101) for *Hymns A & M*, 1861; there the last 3 sts. are entirely Baker's. This vn. became standard; though 2 sts. are often omitted in non-Anglican books. The familiar tune was written by a vicar who later became Bishop of Dunedin (T. Jenner); since Bullock was Dean of Halifax, N.S., soon after its publication in *Hymns A & M* it became a hymn with words by a dean & tune by a bishop, both living and neither living in his home country: in this, unique in hymnody. In *Songs of Praise*, 1931, it was rewritten again by P. Dearmer (88).

US & CAN: BP325: Can355: H398 • ENG: AM242: An13: CH236/- : CP248: E508: M677

WILLIAM BULLOCK, b. Prittlewell, Essex, 12 i 1797; Sch. Blue Coat School (Christ's Hospital), London and for Royal Navy; above incident occurred when he was on H.M.S. *Snap* surveying coast of Newfoundland. Ord. C/E 1822, and returned almost at once to Newfoundland, where he stayed until '51, being parson, magistrate, doctor and coroner for the parish; then Rector of Digby, N.S., Rector of St. Luke's, Halifax '58, and Dean of the (new) cathedral, Halifax, N.S., '64. † there 16 iii 1874 (77).

781. WE MEET YOU, O CHRIST, IN MANY A GUISE

4 st. 10 10. 11 11   PCH 494

F. H. Kaan (202), *Pilgrim Praise*, 1966, 1971; this highly allusive poem is perhaps the most characteristic work of this talented author.

US & CAN: Can104: H*36 • ENG: B*91: NC263

782. WE PLOUGH THE FIELDS AND SCATTER

3 st. 7.6.7.6 D with refrain 6.6.8.4

J. Montgomery-Campbell, in Bere's *Garland of Song*, 1861. It is a translation of part of a song in the sketch 'Paul Erdmanns Fest' by M. Claudius, 1782. The song is in 17 st. beginning 'In Anfang war's auf Erden,' from which J. M-C took sts. 3, 5, 7, 9, 10, 13, running sts. together in pairs and adding a refrain which is taken from the altered German version of c. 1800. *Hymns A & M* printed it in 1868 with J. B. Dykes' harmonization of the original tune, and it at once became a popular harvest hymn.

US & CAN: BP563: Can383: CW594/138: H364: M515: P464/524/- : Pm460: CLB317 • ENG: AM383/483: An654: B732: BB444: CH618/620: CP646: E293: M963: NC264

MATTHIAS CLAUDIUS, b. Reinfeld, Germany, 15 viii 1740, son of a Luth. pastor; Sch. Univ. Jena. Began with intentions of the ministry but health & academic difficulties prevented this; lived at Wandsbeck, Hamburg and edited *Wandsbecker Bote* (newspaper); friend of Goethe; poet, playwright, author; † Hamburg, 21 i 1815 (74).

JANE MONTGOMERY-CAMPBELL, b. London 1817; taught singing in her father's parish school, and wrote poetry & songs & a *Handbook for Singers* (teacher's manual). † Bovey Tracy, S. Devon, 15 xi 1878 (61).

783. WE PRAISE THEE, O GOD, OUR REDEEMER, CREATOR

3 st. 12.11.12.11 anap.

J. B. C. Cory, 1902 (age 20) at suggestion of J. Archer Gibson, Organist of Brick Presbyterian Church, New York, who wanted alternative & less boisterous words for the tune of WE GATHER TOGETHER (777). Text revised in *Pilgrim Hymnal*, 1958, now standard. (Statements that this is an alternative translation of the Dutch hymn are in error). First in a hymnal, *Presbyterian Hymnal*, 1933.

US & CAN: BP571: B15: L450: P461/17/627: Pm22 • ENG:

JULIA BULKLEY CADY CORY, b. New York, 1882, d. of J. Cleveland Cady, architect. † 1963.

784. WE PRAY THEE, HEAVENLY FATHER

4 st. 7.6.7.6 D

V. S. S. Coles, written before his ordination, 1869 (age 24) and pub. in *Church Hymns*, 1871.

US & CAN: CLB351 • ENG: AM321/401: An389: BB219: E334: PL64

VINCENT STUCKEY STRATTON COLES, b. the Rectory, Shepton Beauchamp, Som., 27 iii 1845; Sch. Eton & Balliol, Oxf.; Ord. C/E 1869; curate at Wantage; Rector, Shepton Beauchamp, '72; Librarian, Pusey House, Oxford, '84, and Principal, '97; Warden of the Community of the Epiphany, Truro, Cornwall, 1910. † Shepton Beauchamp, 19 vi 1929 (84).

785. WE SAW THEE NOT WHEN THOU DIDST COME

5 st. 8.8.8.8.88

J. H. Gurney (174) in his *Psalms & Hymns*, 1851; opening words taken from a similar hymn by Mrs. Anne Richter in *Songs from the Valley* (Kirkby Lonsdale, Lancs, 1834). But apart from that line it is a new composition. Partly revised in *Hymns A & M*, 1875. Rev. again by A. Petti in *NC* as WE DID NOT SEE YOU WHEN YOU CAME.

US & CAN: • ENG: AM174/- : An514: B132: BB74: CH72/- : E509: M148: NC261‡

WE SING THE MIGHTY POWER OF GOD: see 320.

786. WE SING THE GLORIOUS CONQUEST

4 st. 7.6.7.6 D   PCH 247

J. Ellerton (80), 28 Feb. 1871 for *Church Hymns*, 1871; on the Conversion of St. Paul.

US & CAN: H114 • ENG: AM406/541: An453: E207

787. WE SING THE PRAISE OF HIM WHO DIED

5 st. LM-alt.   PCH 104

T. Kelly (406), *Hymns . . . not before Published* (Dublin), 1815; st. 3 revised by him later, as now given.

US & CAN: BP170: Can110: H340: L494 • ENG: AM200/215: An162: B150: BB95: CH109/258: CP132: E510: M196

788. WE THREE KINGS OF ORIENT ARE

5 st. 7.7.8.6 troch. and dact., with ref. 87.8.7 iamb. and troch.

J. H. Hopkins (words & tune), *Carols, Hymns & Songs*, 1863, in dialogue style; the first modern American Christmas carol.

US & CAN: CW204/- : H51: M402: P -/176/- : Pm143: CLB237: W300 • ENG: NC267 and most carol books

JOHN HENRY HOPKINS, b. Pittsburgh, 28 x 1820; his father was an ironmaster, who after becoming teacher, lawyer and priest, became second Bp. of Vermont and presiding Bp., 1865. J. H. H. Sch. Univ. Vermont; worked as reporter in New York; tutor to children of Bp. Elliott of Savannah, Ga., then entered General Theol. Sem., New York, and Ord. Episc. 1850. He was the first instructor in music at Gen. Th. Sem., and founded & edited *Church Journal*, '53-'68. Ord. Episc. 1872 after much work in ecclesiology (study of church ornament & furniture); Rector of Trinity Ch., Pittsburgh, N.Y., '72, of Christ Ch., Williamsport, Pa., '76-'87. † Hudson, N.Y., 14 viii 1891 (70).

N.B.: NOTES 789 and 790 should be read together.

789. WE WOULD SEE JESUS, FOR THE SHADOWS LENGTHEN

7 st. 11.10.11.10

This, though little used now, needs noting because of its similarity to the next one, with which it may be confused.

It appears in the novel *Dollars & Cents* (New York, 1852), pub. in London, 1853, as *Speculation*, by Anna Bartlett Warner (359), writing under pen-name Amy Lothrop. It appeared in Hastings, *Church Melodies*, 1858; all 7 st. were in *Hymnal Companion*, 1877, and 5 st., using st. 7 as st. 2, are in *Worship Song*, 1905. In 1871 source the hymn is marked 'anon'; and in *W.S.* is ascribed to 'Ellen Ellis' (a person whose existence is doubted by *Julian*, pp. 1595, 1725). 'Ellen Ellis,' however, appears in several later hymnals.

US & CAN: CW400/- : P263/-/- ● ENG:

790. WE WOULD SEE JESUS: LO, HIS STAR IS SHINING

5 st. 11.10.11.10

J. E. Park, for *Worship and Song*, 1913; John 1:21. He took the first words from (Scripture and) the preceding hymn.

US & CAN: B98: CW209/- : M90: P -/183/- : Pm152 ● ENG:

JOHN EDGAR PARK, b. Belfast, N. Ireland, 7 iii 1879; Sch. Queen's, Belfast, Royal Univ., Dublin, then Edinburgh; Leipzig; Munich; Oxford; Princeton, N.J.; Ord. Presb. (U.S.), 1902; worked in lumber camps in the Adirondacks; then became Congregationalist and served Second Congl. Ch., West Newton, Mass., 1906; President, Wheaton Coll., Mass., 1926. † Cambridge, Mass., 4 iii 1956 (76).

791. WEARY OF EARTH AND LADEN WITH MY SIN

8 st. 10 10. 10 10

S. J. Stone (685), *Lyra Fidelium*, 1866. Full text in *A & M (S)*.
US & CAN: H58: L366 ● ENG: AM252/- : E91: M355

WELCOME, DAY OF THE LORD
WELCOME, HAPPY MORNING   **see 872.**
WELCOME, MORNING OF JOY

792. WERE YOU THERE WHEN THEY CRUCIFIED MY LORD?

Negro Spiritual: perhaps among the generality of hymn-singers the most celebrated of them all, and certainly the first to appear in a standard hymnal. See 223.

US & CAN: Can460: B108: CW -/161: H80: L500: M436: P -/201/- : Pm179: CLB264: W302 ● ENG: E*29: M*93: NC266: PL190

793. WE'VE A STORY TO TELL TO THE NATIONS

4 st. 10.8.8.7 anap., with refrain 9.8.9.7 anap.

H. E. Nichol, writing as Colin Sterne, 1896 leaflet; *Sunday School Hymnary*, 1905.

US & CAN: B281: CW530/- : M410: P -/504/- ● ENG: B400

HENRY ERNEST NICHOL, b. Hull, Yorks, 10 xii 1862: apprenticed to a civil engineering firm, 1877, but changed to music, '85; Sch. Oxford: B.Mus., 1888. Thereafter became composer, publisher and popularizer of what can best be called Children's Gospel Songs, which became as popular, especially in the north of England, as the Sankey songs became in the adult missions. These appeared in a long series of leaflets for Sunday School Anniversaries; they totalled 130 songs, all in a primitive style. For texts he took the name Colin Sterne—anagram (almost) of his own name. † Skirlaugh, Yorks, 30 viii 1926 (63).

794. WHAT A FRIEND WE HAVE IN JESUS

6 st. 8.7.8.7 (now always 8.7.8.7 D)

J. Scriven, in Hastings' *Social Poems, Original & Selected*, 1865. During the author's lifetime authorship always kept secret, and divulged only

near the time of his death when he said he had written it for his mother in a time of great sorrow. Probably the best known hymn of Canadian origin.

US & CAN: BP431: Can114: B403: CW331/224: H422: L459: M261: P257/385/- : Pm335 ● ENG: An612: CH701/- : CP371: M538

JOSEPH MEDLICOTT SCRIVEN, b. Seapatrick, Co. Down (Ireland), 10 ix 1819; Sch. for army but abandoned career for reasons of health. Then Sch. Trinity Coll., Dublin. His fiancée was drowned the evening before their wedding; in 1844 moved to Canada, served as tutor to family of Lieut. Pengelley, at Bewdley, Ont. Here again a second fiancée (Pengelley's daughter) died just before they were to be married. He was a member of the Plymouth Brethren and thereafter gave all his time to philanthropic work for handicapped and destitute persons. In later years failing health induced depression and when he was found dead near Rice Lake it was not known whether this was accident or suicide. † Bewdley, Ont., 10 viii 1886 (66).

795. WHAT CHILD IS THIS, WHO LAID TO REST

3 st. 8.7.8.7 iamb., with refrain 6.8.6.7

W. C. Dix (35) in Bramley & Stainer, *Christmas Carols New and Old*, 1871, to carry the tune GREENSLEEVES. Now much better known in U.S. than in Britain. (Note: The *Hymnal-1940 Companion* is astray in calling this 'The Manger Throne': that is another carol by the same author in the same source.)

US & CAN: CW200/133: H36: L48: M385: P -/159/630: Pm140: W303 ● ENG:

796. WHAT DOTH (DOES) THE LORD REQUIRE . . . ?

5 st. 6.6.6.6.3.3.6, dact., iamb. and anap.   **PCH 470**

A. F. Bayly (537) in *Rejoice, O People*, 1950; later revised into 'you' form, with other modifications, for *100 Hymns for To-Day*, 1969, and sometimes abr. to 3 st. Refrain quotes Micah 6:8.

US & CAN: H*37: W304 ● ENG: AM*99: B*94

797. WHAT GRACE, O LORD, AND BEAUTY SHONE

5 st. CM

E. Denny, *Selection of Hymns*, 1839; 'The Forgiving One: Ps. 45:2.'

US & CAN: BP162: CW219/- : M178: P113/180/- ● ENG: CH87/216: M115

SIR EDWARD DENNY, Bt., b. Tralee Castle, Kerry, Ireland, 2 x 1796; succeeded his father as 4th Baronet, 1831, when almost the whole of the town of Tralee belonged to him and his rental income was £13,000 a year. Like many Kerry gentry he joined the Plymouth Brethren, and became their foremost hymnodist, editing 2 collections in which many of his own hymns appeared. At the time of the writing of *Julian's* note he is still written of in the present tense, but he † Tralee, 13 vi 1889 (92).

798. WHAT STAR IS THIS THAT BEAMS SO BRIGHT?

6 st. LM

Latin: QUAE STELLA SOLE PULCHRIOR, C. Coffin (52), *Paris Breviary*, 1736.

Tr. J. Chandler (52), *Hymns of the Primitive Church*, 1837. All hymnals agree on the first line but on no other line in the hymn. Nearest to orig. is in EH; furthest away is vn. in *Hymns A & M*; but all vns. derived from same source.

US & CAN: CW -/142: H47: P -/-/632: Pm144: W305 ● ENG: AM77/- : BB69: E44: NC270

799. WHAT WONDROUS LOVE IS THIS . . . ?   **PCH 399**

The melody and words of this appear in *Southern Harmony* (U.S.), 1835; there and in other kindred books the text is anon., but W. Hauser in *The Hesperian Harp*, 1848, attributes text to the Rev. Alexander

HYMNS 800—808

Means, a Methodist minister of Oxford, Georgia, and against the tune in *Sacred Harmony* stands an unintelligible ascription to 'Christopher.' G. Pullen Jackson in *The Story of the Sacred Harp, 1844-1944* (Nashville, 1944), says that the tune and the word-structure are derived from a secular ballad:

My name was Robert Kidd when I sailed, when I sailed. . . .

This is so far the most travelled of these American Folk Hymns, or 'White Spirituals' from the valleys of the Southern Appalachians (E. Tennessee, E. Kentucky, W. North Carolina) which, until the early 1950's, were almost unknown outside the very close communities that used them. The texts of the hymns to which they were set are often 18th-cent. Calvinist (cf. AMAZING GRACE, 31), more or less faithfully transcribed; but the melodies, though usually showing unmistakable Celtic influences, are always original and often of great beauty.

The first standard hymnals to include this were *M(U.S.)* 1966, and, in Britain, *Cambridge Hymnal*, 1967.

US & CAN: B106: CW -/157: H*69: M432: W306 ● ENG: M*94

WHATE'ER MY GOD ORDAINS IS GOOD: see 886.

800. WHEN ALL THY MERCIES, O MY GOD

13 st. CM   **PCH 47**

J. Addison (295), *The Spectator*, 9 viii 1712; 'Gratitude.' Exists in full text now only as Hymn 1 in the 5 hymns additional to the *Scottish Paraphrases* in the *Scot. Psalter* 1929 (see 76); elsewhere always abr. to 8 st. or fewer; it hardly makes its effect in fewer than 6. Last line of st. 1 was used by C. Wesley (1) in final line of 'Love divine' (442).

US & CAN: BP99: Can207: B468: H297: L440: M70: P81/119/- : Pm84 ● ENG: AM517/177: An568: B77: BB22: CH26/150: CP49: E511: M413

801. WHEN GOD OF OLD CAME DOWN FROM HEAVEN

11 st. CM

J. Keble (83), *The Christian Year*, 1827; Pentecost. *Hymns A & M*, 1861, included sts. 1, 3, 4, 6, 7, 9, 11 and this selection is more or less standard.

US & CAN: Can483 ● ENG: AM154: CH181/331: CP211: E158: M276

802. WHEN, HIS SALVATION BRINGING

3 st. 7.6.7.6 D

J. King, Gwythers' *Psalmist*, 1830. Refrain peculiar to *Hymns A & M* (1916).

US & CAN: P149/186/- ● ENG: AM728/437: M835

JOHN KING, b. Hull, 1789, was incumbent of Christ Church, Hull; apart from this, which we are told in source of his hymn, nothing is known of him except that he † Hull, 12 ix 1858.

803. WHEN I NEEDED A NEIGHBOUR, WERE YOU THERE?

7 st. stress 4-3 with refrain 4-1.

S. Carter (173), *9 Ballads or Carols*, 1964 and other later collections of his songs.

US & CAN: H*38 ● ENG: AM*100: B*97: M*97: PL298

804. WHEN I SURVEY THE WONDROUS CROSS

5 st. LM-alt.   **PCH 38**

I. Watts (10), *Hymns . . .* , 1707, Book III: 'Crucifixion to the world by the Cross of Christ,' Gal. 6:14. Nowhere else is it so important to note the title and leading text of a hymn, since once it is noted, the omission of st. 4, still very common, becomes totally indefensible: the core of the thought of the hymn is there. In first ed., the second line read

'Where the young Prince of glory died.' In all subsequent edns. this was altd. by author as now familiar. No alterations apart from this are really tolerable, least of all 'When I behold . . .' which is creeping in at the time of writing. The doxology in *AM(S)* is, of course, spurious and out of place.

US & CAN: BP178: Can109: B111: CW228/171: H337: L503: M435: P152/198/635: Pm177: CLB458 ● ENG: AM108: An164: B151: BB97: CH106/254: CP131: E107: M182: NC273: PL177

805. WHEN MORNING GILDS THE SKIES

2 versions of this are now in use, both being translations (one perhaps more a paraphrase) of an anonymous German song beginning BEIM FRUHEN MORGENLICHT, itself found in 2 different forms in Porter's *Katholisches Gesangbuch*, 1828, (Diocese of Wurzburg); and Ditfurth's *Frankische Volkslieder*, Leipzig, 1855. In 1828 source it is 14 st., in 1855, 13 st., in both 66.7.66.7.

Tr. (a)   E. Caswall (26), Formby's *Catholic Hymns*, no date (c. 1854), 6 st. 66.6.66.6; in his *Masque of Mary*, 1858, remaining sts. of 1828 text were added. From this a 6 st. cento was made for *Hymns A & M*, 1868, which was expanded to 8 st. in edn. of 1875. Caswall's original trsln. is used for the 8 st. version in *EH* but *A & M* version (with alterations) is usually taken by other books.

     (b)   R. Bridges (9), *Yattendon Hymnal*, 1899, 5 st. 66.7.66.7 D (i.e. 10 st. of orig.), designed to be a nearer translation and restored to orig. meter by writing *prais-ed* for *prais'd* in refrain lines (which otherwise are taken from [a]). After this version brought the Genevan tune for Ps. 3, which Bridges used, into currency, Caswall's vn. was found (e.g. in *A & M*, 1916) in 12-line sts. with 'prais-ed.' Conversely, the Bridges version, though occasionally printed in full (as *CP*), is often now abr. to 6 st. of 6 lines (or 3 of 12), and may appear either with 'prais'd' for the tune first associated with Caswall's version, or as he first wrote it.

US & CAN: BP230 (a) CW135 (a)/296 (a) H367 (b) L416 (b) M91 (a) P3 (a)/ 4k (a)/637 (a) Pm35 (a) CLB469 (a) ● ENG: AM303 (a)/223 (a) An271 (a) B685 (a) BB285 (b) CH167 (a)/370 (a) CP193 (a), 194 (b) E512 (b) M113 (a)

806. WHEN MOTHERS OF SALEM THEIR CHILDREN BROUGHT TO JESUS

4 st. 6.7.8.6.88.6.5 (one irregular line)

W. M. Hutchings, for Anniversary service of St. Paul's Chapel Sunday School, Wigan, Lancs, and (rev.) *Juvenile Missionary Magazine*, 1850.

US & CAN: BP159: P446/-/- ● ENG: B401: CH659/- : M866

WILLIAM MEDLEN HUTCHINGS, b. Devonport, 28 viii 1827, a Congregationalist and, for a time, printer and publisher in London. † Camberwell, London, 21 v 1876 (48).

807. WHEN MY LOVE TO CHRIST (GOD) GROWS WEAK

6 st. 77.77

J. R. Wreford (439) for J. R. Beard's *Collection of Hymns . . .* , 1837 (designed for Unitarians). In *Hymns of the Spirit* (Boston, 1864: see 7) first line changed to '. . . to God . . .' which is now mostly kept except in *An*.

US & CAN: Pm162 ● ENG: An168: CP124: M178

808. WHEN ON MY DAY OF LIFE THE NIGHT IS FALLING

7 st. 11.10.11.6   **PCH 367**

J. G. Whittier (11), 1882; in *The Bay of Seven Islands*, 1883; a hymn for old age written when he was himself 75.

US & CAN: BP535 ● ENG: BB777: CH589/- : CP770: M642

809. WHEN OUR HEADS ARE BOWED WITH WOE

6 st. 77.77

H. H. Milman (524), in Heber's *Hymns . . .* , 1827; for 16th Sunday after Trinity; Luke 7:11-17.

US & CAN: H79 ● ENG: AM399/- : CH329/- : E513: M978

810. WHEN THE LORD OF LOVE WAS HERE

6 st. 77.5.77.5

S. Brooke (384), *Christian Hymns*, 1881; st. 4 sometimes omitted.

US & CAN: CW215/- : P141/-/- ● ENG: B133: CH85/- : CP110: M147

811. WHEN THIS PASSING WORLD IS DONE

9 st. 77.77.77: irregular syllables in one st.

R. M. McCheyne, Scottish Christian Herald, 20 v 1837; always abr. to 4 st.

US & CAN: BP541 ● ENG: B616: CH582/- : CP772: M643

ROBERT MURRAY McCHEYNE, b. Edinburgh 21 v 1813; Sch. Edinburgh High Sch. & Univ.; Ord. C/Scot. 1835; asst. minister at Larbert & Dinipace, Stirlingshire; minister, St. Peter's, Dundee, 1836. Sent to Palestine, '39, as member of commission of enquiry into possibility of missions to Jews. Much engaged in evang. missions in Scot., and Eng., and one of the most renowned preachers of his day. Ill-health constantly interrupted his ministries, but his name remains a legend in Scotland. † Dundee, 25 iii 1843 (29).

812. WHEN WILT THOU SAVE THE PEOPLE?

3 st. 7.6.7.6.888.5   **PCH 213**

E. Elliott, posth. in *More Verse & Prose*, 1850; first as a hymn in *Congl. Church Hymnal*, 1887, with famous & expressive tune by J. Booth. An utterance of social passion direct from English Chartists.

US & CAN: CW563/- : H496: P375/- ● ENG: B654: CP567: E566: M909

EBENEZER ELLIOTT, b. Masbro, Rotherham, 17 iii 1781. His father, known as 'Devil Elliott' was an extreme radical in politics and extreme Calvinist in religion. E. E. disfigured in youth by smallpox, and during early years something of a recluse; entered iron trade in Sheffield, 1821, and himself active in literature & politics, especially in writing rhymes (comparable to some Tennessee folk songs of 20th century) depicting the misery of the poor and the iniquity of the Corn Laws (for which he came to be known as the Corn Law Rhymer). His writings are thought to have contributed to the repealing of the Bread Tax in 1846. † Great Houghton, nr. Barnsley, Yorks, 1 xii 1849 (68).

813. WHERE CROSS THE CROWDED WAYS OF LIFE

6 st. LM alt.   **PCH 537**

F. M. North, *The Christian City*, June 1903 and *Methodist Hymnal* (U.S.). Editors of *MH* had asked him to write a missionary hymn, and after demurring, he wrote this for the city; its opening was suggested by the American Rev. Vn. of Matt. 22:9—'Go ye therefore unto the partings of the highways.' Predating 'O God on earth and altar' and 'Judge eternal' by a year or two, this is probably the earliest Christian hymn of the modern city. First in Britain in Supplement (1920) to the *Fellowship Hymn Book*. In *CLB* begins 'On all the crowded . . .' and thus misses the allusion intended by the author.

US & CAN: BP496: Can303: B311: CW519/268: H498: L351: M204: P410/507/642: Om423: CLB498‡ ● ENG: B533: CH -/512: M895

814. WHERE HIGH THE HEAVENLY TEMPLE STANDS

6 st. LM-coup.   **PCH 100**

Scottish Paraphrases, 1781, #58, 2nd version (76), attributed, but uncertainly, to M. Bruce; Hebr. 6:14ff.

US & CAN: BP213: P -/389/- ● ENG: AM210/204: An213: B178: BB498: CH140/295: CP184: E*316

815. WHEREFORE, O FATHER, WE, THY HUMBLE SERVANTS

2 st. 11.11.11.5 (Sapphic)

W. H. H. Jervois, *English Hymnal*, 1906.

US & CAN: H205 ● ENG: AM -/416: An368: BB220: E335

WILLIAM HENRY HAMMOND JERVOIS, b. 10 x 1852, Isle of Alderney; Sch. Rugby & Trinity, Oxf.; Ord. C/E, 1879; Vicar of St. Mary Magdalene, Munster Square, London, 1896-†. Member of ed. cttee. of *English Hymnal*, and, since he died just before the book was completed, *EH* is dedicated to him. † London, 5 viii 1905 (52).

816. WHILE SHEPHERDS WATCHED THEIR FLOCKS BY NIGHT (WHILE HUMBLE SHEPHERDS WATCHED THEIR FLOCKS)

6 st. CM   **PCH 22**

Tate & Brady (53), *New Version of the Psalms*, 1696, one of the 6 hymns authorized for use and appended to the Psalter. Being a close paraphrase of the Nativity passage in Luke 2, it was taken into *Scot. Paraphrases* (76) as #37, with alterations including variant opening line. Only one other alteration is made in the otherwise universal text: 'a Saviour' for 'the Saviour' in st. 3 (important and right). So many tunes, many of them English folk hymn tunes, are known to this that it is of interest to note that that suggested in the first musical ed. of the *New Version* (*Supplement to the New Version*, 1708) is ST. JAMES—at that time a brand-new tune (1699).

US & CAN: BP127: Can405: B97: CW185/126: H13: L24: M394: P120/169/643: Pm146: CLB214: W309 ● ENG: AM62: An123: B113: BB61: CH42†/174†: CP80: E30: M129: NC277: PL157

817. WHO ARE THESE LIKE STARS APPEARING?

8.7.8.7.77

German: WER SIND DIE VOR GOTTES THRONE, 20 st., by H. Schenck (his only hymn) in *Neu-vermehrtes Gbch*, Frankfurt, 1719; Rev. 7: 13-17.

Tr. F. E. Cox (352) in *Sacred Hymns from the German*, 1841, 15 st., orig. met. Accepted selection is sts. 1, 3, 4, 5, 9, first made in Alford's *Psalms & Hymns*, 1844.

US & CAN: Can504: H130: CLB300 ● ENG: AM427/570: An465: BB236: CH222/- : E204

THEOBALD HEINRICH SCHENCK, b. Alsfield, Hesse, 1656; Sch. Univ. Giessen, became pastor there, 1689; remained until † 11 iv 1727 (70).

818. WHO FATHOMS THE ETERNAL THOUGHT?

CM   **PCH 366**

J. G. Whittier (11), from 'The Eternal Goodness' in *A Tent on the Beach . . .* , 1867. Selections from this 22-st. poem have been made into hymns, those current being:

    (a) WHO FATHOMS THE ETERNAL THOUGHT, beginning at st. 4;

    (b) I BOW MY FOREHEAD TO THE DUST, beginning at st. 9, set in CMD, and using a quite different seln. of sts. from (a) and (c);

    (c) I KNOW NOT WHAT THE FUTURE HATH, norm. using sts. 16-20.

US & CAN: BP518 (a): B492 (c): L593 (c): M290 (c): P282 (b)/109 (b)/- ● ENG: CH558 (a)/- : CP476 sts. 3-6 (c): M513 (a)

819. WHO IS HE, IN YONDER STALL?

8 st. 77 with ref. 88.77

B. R. Hanby (almost certainly) in *The Dove, a Collection of Music for Day & Sunday Schools*, Chicago, 1866, but not now in common use in U.S. Hanby's original tune (there is no doubt about his composership) was replaced in *EH* with the old carol RESONET IN LAUDIBUS which turned out to fit it exactly. (It cannot be supposed that Hanby chose his unusual meter with that carol tune in mind: it must be a coincidence.)

US & CAN: ● ENG: An284: B134: BB75: CH77/221: E612: M151

BENJAMIN RUSSELL HANBY, 1833-67, places unknown, was co-editor with G. F. Root of *Chapel Gems*, 1866. He was Sch. for the ministry but made music his life's work; when he died he was already well known as a Sunday School composer.

820. WHO IS ON THE LORD'S SIDE?

5 st. 6.5.6.5 Ter.

F. R. Havergal (252), 13 Oct. 1877; in *Loyal Responses*, 1878. St. 2 norm. om.

US & CAN: BP480: CW367/- : P272/355/- ● ENG: AM683/- : An592: B534: CH519/479: CP528: M820

821. WHO WOULD TRUE VALOUR SEE
HE WHO WOULD VALIANT BE

3 st. 6.5.6.5.666.5   PCH 434

(a) WHO WOULD . . . , J. Bunyan, in 1684 edn. of *The Pilgrim's Progress* (not in 1678 edn.), just before conclusion of pt. 2. Written approximately in meter of the old carol 'Remember O thou man' (see *Oxford Book of Carols*, 42), whose tune was very popular at the time. First in hymnal, *Hymns Ancient & Modern* 1916 Supplement (which jibbed only at 'hobgoblin') and *Congregational Hymnary*, 1916 (true text). This late appearance undoubtedly due to the existence of (b) below.

(b) HE WHO . . . , P. Dearmer (88), written in imitation of Bunyan's poem for *English Hymnal*, 1906, same length and using some of its lines, but a totally different composition. It was done because, as he said, 'Bunyan would never have sanctioned the unaltered form as a hymn.' This was true: Dearmer claims with justice that, e.g., his 'giant' is more biblical than 'hobgoblin' in st. 3. The instant popularity of this, with Vaughan Williams' arrangement of a folk song, caused others to ask whether the original could not equally well be sung as a hymn, with the new tune. (But Dearmer's argument must be pondered.) The consequence was that most British books now print (a) (A & M, by the way, offers the 'Remember O thou man' tune with it), while U.S. books (always shy of pre-Watts hymnody) use (b).

US & CAN: BP520 (b) Can293 (a): B284: CW364/252: H563: L563: M155: P276/345/414: Pm371 (all [b]) ● ENG: AM676/293: B561: BB371: CH 576/443: CP486: E402 (b): M620: NC279: PL285 (exc. *EH*, all [a])

JOHN BUNYAN, bapt. 30 xi 1628 at Bedford, b. Harroden, Bedford; apprenticed to his father's trade (tinker). Served in Parliamentary forces 1644; married a poor woman whose dowry consisted of 2 religious books, which began a spiritual awakening in him. After a period of spiritual search, began preaching; recognized as Bapt. minister, 1657. Imprisoned for refusing to conform to Angl. Ch., 1660-72, during which time he wrote *Grace Abounding* (1666) and *The Holy City*. Released '72, but in prison again 6 months '75, when he wrote *The Pilgrim's Progress*, the only work of fiction by a 17th century Puritan, which sold 100,000 copies in 10 years. His fame now principally rests on this. † Bedford, 31 viii 1688 (59).

822. WHOM OCEANS PART, O LORD, UNITE

5 st. LM coup.

H. Elvet Lewis (430), for a Colonial Missionary Society Anniversary, before 1914. *Congregational Hymnary*, 1916.

US & CAN: CW525/- ● ENG: B656: CH628/- : CP343

823. WILL YOUR ANCHOR HOLD IN THE
STORMS OF LIFE?

4 st. 10 10. 10 10 troch. and dact., with refrain 99.9 10 dact.

P. J. Owens (779). The familiar form of this is due to Sankey's *Sacred Songs & Solos*, 1874.

US & CAN: BP515: Can191 ● ENG: B568: CH -/412: M634

824. WISE MEN SEEKING JESUS

7 st. 6.5.6.5

J. T. East, *Methodist School Hymnal*, 1911.

US & CAN: BP151: Can122: CW203/- ● ENG: B135: CH -/222: CP96: M862

JAMES THOMAS EAST, b. Kettering, Northants, 28 i 1860; Ord. Meth. (Wesleyan) 1886; served in Meth. ministry till retirement, 1924. The only other information given about him in several reference books is that his great grandmother was the sister of John Bunyan (821); i.e., born more than 200 years before him. This probably needs scrutiny. † Blackburn, Lancs, 28 v 1937 (77).

825. WITH JOY WE MEDITATE THE GRACE

6 st. CM

I. Watts (10), *Hymns . . .* , Book I, 1707; 'Christ's Compassion to the weak and Tempted. Heb. 4:15-16; 5:7; Matt. 12:20.' Full text in *CP*; final line sometimes altd.

US & CAN: ● ENG: An281: B179: BB134: CP97: M236

826. WORKMAN OF GOD, OH, LOSE NOT HEART

CM   PCH 210

F. W. Faber (175), *Jesus & Mary*, 1849; 'The Right must Win,' in 19 st. beginning OH IT IS HARD TO WORK FOR GOD. Only one current hymnal has st. 1 (*AMS*). Others begin at st. 11, but the orig. here read WORKMEN OF GOD. . . . Sts. are selected from all over the poem— thus: *AM*—1, 2, 8, 11, 14, 19; *B(Brit.)*—11, 8, 2, 12, 19; *CH(both)*—11, 12, 2, 8, 14, 19; *CP*—11, 2, 8, 12, 19: *M(Brit.)*—11, 12, 8 (altd.), 14, 19. *Pm* has unusual and good seln.: 15, 11, 12, 13, 19. *Worship Song* (1905) had fullest selection—12 st. in 2 hymns.

US & CAN: Pm369 ● ENG: AM739/- : B535: CH520/670: CP544: M489

827. YE CHOIRS OF NEW JERUSALEM

Latin: CHORUS NOVAE JERUSALEM, Fulbert of Chartres, c. 1000 A.D., 6 st. LM-coup.

Tr. (a) CM, R. Campbell, 6 st., *Hymns & Anthems*, 1850;
     (b) revision of (a) by compilers of *Hymns A & M*, 1861;
     (c) LM, J. M. Neale (2), 6 st., *Hymnal Noted*, 1854, rev. from earlier vn. in *Medieval Hymns*, 1851, beginning THOU NEW JERUSALEM ON HIGH;
     (d) SING, CHOIRS OF NEW JERUSALEM, A. Petti, *NCH*, CM, based on (a).

US & CAN: Can463 (b) ● ENG: AM125 (b)/128 (b): An191 (b): BB116 (b): E139 (a), 122 (c) NC213 (d)

ROBERT CAMPBELL, b. Trochraig, Ayrshire, 19 xii 1814; Sch. Univ. Glasgow, & became an advocate. Began translating Latin hymns, 1848; collected them in source above; became R.C., 1852. † Edinburgh, 29 xii 1868 (54).

828. YE GATES, LIFT UP YOUR HEADS ON HIGH

2 st. CMD with coda   **PCH 13**

Scot. Psalter, 1650 (323), Ps. 24, vv. 7-10. This fragment, since composition of famous tune ST. GEORGE'S, EDINBURGH, about 1820 (which causes it always to appear in this meter), came to have special eucharistic significance in Ch. of Scot., at the 'Greater Entrance' (bringing-in of the Elements). After falling into disuse this custom was revived in the 1940s under the influence of the Iona Community.

US & CAN: BP10: Can4 ● ENG: B172: ScPs24/CP566: CP730

829. YE HOLY ANGELS BRIGHT

4 st. 6.6.6.6.4.44.4   **PCH 430**

J. H. Gurney (174), based on Richard Baxter (116). The original, with this opening line, is Baxter's 'A Psalm of Praise to the tune of Psalm 148,' in his *The Poor Man's Family Book*, 1672, in 16 stanzas. The well-known form is a new hymn, though entirely in the spirit of the original and very well constructed. Baxter's surviving lines are st. 1, line 1, st. 2, lines 5-8, and st. 4 lines 1-4, with alterations of detail. The rest is Gurney, whose hymn is based on Baxter's first 5 stanzas (omitting his 4th), and in this form it appeared in his *Psalms and Hymns*, 1838, and was made popular when later in the 19th cent. associated with Darwall's tune.

    The Canadian *Hymn Book*, 1971, alone uses Baxter's original sts. 1-3 and 5, and this makes a very acceptable piece, although, being only a quarter of the original, it is less tightly organized than Gurney's version.

US & CAN: Can 6‡: H600: L409: Pm23: CLB532‡ ● ENG: AM546/371: An24: B36: BB286: CH39/363: CP5: E517: M26: NC282

830. YE SERVANTS OF GOD, YOUR MASTER PROCLAIM

6 st. 5.5.5.5.6.5.6.5

C. Wesley (1), *Hymns for Times of Trouble & Persecution*, 1744, the title being 'Tumult.' Rarely has a famous hymn been so completely changed in character by abridgment (though one can compare the same author's O FOR A THOUSAND TONGUES, see 510). Here sts. 2 and 3 of the original refer to the fears of British Protestants on the eve of the 1745 Rebellion (which had it been successful might have gravely threatened the whole Protestant interest, then regarded as congruent with the British way of life). Without these 2 sts. it is a hymn of praise so generalized as to have become hackneyed through constant casual use. The two missing sts. are these:

> The waves of the sea / have lift up their voice,
> sore trouble that we / in Jesus rejoice;
> the Floods they are roaring / but Jesus is here;
> while we are adoring / He always is near.

> Men, Devils, engage / the Billows arise,
> and horribly rage / and threaten the skies;
> their Fury shall never / our stedfastness shock,
> the weakest Believer / is built on a Rock.

The language here echoes Ps. 93.

US & CAN: BP238: Can35: B292: CW258/76: L446: M409: P198/27/645: Pm206: CLB447 ● ENG: AM704/226: An336: B37: BB287: CH168/372: CP66: E*94: M426

831. YE SERVANTS OF THE LORD

5 st. SM

P. Doddridge (64), posth., *Hymns . . .* , 1755; 'The Active Christian: Luke 12:35-8.'

US & CAN: ● ENG: AM268/229: An606: B197: BB372: CH156/319: CP493: E518: M581

832. YE WATCHERS AND YE HOLY ONES   **PCH 266**

4 st. LM-coup. with interpolated lines, 8 syll. after first coup., 20 after 2nd.

A. Riley (112), *English Hymnal*, 1906, to carry R. Vaughan Williams' then new arrangement of the tune LASST UNS ERFREUEN (EASTER ALLELUIA). A festive song in which st. 2 refers to the Blessed Virgin. It was once pointed out (by Canon Adam Fox of Westminster Abbey) that one quarter of this text is in the Hebrew language (30 words out of 121). It was this hymn that made the tune, now associated with several others, popular. The text is now found more often in U.S. than in Britain and it is interesting to note how this very tractarian text has appealed to so many American Protestant editors.

US & CAN: Can7: H599: L437: M19: P -/34/- : Pm30: W313 ● ENG: BB288: E519

PART II: HYMNS OF FOREIGN ORIGIN IN MULTIPLE ENGLISH TRANSLATIONS

833. AD COENAM AGNI PROVIDI

LM   **PCH 146**

Anon., before 1000 A.D. This was revised by order of Pope Urban VIII as AD REGIAS AGNI DAPES, first printed 1632.

    (a) THE LAMB'S HIGH BANQUET WE AWAIT, J. M. Neale (2), *Hymnal Noted*, 1854, 7 st. LM-coup.

    (b) Revision of (a) with same opening line by compilers of *Hymns A & M*, 1861.

    (c) Revision of (a) with same opening line by R. Bridges, *Yattendon Hymnal*, 1899.

Both in original and in translations this hymn contains an unusual richness of medieval Easter imagery including the white robes of baptism, the Exodus typology, and the Altar as symbolic of the Cross. Especially suitable for Easter Vigil.

    (d) AT THE LAMB'S HIGH FEAST WE SING, R. Campbell (827), *St. Andrew's Hymnal*, 1850, 4 st. 77.77 D; small alterations in various books.

US & CAN: Can472 (b): H89 (d): L95 (d): CLB275 (d): W29 (d) ● ENG: AM128/129 (b), 127/139 (d): BB113 (c): E125 (a), 128 (d): NC18 (d):

PL197 (d)

ADORO TE DEVOTE LATENS DEITAS: see 186 IV.

834. AETERNA REX ALTISSIME

7 st. LM

Latin, prob. 6th cent., anon.; earliest source, Wurzburg ms., 13 cent.

Tr.:   (a) ETERNAL MONARCH, KING MOST HIGH, J. M. Neale (2), 6 st. LM, text taken from Sarum Breviary (6 st.).

    (b) O THOU ETERNAL KING MOST HIGH, derived from (a), rewritten by compilers of *Hymns A & M*, 1861, 6 st. LM (in *AMR* reduced to 3 st.).

    (c) CHRIST ABOVE ALL GLORY SEATED, J. R. Woodford, *Hymns arranged for the Sundays of the Year*, 1865, 6 st. 8.7.8.7.

US & CAN: Can479 (a): P -/-/324 (c) ● ENG: AM144/145 (b): An198 (c): BB121 (c): E141 (a): M225 (c)

JAMES RUSSELL WOODFORD, b. Henley on Thames, Oxon., 30 ix

1820; Sch. Merchant Taylors Sch., & Pembroke, Camb.; Ord. C/E 1843; Rector of Kempsford, Glos., '55-'68; Vicar of Leeds, '68-'73; Bp. of Ely, '73-† there 24 x 1885 (85).

835. ALLELUIA PIIS LAUDIBUS

12 st. 12 12. 7 (mostly dact.)

Latin: Mozarabic Breviary, 5th cent.

Tr.: (a) SING ALLELUIA FORTH IN DUTEOUS PRAISE, J. Ellerton (80), *Churchman's Family Magazine*, 1865, 12 st. 10 10. 7, in full with explanatory note. Selections from this distinguishable by inclusion of Trinitarian stanzas.

(b) SING ALLELUIA FORTH IN DUTEOUS PRAISE: abr. by author to 9 st. in *Hymns A & M*, 1868, omitting sts. above mentioned.

(c) as above, reduced to 8 st. for *Church Hymns*, 1871.

(d) SING ALLELUIA FORTH IN LOYAL PRAISE, P. Dearmer (88), 4 st. 10 10. 7, for *Songs of Praise*, 1925, expanded to 6 st. in edn. of 1931, a paraphrase.

(e) SING ALLELUIA FORTH IN DUTEOUS PRAISE, compilers of *Hymnal-1940* (U.S.).

US & CAN: Can5 (a4): H583 (e) ● ENG: AM296/283 (b9): B27 (b8): BB282 (b7): CH -/542 (b6): CP27 (d6): M671 (a6)

836. AUDI BENIGNE CONDITOR

Latin: St. Gregory the Great (d. 604), medieval mss., LM.

Tr.: (a) O MAKER OF THE WORLD, GIVE EAR, J. M. Neale (2), *Hymnal Noted*, 1852.

(b) O MERCIFUL CREATOR, HEAR, rewritten from (a) by compilers of *Hymns A & M* 1875.

(c) O KIND CREATOR, BOW THINE EAR, T. A. Lacey (502), *English Hymnal*, 1906.

(d) O MAKER OF THE WORLD, GIVE EAR, using first line of (a) but otherwise rewritten by compilers of *Hymns A & M*, 1950.

All in 5 st. LM.

US & CAN: ● ENG: AM87 (b)/84 (d): BB346 (c): E66 (c)

837. AURORA LUCIS RUTILAT

Latin: 11 st. LM, of which 9 are the early form of the hymn and the last 2 are a double doxology which is probably medieval, the original being early.

Tr.: 2 trs. of the whole are now in use. Both respect the medieval division of the original into 2 parts, the second beginning SERMONE BLANDO ANGELUS. In modern use a third version appears at st. 10, CLARO PASCHALI GAUDIO. These 3 parts are here referred to as i, ii and iiA.

(a) LIGHT'S GLITTERING MORN BEDECKS THE SKY, J. M. Neale (2), *Hymnal Noted*, 1852; in 15 st. (ii) begins at st. 8, WITH GENTLE VOICE THE ANGEL GAVE. Sts. 6-7 are repeated as 14-15, thus the 13 st. orig. is preserved. This is nowhere in use now. However, with same first line the rewritten version in *Hymns A & M* 1861 is, in whole or in part, in wide use. Here (ii) begins with last st. of what was pt. i in orig. and in Neale: THE APOSTLES' HEARTS WERE FULL OF PAIN, and (iiA) begins with a new vn. of Neale's st. 11 (orig. 9), THAT EASTER DAY WITH JOY WAS BRIGHT. (This section now very popular in U.S.). Pm begins iiA with a st. from *Methodist Hymnal*, 1935, JOY DAWNED AGAIN.

(b) THE DAY DRAWS ON WITH GOLDEN LIGHT, T. A. Lacey (502), *English Hymnal*, 1906, 15 st., exactly the same pattern as (a) spread over 2 hymns, the second being ii, but both divided into 2 parts at sts. 3 and 9 of original respectively. (ii) begins HIS CHEERING MESSAGE FROM THE GRAVE.

US & CAN: In America, all (a iiA): Can474: H98: L94: P -/-/581: Pm 188‡: CLB270: W260 ● ENG: AM126/602 (a): B159 (a i): BB107 (a i), 108 (a i,ii), 111 (a iiA): 104 (b ii) E123-4 (b)

838. AUS TIEFER NOTH SCREI ICH ZU DIR PCH 2

German: M. Luther (112), *Etlich Christliche Lieder*, 1524 & *Enchiridion*, 1524, in 4 st. 8.7.8.7.88.7; rev. by him in *Geistliche Gesangk Buchlein*, 1524, in 5 st.; paraphrase of Ps. 130, sung by him & Melanchthon (487) at a critical point in their journey to Worms.

Tr.: (a) FROM DEPTHS OF WOE I RAISE TO THEE, R. Massie (112), *Martin Luther's Spiritual Songs*, 1854; 5 st.

(b) OUT OF THE DEPTHS I CRY TO THEE, C. Winkworth (14), *Lyra Germanica* I, 1855; 4 st. 8.6.8.6.88.7.

(c) OUT OF THE DEPTHS I CRY TO THEE, C. Winkworth (14), *Chorale Book for England*, 1863; 4 st. 8.7.8.7.88.7.

(d) OUT OF THE DEPTHS I CRY TO THEE, E. T. Horn III (127), for Lutheran *Service Book & Hymnal*, 1958, 4 st. 8.7.8.7.88.7.

US & CAN: CW -/89 (c): L372 (d): M526 (c) ● ENG: B457 (c): CH407 (a) /- : CP381 (c): M359 (b)

839. BEATA NOBIS GAUDIA

Latin: 9th cent., 6 st. LM, Pentecost.

Tr.: (a) JOY BECAUSE THE CIRCLING YEAR, J. Ellerton (80) & R. Mant (95), *Church Hymns*, 1871, and *A & M*, 1875; 6 st. 77.77.

(b) O JOY BECAUSE THE CIRCLING YEAR, rev. from (a) by compilers of *Hymns A & M*, 1904, and further by those of 1950 (6st., 4 st.) to restore orig. meter (LM).

(c) REJOICE, THE YEAR UPON ITS WAY, R. E. Roberts, *English Hymnal*, 1906, 6 st. LM: now most popular, though elsewhere abr.

US & CAN: BP267 (a): Can 486 (c) ● ENG: AM153 (a) /151 (b): B238 (c): BB162 (c): CH -/330 (c): E151 (c)

RICHARD ELLIS ROBERTS, b. Islington (London), 26 ii 1879; Sch. St. John's, Oxf.; on staff of *Pall Mall Gazette*, 1903-5; literary critic, essayist, poet; literary editor, *New Statesman*, 1930. Lived in U.S.A. in later years, and † Carmel, California, 5 x 1953 (74). Cf. 21.

840. BEFIEHL DU DEINE WEGE PCH 195

German: P. Gerhardt (18) in Frankfurt ed. (1656) of *Praxis Pietatis Melica*, 12 st. 7.6.7.6 D, and from a very early stage associated with the tune known to us as PASSION CHORALE. It is an acrostic on Luther's version of Ps. 37.

Tr.: (a) COMMIT THOU ALL THY GRIEFS, a free paraphrase by J. Wesley (1) in *Hymns and Spiritual Songs*, 1739, 8 st. SMD (64 lines). Modern books print this in various ways; some in 2 parts, beginning pt. 2 at GIVE TO THE WINDS THY FEARS; others begin pt. 2, or print part 2 (abr.) only, PUT THOU THY TRUST IN GOD; but that quatrain, of unknown authorship, is no part of the original and first appeared in the *Mitre Hymn Book*, 1836, (see 83) with altd. versions of 3 other quatrains. This in turn generated the 16-line version found in *Hymns A & M*, 1916, 1950; but the PUT THOU quatrain also appears in hymnals that otherwise preserve closer versions of J. W.'s text. (Books with PUT THOU ... marked ‡ below). The fullest text is in *M(Brit)*.

(b) COMMIT THOU ALL THAT GRIEVES THEE, a closer version of selected stanzas from Gerhardt by A. W. Farlander and W. Douglas (659), 4 st. 7.6.7.6 D, made for *Hymnal-1940* (US) and found only there.

(all [a] except *H*)

US & CAN: BP503 (a ii): B224‡: H446 (b): L579‡ ● ENG: AM692‡/310‡ An 482: B574: BB313‡: CH546-7‡/669‡: CP487: M507

841. CAELESTIS FORMAM GLORIAE

Latin: *Sarum Breviary*, LM; The Transfiguration.

Tr.: (a) O WONDROUS TYPE, O VISION FAIR: compilers of *Hymns A & M*, 1861, using only 2 lines of a tr. by J. M. Neale (2), *Hymnal Noted*, 1854. (*BP* begins O WONDROUS LIGHT ...).

(b) AN IMAGE OF THAT HEAVENLY LIGHT, R. E. Roberts (839), *English Hymnal*, 1906.

US & CAN: (all a): BP209: H119: L147: P142/182/531 • ENG: AM760/558 (a): An274 (a): CH89/217 (a): E233 (b)

842. CONDITOR (CREATOR) ALME SIDERUM

Latin: anon., perhaps 7th cent., 6 st. LM.

Tr.: (a) CREATOR OF THE STARRY FRAME, E. Caswall (26), *Lyra Catholica*, 1849; st. 1 altd. by author in *Hymns & Psalms*, 1873, to DEAR MAKER OF THE STARRY SKIES (thus *PL*).
(b) CREATOR OF THE STARS OF NIGHT, J. M. Neale (2), *Hymnal Noted*, 1852.
(c) CREATOR OF THE STARRY HEIGHT, based on (b), compilers of *Hymns A & M*, 1861.
(d) DEAR MAKER OF THE STARRY SKIES, based on (a), R. A. Know (866), *Westminster Hymnal*, 1950.
(e) CREATOR OF THE STARS OF NIGHT, based on (b), compilers of *Hymnal-1940* (U.S.).
(f) CREATOR OF THE STARS OF NIGHT, based on (b), I. Udulutsch, *NCH*, 1971.
(g) CREATOR OF THE STARS OF NIGHT, based on (b), P. Scagnelli, *Catholic Liturgy Book*, 1975.

US & CAN: BP117 (e): CW -/103 (e): H6 (a): M78 (e): P -/-/348 (e): CLB 200 (g): W65 (d) • ENG: AM45 (c): BB31 (c): E1 (b): PL125 (a): HC46 (f)

843. CORDE NATUS EX PARENTIS   PCH 155

Latin: Prudentius, *Cathemerinon*, 4th cent.; a long poem in 8.7.8.7.8.7 (a mater probably invented by Prudentius) beginning DA PLECTRUM PUER CHOREIS, which was a poem about Christian belief written, as was the manner of Christian Latin poets at that time, in the style of a secular epic. CORDE NATUS . . . is st. 4 of this, and 11 cent. mss. at the British Museum & at St. Gall contain the first appearances of a 9 st. hymn beginning there and adding the refrain-line *saeculorum saecula* which is retained in most modern translations (though not in [c]).

Tr.: the first in common use was that of J. M. Neale (2), *Hymnal Noted*, 1852, opening OF THE FATHER SOLE-BEGOTTEN, later altd. by him to OF THE FATHER'S LOVE BEGOTTEN. This was in 5 st. plus a doxology which was not in orig.

(a) The older tr. now in use, OF THE FATHER'S LOVE BEGOTTEN, is a revision of Neale by H. W. Baker (101) in *Hymns A & M*, 1861; 3 missing sts. were supplied by Baker.
(b) A complete tr. of the medieval text in 9 st., OF THE FATHER'S HEART BEGOTTEN, was made by R. F. David in the *English Hymnal*, 1906, and is found only there in its entirety.
(c) SING YE FAITHFUL, SING WITH GLADNESS, J. Ellerton (80), in Brown-Borthwick's *Sixteen Hymns for Church and Home* (1870), recently revived in 2 books after long disuse, originally had the 'evermore and evermore' refrain, but now appears without it, 8.7.8.7.8.7. Julian says it is based on the Prudentius poem, but it uses a quite different selection of sts. from (a) and (b) above, and most of it is more reminiscent of certain sts. from the Fortunatus PANGE LINGUA (868).

Modern hymnals prefer (a), but *B(Brit.)* and *CP* switch to (b) for st. 8, 'Now let young and old . . .'; and *An* does so for st. 3. A 5th version, with spurious doxology, is normal in Britain, either sts. 1, 3, 5, 4, 9 of (a) in *BBC, CH*; or sts. 1, 2, 5, 4 of (a) but with st. 8 of (b) before st. 4 of (a) in *B, CP*. The 3 st. version often found in U.S. uses sts. 1, 4, 9 of (a) and has no reference to Christmas. *AMR*, shorter vn. (#58), has sts. 1, 3, 4. Elsewhere other selections.

US & CAN: BP137, 239 (c): Can429: B62: CW -/39: H20: L17: M357: P -/7/534: Pm111: CLB442: W216 • ENG: AM56/58, 591: An109: B85: BB57: CH60/198: E613 (b): E*89 (c): M83: NC66: PL140

AURELIUS CLEMENS PRUDENTIUS, b. 348 in Spain of good family; became a judge in 2 important cities, then chief of Imperial Guard to Emperor Honorius. Turned to Christianity at age 57, and became one of the leading Christian Latin poets of his time. † about 413.

ROBERT FURLEY DAVIS, b. Nottingham, 12 i 1866; Sch. St. John's, Oxf.; became schoolmaster & scholar, and with R. M. Pope ed. translations of Prudentius, as well as writing commentaries on other classical works. † Belfast, 14 ii 1937 (71).

844. DEUS TUORUM MILITUM

Latin: prob. 8th cent. or earlier; 4 st. with doxology: also found in a later 8 st. vn. Shorter vn. used for translation.

Tr.: (a) O GOD, THY SOLDIERS' CROWN AND GUARD, J. M. Neale (2), *Hymnal Noted*, 1852. *EH* uses this with later doxology.
(b) O GOD, THY SOLDIERS' GREAT REWARD, compilers of *Hymns A & M*, 1861, based on (a) but mostly rewritten.
(c) O GOD, THY SOLDIERS' FAITHFUL GUARD, in 3 st., by compilers of *BBC Hymn Book*, 1951, based on (b).

US & CAN: • ENG: AM442/516 (b): BB232 (c): E181 (a)

845. DIE NACHT IST KOMMEN

German: P. Herbert, *Kirchengesang* (Bohemian Brethren), 1566, in 6 st. 11.11.11.5 (Sapphic).

Tr.: (a) NOW GOD BE WITH US FOR THE NIGHT IS CLOSING, C. Winkworth (14), *Chorale-Book for England*, 1863, 6 st.; st. 4 always, st. 3 sometimes omitted; when st. 3 is retained, always reads 'holy' for 'pious.'
(b) NOW IT IS EVENING, TIME TO REST FROM LABOUR: G. R. Woodward (737), *Songs of Syon*, 1910, 5 st. Sapph., a freer Paraphrase.
(c) NOW IT IS EVENING: TIME TO REST FROM LABOR, st. 1 using most of (b), the rest by compilers of *Hymnal-1940* (U.S.) in 4 st. Sapph.

US & CAN: BP559 (a): Can369 (a): CW147/- (a): H167 (c): L225 (a): P -/53/- (a): Pm59 (a): CLB328 (b) • ENG: B697 (a): CH280/643 (a): BB418 (b): CP615 (a): PL316 (b)

PETRUS HERBERT, b. Fulneck, Moravia (date unknown), one of 3 editors of Moravian Brethren's hymnals in mid-16 cent.; visited Calvin in Switzerland 1560-1; studied at Tubingen, '61-4; one of three deputies planning union of Moravians with Lutherans, '65. Wrote over 70 hymns. † Eibenschutz, 1571.

846. DIES IRAE, DIES ILLA   PCH 153

Latin: the text usually translated or used in Latin in musical settings of the Requiem Mass is in a 14th cent. ms. in the Bodleian Library, Oxford, and consists of 57 lines; 51 are in 888 all rhymed, then follow 6 lines:

Lacrymosa dies illa
qua resurget ex favilla
iudicandum homo reus,
huic ergo parce Deus.
pie Jesu Domine
dona eis requiem.

These last lines were probably added when the poem, originally for private devotion, was adapted for public use.

The 17-stanza poem, without this appendix, is usually attributed to Thomas of Celano, 13th cent., but the appended lines, though added later to this poem, are actually earlier than it. *Julian* lists 91 English translations and 61 American up to 1892, the earliest being 1621; but of the following only (a) is in common use as a rendering of the complete poem.

Tr.: (a) DAY OF WRATH AND DAY OF MOURNING, W. J. Irons. It was made in 1848 after hearing the original sung at the funeral service of Archbishop Affre of Paris, who had been killed in the 1848 revolution; printed 1849 in his *Introits and Hymns for Advent*, privately produced for Margaret Chapel, London (cf. 500); also printed with plainsong tune at end of his *Metrical Psalter*, 1855. This is 18 st. 888, taking in full text. *EH* alters opening lines, beginning DAY OF WRATH AND DOOM IMPENDING, to accommodate a better trsln. of the 3rd line, *Teste David cum Sibylla*.

(b) DAY OF JUDGMENT, DAY OF WONDERS, J. Newton, *Olney Hymns* (37), 1779; in 7 st. 8.7.8.7.4.7; a shorter paraphrase.

(c) THAT DAY OF WRATH, THAT DREADFUL DAY, Sir Walter Scott, in *The Lay of the Last Minstrel*, 1805, a 3 st. fragment in LM-coup. First as a hymn in Collyer's *Collection*, 1812 and in Cotterill (333), 8th ed., 1819. 'Noble Angus' sings it in Scott's poem having completed his pilgrimage to Melrose Abbey.

US & CAN: B502 (b): H468 (a) ● ENG: AM398/466 (a), 206/228 (c): CH161 (c)/- : E351 (a), 487 (c): M646 (a), 645 (c)

THOMAS OF CELANO, b. about 1190, became one of the earliest followers of St. Francis of Assisi (13) and his first biographer; he wrote his first version of the biography at request of Pope Gregory IX, 1228, and the second, at request of the General of the Franciscan Order, 1246-7; then in 1253, 'The Miracles of St. Francis'; all 3 were in rhythmical Latin prose. † about 1260.

WILLIAM JOSIAH IRONS, b. Hoddesdon, Herts, 12 ix 1812, son of J. Irons, a well-known Nonconformist preacher. Sch. Queen's, Oxf.; Ord. C/E, 1835; rector of St. Peter's, Walworth (London); Vicar of Brompton, Rector of Waddingham, then 1872-3, Rector of St. Mary, Woolnoth, London (where J. Newton had been until 1807—see 37). Prebendary of St. Paul's, 1860-83; Bampton Lecturer, Oxford, '70—*Christianity as Taught by St. Paul*. † London, 18 vi 1883 (70).

SIR WALTER SCOTT, b. Edinburgh, 15 viii 1771; Sch. Edinburgh High Sch. & Univ.; studied law & became advocate; Sheriff-Depute of Selkirk, 1799; Clerk of Session, Edinburgh, 1806. The most eminent Scottish man of letters of his generation, he became famous as a poet with the *Lay of the Last Minstrel*, 1805, and *Marmion*, 1808; later became partner in a publishing business, that of James Ballantyne (Edinburgh) and began writing novels, beginning with *Waverley*, 1814. Went to live at Abbotsford to write, and entertained every distinguished person within reach; organized the visit of King George IV to Edinburgh. In 1826 the publishing house failed, with debts of £250,000; for the next years Scott set himself to pay the debt by writing. The effort shortened his life but the debt was paid in full just after his death. Biographer in *Everyman's Dictionary of Literary Biography* says, 'in his greatness and his wide humanity Scott takes a place beside Homer and Shakespeare.' † at Abbotsford, near St. Boswell's, Roxburghshire, 21 ix 1832 (61).

847. EIN' FESTE BURG IST UNSER GOTT

4 st. **PCH 4, 330**

German: M. Luther, 8.7.8.7.55.56.7 (111). It is not possible to date the first appearance of this with certainty; it is always said to have been printed first in Klug's *Geistliche Lieder*, 1529, but no copy exists from which that can be verified. Nor can it be said exactly when it was written. St. 3, 'Und wenn die Welt voll Teufel war,' suggests Luther's famous words before the Diet of Worms, 1520, 'If the houses were tiled with devils, still I would go on'; but the hymn is so different in style from Luther's creedal series of 1524 that it is easier to believe either that it emerged from his early struggles of c. 1520 (it is indeed much more, both in text and tune, like his very first hymn, EIN' NEUES LIED) or from his later experiences, such as the burning alive of the Bavarian pastor Leonard Kisser in 1527, or the critical period in the Diet of Speyer, 1529. Its text is based on Ps. 46 and it has been constantly sung by people under stress of religious persecution, from which it got its nickname, 'The Battle Hymn of the Reformation.' Bernhard Fick in 1897 assembled 80 translations of it in 53 languages; many of these were in English, but tradition has now settled down to two, with one exception surviving from an earlier tradition and now going out in favour, and one other made very recently.

Tr.: (a) A SAFE STRONGHOLD OUR GOD IS STILL, T. Carlyle, *Fraser's Magazine*, 1831; now in all English books except

AM(S). In the article containing the translation, Carlyle says that the orig. German is 'like the sound of Alpine avalanches, or the first murmur of earthquakes.' One of the earliest hymnals to use it was the 1876 edition of *Hymns for the People Called Methodists*; it began to rout all its English competitors when it was used in the *English Hymnal*, 1906.

(b) A MIGHTY FORTRESS IS OUR GOD, F. H. Hedge, published in *Hymns for the Church of Christ*, 1853, of which he was co-editor, written the previous year; though written later this was in use as a hymn before (a).

(c) GOD IS A STRONGHOLD AND A TOWER, E. Wordsworth, for *Hymns A & M*, 1904, surviving in editions of 1916, 1922, but dropped in favor of (a) in 1950.

(d) OUR GOD'S A FORTRESS FIRM AND SURE, J. Macpherson, Canadian *Hymn Book*, 1971.

All these trs. adjust Luther's original meter to 8.7.8.7.66.66.7 because of the fashion of singing the tune in the version of J. S. Bach (or in versions rhythmically derived from it). But note a new hymn, taking off from Luther's opening lines, but going into quite different territory thereafter, which begins with opening line of (b) but accommodates the original meter of the tune, at *Worshipbook 276*.

In US & CAN line below, all (b) except ‡.
In ENG line, all (a) except ‡.

US & CAN: BP86: Can135‡: B137: CW155/31: H551: L150: M20: P266/19/274, 276‡: Pm363: W2 ● ENG: AM678‡/183: An401: B562: BB297: CH526/406: CP485: E362: M494

THOMAS CARLYLE, b. Ecclefechan, Dumfriesshire, 4 xii 1795; Sch. Annan Gram. Sch. & Univ. Edinburgh; began training for ministry but abandoned it and became teacher of mathematics at Kirkcaldy, Fife; returned to Edinburgh to study law; abandoned that & became a private tutor, 1822; began his literary career with articles on Schiller in *London Magazine*, 1823. Went to London, joined the literary circle there, became the foremost man of letters of his time, writing on philosophy (*Sartor Resartus*), history (*History of the French Revolution; Oliver Cromwell's Letters and Speeches*) & many other subjects. Refused a barony in England but accepted the Prussian O.M. † London, 4 ii 1881 (85).

FREDERIC HENRY HEDGE, b. Cambridge, Mass., 12 xii 1805; studied in Germany from age 13; then Sch. Harvard Univ. & Div. Sch.; Ord. Unit., served at W. Cambridge, Mass., Bangor, Maine, '35-'50; Providence, R. I., '50; Brookline, Mass., '57, and at the same time prof. Ch. History, Harvard; from '72 also prof. of German. † 21 viii 1890 (84).

ELIZABETH WORDSWORTH, b. Harrow on the Hill (London), 1840, d. of Bishop Wordsworth (270); became Principal of Lady Margaret Hall, Oxford, 1879-1905. † Oxford, 30 xi 1932 (92).

JAY MACPHERSON, b. London, Ont., 31 v 1931; Sch. Carlton Univ., Ottawa and Univ. Toronto; member of Faculty of English, Victoria Coll., Toronto, since 1954. Noted Canadian poetess.

848. ES IST EIN' ROS' ENTSPRUNGEN

7.6.7.6.6.7.6

German: first found in 23 st. in *Speyer Gbch.*, 1600, then in 6 st. in *Andernach Gbch*, 1608, from which English versions are taken.

Tr.: (a) A SPOTLESS ROSE IS BLOWING, C. Winkworth (14), *Christian Singers of Germany*, 1869, 2 st.

(b) BEHOLD A BRANCH IS GROWING, Harriet R. Krauth, 1875, 4 st.; with a 5th by John Caspar Mattes (1876-1948), 1914, makes a 5 st. vn. in *Oxford American Hymnal*, 1930.

(c) THE NOBLE STEM OF JESSE, G. R. Woodward (737), Cowley Carol Book, 1902, 4 st.

(d) LO, HOW A ROSE E'ER BLOOMING, T. Baker (777), 2 st.

(e) LO, HOW A ROSE E'ER BLOOMING, composite translation using (d) with 2 st. from (b): st. 3 (Krauth) and st. 5 (Mattes).

(f) I KNOW A ROSE TREE BLOOMING, compilers of *Hymnal-1940* (U.S.).

(g) THERE IS A FLOWER SPRINGING, Ursula Vaughan Williams

(wife, now widow, of R. Vaughan Williams, 579), in *Oxford Book of Carols*, amplified edn., 1964.

   (h) A NOBLE FLOWER OF JUDAH, A. Petti for *New Catholic Hymnal* (1971), 4 st.

US & CAN: BP135 (e): H18 (f): L38 (e): P -/162 (d)/455 (d): Pm131 (d): W164 (d) ● ENG: NC12 (h)

849. FINITA IAM SUNT PRAELIA

Latin: *Symphonia Sirena Selectarum*, Cologne, 1695, in 5 st. with 3 alleluias preceding, 88.44.8 (LM with internal rhyme in line 3, line 4 always being 2 alleluias).

Tr.; (a) FINISHED IS THE BATTLE NOW, J. M. Neale (2), *Medieval Hymns*, 1851, 5 st., meter slightly irregular, line 1 being 7 syllables, but otherwise 88.44.4, with 2 alleluias preceding each st. and the final line showing one Alleluia. Apart from its metrical difficulty, which later Neale wd. have avoided, it is a finer trsln. than the well known one, and *PL* has adapted it to the orig. meter, beg. FINISHED THE STRIFE AND BATTLE NOW.

   (b) BATTLE IS O'ER, HELL'S ARMIES FLEE, R. A. Knox (866), *Westminster Hymnal*, 1940; this keeps the orig. met. exactly.

   (c) THE STRIFE IS O'ER, THE BATTLE DONE, in all listed hyls. exc. *PL*. F. Pott (45), *Hymns Fitted to the Order of Common Prayer*, 1861, and *Hymns A & M*, 1861, in slighted altd. vn. (*EH* has orig. vn.): 3 opening alleluias (before 1st st. only) then 888.4, last line always alleluia. Minor alts. in difft. books.

US & CAN: BP202: Can468: CW238/182: H91: L90: M447: P164/203/597: Pm181: CLB278: W273 ● ENG: AM135: An192: B163: BB114: CH122/266: CP148: E625: M215: NC217: PL200 (a)

850. GOTT IST GEGENWARTIG   **PCH 202**

German: G. Tersteegen (741), *Geistliche Blumengartlein*, 1729, 8 st., 66.8.66.8.33.66.

Tr.: (a) LO, GOD IS HERE: LET US ADORE, J. Wesley (1), *Hymns & Sacred Poems*, 1749, 6 st. 8.8.8.8.88 (om. sts. 7-8 of orig.). Now abr. to 4 st. or fewer.

US & CAN: BP89: Can21: L162: Pm499 ● ENG: AM526/248: B16: BB264: CP261: E637: M683

   (b) GOD REVEALS HIS PRESENCE, F. W. Foster & J. Miller, *Collection of Hymns* (Moravian), 1789, 5 st. orig. met. (using sts. 1, 2, 4, 7, 8 of orig.); always now in 3 st. and as altd. by W. Mercer in *Church Psalter & Hymn Bk.*, 1855.

   (c) GOD IS IN HIS TEMPLE, W. T. Matson (419), in *English Hymn Book* (ed. R. W. Dale), 1879; not a trsln. but a 3-st. imitation in Trinitarian form, using meter of orig.

US & CAN: (all [a]) BP322: Can16: B16: CW123/61: H477: L164: P51/3/384: Pm3 ● ENG: An5 (a): B41 (b): CH234/355 (a): CP224 (b): M31 (a)

FREDERICK WILLIAM FOSTER, b. Bradford (England), 1760, Sch. Moravian Settlement, Fulneck, Yorks, and Moravian Coll., Barby, Germany. Asst. Master, Fulneck 1791, later pastor & provincial superintendent. Bishop, 1818. Ed. many Morav. hymnals of which the one above was the first. † Ockbrook, Derbyshire, 1835 (75).

JOHN MILLER, orig. JOHANN MÜLLER, b. Grosherrensdorf, nr. Herrnhut, Germany, 1756; Sch. Morav. School, Niesky & Morav. Coll., Barby. Went to Fulneck, 1781, as chaplain to church school; later minister of congregation at Pudsey (after 1788). Collaborated with Foster in hymnal editing for Moravians. † Fulneck, 1810 (54).

851. HORA NOVISSIMA PESSIMA TEMPORA SUNT, VIGILEMUS   **PCH 162**

Latin: Bernard of Cluny (or of Morlaix), 12 cent., a poem of 2,966 lines written in unvarying dactylic hexameters, metrically unique in literature. Its subject is the contrast between the corruptions of medieval society and the glories of heaven; most of it is given to a caustic de-

scription of the former but we are concerned only with that section which describes the latter. A fragment of 95 lines was transcribed by Dean (later Archbishop) Trench in his *Christian Latin Poetry*, 1849, taken from this final section, and this was the basis for the first English translation in verse.

Tr.: J. M. Neale, in *Medieval Hymns*, 1851, 96 lines, 7.6.7.6D, using the cento of Trench; this translation was expanded to 276 lines (using 218 lines of the Latin) in a separate publication, *The Rhythm of St. Bernard of Morlaix*, 1858, which was included in the 2nd edition, 1863, of *Medieval Hymns*. This edition included the preface to the 1858 booklet, but with alterations, in one of which the author seems to have misled the reader. In saying that he was encouraged to expand his original translation by 'the great popularity of my translation, evinced from the very numerous hymns compiled from it', he obscures the fact that it was *Hymns Ancient & Modern*, 1861 which began to make popular the centos which are now so well known. Observing the division into informal sections laid out in Neale's work, the editors of *Hymns A & M* presented 3 groups of sts., beginning 'Brief life is here our portion'. 'For thee, O dear, dear country' and 'Jerusalem the golden' as the three parts of #142 in the 1861 edn., and another group, from the opening of Neale's trsln., 'The world is very evil', as #298 in the 1868 ed. Upon this editorial pattern all later centos are founded. In modern hymnals stanzas are sometimes switched from one part to another, and alterations to the words (mostly for the worse) are introduced. *EH*, in all parts, has the most reliable text. Broadly speaking, one now finds the sections in instalments of 32-40 lines, normally 7.6.7.6D, but section II ('Brief life . . .'), because of a musical association begun in 1861, often 7.6.7.6.

Pt. 1: THE WORLD IS VERY EVIL (using 1st line of orig. trsln.)

US & CAN: ● ENG: AM226/276: E495

Pt. 2: BRIEF LIFE IS HERE OUR PORTION

US & CAN: H596: L527: P -/430/- ● ENG: AM225/275: BB241: CH597/-: CP350: E371: M652 (i)

Pt. 3: FOR THEE, O DEAR, DEAR COUNTRY

US & CAN: H598: L534: P -/429/- ● ENG: AM227/277: CH598/-: CP351: E392

Pt. 4: JERUSALEM, THE GOLDEN

US & CAN: BP528: Can 184: CW569/-: H597: L584: M303: P435/428/-: Pm309 ● ENG: AM228/278: An432: B406: BB248: CH599/537: CP352: E412: M652 (ii)

BERNARD OF CLUNY was a monk at the monastery of Cluny when Peter the Venerable was Abbot (1122-56), and while there must have met P. Abelard (34) who was offered shelter there c. 1140. Nothing else is certainly known about him. His association with Morlass (miscalled Morlaix) is only conjectural. As to his ancestry, a guess is offered by a literary critic (anonymous) in a 1908 reprint of Neale's *Rhythm*, who, commenting on the unusual meter of the Latin poem, says it 'more nearly resembles one to be found in modern Welsh than anything naive to English soil,' saying it is reminiscent of Glan Geirionydd's *Morfa Rhuddlan*. It is possible that Bernard came of a Celtic background, there being much traffic in those days between the Gallic and Celtic traditions of monasticism.

ARCHBISHOP RICHARD CHENEVIX TRENCH of Dublin, referred to above, b. Dublin, 9 x 1807; Sch. Harrow & Trinity, Camb.; prof. Divinity, King's, London, 1846-58 (when he produced his *Christian Latin Poetry*); Dean of Westminster '56-'63 (when Neale wrote about him), and Abp. Dublin, '64-'84; one of the foremost scholars of his day, he made several contributions to hymnody. † Westminster (London), 28 iii iii 1886 (78).

852. HYMNUM CANAMUS GLORIAE   **PCH 157**

Latin: Bede of Jarrow, 8th cent., 11 st. LM

Tr.: (a) SING WE TRIUMPHANT HYMNS OF PRAISE, mostly B. Webb (545), 7 st. LM-coup., in Neale's *Hymnal Noted*, 1854 (occasionally ascribed to Neale who wrote last 2 st.).

(b) A HYMN OF GLORY LET US SING, Mrs. Charles (479), *The People's Hymnal*, 1867. *Worshipbook* (U. S.) uses sts. 1 and 5 of this and st. 7 of (a).
Other refs. use sts. 1, 2, 3, 7 of (a) except -

(c) NEW PRAISES BE GIVEN, R. A. Knox (866), 7 st. 11 11. 11 11 anap. in *Westminster Hymnal* (1940).

US & CAN: BP206 (a): P -/-/273 (b, a): CLB290 (c) ● ENG: BB130 (a): CH -/305 (a): CP150 (a): E146 (a)

ST. BEDE OF JARROW (known as 'The Venerable'), b. about 673; probably joined the community at Jarrow (co. Durham) as a boy at the time of its foundation, c. 681; Ord. deacon very early, about 692; priest, about 703; never left Northumbria. Author of many books; early text-books for pupils at the monastery on spelling and metrics; *De Temporum Ratione* which did much to establish the custom of dating events from the Incarnation; *De Temporibus*, to clarify the calculation of the date of Easter; *Lives* of many saints, and, most important, *Historia Ecclesiastica Gentis Anglorum*, the first history of the English Church, completed 731. † Jarrow 735.

853. IAM DESINANT SUSPIRIA   PCH 173

Latin: C. Coffin (52), *Paris Breviary*, 1736. 8 st. LM

Tr. (a) GOD FROM ON HIGH HATH HEARD, J. R. Woodford (834), *Hymns arranged for Sundays . . .*, 1852. 8 st. 6.6.6.6.

(b) GOD FROM ON HIGH HATH HEARD, revision of (a) by compilers of *Hymns A & M*, 1861, 8 st. SM.

(c) LET SIGHING CEASE AND WOE, W. J. Blew, *Church Hymn & Tune Book*, 1852, 8 st. SM.

US & CAN: ● ENG: AM58/63 (b): BB49 (a): CP82 (a) E27 (c): M140 (a)

WILLIAM JOHN BLEW, b. Ealing (London) 13 iv 1808; Sch. Ealing Gram. Sch. and Wadham, Oxf.; Ord. C/E 1832; Vicar of St. John's, Gravesend, Kent. Translator & hymn writer; ed. of several hymnals. † Gravesend, 27 xii 1894 (86).

854. THE HYMNS OF THE HOURS

IAM LUCIS ORTO SIDERE
NUNC SANCTUS NOBIS SPIRITUS
RECTOR POTENS, VERAX DEUS
RERUM DEUS TENAX VIGOR

This group of Latin hymns, all LM, all anon., all probably from the 8th cent., formed the devotions for four of the 'Little Hours' in the monastic life of the medieval church. IAM LUCIS is for dawn (Prime or Matins), NUNC SANCTE for Terce (9 a.m.), RECTOR POTENS for Sext (noon) and RERUM DEUS for None (3 p.m.); they would be flanked by the midnight devotions (see 862) and Compline (878); at these 'Little Hours' of daily worship the worshiper was encouraged to remember the events of Good Friday (to which the hymns do not refer) and the disciplines of waking, working, eating and resting (to which they do).

There are 2 major translations of the whole group: that of J. H. Newman (196) in *Tracts for the Times*, #75, 1836 and that of J. M. Neale (2) in *Hymnal Noted* 1852. Neale's is found much altd. in early eds. of *Hymns A & M* and elsewhere. These are always in LM: Newman's in various meters. Other trs. are noted below as they come.

I. IAM LUCIS: 4 st. plus doxology; (‡ - plus doxology)   PCH 139

Tr. (a) Newman: NOW THAT THE DAYSTAR GLIMMERS BRIGHT, 4 st.‡. CM

(b) Neale: NOW THAT THE DAYLIGHT FILLS THE SKY, 4 st.‡. LM

(c) Revision of (b) in *A & M, 1861*, 4 st‡.

US & CAN: BP543 (b): Can361 (b): H159 (b): L241 (a) CLB325 (b) ● ENG: AM1 (c)/1 (b): An44 (c): CH260 (a)/-, 258/45 (b): E254 (b): PL307 (c)

(Note: a translation of this original made by John Austin and Richard Crashaw is in their *Devotions* of 1668 and was included in the hymns

appended to Tate & Brady's *New Version* 1696).

II. NUNC SANCTE, 2 st.‡   PCH 140

Tr.: (a) Newman: COME, HOLY GHOST, WHO EVER ONE, 2 st.‡.

(b) Neale: COME, HOLY GHOST, WITH GOD THE SON, 2 st.‡.

US & CAN: H160 (b) ● ENG: AM9 (a) /11 (a): E255 (b): PL305 (a)

IV. RERUM DEUS

2 st.‡ LM   PCH 142

Tr.: (a) Neale: O GOD, CREATION's SECRET FORCE, 2 st‡. LM.

(b) J. Ellerton (80) and F. J. A. Hort: O STRENGTH AND STAY, UPHOLDING ALL CREATION, 2 st‡. 11.10.11.10, *Church Hymns*, 1871.

(c) The Benedictine Nuns of Malling: O GOD, CREATION'S STRENGTH AND STAY, 2 st. LM, *Praise the Lord*, 1972.

(d) R. Wright, ETERNAL LOVING LORD OF ALL, 2 st‡. LM, *Praise the Lord*, 1972.

US & CAN: H162 (a): L219 (b) ● ENG: AM11 (a) /14 (a): AM12/17 (b): E262 (a), E271 (b): PL309 (d), 310 (c)

855. IN TE CHRISTE CREDENTIUM   PCH 321

Latin: St. Columba, in LM-coup., 6th cent.; full text preserved in *Oxford Book of Medieval Latin Verse*. St. C. had written a hymn on the Trinity, *Altus Prosator*, which a contemporary had criticized for lack of emphasis on the Work of Christ. He then wrote this to replace it. 2 sections of it were translated by Duncan MacGregor for the celebrations (1897) of the 1300th anniversary of C's death, and published in his *Columba* (1898); they were just too late to get into the *Church Hymnary* of that year but appeared in the Church Hymnal (Ireland) 1919 as (Pt. 1), HAVE MERCY, LORD, HAVE MERCY and (Pt. 2) CHRIST IS THE WORLD'S REDEEMER. In *Church Hymnary*, 1927, Pt. 1 begins at line 9, O GOD, THOU ART THE FATHER.

Pt. I: US & CAN: P -/93/504: Pm248 ● ENG: CH454/397: E*758

Pt. II: US & CAN: P123/136/- ● ENG: CH179/301: E*756

ST. COLUMBA, b. about 521 of aristocratic Irish family; trained in monastic life & became founder of several monastic communities in Ireland. About 563, went to Island of Iona from which he evangelized W. Scotland and neighbouring islands; converted King Brude of the Picts & baptized King of the Scots, thus influencing the two major tribes then in possession: with St. Aidan of Northumbria, regarded as the founder of Scottish Christendom. † 597.

DUNCAN MACGREGOR, b. Fort Augustus, Inverness-shire, 18 ix 1854; Sch. parish schools and Univ. Aberdeen; served as parish missionary esp. to northern isles, then Ord. Ch/Scot., 1881 at Inverallochy, Aberdeenshire, where he remained until † there 8 x 1923 (69).

856. INSTANTIS ADVENTUM DEI

Latin: C. Coffin (52), *Paris Breviary*, 1736, 6 st. LM

Tr.: (all in SM).

(a) THE COMING OF OUR GOD (LORD): derived from tr. of R. Campbell (827) in *St. Andrew's Hymnal*, 1850.

(b) THE ADVENT OF OUR KING: Compilers of *Hymns A & M*, 1861, based on J. Chandler (52) in Hymns of the *Primitive Church*, 1837; this vn. used in *Hymns A & M* up to 1950 (wh. omits st. 5) and *BBC* (wh. uses sts. 1-4).

(c) THE ADVENT OF OUR GOD: Harriet Packer, *English Hymnal*, 1906.

(d) THE ADVENT OF OUR GOD: P. Dearmer (88), *Songs of Praise*, 1931.

(e) THE ADVENT OF OUR GOD: Compilers of Canadian *Hymn Book*, 1871, using (d) sts. 1 and most of 2 & 5; (b) st. 2 line 1, st. 4 with one small misprint and (c) with small alts. in sts. 3, 6.

US & CAN: Can397 (e): L 3 (b) ● ENG: AM148 (b): An 88 (b): BB39 (b): E11 (c): NC223 (a): PL134 (a)

857. JESU DULCIS MEMORIA (or DULCIS JESU . . .)

PCH 163

Latin: still widely attributed to St. Bernard of Clairvaux (12th cent.) but the best modern scholarship regards this as so improbable as to be discountable. Bernard disapproved of poetry and is unlikely to have written any, let alone anything so passionate as this. Since the first mss. of it circulated from Britain, it is inferred that the author was an anonymous English Cistercian. (See F. J. E. Raby in *Bulletin of the Hymn Society of Gt. Britain*, Oct. 1945, quoted in Frost, *Historical Companion to Hymns Ancient & Modern*, 1961 and W. Connolly, *Hymns of the Roman Liturgy*, 1957, at #41).

The earliest ms. has 42 st., LM (12th cent.). A 13th cent. ms. adds sts. to make it up to 50, it is thought for purposes of the Rosary. The first printed text known (Benedictine, 1719) has 48. But various sections and centos from the poems were used in later Latin rites, and copyists and editors added more stanzas, so that in any complete writing of the hymn (none actually exists) there would be 79. In English versions, which are taken from the liturgical fragments, some sts. are from the later sources and some from the original 42 st. version.

Taking *EH* 419, the longest selection in current use, having 15 st. in 3 parts, the following sts. are from later sources: 5, 'Jesus, our only joy'; 7, 'When once thou visitest'; and 10, 'Thee may our tongues.' The 3 parts of *EH* 419, 'Jesus the very thought...', 'O Jesus, King...', 'O Jesus thou the beauty art...' were used respectively at the offices of Vespers, Matins and Lauds of the Holy Name. The short section mentioned in (d) and (e) below was used at the Office of the Transfiguration. The opening sts. also formed a hymn for the Circumcision.

Only (a) below is derived from a complete translation; all others are centi or fragments.

Trs.:   (a) JESUS THE VERY THOUGHT OF THEE, E. Caswall (26), in CM, *Lyra Catholica*, 1849, using the liturgical centi above, and *Masque of Mary*, 1858, using the full 42 st. text of 12th cent. *EH* uses the 1849 text complete (15 st.): others have different selections of sts., and (iv) below is from the 1858 text.

      (i) JESUS THE VERY THOUGHT OF THEE, 5 or 6 st.
      (ii) O JESUS, KING MOST WONDERFUL, 5 or 6 st.
      (iii) O JESUS THOU THE BEAUTY ART, 5 st.
      (iv) JESUS, THY MERCIES ARE UNTOLD, 4 st.

In refs. below all signify (i) and (ii) except *EH* which has (i) to (iii) in full orig. vn. (1849), and *AM*‡, BB‡ which refer to (iv).

US & CAN: BP243, 245: Can 120-1: B73: CW392/282: H462: L481,468: M82: P309/401/- : Pm226 ● ENG: AM178/189, 189‡/201‡: An536, 542: B205, 188: BB322, 324‡: CH422-3/377-8: E419: M108,107: NC122

    (b) JESUS, THE VERY THOUGHT IS SWEET, J. M. Neale (2), 9 st. in *Hymnal Noted*, 1852, LM. Another eucharistic vn. is in 1854 edition with same sts. 1-3 but refs. use 1852 text. *EH* has full text, others abr.

US & CAN: ● ENG: AM177/188: CH421/-: E238: M106

    (c) JESUS, THOU JOY OF LOVING HEARTS, R. Palmer (370), paraphrasing 5 st. in *Sabbath Hymn Book*, 1858 (eucharistic, much as Neale [ii] above). In some books, O JESUS, JOY....

US & CAN: BP231: Can343: B72: CW419/320: H485: L483: M329: P354/215/510: Pm290: W149: CLB362 ● ENG: AM190/387: An380: B207: BB323: CH420/571: CP291: M109

    (d) LIGHT OF THE ANXIOUS HEART, J. H. Newman (196), in *Tracts for the Times* #36, 1836, 3 st. SM, taking text from Roman Breviary, 1568, & using material mostly not in orig. text.

US & CAN: ● ENG: CH249/13

    (e) LIGHT OF THE ANXIOUS HEART, R. Campbell (827), using 1568 text as (d), *Hymns A & M*, 1850, SM: this uses 2 sts. as (d) (1 and 3) with a doxology from liturgical redactions.

US & CAN: L475

858.   JESU, GEH' VORAN

4 st. 55.88.55

German: N. L. von Zinzendorf (371) had 2 hymns, each 11st., in his *Sammlung*, 1725, (i) SEELENBRAUTIGAM (perhaps the only hymn in

existence whose opening line consists of only one word), wh. was tr. by J. Wesley (1) as (a) below, and (ii) GLANZ DER EWIGKEIT. After his death the Moravian C. Gregor, ed. of *Bruder Gesangbuch*, 1778, made a cento using (i) sts. 10, 4, 11 and (ii) st. 11 (placing this second). From this 4 st. hymn, English trs. (b) and (c) were made.

Tr.:   (a) O THOU TO WHOSE ALL-SEARCHING SIGHT, J. Wesley (1), *Collection of Psalms & Hymns*, 1738, using sts. 1-2, 10-11, of SEELENBRAUTIGAM and inserting a st. from Freylinghausen's WER IST WOHL: LM.
    (b) JESUS, STILL LEAD ON, J. L. Borthwick (70), *Free Church Magazine*, 1846, 4 st. orig. meter.
    (c) JESUS, LEAD THE WAY, A. W. Farlander (659), *Hymnal-1940*, 4 st. orig. met.

US & CAN: BP501 (b): B500 (b): CW357/242 (b): H425 (c), 411 (a): L532 (b): M213 (a): P -/334 (b)/441 (c): W146 (c): CLB 342 (a) ● ENG: AM 669 (b)/206 (b): B544 (b): CH567 (b)/- : CP490 (b): M505 (a), 624 (b)

859.   JESU, MEINE FREUDE

6 st. 66.5.66.5.7.86

German: J. Franck (162), in C. Peter's *Andachts Zymbeln*, 1655.

Tr.:   (a) JESU, PRICELESS TREASURE, C. Winkworth (14), *Chorale Book for England*, 1863; om. st. 3. Norm. sel, from this, sts. 1, 2, 5.
    (b) JESUS, ALL MY GLADNESS, A. W. Wotherspoon, *Scottish Mission Hymnbook*, 1912; translated all 6 st. Norm. sel., 1, 4, 6.

(all [a] except *H*)

US & CAN: CW -/289: H453‡: L575: M253: P -/414/442: Pm222 ● ENG: An640: B768: BB518: CP759: M518: NC119

ARTHUR WELLESLEY WOTHERSPOON, b. 6 i 1853, Kilspindie, Perthshire; Sch. Perth Academy & Univ. St. Andrews; Ord. C/Scot., 1883, served at Oatlands, Glasgow (first minister); President Scottish Church Society, 1910. † Edinburgh, 15 iii 1936 (83).

860A.   LIEBSTER JESU, WIR SIND HER (Clausnitzer)

3 st. 7.8.7.8.77

German: T. Clausnitzer (772), *Altdorffisches Gesang-Buchlein*, 1663.

Tr.:   (a) BLESSED JESUS, AT THY WORD, C. Winkworth (14), 3 st. *Lyra Germanica* II, 1858.
    (b) DEAREST JESUS, WE ARE HERE, G. R. Woodward (737), 3 st. paraphrase for Eucharist, *Songs of Syon*, 1910 (abr. to 2 st. in *AMR*).
    (c) LOOK UPON US, BLESSED LORD, R. A. S. Macalister (626), *Church Hymnary*, 1927.

US & CAN: BP290 (a): CW -/212 (a): M257 (a): P -/-/309 (a): Pm212 (a): W37 (b) ● ENG: AM713 (b)/408 (b): An2 (a): BB257 (a): CH203 (c)/129 (c): PL254 (a)

860B.   LIEBSTER JESU, WIR SIND HER (Schmolck)

7 st. 7.8.7.8.77—based on 860A, for same melody, but for Baptism.

German: B. Schmolck (400), *Heilige Flammen*, 3rd edn., 1706.

Tr.: C. Winkworth, 7 st. (always abr. in modern books, even to 1 st.), *Lyra Germanica* II, 1858, BLESSED JESUS, HERE WE STAND. In *CLB* DEAREST JESUS....

US & CAN: H186: P -/-/310: Pm279: CLB331 ● ENG: CH307/552: E336: M752

861.   LUCIS CREATOR OPTIME

4 st. with doxology, LM

Latin: medieval, possibly by Gregory the Great (836); mss. of 11th cent.

Tr.:   (a) O BLEST CREATOR OF THE LIGHT, J. Chandler (52), *Lyra Catholica*, 1849.

(b) BLEST CREATOR OF THE LIGHT, by compilers of *Hymns A & M*, 1861, based on (a) but rewritten in 77.77.

(c) O BLEST CREATOR OF THE LIGHT, J. M. Neale (2), *Hymnal Noted*, 1852—shares first line but little else with (a).

Office Hymn for Sunday evening.

US & CAN:H163 (c) ● ENG: AM38 (b)/44 (a): E51 (c)

LAUDA SION SALVATOREM: see 867 III.

862. NOCTE SURGENTES VIGILEMUS OMNES

3 st. 11.11.11.5 Sapphic   **PCH 145**

Latin: Gregory the Great (836): British museum ms., 11th cent. Hymn for Matins, which originally implied being sung in the small hours of the morning (*NOCTE*), but trs. always soften this down for use after sunrise.

Tr.: (a) FATHER WE PRAISE THEE, NOW THE NIGHT IS OVER, P. Dearmer (88), *English Hymnal*, 1906.

(b) LET HEARTS AWAKEN, NOW THE NIGHT IS ENDED, C. S. Phillips, *Plainsong Hymn Book*, 1932.

US & CAN: (all a) BP546: Can359: CW102/62: H157: L*788: M504: P24/43/365: Pm41: CLB326: W78 ● ENG: (all a except ‡) AM -/10‡: An40‡: B675: BB405: CH263/43: CP588: E165: PL306

CHARLES STANLEY PHILLIPS, b. Boston, Lincs., 1883; Sch. King's, Camb.; Ord. C/E 1908; after curacies, Lecturer & Chaplain, Selwyn Coll., Camb., 1914; Fellow '16; Vicar of Radley, Berks, '19; Vicar of King Cross, Halifax, '21; Rector of Milton, Cambridge, '27; Chaplain from foundation of College of St. Nicolas (which later became Royal Sch. of Church Music), '27; Vicar of Stalisfield, Kent, '41 and of Sturry, Kent, '47. Author of books on hymnody; member of ed. cttee., *Hymns A & M*, 1950. † Dormans, Surrey, 28 xi 1949 (66).

863. NUN RUHEN ALLE WALDER

77.6.77.8   **PCH 193**

German: P. Gerhardt (18), *Praxis Pietatis Melica*, 1648, 9 st.

Tr.: (a) NOW ALL THE WOODS ARE SLEEPING, C. Winkworth (14), *Lyra Germanica* I, 1856 reprint, replacing translation in 1855 edn. not in original meter); now always abr. to 5 st. or fewer.

(b) THE DUTEOUS DAY NOW CLOSETH, R. Bridges (9), *Yattendon Hymnal*, 1899, 4 st., a paraphrase which after st. 1 owes little to original.

(c) NOW WOODS AND WOLDS ARE SLEEPING, G. R. Woodward (737), *Songs of Syon*, 1910, 4 st.; trs. of sts. 1, 3, 8, 9 of original (U.S. books read NOW WOODS AND FIELDS . . .).

US & CAN:BP557 (a): H181 (b): L228 (b): P505/66/- (c): Pm53 (b) ● ENG: AM -/34 (b): An57 (a): B707 (b): BB427 (b): CH284/57 (b): CP629 (b): E278 (b): M946 (a)

NUNC SANCTE NOBIS SPIRITUS: see 854.

864. O ESCA VIATORUM

                                                                PCH 169

Latin: formerly thought to be by St. Thomas Aquinas, but now thought to be by an anon. German Jesuit; first found in *Mainz Gbch*, 1661, with a German translation, 3 st. 77.6.77.6.

Tr.: (a) O BREAD TO PILGRIMS GIVEN, R. Palmer (370), *Sabbath Hymn Book*, 1858, 3 st. 7.6.7.6 D, usually found with minor alterations.

(b) O FOOD THAT WEARY PILGRIMS LOVE, by compilers of *Hymns A & M* for a set of introits to be issued with edn. of 1861; included in 1868 edn. 3 st. 88.6.88.6.

(c) O FOOD OF MEN WAYFARING, A. Riley (112), *English Hymnal*, 1906, 3 st. orig. meter.

(d) O FOOD OF TRAVELLERS, ANGELS' BREAD, W. H. Shew-

ring, *Westminster Hymnal*, 1940 (altd. in *PL*): 3 st. LM.

US & CAN:H192 (c): L271 (c): CLB371 (c) ● ENG: AM314/389 (b): BB209 (c): CP292 (a): EH321 (c): M768 (a): PL74 (d)

865. O LUX BEATA, TRINITAS

2 st. LM with doxology   **PCH 327**

Latin: Ambrose (689).

Tr.: (a) O TRINITY, O BLESSED LIGHT, W. Drummond, *Primer or Office of the Blessed Virgin*, 1619.

(b) O TRINITY OF BLESSED LIGHT, J. M. Neale (2), *Hymnal Noted*, 1852.

(c) O TRINITY OF BLESSED LIGHT, compilers of *Hymns A & M*, 1861, based on (b).

US & CAN:H271 (b): L133 (b): P59/245/- (b) ● ENG: AM14/15 (c): CH4/56 (a): E164 (b)

WILLIAM DRUMMOND OF HAWTHORNDEN, b. 13 xii 1585, of aristocratic Scottish family; Sch. Edinburgh High Sch. and Univ.; studied law but succeeded to ancestral estate of Hawthornden, 1610 and lived as poet & man of letters; he was a mechanical genius & patented 16 inventions. † Hawthornden, Scotland, 4 xii 1649 (63).

866. O PATER SANCTE, MITIS ATQUE PIE

4 st. 11.11.11.5 Sapphic   **PCH 147**

Latin: earliest ms., British Museum, 11th cent.

Tr.: (a) FATHER MOST HOLY, MERCIFUL AND LOVING, A. E. Alston, in *Hymns A & M*, 1904.

(b) FATHER MOST HOLY, MERCIFUL AND TENDER, P. Dearmer (88) in *English Hymnal*, 1906.

(c) FATHER MOST HOLY, GRACIOUS AND FORGIVING, R. A. Knox, *Westminster Hymnal*, 1940.

US & CAN: Can489 (a): L134 (b): CLB415 (a) ● ENG: AM -/158 (a): An 226 (a): BB167 (a): E160 (b): PL220 (c)

ALFRED EDWARD ALSTON, b. Victoria, B.C., 25 vi 1862; Sch. in England at St. Paul's School & Gloucester Theol. Coll.; Rector of Framingham-Earl, Norfolk, 1887- † there 13 v 1927 (64).

RONALD ARBUTHNOT KNOX, b. 17 Feb. 1888, son of the Bishop of Manchester; Sch. Eton & Trinity, Oxf.; President, Oxford Union; Fellow of Trinity; Ord. C/E, Chaplain of Trinity, 1912-17; then Ord. R.C. 1919, and Chaplain to Catholics in Oxford, 1925—where he wrote a number of detective stories to raise money for chaplaincy furnishings; already a well known writer of theological polemic, he became domestic Prelate to the Pope, 1936, with title of Monsignor, & retired to Somerset 1939 to devote himself to his translation of the Vulgate Bible which appeared 1944 (N.T.) and 1950 (O.T.); also wrote commentaries, published sermons, and wrote a major work of Ch. History, *Enthusiasm* (1948); very well known as preacher & leader of retreats, he was also a notable literary humorist, a composer of crosswords ('Ximenes' in the *Observer* for many years), and had a special faculty for cryptograms—all three of which gifts are manifested in his early work, *Essays in Satire*. He was one of the foremost R.C. intellectual leaders of his time, with Chesterton (513), Hilaire Belloc and Maurice Baring. † 24 viii 1957 (69).

867. THE EUCHARISTIC CYCLE OF CORPUS CHRISTI

I. PANGE LINGUA GLORIOSI CORPORIS MYSTERIUM
II. VERBUM SUPERNUM PRODIENS
III. LAUDA SION SALVATOREM
IV. ADORO TE DEVOTE LATENS DEITAS.

Latin: the first three of these were written by St. Thomas Aquinas, ca. 1263, at the request of Pope Urban IV for the liturgy of Corpus Christi as a single group. All share their first lines with hymns already well known in medieval devotion; all share a very dense theological diction which makes them unusually difficult to translate: therefore translations, especially of (I), differ from book to book. ADORO TE (IV) has to be considered separately although it is included in this group because for a long while it too was believed to be by St. Thomas. See below.

I. PANGE LINGUA   PCH 164

6 st. 8.7.8.7.8.7, often appearing as 2 separate hymns, dividing before st. 5, TANTUM ERGO SACRAMENTUM, the last 2 st. being used at the Adoration of the Blessed Sacrament. Latin text at *CLB* 374, *W* 225.

Tr.: (a) SING MY TONGUE THE SAVIOUR'S GLORY, E. Caswall (26), *Lyra Catholica*, 1849. Altd. in *M** and *CLB*.

  (b) OF THE GLORIOUS BODY TELLING, J. M. Neale (2), *Hymnal Noted*, 1854.

  (c) NOW MY TONGUE THE MYSTERY TELLING: compilers of *Hymns A & M*, 1861, based on (a) and (b).

  (d) NOW MY TONGUE THE MYSTERY TELLING: compilers of *Hymnal-1940* (U.S.), based on (c).

  (e) I SHALL PRAISE THE SAVIOUR'S GLORY: A. Petti, *New Catholic Hymnal*, 1971, based on (c).

  (f) SING, MY TONGUE, ACCLAIM CHRIST PRESENT; Benedict Avery, 1955.

US & CAN: H199 (d): CLB375 (f), 367 (a): W225 (a) ● ENG: AN309/383 (c): B326 (a): BB208 (c): CH -/578 (c): CP314 (a): E326 (b): M*63 (a‡): NC 108 (e): PL334 (b)

II. VERBUM SUPERNUM PRODIENS, 6 st. LM, sometimes divided at st. 5, O SALUTARIS HOSTIA (as I). Shares first line with second Office Hymn of Advent (*EH* 2). Latin Text at *CLB* 372.

Tr.: (a) THE WORD DESCENDING FROM ABOVE, E. Caswall (26), *Lyra Catholica*, 1849, now always found in altd. form.

  (b) THE WORD OF GOD PROCEEDING FORTH, J. M. Neale (2), *Hymnal Noted*, 1854.

  (c) FORTH FROM ON HIGH THE FATHER SENDS, J. Quinn, *Hymns for All Seasons*, 1969.

  (d) THE WORD OF GOD PROCEEDING FORTH, A. Petti, *New Catholic Hymnal*, 1971, based on (a) and (b).

  (e) composite: sts. 1-2 Neale & Caswall, sts. 3-5 G. M. Hopkins (1889).

NOTE: (b) below always means (b) with insertions from (a) and ‡ means only O SALUTARIS translated.

US & CAN: Can342 (b‡): H209 (b‡): L277 (b‡): W212 (a‡): CLB373 (b) ● ENG: AM311/384 (b): BB212 (b‡): CH -/581 (c): E330 (b): NC246 (d): PL233 (a‡), 186 (e)

III. LAUDA SION SALVATOREM: 9 st. 88.6.88.6, then 2 st. 888.6.888.6, then 1 st. 8888.6 D; often divided at st. 10 and/or st. 12. Sequence.

Tr.: (a) LAUD, O SION, THY SALVATION, *E* 317: compiled there mainly from the *People's Hymnal*, 1867, which itself contains elements from the tr. by E. B. Pusey (see 83), 1847, A. D. Wackerbarth, 1843, and J. D. Chambers (16), 1857. Final version is the work of compilers of *English Hymnal*, 1906, which alone contains it.

  (b) PRAISE THY MASTER, *AMR* 622; sts. 1-9 by C. S. Phillips (862) in *Plainsong Hymn Book*, 1932, sts. 10-12 by compilers of *Hymns A & M*, 1875, which contained only those sts. Only *AMR* carries this full text.

IV. ADORO TE DEVOTE LATENS DEITAS (VERITAS): PCH 165

7 st. 6.5.6.5. D, written 11 11. 11 11 with one up-beat syllable at beginning of line 1 which is sometimes elided in the version ADORO DEVOTE. . . .

Although this is still ascribed to St. Thomas in the hymnals, and stated to be part of the eucharistic cycle above, the first of these statements is improbable and the second untrue. This was proved by Dom André Wilmart in *Recherches de Théologie ancienne et médiévale* (Louvain), vol. i, 1929, and confirmed by F. J. E. Raby in the *Bulletin of the Hymn Society of Great Britain*, April 1943. This text was associated with the other 3 first in the *Roman Breviary* of Pope Pius V, 1570. Its character, that of a personal devotion, is quite different from that of the others which are firmly theological & objective. These two scholars date it about 1323, from the earliest available mss. (May it have been written by a disciple in celebration of the Canonization of St. Thomas?) A tradition that St. Thomas composed it on his deathbed is entirely unreliable. Latin text in full at *W* 5.

Tr.: (a) THEE WE ADORE, O HIDDEN SAVIOUR, THEE, 4 st. 10 10. 10 10 (om. sts. 2, 3, 4,) J. R. Woodford (834), *Hymns arranged . . .*, 1852; though not in orig. meter, this is the most widely used version.

  (b) HUMBLY I ADORE THEE, 7 st., orig. met., J. M. Neale (2), *Hymnal Noted*, 1854.

  (c) HUMBLY I ADORE THEE, 4 st., orig. met., (om. sts. 2, 3, 6), compilers of *Hymnal-1940* (U.S.), partly based on (b).

  (d) HUMBLY WE ADORE THEE, 5 st. orig. met., but so remote from orig. as to be virtually a new hymn; M. Farrell, *Praise the Lord*, 1972.

  (e) GOD WITH HIDDEN MAJESTY, 5 st. orig. met., irreg., (om. 2, 6), A. Petti, *New Catholic Hymnal*, 1971.

  (f) GODHEAD HERE IN HIDING, 7 st., orig. met., G. M. Hopkins, *Collected Poems* (ed. R. Bridges (9), 1918; first as a hymn in *Westminster Hymnal*, 1940.

(Note also the exquisite version by R. Crashaw, *Steps to the Temple*, 1646, Westminster Hymnal #61 and *PCH* 165).

US & CAN: (all [a] except where marked) Can329: CW -/319: H204: L272 (c): P -/-/599: W5 (f) ● ENG: AM312/385: B330: BB217: CH319/584: E331: NCH79 (e): PL65 (d)

ST. THOMAS AQUINAS, b. Roccasecca, Italy, about 1225, youngest son of Count Landulf of Aquino, a relative of the King of France. At age 5, Sch. Monte Cassino Benedictine School; then (1240) Naples, where he decided to seek admission to the Dominican order which had been founded 1220. Family opposed this and kept him under restraint for 15 months; but he joined the Order in 1244. Pursued further studies at Paris, then taught at the new Dominican Hall of Studies, Cologne. Returned to Paris, 1252; taught at Anagni and Orvieto, 1259-65; at Rome, '65-7; at Paris again, '69; then went to Naples where he worked on the completion of his *Summa Theologiae*, his greatest work. A voluminous and authoritative writer, his grasp of theology & philosophy, and ability to organize & communicate them, earned him the title of 'The Angelic Doctor'; his was probably the most massive intellect of the medieval church. On his way to the Council of Lyons, † at Monastery of Fossanuova, 7 iii 1274, aged about 49. Canonised 1323.

GERARD MANLEY HOPKINS, b. Straford, Essex, 28 vii 1844; Sch. Highgate School & Oxford, where he was converted to R.C. faith; taught at a school in Birmingham, then prepared for & took Jesuit vows. Ord. R.C., 1877; worked in London, Oxford, Liverpool, Glasgow; taught at Stonyhurst School, Lancs.; Prof. Classics at University Coll., Dublin. Wrote a modest amount of poetry which was unknown in his lifetime and published nearly 30 years after his death by his friend and admirer R. Bridges (9) in 1918. Immediately on publication he was acknowledged to be a major English poet, and a new generation came to appreciate a style which during his own lifetime, even had his poems been published, English taste would have found unfashionably austere. † Dublin, 8 viii 1889 (45).

JAMES QUINN, b. Glasgow, 21 iv 1919; Ord. R.C. (S.J.), and a member of the Lauriston Fathers in Edinburgh, Scotland; produced in 1969 *Hymns for All Seasons*, which was the first one-man R.C. hymnal in English, and provided a new standard of excellence in English translations of Latin hymns, which is what the book mostly contains.

868. PANGE LINGUA GLORIOSI PRAELIUM (LAUREAM) CERTAMINIS

10 st. 8.7.8.7.8.7   PCH 156

Latin: Venantius Fortunatus, 6th cent. In later medieval liturgical use, exemplified in the *Roman Breviary*, 1632, a doxology is added and the opening line reads . . . LAUREAM CERTAMINIS. In this use the hymn was divided after st. 5 and again after st. 7; Part 2 beginning LUSTRA SEX QUI IAM PERACTA, and Part 3, CRUX FIDELIS. Still in Neale's trsln. 'When, O Judge of this world . . .' is not found before 1632, and is not in modern books; st. 6 of his tr. also omitted now. (The most recent revision of the Roman Breviary or *Liturgia Horarum* restores the hymns for the most part to their pre-1632 texts.)

Tr.: (all except [g] in original meter)

(a) SING, MY TONGUE, THE GLORIOUS BATTLE WITH COMPLETED VICTORY RIFE, J. M. Neale (2), *Medieval Hymns*, 1851, 12 st.; modern hymnals use only pt. 2, THIRTY YEARS AMONG US DWELLING.

(b) SING, MY TONGUE, THE GLORIOUS BATTLE, SING THE ENDING OF THE FRAY, revision of (a) by compilers of *Hymns A & M*, 1868, 10 st. abr. to 9 st. in 1950.

(c) SING, MY TONGUE, HOW GLORIOUS BATTLE GLORIOUS VICTORY BECAME; compilers of *Scottish Mission Hymnal*, 1912 (see 858b); st. 1-3 and doxology, plus st. 4 from (a), st. 8.

(d) SING, MY TONGUE, THE GLORIOUS BATTLE: SING THE ENDING OF THE FRAY; revision of (a) and (b) by P. Dearmer (88), *English Hymnal*, 1906, st. 1-5 only, appearing as #95 in that book (#96 is [a], Pt. 2-3).

(e) SING, MY TONGUE, THE GLORIOUS BATTLE: SING THE ENDING OF THE FRAY; further revision of (a), (b) and (d), by P. Dearmer for *Songs of Praise*, 1931, sts. 1, 4, 7, 8, doxology.

(f) SING, MY TONGUE, THE GLORIOUS BATTLE: SING THE WINNING OF THE FRAY, revision of (a) by compilers of *Hymnal-1940* (U.S.); sts. 1, 4, 7, 8, 9 doxology.

(g) SEE THE DESTINED DAY ARISE, R. Mant (95), *Ancient Hymns*, 1837: earlier than all the others but a free paraphrase, 7 st. 77.77 (now 5 st.).

US & CAN: Can446 (a): H66 (f), 67 (g): L*728 (e): W225 (f) ● ENG: AM97 (b), 113/101 (g): An161 (b): B146 (e): BB90 (b): CH108/256 (c): CP125 (e): E95 (d), 96 (a), 110 (g): PL181 (b)

VENANTIUS FORTUNATUS, b. Treviso, Venetia, c. 535; Sch. at Revanna; became a poet & traveling singer; later in life, on a journey of pilgrimage to the tomb of St. Martin of Tours, met Queen Rhadegunda, then separated from her husband, King Clotaire of Neustria, and under her influence settled at Poitiers, took vows, and was Ord. priest; in 599 made bishop of Poitiers; his writings in sacred poetry are the only literature of that kind surviving from the otherwise barren 7th century—an age whose only other figure of intellectual distinction was Justinian (d. 565). † Poitiers, 609.

869. PHOS HILARON   PCH 177

Greek: the hymn of the lamplighting ceremony in the early church; quoted by St. Basil (329-90) as of unknown authorship even then, but as well known; some believe it goes back to the days of the catacombs, when light in darkness had special significance. Probably safe to say it was known in 2nd century. The Greek original is in 13 lines, unmetrical, and *PCH* gives a modern translation which fits the original tune.

Tr.: (a) HAIL, GLADDENING LIGHT, unmetrical but not far from Greek original, by J. Keble (83), *British Magazine*, 1834, the earliest tr. in English; first as a hymn in *Hymns A & M*, 1868.

US & CAN: ● ENG: AM18: An54: B695: BB416: CH281/54: CP612: M931

(b) O GLADSOME LIGHT, O GRACE OF GOD, 66.7.66.7, R. Bridges (9), *Yattendon Hymnal*, 1899, written for the tune of the Genevan Nunc Dimittis (1545) in 3 st.; so different from (a) that many books have both.

US & CAN: Can365: CW -/292: H176: P app82/61/494: Pm49: W197 ● ENG: B699: CH -/55: CP611: E269: M936

870. QUICUNQUE CHRISTUM QUAERITIS   PCH 154

Latin: Prudentius (843) in 52 st., LM. Appeared in the *Roman Breviary* (1632) in 4 separate centos, 2 of which remain in English use.

I. O SOLA MAGNARUM URBIUM, 4 st. with doxology, LM, being sts. 20, 2, 18, 8 of orig.:

Tr.: (a) BETHLEHEM OF NOBLEST CITIES, E. Caswall (26), *Lyra Catholica*, 1849, 5 st. 8.7.8.7, thus beginning, but variously altd. in later books (*EH* nearest to his original).

(b) EARTH HAS MANY A NOBLE CITY, compilers of *Hymns A & M*, 1861, 5 st. 8.7.8.7 based on (a) but mostly rewritten.

(c) BETHLEHEM, MOST NOBLE CITY, 4 st. 8.7.8.7, A. Petti in *New Catholic Hymnal*, 1971.

US & CAN: (all b) BP146: Can431: CW -/140: H48: L51: M405: CLB233: W70 ● ENG: AM76 (b): An127 (b): BB64 (a): CH -/199 (a): E40 (a): NC21 (c): PL158 (a)

II. SALVETE FLORES MARTYRUM, 3 st. with doxology, sts. 32-4 of original.

Tr.: (a) SWEET FLOWERETS OF THE MARTYR BAND, LM, H. W. Baker, *Hymns A & M*, 1868.

(b) ALL HAIL YE LITTLE MARTYR FLOWERS, A. Riley (112), *English Hymnal*, 1906.

(c) O MARTYRS, YOUNG AND FRESH AS FLOWERS, J. M. C. Crum (494), *Hymns A & M*, 1950.

US & CAN: ● ENG: AM68 (a)/538 (c): E34 (b)

RECTOR POTENS VERAX DEUS:
RERUM DEUS TENAX VIGOR: see 854.

871. SALVE CAPUT CRUENTATUM   PCH 194

Latin: this is the 7th section, 5 st. 88.88.8 D (4 lines troch., 5th iamb.), of a long Latin poem, attributed by some (improbably) to Bernard of Clairvaux (857), by others to the 15th cent. mystic A. von Loewen. Each of the 7 sections is devoted to one of the Aspects of the Crucified: Feet, Knees, Hands, Side, Breast, Heart, and (this one) Face (Section III is translated as [f] below).

German: O HAUPT VOLL BLUT UND WUNDEN, P. Gerhardt (18), 10 st. 7.6.7.6 D in *Praxis Pietatis Melica*, 1656.

English:

(a) O SACRED HEAD, NOW WOUNDED, J. W. Alexander, *Christian Lyre*, New York, 1830, 8 st. 7.6.7.6 D, from the German. The 2 missing sts. (3, 6) added 1849 and given in Schaff's *Christ in Song*, 1870. Norm. sel. now sts. 1, 2, 4, 10; often begins, O SACRED HEAD, SORE WOUNDED.

(b) O SACRED HEAD, SURROUNDED, H. W. Baker (101), for *Hymns A & M*, 1861, 3 st. 7.6.7.6 D, cento from sts. 1-3 of Latin.

(c) O SACRED HEAD, SORE WOUNDED, R. Bridges (9) in *Yattendon Hymnal*, 1899, 5 st. 7.6.7.6 D, from Latin: full text in *EH*.

(d) O SACRED HEAD, ILL-USED, R. A. Knox (866), *Westminster Hymnal*, 1940, 5 st. 7.6.7.6 D, from Latin (1 st. om. in *PL*).

(e) DEAR FACE, WITH PAIN TRANSFIGURED, A. Petti, *New Catholic Hymnal*, 1971, 4 st., 7.6.7.6 D, from Latin.

(f) WIDE OPEN ARE THY HANDS, tr. C. P. Krauth, 3 st. SMD, in *Service Book & Hymnal* (Lutheran) 1958, from Latin of section III.

US & CAN: BP171 (a): CW231/163 (a): H75 (c): L88 (a), 66 (f): M418 (a): P151/194/524 (a): Pm170 (a): CLB260 (c): W211 (b) ● ENG: AM111 (b): An158 (a): B145 (a): BB86 (c): CH107/253 (a): CP127 (a): E102 (c): M202 (a): NC50 (e): PL179 (d)

JAMES WADDELL ALEXANDER, b. Hopewell, Va., 13 iii 1804; Sch. Coll. of New Jersey, Princeton, and Princeton Theol. Sem.; Ord. Presb., 1827, served at First Presb. Ch., Trenton, N.J.; Prof. of Rhetoric, Coll. of N.J., '32: Duane St. Presb. Ch., New York, '44; Prof. Ch. Hist., Princeton Th. Sem., '49; Fifth Avenue Presb. Ch., New York, 51-† Sweetsprings, Va., 31 vii 1859 (55).

CHARLES PORTERFIELD KRAUTH, b. Martinsburg, Va., 17 iii 1823; Sch. Gettysburg Luth. Sem., 1841; Ord. Luth.; Prof. Systematic Theol., Mt. Airy Luth. Sem., Philadelphia, '64; faculty member & trustee, Univ. Pennsylvania. Ed. *The Lutheran, The Missionary, Lutheran Church Review*. † Philadelphia, 2 i 1883 (59).

872. SALVE FESTA DIES

Latin: Venantius Fortunatus (868) wrote a poem, *Tempore Florigero* ('In Springtime') in elegiac couplets & dedicated it to Bp. Felix of Nantes, who d. 592. It was an Easter poem not designed for singing. Medieval liturgical books from c. 950 adapted it for Easter singing by rearranging the sts.: the original opening couplet appears as st. 2 of the Ascension centos below and the refrain-st. (which begins the hymn and follows each st.) is st. 39 of original. Later it was developed and imitated to make hymns for other seasons, until the *Sarum Processional* had 7 hymns, for Easter, Ascension, Pentecost, Dedication, Corpus Christi, the Visitation and the Holy Name. Probably the last 4 were of English origin.

Tr.: there are 3 English trslns. of the 4-hymn sequence (first 4 above), which broadly use the same original centi. All 3 use the burden-stanza form in which st. 1 is repeated after all the other sts.

   (a) HAIL FESTAL DAY, WHOSE GLORY NEVER ENDS, A. J. Mason, *Hymns A & M*, 1904, all lines iambic 10 10, in 4 sections, as above: *AM(S)* 650 (10 st.), 652 (11 st.), 653 (6 st.), 747 (8 st.). This was replaced in 1950 by (c).

   (b) HAIL THEE, FESTIVAL DAY, in 4 sections as above, by various authors in orig. meter for *English Hymnal*, 1906: *EH* 624 (10 st.) by M. F. Bell, 628 (9 st.) by P. Dearmer (88), 630 (8 st.) by G. Gillett (342) and 634 (8 st.) by M. F. Bell. Sect. iii is at *CH³* 328: sect. i is at *H(U.S.)* 102.

   (c) WELCOME, MORNING OF JOY, C. S. Phillips (862), orig. meter, in *Plainsong Hymn Book*, 1932: *AMR* 600 (10 st.), 608 (10 st.), 612 (8 st.), 618 (8 st.).

Other translations and imitations:

   (d) WELCOME, HAPPY MORNING, J. Ellerton (80), *Supplemental Hymn & Tune Book*, 1871; Easter section only; 6 st. 6.5.6.5 D with refrain 6.5.6.5, using first 2 lines (of 6-line sts.) as lines 5-6 of succeeding stanzas, but now more often using only 1st line as refrain and usually abr. to 5 st. or fewer.

US & CAN: Can462: CW246/ : H87: L93: M452: P169/207/- : W109 ● ENG: AM487/- : An195: B165: CH115/272: CP139: M212

   (e) HAIL THEE, FESTIVAL DAY, P. Dearmer, adapted from (b) above, 11 st., sts. 2-5 being seasonal, sts. 6-11 general for festivals; only one of sts. 2-5 to be used for each festival, and alternative refrain-stanzas provided for each. *Songs of Praise*, 1931, #389.

   (f) WELCOME, DAY OF THE LORD, P. Dearmer (88), refrain plus 5 st., for Sunday Morning. *Songs of Praise*, 1931, #390.

ARTHUR JAMES MASON, b. Laugharne, S. Wales, 4 v 1851; Sch. Repton Sch. & Trinity, Camb.; Fellow, 1873; Ord. C/E, '74; accompanied Bp. Benson when he became first bp. of Truro; Vicar of All Hallows, Barking (London), '84; Canon of Canterbury, '95 and Lady Margaret Prof. of Divinity, Camb.; Master of Pembroke Coll., Camb., 1903-12, Vice-Chancellor, Univ. Camb., 1908-10. Ed. *Cambridge Patristic Texts*. M. & A. S. Walpole (d. 1920) worked 20 years on preparation of *Early Latin Hymns*, from which many trs. were taken in *Hymns A & M*, 1904. † Canterbury, 24 iv 1928 (76).

MAURICE FREDERICK BELL, b. London, 26 ix 1862; Sch. Hertford Coll., Oxf.; Ord. C/E 1886; Vicar of St. Mark's, Regent's Park, London, 1904. Made several trslns. for *English Hymnal* 1906 and wrote on church music. † Henfield, Sussex, 6 iv 1947 (84).

873. SCHONSTER HERR JESU

6.6.8.6.6.8, Irreg.

German: Anon. in *Munster Gbch*, 1677. 5 st. in *Schlesicher Volkslieder*, 1842, much altered, using sts. 1, 3, 2, 5 with a new st. inserted after st. 1; (this is in English version the 'woodlands' stanza). Tune in 1677 was that given at *EH*323 (F minor); tune from 1842 the more famous one, associated with romantic and totally imaginary legends about Crusaders (Both tunes are in P[1955]).

Tr.: (a) FAIREST LORD JESUS, (4 st.), anon., *Church Chorals*, Philadelphia, 1850. This is often used, abr. to 3 st., in U.S.

   (b) BEAUTIFUL SAVIOR, J. A. Seiss in *Sunday School Hymn Book*, Philadelphia 1873 (Lutheran). This is in *L* and last st. is used as 4th and last in *B(U.S.)*.

   (c) FAIREST LORD JESUS, attrib. to Lillian Stevenson in *Cantate Domino*, 1930. This is in effect an adaptation of (a) with the 2 missing sts. translated, and is used in British books.

US & CAN: BP232 (c): Can46 (c): B48 (a): CW261/286 (a): H346 (a): L434 (b): M79 (a): P194/135/360 (a): Pm327 (a) ● ENG: B202 (c): BB38 (c): CP175 (c): CH -/375 (c)

LILLIAN SINCLAIR STEVENSON, b. Rathgar, Co. Dublin, 1870; † Beaconsfield, Bucks, 3 ii 1960.

874. SOL PRAECEPS RAPITUR   PCH 467

Latin: Anon. in *Traité abr. Sainte Volonté de Dieu*, 1805, 4st. 6.6.6.6.7.8 iamb. and troch., with plainsong tune derived from that associated with PANGE LINGUA (868).

Tr.: (a) THE SUN IS SINKING FAST, 7 st. 6.4.6.6, E. Caswall (26), *Masque of Mary*, 1858, slightly altd. in *Hymns A & M*, 1861.

   (b) FAST SINKS THE SUN TO REST, 4 st. orig. met., C. S. Phillips (862), *Plainsong Hymn Book*, 1932, only at ‡ below.

US & CAN: H183 ● ENG: AM17/30, 37‡: B709: BB428: CH272/50: CP 614: E280: M939

875. SPLENDOR PATERNAE GLORIAE

Latin: Ambrose (689); in all medieval mss., 8 st. LM plus doxology.

Tr.: (a) O JESUS, LORD OF HEAVENLY GRACE, J. Chandler (52), *Hymns of the Primitive Church*, 1837, 8 st.

   (b) O JESUS, LORD OF LIGHT AND GRACE, compilers of *Hymns A & M*, 1861, based on (a), 7 st.

   (c) O SPLENDOUR OF GOD'S GLORY BRIGHT, R. Bridges (9), *Yattendon Hymnal*, 1899, 9 st.; full text, *EH*.

   (d) O SPLENDOUR OF GOD'S GLORY BRIGHT, compilers of *Hymns A & M*, 1904: no connexion with (c) but tenuously based on (a).

   (e) O SPLENDOR OF GOD'S GLORY BRIGHT, L. F. Benson (559), in *The Hymnal* (U.S. Episc.), 1911.

   (f) O SPLENDOR OF GOD'S GLORY BRIGHT, composite, using 3 st. of (e) and one (as st. 3) of (d), 4 st.

   (g) LORD JESUS, GOD OF HEAVENLY GRACE, A. Petti, *New Catholic Hymnal*, 1971, based on (a).

US & CAN: BP549 (a): CW -/283 (d): H158 (c): L206 (c): M29 (f): P32 (e)/ 46 (f)/529 (f): Pm39 (c) ● ENG: AM2 (b)/2 (d): An33 (a): B21 (d), 680 (a): BB409 (d): CP587 (a): E52 (c): M932 (c): NC140 (g)

876. STABAT MATER DOLOROSA   PCH 166

Latin: poem in 10 st. 88.7 D, author uncertain, thought by some to be Pope Innocent III, more prob. Jacopone da Todi. In *Roman Missal* 1727, but in popular use since Flagellants in mid-13th cent. Later used liturgically as Sequence.

Trs.: (a) AT THE CROSS HER STATION KEEPING, norm. in 5 st., orig. met.; form usually met. which owes 2 opening lines to E. Caswall (26), 17 lines to R. Mant (95) and 7 lines to compilers of *Hymns A & M*, 1861 and 1875. Version in *EH* has some lines from Aubrey de Vere (R.C. poet, 1814-1902). This vn., in whichever form, uses sts. 1-5 or orig.

   (b) NEAR THE CROSS HER VIGIL KEEPING, L. F. Benson (559) in *Hymns Original and Translated*, 1925, same selection, 5 st. orig. met.

   (c) AT THE CROSS HER VIGIL KEEPING, A. Petti in *New Catholic Hymnal*, 1971, 15 st. 88.7.

US & CAN: Can455 (a): CW -/164 (b): H76 (a): L84 (a) ● ENG: AM117/ 118 (a): BB80 (a): CH99/246 (a): E115 (a‡): M689 (a): NC17 (c): PL229 (a)

JACOPONE DA TODI (Jacobus de Benedictis), b. Todi, Umbria, early 13th cent.; dramatic circumstances, associated with the death of his wife at an accident in a theatre, sent him into the Franciscan Order where he became a lay brother; wrote much poetry in Italian, and known as eminent satirist of manners & morals of his time: what he said about the hierarchy sent him to prison more than once; released for the last time only after the fall of Pope Boniface VIII. † Todi, 1306.

877. STILLE NACHT, HEILIGE NACHT

German: J. Mohr, Christmas Eve, 1818, in 6 st., stress 4-4-4-4-3-3 troch. & dact. The reliable story is that the church organ at Oberndorf, Upper Austria, broke down on Christmas Eve, and the pastor (Mohr) wrote the carol, inviting his organist (Gruber) to set it, which he did for voices & guitar. Pub. *Leipziger Gbch*, 1838, after being scored for organ, orchestra and choir by composer in 1833.

This song waited 100 years to gain recognition outside its own country and the German-speaking communities in the U.S.A., and it is only since 1927 in Britain and about 1930 in the U.S.A. that hymnals outside those traditions have taken it. The present writer's father possessed a record of the song sung in German by Ernestine Schumann-Heink in the mid-1920s (the record was probably made a number of years earlier), which was put out, with Bizet's *Agnus Dei* on the other side, by His Master's Voice Company; but during research for *The English Carol* the author elicited from EMI Corporation (by then the parent company) that they had no knowledge of this. In the late 1930's secular media assisted it to popularity (it achieved the status of a 'hit' in the film *The Bells of St. Mary's* when there sung by Bing Crosby), but it was only after that that it achieved the popularity it now enjoys as one of the best known carols in any language. The first English hymn book to carry it was the *Church Hymnary*, 1927.

Tr.: (a) SILENT NIGHT, HOLY NIGHT, often listed anon., but now known to be by J. F. Young in *Sunday School Service & Tune Book* (U.S.A.), 1863.
  (b) STILL THE NIGHT, HOLY THE NIGHT, Stopford A. Brooke (340) in his own collection, *Christian Hymns*, 1881; this was much altd. when included in *Church Hymnary*, 1927 and other editors who use this version follow those amendments.
  (c) SILENT NIGHT, HOLY NIGHT, unidentifiable, in *English Hymnal Service Book*, 1962, first 2 sts. owing something to (a), 3rd st. new.
  (d) SILENT NIGHT, HOLY NIGHT, G. B. Timms, *English Praise*, 1975.

US & CAN: BP122 (a): Can416 (a): B89 (a): CW188/118 (a): H33 (a): L16 (b): M393 (a): P132/154/567 (a): Pm139 (a): CLB219 (a): W244 (a) ● ENG: An113 (a): B108 (b): CH49/176 (b): CP714 (b): E*328 (c)/*14 (d): M123 (b): PL155 (a)

JOSEPH MOHR, b. Salzburg, Austria, 11 xii 1792; as a boy, chorister in Salzburg Cathedral; foster-child of a R.C. priest, D. J. N. Niernle, and himself Ord. R.C., 1815; in 1817-19 was asst. priest at St. Nicholas, Oberndorf, where above incident occurred. Vicar of Hintersee, 1828-† Wagrein, 4 xii 1848 (55).

JOHN FREEMAN YOUNG, b. Pittston, Maine, 30 x 1820; Sch. Wesleyan Univ. & Virginia Theol. Sem., Alexandria; Ord. Meth., 1845; served in various parts of the U.S. until made 2nd Meth. Bp. of Florida, 1867, which post he held until † New York, 15 xi 1885 (65).

GEORGE BOORNE TIMMS, b. Derby, 4 x 1910, Prebandary of St. Paul's, London; Editor in Chief of *English Praise*, 1975, and translator of a number of hymns in that book.

878. TE LUCIS ANTE TERMINUM   PCH 143

Latin: 2 st. with doxology, in all mss. after 7th cent., Office Hymn for Compline (cf. 854). All trs. keep original meter and shape.

Tr.: (a) BEFORE THE ENDING OF THE DAY, J. M. Neale (2), *Hymnal Noted*, 1852; but current version uses first 2 lines from tr. by R. Campbell (827), in his *Hymns & Anthems*, 1850.
  (b) BEFORE THE ENDING OF THE DAY, compilers of *Hymns A & M*, 1861, much altd. from (a).

(c) BEFORE THE LIGHT OF EVENING FADES, R. Wright, *Praise the Lord*, 1972.
(d) BEFORE THE ENDING OF THE DAY, compilers of *Hymnal-1940* (U.S.) (659).

US & CAN: Can371 (a), 2 st.: H164 (d): L*790 (a): CLB327 (a) ● ENG: AM 15/16 (b): BB413 (a): E264 (a): PL312 (c)

879. URBS BEATA HIERUSALEM   PCH 158

Latin, perhaps 6th cent., 9 st. 8.7.8.7.8.7; first in British Museum ms., 11 cent.

Tr.: (a) BLESSED CITY, HEAVENLY SALEM, J. M. Neale (2), in *Medieval Hymns*, 1851, but in *Hymnal Noted*, 1852, set out in 2 parts, the 2nd beginning CHRIST IS MADE THE SURE FOUNDATION (ANGULARIS FUNDAMENTUM), each ending with doxology which thus appears as st. 5 and st. 10. Modern hymnals give different selections. Some print all 9 in 1851 form (*AM-S*); some print in 2 parts in 1852 form (*EH* in full as 2 hymns). The longer form in *AM-R* has 3 parts (3rd beginning at orig. st. 7). Others give as 2 separate hymns (*H* [*U.S.*], om. st. 9: *L*, om. st. 6). Others again select sts. from both parts to make one hymn: *An* having sts. 1, 2, 3, 5, 7, 8; *CP*, 1, 5, 6, 7, 8; *M**, 1, 5, 7, 8. Yet others use only pt. 2, CHRIST IS MADE . . . —*BBC*, sts. 5-9; *CH*, *NC*(altd.), 5, 7, 8, 9, which is also the selection in *BP*, *Can.*, *M(U.S.)*, *P* (all 3) and *Pm*.

US & CAN: BP304: Can145: H383-4: L254, 242: M298: P336/433/325: Pm263: CLB473: W43 ● ENG: AM396/474,620: An660: BB445: CH207/ 10: CP237: E169,170: M*7: NC32‡

  (b) CHRIST IS OUR CORNER-STONE, J. Chandler (52), *Hymns of the Primitive Church*, 1837, in 6 st. of 6.6.6.6.4.44.4, now abr. to 4 st.

US & CAN: P472/-/- ● ENG: AM239/243: An456: B267: BB258: E*56: M702

880. VENI CREATOR SPIRITUS   PCH 160

Latin: 6 st. LM-coup.; anon.; probably 9th cent., variously ascribed but never with certainty. Earliest extant ms. is of 11th cent. Julian lists 35 translations by 1907. Latin text at *CLB* 298, *W* 289.

Tr.: (a) COME, HOLY GHOST, ETERNAL GOD, in the *Book of Common Prayer*, 1662, Service for the Ordering of Priests: 16 st. CM, this altered from 14 st. version in Prayer Book of 1549. This is the earliest English singing version and is now preserved only at *AM-S*, 508.
  (b) COME, HOLY GHOST, OUR SOULS INSPIRE, J. Cosin, *Collection of Private Devotions*, 1627, in 9 couplets, 88: included in 1662 *Prayer Book* at same point as (a) and as alternative to it. Designed originally for reading, set in Prayer Book for Responsive reading, and only brought into singing use by *Hymns A & M*, 1861, which had to adapt the LM plainsong tune to carry the odd number of couplets. This alone indexed below:

US & CAN: BP256: H217: L117: M467: P -/237/335: Pm575 ● ENG: AM157: An216: B226: BB151: CH182/342: E153: CP199: M779: NC43‡: PL8‡,9

  (c) CREATOR SPIRIT, BY WHOSE AID, J. Dryden, *Miscellaneous Poems*, 1693, 39 lines in 7 unequal sts., all lines 8 syllables; a vn. in 5 st. 88.88.88 first made by J. Wesley (1) in *Psalms & Hymns*, 1742; variants in more recent hymnals until *English Hymnal*, 1906, standardized text in 4 st. (*Oxford Hymn Book*, 1908, retains a longer vn. with one st. in 7 lines).

US & CAN: H371: L124: W62 ● ENG: B230: CH184/118: CP200: E156: M293

  (d) COME, HOLY GHOST, CREATOR BLEST; originally by E. Caswall (26), successively altd. by R. Mant (95) and compilers of *Hymns A & M*, 1875; 7 st. LM-coup. (4 st. in U.S.).

US & CAN: CLB299: W50 ● ENG: AM347/-

(e) COME, O CREATOR SPIRIT, COME, R. Bridges (9), *Yatten-don Hymnal*, 1899, 6 st. LM-coup.

US & CAN: CW -/197 • ENG: AM -/152: E154: PL9

(f) O HOLY SPIRIT, BY WHOSE BREATH, J. W. Grant, Canadian *Hymn Book*, 1971. 4 st. LM-coup.: in *CLB* conflated with (d).

US & CAN: Can246: CLB298: W205 • ENG:

JOHN COSIN, b. Norwich, 30 xi 1594; Sch. Caius, Camb., Ord. C/E, chaplain to Bp. of Durham, 1624; Archdeacon of East Riding of Yorkshire, '25; Master of Peterhouse, Camb., '35; Vice-Chancellor of Camb. Univ., '39; exiled to France during Commonwealth period '49-'60; Bp. of Durham '61-† Westminster (London), 15 i 1672 (77).

JOHN DRYDEN, b. Aldwinkle, Northants, 9 viii 1631; Sch. Westminster & Trinity, Camb.; became leading poet & dramatist of his generation (post-Restoration England), and in later life often aroused controversies through his satires, such as *Absalom and Achitophel*, 1682. Much involved in political writing, and in sharp disputes about a possible R.C. royal succession in England, which aroused his sympathy. Deprived of all appointments at accession of William III, 1689, but continued to write. His famous *Ode on St. Cecilia's Day* was published almost at the end of his life (1697). † London, 1 v 1700 (68).

JOHN WEBSTER GRANT, b. Truro, Nova Scotia, 27 vi 1919; Sch. Pictou Academy, Dalhousie Univ., Pine Hill Divinity Hall, Halifax, and, after service as chaplain in World War II, Keble, Oxf.; Ord. United Ch. of Canada; Lecturer Pine Hill, '48; Prof. Ch. History, Union Coll., Vancouver, '49; Editor in Chief, Ryerson Press, '59; Prof. Ch. History, Victoria Univ., Toronto, '63. Member of ed. cttee., Canadian *Hymn Book*, 1971.

881. VENI SANCTE SPIRITUS PCH 152

Latin: 5 st. 77.7.77.7; the two most probable ascriptions are to Pope Innocent III and Stephen Langton (Archbishop of Canterbury, d. 1228). Much depends on dating of earliest mss.; if (as *Julian*) earliest is c. 1150, this is too early for Langton.

All trslns. original meter except (f) & (g).

Tr.: (a) HOLY SPIRIT, LORD OF LIGHT, E. Caswall (26), *Lyra Catholica*, 1849.

(b) COME, THOU HOLY PARACLETE, J. M. Neale (2), *Hymnal Noted*, 1854, in which, as in Latin orig., all 3rd & 6th lines rhyme throughout.

(c) COME, THOU HOLY SPIRIT, COME, compilers of *Hymns A & M*, 1861, based on (a).

These three above are occasionally mixed: *B(Brit.)* contains 2 lines of (b) in st. 1 of a version which is otherwise (c).

(d) HOLY SPIRIT, GOD OF LIGHT, A. Petti, *New Catholic Hymnal*, 1971.

(e) HOLY SPIRIT, FONT OF LIGHT, J. W. Grant (880), Canadian *Hymn Book*, 1971.

(f) COME, HOLY GHOST, IN LOVE, 5 st. 66.4.666.4, R. Palmer (370) in *Sabbath Hymn Book*, 1858.

(g) HOLY GHOST, MY COMFORTER, C. Winkworth (14), *Christian Singers of Germany*, 1869, taken from German tr. of Latin orig., HEIL'GER GEIST, DU TROSTER MEIN, 10 st., 777.

US & CAN: Can248 (e): H109 (c): L121 (f): CLB294 (e): W56 (c) • ENG: AM156 (c): An225 (c): B228 (c): CH186/105 (b): CP203 (b),202 (f): E155 (b): M287 (g), NC93 (d): PL216 (a)

POPE INNOCENT III: b. Anagni, Italy, 1161; after being cardinal at a very early age, became Pope at age 37, 1198, and under him the papacy reached the zenith of its prestige, owing to his unusually high & blameless character. Convened Fourth Lateran Council, 1215. † Perugia, 1216.

882. VEXILLA REGIS PRODEUNT

Latin: Venantius Fortunatus (868) in 8 st. LM. In later liturgies, before 12th cent., 2 sts. were added at the end, 'O Crux, ave . . .' and a doxology; and fairly soon after this, sts. 2, 7, 8 of orig. were dropped from use—in one ms. being actually written and erased. See Biography of

V. F. While he was at Poitiers, where Queen Rhadegund founded a nunnery, the day came for the consecration of the new institution, for which the Queen desired to present certain relics including a fragment of the True Cross. She obtained this fragment from the Emperor Justin II, and it was sent to the Bishop of Tours. It travelled from there to Poitiers in a barge procession with torches, the Queen heading it for the last 3 miles, together with V. F. himself. The arrival of this procession, 19 November 569, was the first time VEXILLA REGIS was heard.

Tr.: (a) THE ROYAL BANNERS FORWARD GO, J. M. Neale (2), *Medieval Hymns*, 1851. He uses the full 10 st. text but omits st. 2 and brackets the spurious sts. (placing them as sts. 6-7 of the 9 st. whole). The text of his sts. 1-7 (including the spurious sts.) is unaltered in *EH*, and, with further omission of st. 6, in *M(Brit.)*.

(b) THE ROYAL BANNERS FORWARD GO, compilers of *Hymns A & M*, 1861, who used 6 st., basing their version on (a) sts. 1-7, omitting 6. Some others follow this with minor alterations: *PL* uses it but restores the missing st. 6 in Neale's version.

(c) THE ROYAL BANNERS FORWARD GO, anon. in *Clarendon Hymn Book*, 1936 (hymnal prepared for use at Charterhouse, England), using sts. 1-4 of orig., and being the only version in current use that includes st. 2, which was omitted by the medieval liturgists.

(d) THE FLAMING BANNERS OF OUR KING, J. W. Grant (880), Canadian *Hymn Book*, 1971, freely & eloquently translating sts. 1, 3, 5, 6, 7 of later text.

Among other translations not noted here, see especially the anonymous one from *The Office of the Blessed Virgin*, 1687, in *Oxford Hymn Book*, 1908.

US & CAN: Can445 (d): H63 (b): L75 (b): CLB262 (b) • ENG: AM96 (b): B147 (b): BB91 (b): CH -/257 (c): CP126 (c): E94 (a): M184 (a): PL183 (b)

883. VICTIMAE PASCHALI PCH 1

Latin prose sequence for Easter, by Wipo of Burgundy, 10th cent. (Latin text at *W* 290); Luther's CHRIST LAG (111) is founded on it.

Tr.: (a) CHRIST THE LORD IS RISEN TO-DAY, CHRISTIANS HASTE YOUR VOWS TO PAY, by J. E. Leeson (444), *Hymns*, 1851 (ed. R. Formby for R.C. congregations), 4 st. 77.77 D.

(b) CHRISTIANS TO THE PASCHAL VICTIM, *English Hymnal*, 1906, based on prose translation in *Antiphoner & Grail*, 1880, and made to fit original plainsong tune, keeping rhythm of Latin. All sources using it with plainsong tune agree on translation, but (Lutherans) *Worship Supplement* adds a congregational antiphon from another source.

US & CAN: H97 (b): L*741 (b): CLB268 (a) • ENG: AM131 (a)/138 (b): An183 (a): E130 (b)

884. VON HIMMEL HOCH DA KOMM ICH HER
PCH 3

German: M. Luther (111), *Geistliche Lieder*, 1535; originally written for a family Christmas play in which his son Hans would take the part of the angel (sts. 1-5) and the family respond with the rest. 15 st. LM.

Tr.: (a) FROM YONDER WORLD I COME TO EARTH, J. Hunt, *Spiritual Songs of Martin Luther*, 1853, in full. In modern use, 8 st. selection begins O LET US ALL BE GLAD TO-DAY, using sts. 6-11, 13-14.

(b) FROM HEAVEN ABOVE TO EARTH I COME, C. Winkworth (14), *Lyra Germanica* II, 1858, in full. Most hymnals use this, but some begin at st. 7, GIVE HEED, MY HEART . . . (‡). Others always abridge.

(c) FROM HEAVEN HIGH I COME TO YOU, W. Douglas (659), for *Hymnal-1940* (U.S.), where #22 uses sts. 1-3 of orig., and #23, NOW LET US ALL RIGHT MERRY BE, sts. 6, 7, 13, 15.

(d) FROM HEAVEN HIGH I COME TO EARTH, R. Bainton.

US & CAN: Can411 (b): CW -/132 (b): H22-3 (c): L22 (b): Pm121 (b): CLB229 (d): W89 (d) • ENG: An98 (b‡): BB48 (b‡): CH56/188 (b‡): CP78 (a): M126 (b‡)

JOHN HUNT, b. Bridgend, Perth, 21 i 1827; Sch. Univ. St. Andrews; Ord. C/E 1855; curacies Deptford, Co. Durham and St. Mary's, Lambeth (London); then Vicar of Otford, Kent '78-†. On editorial staff of *Contemporary Review*; author of *Religious Thought in England*, 3 vols., 1878 and *Religious Thought in England in the XIX Century*, 1896. † Otford, 12 iv 1907 (80).

885. WACHET AUF! RUFT EINE STIMME

3 st. 89.8.89.8.66.4.44.8   **PCH 188**

German: P. Nicolai, *Frewden-Spiegel*, 1599, 'Of the Voice at Midnight, and the Wise Virgins who meet their Heavenly Bridegroom.' Matt. 25; also scriptural refs. to Rev. 19:6, 21:21; 1 Cor. 2:9; Ezek. 3:17; Is. 52:8. Written (like 888) probably at a time of great personal distress when his parish was stricken by plague.

All trs. of this monumental and heraldic composition keep orig. meter; it has gradually come forward toward popularity in Britain and the U.S.A. during the 20th century, and this and 888 are probably the most complex stanzas ever to be set to tunes which became popular. It has been continuously known to Lutheran congregations, as well as other, in original tongue or in non-English translations.

Tr.: (a) WAKE, AWAKE, FOR NIGHT IS FLYING, C. Winkworth (14), *Lyra Germanica*, II, 1858; a revised version of this is in *Hymnam-1940* (U.S.).
       (b) SLEEPERS, WAKE, THE WATCH-CRY PEALETH, in *AM-R* (1950) altered from WAKE! THE STARTLING WATCH-CRY PEALETH, by F. E. Cox (352), *Lyra Messianica*, 1864.
       (c) WAKE, O WAKE! WITH TIDINGS THRILLING, F. C. Burkitt (593), *English Hymnal*, 1906.
       (d) 'SLEEPERS, WAKE!' THE WATCH ARE CALLING, J. Macpherson (848), Canadian *Hymn Book*, 1971, to some extent based on (a).

US & CAN: Can394 (d): CW -/112 (a‡): H3 (a‡): L7 (a): M366 (a): P -/-/614 (a): Pm108 (a‡): W291 (a‡) • ENG: AM -/55 (b): An77 (a): BB40 (a): CH162/315 (a): CP760 (c): E12 (c): M255 (a)

PHILIPP NICOLAI, b. 10 viii 1556, Mengeringhausen, Waldeck (Germany); Sch. Erfurt & Univ. Wittemberg; Ord. Luth.; assisted his father at home, then preached at Herdecke until removed by Catholics. Became deacon, then pastor, at Niederwindungen, then chief pastor & court preacher, Altwildungen; pastor at Unna, Westphalia, 1596, where his 2 famous hymns were written; forced to flee by Spanish invasion. Pastor at Hamburg, 1601, where † 26 x 1608 (52).

886. WAS GOTT THUT, DAS IST GUT GETHAN

German: S. Rodigast, *Der Hannoverische Gesangbuch*, 1676, 6 st. 8.7.8.7.44.88.

Tr.: (a) WHATE'ER MY GOD ORDAINS IS JUST, C. Winkworth (14), *Chorale-Book for England*, 1863, 5 st. orig. meter, revised from earlier version (same opening line) in *Lyra Germanica*, II, 1858, in 6 st.
       (b) WHAT OUR FATHER DOES IS WELL, free paraphrase by H. W. Baker (101) for *Hymns A & M*, 1875; 4 st. 77.77.77.

US & CAN: BP100 (a): L582 (a): P291 (a)/366 (a)/633 (a): Pm96 (a) • ENG: AM389 (b)/- : An515 (a): CH540 (a)/-

SAMUEL RODIGAST, b. Groben, Germany, 1649; Sch. Univ. Jena; famous educator and scholar; asst. prof. philosophy at Jena, but refused full professorship there & rectorships elsewhere; but finally became Rector of Berlin Gymnasium, 1698. † Berlin, 1708.

887. WER NUR DEN LIEBEN GOTT LASST WALTEN

German: G. Neumark, 1641, as a thanksgiving when, after a period of poverty & depression he obtained a post as tutor in the family of Judge

Stephen Henning at Kiel; 'A Hymn of Consolation: that God will care for and preserve his own in his own time. Ps. 55:22.' 7 st. 9.8.9.8.88. Both translations in use are by the same hand.

Tr.: (a) LEAVE GOD TO ORDER ALL THY WAYS, C. Winkworth (14), *Lyra Germanica* I, 1855, 7 st. 8.8.8.8.88.
       (b) IF THOU BUT SUFFER GOD TO GUIDE THEE, *Chorale-Book for England*, 1863, 7 st., revised from (a) to accommodate orig. meter. Norm. sel. is now sts. 1, (2), 3, 7.

all (b) except ‡.

US & CAN: B203: CW404/51: H*15: L568: M210: P105/44/431: Pm83 • ENG: An523: B580: CH541/668: CP389: M504‡

GEORG NEUMARK, b. Langensalza, Germany, 16 iii 1621; Sch. Schleusingen & Gotha. Intended to study law at Konigsberg, but on his way there (aged 19, 1640) was set on by robbers who took everything he had. Supported himself as a wandering musician; finally obtained teaching post at Kiel, where he wrote his famous hymn & the tune that goes with it. Eventually arrived at Konigsberg, but again lost everything, this time through a fire. Travelled on by Danzig and Hamburg, to Weimar, where became a registrar & librarian, and † there 8 vii 1681 (60).

888. WIE SCHON LEUCHTET DER MORGENSTERN

7 st. 88.7.88.7.44.44.8

Note: this hymn as it appears in many current hymnals is not always rightly ascribed.

German: P. Nicolai, in *Frewden Spiegel*, 1599, has a hymn in 7 st. beginning thus, which he probably wrote in the same circumstances (1597) as 885; it is entitled 'A Spiritual Love Song of the Believing Soul Concerning Jesus Christ her heavenly Bridegroom (Ps. 45)'; it has much in common with 885 and nothing to do with the Epiphany season.

Tr. of this was by C. Winkworth (14) in the *Chorale-Book for England*, 1863, in 4 st. beginning O MORNING STAR, HOW FAIR AND BRIGHT; the others sts. begin (ii) 'Thou heavenly brightness . . . ,' (iii) 'But if thou look on me . . . ,' (iv) 'Here will I rest. . . .'

Nearly 200 years later J. A. Schlegel (70) wrote a hymn imitating Nicolai and using his tune, beginning WIE HERRLICH STRAHLT DER MORGENSTERN, and published it in *Sammlung geistliches Gesange*, 1766, in 5 st.

Tr. of this is also by C. Winkworth in above source, the 5th st. beginning HOW BRIGHTLY BEAMS THE MORNING-STAR, and the other sts. beginning (ii) 'Thou here my comfort . . . ,' (iii) 'Through thee alone . . . ,' (iv) 'O God our Father . . . ,' and (v) 'O praise to him who came to save.'

In the *Church Psalter & Hymn Book*, 1855, its editor, W. Mercer (500), wrote a hymn in 4 st. taking his opening words from Nicolai and approximately matching C. W.'s tr. of Schlegel in st. 1, but going on from there to write a new hymn for the Incarnation. This begins HOW BRIGHT APPEARS THE MORNING STAR, then (ii) 'Though circled by the hosts on high,' (iii) 'Then to the world I'll make my boast,' (iv) 'Rejoice, ye heavens; thou earth, reply.' In this there is nothing of Nicolai after the opening line.

All these hymns go to Nicolai's tune, which through the 17th and 18th centuries was even more popular in Germany than WACHET AUF, and which has generated a number of other texts (some of which in translation can be read in the Lutheran *Service Book & Hymnal*, 1958, which has Schlegel and three other texts). But the contribution of Nicolai to texts in current hymnals is fairly slight.

In order to sort out the provenances of current versions the following analysis is offered, assuming that (a) is Schlegel/Winkworth, (b) is Mercer, (c) is Nicolai/Winkworth and (d) is (c) but with st. 1 tr. by M. Harbaugh. Nicolai, with full German text and full English translation, is at *PCH* 189 (7 st.).

In order of appearance of stanzas in each entry:

BP152	(a) 1, 5	Schlegel	2 st.
Can117	(a) 1, 5	Schlegel	2 st.
CW -/287	(a) 1, 3, 5	Schlegel	3 st.
H329	(b) 1, 2, 4	Mercer	3 st.
L404	(a) 1, 3, 5 altd.	Schlegel	3 st.
M399	(c) 1, 2	Nicolai	2 st.
P(33)321	(c) 1, 2	Nicolai	2 st.
P(55)415	(c) 1, 2	Nicolai	2 st.
P(72)521	(c) 1, 2, (b) 4 altd.	Nicolai-Mercer	3 st.
CLB443	(c) 1, 2, (b) 4 altd.	Nicolai-Mercer	3 st.
W	(c) 1, 2, (b) 4 altd.	Nicolai-Mercer	3 st.

ENGLISH:

An130	(a) 1, 2, 5, (b) 4	Schlegel-Mercer	4 st.
BB141	(a) 1, 5	Schlegel	2 st.
CH -/202	(a) 1, 5	Schlegel	2 st.
M*33	(d) 1, (c) 2, 4	Nicolai	3 st.
E*10	(b) 1, 2, 4	Mercer	3 st.
NC94	(a) 1, 3, 5 altd.	Schlegel	3 st.

JOHANN ADOLF SCHLEGEL, b. Meissen, Germany, 17 ix 1721; Sch. Pforta and Univ. Leipzig; private tutor 1746-8; returned to Leipzig for literary work, then appointed master in school at Pforta, '51 and diaconus of the church; chief pastor of Trinity Church, Zerbst & prof. theology & metaphysics at Gymnasium there, '54; pastor of Markt Ch., Hanover, '59, Neustadt Ch. there, '75; Superintendent of district of Hoya, '82, dist. of Kalenberg, '87. † Hanover, 16 ix 1793 (72 less one day).

APPENDIX

Article 623 refers to the hymn ROCK OF AGES, and to a paper in the *Gospel* Magazine for March 1776 at the end of which the full text of the hymn first appears. The article is transcribed here, being included in the 1849 edition of Toplady's works (copied from the first edition of 1794), pages 448-450.

QUESTIONS AND ANSWERS RELATIVE TO THE NATIONAL DEBT

Qu. 1. SUPPOSING this debt to be only 130 millions of pounds sterling at present (although it is much more), and that it was all to be counted in shillings: that a man should count at the rate of 100 shillings per minute, for twelve hours each day until he had counted the whole; how much time would he take in doing it?

Ans. 98 years, 316 days, 14 hours, and 40 minutes.

Qu. 2. The whole of this sum being 2600 millions of shillings, and the coinage standard being 62 shillings in the Troy pound, what is the whole weight?

Ans. 41 million, 935 thousand, 484 Troy pounds.

Qu. 3. How many carts would carry the weight, supposing a ton in each?

Ans. 20,968 carts.

Qu. 4. Supposing a man could carry 100 pound weight from London to York; how many men would it require to carry the whole?

Ans. 419 thousand, 355 men.

Qu. 5. If all these men were to walk in a line at two yards distance from one another, what length of road would they all require?

Ans. 476 miles, half a mile, and 70 yards.

Qu. 6. The breadth of a shilling being one inch, if all these shillings were laid in a straight line close to one another's edges, how long would be the line that would contain them?

Ans. 41,035 miles; which is 16,035 miles more than the whole circumference of the earth.

Qu. 7. Supposing the interest of this debt to be only 3½ *per cent per annum*, what does the whole annual interest amount to?

Ans. Four million 550 thousand pounds sterling.

Qu. 8. How doth the government raise this interest yearly?

Ans. By taxing those who lent the principal, and others.

Qu. 9. When will the government be able to pay the principal?

Ans. When there is more money in England's treasury alone than there is at present in all Europe.

Qu. 10. And when will that be?

Ans. Never.

SPIRITUAL IMPROVEMENT OF THE FOREGOING

Qu. What is the moral law of God?

Ans. The transcript of his own most holy nature, and the standard of human purity and obedience.

Qu. Will this law make any allowance of human infirmity, or admit any abatement of the perfect conformity which it demands?

Ans. It makes no allowance for the former, nor will it dispense with a single grain of the latter.

Qu. How does that appear?

Ans. It appears from the undeniable current of Scripture: where the language of the law is, Be ye perfect, as your Father in heaven is perfect (Matt. 5:48). Cursed is every one who continueth not in all things that are written in the book of the law to do them. Gal. 3:10. The indispensable requisition is, Thou shalt love the Lord thy God with all thy heart, and with all thy soul, and with all thy strength, and with all thy mind; and thy neighbour as thyself. Luke 10:27. Hence, in the eye of the law and the estimation of the law-giver, the risings of wrath are tantamount to murder; the calling any man a fool exposes us to the penalty of hell-fire; an impure thought brings us under the condemnation of actual adultery. Matt., c. 22, 28.

Qu. What is the grand inference from these alarming premises?

Ans. That inference which the apostle terms an evident one, and evident indeed is, *viz.*: that no man is justified by the law in the sight of God. Gal. 3:11. For a single breach of the law renders us guilty of the whole: James 2:10. And one idle word lays us open to the vengeance of God, according to the tenor of the covenant of works. Matt. 12:36.

Qu. Supposing a person was to break the law once in 24 hours; to how many would his sins amount in a life of ten, twenty, thirty, forty, fifty, sixty, seventy, or eighty years?

Ans. If he was to fail in moral duty but once a day his sins at ten years of age would amount to 3 thousand 6 hundred and 50. At twenty years' end, the catalogue would be 7 thousand 3 hundred. At thirty, to 10 thousand nine hundred and 50. At forty, to 14 thousand 6 hundred. At fifty, to 18 thousand 2 hundred and 50. At sixty, to 21 thousand 9 hundred. At seventy, to 25 thousand 5 hundred and fifty. At eighty, to 29 thousand 2 hundred.

Qu. What if a person's sins are supposed to bear a double proportion to the foregoing estimate? That is, let us imagine him to sin twice a day, or once every twelve hours.

Ans. In that case his sins at the age of ten years will be multiplied to 7 thousand 3 hundred. At twenty, to 14 thousand 6 hundred. At thirty, to 21 thousand 9 hundred. At forty, to 29 thousand, 2 hundred. At fifty, to 36 thousand 5 hundred. At sixty, to 43 thousand 8 hundred. At seventy, to 51 thousand 1 hundred. At eighty, to 58 thousand 4 hundred.

Qu. We must go further still. What if a man's sins keep exact pace with every hour of his life? *i.e.*, we will suppose him to sin 24 times a day.

Ans. His sins will then amount, in a life of ten years, to 87 thousand, 6 hundred. At twenty years of age they will accumulate to 175 thousand, 2 hundred. At thirty, to 262 thousand 8 hundred. At forty, to 350 thousand 4 hundred. At fifty, to 438 thousand. At sixty, to 525 thousand 6 hundred. At seventy, to 613 thousand 2 hundred. At eighty, to 700 thousand and eight hundred.

Qu. Is there a single minute from the first of our existence to the very article of death, wherein we come up to the whole of that inward and outward holiness which God's all-perfect law requires?

Ans.   Most certainly not.

Qu.   Of how many sins then is each of the human race guilty, reckoning only at the rate of one sin for every minute?

Ans.   At ten years old we (according to that method of calculation) are guilty of no fewer than 5 millions 256 thousand sins. At twenty, of 10 millions and 512 thousand. At thirty, of 15 millions 568 thousand. At forty, of 21 millions and 24 thousand. At fifty, of 26 millions and 280 thousand. At sixty, of 31 millions and 536 thousand. At seventy, of 36 millions and 792 thousand. At eighty, of 42 millions and 48 thousand.

Qu.   May we not proceed abundantly further yet? Sixty seconds go to a minute. Now, as we never in the present life rise to the mark of legal sanctity, is it not fairly inferrable that our sins multiply with every second of our sublunary duration?

Ans.   It is too true. And, in this view of the matter, our dreadful account stands as follows.—At ten years old, each of us is chargeable with 315 millions, and 36 thousand sins.—At twenty, with 630 millions, and 720 thousand.—At thirty, with 946 millions, and 80 thousand.—At forty, with 1261 millions, 440 thousand.—At fifty, 1576 millions, and 800 thousand.—At sixty, 1892 millions, and 160 thousand.—At seventy, 2207 millions, and 520 thousand.—At eighty, with 2522 millions, 880 thousand.

Qu.   When shall we be able to pay off this immense debt?

Ans.   Never. Eternity itself, so far from clearing us of the dreadful arrear, would only add to the score by plunging us deeper and deeper even to infinity. Hence the damned will never be able to satisfy the justice of the Almighty Creditor.

Qu.   Will not divine goodness compound for the debt by accepting less than we owe?

Ans.   Impossible. Justice, holiness, and truth, will and must have their own, even to the very uttermost farthing. God himself (with profoundest veneration be it spoken) must become an Antinomian, and renounce himself, ere he can forego his essential attributes, and repeal his inviolable law, by offering violence to those, and by making void the claims and the threatenings of this.

Qu.   Who then can do us any good in this respect?

Ans.   Not all the angels in heaven, nor all the men that ever did or ever shall exist. Others cannot help us, nor can we help our own selves.

Qu.   If so, are we not lost, without remedy and without end?

Ans.   In ourselves we are. But (sing, O heavens!) God's own arm brought salvation.

Qu.   How so? What is there wherewith to counterbalance such an exceeding and astonishing weight of guilt?

Ans.   'Christ hath redeemed us from the curse of the law; being made a curse for us.' Gal. 3:13.—This, this will not only counter-balance, but infinitely over-balance, all the sins of the whole believing world.

Qu.   If the personal short-comings and misdoings of each sinner in particular amount to so vast a multitude, who can calculate the extent of the whole national debt, the entire aggregated sum, which (abstracted from her union with Christ) lies on the Church at large, that elect nation whom he has redeemed from among men?

Ans.   The arithmetic of angels would be unable to ascertain the full amount.

         O thou covenanting, thou incarnate, thou obeying, thou bleeding, thou dying, thou risen, thou ascended, thou interceding Son of God: not all the seraphs thou hast created, not all the innumerable saints thy love hath ransomed, will be able to comprehend, much less to display, along the endless line of eternity itself, the length, the breadth, the depth, the height, of a sinner's obligations to thee.

Qu.   If, on one hand, we are each constrained to cry out with the believers of old, Enter not into judgment with thy servant, O Lord, for in thy sight shall no flesh living be justified by works of human performance; —Who can tell how oft he offendeth?—How shall man be just with God?—If thou contend with him for his transgressions, he cannot answer thee for one of a thousand;—My sins are more in number than the hairs of my head;—Forgive us our debts, and cast all our sins into the depths of the sea; what has faith to say?

Ans.   Faith, on the other hand, can reply in the very words which the Holy Ghost teacheth, the blood of Jesus Christ cleanseth from all sin; and there is now no condemnation [i.e.: not one condemnation] to them that are in Christ Jesus. So that we may sing, with Dr. Watts,

         "Believing sinners free are set,
             For Christ hath paid their dreadful debt."
         We may add, with another sweet singer in Israel,
             "Who now shall urge a second claim?
             The law no longer can condemn;
                 Faith a release can shew:
             Justice itself a friend appears;
             The prison-house a whisper hears,
                 Loose him, and let him go!"

Qu.   What return can believers render, to the glorious and gracious Trinity, for mercy and plenteous redemption like this?

Ans.   We can only admire and bless the Father, for electing us in Christ, and for laying on him the iniquity of us all:—the Son, for taking our nature and our debts upon himself, and for that complete righteousness and sacrifice whereby he redeemed his mystic Israel from all their sins;—and the co-equal Spirit, for causing us (in conversion) to feel our need of Christ, for inspiring us with faith to embrace him, for visiting us with his sweet consolations by shedding abroad his love in our hearts, for sealing us to the day of Christ, and for making us to walk in the path of his commandments.

ROCK OF AGES, CLEFT FOR ME
LET ME HIDE MYSELF IN THEE . . .

CHRONOLOGICAL INDEX

Note: Many dates before c. 1450 are speculative and are printed in italic when there is uncertainty; after that date, only assured dates are given.

FOURTH CENTURY
329-389, Gregory Nazianzen, 533
339-397, St. Ambrose, 865
348-410, Prudentius, 844
375-414, Synesius, 426
389-461, St. Patrick, 626

FIFTH CENTURY
? - ? Sedulius, 211

SIXTH CENTURY
521-597, St. Columba, 855
535-609, Fortunatus, 868
540-604, St. Gregory, 836

SEVENTH CENTURY
673-735, St. Bede, 852

EIGHTH CENTURY
784-856, Rhabanus Maurus, 112
750-821, *Theodulph, 15*

ELEVENTH CENTURY
1079-1142, Abelard, 35
1090-1153, St. Bernard of Clairvaux, 857

TWELFTH CENTURY
1135-1204, Maimonides, 694
1161-1215, Innocent III, 876
? - ? , Bernard of Cluny, 851
1182-1226, St. Francis of Assisi, 13

THIRTEENTH CENTURY
1225-1275, St. Thomas Aquinas, 867
1230-1306, Jacopone da Todi, 846

FIFTEENTH CENTURY
? -1434, Bianco of Siena, 123
1380-1471, St. Thomas à Kempis, 402
? -1460, Laufenberg, 425
? -1494, Tisserand, 562

1480-1534, Weisse, 113
1483-1546, Luther, 111
1497-1560, Melanchthon, 487

---

	birth	death		birth	death
1506	Xavier, 465		1637	Ken, 63	
1528	Selnecker, 487		1640	Schutz, 642	
1534		Weisse, 113	1647		Heerman, 9
1541		Decius, 14	1648		Lowenstern, 431
1546		Luther, 111	1649		Rinkart, 492
1552	Spenser, 457		1650	Neander, 19	
		Xavier, 465	1652	Tate, 53	
1556	Nicolai, 885		1654	Canitz, 135	
1560		Melanchthon, 487	1656	Schenck, 817	
1571		Herbert, P., 845	1659	Brady, 53	
1579	Rous, 323				Rous, 323
1583	Dickson, 344		1661		Rutherford, 712
1585	Heermann, 9		1663		Dickson, 344
1586	Pestel, 77		1667		Rist, 89
	Rinkart, 492				Taylor, 167
1590	Weissel, 398		1671	Neumeister, 645	
1592		Selnecker, 487	1672	Schwedler, 56	
1593	Herbert, G., 137			Addison, 295	
1594	Lowenstern, 431			Schmolck, 400	
	Cosin, 880				Cosin, 880
1599		Spenser, 457	1674		Milton, 394
1600	Rutherford, 712			Watts, 10	
1607	Gerhardt, 18		1676		Gerhardt, 18
	Rist, 89			Coffin, 52	
1608	Milton, 394			Rodigast, 886	
		Nicolai, 885	1677		Franck, 162
1611	Olearius, 151				Scheffler, 548
1613	Taylor, Jeremy 167		1680	Browne, 124	
1614	More, 229				Neander, 19
1615	Baxter, 115		1681		Neumark, 887
1618	Franck, 162		1684		Olearius, 151
1619	Clausnitzer, 772				Crossman, 345
1621	Neumark, 887				Clausnitzer, 772
1624	Crossman, 345		1687		More, 229
	Scheffler, 548		1688		Bunyan, 821
1628	Bunyan, 821			Rothe, 488	
1630	de Santeuil, 101		1690		Schutz, 642
1632		Herbert, G., 137	1691		Baxter, 115
1635		Weissel, 398	1692	Byrom, 119	

115

birth	death	birth	death
1694	Mason, J., 300	Mahlmann, 227	
1697	de Santeuil, 101	Scott, Sir. W., 846	
K. von Schlegel, 70		1773 Auber, 589	
Tersteegen, 741		1774 Bahnmaier, 659	
1699	Canitz, 135	1775 Cawood, 34	
1700 Zinzendorf, 371		1776 Mant, 95	
1702 Doddridge, 64		1778	Toplady, 3
1703 Wesley, J., 1			Steele, 185
1707 Wesley, C., 1		1779 Moore, 148	
1708	Rodigast, 886	Doane, 197	
1711	Ken, 63	Cotterill, 333	
Wade, 500		Wardlaw, 541	
1712 Hart, 126		Grant, 575	
1715	Tate, 53	1780 Croly, 657	
Gellert, 352		Marriott, 744	
1717 Steele, 185		1781 Elliott, Eb., 812	
Williams, W., 258		1783 Heber, 93	
1718 Cennick, 69		Taylor, Jane, 420	
1719	Addison, 295	1784 Barton, 382	
Franz, 288		1785 Kirke White, 578	
1721 Bakewell, 260		1786	Wade, 500
1722 Williams, P., 258			Shirley, 673
1725 Newton, 37		Denny, 795	
Shirley, 673		1787 Whately, 248	
1726 Perronet, 17		Reed, 656	
	Brady, 53	1788	Wesley, C., 1
Madan, 260			Logan, 76
1727	Schenck, 817	1789 Conder, 92	
1728 Stennett, 445		Elliott, Charlotte, 118	
1730	Schwedler, 56	Ingemann, 748	
1731 Cowper, 235		King, 802	
1732	Browne, 124	1790	Robinson, 135
1734 Haweis, 564			Madan, 260
Allen, 673			Franz, 288
1735 Robinson, R., 141		1791	Wesley, J., 1
1737	Schmolck, 400		Williams, W., 258
1738 Medley, 313		Edmeston, 386	
1740 Toplady, 3		Milman, 524	
Fawcett, 87		1792	Perronet, 17
Claudius, 782		Keble, 83	
1741 Lavater, 528		Bowring, 230	
1743 Barbauld, 602		Carlyle, T., 847	
1744 Hill, 404		Mohr, 877	
1745 Heath, 474		1793 Clare, 4	
1746 Bruce, 76		Lyte, 5	
1748	Watts, 10	1794 Tappan, 756	
Logan, 76		1795 Cummins, 356	
Bromehead, 344			Stennett, 448
1749	Coffin, 52	1796	Williams, P., 258
1751	Doddridge, 64	Bathurst, 508	
Cameron, 76		1797 Mote, 469	
Oswald, 532		Bullock, 780	
1752 Dwight, 316		1798 Binney, 171	
1755	Cennick, 69	Osler, 361	
1756	Newmeister, 645	1799	Medley, 313
1757 Blake, 40		Pusey, 431	
1758	Rothe, 488	1800	Cowper, 235
Carlyle, J., 438			Lavater, 528
1760	Zinzendorf, 371	Bridges, M., 78	
1762 Hupton, 146		Wreford, 439	
1763	Byrom, 119	1801 Newman, 196	
1767	Bruce, 76	Spitta, 522	
1768	Hart, 126	1802 Williams, I.,	
1769	Gellert, 352	Gurney, 174	
	Tersteegen, 741	Oakeley, 500	
Kelly, 406		Bacon, 511	
1770 Cooper, 183		1803 Buckoll, 135	
1771 Montgomery, 6		Hickson, 227	

birth	death	birth	death
		Lynch, 163	
1804	Carlyle, J., 438	Downton, 205	
	Allen, 673	Mudie, 314	
Kennedy, 56		Pyrnne, 360	
Copeland, 449		Duffield, 661	
Alexander, J. W., 871		Prentiss, 455	
1805 Chambers, 16		Coxe, 572	
Adams, 478		**1819**	Bakewell, 260
1805 Browne, T. B., 600		Longfellow, 7	
Hedge, 847		Kingsley, 215	
1806	Kirke White, 578	Gill, 421	
Chandler, 52		Howe, 454	
Russell, 89		Lowell, 585	
1807	Newton, 37	Maude, 733	
Whittier, 11		Scriven, 794	
Wordsworth, C., 27		**1820**	Haweis, 564
Rawson, 99		Ingelow, 41	
Trench, 850		Crosby, 84	
1808 Bonar, 81		Walworth, 288	
Chorley, 249		Warner, 359	
Palmer, 370		Webb, 545	
Chatfield, 426		Hopkins, J. H., 788	
Smith, S. F., 458		Woodford, 834	
Anstice, 536		Young, 877	
Blew, 853		**1821** Baker, H. W., 101	
1809 Blackie, 47		Threlfall, 293	
Holmes, O. W., 427		Greenwell, 304	
Leeson, 444		Plumptre, 534	
Fuller-Maitland, 578		Dexter, 638	
Tennyson, 620		Rorison, 745	
Crewdson, 727		**1822** Johnson, 120	
1810 Alford, 150			Heath, 474
Sears, 339		Smyttan, 209	
Parker, T., 563		Hughes, T., 516	
1811	Cameron, 76	Longstaff, 675	
Monsell, 193		**1823**	Cotterill, 333
Mercer, 248		Twells, 57	
1812 McLeod, 154		Burns, 60	
Cox, 352		How, 75	
Burleigh, 387		Thring, 191	
Stowe, 663		Waring, 332	
Irons, 846		Findlater, 522	
1813 Borthwick, 70		**1824**	Taylor, Jane, 420
Wolcott, 106		Bright, 43	
Bateman, 121		Willis, 178	
Brooks, C. T., 227		Smith, W. C., 329	
Luke, 322		Macdonald, 539	
Armstrong, 570		Palgrave, 567	
McCheyne, 811		Romanis, 624	
1814 Caswall, 26		Cousin, 712	
Faber, 175		Hensley, 750	
Duncan, 369		**1825**	Barbauld, 602
Everest, 676			Marriott, 744
Campbell, 827		Whiting, 169	
1815	Claudius, 782	Tuttiett, 182	
1816 Hopper, 366		Procter, 466	
Pennefather, 368		Bickersteth, 517	
Bode, 529		Midlane, 618	
Phelps, 633		**1826**	Heber, 93
1817	Fawcett, 87		Mahlmann, 227
	Dwight, 316		Bromehead, 344
Noel, 58		Ellerton, 80	
McDougall, 102		Lowry, 318	
Small, 343		Maclagan, 342a	
Smith, E. L., 527		**1827**	Blake, 40
Montgomery-Campbell, 782		Winkworth, 14	
1818 Neale, 2		Blunt, 281	
Alexander, C. F., 24		Collins, 362	
Alderson, 42			

birth	death	birth	death
	Gladden, 549		Chesterton, 513
Caird, 32			Stocking, 550
Routley, 25			Wotherspoon, 859
1918	Gilmore, 276	Wren, 413	
	Hawks, 318	1937	Greenaway, 553
	Spring-Rice, 324		East, 824
	Holland, 378		Davis, R. F., 843
	Butler, H. M., 399	1938	Turton, 568
	Tilak, 586	1939	Whitmarsh, 12
Brooks, R. T., 682			Rees, T., 232
1919 Grant, J. W., 880			Grubb, 592
	Ainger, 234		Hoyle, 732
	Collins, 362	1940	Copenhaver, 280
1920	Rawnsley, 190	1941	Oxenham, 331
		1942	Lee, 471
Quinn, 867		1943	Piggott, 204
1921 Ferguson, 36		1944	Burke, 429
1922	Wortman, 245		Douglas, 659
1923	Thomson, 568	1945	Riley, 112
	MacGregor, 855	1946	Hardy, 505
1924	Thomas, 98		Knapp, 416
	Wright, 448	1947	Lew, 683
	Baring-Gould, 493	1948	Shillito, 66
	Muirhead, 684		Gillett, 342b
	Sharp, C., 697		Mattes, 848
1925	Dugmore, 30	1949	Phillips, 862
	Bourne, 415	1950	Kerr, 244
	Brownlie, 531		MacAlister, 626
	Krauth, 848	1951	Mathews, 176
1926	Mann, N., 604		Macnicol, 586
	Nichol, 793		Rowley, 326
		1952	Robbins, 609
1927 Bridge, B., 725			Tweedy, 170
1928	Mann, F., 467	1953	Merrington, 238
	Tarrant, 491		Struther, 428
	Landsberg, 604		Lewis, Elvet, 430
	Chope, 829		Roberts, R. E., 839
	Mason, A. J., 872	1954	Merrill, 482
1929	Studdert-Kennedy, 62		Fletcher, 561
	Parker, W. H., 290	1955	Alington, 253
	Hosmer, 483	1956	Newbolt, 396
	Bates, 496		Park, 790
Kaan, 202		1957	Knox, 866
1930	Bridges, R., 9		Watt, 306
	Benson, L. F., 559	1958	Bell, G. K. A., 108
1931	Byrne, 72		Olson, 104
	McBean, 102		Crum, 494
	Mathams, 348		Vaughan Williams, 579
	Davis, O. S., 775	1959	Briggs, 110
	Lacey, 502		Housman, 177
1932	Gurney, D. F., 555		Moment, 452
	Lowry, S. C., 650	1962	Roberts, K. E., 21
	Budry, 732		Bax, 764
	Wordsworth, E., 847		Cory, 783
1933	Draper, 13	1964	Vories, 392
	Masterman, 31		Holmes, J. H., 718
	Cook, 277	1965	Farjeon, 456
	van Dyke, 377	1967	Hughes, D., 156
	Robinson, J. A., 755	1969	Fosdick, 239
1934	Pollard, 275		Bowie, 414
	Woodward, 737	1971	Bunn, 263
	Baker, T., 777	1973	Edgar, 250
1935	Hull, 72	1974	Taylor, W. R. O., 683
	Burkitt, 593	1975	Harkness, 292
	North, 813	1976	Micklem, 724
1936	Dearmer, 88		
	Kipling, 241		

INDEX OF AUTHORS

(the author's biography will be found at the first number listed)

Jacopo da Todi, 876
Jervois, W. H. H., 815
Johnson, S., 120, 180, 395
Jones, R. G., 237

Kaan, F., 202, 409, 489, 643, 644, 781
Keble, J., 83, 423, 480, 668, 723, 869, 881
Kelly, T., 406, 695, 703, 787
Ken, T., 63
Kennedy, B. H., 56
Kerr, H. T., 244
Kethe, W., 20
King, J., 802
Kipling, R., 241, 382
Kingsley, C., 215
Kirke-White, H., 578
Kitchin, C., 396
Knapp, S., 416
Knox, R. A., 866, 849, 852, 871

Lacey, T. A., 502, 836, 837
Landsberg, M., 604
Langton, S., 881
Lathbury, M. A., 93, 158
Laufenberg, H. von, 425
Lavater, H., 528
Leeson, J. E., 444, 632, 883
Lee, H., 471
Lew, T. T., 683
Lewis, H. Elfed, 430
Littledale, R. F., 123
Logan, J., 76
Longfellow, S., 7, 291, 315, 490
Longstaff, W. D., 675
Lowell, J. R., 585
Lowen, H. von, (871)
Lowenstern, H. von, 431
Lowry, D. C., 650
Luke, J., 322
Luther, M., 111, 127, 838, 847, 884
Lynch, T. T., 163, 255, 702
Lyte, H. F., 5, 240, 353, 405, 595, 597, 599, ?630

MacAlister, R. A. S., 626, 860
McBean, L., 102
McCheyne, R. M., 811
MacDonald, G., 539
McDougall, M., 102
McGregor, G., 855
MacLagan, W. D., 342
McLeod, N., 154
MacNicol, N., 586
McPherson, J., 885
Madan, M., 260
Mann, F., 467
Mann, N., 604
Mant, R., 95, 199, 839, 876
Marckant, J., 543
Marriott, J., 744
Mason, A. J., 872
Mason, J., 300
Massie, R., 111, 838
Masterman, J. H. B., 31
Mathams, W., 348
Matheson, G., 446, 547
Matson, W. T., 419, 850

Matthews, B., 176
Maude, M. F., 733
Medley, S., 313
Melanchthon, P., 487
Mercer, W., 249, 500, 888
Merrill, W. P., 482, 622
Merrington, E. W., 238
Micklem, N., 724
Midlane, A., 618, 728
Miller, E. H., 317
Miller, J., 850
Milman, H. H., 524, 619, 809
Milton, J., 394, 706
Mohr, J., 877
Moment, J. J., 452
Monsell, J. S. B., 193, 312, 432, 576, 581, 616, 641, 642
Montgomery, J., 6, 46, 69, 152, 200, 224, 233, 261, 269, 397, 417, 435, 518, 563, 596, 652, 655, 660
Montgomery-Campbell, J., 782
Moore, T., 148
More, H., 229
Mote, E., 469
Moultrie, G., 388
Mudie, C. E., 314
Muirhead, L. B. C. L., 684
Myers, F. W. H., 271

Neale, J. M., 2, 8, 15, 29, 50, 51, 117, 147, 166, 192, 254, 350, 364, 390, 402, 502, 520, 562, 571, 662, 686, 687, 690, 694, 760, 827, 834, 836, 837, 841, 842, 843, 844, 849, 851, 854, 857, 861, 865, 867, 868, 878, 879, 881, 882
Neander, J., 19, 605
Nelson, H., 54
Neumark, G., 887
Neumeister, E., 645
Newman, J. H., 196, 384, 603, 854, 857
Newton, J., 37, 49, 74, 136, 161, 220, 301, 451, 625, 846
Nichol, H. E., 793
Nicolai, P., 885, 888
Noel, C. M., 58
North, F. M., 813

Oakeley, F., 500
Oakley, C. E., 284
Olearius, J., 151
Olivers, T., 692
Olson, E. W., 104
Osler, E., 519, 601
Oswald, H. S., 532
Owens, P., 779, 823
Oxenham, J., 331

Packer, H., (855)
Palgrave, F. T., 567
Palmer, R., 370, 459, 857, 881
Park, J. E., 790
Parker, T., 565
Parker, W., 290, 679
Peacey, J. R., 195
Pennefather, W., 368
Perronet, E., 17
Pestel, T., 77

Petti, A., 827, 867, 870, 871, 875, 876, 881
Phelps, S. D., 633
Phillips, C. S., 862, 867, 872, 874
Pierpoint, F. S., 201
Piggott, W. Charter, 204
Plumptre, E. H., 534, 614, 731, 749
Pollard, A., 275
Pollock, T. B., 374
Pope, A., 621
Pott, F., 45, 209, 848
Potter, T. J., 97
Prentiss, E. P., 455
Procter, A. A., 466
Prudentius, 843, 870
Pusey, P., 431

Quinn, J., 867

Rabanus, Maurus, 112
Rankin, J. E., 226
Rawnsley, H. D., 190
Rawson, G., 99, 143, 179
Reed, A., 656
Rees, B. A., 273
Rice, C. S., 324
Riley, A., 112, 832, 864, 870
Rinkart, M., 492
Rippon, J., 17
Rist, J., 91
Robbins, H. C., 609
Roberts, D. C., 242
Roberts, K. E., 21
Roberts, R. E., 839
Robinson, J. A., 755
Robinson, R., 141, 453
Robinson, R. H., 286
Rodigast, S., 886
Romanis, W., 624
Rorison, G., 745
Rossetti, C., 335, 441, 481
Rothe, J. A., 488
Routley, E., 25
Rowley, F. H., 326
Russell, A. T., 91, 701
Rutherford, S., 712

Salmot, T., 670
Santeuil, J. B. de, 101, 164
Scheffler, J., 548, 721
Schenck, H., 817
Schlegel, J. A., 888
Schlegel, K. A., 70
Schmolck, B., 400, 470, 588, 860
Scholtes, P., 774
Schutz, J., 640
Schwedler, J. C., 56
Scott, L., 319
Scott, R. B. Y., 503
Scott, W., 846
Scottish Paraphrases, 76, 79, 86, 133, 186, 272, 297, 299, 328, 709, 715, 765, 814
Scottish Psalter, 323, 325, 542, 607, 705, 753, 828
Scriven, J., 794
Sears, E. H., 338
Sedulius, C., 211
Seiss, J. A., 873
Selnecker, N., 487

Sharp, C., 697
Shillito, E., 66
Shirley, W., 673
Shurtleff, R., 385
Shuttleworth, F. C., 184
Small, J. G., 343
Smith, E. A., 528
Smith, E. L., 309
Smith, L. G., 100
Smith, S. F., 458, 708
Smith, W. C., 329
Smyttan, J., 209
Spenser, E., 457
Spitta, C. J. P., 522
Steele, A., 185
Stennett, S., 445
Stevenson, I., 287
Stock, S. G., 391
Stocking, J. T., 550
Stone, S. J., 685
Stowe, H. B., 663
Struther, J., 428
Studdert-Kennedy, G. A., 62
Symonds, J. A., 730
Synesuis, 426

Tappan, W. B., 756
Tate and Brady, 53, 347, 747, 816
Taylor, Jane, 420
Taylor, Jeremy, 167
Taylor, W. R. O., 683
Tennyson, A., 620, 666, 669
Tersteegen, G., 741, 850
Theodulph of Orleans, 15
Thomas à Kempis, (8), 402, 852
Thomas Aquinas, 867
Thomas of Celano, 846
Thomas, H. A., 98
Thomson, M. A., 577
Threlfall, J., 293
Thring, G., 191, 214, 515, 628, 709, 743
Tilak, N. V., 586
Tisserand, J., 562
Toplady, A. M., 3, 623
Trench, R. C., 851
Troutbeck, J., 89
Tucker, F. B., 22, 34
Turton, W. H., 568
Tuttiett, L., 182
Tweedy, H. H., 170
Twells, H., 57, 485

Vaughan, H., 475
Vaughan Williams, R., 579
Vories, W. M., 392

Wade, J. F., 500
Walford, W., 670
Walworth, C. A., 288
Wardlaw, R., 541
Waring, A. L., 332
Warner, A., 359, 789
Watt, L. McB., 306
Watts, I., 10, 36, 73, 86, 122, 128, 131, 145, 210, 218, 219, 245, 283, 296, 297, 320, 327, 328, 367, 375, 376, 433, 468, 472, 477, 592, 671, 696, 726, 736, 804, 825
Webb, B., 545, 852

A BRIEF BIBLIOGRAPHY

Many of the books in this list may well be out of print; only those books are included which would have some appeal or usefulness for the reader who wants to pursue research or to increase his enjoyment of hymnody.

A bibliography of 'Companions to Hymnals' appears on page *xii* and is not repeated here, except where a Companion to a book outside the reference list should be recorded.

In each section books are listed in reverse order of publication date.

1. HISTORIES OF HYMNODY

1963   *A Survey of Christian Hymnody*, W. J. Reynolds, Holt Rinehart Winston, Inc.

1962   *The Story of the Church's Song* (orig. pub. by Church of Scotland, Edinburgh, 1927, same title), Millar Patrick, rev. J. R. Sydnor, John Knox.

1956   *Christian Hymnody*, E. Keith, Convention Press, Nashville, Tenn.

1952   *Hymns and Human Life* [346]* (rev. '58), E. Routley, John Murray (London).

1940   *Three Centuries of American Hymnody*, H. W. Foote, Harvard Univ. Press.

1937   *Hymnody Past and Present* [418], C. S. Phillips, S. P. C. K.

1915   *The English Hymn* [624], L. F. Benson, John Knox.

n.d.   *The Hymn Lover* [525] (One of the earliest surveys of hymnody:
(1889)   especially interesting in its account of American hymnody which its author introduced to England), W. G. Horder, Curwen, London.

2. SPECIAL SUBJECTS

1966   *Hymns Unbidden* (studies of the influence of Watts, Wesley and other evangelical hymn writers on other literature, especially Blake), M. W. England and J. Sparrow, New York Public Library.

1965   *Anatomy of Hymnody* (The only available study of hymn meters: indispensable), A. C. Lovelace, Abingdon.

1960   *A Hundred Years of Hymns Ancient and Modern* [90] (bibliographical history of the most famous of all hymnals), W. K. Lowther-Clarke, Clowes.

1956   *Sursum Cords* (Study of German writers and their translators), S. H. Moore, Independent Press, London†.

1954   *French Diocesan Hymns and their Melodies* (Latin texts and tunes of hymns of the 18th century RC Liturgical Revival [52]), C. E. Pocknee, Faith Press, London.

1949   *Four Centuries of Scottish Psalmody*, Millar Patrick, Oxford Univ. Press, London.

1932   *Processions* (Manual of practice and custom), C. Dunlop, Oxford Univ. Press, London.

1931   *Unitarian Hymn Writers*, H. W. Stephenson, Lindsey Press, London.

1929   *A Forgotten Psalter* (Essays on folk song, church music, shanties and the Genevan Psalter), R. R. Terry, Oxford Univ. Press, London.

3. SPECIAL AUTHORS

ISAAC WATTS

1974   *Isaac Watts Remembered* [112], D. Fountain, Worthing, Eng. H. E. Walter.

1974   *Isaac Watts, Hymns & Songs, Publication History & Bibliography* [479], S. Bishop, Pierian Press, Ann Arbor, Mich.

*For books of less than 120 pages or more than 300 the number of pages is given thus.

†Independent Press: stock now held by Tavistock Bookshop, 86 Tavistock Place, London WC1H 9RT.

1962   *Isaac Watts, Hymns & Spiritual Songs: textual criticism* [387], S. Bishop, London, Faith Press.

1962   *Isaac Watts, Hymnographer* [304], H. Escott, Independent Press†, London.

1948   *Isaac Watts* (biography) (in U.S.A., 1943), A. P. Davis, Independent Press†.

THE WESLEYS

1972   *John Wesley and the German Hymn* [413], J. L. Nuelsen, tr. A. S. Holbrook, A. Holbrook, Calverley, Eng., LS28 5RQ.

1966   *A Rapture of Praise* (anthology), Hodges & Allchin, Hodder & Stoughton, London.

1966   *Wesley's Prayers & Praises* (anthology), J. A. Kay, Epworth Press, London.

1962   *Representative Verse of John & Charles Wesley* [413] (large selection of hymns with textual & Bibl. commentary), F. Baker, Epworth.

1953   *The Hymns of Charles Wesley* (brief & scholarly account), R. N. Flew, Epworth.

1948   *The Eucharistic Hymns of John and Charles Wesley*, H. E. Rattenbury, Epworth.

1945   *The Hymns of Methodism* (3rd ed.) (excellent study of scriptural and literary associations), H. Bett, Epworth.

1942   *The Evangelical Doctrines of Charles Wesley's Hymns*, H. E. Rattenbury, Epworth.

J. M. NEALE

1962   *The Influence of J. M. Neale* (not confined to hymnody), A. G. Lough, S. P. C. K.

J. ELLERTON

1896   *John Ellerton, a Sketch of his Life and Works* (with 200 pp. of E's own writings), H. Housman, S. P. C. K.

4. CRITICISM AND APPRECIATION

1964   *Hymns To-day and To-morrow* (available in paperback), E. Routley, Abingdon.

1942   *The Hymns of Wesley and Watts* (a classic appreciation, with much wit & insight, in a small colln. of essays pub. after author's death), B. Manning, Epworth, London.

1936   *Collected Essays, Papers, &c.* (Rare; a special collection made for the Church Music Society, in England, by author's widow incl. much about hymns & church music by a great authority), R. Bridges [9], Oxford Univ. Press, London.

1861   *National Hymns: How they are Written and How they are Not Written* (a collector's piece: being an account of the entries in a competition for 'A national hymn,' with hilarious texts and comments), R. G. White, Rudd & Carleton, New York.

5. PRACTICAL

1973   *These are the Hymns* [93] (about the choice of hymns: paperback), A. Dunstan, S. P. C. K.

1960   *The Hymn and Congregational Singing*, J. R. Sydnor, John Knox.

6. JOURNALS

The Hymn, being the Journal of the Hymn Society of America; important occasional papers also published. Enquiries to the Society at Wittemberg University, Springfield, Ohio, 45501.

The Bulletin of the Hymn Society of Great Britain & Ireland, obtainable by subscription (in 1975, £7.50 p.a.); enquiries to the Royal School of Church Music, Addington Palace, Croydon, England, CR9 5AD.